Troubleshoot and Optimize Windows 8 Inside Out

Mike Halsey

Published with the authorization of Microsoft Corporation by:
O'Reilly Media, Inc.
1005 Gravenstein Highway North
Sebastopol, California 95472

ISBN: 978-0-7356-7080-8

1 2 3 4 5 6 7 8 9 LSI 8 7 6 5 4 3

Printed and bound in the United States of America.

Microsoft Press books are available through booksellers and distributors worldwide. If you need support related to this book, email Microsoft Press Book Support at *mspinput@microsoft.com*. Please tell us what you think of this book at *http://www.microsoft.com/learning/booksurvey.*

Acquisitions and Developmental Editor: Kenyon Brown
Production Editor: Holly Bauer
Editorial Production: Online Training Solutions, Inc.
Technical Reviewers: Todd Meister, George Grigorita, Randall Galloway
Copyeditor: Victoria Thulman
Indexer: Jan Bednarczuk
Cover Design: Twist Creative • Seattle
Cover Composition: Zyg Group, LLC
Illustrator: Rebecca Demarest

Contents at a Glance

Part 4: Disaster Recovery

Part 5: Using Advanced Utilities

Part 6: Appendices

Table of Contents

Part 3: Using Advanced Technical Fixes

Part 6: Appendices

Introduction

When you buy a new television set or games console, you expect to be able to plug it in and have it work without incident, every day of every year, until it dies. Computers, however, are infinitely customizable, and every one of those changes adds or modifies files in the core operating system. When you buy a computer, you hope never to encounter a problem, but you might because of the flexibility you demand of these devices.

If you do encounter a problem, the sheer number of combinations of software, hardware, updates, settings, customization options, and plug-ins can make diagnosing and repairing that problem challenging. How do you repair a problem in an operating system that's made up of thousands of files and that has an extremely complex structure and format?

That's where this book comes in. Think of it as an introduction, a complete guide, and a master class all in one volume—not just regarding the structure of the operating system and its related files, but also regarding what commonly goes wrong and why, and how you can embark on the troubleshooting process.

Beginning with the assumption that preventing problems from occurring is the best starting point, *Troubleshoot and Optimize Windows 8 Inside Out* guides you through the technical maze of Microsoft's latest operating system and explains troubleshooting in ways that are relevant to you.

Who This Book Is For

This book offers a comprehensive look at how to troubleshoot problems and optimize Windows 8. It serves as an excellent reference for users who need to understand how to accomplish what they need to do. In addition, this book provides useful information to advanced users and IT professionals who need to understand the bigger picture.

Assumptions About You

You have already have been repairing or supporting computers and users in some fashion, whether privately (within your circle of friends and family), for a business or organization (either formally or informally), or within an enterprise environment. You are also keen to expand your skills and knowledge, and broaden and deepen your technical understanding of Windows 8 and how it works and interacts with hardware, software, and the Internet.

This book addresses some IT professional subjects that are covered in more detail elsewhere and for which there are sometimes Microsoft certification qualifications, but you will not need prior knowledge or understanding of these subjects. I focus on techniques and topics that are likely to appeal to readers who have already mastered the many basics of the Windows operating system.

How This Book Is Organized

This book gives you a comprehensive look at the features in the Windows 8 operating system that you will need to prevent, mitigate, diagnose, and repair problems and errors. This book is structured with a logical approach to troubleshooting.

Part 1, "Preventing Problems," examines the ways in which Windows 8 computers can be installed and configured so that you can prevent problems from occurring or minimize the impact of those problems.

Part 2, "Applying Easy Technical Fixes," details the many ways in which problems and errors can be repaired quickly and simply, sometimes by remotely giving instruction to the user.

Part 3, "Using Advanced Technical Fixes," details the process of how you begin diagnosing and troubleshooting complex problems, and identifies what to look for in the operating system, and tools and utilities to help with this.

Part 4, "Disaster Recovery," assumes that a significant problem has already occurred that needs to be fixed quickly but cannot be easily addressed from within the operating system itself.

Part 5, "Using Advanced Utilities," examines the advanced administration and configuration tools for Windows 8 in depth, looking at how they can be used for advanced troubleshooting and optimization, and how you can use them to configure Windows 8 to further prevent and mitigate problems.

The three appendixes detail the different Windows 8 editions, and their features and hardware requirements; a complete list of Windows 8 keyboard shortcuts, which can make life much simpler for some users; and an introduction to Windows RT.

Windows 8 Editions

Windows 8 is available in several different versions, known as *editions.* As you read through the book, I indicate which features are relevant to particular versions of the operating system. Following is a brief description of each Windows 8 edition. See Appendix A, "Windows 8 Editions and Features," for more information about particular features provided in each edition.

Windows 8

Windows 8 is the main consumer version of the operating system. It contains all the features you need when using Windows 8 at home, including the updated File Explorer, Task Manager, better multimonitor support, and the ability to easily change the language option, which previously was available only to users purchasing the Enterprise and Ultimate Editions of Windows.

Windows Pro

Windows 8 Pro is for tech enthusiasts, and business and technical professionals. It provides features for encryption, virtualization, computer management, and domain connectivity. The Windows Media Center functionality is available as an add-in to Windows 8 Pro, known as the *Media Pack*.

Windows 8 Enterprise

Windows 8 Enterprise is available only through Microsoft's volume licensing subscription service. It includes additional features that are specific to using Windows 8 in a Windows server environment, for which additional management and security controls are required. It also includes the Windows To Go feature by which Windows 8 installations can be distributed on USB flash drives.

Windows RT

Windows RT is the ARM processor variant of Windows 8; it does not include all of the management features of Windows 8 Pro or Enterprise. It does include a desktop, although the only software that can be run on it are File Explorer, Windows Internet Explorer, and the bundled, full editions of the Microsoft Office programs, that is, Microsoft Word, Excel, PowerPoint, and OneNote.

Features and Conventions Used in This Book

This book uses special text and design conventions to make it easier for you to find the information you need. The following table describes these conventions.

Convention	Meaning
Abbreviated commands for the ribbon	For your convenience, this book uses abbreviated commands. For example, "Click Home\Insert\Insert Cells" means that you should click the Home tab on the ribbon, then click the Insert button, and then finally click the Insert Cells command.
Boldface type	**Boldface** indicates text that you type.
Initial Capital Letters	The first letters of the names of tabs, dialog boxes, dialog box elements, and commands are capitalized, for example, the Save As dialog box.
Italicized type	*Italicized* type indicates new terms or terms being emphasized.
Plus sign (+) in text	Keyboard shortcuts are indicated by a plus sign (+) separating key names. For example, Ctrl+Alt+Delete means that you press the Ctrl, Alt, and Delete keys at the same time.

Design Conventions

INSIDE OUT **This statement illustrates an example of an "Inside Out" heading**

These are the book's signature tips. Here, you get the straight scoop on what's going on with the software—inside information about why a feature works the way it does. You'll also find handy workarounds to deal with software problems.

CAUTION !

Cautions identify potential problems that you should look out for when you're completing a task or that you must address before you can complete a task.

Note

Notes offer additional information related to the task being discussed.

Your Companion Ebook

With the ebook edition of this book, you can do the following:

- Search the full text
- Print
- Copy and paste

To download your ebook, please see the instruction page at the back of this book.

Support and Feedback

The following sections provide information on errata, book support, feedback, and contact information.

Errata & Support

We've made every effort to ensure the accuracy of this book and its companion content. Any errors that have been reported since this book was published are listed on our Microsoft Press site at *http://oreilly.com*:

http://go.microsoft.com/FWLink/?Linkid=260982

If you find an error that is not already listed, you can report it to us through the same page.

If you need additional support, send email to Microsoft Press Book Support at *mspinput@microsoft.com*.

Please note that product support for Microsoft software is not offered through the preceding addresses.

We Want to Hear from You

At Microsoft Press, your satisfaction is our top priority and your feedback our most valuable asset. Please tell us what you think of this book here:

http://www.microsoft.com/learning/booksurvey

The survey is short, and we read every one of your comments and ideas. Thanks in advance for your input!

Stay in Touch

Let's keep the conversation going! We're on Twitter: *http://twitter.com/MicrosoftPress*.

Acknowledgments

It is sometimes very difficult to write books, even when you know the subject matter backward, forward, and every direction in between. Writing a troubleshooting and optimizing book presents further problems when you want to make sure you have all the bases covered. I would like then to dedicate this edition to all the people who have swelled my mailbag in recent years with an enormously wide assortment of Windows-related issues and other computer problems, errors, and crashes. You're all in here, somewhere. :)

Keep 'em coming!

PART 1

Preventing Problems

CHAPTER 1

Finding Your Way Around Windows 8

The Start screen introduced in Windows 8 provides you with an efficient way to access the information, tools, and apps you work with most. IT professionals, PC enthusiasts, and users who work with the administrative and management tools in Windows will find the easily customizable aspect of the Start screen especially helpful. Just a couple of clicks are necessary to add all the administration options to the Start screen, a task not easily accomplished in earlier Windows versions. So that you can find your way around Windows 8, this chapter explains where to locate the tools and utilities you commonly need when you're troubleshooting and optimizing Windows, your software, and your hardware. This chapter also explains what new tools and features have been added to assist you and how to use these with the new Start screen.

Finding the Desktop

When you start Windows 8, you're presented with the Start screen, which is populated with Tiles. Each Tile represents an app or a program in the same way a desktop icon represents a program. One of the Tiles you see is the Desktop Tile. Note that the desktop isn't loaded until you actually need it. If you don't use the desktop at all in a computing session, Windows 8 will run slightly more quickly, because you don't have the memory and processor overheads of loading and running the desktop. Figure 1-1 shows the desktop.

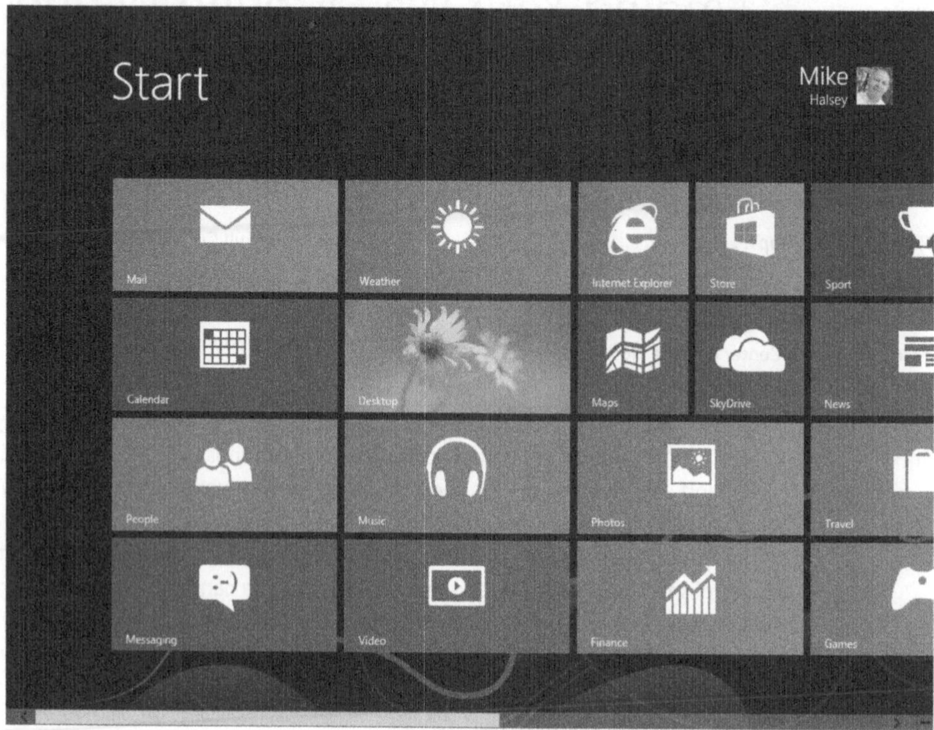

Figure 1-1 You can open the desktop in Windows 8 by clicking the Desktop Tile on the Start screen.

Using Charms

The Start button in the lower-left corner of the desktop, which has been a part of many versions of Windows, has been replaced by the Start screen. Charms are buttons that provide access to Windows tasks such as Start, Search, Sharing, Devices, and Settings. You can access charms, which appear on the right side of your screen, from both the Start screen and the desktop. To display the charms, use one of the following three methods:

- On touch devices, from the right edge of the screen, swipe inward with your finger.
- Move your mouse to the hot corners in the upper-right or lower-right corners of your screen.
- Press the Windows logo key+C on your keyboard.

Using the Taskbar

The Windows 8 taskbar has several helpful features in addition to charms. For example, you can pin program icons to it for quick access to the programs, thus saving trips back and forth between the desktop and the Start screen. To pin program icons, on the Start screen, right-click an icon, and then from the option menu that appears at the bottom of the screen, select Pin To Taskbar.

INSIDE OUT Accessing a program's properties

Sometimes you may need to access the properties for a desktop program. In Windows 8, you do this by using the All Apps view on the Start screen. With a program's icon visible, right-click the icon to open the program's file location. Then right-click the app icon to access its properties.

Jump Lists are a convenient way to access commonly used features within a program or run a second instance of a program. Many Jump Lists also contain lists of recently accessed files, and you can pin files to Jump Lists so that the files always appear when the Jump List is opened. You access Jump Lists in Windows 8 by right-clicking the icon.

Additionally, you can pin websites to the taskbar by dragging the site's icon from the Windows Internet Explorer address bar onto the taskbar. Many websites have Taskbar Jump Lists code embedded into them containing specific links to different areas of the website. These links can appear and be operated form a Jump List if you drag the website's icon onto the Taskbar to pin it there.

INSIDE OUT Be careful which icon you place first on the taskbar

Even though the Start menu is gone, you may still have the urge to move your mouse to the lower-left corner of the screen to open it. My best advice is to ensure that the first icon on the taskbar is something that opens quickly, such as File Explorer, because you'll be opening it quite a bit at first.

Accessing Action Center and the Notification Area

At the far right of the taskbar is the white flag icon for Action Center (see Figure 1-2). The Action Center is the central location for all Windows 8 notifications regarding alerts, warnings, security, maintenance, and backup. You'll know when a message is waiting for you because the Action Center icon displays a small red-and-white notification cross to get your attention.

Figure 1-2 The Action Center icon and other icons are in the notification area.

To the left of the Action Center icon is a small arrow. Click this arrow to display hidden icons. You can find any software running in the background that has its own icon here.

If you have a touchscreen-enabled device, Windows 8 will add the on-screen keyboard icon to the notification area as well.

Finding the Full Control Panel

When you want to handle administrative tasks, you use Control Panel. You can configure many aspects of your computer's administration in the desktop Control Panel, but Windows 8 offers an alternative way to quickly configure common system settings as well. To take advantage of this, click the Settings charm to display just a few settings (see Figure 1-3). If you don't see what you need, click the Change PC Settings link to open PC Settings.

Figure 1-3 Clicking the Settings charm from the desktop displays a Control Panel link.

By default, Control Panel opens in the Categories view, but you can show the Large Icons or Small Icons view instead by clicking the View By option, located in the upper-right part of the window. Showing large or small icons displays all Control Panel items, as shown in Figure 1-4.

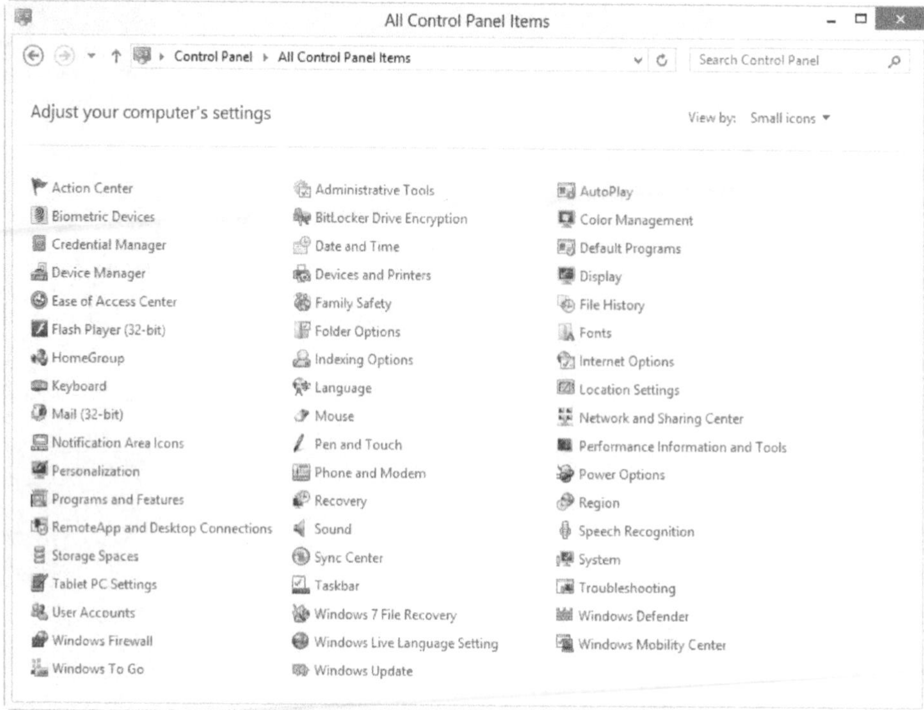

Figure 1-4 The Small Icons view of Control Panel in Windows 8 shows all Control Panel items.

Finding the Computer Management and Administrative Tools

In Windows 8, you have several options for accessing Administrative Tools. You can access them from Control Panel by clicking the link to the Computer Management console (see Figure 1-5), or you can access this console and other features directly from the desktop and the Start screen by right-clicking in the lower-left corner of the screen, which opens the WinX menu. The WinX menu is also available by pressing Windows logo key+X.

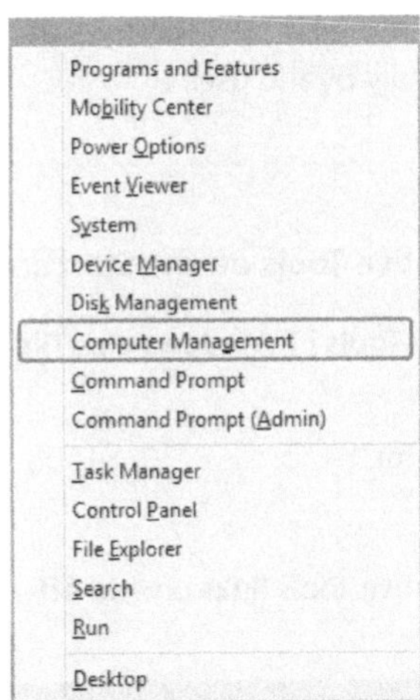

Figure 1-5 The Win X menu appears in the bottom left of the screen and is not customizable, ensuring that the available options are always in the same place.

The Administration menu contains links to the common management tools in Windows in addition to some features such as the Command Prompt (also with a separate Admin link because you cannot right-click in this menu) and the Run dialog box.

Though the Win X menu is locked by default to prevent software packages from plugging into it and using it as a surrogate Start menu, some third-party packages do exist that allow you to customize the menu, though I wouldn't necessarily recommend doing this. You can find the menu's main settings and links in File Explorer. Go to C:\Users\Your user name\AppData\Local\Microsoft\Windows\WinX. (Note that on the View tab on the ribbon in File Explorer, you need to select the Show Hidden Items check box to display the AppData folder.) In the WinX folder, you have folders called Group1, Group2, and so on, each of which represents an item group in the menu (see Figure 1-6). Item groups are delineated by a horizontal line.

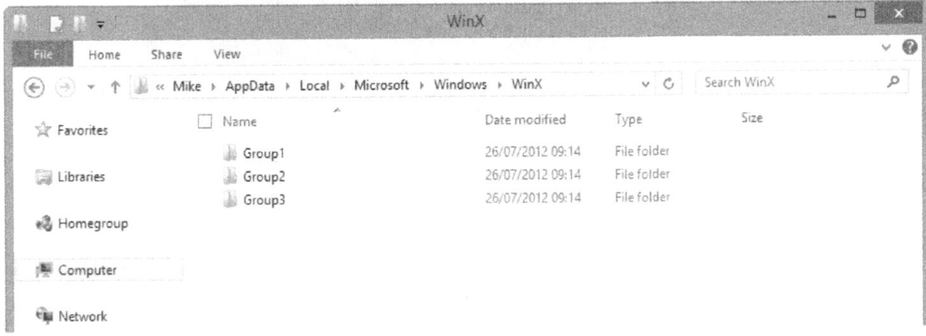

Figure 1-6 Modify the Administrator menu options.

Some software exists to allow you to customize this menu, but security that Microsoft has introduced prevents it from being changed manually by the user.

INSIDE OUT Displaying the Administrative Tools on the Start screen

If you want, you can show all the Administrative Tools in Windows 8 as Tiles on the Start screen. To do this, follow these instructions:

1. **On the Start screen, click the Settings charm.**
2. **In the upper-right screen, click Tiles.**

   An option appears to turn the Administrative Tools links on and off, as shown in Figure 1-7.

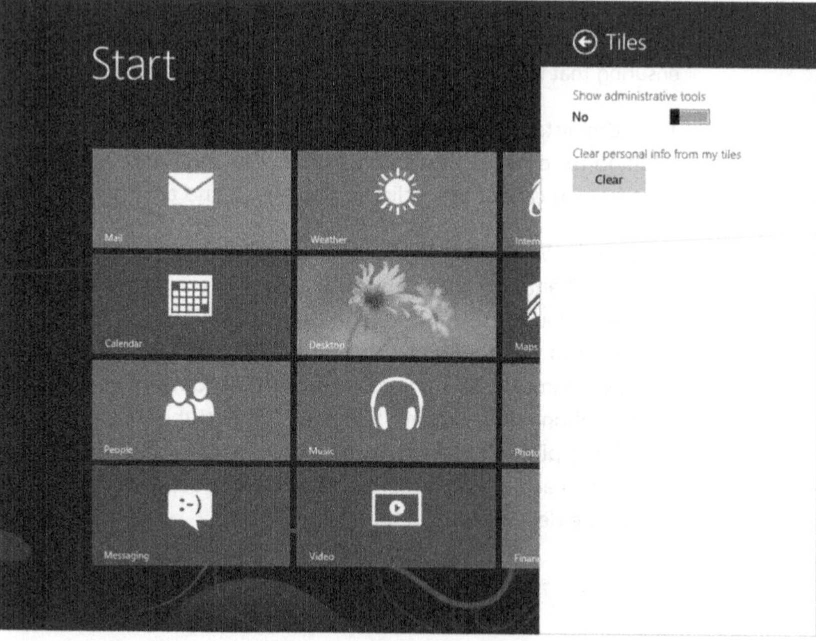

Figure 1-7 You can display the Administrative Tools on the Start screen.

Searching in Windows 8

The Search feature in Windows 8 is very easy to use. You can access Search in several ways: from the Administration menu; by clicking the Search charm; or by opening the Start screen, which you can do at any time by pressing the Windows logo key on your keyboard and then typing your search query. I find this last approach to be the easiest.

To display search results automatically, start typing while on the Start screen. Results are separated into three categories—Apps, Settings, and Files—and you can see the categories in the upper-right area of the Search bar. When you are troubleshooting and optimizing Windows 8, you most often will want to click Settings in the upper right of the search results screen to display all the Settings results.

INSIDE OUT Search in File Explorer

The search box in File Explorer prioritizes content according to the current view you are in. If you are in the Administrative Tools view, for example, and execute a search, the search results prioritize results to show tools matching criteria in Administrative Tools.

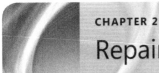

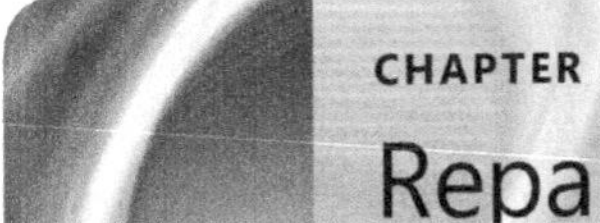

CHAPTER 2

Repairing Common Issues in Windows 8

Unless you're repairing an earlier computer and charge by the hour, time is of the essence when troubleshooting and repairing a problem. IT Support personnel typically spend no longer than half an hour troubleshooting before giving up and reimaging the machine. Repairing a computer is always the better option, however, because settings, updates, and software will need changing and configuring after an image is restored. Thus, in this chapter, I show you how you can use just half an hour of your time (or less) to repair problems that range from system instabilities to an unresponsive system that results in the blue screen (see Figure 2-1).

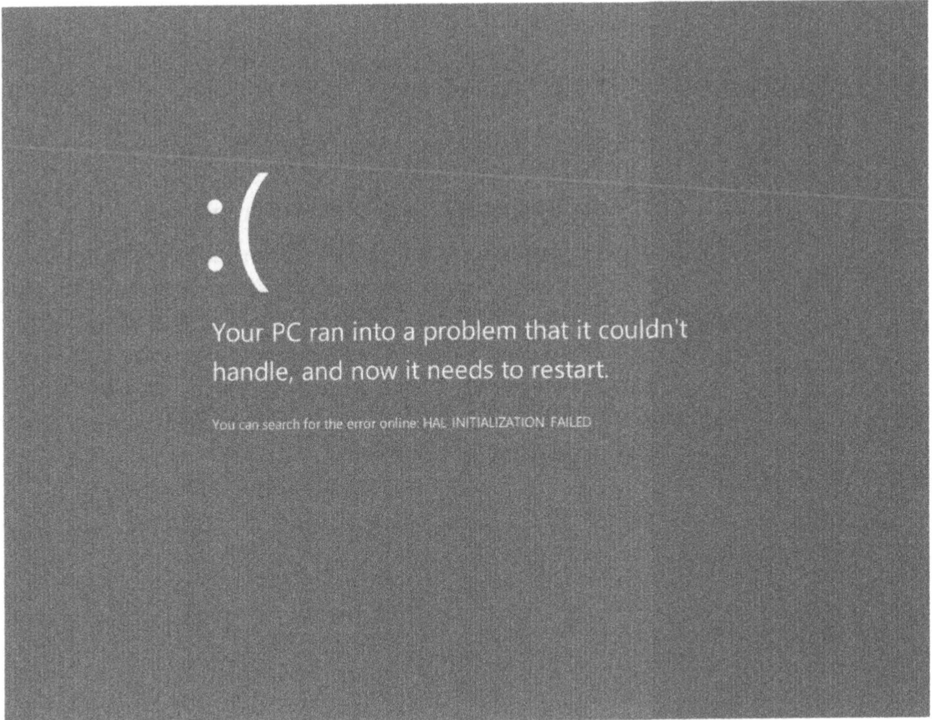

Figure 2-1 The blue screen lets you know that the system is not responding.

Windows is one of the most widely supported computing platforms available. Many programs, apps, peripherals, and pieces of internal (and external) hardware exist for Windows. This openness is a significant strength, but sometimes the operating system interacts with third-party software and hardware in unpredictable ways. When Windows does act unexpectedly, how do you get it back up and running just as it was before, without the issues, as quickly as possible? This is the single question that PC enthusiasts and IT professionals have asked me most since I wrote *Troubleshooting Windows 7 Inside Out* (Microsoft Press, 2010). As a result, I am starting this book by answering that question.

The most common problems that arise in Windows are usually the quickest and easiest to fix, and I review some of them here to help you become familiar with them, though in Chapter 11, "Troubleshooting Windows 8 Issues," I cover many more. These problems are often caused by the software you install and the hardware you plug into your computer—although Microsoft might understand how to make things work seamlessly with Windows, third-party hardware and software companies might not have the same level of knowledge, or worse, for reasons of cost cutting or expediency, might not really care. You might experience problems with the following:

- Starting the computer
- Security
- Configuration

In this chapter, I discuss how you can quickly address issues for each of these.

INSIDE OUT

Windows RT and common problems

Third-party products and some software you download from Windows Update can cause issues if the code has been written poorly, such as a badly designed app or hardware driver. Even Windows RT isn't completely immune, despite most tablets not supporting external hardware and the operating system supporting only new apps. ARM processors are new to Windows computers. Until recently, they were used primarily for smartphones and tablets running Apple iOS and the Google Android operating system. ARM processors are incompatible with the Intel chips found in desktop PCs, which is why a separate version of Windows 8 has been released for them.

Determining What's Changed

The first question to ask yourself if you encounter a problem is, "What's changed?" For example, if your computer has been stable every day for the last three weeks, performing the same tasks in the same way, yet you are encountering an issue, some aspect of your system has possibly changed to cause it. Your first job is to diagnose what that change is. Ask yourself these questions:

- Have I just performed a Windows Update? (This should always be the first question.)
- Have I installed new hardware?
- Have I installed new software?
- Have I updated the driver for a hardware device?
- Have I updated any of my software?
- Am I using two software applications at the same time in a way I don't normally use them?
- Am I trying to perform several complex jobs at the same time?
- Have I experienced an interruption to the power supply recently?
- Have I been eating or drinking at the computer?
- Has anybody else used my computer?

If you continue with this list, you eventually get to "Did I remember to plug it in?" and "Is there a power outage in my neighborhood?" At this point, you reach the oldest question in technical support: "Have I tried turning it off and on again?" You might be amazed at just how often restarting the computer fixes problems. A simple restart fixes many problems because human error is often the issue. When you restart a computer, you're likely no longer doing whatever it was you were doing before. Any software program you were running will probably close; any hardware you were using will probably be inactive; and you are effectively starting with a clean slate.

Sometimes, however, an issue will cause a lasting impact on the computer, hardware drivers, software, or the operating system, and after you restart, something will go wrong—Windows will either work in unexpected ways when you try to use it, or in the worst case, not load. This is a very common complaint to IT departments, so it's a good place to start the discussion.

Fixing Common Startup Problems

The operating system has a utility called Startup Repair, which the operating system uses to attempt to fix itself, and it is often successful. If you can't start your copy of Windows 8, try restarting your computer a few times; Startup Repair should automatically run.

The Startup Repair utility sits on a hidden system partition and is created when Windows 8 is first installed. It will run a series of checks on the components that start the operating system and reset everything to its default configuration.

If somebody calls you to say that his or her computer won't start, ask that user how many times he or she has tried to start it. Usually you need to attempt to start your computer three times before Startup Repair runs.

If Startup Repair doesn't start, you will need to enter the Startup Repair options manually. You access these options from the boot options menu. To open this menu, press F8 when you start the computer, right after the BIOS or Unified Extensible Firmware Interface (UEFI) screen appears. A message appears on your computer screen (although you might not see it on a new computer) informing you that the software on the motherboard knows how to get the hardware and the operating system talking to each other and is working.

INSIDE OUT Windows Fast Start and the boot options menu

Unless you have a dual-boot system on your computer, you might find it challenging to get the boot options menu to appear. Thus, it is always wise to create a recovery drive or a system repair disc, and I will show you how to create these in Chapter 6, "Optimizing Backup and Restore."

You have two other ways to access the startup options, shown in Figure 2-2, if you are not able to press F8 or Shift+F8 in time (pressing F8 or Shift+F8 accesses the boot options menu):

- Hold down the Shift key while clicking the Restart button to force Windows 8 to stop at the boot options menu when it restarts.
- Open PC Settings from the Charms menu. In the General section, in the Advanced Startup section, click Restart Now. When the boot options menu opens, click the Troubleshoot option.

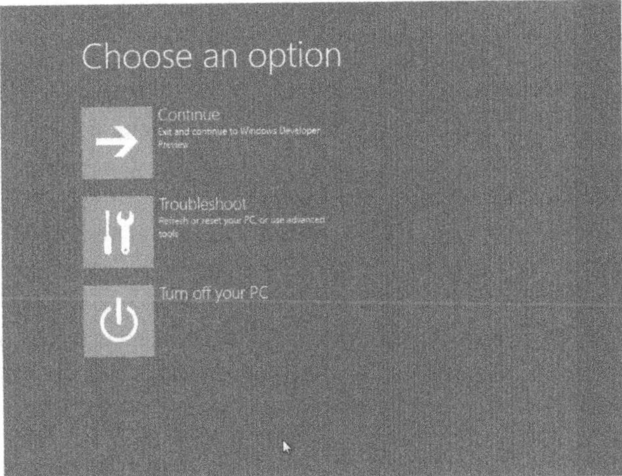

Figure 2-2 The boot options menu provides access to startup and troubleshooting options.

When you click the Troubleshoot option, the Troubleshoot window opens and presents two new features in Windows 8: Refresh Your PC and Reset Your PC (see Figure 2-3). You should use the Reset Your PC option only if you want to wipe all your user accounts, programs, apps, hardware drivers, and files off the computer. You might want to do this, for instance, if you're selling the computer or giving it to a friend.

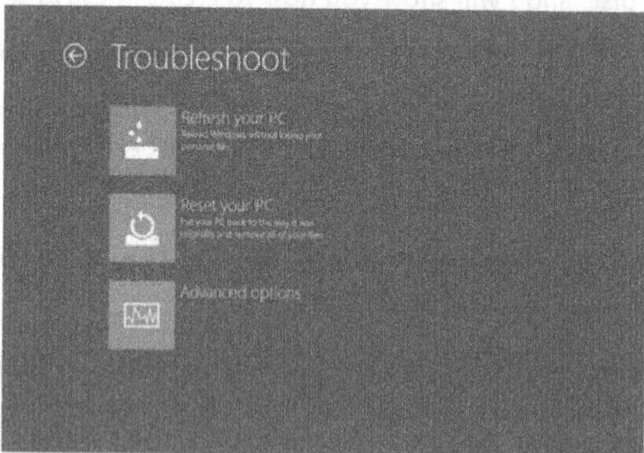

Figure 2-3 Know the difference between Refresh Your PC and Reset Your PC, which are the first options in the Troubleshoot menu.

The Refresh Your PC option is a way to restore a system image of Windows, complete with all your current settings, files, and apps intact. This option is not the same as creating a system image, however, but you can still do that, too. The main difference between Refresh Your PC and creating a system image is that to refresh a copy of Windows 8, the image required already exists without any user involvement in the form of a .wim file (Windows image file) that forms part of the Windows 8 installer and that is copied over to your hard disk as part of that install to act as a backup of the original system files. Refresh takes a snapshot of your installed programs, apps, and user accounts but not your program settings. After you restore from a refresh image, you will need to change your custom options in your software, set up email accounts, and make other changes that Refresh Your PC doesn't save.

When you create a system image of Windows 8, you are taking a snapshot of your installation, complete with programs, apps, settings, and configuration options as they existed at the time they were imaged. Restoring the system image will restore Windows 8 exactly as it was at the time the image was taken. I discuss both of these system image approaches more fully in Chapter 7, "Performing Maintenance on Windows 8."

INSIDE OUT Creating a custom refresh image

You can create a custom refresh image in Windows 8, Windows 8 Pro, and Windows 8 Enterprise by using the following simple command at the Command Prompt. (You will need to be signed in as an Administrator to run the command.)

recimg -CreateImage C:\<*Folder*>

In this case, C:\<*Folder*> is the location on your hard disk where you want the image to be located.

Remember that if you create a custom refresh image, that image will be the snapshot that is restored, including all your installed desktop software.

One of the great advantages of Refresh Your PC is that it's very easy to use. Suppose you work at a support desk and someone calls to say he can see the Start screen or desktop, but Windows 8 is malfunctioning. You can talk him through six simple keystrokes to start the process of restoring the system. This saves both of you valuable time.

Sometimes, however, you don't want to have to wait for an image to be restored using the refresh option, and using System Restore will suffice in those cases, especially if the problem occurs after a software or hardware installation, a manual driver update, or a Windows Update.

After you click Troubleshoot, choose Advanced Options, which opens the menu shown in Figure 2-4. Here, you see System Restore and the System Image Recovery option.

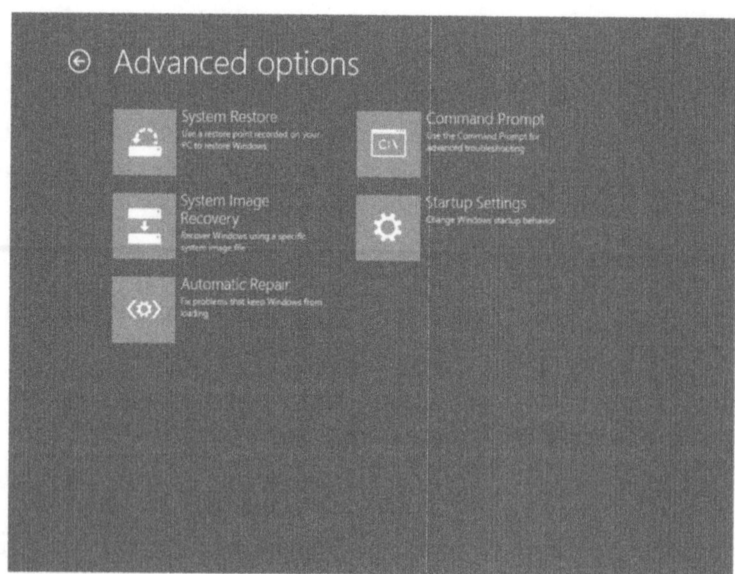

Figure 2-4 You can find System Restore in the Advanced Options menu.

If the boot system has been corrupted to prevent you from starting Windows, you must manually rebuild the system from the Command Prompt option in the Advanced Options menu. I show you how to do this in Chapter 20, "Using Advanced Repair Methods."

Refreshing Windows 8

I've talked a bit in this chapter about a new feature called Refresh Your PC that reinstalls Windows 8 while keeping all your apps, settings, and files intact. Even if you have a custom image set, refresh restores your desktop software. The following provides the step-by-step process for using refresh.

1. Open the charms by pointing to the lower right of the screen or pressing Windows logo key+C on your keyboard. The Start screen is shown in Figure 2-5.

Figure 2-5 The Start screen displays charms on the right edge of the screen.

2. Click the Settings charm.

3. In the pane that appears, at the lower right corner, click the Change PC Settings option, which is shown in Figure 2-6.

   The PC Settings screen appears.

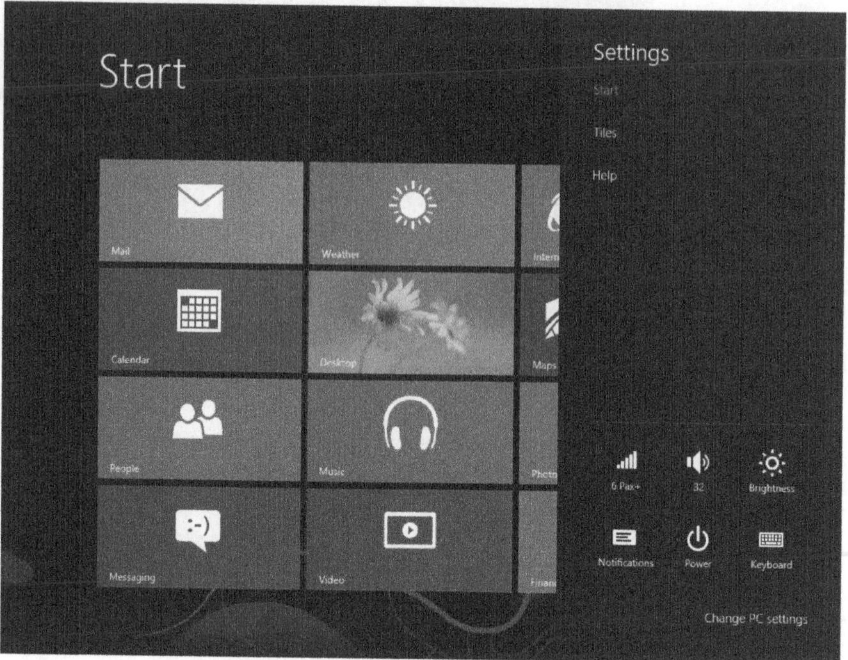

Figure 2-6 Clicking the Settings charm displays the Settings pane.

4. On the left side of the PC Settings screen, shown in Figure 2-7, click General.

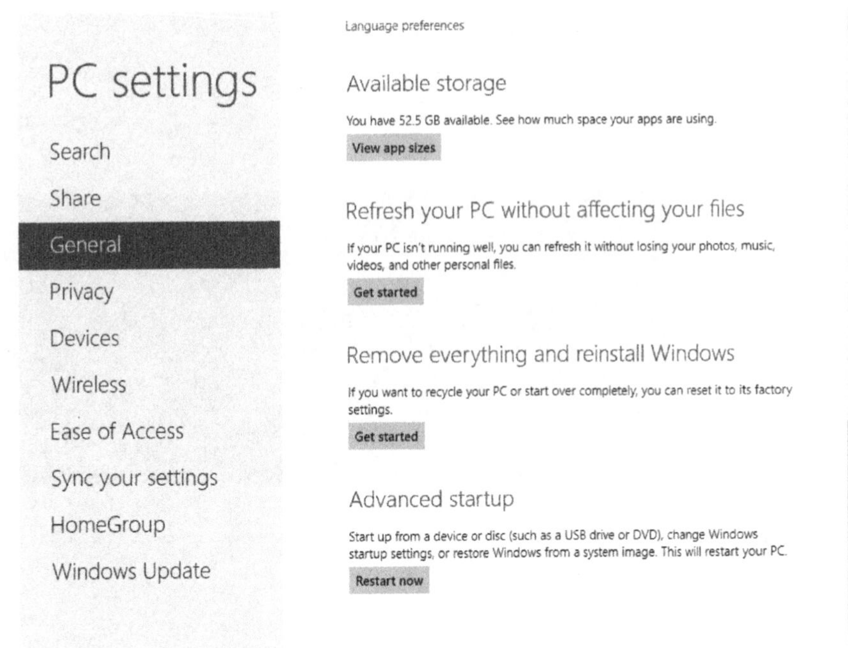

Figure 2-7 The PC Settings screen offers configuration options.

5. In the pane on the right side of the screen, in the Refresh Your PC Without Affecting Your Files section, click Get Started.

   The notification shown in Figure 2-8 appears, explaining what Refresh Your PC is and what it does.

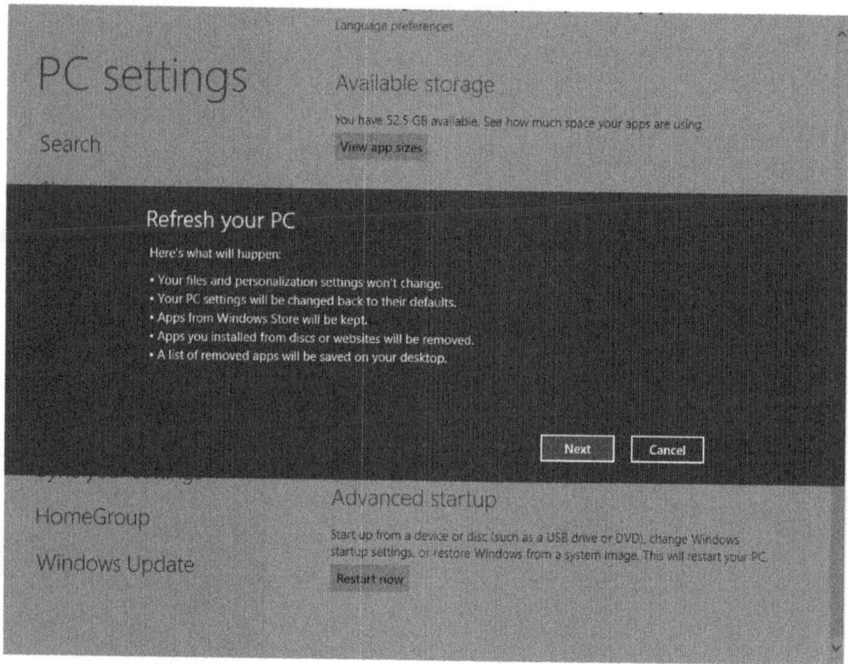

Figure 2-8 The blue Refresh Your PC bar explains what the option does.

6. To refresh the PC, click Next.

   The computer will restart to a black screen with the blue Windows logo, and you will see a percentage figure appear displaying the current status of the Refresh process.

Fixing Common Security Problems

Security problems can happen for many different reasons and can cause a wide range of issues, from inaccurate Windows reporting, to the inability of users to access their files, to encryption locking you out of your files or computer. Some security problems are caused by a malware infection, which can be tricky to resolve.

> **Note**
>
> **It is normally a good idea, when traveling with a BitLocker-encrypted laptop or tablet, to have with you, but kept separately from the device, a USB flash drive containing the encryption key or keys so that you can start your computer if an error or security problem causes Bitlocker to lock the boot loader.**

Security problems can often be resolved by refreshing the computer (as in the case of inaccurate Windows reporting) or running a System Restore—if the configuration worked well earlier, restoring those settings should work again.

Fixing Common Configuration Problems

Very often, configuration problems are caused by new software installation or updates to existing software, a new hardware device, updates to existing drivers, or automated updates. When you encounter a configuration problem, you can sometimes handle it by undoing what you've just done, that is, uninstalling software, rolling back a hardware driver (see Chapter 11 for instructions on how to do this), or performing a System Restore again to rectify an update.

Sometimes, configuration problems manifest as USB devices that no longer work. The best way to fix this is to unplug the device and then plug it into a different USB port. This will force Windows to reload the drivers for that device.

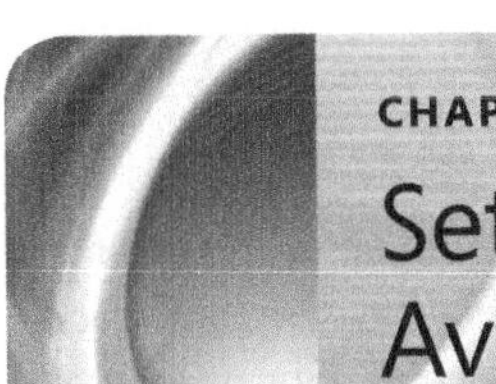

CHAPTER 3

Setup and Backup Strategies for Avoiding Major System Issues

YOU CAN EASILY PREVENT MANY PROBLEMS, but where do you start? A plethora of hardware and software packages exist for Windows 8, and predicting how these packages will interact with each other and with Windows can be challenging. Windows 8 comes with a number of troubleshooting, repair, and diagnostic tools to help you, such as System Restore, image backup (not just one type but two types, including Refresh Your PC), a reset option, file versioning, automated troubleshooters, and the Action Center. However, a good preventative strategy involves not only taking advantage of available tools but also preparing for problematic scenarios. Spending a little additional time setting up your system can save you the time, money, and resources required later on to diagnose and fix issues.

In this chapter, I show you how you can set up Windows 8 after installation to help give you the smoothest running and most robust experience you can have with the operating system. This includes tweaking and optimizing some controls within the operating system in addition to making sure everything is properly backed up at a time when all is running well.

Backing Up a Clean Install of Windows

Windows 8 and your installed software constantly make small changes and adjustments to their files and settings as you work. The more you use the computer, the more changes are made. Over time, it is possible that some of these file changes, especially those made by third-party software and services, can cause conflicts that in turn cause components to malfunction, and these conflicts are extremely difficult to undo. If you back up your copy of Windows 8 after the changes are entrenched, you preserve those problems, and you're stuck with them.

The benefit of taking time to back up a clean, unused Windows 8 installation is that when something goes wrong, your backup will be an exact copy of a fully working setup, including all of your software and settings. There will be no need to reinstall everything one piece at a time. Plus, you need to make the initial backup only once.

If you have a desktop PC and access to two or more hard disks, you're in an even better position during a system catastrophe if you split your Windows installation, files, and backups across the disks. For example, if you encounter a serious problem with your primary hard disk, you won't also lose your backup copy of Windows. You can also use two hard disks to keep identical copies of your files and data—again, just in case.

Laptops and most PC systems include only one physical disk and now commonly come with solid-state drives, which can be smaller than conventional hard disks, so you typically won't have the option of splitting your data across different physical drives. But if the idea of splitting things up interests you, you might want to purchase a separate USB external hard disk.

INSIDE OUT Divide your stuff into partitions

Think of a hard disk as one big plate for all the food at a party buffet. No matter how careful you are in laying out the food, the food will likely end up mixed together, and if somebody spills the garlic mayonnaise, it'll go over everything.

What you really need are different plates to separate the food. If you use one long plate that's split into several compartments, you can put a different treat in each space, and these compartments will help keep the garlic mayonnaise off the chocolate profiteroles.

It's a similar situation with computer hard disks. You can split your hard disk into partitions; for example, one for Windows 8, a second for your files and data, and a third for backups, including a backup of your Windows 8 installation (see Figure 3-1). Splitting them between partitions keeps them safe from system, driver, or software errors that can render your Windows 8 installation unusable.

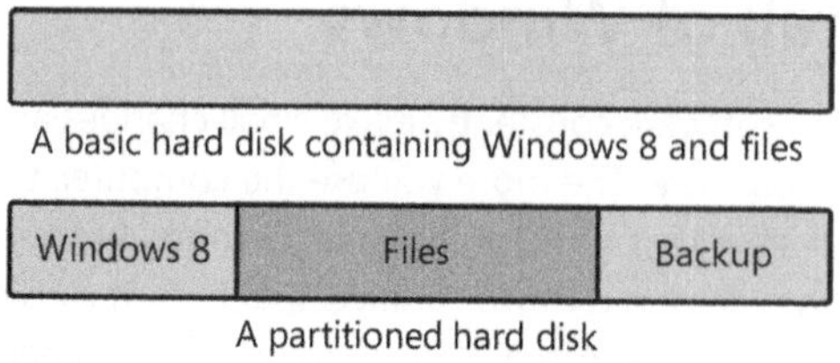

Figure 3-1 Split your hard disk into partitions for safety.

Performing a Clean Install or Upgrading

Whenever a new version of Windows is released, one of your biggest questions is whether to format the hard disk and start with a clean installation, or upgrade the existing copy of Windows in which you already have all your software, drivers, and files working. I always recommend performing a format of the hard drive and a clean install of the new operating system.

CAUTION!

Whenever you perform a clean install or especially an upgrade of Windows, you must first ensure that you have a complete and up-to-date backup of all your files, data, and documents.

Performing a Clean Install of Windows 8

If you are upgrading from Windows 7 or Windows Vista, I suggest you delete the partition that Windows resides on and the 100-megabyte (MB) System Reserved partition that goes with Windows 7 and Windows Vista, because you can encounter backup and restore problems caused by the System Reserved partition.

It is wise to delete the partition of your previous installation and the System Reserved partition because subtle changes are made to the Windows boot system with each incarnation of the operating system. One of the biggest changes is a modified boot system, which now contains a System Reserved partition of 350 MB—significantly larger than the 100-MB System Reserved partition used by Windows 7. This increased size is required to store all the boot and system rescue files required by Windows 8.

Note

If you have multiple hard disks installed in the computer, it is always wise to open the case and physically unplug all but the primary hard disk. This ensures that the System Reserved partition and Windows 8 are always on the same drive. If they end up on separate drives, and you remove the drive containing the system partition, you will always prevent Windows 8 from starting. After Windows 8 is installed, you can turn off your computer and plug the second drive back in.

INSIDE OUT **Wiping and re-creating the Windows 8 System Reserved partitions when installing**

When you install Windows 8 and choose a Custom Installation, you will be asked on what physical hard disk you want to install the operating system (see Figure 3-2). If you are wiping out a previous Windows installation, I recommend using the Drive Options to delete both the Windows partition *and* the 100-MB System Reserved partition, if you have one.

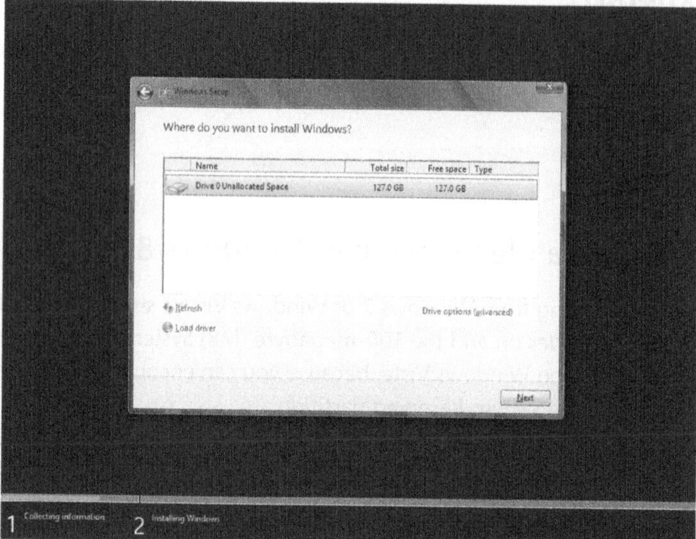

Figure 3-2 This is what a hard disk looks like when all partitions are deleted.

Then you can create a new Windows partition on this disk, and the Windows 8 installer will create a new System Reserved partition.

Upgrading to Windows 8 from Windows 7, Windows Vista, or Windows XP

If you do upgrade from an earlier version of Windows, what can you take with you from your previous Windows installation—files, user accounts, settings, or even programs? For the upgrade to Windows 8, you can transfer only specific aspects, so you might find that if you are upgrading from Windows Vista, for example, it is more advantageous to do a clean installation because you can't migrate your software. Table 3-1 presents a synopsis of what can be upgraded.

Table 3-1 **Items That You Can Upgrade to Windows 8**

	When Upgrading From...		
You Can Transfer	**Windows 7**	**Windows Vista**	**Windows XP**
Applications	Yes	No	No
Windows settings	Yes	Yes	No
User accounts and files	Yes	Yes	Yes

Note

Many differences exist between the 32-bit (x86) and 64-bit (x64), and it is important to note that the Windows Installer will not allow you to move from an x64 operating system to an x86 operating system or vice-versa.

When you upgrade, some aspects of the system will work as expected, but some may not. The Windows 8 Upgrade Advisor runs automatically and informs you of any potential problems and incompatibilities with your software and hardware. If you have Microsoft Security Essentials installed, you will need to uninstall it before upgrading, because antivirus is built in to Windows 8, and Security Essentials won't work with Windows Defender. If software worked in Windows 7, it has a great chance of working in Windows 8 just as well, or in a few cases (as I've found myself), even better! It is always a good idea to refer to the Upgrade Advisor that appears during the upgrade process, because it will inform you of what software and drivers on your computer can be migrated successfully, what might need to be uninstalled first, and what might need upgrading afterwards.

Determining Partition Size

The size of your hard disk and how you intend to use your computer will determine how big you should make your partitions. I suggest that you have, at a minimum, a three-partition structure: one for Windows 8, one for files, and one for a backup copy of Windows.

You may want to make your backup partition slightly larger than your Windows 8 partition; doing so will give you some extra space to keep a copy of essential hardware drivers and software. However, if you are creating both the Windows 8 and backup partitions before installing the operating system, at which point you won't know exactly how big your installation will be, you can either just store your backup on a separate files installation or make your backup installation the same size as your Windows 8 installation.

> **Note**
>
> **If you want to keep a custom system image and a custom refresh image (which I recommend), your backup partition will need to be twice the size of your Windows 8 installation.**

You can use Table 3-2 as a guide for how large your Windows 8 partition should be. Please note these figures are suggestions only. If you use development software (web, programming, or design), you might find you will need more space for your programs.

Table 3-2 **Recommended Windows 8 Partition Sizes for Various Usage Scenarios**

PC Usage	Windows 8 Partition Size	Entry in Partition Size Box
Business user	30 gigabyte (GB)	30720
Light home user	30 GB–50 GB	30720–51200
Power user	50 GB–200 GB	51200–204800
Developer	100 GB	102400
Video/photo editor	100 GB–200 GB	102400–204800
Gamer	100 GB–300 GB	102400–307200

So what do you do about creating partitions for your files and the Windows image backup? Practically, if you have more than one physical hard disk in your computer, always put the image backup on the secondary drive and consider putting the files there also. This ensures that if the hard disk containing Windows fails, you don't lose your files or backup, and if the disk containing the files and backup fails, you still have a working copy of Windows.

However, if you are on a single-disk system—which is much more likely given that most new Windows 8 computers are all-in-one desktops, laptops, or tablets that have less interior space in the case and, as such, less configurability—your backup would most likely be kept on the same partition you create for file and data storage.

This approach is generally fine on a desktop or all-in-one computer that ships with a hard disk of 1 terabyte (TB) or more, but what if you are installing Windows 8 on an Ultrabook or a tablet that comes with only a 128-GB solid-state drive? In this circumstance, I suggest skipping the backup partition and instead creating a backup image on a DVD, or better still, on an external USB flash drive.

INSIDE OUT **Deleting the OEM restore partition**

Computer manufacturers, known as original equipment manufacturers (OEMs), often put a hidden restore partition on your computer. This could contain, for example, a copy of Windows 7 or Windows Vista. If you are performing a clean installation of Windows 8 and don't mind losing the earlier version of Windows, which frankly will be of little use to you from this point on anyway, you can delete this backup partition by using the Windows Installer.

What to Do When Windows 8 Is Installed

After Windows 8 is installed, you need to complete the following important tasks before you install all your software and use the operating system:

- Windows 8 is the first version of Windows that comes with antivirus protection. If you prefer using antivirus software different from Windows Defender, you should install this protection first.
- Install only software and Windows Store apps you will definitely use regularly. Avoid loading software you will use only rarely or might not use at all; when you are ready to use it, you might find that it's been upgraded anyway.
- Try to avoid installing shareware or trial version software. Although many amateur software authors do write some excellent applications, that software rarely goes through the same quality control process as commercial packages. Shareware and similar software can cause problems on a PC.
- Update all the installed software to get any upgrades. This is especially important for Adobe Acrobat Reader, because PDF files are often used to hide viruses.
- Activate your software and enter the required product keys to keep the software from becoming unusable if you need to restore it from a backup.

For a new installation of Windows 8, I recommend the following steps:

1. Ensure that Windows 8 is activated. If you don't activate Windows 8, it might become inoperable if you at some point restore from a backup. To activate Windows 8 from Control Panel, click System And Security, and then click System. The option to activate Windows 8 is at the bottom of the window.

2. Run Windows Update to make sure you have the latest updates to the operating system. You can access Windows Update on the Start screen or the PC Settings screen. You may have to run Windows Update several times, because some updates will not appear in Windows Update until other previous updates are installed.

   Windows will inform you that your computer needs to be restarted after updating. Modify Windows 8 settings to your preferences (regional settings, for example). Read the following section for details about how to do this.

CAUTION!

It's important not to use the computer very much while getting Windows 8 ready to create a system image backup. By keeping your activity to a minimum, you ensure that software that may change system files, or that performs actions that can cause bloat or instability, don't produce problems that will be copied into your backup image.

Useful Windows 8 Settings to Change

You'll find that you don't need to tweak many settings in Windows 8, but a few tweaks will enhance the computer's performance and make the operating system run better in general. You access these settings in the desktop Control Panel, shown in Figure 3-3. On the Start screen, type the word **control** to search for it.

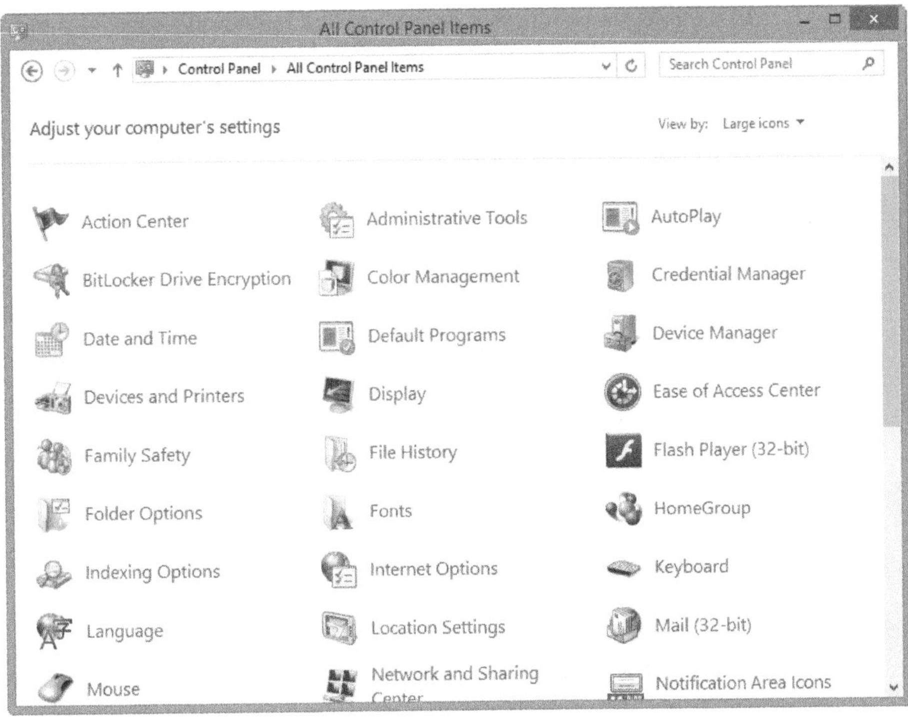

Figure 3-3 The desktop Control Panel in Windows 8 showing all icons on the Large Icons view.

Windows 8 uses a space on your hard disk drive called virtual memory to help better manage the computer's physical memory and to load programs quickly. By default, Windows manages the size of the virtual memory file (also known as the paging file), but this file can grow and shrink, ultimately slowing down access to the files and data on the hard disk.

To change the virtual memory size, follow these steps:

1. In Control Panel, click System And Security, and then click System.

   A new list of options appears.

2. Under Control Panel Home on the left side of the window, click Advanced System Settings.

3. In the System Properties dialog box, click the Advanced tab, as shown in Figure 3-4.

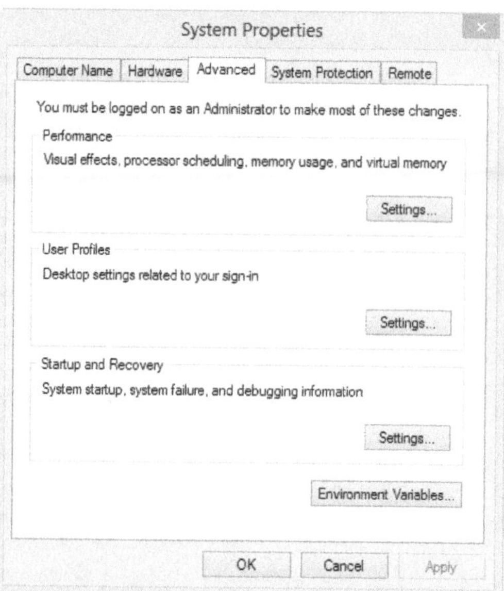

Figure 3-4 The Advanced tab in the System Properties dialog box in Control Panel.

4. In the Performance section, click Settings to open the Performance Options dialog box.

5. In the Performance Options dialog box, click the Advanced tab, and then click Change.

   The Virtual Memory dialog box appears, in which you can change the virtual memory settings (see Figure 3-5).

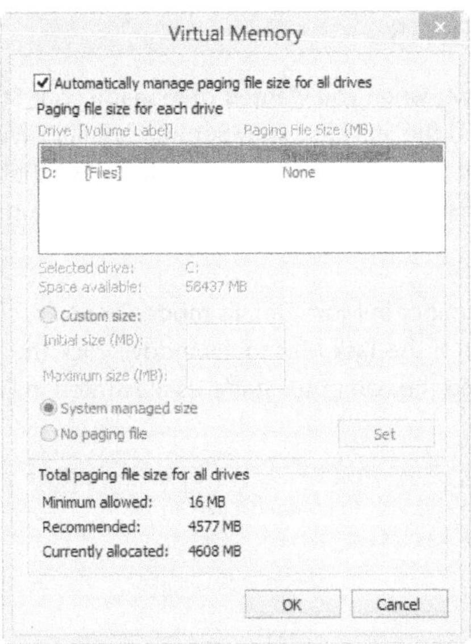

Figure 3-5 Set the virtual memory page file size in the Virtual Memory dialog box.

Clearing the Automatically Manage Paging File Size For All Drives check box lets you select the Custom Size option. When you select Custom Size, you instruct Windows to keep this paging file the same size all the time, which can help keep the speed with which you access your files fast by ensuring the file size is static, preventing fragmentation of the hard disk file.

The recommended amount of disk space is displayed toward the bottom of the Virtual Memory dialog box (4577 MB in the example in Figure 3-5). Enter the recommended paging file size for your computer in both the Initial Size (MB) box and Maximum Size (MB) box, click Set, and then click OK to close the dialog box.

In Control Panel, you can also change regional and language settings and get access to Device Manager to check that the drivers for all of your hardware are installed. You can see in Device Manager whether a driver is not installed or incorrectly installed, because the device will be listed with a red warning cross or a yellow warning triangle next to its icon.

Managing Startup Programs

In previous versions of Windows, when you wanted to manage your Startup programs, you launched MSConfig and clicked the Startup tab. MSConfig is still in Windows 8, but it no longer manages programs that run when the computer starts. For that, you use Task Manager. Task Manager allows users to easily manage which programs run when they start their computers.

You'll want to run the Task Manager in More Details mode. To do so, click the More Details button in the lower-left corner of the Task Manager window. Click the Startup tab to display a list of software that runs when the computer starts, as illustrated in Figure 3-6.

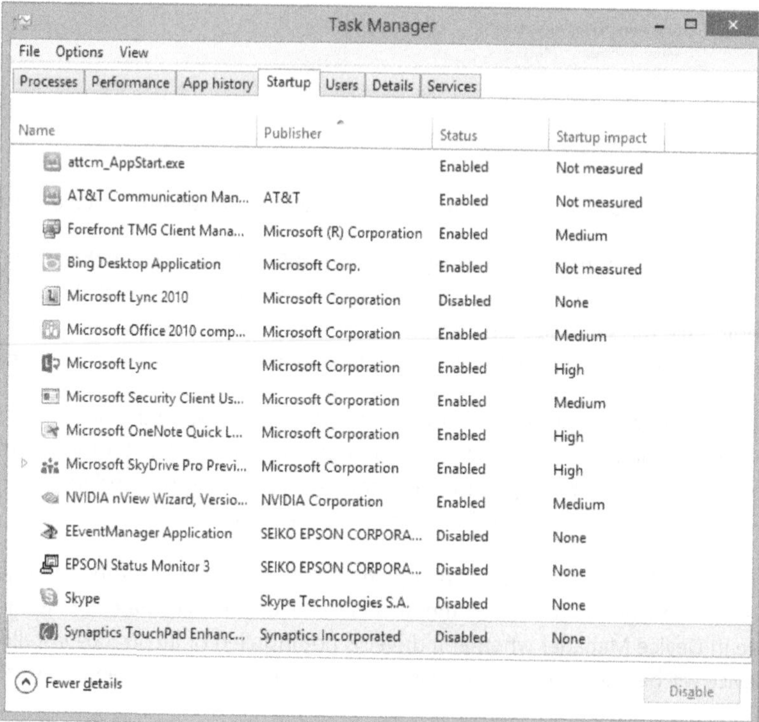

Figure 3-6 The improved Task Manager in Windows 8 now manages Startup software.

When you want to disable a program, click it, and then in the lower-right corner of the window, click Disable. On this tab, take note of the new Startup Impact column, which helps you make more informed decisions about what to disable and what to leave enabled because it indicates how long each program will need to load when Windows first starts.

Moving Files to Their Own Partition

To ensure that you do not lose all your files in the event that Windows becomes corrupt, keep your important files and documents in a partition that is separate from the partition your copy of Windows resides on. (I show you how to recover files from a failed Windows installation in Part IV of this book, "Disaster Recovery.")

You have several options for moving your files and data away from the partition with Windows 8. You can change all the default store folders for libraries, one at a time, but this can be an arduous task. Here's a much more efficient way to do it:

1. Open File Explorer.
2. On the left side of the address bar, click the folder arrow, as depicted in Figure 3-7.

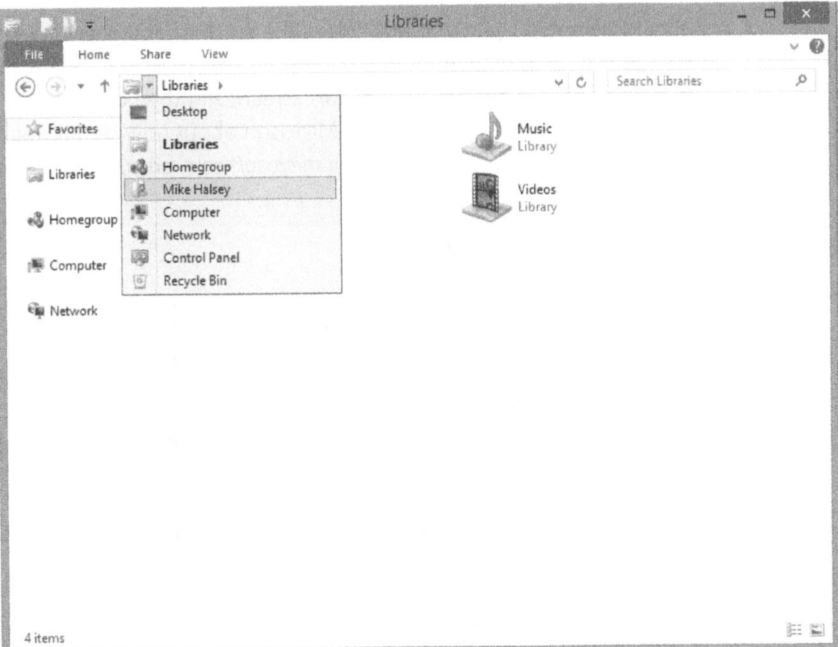

Figure 3-7 Click the folder arrow to begin the process of moving your files to a new partition.

3. On the drop-down menu that appears, click your user name.

4. Select your user folders. I always recommend Downloads, Favorites, My Documents, My Music, My Pictures, and My Videos.
5. On the Home tab of the ribbon in the Clipboard group, click Cut.
6. Go to the hard disk or partition on which you want the user folders stored.
7. On the Home tab, in the Clipboard group, click Paste.

CAUTION!

Be sure to click Cut and not Copy in step 5. The Copy command does not move the files; it only duplicates them.

It should be noted that I'm listing this as the quickest and easiest way to move your user files. This will remove them from the indexing system in Windows 8, however, so you should search for indexing options on the Start screen, and then click Modify to add them back into the Index. For information from Microsoft about how best to manage libraries, you can read a Microsoft FAQ at *http://technet.microsoft.com/en-us/library/ee449413(v=ws.10).aspx.*

Backing Up Windows 8

In Windows 8, you have two options for creating an image backup: you can create a custom refresh image, discussed in Chapter 1, "Finding Your Way Around Windows 8"; or you can create a full image backup, which I would recommend doing. If Windows stops responding and you can't load the refresh option from the boot loader, you will need a full image containing both Windows 8 and the boot loader that you can reinstall from a USB flash drive or from a DVD startup repair disc.

You can find the image backup creation tool by following these steps:.

1. Show all Control Panel items by opening Control Panel *and* changing the View By setting to Large Icons or Small Icons.

2. Click Windows 7 File Recovery to open the Windows 7 File Recovery window (see Figure 3-8).

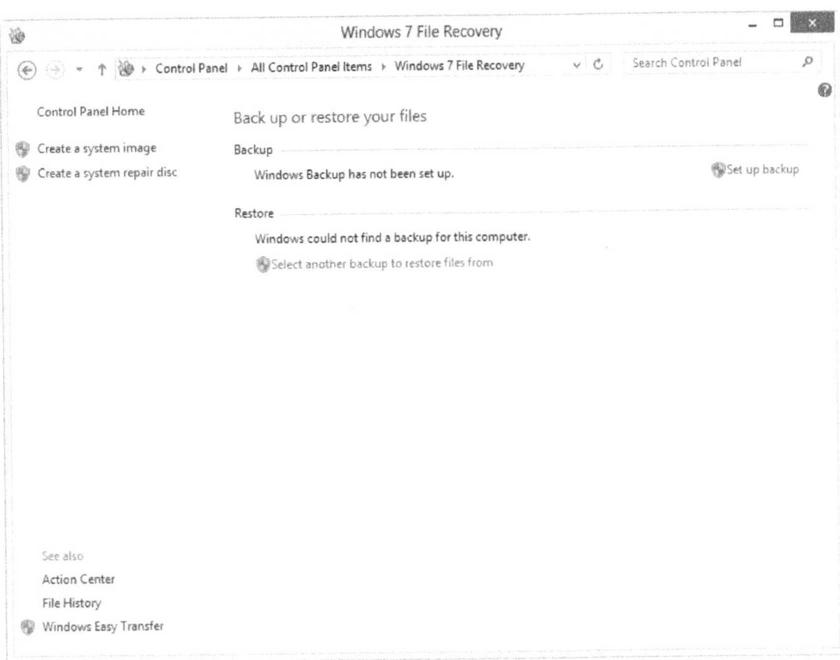

Figure 3-8 Use Windows 7 File Recovery to create a full image backup.

3. In the pane on the left side of the window, click Create A System Image.

4. In the Create A System Image dialog box, on the Where Do You Want To Save The Backup page, select the location where you want to store your Windows image backup, as shown in Figure 3-9, and then click Next.

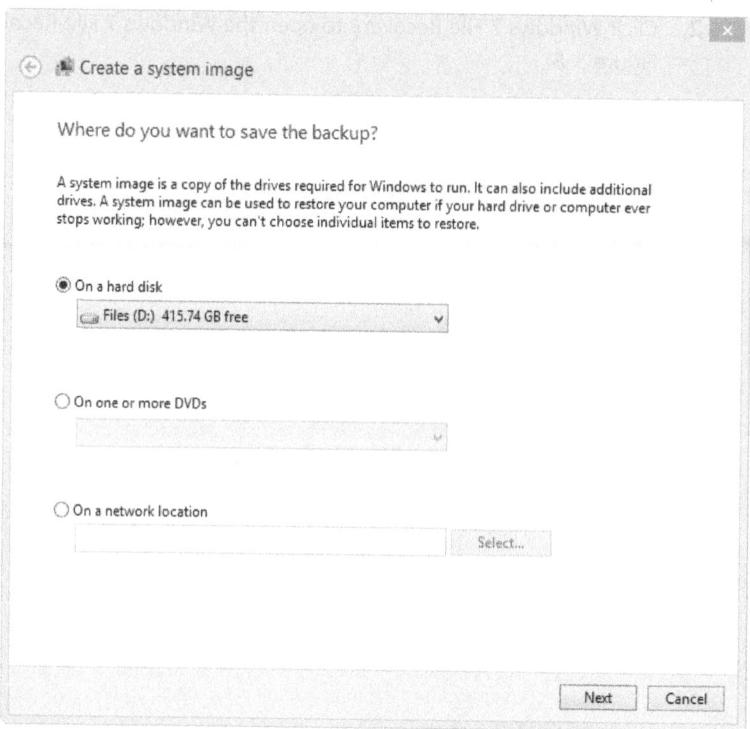

Figure 3-9 Create a system image backup in this dialog box.

Windows 8 automatically selects your Windows and System Reserved partitions for backup.

5. Click Next again to start the backup process.

INSIDE OUT Network backup precautions

Don't back up your operating system to a network location if your computer connects to the network only via wireless network, because you will be unable to see the backup if you need to restore it. Only do a network backup if you connect via a physical network cable. This is because you restore the image from the boot system of the installation DVD, and Wi-Fi networks cannot be seen by Windows in this mode.

Windows 8 is now backed up, although I would advise you to create a refresh image as well. The refresh image can usually be stored on your Files partition if no space exists for it on your Backup partition. If you have a serious problem with Windows 8, you can restore the refresh image quickly and easily. I show you how to do this in Chapter 14, "Easy Ways to Repair Windows 8."

CHAPTER 4

Using the Basic Windows Utilities

The Windows 8 user interface (UI) has two main objectives: to be tablet-friendly and to simplify the user experience. The accessibility of features is one way it achieves this. PC Settings, for example, which is like a mini Control Panel, includes the options that most people need, most of the time. Most of the settings offered in PC Settings are fairly straightforward, but a couple, which are useful for maintaining and troubleshooting a healthy computer, require some explanation: Refresh Your PC and Windows Update. This chapter looks first at those Windows 8 utilities and then delves into other basic utilities available for users, such as the desktop utilities, Windows Firewall, and Windows Defender.

Refresh Your PC

Refresh Your PC can be used by a user to restore Windows 8 to a working copy while keeping files, apps, software (if a custom image has been set), and Windows settings intact. The Refresh Your PC option is located in the General section under PC Settings, as shown in Figure 4-1.

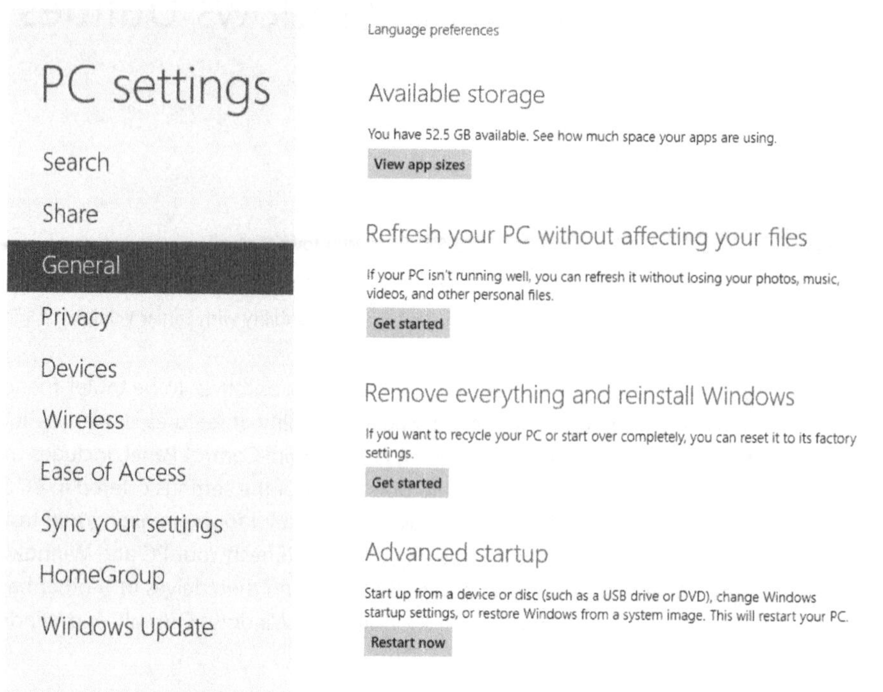

Figure 4-1 You can find the Refresh Your PC option in the General section in PC Settings.

As mentioned in Chapter 2, "Repairing Common Issues in Windows 8," Refresh Your PC doesn't take a complete, current snapshot of your working Windows installation. Although it saves all your installed desktop apps and installed Windows 8 apps, it doesn't save any of the settings for your desktop software. The effect of this is that after performing a Refresh Your PC, you have to set up your desktop apps again, including entering email account information in Microsoft Outlook or any other email client.

Refresh Your PC is an unsuitable option for any user who uses the desktop exclusively in the workplace; unless the user engages apps exclusively or most of the time, a system image backup is a better option.

Windows Update

The Windows Update option in PC Settings is enabled by default in Windows 8. All you do is click Check For Updates Now. Figure 4-2 shows this option.

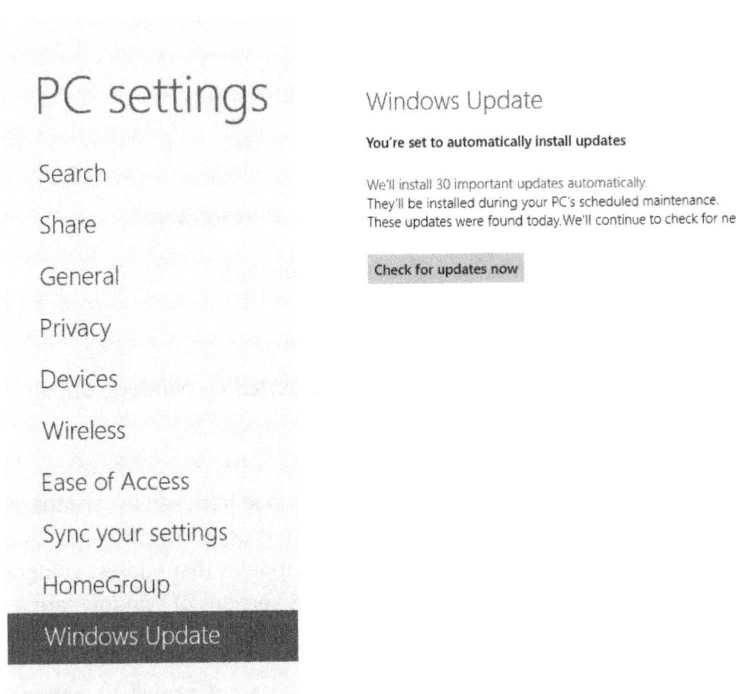

Figure 4-2 The simple-to-use Windows Update in PC Settings.

When Windows Update is set to automatically update the computer, users may not always see all the updates and upgrades available for components or software, such as those for Windows Internet Explorer or Windows Live Essentials, until these upgrades become mandatory. As a result, you may want to manually check for updates periodically, because these optional updates can provide great advantages to the Microsoft software you have installed on your computer.

Note that by the time the first service pack launches for a Windows operating system, additional security and software updates could be included as part of it. These updates address issues related to the following:

- Virus and malware attacks
- Hacking attacks
- Security vulnerabilities
- Issues found in Windows
- Incompatibilities with third-party and Microsoft software
- Updates for programs and features in Windows 8
- Updated drivers for hardware
- Updates for other Microsoft software supported by Windows Update
- Code updates for earlier versions of code

Most updates address security vulnerabilities and code from earlier versions of the Windows operating system. The Windows operating system is used worldwide, so it's a huge target for hackers who want to exploit software. Code updates that address vulnerabilities resulting from maintaining compatibility with previous versions of Windows are a large part of service packs.

For a stand-alone computer or a computer that is part of a small, unmanaged network, I recommend turning on the feature to automatically update Windows, shown in Figure 4-3. This feature can help prevent problems on your computer by automatically updating Windows components as updates become available. To access Windows Update, go to Action Center, or in Control Panel, go to System And Security.

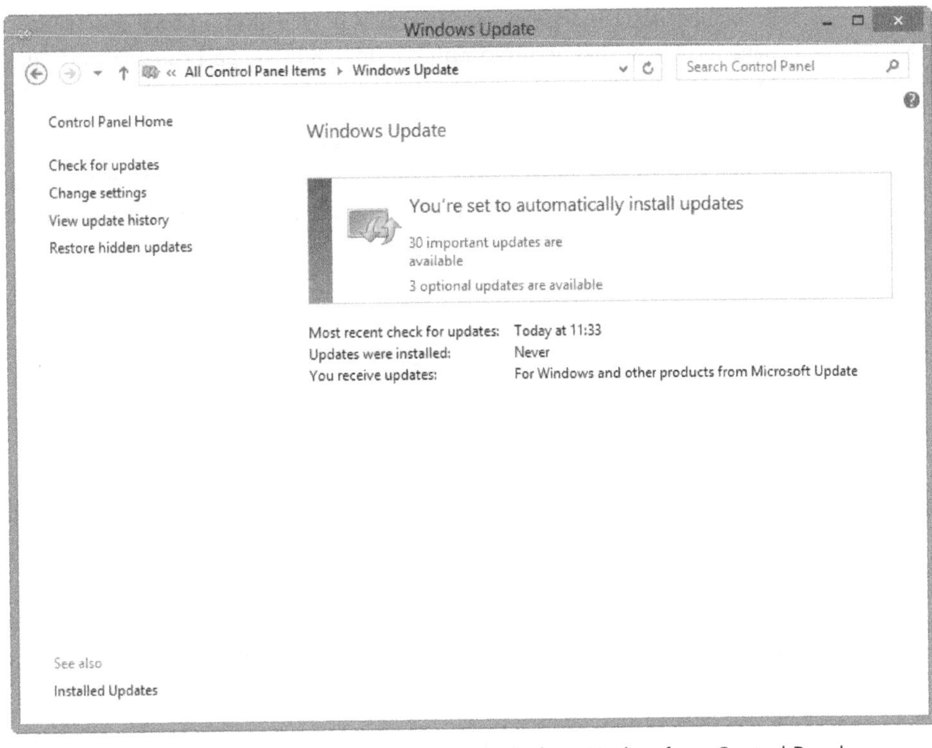

Figure 4-3 Automatically install updates by using Windows Update from Control Panel.

Desktop Utilities

From the desktop, you have many choices with respect to utilities and tools for managing, maintaining, and gaining valuable information about the status of your computer.

Action Center

Action Center is a hub for controlling essential Windows 8 features and the central location for all important diagnostic and maintenance messages from the operating system, such as messages informing you about out-of-date antivirus software or messages alerting you that updates are waiting to be installed. It is also the central place for controlling essential Windows 8 features such as the User Account Control and Network Access

Protection. You can view archived Action Center messages from the main Action Center pane; problems that occurred with Windows 8 in the past can give you clues to a solution for a current problem.

You access Action Center by clicking the Action Center icon (a white flag) on the far right of the Windows 8 taskbar on the desktop (see Figure 4-4). If any messages are pending, the white flag will appear with a red circle and a white cross. A pop-up window includes an Open Action Center link.

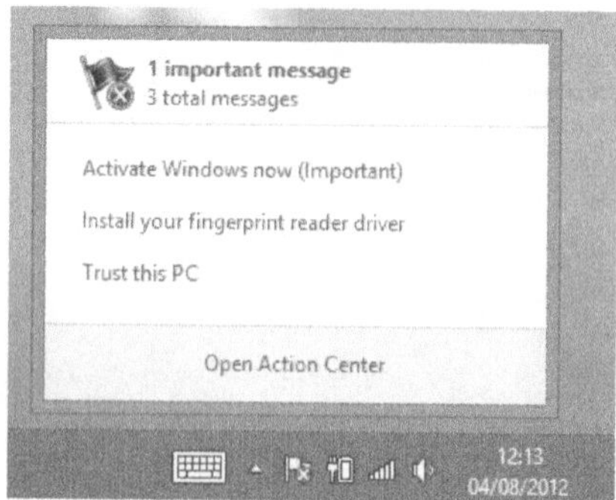

Figure 4-4 Action Center notifications on the Windows 8 desktop provide important information.

You can control the types of messages and alerts you receive from Action Center; for example, you can turn off all messages about Windows backup if you use third-party backup software. Some third-party software, especially antivirus packages, automatically add themselves to Action Center, and you can monitor that software from there.

All messages in Action Center display a colored band to their left (see Figure 4-5) that denotes the message's priority; green indicates that all is well, yellow messages signify that information is available, and red bands designate that something needs your attention.

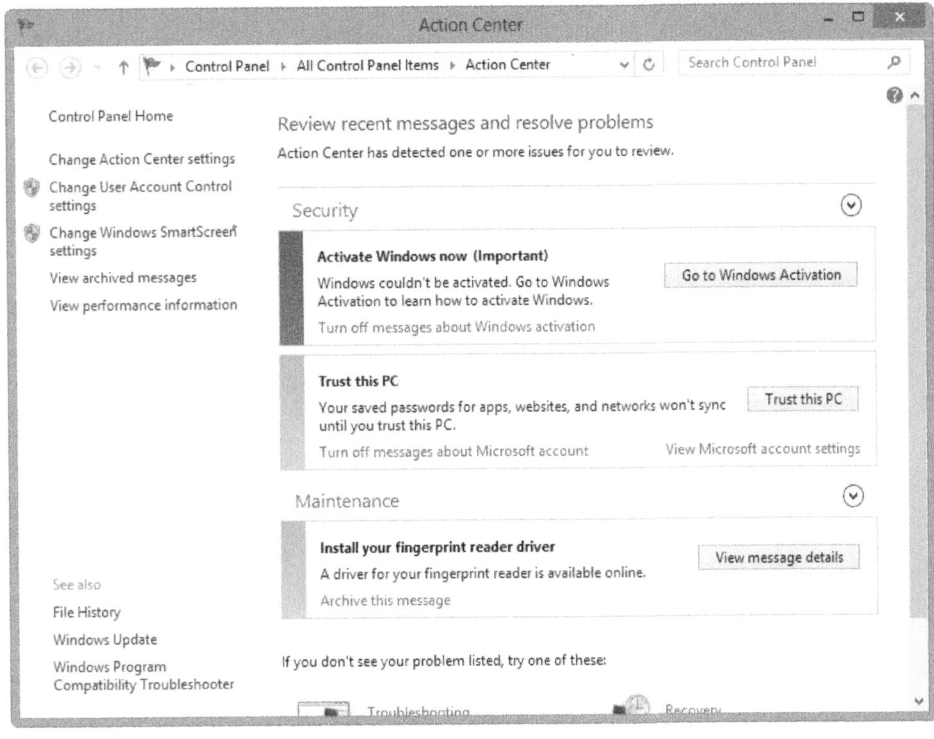

Figure 4-5 Colored bands in Action Center indicate message priority.

To control which messages appear in Action Center, in the pane on the left in the Action Center pane, click Change Action Center Settings. In Change Action Center Settings, select the items you want Windows to notify you about when problems arise, as shown in Figure 4-6.

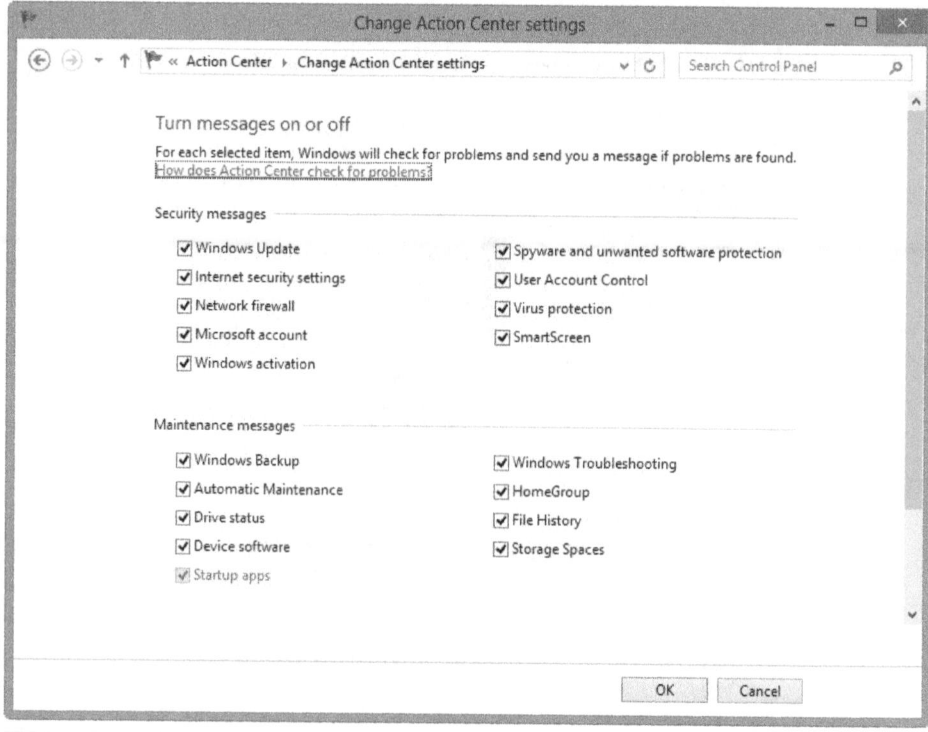

Figure 4-6 Changing Action Center settings.

Error Logs and Check For Solutions

When your operating system experiences an error, such as a program or a driver that is not responding, the operating system stores information about the errors in a log and displays the log in Action Center. In Action Center, you will see a Check For Solutions option under Maintenance. Click this option to search for a matching error log that may provide a solution in the Microsoft Solution Center, which is an online store of problems and error messages where Microsoft has help documents, documentation, and sometimes automatic fixes you can download and run. In the Maintenance section, you can also change the settings to have Windows 8 check for solutions to problems automatically and establish when and how often it checks. Sometimes, in a corporate environment, the IT department turns off these settings to conserve Internet bandwidth or to comply with its own update management policy.

View Reliability History

In Action Center, you can view the operating system's reliability history, which is a record of events that have occurred that will affect the reliability of Windows in some way. These events range from software installs to blue screens indicating the system is not responding. This information is displayed graphically to help you see the status of Windows 8 at a glance. To view this information, find the Maintenance section (see Figure 4-7), and under Check For Solutions To Problem Reports, click View Reliability History. Windows 8 tracks problems caused by software, drivers, and Windows components, and represents this information in a chart.

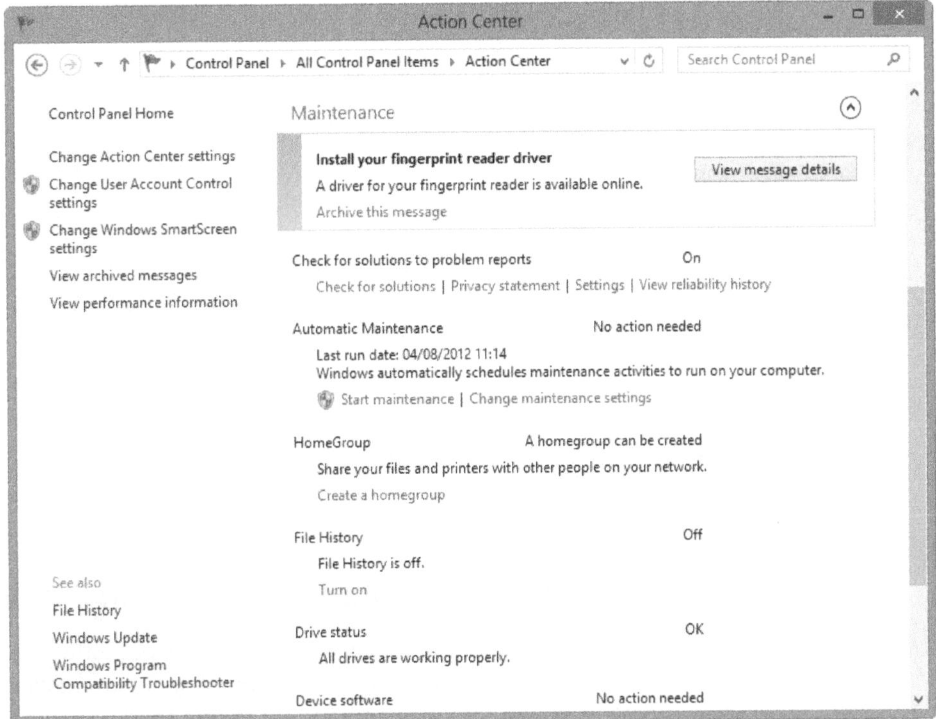

Figure 4-7 In the Maintenance section, click View Reliability History to view a graphical representation of everything from software installs to blue screen errors.

Automatic Maintenance Tool

In Action Center, the Automatic Maintenance tool (see Figure 4-8) checks for and installs software updates, security scans, and system diagnostics on a daily schedule to keep Windows 8 healthy. Performing all the tasks simultaneously also helps reduce battery drain when you are using a laptop or tablet computer. You can configure Automatic Maintenance to temporarily wake up a computer from sleep to perform these tasks (but only if the computer is plugged into an electrical outlet).

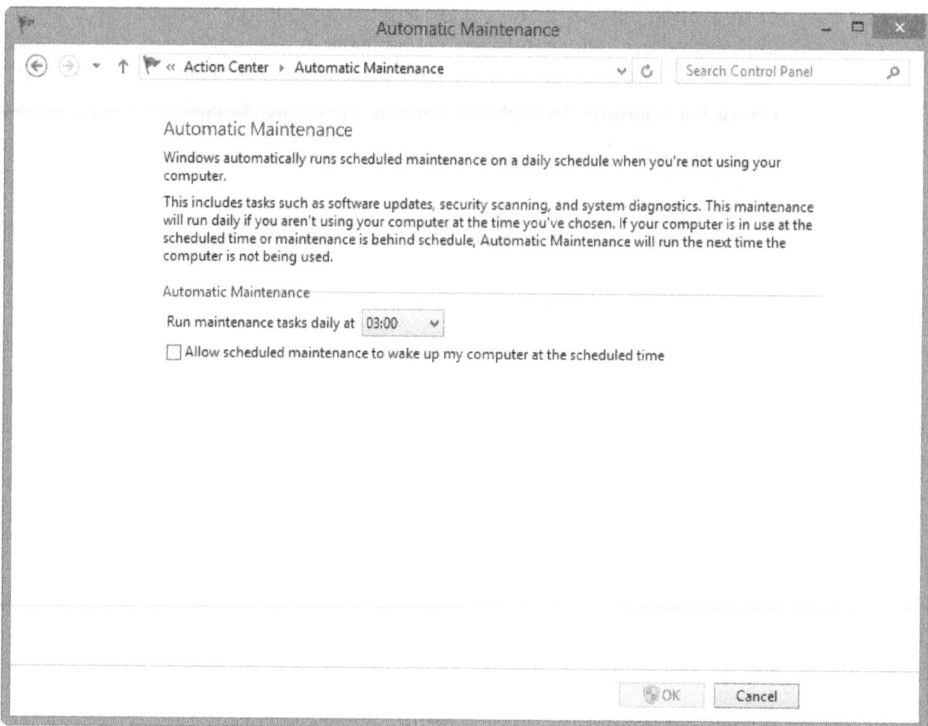

Figure 4-8 You can configure Automatic Maintenance.

Controlling Windows Update Through Group Policy

Sometimes an update introduces an incompatibility with previous software or hardware, preventing that software or hardware from working properly or making Windows 8 unstable when software runs. In a corporate environment or on a small Windows Server network with multiple users, you can disable the Windows Update service and instead use Windows Server Update Services (WSUS) or System Center Configuration Manager (SCCM) to download and test all updates before they are rolled out across the network.

You can disable Windows Update in corporate environments by using a utility called Group Policy Editor. To access Group Policy Editor, open the Start screen and search for GPEdit.msc (not case-sensitive). The Local Group Policy Editor window appears, as depicted in Figure 4-9. You can read more about Group Policy at *http://technet.microsoft.com/en-us/windowsserver/bb310732.aspx*.

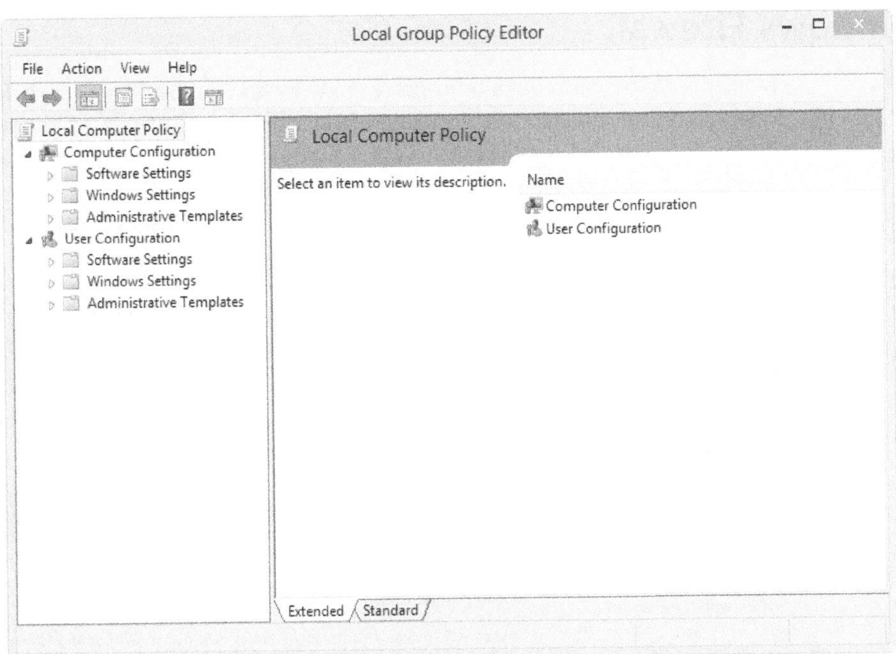

Figure 4-9 You can disable Windows Update by using Local Group Policy Editor.

INSIDE OUT Group Policy Editor availability in Windows 8

As with previous versions of Windows, the Local Group Policy Editor is available in Windows 8 Pro and Enterprise editions. It is also available in Windows RT but not in the basic Windows 8 edition.

By using the Group Policy Editor, you can independently control policies for the computer and for individual users. This is important because you want to grant systems administrators full control of the computer but limit access for other users. To control Windows Update and set the policy for all users, in the Local Group Policy Editor, click Computer Configuration, click Administrative Templates, click Windows Components, and then click Windows Update. In this window, you can configure Windows Update to stop receiving automatic updates or to receive updates only from your company's server. You also have other options that are available for controlling Windows Update, such as controlling if and when a computer will restart after updates are installed.

Windows Firewall

Many people prefer to use a third-party firewall with Windows. Third-party firewalls can offer more features and more protection than the standard Windows Firewall, but they can also be intrusive and complicated to use. For advanced computer users, the standard firewall that comes with Windows 8 is perfectly adequate; in fact, some antivirus and security suites don't include their own firewall, recognizing the effectiveness of the one that ships by default with Windows 7 and Windows 8.

Figure 4-10 shows that Windows Firewall is a two-way firewall that will block incoming and outgoing traffic, unlike the inbound-only block included in Windows XP. I recommend that you always have a firewall turned on, whether it's Windows Firewall or a third-party product. This is an essential security strategy that can prevent many types of problems and attacks on your computer.

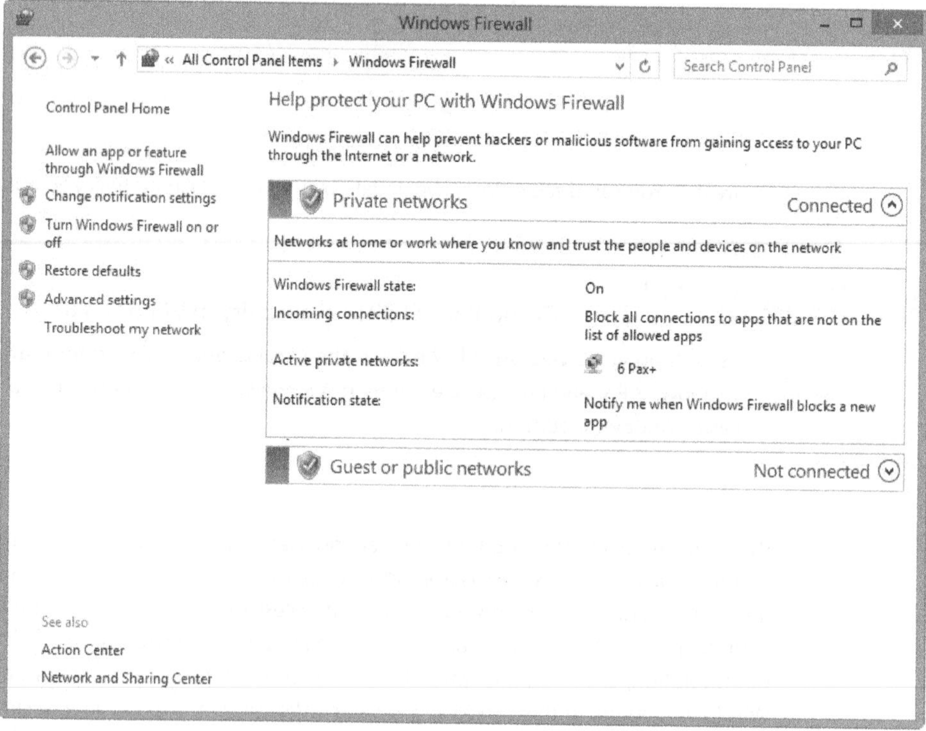

Figure 4-10 Turn Windows Firewall on to prevent attacks on your computer.

By default, Windows Firewall settings provide adequate protection for most situations; however, more advanced controls might be necessary in certain environments, such as in a home where residents play Internet games or share files, or in an office where Windows Firewall could block access to a network or file share.

To manage certain Windows issues, such as network connection problems in which a program or service cannot communicate outside of your network or with your network, you might need to set more appropriate permissions for a particular program or service. To change these permissions, you need to access the advanced settings. In the pane on the left of the Windows Firewall main window, click Advanced Settings. The Windows Firewall With Advanced Security window opens with a broad array of options for controlling your firewall and regulating access to and from your computer. I show you how to use the Advanced Firewall in Chapter 34, "Exploring Windows 8 Firewall." It should be noted that the Advanced Firewall is not a feature of Windows RT.

INSIDE OUT **Basic Windows Firewall control**

Windows Firewall alerts you when a program is requesting permission to pass through the firewall. If you accidentally give permission to a program and later want to deny it access, you can do this on the main Windows Firewall options pane by clicking Allow A Program Or Feature Through Windows Firewall. A list of programs that have firewall access appears. Clear the check boxes for the programs and features you want to block.

Windows Defender

Windows Defender is a full version of Microsoft's free Security Essentials antivirus product. Figure 4-11 shows the new Windows Defender antivirus tool. Windows Defender is easily accessible from the desktop app and Action Center. You can find it by opening the Start screen and searching for it.

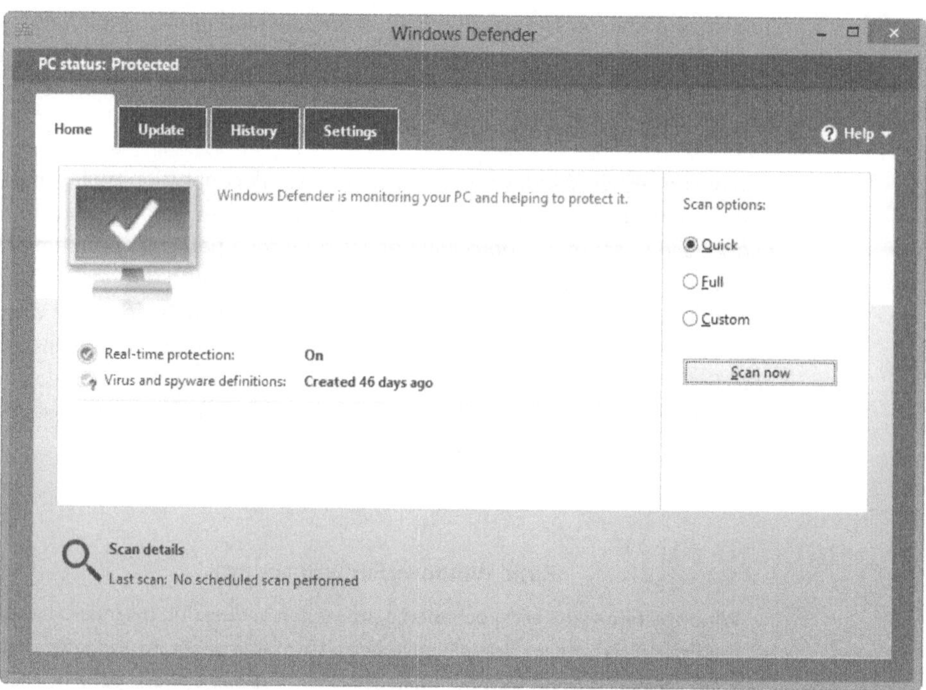

Figure 4-11 Windows Defender is a global antivirus tool.

It's great to see full-featured antivirus functionality finally packaged with Windows, although you can install and use a third-party package instead. If you do elect to go with third-party antivirus protection, you might find that the package conflicts with Windows Defender; thus, you will want to turn Windows Defender off, which you can do with the Intel versions of Windows 8; Windows RT does not support third-party antivirus software, so this option is not available. To access this feature, open Windows Defender, click the Settings tab, and then click Administrator, as shown in Figure 4-12. Clear the check box to turn the feature off.

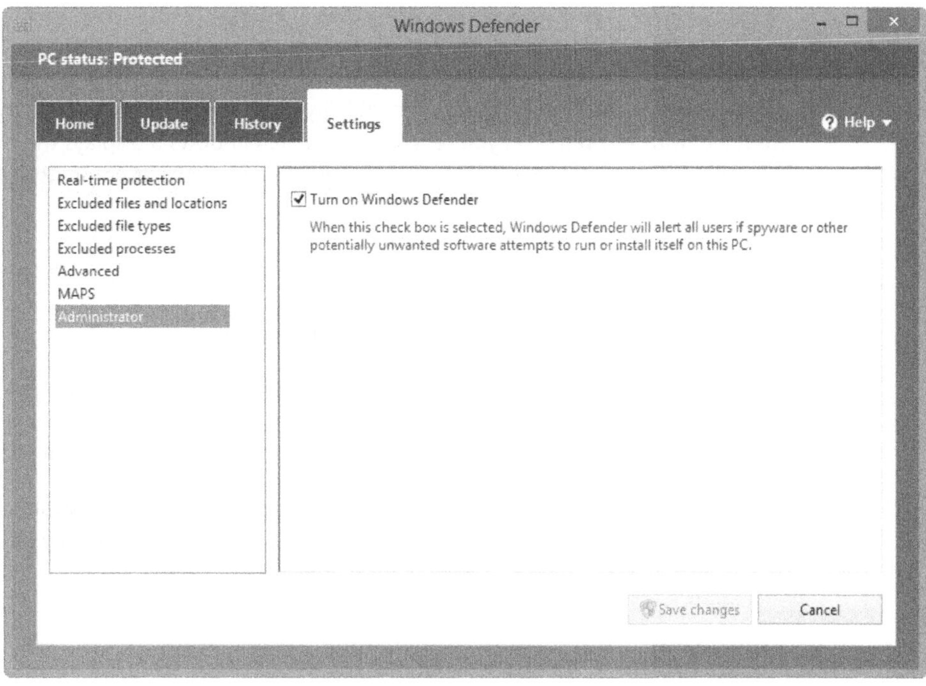

Figure 4-12 You can disable Windows Defender in the Administrator section.

Compatibility with Earlier Versions of Software

Windows 8 is capable of running programs designed for every version of Windows and even some programs designed for MS-DOS, too. However, you might encounter software that does not install or function as expected. There are several ways to get around problems caused by incompatible software.

Windows 8 maintains the same software and hardware compatibility as Windows 7. Everything that runs on Windows 7 will run on Windows 8. If you need a virtual machine such as XP Mode to run some earlier software, which will avoid incompatibility issues, you need a virtual machine such as Microsoft Client Hyper-V, which is built into the Pro and Enterprise editions of Windows 8. You can read more about Hyper-V at *http://technet.microsoft.com/en-us/library/hh857623.aspx*.

The Program Compatibility Assistant

Windows 8 is extremely good at detecting software that won't install or run properly, via a new feature called the Program Compatibility Assistant. If you experience a compatibility problem with software that you're trying to install, Windows 8 displays the Program Compatibility Assistant, which offers some settings you can use to attempt installing the program correctly.

INSIDE OUT Setting compatibility manually

Because software is run from the new Start screen or from the desktop, you access the compatibility settings for an individual program by opening the Start screen, right-clicking the program, and then from the App bar, clicking Open File Location.

After you're in the file location for the program, right-click the program's icon and click Properties. In the settings pane that appears, click the Compatibility tab. Figure 4-13 shows the various settings that can be configured on this tab.

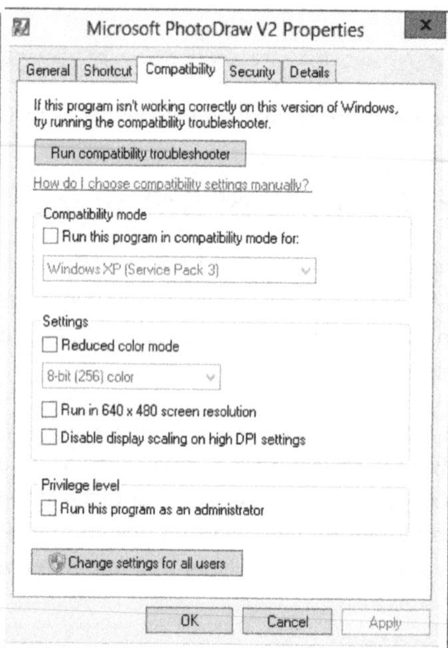

Figure 4-13 You can manually set a program's compatibility.

CAUTION!

Compatibility settings include addressing versions of Windows that go back to Windows 95. However, if a feature has been withdrawn, replaced, or significantly changed in Windows, such as Direct 3D used by Microsoft Photodraw (see Figure 4-13), the software will report problems and errors.

INSIDE OUT Administrator mode

The default user account in every version of Windows releases prior to Windows Vista is administrator. In an administrator user account, everything in Windows can be changed, moved, or deleted with impunity. Hackers are well aware of this and write viruses to take advantage of it. User Account Control (UAC) adds a layer of security to prevent these changes from being made automatically by malicious or poorly written software, but it can prevent some programs from running correctly.

Some programs require access to root Windows files and areas that UAC protects. If a program can't write files to these parts of the Windows operating system, the software can become unresponsive. You should be careful elevating any program to administrator, especially one you do not know well, because bypassing the essential UAC security feature can potentially cause damage. Some programs, however, must have administrator permissions to operate properly. You can read more about User Account Control at *http://technet.microsoft.com/en-US/library/0d75f774-8514-4c9e-ac08-4c21f5c6c2d9.aspx.*

One of the problems facing users who want to use earlier software and hardware is that the very useful—and free—Windows XP Mode that ran in Windows 7 Professional, Enterprise, and Ultimate editions isn't supported and won't install in Windows 8. However, Windows 8 has an equivalent: full Hyper-V hypervisor, which is a virtualization client type that allows a virtual machine to take full advantage of your computer hardware, as opposed to previous virtual machine types that only simulated computer hardware. I discuss this in depth in Chapter 10, "Working in a Virtual Environment," including how to use and manage Windows XP and earlier software.

CHAPTER 5

Optimizing Windows 8 Security

VARIOUS VERSIONS OF WINDOWS AND WINDOWS INTERNET EXPLORER are used by hundreds of millions of people worldwide. Because Windows is compatible with earlier versions of software, users sometimes run a range of earlier software on hardware as they prepare to update their systems. Companies sometimes resist updating software regularly because doing so can be expensive and they are concerned about risk; if a system works now, why fix it? However, the popularity and compatibility of Windows—a huge strength of Windows—can also be a vulnerability that you need to address with good security practices. I discuss optimizing security in this chapter.

Microsoft has announced that Windows 8 will be the last version of the operating system to come in a 32-bit (x86) version, so the next versions of Windows will be very robust, though much less compatible with earlier software and hardware.

Windows 8 is the first version of Windows to come with full-featured, built-in antivirus protection. The addition of Microsoft Security Essentials, the company's well-known free antivirus package, is now called Windows Defender.

Security, Windows XP, and Virtualization

Computers today come with multicore processors. Your computer might have an Intel Core 2 Duo chip with two cores or a quad-core processor (four cores). Server chips commonly now have 6, 8, or even 12 cores.

Each core is its own processor—essentially the heart of its own PC—and is capable of running a full operating system and accompanying software on its own. Virtual machines on a computer running Microsoft Client Hyper-V (also called a host) can take advantage of this, running your host operating system on one core while allowing other virtual machines to run on other cores. It is not necessary to have a multicore processor to run a virtual machine, however.

As Microsoft moves away from supporting former software versions in future operating systems, it will include virtualization software. Windows 7 Professional included the free Windows XP Mode, a full licensed copy of Windows XP that integrated with the Windows 7 desktop and allowed users to continue to run their earlier software without problems.

With Windows 8, Windows XP Mode is no longer available, but the 64-bit Pro and Enterprise editions include Client Hyper-V virtualization software instead, which is a more powerful application that was first seen in Windows Server.

All support for Windows XP will end as of April 2014. This means that beyond that date, there will be no more security updates available for the operating system. If you are using Windows XP even in a virtual machine and it requires a connection to the Internet, or you need to use the web browser in Windows XP to get online, you need to be aware that after all support ends, your operating system will be vulnerable to attack.

Thus, I discuss how to use Windows XP in a virtual machine safely with Windows 8 in Chapter 10, "Working in a Virtual Environment," but my best advice is that you should seek alternative software packages if the earlier Windows XP software you use in Windows 8 really won't work properly.

Antivirus Software

Many antivirus options exist for Windows 8—some are built in, such as Windows Defender, and others are third-party tools, such AVG or Kaspersky Internet Security, which you can use depending on your unique situation. Although I believe that there's nothing wrong with Windows Defender in Windows 8 and it will provide excellent protection as long as you're not careless online, people commonly want to use an alternative, especially if they are accustomed to a particular package. The following sections describe a few of these packages.

Windows Defender

As mentioned earlier, Windows 8 is the first version of the Microsoft desktop operating system to come with built-in antivirus capability, called Windows Defender.

Windows Defender, because it is free and stays out of the way, both in terms of alerts and also in terms of scanning, is a very lightweight package. The scanning engine, for example, will run full scans of your computer only when you are not actively using it. On powerful desktop computers, this timing doesn't make a noticeable difference on performance; however, on less powerful laptops and tablet computers, the effect on performance can be quite pronounced.

Suppose you want to use a third-party security package instead of Windows Defender. If you want to use a third-party antivirus package in place of Windows Defender, you will need to deactivate Windows Defender so that your new antivirus package and Windows Defender do not conflict with one another.

To deactivate Windows Defender, on the Start screen, type **defender** to search for it. When you locate it, open it, click the Settings tab, and then click Administrator, as illustrated in Figure 5-1. Clear the Turn On Windows Defender check box. Note that this option is not available in Windows RT.

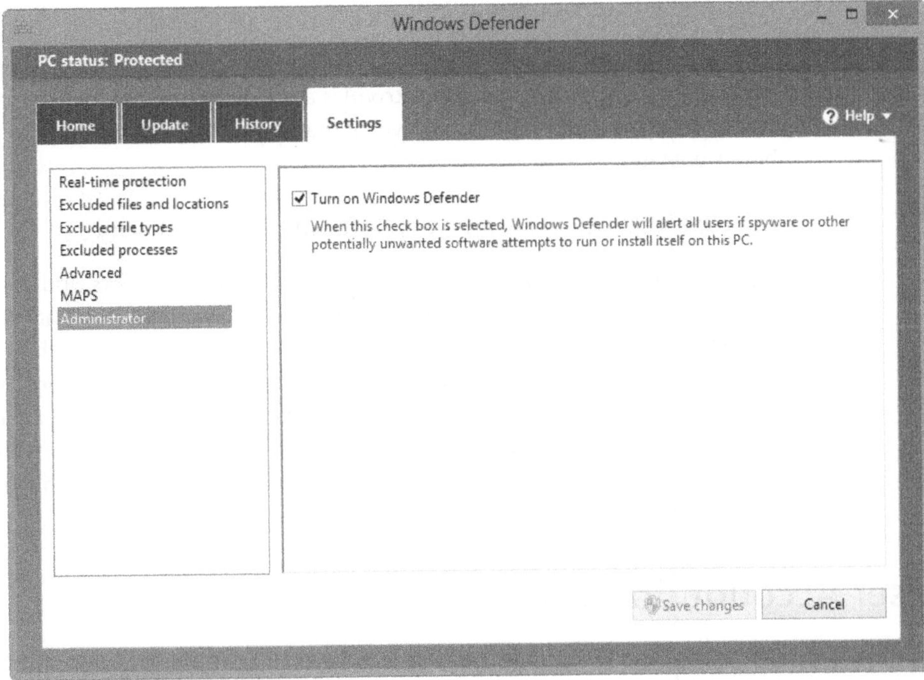

Figure 5-1 Use the Settings tab in Windows Defender to turn Windows Defender off.

Before you turn off Windows Defender, download an alternative antivirus package. Here are some of my own recommendations, based on features and effectiveness.

AVG AntiVirus FREE (*http://www.free.avg.com*) has long been a favorite in the free antivirus category for its overall effectiveness in blocking malware and providing warnings about dangerous websites. The current version of AVG is effective, but the the free version constantly advertises the version you pay for. If you can tolerate pop-up advertising, AVG AntiVirus FREE is an excellent choice to protect your computer.

Trend Micro Titanium Internet Security

Trend Micro (*http://www.trendmicro.com*) is a purchasable security suite for everyday computer users that offers award-winning protection and an interface that is very easy to use. The current version does not contain its own firewall, recognizing that the Windows Firewall is adequate protection, which helps the product have a minimal impact on your computer's performance.

Kaspersky Internet Security

For IT professionals and enthusiasts who want more control over their computer's security, Kaspersky (*http://www.kaspersky.com*) is a good option. It includes an excellent scanning engine with a significant level of granularity and control over the product and how it operates.

Microsoft Windows Malicious Software Removal Tool

If you review the updates your computer receives through Windows Update, you might notice the Microsoft Windows Malicious Software Removal Tool. This is an antimalware tool that you can use in addition to Windows Defender that is updated monthly by Microsoft and runs automatically on your computer. It can also be downloaded from the Microsoft website (*http://www.microsoft.com/en-us/download/details.aspx?id=16*). It checks your computer for viruses and malware, tries to remove any it finds, and reports this information to Microsoft. Although the tool is useful, it should not be considered a replacement for separate antivirus and antimalware products.

User Account Control

User Account Control (UAC) is an essential addition to Windows. It prevents changes from being made to the operating system, including software installations, without an administrator's permission. Every time a change occurs that could potentially harm either the computer or user accounts, a UAC dialog box appears to alert you, and all apps and programs are temporarily minimized.

INSIDE OUT Why do administrators need to run things as Administrator?

People with administrator accounts in Windows have permission to perform any action they want, but UAC will still alert them when changes might have a detrimental effect on the computer. However, if an administrator wants to run a program, for example, the Command Prompt, he still needs to right-click it and select Run As Administrator.

This functionality exists to prevent malware from bypassing UAC Security, because most computers are used by their main user (Administrator) much of the time. Administrators are granted elevated privileges; without UAC Security, malware would also be granted elevated privileges.

To access UAC, on the Start screen, type **UAC**. UAC will appear in the Settings results. You can also access it in Control Panel, in the System And Security section. Figure 5-2 shows the UAC window.

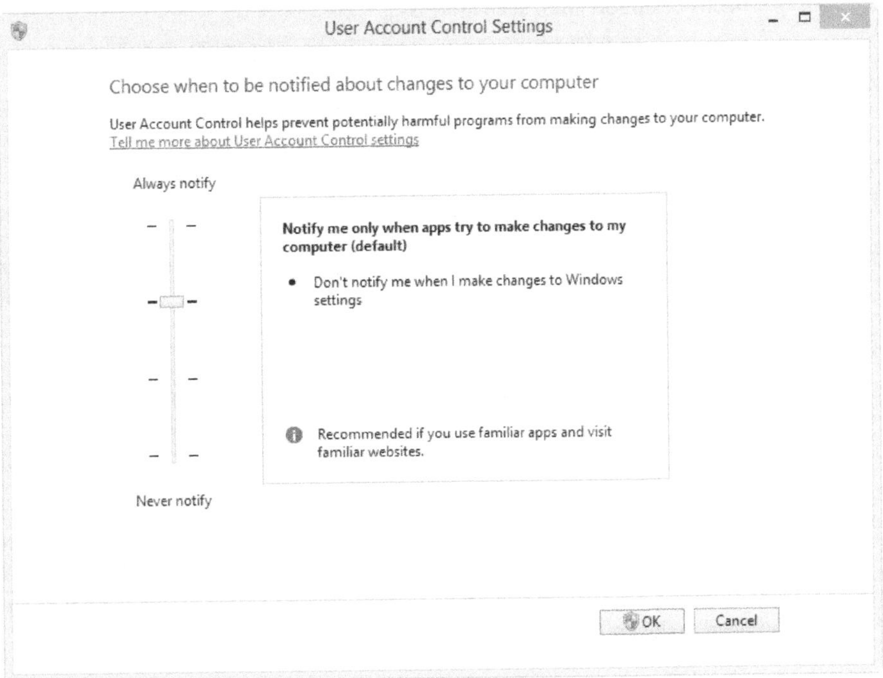

Figure 5-2 Set the UAC level in User Account Control Settings in Windows 8.

UAC has four settings, or levels, in Windows 8:

- **Never Notify** UAC is turned off, so you are not alerted to any changes to your computer or to any software attempts to access critical operating system files.
- **Apps Only** You are notified only when programs try to make changes to your operating system settings. You are not notified about other setting changes.
- **Default** This is the standard and recommended setting. You are notified when programs and other features try to change system settings, but not when you make changes yourself.
- **Always Notify** You are notified when any system setting changes.

INSIDE OUT What triggers UAC?

Windows will give you a visual clue as to what programs and settings are likely to trigger a UAC alert by placing a blue and yellow UAC shield icon over or next to program icons or option links. See Figure 5-3.

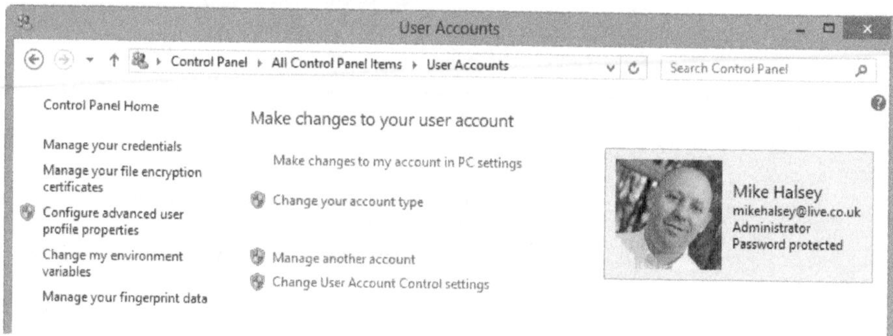

Figure 5-3 Some controls in Windows have a UAC icon to indicate they will change settings for all users

Some users do disable UAC; in Windows Vista, the only option is to either always notify the user of all system setting changes or never notify the user. However, in Windows 8, I recommend leaving the system turned on, because UAC is an essential defense against viruses, malware, and other malicious software on your PC.

BitLocker and BitLocker To Go

Microsoft BitLocker is a feature of the Pro and Enterprise editions of Windows 8 that you use to implement full-disk encryption of your copy of Windows and all your files and data. It supports multiple partitions and hard disks across a computer and can work in conjunction with a Trusted Platform Module (TPM) chip on your computer's motherboard to securely store the encryption keys. This means that even if your hard disks are physically removed from the computer, those hard disks cannot be decrypted.

To access BitLocker on your computer, open the Start screen and search for **Bitlocker**, or find it in Control Panel. The following scenarios explain how to use Bitlocker:

- **Encrypting a hard disk or partition with hardware support** If your computer's motherboard has a TPM chip, it stores the cryptographic keys needed to encrypt and decrypt your hard disk or partition. This encryption key (or cipher) is unique to this chip, so if an encrypted disk is removed, that disk can never be decrypted on another computer because the encryption key is still on the old computer.
- **Encrypting a hard disk or partition without hardware support** If your computer does not have a TPM chip on the motherboard, the cryptographic keys are stored within Windows and are not linked to specific hardware. Using this method, you can use the password to access the hard disk if it is plugged into another computer running Windows 8 or Windows 7.
- **Encrypting a USB flash drive or external hard disk** This method of encryption is similar to the non-TPM–based hard disk scenario described in the preceding bullet. Windows uses standard BitLocker cryptographic keys to ensure that an encrypted flash drive or hard disk can be used on other computers running Windows 7 or Windows 8. This method uses the Windows 8 Microsoft BitLocker To Go feature. To read a BitLocker To Go protected external drive in Windows XP, you can use the BitLocker To Go Reader software that is automatically placed on the drive. The BitLocker To Go Reader does not allow writing to an encrypted disk or USB flash drive.

INSIDE OUT **What is 128-bit AES encryption?**

Advanced Encryption Standard (AES) is a method of encrypting a hard disk, a partition, an external disk, or files. It divides data into block sizes of 128 characters (bits of data) and then performs encryption on each block 10 times to secure it, scrambling the data so that it cannot be read without being unscrambled.

The blocks of data can be decrypted only with a cipher and a password combination, which is never openly displayed. When you type your password to decrypt data, your password is converted into a hash key—a random string of characters created by an established algorithm (or formula) that can never be converted back into the password. The server or computer that contains the AES encryption algorithm does the same with the password it has stored in its password vault. If the two hash codes match, the password is accepted.

Administering Your TPM Chip

The main BitLocker Drive Encryption window displays a TPM Administration link in the bottom-left corner of the window, which you can click to administer the TPM chip on your motherboard. This chip needs to be activated before you can use BitLocker; however, when you turn BitLocker on, Windows 8 can activate it for you automatically.

However, if BitLocker already has been used on the computer, perhaps if you were using Windows Vista or Windows 7 with BitLocker enabled, you might want to clear the TPM chip to reset its stored passwords if the passwords are no longer relevant or required, which you can do on the Actions menu of Trusted Platform Module Management. You can also reset a lockout from the TPM chip if you have had a security problem. The TPM administration pane is shown in Figure 5-4.

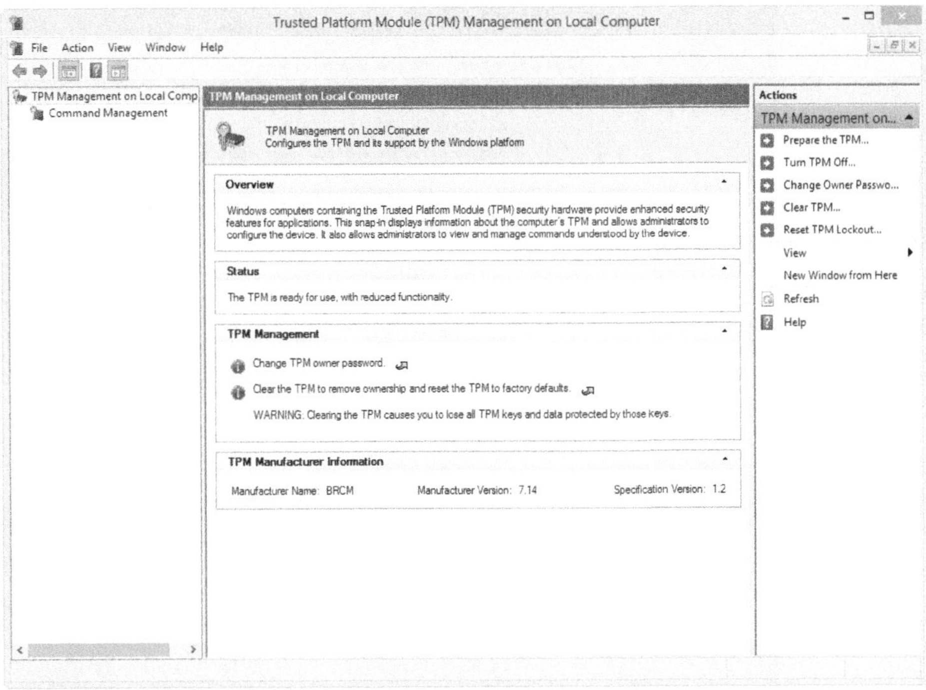

Figure 5-4 You can administer the TPM chip in Windows 8.

Enabling BitLocker

In the main BitLocker window, all the hard disks that physically reside inside your computer are displayed. In the Bitlocker To Go section, all the hard disks that are attached to your computer via USB flash drive are displayed. Each hard disk has a link next to it labeled Turn On BitLocker, as shown in Figure 5-5.

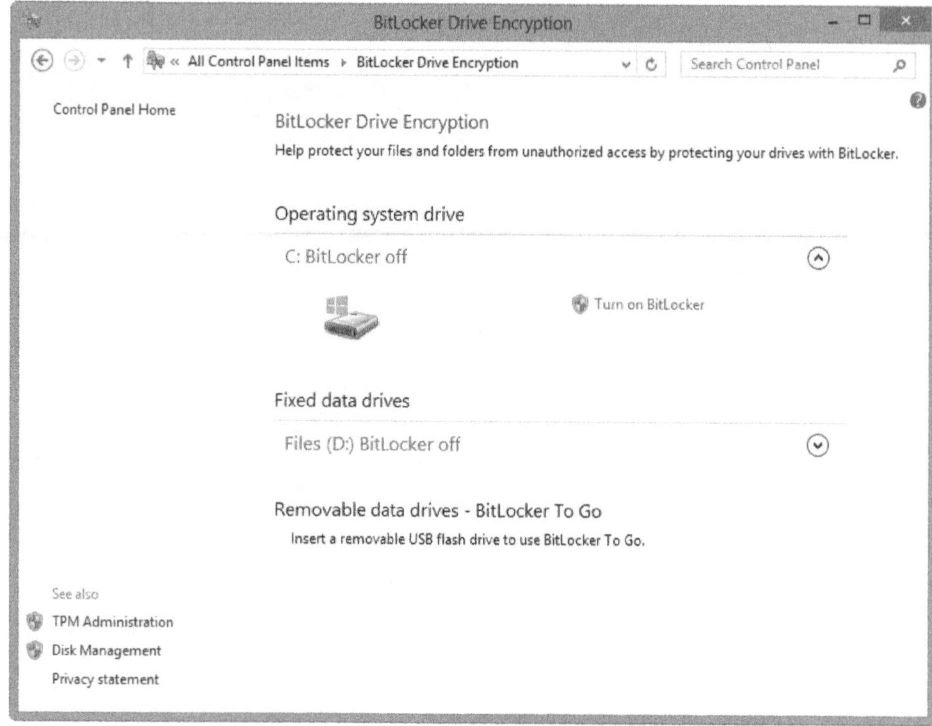

Figure 5-5 You can turn on BitLocker in the main BitLocker tool in Control Panel.

You will need to have your main Windows drive completely encrypted by BitLocker before Windows will allow you to encrypt any other drives; however, Windows will allow you to select all or several drives at the same time when you are decrypting drives.

> **Note**
>
> **If you have a lot of data on the hard disk, encryption of it will take a while, possibly overnight. Moving the data you do not want to have encrypted off the hard disk temporarily will speed up the process.**

CAUTION!

BitLocker provides an extremely high level of security and encryption. If you forget the password or your TPM-equipped motherboard fails and has to be replaced, you may never be able to access that data again. *Do not* encrypt data by using BitLocker if you do not have a backup copy of that data elsewhere.

Although it can take a while to encrypt your computer with BitLocker, you are free to shut down the computer or put it to sleep. The encryption or decryption process will pause upon shutdown or when going into Sleep mode and resume the next time the computer is used.

INSIDE OUT Alternatives to BitLocker To Go

You cannot write to a USB flash drive or external hard disk that has been encrypted with BitLocker To Go. What are your alternatives?

TrueCrypt (*http://www.truecrypt.org*) is a free, third-party program for encrypting your files and data. You can carry a copy of the TrueCrypt software on your flash drive or hard disk for installation on a host PC. This software is compatible with all versions of Windows and the Apple computers, and it will allow you to read and write files on the disk.

The limitation of TrueCrypt is that you might not be allowed to install the software on computers for which specific policies are set up to prevent users from installing software. If you intend to use TrueCrypt in a business or educational environment, you should first verify with the organization's IT department that it is indeed supported.

Cloud storage is another way to store files in one place and access them from different locations. The Microsoft SkyDrive service (*http://www.skydrive.com*) offers 7 gigabytes (GB) of free storage space.

The advantages of cloud storage are that you never need to carry a physical device with you, your files will always be safe and encrypted, and you can access your data anywhere you have an Internet connection.

The downside of cloud storage is that you *must* have a working Internet connection to access the files. If you commonly work remotely with a laptop in places where you don't have access to the Internet, or if you lose Internet connection, you will not have access to your cloud-based files.

Why Use BitLocker?

I recommend BitLocker for use on laptop computers and sometimes for use on USB flash drives and external hard disks. There might even be legal requirement to do so. Depending on the country in which you're working, if you carry critical information such as personal data about other people, you might be subject to data protection laws that make it illegal to transport unencrypted data.

BitLocker is also useful for everyday computer users who not only carry a great deal of personal information in their files, but who also commonly store passwords for websites in Internet browsers. If you have a laptop running the Windows 8 Enterprise or Pro edition, encrypting your hard disk is well worth it. If you are considering buying a laptop and can afford to do so, purchase one with a TMP chip and Windows 8 Pro or Enterprise. I believe the peace of mind is worth the extra expense incurred. Business users who carry sensitive or customer-related data on laptops should encrypt the data by using BitLocker or another encryption software.

Tips for Keeping Your Computer Safe

If you have antivirus software installed in Windows 8 and UAC enabled, your operating system should be secure. However, user errors can often compromise security. Here are my top tips for avoiding the user errors that can undermine your computer's security:

- **Keep your antivirus software current** Always ensure that first and foremost, you are protected from external attacks by installing antivirus software.
- **Ensure that you have a good, up-to-date firewall** Just as important as antivirus software is a firewall. This is your first line of defense against attack. Make sure that it's kept up to date. If you're running Windows XP in a virtual machine, don't rely solely on the built-in firewall; it's not enough.
- **Keep Windows up to date** Turning on Windows Update and leaving it on is essential. Updates are released by Microsoft on a monthly basis, and although some might require you to restart your computer, this slight inconvenience is worth the added security and peace of mind.
- **Keep your software up to date** Ensure that you regularly check for general and security updates for the software you use the most. You can find these on the manufacturers' websites.

- **Always check email attachments before opening them** It's always a good idea to check all email attachments for viruses. Save them to your hard disk first, and then in File Explorer, right-click the file and select Scan With [*your antivirus software*] before you open it.

  If you receive a suspicious-looking email attachment from someone you know, you could email that person to ask if she did intend to send it to you. It could be that a virus on her computer has forwarded itself to people in her address book, in which case she would probably like to be notified.

- **Use a secure Internet browser** Browsers such as the latest versions of Firefox or Internet Explorer provide much of the protection you need. In Windows 8, the protected mode in Internet Explorer that denies the access of any software running in the browser to the rest of the operating system, and the Start screen filter that detects malicious software and websites, are an extra security bonus.

- **Get spam and phishing filtering for your email software** Spam is a nuisance, but phishing emails are the messages that purport to be from a real bank or credit card company asking you to provide your personal details to a website. I've seen some of the most net-savvy people get caught by these. Microsoft Forefront might be an option.

- **Never click anything you don't explicitly want to click** If you haven't gone to a website with the express intention of clicking items—for instance, to install a browser plug-in or get a specific download—don't click anything. *Never* click anything unless you know exactly what it is. Beware of reputable websites such as YouTube on which viruses are occasionally posted disguised as a codec that is required to play a video. If you are ever in doubt, simply *don't* click it!

- **Look for the padlock or the green bar** When shopping online or visiting any website that requires you to enter personal information, look for the padlock, which is a visual method for your browser to tell you that the website is encrypting any data sent back and forth by using a valid security certificate. The browser you use will determine where this is located. One security convention in browsers, for example, is to color-code the address bar. The address bar is displayed as green if the site is okay, and orange or red if you should use caution or avoid the site.

> **Note**
>
> **Not all web browsers will use color-coded address bars, and they might display the padlock in different ways and in different areas of the browser. Refer to the Help menu for your specific browser for more advice about this.**

- **Never give private details online unless you must** Shopping for a credit card or car insurance may require revealing personal details online, but many websites will unnecessarily ask for personal details. At best, these details are used to send you spam; at worst, they are used to steal your identity.
- **Keep backups** Ensure that you keep regular backups of your data somewhere away from your Windows installation, perhaps on an external USB storage device, for instance. Windows has a built-in backup utility, but third-party packages offer backup solutions, too.
- **Keep your backups in a safe place** It is not wise to keep your backups on your computer or in the same location as your computer. Cloud storage is a useful and secure place for storing backups, but it can be very slow if you have large amounts of files to back up or a slow broadband connection. CDs, DVDs, and blu-ray discs can degrade over time. If affordable, the best solution is an external USB hard disk that is stored offsite and brought back monthly to be updated.
- **Keep the driver CDs and manuals for your computer** Always safeguard the discs and manuals that come with your computer. You should also keep a copy of your Windows (and software) product keys in the same place. These are critical if Windows ever needs to be reinstalled. Make sure you keep them somewhere safe and keep them together.
- **Get a Windows installation DVD for your computer** Many computers do not ship with Windows 8 installation DVDs. This is done as an antipiracy measure. Instead, they come with preconfigured restore partitions. It is always wise to contact the company you bought your computer from and request a Windows 8 installation DVD so that you have it available in the rare case you will need it. There might be a postage charge for sending it, but do bear in mind that some computer vendors will be unable to provide a disc. It's always a good idea to check on this before you decide which company to buy your computer from.

- **Keep Windows maintained** You will have much more fun on your computer if you keep it tidy and maintained. Uninstall programs that you don't need, and use the built-in tools or third-party tools to remove unnecessary files.
- **Erase the hard disk before you discard your computer** When your computer comes to the end of its useful life, be sure to use a utility that will securely erase the hard disk by overwriting the data several times. If you can, also remove the erased hard disk and dispose of it separately. Discarded computers can contain a wealth of sensitive information that makes them a bargain find for identity thieves.

  Windows 8 includes a new Reset Your PC option, which you can find in the General section of PC Settings. This will completely wipe all user accounts, settings, apps, programs, and files, and return your computer to a state where it is suitable to be passed on.

CAUTION!

The Reset Your PC option and deleting files will not *securely* erase them. You should use a specific secure erase program if you want to guarantee that files cannot be recovered later. This can be a slow process, however, so be patient.

The market for computer security is enormous and includes every type of product that you can imagine. One website that I've found invaluable over the years is Gibson Research Corporation at *http://www.grc.com*. Steve Gibson is a highly respected computer security expert. His website includes his ShieldsUP! tools, which he describes as "the Internet's quickest, most popular, reliable and trusted, free Internet security checkup and information service." Many other tools are also available at the website for testing the security of your computer, Internet connection, and firewall. I cannot recommend the tools on this website highly enough.

CHAPTER 6

Optimizing Backup and Restore

WINDOWS 8 COMES WITH MANY WAYS TO BACK UP both your files and the operating system. These myriad options make keeping backups, file version histories, and system images a simple and straightforward process. In this chapter, I show you each backup option, how you use it, and why you should use it.

Storing Your Files Separately from Windows 8

In Chapter 2, "Repairing Common Issues in Windows 8," you learned that it's essential to move your files and data to a partition different from the one on which Windows 8 is installed. If Windows 8 experiences a critical problem and needs to be restored from a backup or reinstalled, you could lose all of your files if they are stored on the same partition as the operating system.

I described how to create a new partition when installing Windows. But what if you want to move your data to a separate partition after you have already installed Windows 8? To help you do this, Windows 8 includes a feature that you can use to grow and shrink the size of partitions and then make additional partitions in the available disk space created.

The Disk Cleanup Wizard

In preparation for moving your data to a new partition, delete any temporary files that consume space. Windows 8 can shrink the partition it's installed on by a finite amount. The more files and programs you have installed on the partition, the less Windows 8 will be able to shrink the drive. To remove unneeded files, perform the following steps:

1. On the Start screen, type **free**. In the Settings results, click Free Up Disk Space By Deleting Unnecessary Files, as shown in Figure 6-1, to open the Disk Cleanup Wizard. Note that this option is not available in Windows RT.

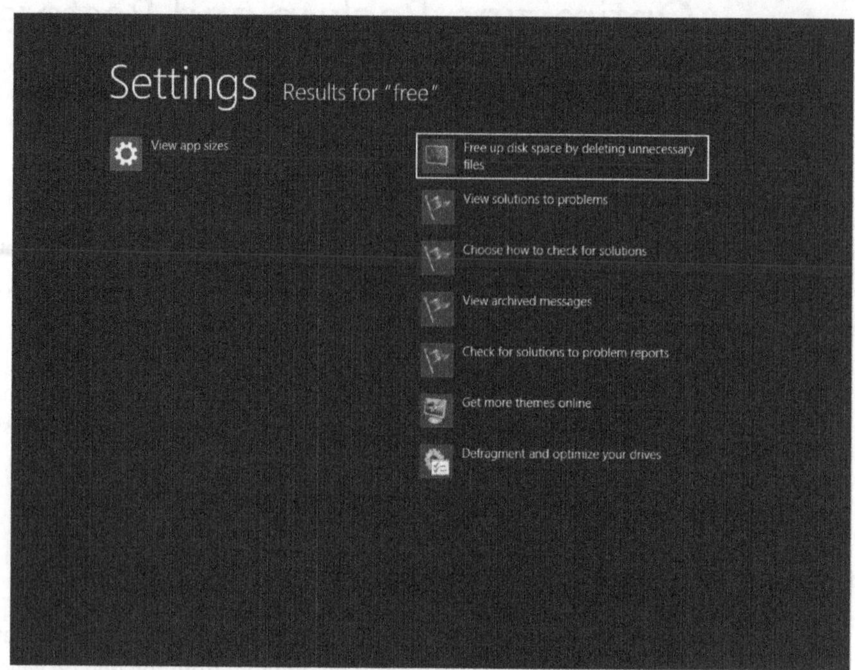

Figure 6-1 Search for the Disk Cleanup wizard to begin the process of removing unneeded files.

2. Run the wizard, indicating which drive you want to clean. (This will usually be the drive C.)

   In the Disk Cleanup dialog box, you will be able to select various options for recovering unused space on your hard disk or in the Windows 8 partition. You can safely choose any of the available options in Disk Cleanup (see Figure 6-2).

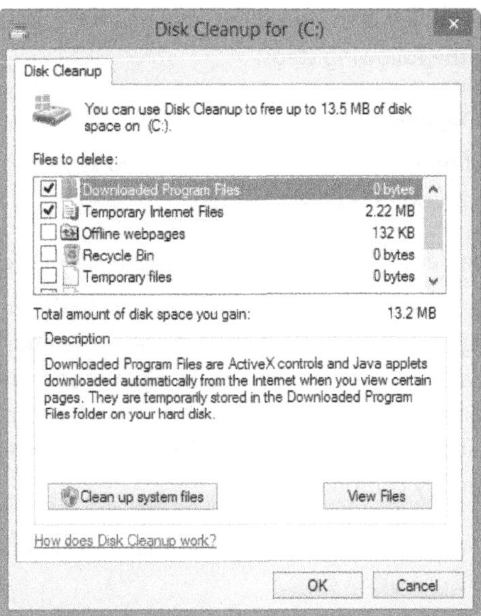

Figure 6-2 You can select custom options for recovering space in the Disk Cleanup wizard.

You might also want to use a third-party utility to help clean up your drives, because sometimes these can offer additional functions and increased usability. I recommend CCleaner from *http://www.piriform.com/ccleaner*.

Shrinking, Extending, and Creating Partitions

Your next step in creating a new partition for your data is to shrink the size of the Windows 8 partition so that you can create space for a separate partition. You do this because the entire current partition was used for your Windows 8 installation. You can also extend a partition if there is any available space into which it can expand, although you will not need to do this for this example.

If your personal files are already on the same partition or drive as Windows 8, you should move them to a separate disk or partition. Having a copy of your personal files on the same partition you are trying to shrink will severely limit how much the partition can contract. To shrink a partition, perform the following steps:

1. Open Computer Management.

   The quickest way to find this is to press Windows logo key+X to open the WinX menu, and then select Computer Management.

2. In Computer Management, expand Storage, and then click Disk Management.

   A list of the available hard disks and partitions appears in the center pane of Disk Management (see Figure 6-3 in the next step). Note in the figure that I have two hard disks on this particular computer and two backup partitions on a different hard disk from the one that contains my main copies of Windows 8 and my files. One backup partition is for files, and one is for a copy of Windows. I also keep a second backup of my files separate from my computer.

3. Right-click the partition you want to shrink, and then select Shrink Volume, as shown in Figure 6-3.

   Windows 8 determines the maximum amount it can shrink the partition.

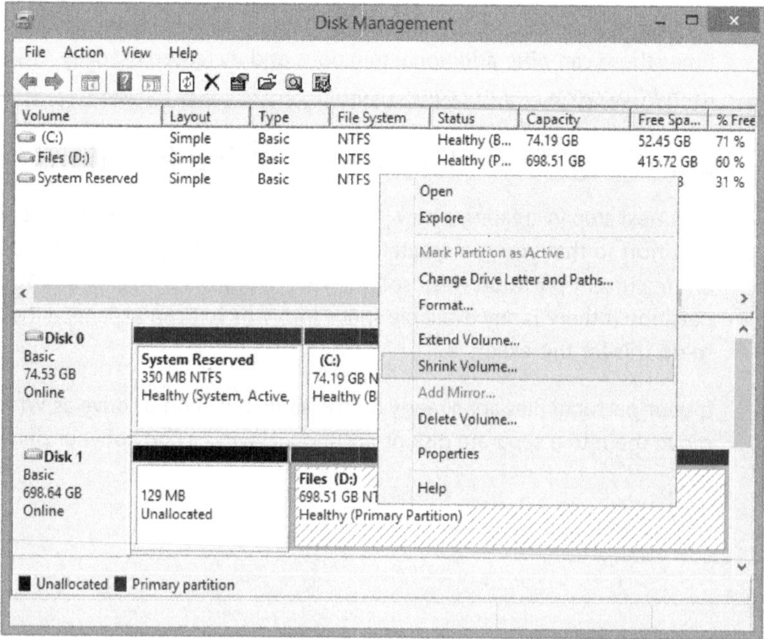

Figure 6-3 You can shrink a partition in Disk Management.

4. Choose a new partition size that will meet your needs and then click OK. (See Chapter 1, "Finding Your Way Around Windows 8," for suggestions about partition size.)

5. In the new unallocated volume that you have created, right-click anywhere in the empty space, and then click New Simple Volume.

   You will want to format the new volume, assign a drive letter, and format the partition, accepting the default file system option, which will allow files to be stored.

Moving the Shell User Folder

If you followed the procedure in the previous section, you now have a spare partition onto which you can move your personal files. But first you need to move the shell user folders to the new partition. Shell user folders are the pointers within Windows 8 that open the correct folder on the correct disk or partition when you click My Documents, My Pictures, and so on. Follow these steps to move the shell user folders:

1. On the Start screen, click the Desktop Tile, and then open File Explorer.

2. At the far left side of the address bar, click the Folder arrow to open a menu of folder locations, as depicted in Figure 6-4, and then click your user name.

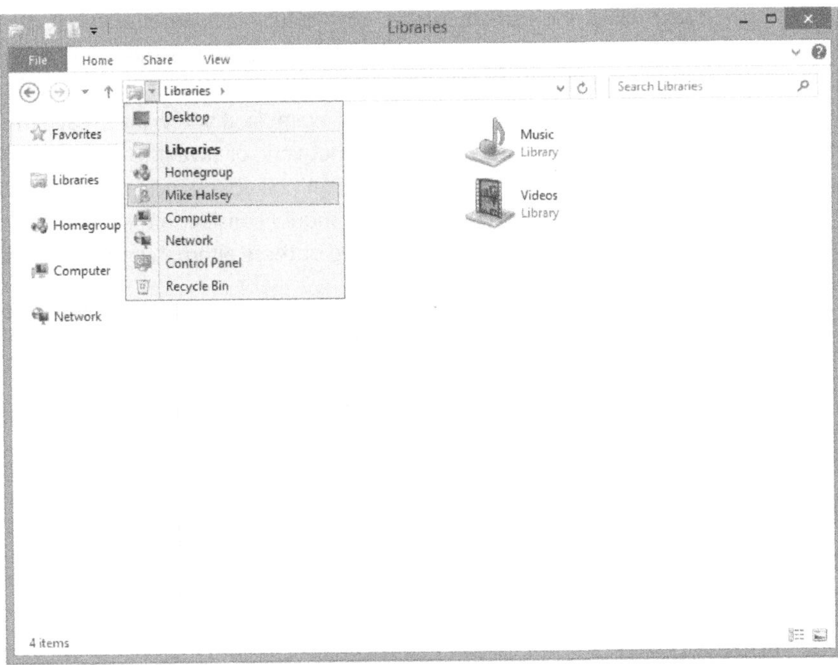

Figure 6-4 You can use File Explorer to find your user folders in Windows 8.

3. In your user folder, select the folders that you want to move.

   I suggest Downloads, Favorites, My Documents, My Music, My Pictures, and My Videos.

4. On the Home tab of the ribbon, click Cut.

5. Navigate to the partition or disk to which you want to move your user folders.

6. On the Home tab, click Paste.

Backing Up Files and Data

Windows 8 has a good, basic utility for backing up your files and folders that's easy to use for most users and worth the time to learn. Of course, you don't have to use the backup utility in Windows 8. The backup software you use is determined by how much flexibility you need and where you store your backups. As an IT professional, I need a bit more flexibility and therefore use a third-party solution. If you exclusively use a cloud service such as Mozy or Carbonite, you may also want to use Windows Backup, because restoring files from these services can be a slow process and is entirely dependent on your Internet speed and any data usage limits you might have.

Backup And Restore saves your files as a secure, compressed archive called a *virtual hard disk*. Backup And Restore can be very useful when you don't want other people looking through the files you've backed up, at least not unless they really know what they're doing, because the file names are not easily visible. However, if you will eventually want to access these files on another computer—for example, if you want to save the backup to a USB drive connected to a home or office network, or save it to an external USB hard disk for working in different locations—you won't be able to access them. If you want to save your backup to an external hard disk, you should consider a third-party backup solution instead of Backup And Restore. I discuss some of these alternatives later in this chapter.

Microsoft renamed the Backup And Restore option offered in Windows 7 to Windows 7 File Recovery. To access it, perform the following steps:

1. Open Control Panel and click Windows 7 File Recovery.

2. In the Backup Or Restore Your Files page of the Windows 7 File Recovery, click the Set Up Backup link (see Figure 6-5).

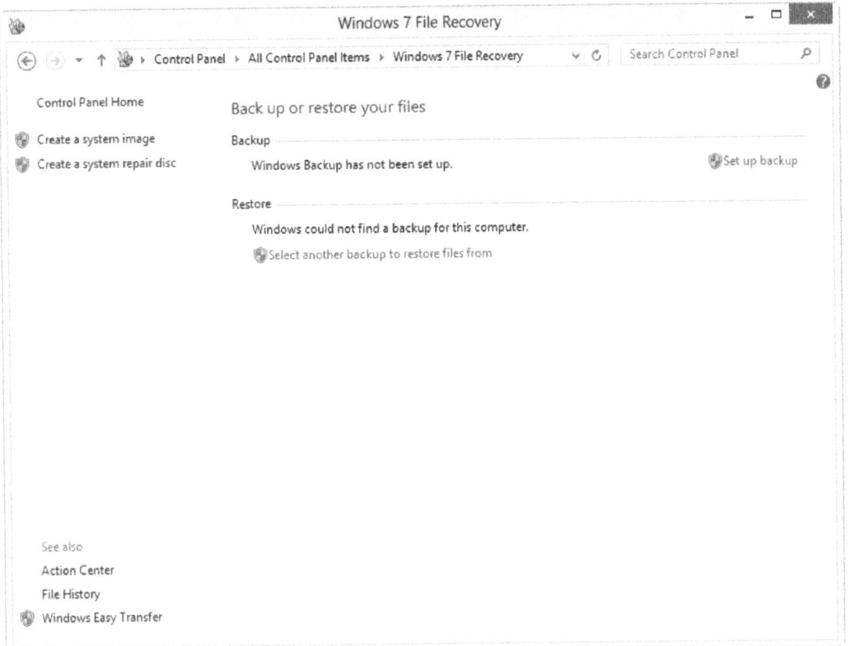

Figure 6-5 You can set up backup options in Windows 7 File Recovery.

The Set Up Backup wizard appears with a list of locations to which you can store your backup. This list includes any hard disks and partitions on your computer. You can also choose to save your backup to a network by clicking Save On A Network.

3. Indicate a location for your backup, and then press Next.

4. Decide how to control what you want to back up. If you want to assign the assignment task to Windows, on the What Do You Want To Back Up page, click Let Windows Choose, which is the default (see Figure 6-6). (Note that the default option can change but will be your second hard disk or partition if you have one.) If you want more control over what is backed up, click Let Me Choose.

   Note that the default option will also create a full backup of your Windows 8 installation. If you already did this separately, click Let Me Choose, and then click Next.

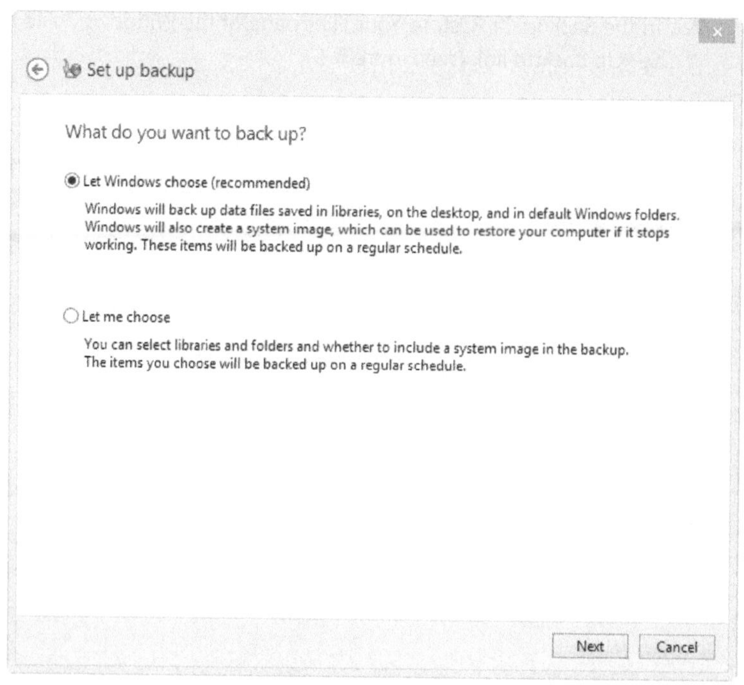

Figure 6-6 You can choose what to back up in the file backup wizard.

5. On the What Do You Want To Back Up page, choose which files and folders you want to back up.

   In Figure 6-7, the bold item (Mike Halsey's Libraries) includes all the standard shell user folders for documents, music, photos, pictures, and videos. Select and clear the check boxes as appropriate to indicate which items to back up. Also note that you can choose whether Windows performs a system image backup of your Windows 8 installation.

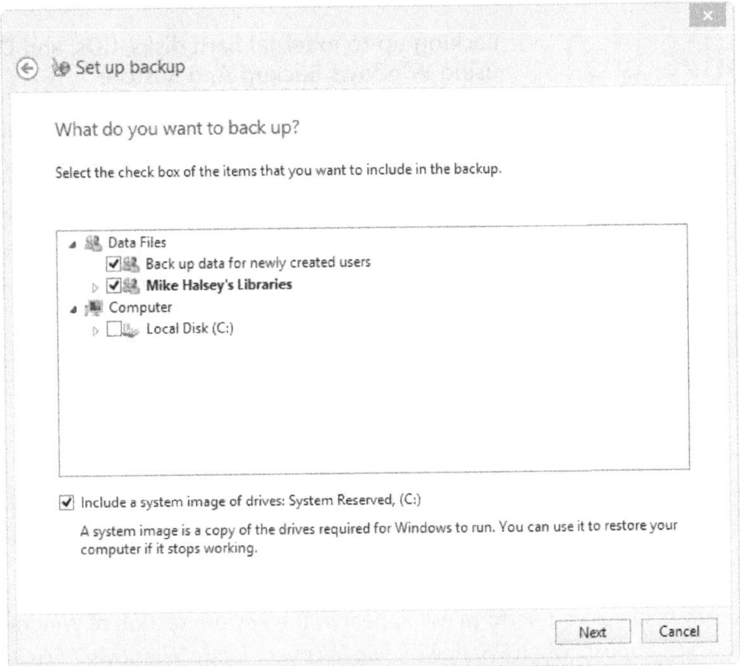

Figure 6-7 You can choose which folders, pictures, and so on to back up.

6. When you are finished selecting the files you want to back up, click Next.

   On the Review Your Backup Settings page, a list appears indicating what you have chosen to back up and the backup schedule. You can change the schedule to suit your own needs and preferences by clicking Change Schedule.

7. When you are ready to perform the first backup, click Save Settings And Run Backup.

CAUTION!

You should let Windows 7 File Recovery make a backup copy of your Windows 8 installation over a network only if your computer is connected to the network by a physical cable. If you connect only via wireless, the restore software will be unable to see the backup if Windows 8 must eventually be restored. This is because the Windows 8 System Image Restore tool doesn't run on the Windows 8 desktop and thus cannot load any wireless hardware drivers. It can rely only on wired networking support provided by the computer's BIOS.

INSIDE OUT **Backing up to external hard disks, CDs, and DVDs by using Windows Backup And Restore**

If you want to back up to an external hard disk on a regular basis, you will need to ensure that the drive is connected to your computer at the scheduled backup times.

Windows Backup and Restore cannot save regular backups to blank CDs, DVDs, or Blu-ray discs; you will need a third-party solution if you want to store your backups to these media. Keep in mind, though, that you can manually copy any backups stored on an external hard disk to an optical disc.

Restoring Files and Data from a Backup

You can restore your files and data from a backup by using Windows 7 File Recovery, which you learned how to access in the section titled "Backing Up Files and Data" earlier in the chapter.

Any backups you perform will appear in the Restore section of Windows 7 File Recovery, which appears when Windows 7 File Recovery loads. Windows 7 File Recovery is automated and will give you the option to restore all of your files and data or only selected items. The restore will find your most recent backup very quickly and will restore all your files to their original locations.

Backing Up to the Cloud

Cloud storage is becoming increasingly popular, and there are many security benefits to keeping a backup of your files online, away from your physical location. The cloud is the ultimate offsite backup. If you are concerned about the privacy and security of files that reside in the cloud, be assured that services from providers such as Microsoft, Google, and Amazon are very trustworthy and maintain tight security.

Note

The rate at which you can back up your files and data to the cloud is dependent on the speed of your Internet connection. If you have a large number of files, you could find that it takes many weeks to complete the initial backup. After the initial backup, however, the backup software backs up only new or modified files and the process is faster.

Cloud-based backup services include Microsoft SkyDrive, Amazon S3, Carbonite, and Mozy. SkyDrive offers 7 gigabytes (GB) of free storage space. Generally, though, you will need to pay a subscription fee to maintain your online backup. The price will depend on the service you use and how much data and the number of files you back up.

Backing Up the Operating System

For many years, system administrators chose to back up Windows by using technologies such as Symantec Ghost or Acronis True Image to create a system image. With Windows Vista, Microsoft introduced system image backup for the first time, though only in the Professional, Enterprise, and Ultimate editions. With Windows 7, system image backup was expanded to every edition of the operating system, including Windows 8.

Windows 8 also offers a second option in Refresh that creates an image that can be restored from within Windows 8 by a user without affecting that user's files, apps, settings, and—if a custom image has been created—that user's desktop software. What are these different image backup solutions, and how do you use them? You explore those questions in the next sections.

Creating a Windows 8 System Image

A system image in Windows is the backup you would restore from when Windows cannot start or is corrupted. You might also want to restore from a system image when you want to clear out all the computer and user settings completely and start again with an operating system that you know is clean and works properly.

INSIDE OUT

What to do before you create a system image backup

Before you create a Windows system image backup, ensure that all your software, drivers, and apps are installed and that all your settings and configuration options are set the way you want them. Try to keep the installation clean, too, by running software such as CCleaner before creating the backup. Doing so cleans out unwanted temporary files and clutter than can slow your copy of Windows.

To create a Windows system image backup, perform these steps:

1. From Control Panel, select Windows 7 File Recovery.
2. In Windows 7 File Recovery (see Figure 6-8), in the Control Panel Home pane, click Create A System Image.

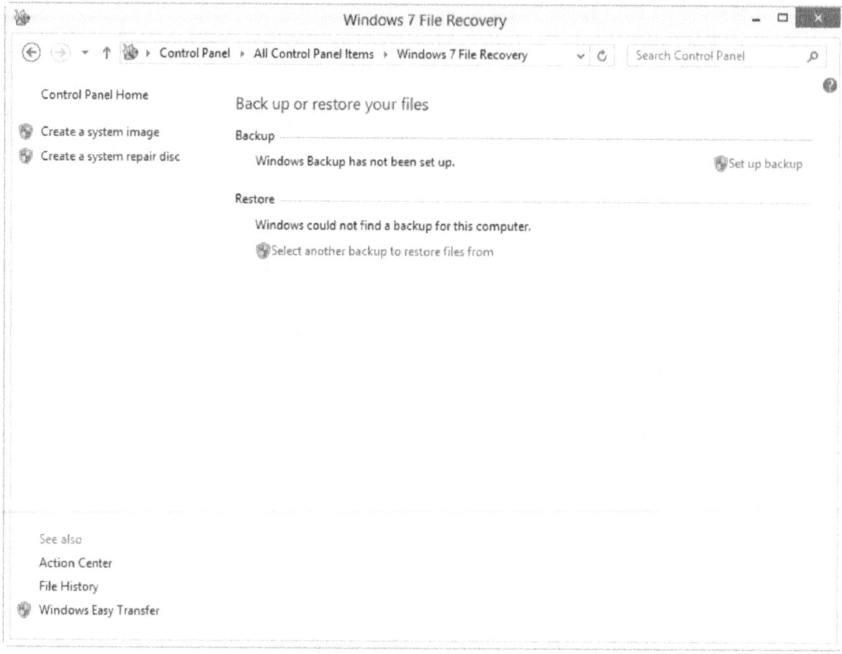

Figure 6-8 The Windows 7 File Recovery window is where you find the option to set up a system image backup.

3. On the Where Do You Want To Save The Backup page of the Create A System Image wizard, select the destination for your system image (see Figure 6-9), and click Next.

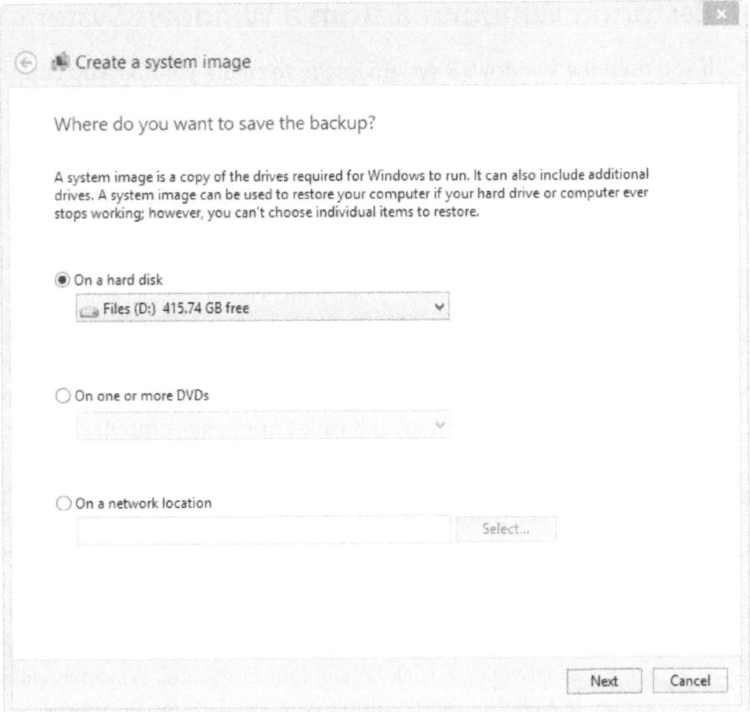

Figure 6-9 You are asked to select a location for your backup.

When the backup has completed, a pop-up window prompts you to create a system repair disc. This is a startup CD or DVD that contains the Windows 8 repair tools.

INSIDE OUT The system repair disc

You can create a system repair disc in several ways. In addition to manually creating a system repair disc, you can use the main Windows 7 File Recovery window. You can also create a system repair disc when you create a full system image of Windows 8.

The benefit of having a system repair disc is that if you ever need to recover Windows 8 from a backup, you won't need to access your original Windows 8 installation DVD. The original media is valuable and should be kept in a location where it will be safe from scratches, loss, and environmental damage.

Restoring Windows 8 from a Windows System Image

If you used the Windows 8 system image to create your backup copy of Windows 8, you will need to start up your computer either from the Windows 8 installation DVD or from a system repair disc that you create.

Restoring Windows 8 from a System Repair or Install Disc

Before you start your machine from a system repair or Windows 8 installation disc, you will need to verify that your computer's BIOS is set to start from the DVD drive before it attempts to start from the hard disk. You can access the BIOS by pressing F2 or Delete on your keyboard when you turn on the computer. The setting to verify is called Boot Order or Boot Priority. You should refer to your OEM's instructions for changing the boot priority because the method for changing it varies from one computer to another.

The system repair disc first determines whether there is a copy of Windows on the computer that won't start. After this is determined, you have the option to repair the faulty installed version of Windows 8 or restore Windows 8 from a previously backed up copy:

- If you are starting your computer from a Windows 8 installation DVD, click through the language options (because you don't need to select a different one), and then on the Install Now page, click Repair Your Computer. Windows will search for operating system installations and then present you with repair options.
- If you are starting your computer from a System Repair Disc, your computer will try to repair Windows 8. If the computer says repairs are completed, you should press a key to restart the computer or press Esc.

INSIDE OUT **The differences between a system repair disc and a Windows 8 installation DVD**

A system repair disc and the Windows 8 install DVD present different options when repairing Windows 8 or restoring it from a backup image. When you start your computer from the Windows 8 installation DVD, you need to click Repair Your Computer on the Install Now page.

1. On the Choose An Option page, click Troubleshoot.
2. On the Troubleshoot page, you are asked if you want to Refresh Your PC or Reset Your Computer, and you are presented with Advanced Options. Click Advanced Options.
3. On the Advanced Options page, click System Image Recovery, as depicted in Figure 6-10.

   Windows finds the system image you created on your hard disk.

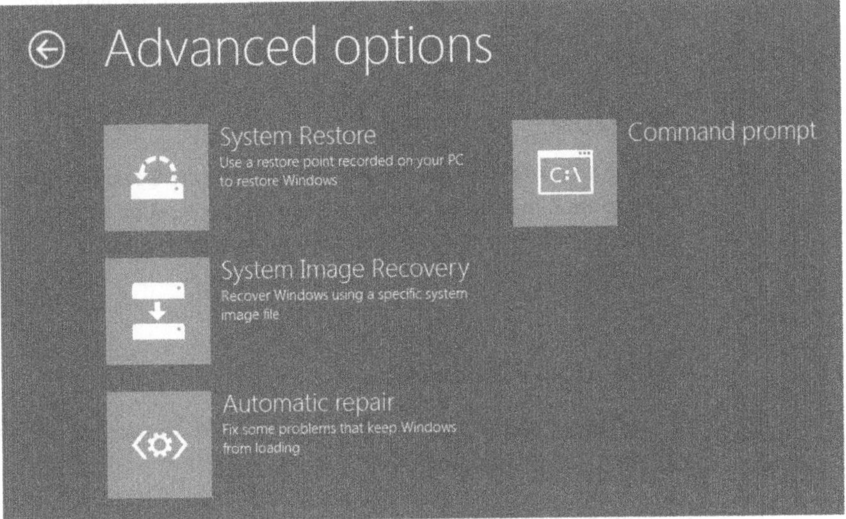

Figure 6-10 The advanced startup options present several recovery and repair options.

4. Select the correct image on the Select A System Image Backup page, and then click Next to restore that image.

Creating a Custom Refresh Image

By default, Windows 8 includes a refresh image of the operating system. However, even though this might save your apps, it will not save your desktop apps. If you want to save your desktop apps, you can create a custom refresh image by performing the following steps:

1. Press Win+X, and on the menu that appears, click Command Prompt (Admin).
2. Type the command **recimg -CreateImage C:*Folder*** to create a custom refresh image, where C:*Folder* is the location where you want to store the image.

It really is that simple to create a custom refresh image in Windows!

CAUTION!

Although a refresh will keep many of your Windows 8 settings intact, settings for some desktop apps, including Microsoft Office, can be reset during the refresh process. A refresh will also reset your pinned apps on the taskbar.

Refreshing Windows 8

There are several ways to access the Refresh Your PC option, the simplest of which is via the Start screen. Follow this procedure to access Refresh:

1. Press Windows logo key+C on your keyboard, and then click the Settings charm.
2. Click Change PC Settings.

3. In PC Settings, click General, and then in the Refresh Your PC Without Affecting Your Files section, click Get Started, shown in Figure 6-11.

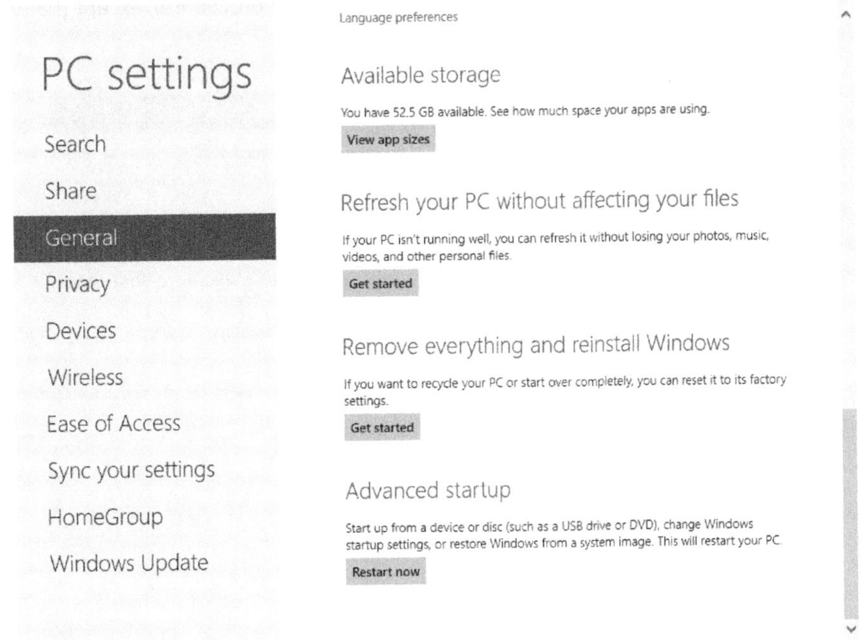

Figure 6-11 The Refresh Your PC option can be found on the General page in PC Settings.

The Refresh Your PC dialog box informs you of what the Refresh Your PC option will do.

4. When you are ready to perform the refresh, click Next.

Your computer will restart, and then the refresh will run.

Refreshing Windows 8 from Control Panel

The process of refreshing your computer from Control Panel is just like refreshing Windows 8 from PC Settings (described in the preceding procedure), except that you click Recovery in All Control Panel Items (see Figure 6-12).

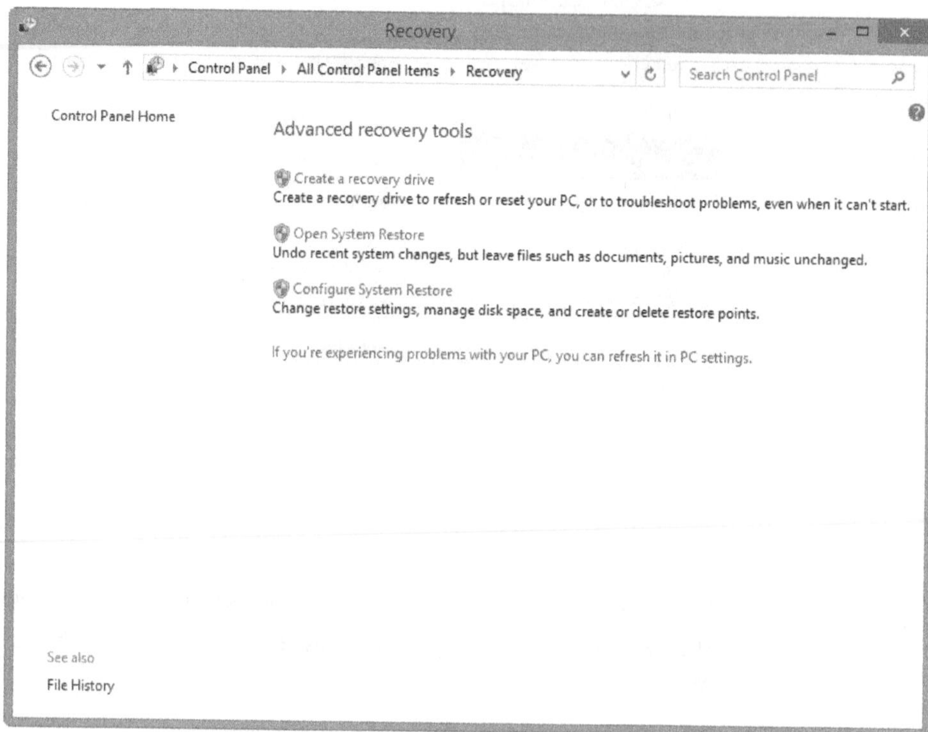

Figure 6-12 The Recovery options in Control Panel include a link for opening Refresh.

Creating a Recovery Drive

You can find the option to create a recovery drive (see Figure 6-13) in Recovery. Sometimes the distinction between CDs, DVDs, and external hard disks can be confusing. A recovery drive will always be a USB flash drive from which you can start your computer, in the event of a disaster, to perform a refresh or a system image restore. In many ways, a recovery drive is the USB equivalent of the system repair disc you learned about earlier.

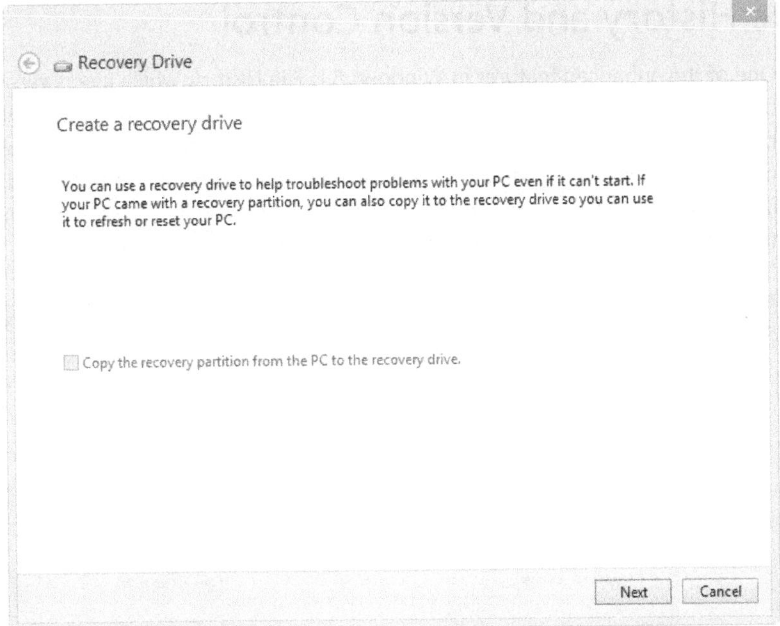

Figure 6-13 Creating a recovery drive in Windows 8 can also include an OEM-created system image.

Most new computers running Windows have a recovery partition instead of an installation DVD. The DVD is very useful for recovery, and you should always get one if you can, but the recovery partition contains everything you need to restore Windows in the event of a disaster.

If your USB flash drive is large enough, you have the option to add the contents of the recovery partition to your flash drive, including the system image that came with the computer when you bought it. The flash drive, therefore, becomes a very valuable resource and one that should be kept in a safe place.

Using File History and Version Control

One of the enhanced features in Windows 8 is File History, which keeps version-controlled backups of your files. You can turn this version control feature on in All Control Panel Items by clicking File History. Previous backup versions can be stored on a local hard drive or on a network location, and there are various advanced settings that you can modify to customize the service to your requirements, as depicted in Figure 6-14. Note that for File History to work, you need to have the Windows 7 file backup schedule turned off.

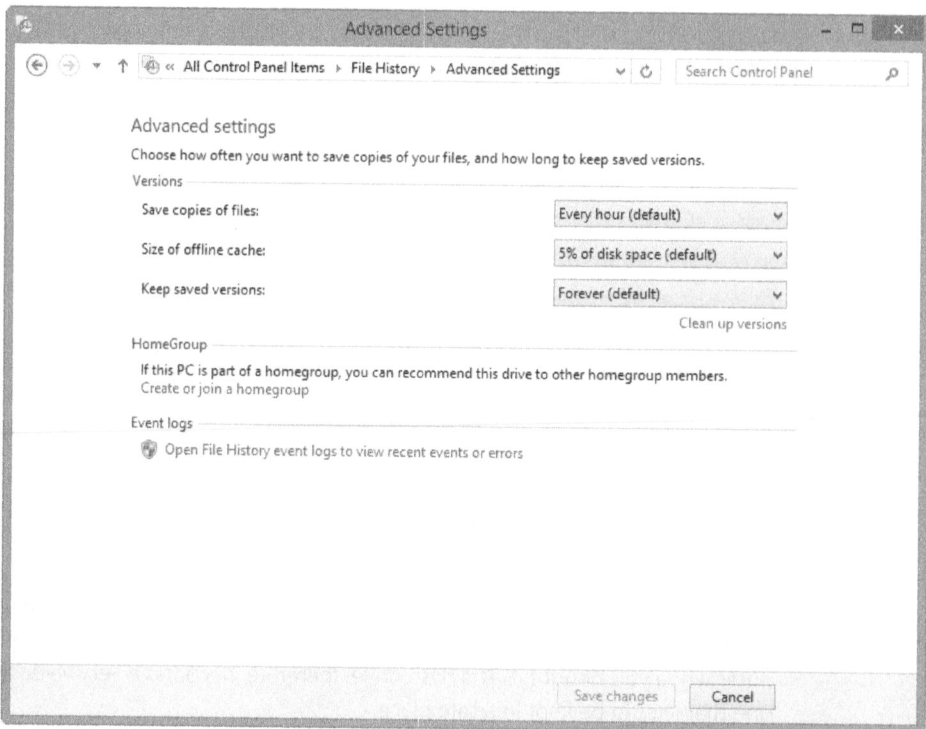

Figure 6-14 The Advanced Settings page for File History presents several useful options.

The settings that you can modify include the following:

- Which folders to exclude from the versioning
- The time when file backups are automatically made
- How much of the hard disk is reserved for file histories
- The length of time Windows should keep saved files

I want to take a moment to discuss music and pictures here, because the topic of how long you should keep saved files is important. If you use your computer at home, you probably play music on it or view pictures and videos. Every time you open one of these files, a file change occurs, even though you don't do a thing to it other than gaze at it. This is because the *last accessed* tag in the file is altered.

As a result, you might find that your File History quickly fills up with versions of your quite large music and image files, while the versions that you *actually* want to keep are deleted. To work around this problem, you can choose to exclude your music and/or picture libraries from the File History.

To restore files by using File History, in File History, in the left pane, click Restore Personal Files.

Storing Multiple Backups

The nineteenth-century playwright and author Oscar Wilde famously said, "To expect the unexpected shows a thoroughly modern intellect," and it's a good motto to live by when deciding how many copies of files, data, and Windows to have backed up and where to keep them. I keep three backups of my files and data:

- One backup is on a second hard disk inside my main computer, intended for quick restore.
- One backup is on a network-attached storage box in my home office.
- I periodically mail an incremental backup (on DVD) to a friend.

This strategy covers all the basics for me, from getting back files in a hurry to guarding against fire and theft. I recommend that you always keep two backups of your files and data. You should keep one with your computer, or close to it, in case you inadvertently lose files that you want back in a hurry. You should store a second backup either with friends or relatives or in a cloud service such as SkyDrive, Carbonite, or Amazon S3. Off-site backup is more important in business, because often the data a business owns is the single most important asset it possesses. It's not worth keeping backup images of your copy of Windows 8 remotely, because in the case of a fire or theft, you would need a replacement computer.

CAUTION!

If you keep critical copies of backups on removable optical discs, be aware that they can degrade over time, eventually becoming unreadable. My advice is to periodically verify that the discs are readable and replace them with other full backups at least once every 12 months.

CHAPTER 7

Performing Maintenance on Windows 8

For the first time, a version of Windows has been produced for both Intel and ARM processors. However, both of these processors work in completely different ways and are incompatible with one another, so the resulting operating systems are very different. This difference is reflected in their names: the Intel version is called Windows 8, and the ARM version is called Windows RT.

Windows RT has advantages over the desktop version. Because it doesn't support traditional desktop programs, less can interfere with its overall smooth running. The operating system is embedded in a chip rather than copied onto an easily erasable hard disk, so it is more robust and harder for malware writers to attack.

This chapter explains the differences between Windows 8 and Windows RT and shows you how to keep your computer healthy.

Maintaining Windows RT

ARM (ARM Holdings, plc.) is a British chip designer whose processors have powered smartphones and tablets internationally for many years. Microsoft has engineered a version of the Windows 8 operating system specifically for these processors.

The advantage of the ARM processor is that it doesn't need maintaining. The automated maintenance tool built into the operating system is all you need to keep Windows running smoothly. Updates aren't delivered to the platform in the same way they are in earlier versions of Windows. Instead, the experience of using a Windows 8 tablet is very similar to that of using a Windows phone with fewer, less frequent updates being delivered than for the Intel version of Windows.

If you are using a Windows 8 tablet with an ARM processor, you will have only a solid-state storage device that will never need defragmenting because the storage is silicon chip–based and, as such, does not suffer from any read slowdown when a file or files are scattered across the disk. All apps are tested for compatibility and malware, so you have fewer stability and security problems, and traditional desktop software won't install.

Using Automatic Maintenance

Windows 8 has an automatic maintenance feature (see Figure 7-1) that performs actions on a specified schedule, including searching for updates, running antivirus scans, and running system diagnostics. You can find Automatic Maintenance in the Maintenance section of Action Center.

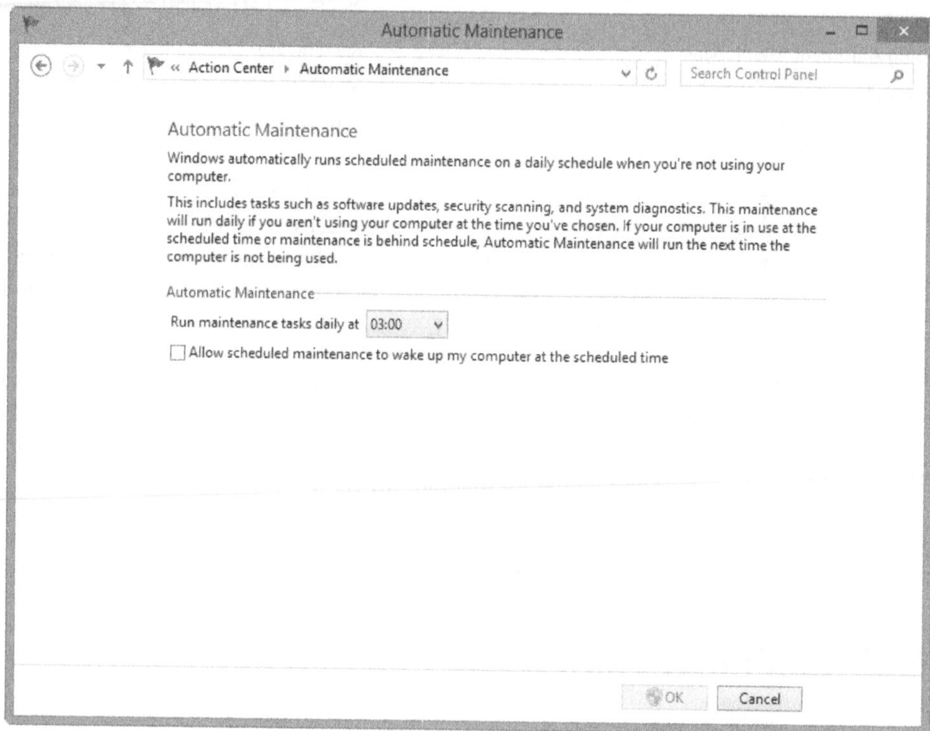

Figure 7-1 The Automatic Maintenance feature in Windows 8 has only a few simple controls.

When you open the Maintenance section in Action Center, you see a link to Change Maintenance Settings. Click this link to find two options: to indicate the time you want the tool to run each day, and whether you want the computer to wake from sleep to perform the maintenance task when the computer is plugged into an electrical outlet. You can tell that maintenance is running when a small static timer icon appears on the Action Center icon on the taskbar.

For casual users, the Automatic Maintenance feature should be all you need to maintain your computer; however, power users and IT professionals may want more control over the removal of temporary files, defragmentation, and so on. I discuss this in the following section.

Defragmenting Your Hard Disks

Does defragmenting your disks actually make a difference to the overall performance of a hard disk? Certainly it does with conventional hard disks. But if you have a solid-state disk drive in your device, defragmenting your disks has no impact at all. These drives are random access, much like the memory in your computer; thus, there's no performance benefit to defragmenting. Because solid-state disks have a finite write life, it can be argued that defragmenting them only reduces their lifespan.

For mechanical hard disks, fragmentation does occur. When your computer writes small files to the disk, the file system puts them in the best available place. However, when you save large files, there may not be enough contiguous space for the entire file to be stored as a single entity. In that case, Windows stores part of the file in one block and other parts in other available spaces, as illustrated in Figure 7-2. This process is called *fragmentation*.

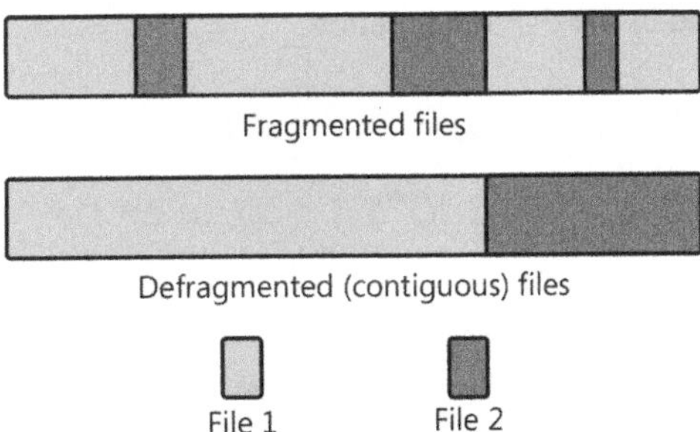

Figure 7-2 A depiction of fragmented and contiguous files.

There's no real risk of data corruption when files are fragmented. However, fragmentation will slow down access to the files slightly. If access speed is important to you, especially regarding Windows operating system files, regularly defragment your computer.

The good news is that Windows 8 can automatically defragment your hard disks. If you want more control—perhaps you prefer determining what hard disks or partitions are defragmented and how often—you can change the defragmentation settings manually.

INSIDE OUT Defragmenting and solid-state disks

If you have a solid-state disk in your computer, I advise you not to defragment it. These drives are random access, so you don't experience an increase in speed, and continually writing to a solid-state disk can shorten the disk's lifespan.

If you are unsure whether you have a solid-state disk in your device, you can find out by checking the defragmenter by opening it as described in this section. Windows tablets and Ultrabooks include solid-state disks by default.

To change the defragmentation settings, on the Start screen, type **defragment** to search in Apps or Settings. The Defragment And Optimize Your Drives link will appear. Click the link to open the Optimize Drives dialog box. When you run the defragmenter, the window displays the fragmentation status of each hard disk and partition in the computer.

Click the Change Settings button to open a smaller Optimize Drives dialog box (see Figure 7-3), in which you can choose when the defragmenter runs, whether you want to be notified if the defragmenter does not run three consecutive times, and which hard disks and partitions are included in the defragmentation.

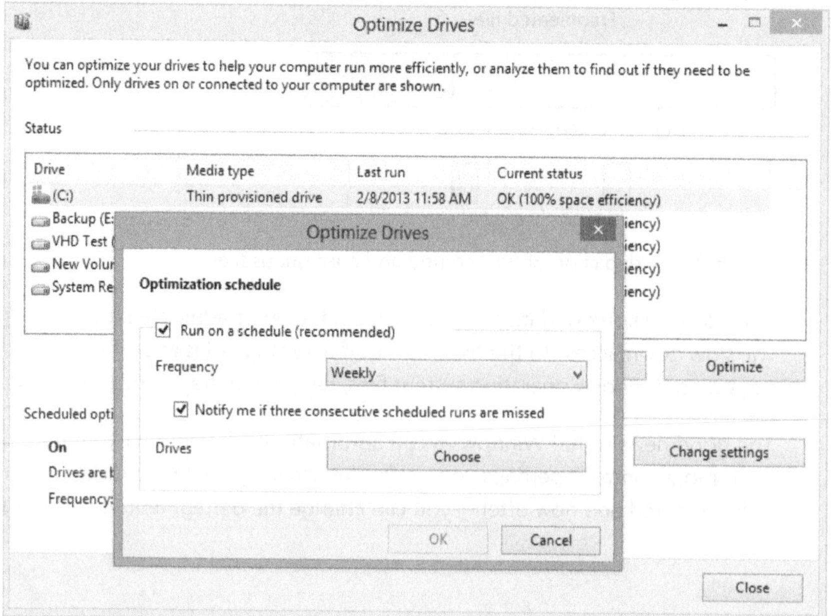

Figure 7-3 The disk defragmenter in Windows 8 offers full control of which hard disks are defragmented and when.

Maintaining Windows 8

Over a period of time, Windows 8 folders become clogged up with all types of old and temporary files, assorted files left over from uninstalled programs, and files that were once used by software you've since uninstalled. These can slow down the computer and certain software. Windows 8 contains a tool called Disk Cleanup that you can use to delete some of these unnecessary files, but other third-party tools are also excellent for keeping Windows 8 healthy such as CCleaner, which I discuss in this chapter in the section titled "CCleaner."

Disk Cleanup

Use Disk Cleanup to delete some of the temporary and other unwanted program files that can slow down Windows 8. To access it, open the Start screen by clicking All Programs. Next, click Accessories, and then click System Tools. You can also find the Disk Cleanup tool by typing **cleanup** on the Start screen. In the Settings results, click Free Up Disk Space By Deleting Unnecessary Files.

You might be prompted to indicate which drive you want to clean; in most cases, you will choose drive C. By default, Disk Cleanup recommends items to delete, but it also offers additional options if you want to reclaim even more space, as shown in Figure 7-4.

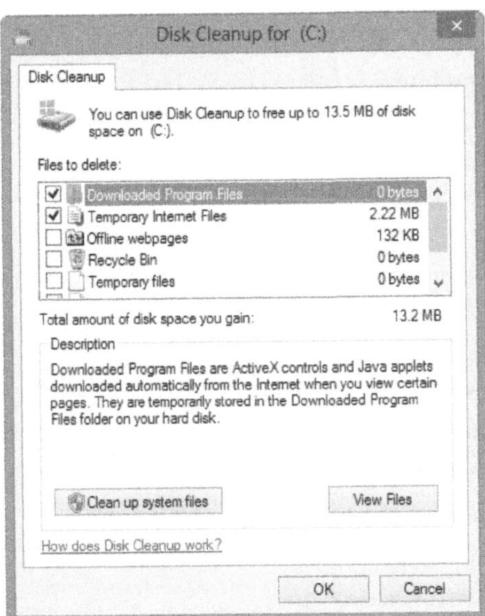

Figure 7-4 The Disk Cleanup tool displays a list of files that can safely be removed from your computer.

Clicking Clean Up System Files displays the More Options tab, which includes the choice to delete operating system restore files. However, you should remove these only if you are very confident that Windows 8 is running completely fine.

Internet and Other Temporary Files

Many of the temporary files on your computer are from your web browser. The method to clear these temporary files differs from browser to browser. For the desktop app of Windows Internet Explorer 10, which ships with Windows 8, you can easily locate the files for removal and cleaning via the Delete Browsing History dialog box. You access this by clicking Settings and then Safety on the menu bar, and then clicking Delete Browsing History. You can also access the Delete Browsing History dialog box in the desktop app of Internet Explorer by pressing Ctrl+Shift+Delete on your keyboard.

In the Delete Browsing History dialog box, shown in Figure 7-5, you can delete temporary Internet files and other items that are not deleted by Disk Cleanup while still preserving the data you want to keep.

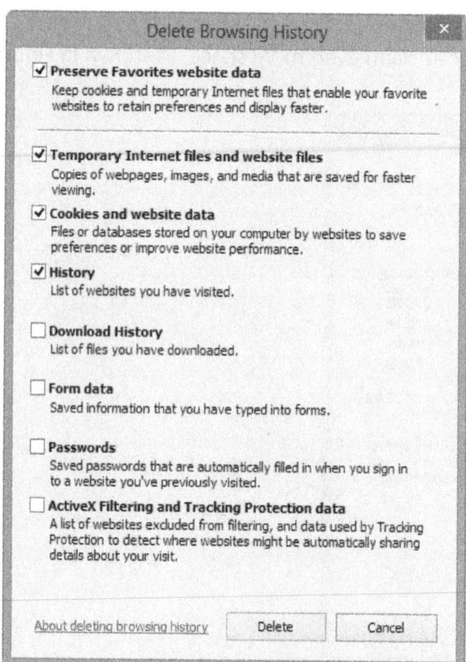

Figure 7-5 You can clean up temporary files in Internet Explorer.

CCleaner

Many third-party companies create tools and utilities for keeping Windows 8 running efficiently. One tool in particular stands out and is considered one of the best programs available for tidying up Windows files: CCleaner (*http://www.piriform.com/ccleaner*). By default, it has very sensible settings, but there are some advanced options, too, which should be used only by advanced users. These advanced features include the ability to clean old and unwanted items from the Windows 8 registry. Note, however, that the use of third-party tools such as CCleaner is not supported by Microsoft, so if you encounter a problem and require technical support, Microsoft will be unable to help you.

INSIDE OUT **Do registry optimizers work?**

The *registry* is a database that stores all Windows settings (user profiles, permissions, and so on) and all the settings for the software you have installed. As settings change and programs are uninstalled, the registry can become fragmented in the same way a hard disk can. There is some debate about whether *optimizing* (defragmenting) this database actually provides any speed improvements. The answer can depend on how old your computer is and how much memory it has.

When Windows starts, it loads many of its files into your computer's memory. The more memory your computer has, the more files it can accommodate. Files loaded into memory can be read much faster than files on the hard disk.

Stability is another issue to consider. A database that becomes very fragmented can eventually become corrupt. This corruption could happen to the registry, too, and defragmenting it could be a good option. However, it's unclear exactly what effect, if any, optimizing your registry has, so although it's a function that some software packages perform, don't be too worried if your clean-up tool is unable to defragment the registry.

The Impact of Installing Too Much Software

Modern computers and operating are capable of running huge numbers of programs and apps and managing the different and sometimes conflicting files from these programs with ease. If you've wondered why the WinSXS folder on your computer is so large, it's because this is where Windows handles all these conflicting versions of files.

There is a case to be made, however, for not installing too much of the wrong type of desktop software, that is, trialware, freeware, and other software written by small software houses and individuals. The reason for this is that although Windows 8 handles its new style apps in a very efficient way, some desktop software packages, especially earlier ones and those written on a tight budget or to a tight schedule, can use workarounds that can cause conflicts with other software. They also can be poorly written to begin with.

My advice is always to keep the amount of smaller desktop packages you have installed to a minimum. Large software houses have the time and resources to devote to making sure their software will not cause problems on your PC, but small software houses can't always give this assurance.

Hardware drivers in your PC can also cause problems when written by smaller hardware manufacturers or third-party companies who decide to write their own drivers for existing hardware. Windows can become unresponsive because of incompatibilities with a software component or a hardware driver. Incompatibility happens because no manufacturer can test every combination of every software package and hardware device for stability. Microsoft offers certification programs for software and hardware in Windows 8, but this certification still cannot test how a specific piece of hardware or software will interact with other hardware and software; this is especially the case for packages that haven't been through the optional certification.

Note

All new apps in Windows 8 will be available exclusively through the Windows Store. All apps sold in the Windows Store are engineered by using approved development tools from Microsoft, and all apps are tested for general stability and malware.

Windows is built on an open platform, and anyone, including enthusiastic amateurs, can write applications for it. This is why Windows is now the most flexible and extensible computing platform in the world. However, you should be aware that some software written for organizations does not go through the sometimes expensive Microsoft certification program. Also, why send your software to Microsoft for certification when only you will be using it? You can see how a limitless number of combinations of hardware and software can be installed on a computer. This can make the whole system unpredictable, and although Microsoft has taken great strides to make Windows 8 as stable as possible, problems can still occur.

My tips for avoiding problems with installed software and hardware are as follows:

- Don't buy any hardware that has not passed Windows 8 certification and does not display the "Certified for Windows 8" logo.
- Avoid shareware and freeware written by small software companies and individuals, if you can.
- Avoid installing trialware that will sit unused on your computer and expire after a while.
- Install only software that you'll actually use!

Keeping Windows 8 Updated

One of the most important strategies you can implement to avoid instabilities with Windows 8 is to turn on Windows Update and have it download updates on a regular schedule. Periodically, incompatibilities are reported and fixed by Microsoft and then distributed through Windows Update on what is frequently referred to as *Patch Tuesday*—the second Tuesday of every month. These updates can fix all types of issues that can cause Windows to become unstable or unresponsive, so it's important to leave Windows Update turned on. Windows Update is discussed in more depth in Chapter 4, "Using the Basic Windows Utilities."

Minimizing Autorunning Software

By default, many programs you install run automatically every time you start your computer, including common favorites such as Adobe Acrobat Reader and Apple iTunes software. Some of these software packages are updaters that sit in your notification area and check the software writers' website periodically for updates to the software. People have been asking Microsoft to allow third-party vendors to distribute their updates via Windows Update for years now, but it has not happened yet. For some software, you might find it advantageous to keep the updater running. In other cases, you might not. Adobe Acrobat PDF files, for instance, are a frequent source of virus infection. If you do not want the Adobe Updater software running every time Windows starts, run it manually at least every month. It can be a good idea to run other updaters also, such as iTunes, only when you actually want to run the software.

Autorunning software doesn't just slow down your computer and increase your carbon footprint (you'd be surprised how much extra money you're paying on your electricity bill by running these things). It also can cause other issues, such as file fragmentation and temporary file clutter, because it runs in the background.

Autorunning software is now managed in the Task Manager, which you can access by pressing Ctrl+Alt+Del on your keyboard or by right-clicking the taskbar. When you're in the Task Manager, click the More Details arrow, and then click the Startup tab (see Figure 7-6). Here you will see what programs are set to run at startup and what impact Windows calculates each has on startup time.

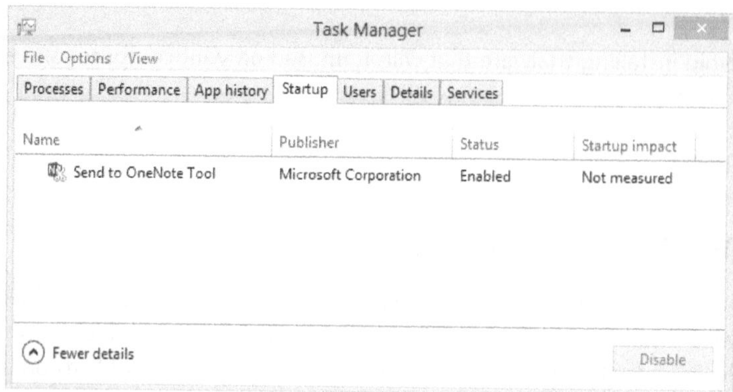

Figure 7-6 You can manage startup programs in the Task Manager.

You might want to deselect some apps to reduce file clutter, processor cycles, and your electricity bill. Remember, the more the computer is doing, the more electricity and battery it will use. You can disable a particular application (or reenable it) by clicking to select it and then clicking Disable.

Periodically Refreshing Windows

With earlier versions of Windows, you needed to format your hard disk and reinstall the operating system regularly as it became unstable. Since the introduction of Windows Vista and its system imaging tool, this process has become almost a moot point. If your computer is used frequently for big and complex jobs, amassing temporary files and incompatibilities can cause problems over time, and you might find that you benefit from refreshing your Windows installation periodically to help keep things running quickly and smoothly.

This restore doesn't need to be a complete reinstall. You can simply restore from a Windows system image that you created, which contains all your settings and software, or use the Windows 8 refresh option. Because this is a clean image, however, you can consider the computer reinstalled.

In Chapter 2, "Repairing Common Issues in Windows 8," I discuss how to back up a working copy of the operating system, complete with all of your programs and hardware installed. You know that the copy you have backed up will be fresh and working fine, so I advise that you restore this backup, update it by using Windows Update, update any programs as necessary, and then back up this new system.

CAUTION!

Remember: don't use the computer too much while preparing it to be backed up. This will help prevent accumulation of temporary files or incompatibilities that would then be part of your backup.

Set some time aside to reinstall Windows, and take your time updating your system thoroughly before locking it down again in a fresh operating system image backup.

CHAPTER 8

Managing Users in Windows 8

DESPITE BEST INTENTIONS, users can be responsible for computer problems in some way, which is why IT support departments have such strict rules about how users operate their computers. IT departments are often ultimately responsible for mitigating losses resulting from user errors. This is why the first part of this book has been devoted to helping prevent problems before they occur. It doesn't matter whether you're reading Part I, "Preventing Problems," to help fix problems with your computer at home, or you manage a corporate network with thousands of computers—either way, downtime costs.

How User Account Control Works

In every earlier version of Windows through Windows XP, users are administrators by default. Being an administrator means that you have complete control over everything in the operating system and can install programs, and delete or move files, without restriction. An administrator in Windows 8 has the same power, but User Account Control (UAC) adds a layer of protection.

The Windows development team at Microsoft recognizes that users will make changes to the operating system, either unintentionally or without understanding the true repercussions. More important, they know that malicious software and viruses will want to do this, too.

UAC helps prevent inadvertent or malicious changes to critical system processes by putting a security layer between the user and any action that Windows determines could cause harm to or destabilize the operating system. When UAC is activated by a questionable action, Windows 8 opens the desktop app in a secure session, where only the UAC dialog box is active and only a user, not software, can make a selection.

UAC is a useful but not foolproof way to protect Windows 8 from attack, however. It's still easy for a user to click Yes without reading or properly understanding the implications of doing so.

Managing User Accounts

There are a great many ways to manage users on a computer and to prevent people from installing unauthorized software, making unnecessary changes, and downloading and opening harmful files from the Internet. But managing user accounts can be a complex process. This section covers some ways to manage user accounts.

Setting an Administrator Password

With UAC, a user can bypass security warnings by clicking in a dialog box. For better security on a multiuser desktop, you can set the main user as an administrator and all other users as standard users. Standard users have far fewer privileges to change Windows. They are even further restricted if you establish a password for the administrator account, which prevents someone from clicking through a UAC dialog box without entering the password.

INSIDE OUT **The pros and cons of setting an administrator password**

On a multiuser computer, protecting the main administrator account with a password prevents other users from logging in as the administrator and upgrading their own accounts from standard users to administrators. But be aware that setting an administrator password can have a downside. Password protection for the administrator account prevents users from making even legitimate changes to Windows or other required software.

To set up additional user accounts on your computer, follow these simple instructions:

1. On the Start screen, press Windows logo key+C.
2. Click the Settings charm.
3. Click Change PC Settings.
4. Click Users, as illustrated in Figure 8-1.

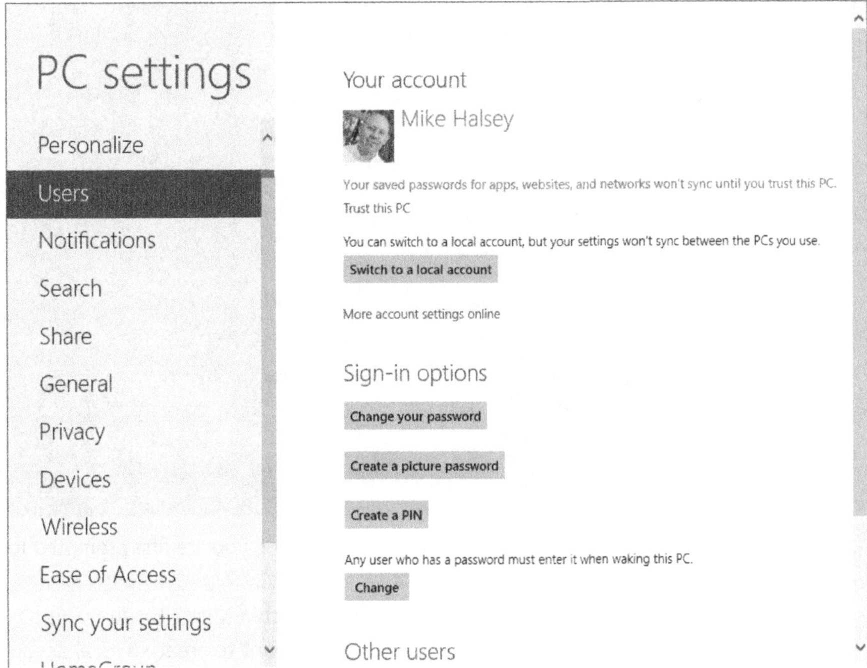

Figure 8-1 You manage and create user accounts in PC Settings.

5. Click the + (plus) button next to Add A User in the Other Users section.

   The Add A User wizard appears, shown in Figure 8-2. You have a choice of whether to allow the user to use his or her Microsoft Account ID on the computer or create a user account specific to the computer. To create a user account specific to the computer, click Sign In Without A Microsoft Account?, and then click Next.

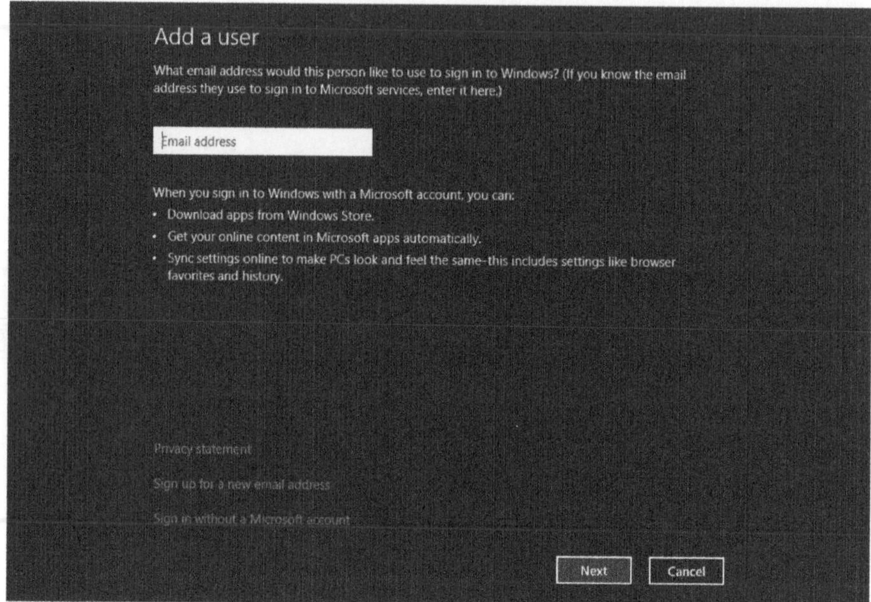
Add a user
What email address would this person like to use to sign in to Windows? (If you know the email address they use to sign in to Microsoft services, enter it here.)
Email address
When you sign in to Windows with a Microsoft account, you can:
• Download apps from Windows Store.
• Get your online content in Microsoft apps automatically.
• Sync settings online to make PCs look and feel the same–this includes settings like browser favorites and history.
Privacy statement
Sign up for a new email address
Sign in without a Microsoft account
Next
Cancel

Figure 8-2 When you add a user account, you are first prompted to use a Microsoft Account ID.

If you want the new user to sign in with a Microsoft Account ID, the wizard asks for the user name and password. If you want to create a local account, proceed to step 6.

CAUTION!

When you sign into a computer that you might use only once, such as a computer at a friend's house or remote office, you might leave Internet Favorites and temporary files on the PC that potentially can be accessed by other users. Deleting the user account when you are finished, or signing in to the guest account, can help prevent this.

6. The next page of the wizard explains the difference between creating a Local Account or a Microsoft Account (see Figure 8-3). Click Local Account to continue.

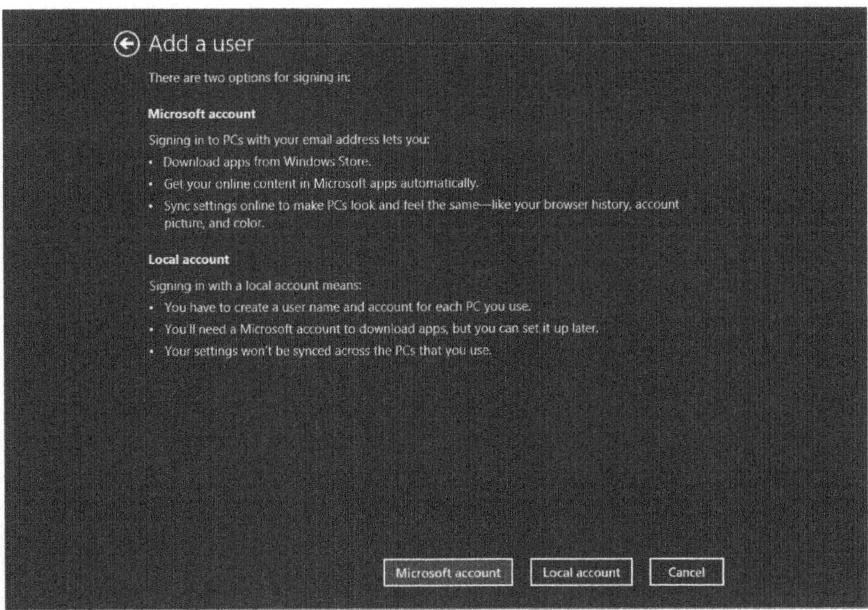

Figure 8-3 When you choose to create a local account, you need to confirm this on the next page of the wizard.

7. In the text boxes shown in Figure 8-4, type a user name and optional password for the account, and then click Next.

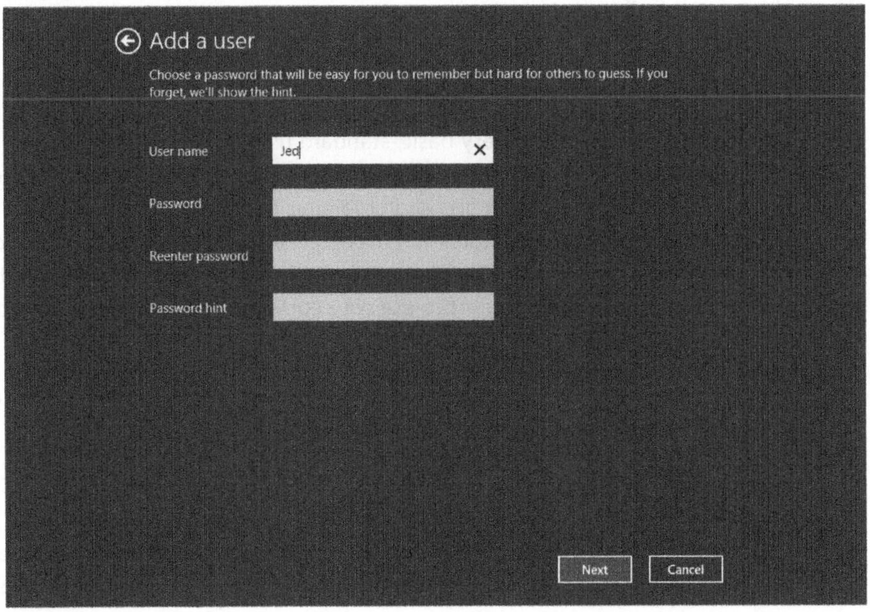

Figure 8-4 You are asked for a user name, password (plus confirmation), and a password hint.

8. On the last page of the wizard, when the account is created, a message saying the new user can sign in is displayed, as shown in Figure 8-5. Click Finish to complete the process.

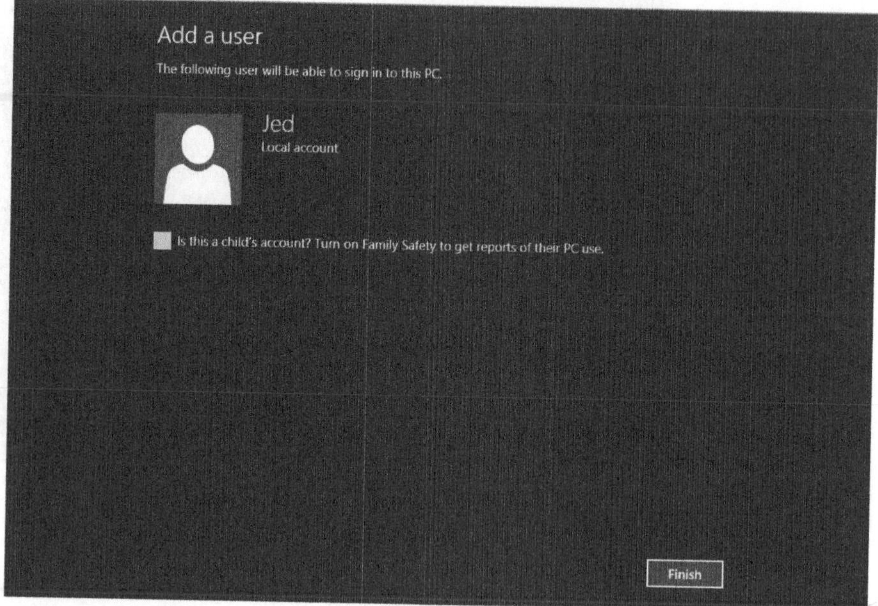

Figure 8-5 You are asked whether the account is for a child, and if so, whether you want Family Safety reports.

The Guest User Account

A *guest account* is a very basic, standard user account, automatically included with Windows 8, that can be turned on and off as needed when you would prefer certain people not have access to your files and programs. The guest account setting in Windows 8 can prevent occasional visitors from making changes to your computer or doing things that can affect other users. The guest account is also useful for quickly creating a user account when someone new wants to use your computer, for example, when you have visitors.

You turn on the guest account from the Users section of Control Panel. To do this, on the Start screen, search for **User**, and in the Settings search results, click User Accounts, and then click Manage Another Account.

> **Note**
>
> **Unless you have a password on your administrator account, anyone logged in with a standard user account will be able to click Yes on UAC security prompts.**

INSIDE OUT Hiding your files from other users

By default, Windows 8 stores your files and data on the same hard disk or partition as your Windows 8 installation. In Chapter 2, "Repairing Common Issues in Windows 8," and Chapter 5, "Optimizing Windows 8 Security," I explain how to move your files away from your Windows installation to secure them in the event Windows 8 becomes unresponsive.

Unfortunately, there's a downside to this strategy when it comes to multiuser systems. When user files are located on the Windows drive, the operating system hides them from other users. When you move those files to another disk or partition, those files become visible to everyone. In this circumstance, a user will initially be barred from viewing files, but if that user has administrator rights, he or she can take ownership of those files and folders and access them.

Windows 8 does not come with a tool for hiding disks or partitions from specific users, but you can set individual user permissions on folders to deny access to other users. Also, there are many third-party tools and tips, most of them free, for hiding disks or partitions and user files.

Family Safety

Windows 8 includes an excellent and full-featured parental control package called Family Safety. This utility, though, has many more uses than just preventing your children from playing games late at night. You can also use it to limit access to certain software packages. You might, for instance, have some work-related software on your home computer that you don't want other users to access.

To access Family Safety in Windows 8, on the Start screen, type **parent**. In the search results, click Set Up Family Safety For Any User.

INSIDE OUT Using Family Safety in Windows 8

To use Family Safety (see Figure 8-6), you must have at least one administrator account and one standard user. You apply Family Safety to the standard user.

The administrator accounts must be password-protected for the feature to work; otherwise, the standard user will be able to log on using an administrator account and then turn the Family Safety off.

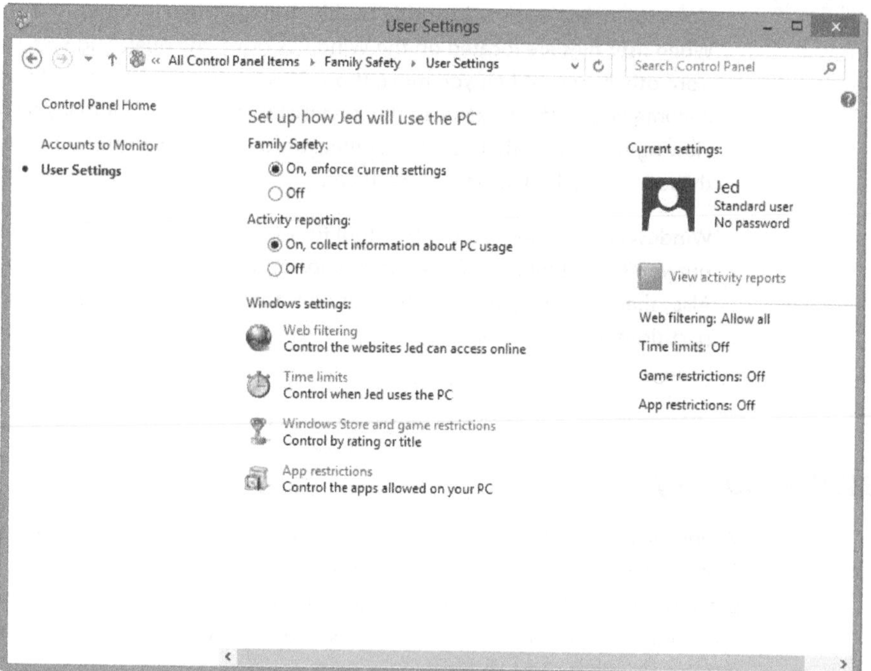

Figure 8-6 You can turn Family Safety on and off in User Settings.

By using the Web Filtering feature in Family Safety (see Figure 8-7), you can prevent children from accessing inappropriate or unsuitable websites.

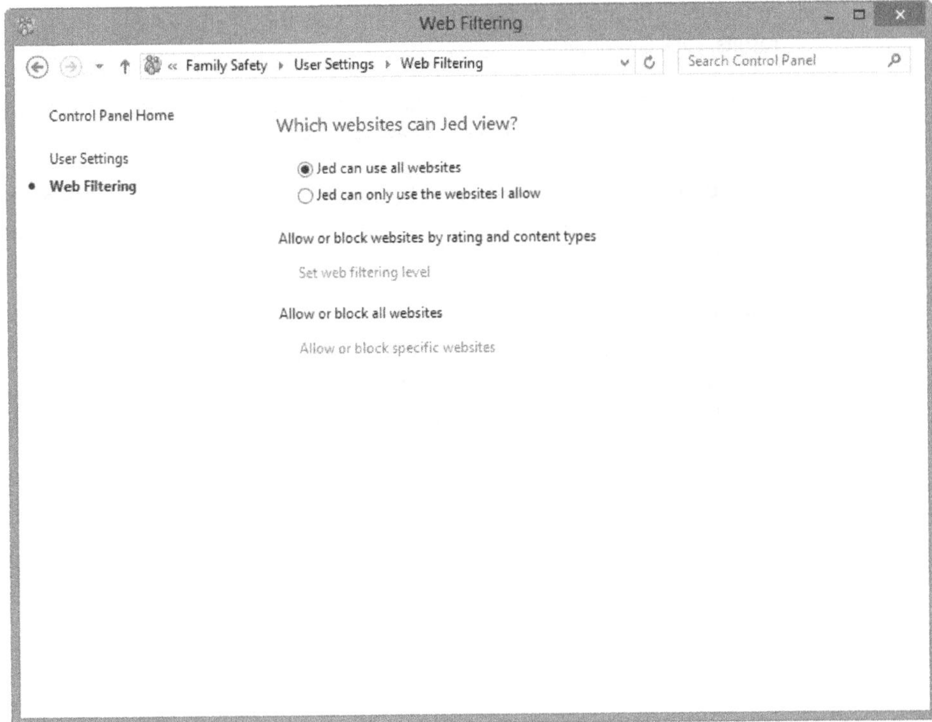

Figure 8-7 With the new Web Filter in Windows 8, you can automatically or manually filter websites.

The web filter has controls to allow access to only those websites that fall within four categories: Child-friendly, General Interest, Online Communication, and Warn An Adult. It can also block file downloads. These categories are very effective in helping prevent malware from infecting a computer.

Group Policies

The Local Group Policy Editor is used almost exclusively in business and corporate IT environments. To access it, on the Start screen, type **gpedit.msc**, and then in the Apps search results, click Gpedit.msc.

The Local Group Policy Editor interface is split into two main sections, Computer Configuration and User Configuration, and functions as follows:

- **Computer Configuration** This section includes settings for the entire computer. You will probably not want to change these unless, for example, you are turning off Windows Firewall or Windows Update in a corporate IT environment.
- **User Configuration** This section provides the settings that apply to specific users. These settings are typically specified remotely by a Group Policy for the server domain, but if you are changing these settings in Windows 8, you must do so on a per-user basis while logged on to that specific user account (see Figure 8-8).

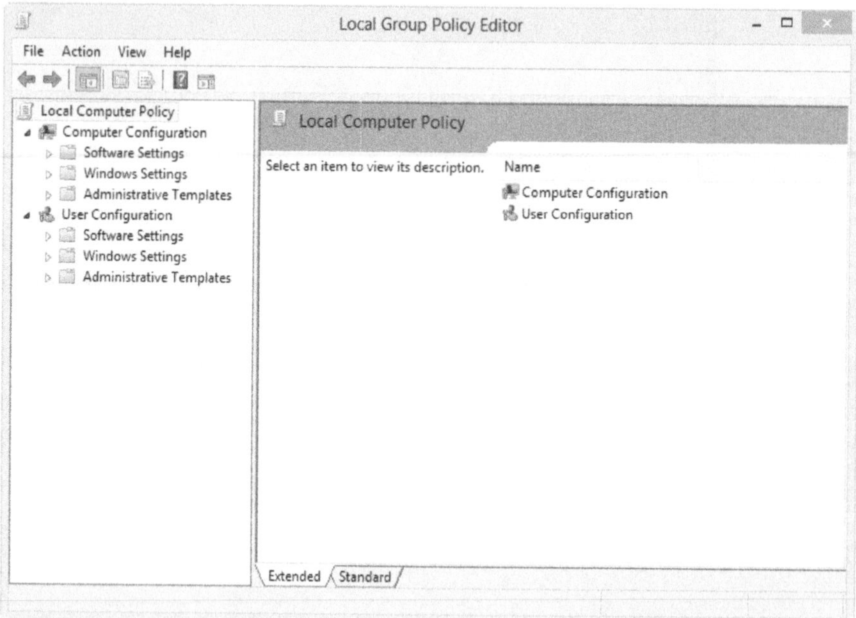

Figure 8-8 You specify settings for a specific user in the Local Group Policy Editor.

Each of these configuration sections is subdivided further into Software Settings, Windows Settings, and Administrative Templates.

You will rarely want to change settings in Local Group Policy Editor unless you are a system administrator on a company network. However, in certain circumstances, changing settings might be appropriate. For example, you might want to enhance security to block user access to the Run command on the Start screen and the Win+X menu, deny users access to common Windows features such as Windows Media Player, or change the default Windows security level for opening email attachments.

Fortunately, all the available options in the Local Group Policy Editor are clearly labeled, and all include detailed descriptions of what happens when you edit them. This can help you understand how each selection will affect you and other users on your computer so that you can make informed choices.

Local Security Policies

Another tool used almost exclusively in business and corporate IT environments is the Local Security Policy window, which is shown in Figure 8-9. To access Local Security Policy, in Control Panel, click Administrative Tools, and then click Local Security Policy (see Figure 8-9). You can read more about the differences between local group and security policies at *http://social.technet.microsoft.com/Forums/en-US/winservermanager/thread/d10b716f-e76a-4d44-94ce-8fe19f5bc1d6*.

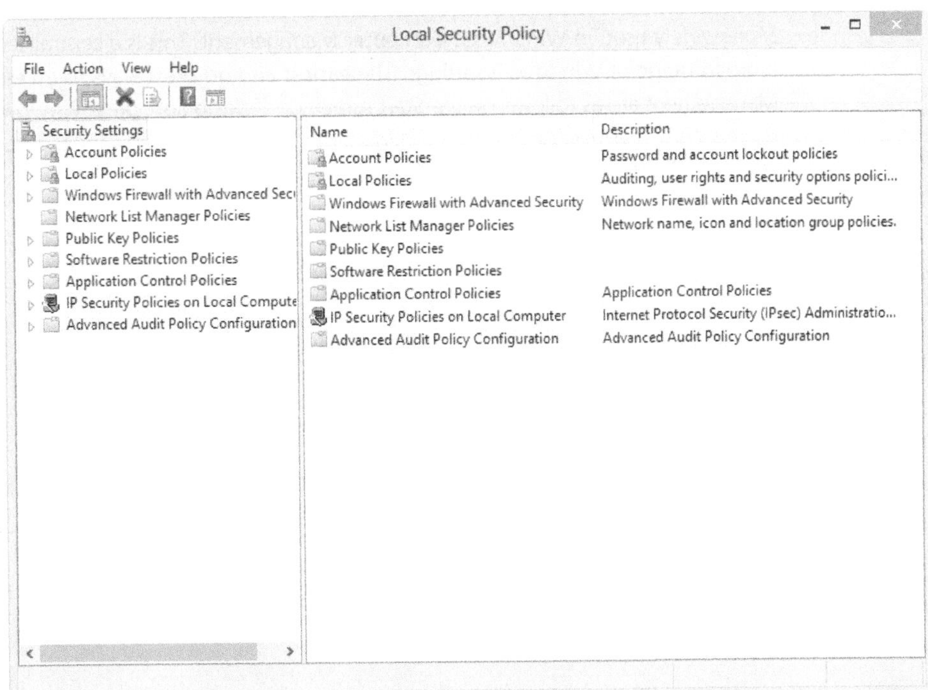

Figure 8-9 The Local Security Policy Settings layout is similar to that of the Group Policy editor.

Most users won't need to change any settings in the Local Security Policy window, and for general computer usage, there's absolutely no need to, because the default security in Windows 8 is extremely robust. However, you can access the following two useful features:

- **Windows Firewall with Advanced Security** Using this feature, you can configure specific rules to allow hardware or software through the Windows 8 firewall. This might include games or access to network storage.
- **Application Control Policies** If you have the Enterprise or Pro version of Windows 8, you have access to a feature called AppLocker. Using this feature, you can control which version of which software can be installed on your computer—especially useful for features such as graphics card drivers for games and some add-ins (for example, Adobe Flash) that will work only with specific software versions. You can use this tool to block the installation of other versions of those applications.

As with the Local Group Policy Editor, all the available options in the Local Security Policy Editor are clear and display detailed descriptions when you click their properties. This makes it easy to understand how each option will affect you and other users on the computer and helps you to make informed choices.

Computer Management

More widely used in Windows is Computer Management. This is a centralized location for a broad range of Windows 8 settings. The easiest and quickest ways to access Computer Management are as follows: on the Start screen or desktop app, press Windows logo key+X; on the Winx menu, click Computer Management. The Computer Management console is shown in Figure 8-10.

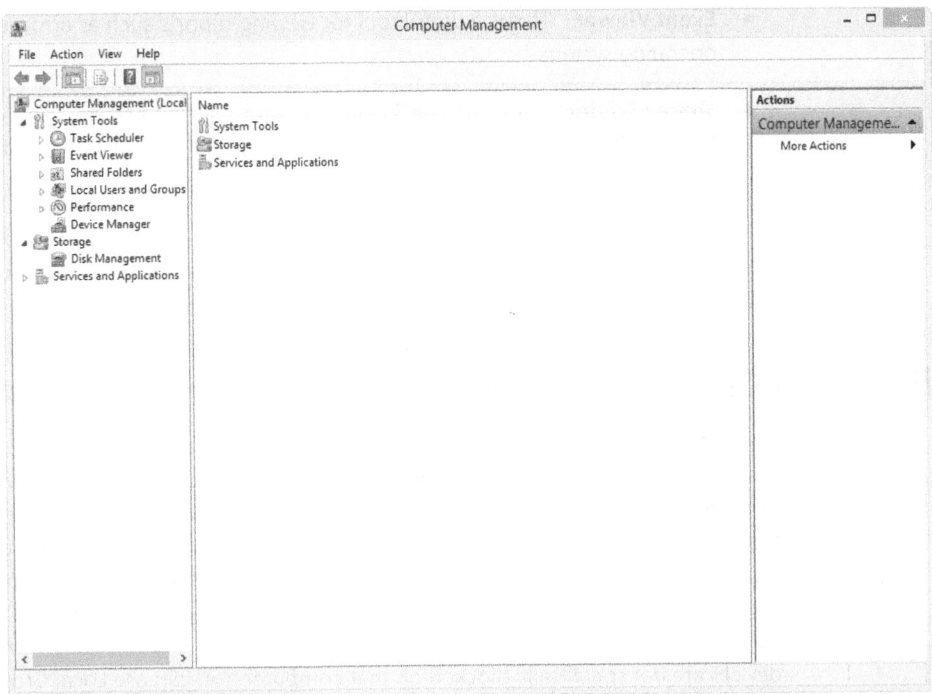

Figure 8-10 The Computer Management console displays all available categories on the left side.

The left pane of the Computer Management console includes links to all the relevant tools and utilities for managing your computer. Following are some that will be of particular interest to you:

- **Task Scheduler** You might find that you want Windows 8 to run certain tasks on a set schedule, such as disk cleanup. You can set any task or program to run on a schedule you define by clicking Task Scheduler in the Computer Management console.

- **Event Viewer** This is a useful tool for viewing reports such as error reports from the operating system.
- **Shared Folders** You can use Shared Folders to permit and deny access to folders that are shared among users on the same computer or across different computers in a home network.

I discuss some of these features in more depth in Chapter 20, "Using Advanced Repair Methods." These and the other features in the Computer Management console are discussed in Chapter 33, "Using Advanced Windows 8 Diagnostic Tools."

Blocking CDs, DVDs, Flash Drives, and External Hard Disks

One of the biggest security problems—certainly one of the biggest in the corporate space—is the use of external flash drives, CDs, DVDs, and external hard disks. If not carefully vetted, these media can transfer viruses and other malware to a computer or be used to steal information. Although computer equipment within an organization can be controlled by using group and security policies, computers external to the company are not subject to the same rules, and these computers can transfer malware to USB hard disks and flash drives. From there, the malware could be transferred to a company computer if these devices are not specifically blocked on that computer. You can use Local Group Policy Editor to deny access to these devices for specific users or for everyone.

To access the Removable Storage Access settings in the Local Group Policy Editor (see Figure 8-11), click User Configuration\Administrative Templates\System\Removable Storage Access.

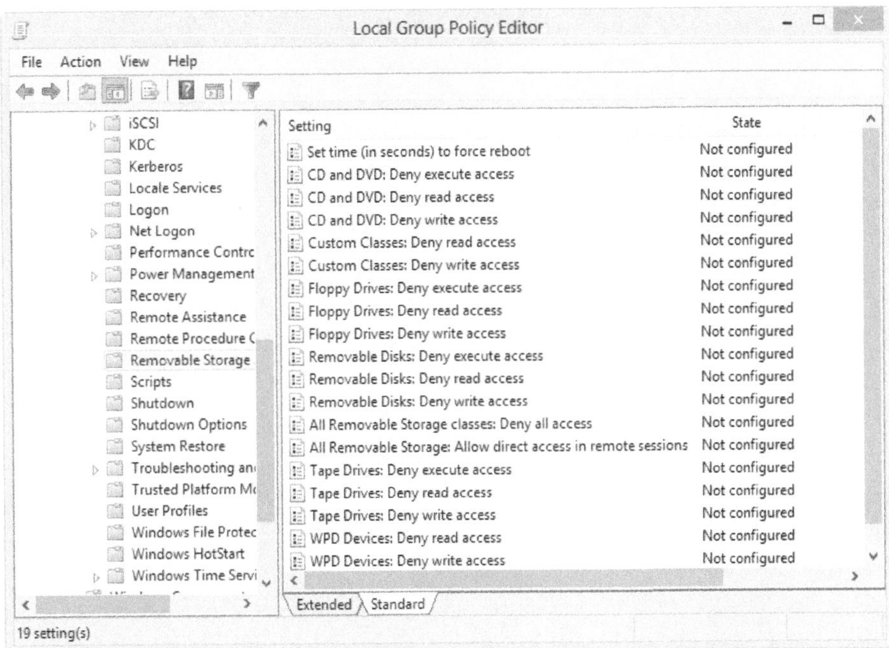

Figure 8-11 You can manage removable storage in the Local Group Policy Editor.

> **Note**
>
> **USB flash drives and external hard disks are classified as *removable* disks. To allow or deny access to a wide range of plug-in drives, right-click any of the settings, click Edit, and then click Disable to block access.**

CHAPTER 9

Maintaining Hardware

YOUR COMPUTER HAS MANY COMPONENTS: the monitor, the motherboard, sockets, the processor, and so on. Sometimes, the hardware is responsible for problems that occur. This chapter discusses the hardware in your computer, what it does, what can go wrong with it, and how you can help prevent problems.

What's in a Computer?

Your computer is a collection of components of all types, shapes, and sizes; some of these components are not intended to be taken apart, and some are put together in such a way that you can quickly and simply swap them out for newer, updated components. The following sections describe these components and how they connect to one another.

The Motherboard

The motherboard is where all of the components in your computer connect. The chips and circuits on this board regulate all the processes and functions of your computer. The motherboard itself rarely fails, but some onboard components, especially those with heat sinks (a metal protrusion much like a radiator that sits on the top of a component) or fans, can cause problems because they get very hot. This heat puts physical stress on the components over time, and a piece of hardware such as a fan will likely fail after a few years, resulting in damage from overheating.

Sockets

Sockets are the ports and slots on the motherboard into which you plug hardware such as TV tuners or graphics cards, or leads that connect to USB devices or a Blu-ray drive. Each component on the motherboard has its own unique plug shape, ensuring that users plug a cable or device into the correct socket, preventing damage to the system. Sometimes, it can be very difficult to push plugs into the sockets on a motherboard. Take care that the motherboard is properly supported when plugging cables and devices into it to avoid putting too much strain on the substratum, which can crack the board.

The BIOS

The basic input/output system (BIOS) is software on a chip (firmware) that is updated infrequently (if ever) because the purpose of the BIOS and the hardware types it is required to work with rarely change. The BIOS regulates the computer and gets it started. It initializes all the hardware and allows the software to communicate with that hardware. The BIOS checks the components for errors during startup, a process referred to as the Power On Self-Test (POST), and reports any issues either through warning lights on the motherboard or, more commonly, through a series of warning beeps. (The particular sound of these beeps depends on the BIOS manufacturer.) BIOS software is made by several companies, including AMI, Phoenix, and Award.

The BIOS beeps can give you clear information about where a fault or potential fault lies with your hardware. When you start your computer, BIOS produces one short beep to indicate that the POST has completed and all is well and that all of the detected hardware is working properly. (Note that the status of USB-attached hardware is not reported by a computer's BIOS.) If you hear combinations of short and long beeps indicating an issue, check the manual for your motherboard or the manufacturer's website for the cause. You can find more information about how to troubleshoot your computer's hardware and its BIOS in Chapter 24, "Diagnosing Hardware Problems."

The BIOS can be reset to its factory default settings easily, and you might need to do this if your computer will not start or cannot detect a specific hardware device. You might also need to reset it to the factory defaults if it does not detect new hardware after you install it. You can do this by locating the reset jumper; refer to the manual that came with your computer for its location. On the reset jumper are three pins sticking outward from the motherboard, which are known as Clear CMOS (CMOS stands for complementary metal oxide semiconductor), and a small connector (known as a jumper) covering two of them.

To reset the BIOS, move the jumper to cover the middle pin and the currently uncovered pin for 10 seconds, and then return the jumper to its original position. You might need to do this because the BIOS can sometimes become stuck and unable to properly update itself. To reset your BIOS on a desktop computer, follow the next set of steps.

CAUTION!

You should always ensure that you are grounded before working inside a computer to avoid an electrostatic discharge that can short out sensitive components. You can do this by wearing an antistatic wristband. If you are in a country that incorporates a ground wire in the electricity circuit, such as the United Kingdom, I recommend leaving the computer plugged into the electric source while you remove the case (be absolutely certain that the power is turned off) and touching your fingers to the power supply inside the case before unplugging the main power lead. If you are not in a country that incorporates a ground wire, the computer must be unplugged when you open the case. This ensures that the computer is properly grounded and prevents static electricity from damaging components.

Note

For all-in-one and laptop computers, refer to the documentation that came with your device regarding how to reset the BIOS.

1. Ensure that the computer is turned off and disconnected from the main power source. Ground yourself to safely discharge any electrostatic buildup by touching an unpainted area on the computer case with your fingertips. You should also use an antistatic wristband, if possible, to protect against continued electrostatic build-up while you're working inside any sensitive electronic device.
2. Open the side of the computer to expose the motherboard, placing the computer on a level, firm surface.

3. Find the battery on the motherboard. It looks like—and, indeed, is—a large watch battery (see Figure 9-1). Unclip the battery to remove it from the motherboard.

Figure 9-1 The BIOS reset jumper and wristwatch-type battery are normally located together on a motherboard.

4. There will be a Clear CMOS jumper somewhere on the motherboard, usually close to the battery, as shown in Figure 9-2; check the motherboard manual for the exact location. The Clear CMOS jumper is a three-pin socket with a small connector covering two of the pins. Remove the connector from the jumper by pulling it straight upward (a small pair of tweezers is useful for doing this) and move the jumper so that it covers the center pin and the previously uncovered pin.

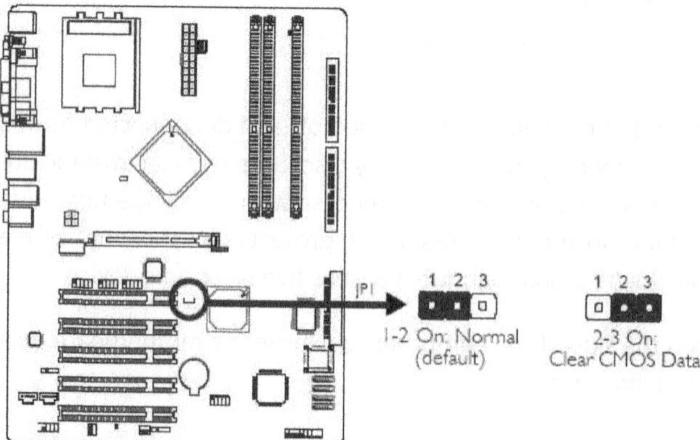

Figure 9-2 This diagram shows a motherboard and the clear CMOS jumper location.

5. Leave the jumper in the Clear CMOS position, as described in step 4, for 10 seconds.
6. Move the jumper back to its original position.
7. Replace the motherboard battery.
8. Reassemble the computer case and reconnect it to the main power supply.

Northbridge and Southbridge Chipsets and the PCH

Two of the hottest components on the motherboard—so much so that they often actually have their own heat sink or fan—are the Northbridge and Southbridge chips. These regulate all the communications between components in the computer; thus, they have a lot of work to do and get very hot.

You should occasionally check that the heat sink or fan is free from dust and obstructions such as stray wires or cables and that there is good airflow inside the computer. You can be reasonably sure of good airflow if no major obstacles are preventing the clean flow of air from the front of the case to the rear.

As mentioned earlier in the chapter, the chip components and their circuitry expand and contract as they heat and cool. Over a long period of time, this can cause physical wear and tear on the chip and will eventually cause it to fail. Fortunately, these chipsets are designed to operate under extremely hot conditions over a very long period of time and are extensively stress-tested by the manufacturers. Normally only an action such as shaking or moving the computer when the components are warming up or cooling down will exacerbate this wear and tear, and this is why laptops and tablets commonly have a shorter lifespan than desktop computers. (It is also why an MP3 player won't last as long as your grandmother's old kitchen radio!).

In newer computers, the Northbridge and Southbridge chips have been replaced with a Platform Controller Hub (PCH). This gives the processor faster communications than the earlier systems had and provides additional faster data links for graphics and data transfer.

Processors

The brain of your computer is the processor. The processor is the hottest component in the computer, and like the Northbridge/Southbridge chipset, it has its own heat sink and fan. There are even water-cooled processors, although these are typically reserved for high-specification gaming computers and certain servers.

You should check that the processor fan and heat sink are free from dust and obstructions such as wires and cables. You should also check that the computer has ample airflow inside the case.

Memory Cards

Memory cards (commonly known as RAM) are thin cards approximately six inches long that protrude from the motherboard. These chips are where Windows 8 and your programs are loaded when the computer is turned on. The chips operate significantly faster than conventional hard disks and even faster than many solid-state drives. If Windows 8 was run entirely from a hard disk, it would be extremely slow. Memory cards can be difficult to fit into the motherboard, so be sure the computer and motherboard are properly supported when inserting or removing memory cards.

Memory cards are also very prone to damage from static electricity. When you touch them (or any component in your computer, for that matter), ensure that you are grounded by touching an unpainted area on the computer chassis (preferably by using an antistatic wristband) to avoid damaging the components via an electrostatic discharge.

Expansion Cards and Riser Cards

As with other components, it can be difficult to correctly place expansion cards and riser cards (mini expansion cards that plug into an expansion slot and commonly allow a card to be mounted sideways when a PC is fitted in a low-profile or media center case). As always, ensure that the computer is level and well supported, because the motherboard can snap under extreme pressure. You should also ensure that expansion cards are correctly screwed in or otherwise secured to the inside of the computer case.

Graphics Cards

Graphics cards are another component that might have their own heat sinks and/or fan. Again, ensure that these are free from dust by using a tool that can blow clean air over the fan (or just a strong puff of breath will work) and that no wires or cables are obstructing the airflow around these cards.

Graphics cards might also require their own power supply. If so, they will have a socket on the top of the card to accommodate this. You should also check that there is a power cable connected to this socket and that the lead is not obstructing any fans.

Optical Drives, Hard Drives, and Solid-State Drives

Optical drives and hard drives are the only components other than fans that contain moving parts; therefore, they can suffer from wear and tear after extensive use and eventually fail. Solid-state drives also fit into the same area of the computer as hard disks (though they tend to be smaller and some require a special mounting cage to enable them to fit properly). Solid-state drives contain no mechanical or moving parts and as such are much more robust than traditional hard disks.

The Power Supply

A computer's power supply will typically have one fan, though some higher power gaming computers may come with a power supply that contains two fans. Although fans are the only moving parts of the power supply, they are among the most common computer components to fail. You might encounter scenarios in which the power supply fans are functioning normally, which can lead you to believe that the entire unit is working properly, however, the power supply itself is no longer capable of providing enough electricity to power the computer. Fortunately, the power supply is one of the least expensive and easiest components to replace. You can do this by unplugging all the leads that run from the power supply to components inside the computer, commonly the motherboard, hard disk or disks, optical drive, and graphics card, and then unscrewing four screws at the back of the case that hold the power supply in place. When swapping this component out, however, be careful that you do not damage anything else in the computer by knocking it.

INSIDE OUT **Is your power supply failing?**

If your computer is unresponsive at what might seem like odd times, such as only after a few hours of the PC being on when it's worked perfectly fine up until that point, or your PC is shutting down unexpectedly, your power supply might be failing. Power supplies are commonly the first component to fail in a desktop computer.

The Computer Case

The case for your computer can contain several fans that can be blocked by dust and carpet fibers. Other moving parts in the case might fail, including the power button, which can stick or break.

Cleaning the Interior of Your Computer

The best way to clean the inside of a computer case is to dislodge dust with an unused paintbrush. You can then use a vacuum cleaner to remove dust from the inside; preferably a battery-powered handheld vacuum, if possible, because this will be much less powerful than a household vacuum cleaner and therefore much less likely to cause damage to components inside your computer through strong suction.

CAUTION!

You should always be very careful when using a vacuum inside your computer. The computer should be turned off and disconnected from the main power supply. Be sure to place the computer on a firm and level surface. Use the paintbrush to dislodge dust as you vacuum, and the suction power on the vacuum should be turned to the lowest level.

Carefully vacuuming the inside of your computer, including all fans and heat sinks, can extend the computer's life and reduce heat buildup and power consumption. When engaging in the cleaning process, always be careful to avoid touching components inside the computer case or dislodging cables from their sockets.

INSIDE OUT **Where should you keep your computer?**

Keeping your computer on or near a carpet can attract dust and carpet fibers. Your computer can also attract dust if you keep it on a laminate or tiled floor. A good location for a main computer case is on a raised platform, at least six inches off the floor, or on a desk. These locations help minimize the buildup of dust and other particles that can be drawn in by the fans and reduce the risk of static electricity buildup.

Maintaining Hardware Health

Different types of computers can require different care. This section covers the three main types of hardware; note that each type varies by manufacturer.

INSIDE OUT **Turn off your computer when cleaning nearby**

If you are dusting or vacuuming the room where your computer is set up, it is a good idea to turn off the computer, because the case fans can draw in any dust that is thrown up by the vacuum.

Desktops

If you have a computer that has a monitor that is separate from the base unit, you can carefully open the side of the base unit box via an access panel (although for very small form factor computers, this might not be possible) without causing any damage. The components are usually accessible for a good blast of air to remove dust and other debris.

Laptops

Laptop and notebook computers have many components that are quite different from those in desktop computers, and these components are often attached permanently to the motherboard. Typically you can find an access port or two on the underside of the laptop, which you can swap out, for example, to upgrade memory or the hard disk. Otherwise, you should not attempt to open a laptop case for cleaning or maintenance. If you need to clean dust from the computer, you can carefully place a vacuum against the heat vents on the sides of the laptop and use low to medium suction.

Ultrabooks and Tablets

Doing any work on the inside of an Ultrabook or a tablet PC will be very difficult. These laptops are so small and light that each component within them is usually custom-designed and very tightly packed inside the case. I do not recommend that you open an Ultrabook or a tablet unless you have documentation, such as a technician's guide provided by the manufacturer, which clearly indicates that you can work inside the computer.

All-in-Ones

An all-in-one device is a desktop computer in which the processor and other components are integrated with the monitor into the same housing unit. They share many similarities with laptops. Thus, I recommend you do not attempt to open them for cleaning or maintenance. You can clean dust from the vents by carefully placing a vacuum against them and using low to medium suction.

SMART BIOS Monitoring of Hard Disk Drives

Most motherboard BIOS software (see Figure 9-3) supports a feature called Self-Monitoring, Analysis, and Reporting Technology, or SMART, which monitors the hard disk drives. SMART monitoring reports hard disk reliability indicators to the BIOS with the goal of anticipating any drive failure before it occurs. The benefit of SMART monitoring is that it allows a user to move any data and files off the drive before the drive fails.

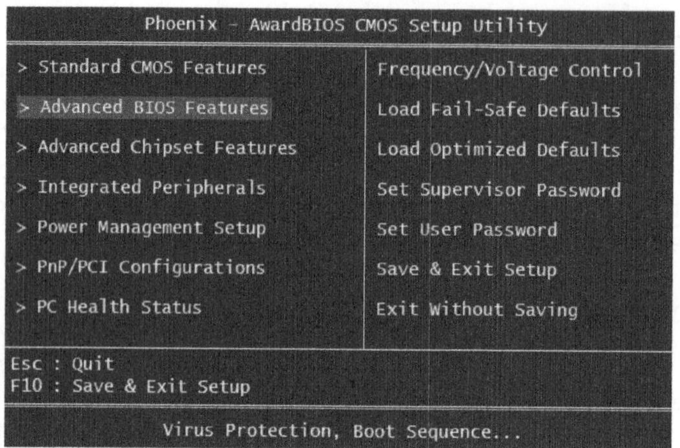

Figure 9-3 This is an example of a BIOS screen from an older computer.

The SMART monitoring feature can be turned off for your hard drives in your computer's BIOS console, though I cannot think of any circumstance where you might want to do this. If you are thinking about switching SMART monitoring off, I advise against it, because this feature can help protect against both hardware failure and data loss.

INSIDE OUT Hard disk monitoring with UEFI motherboards

All new computers running Windows 8 must come with a Unified Extensible Firmware Interface (UEFI)–equipped motherboard. This requirement is mandated by Microsoft, though at the time of this writing, it is still possible to buy systems from small independent retailers and build your own system with a traditional BIOS.

UEFI systems vary considerably, and you may not see a specific SMART Monitoring option. UEFI is very good at communicating with your operating system and reporting on hardware, however, and it will probably be configured to send a message directly to your copy of Windows 8.

Peripherals

Unless you are using a tablet running Windows 8, you will need peripheral hardware to interact with your computer. These important devices need care and attention to prevent them from causing trouble.

Touchscreen-Enabled Devices

If your touchscreen-enabled device doesn't work when you start it, restarting it might fix the glitch. If that doesn't work, you could be experiencing a driver error. Check whether the driver was updated recently by Windows Update by viewing the Update History. Or, if you updated the driver yourself, roll it back to the previous working version. I explain how to do this in Chapter 14, "Easy Ways to Repair Windows 8." If your touch-screen enabled monitor is separate from your PC, check to see whether its connection cable has come loose.

Keyboards and Mice

A commonly reported Windows problem is "my keyboard and/or mouse won't work." Is this problem a result of a fault with the hardware driver for the device, or with the hardware itself? If it is a result of the hardware itself, unplugging the hardware and plugging it back in (perhaps into a different USB port in case that port is also encountering a problem) will almost always fix the problem. However, the problem might be dirty hardware. It's good practice to keep your keyboard clean by using a small brush to sweep between the keys. You can keep your mouse clean by occasionally wiping it with a dry cloth.

Note

While I was providing IT support a few years ago, a client from a major British bank was talking on the phone with a colleague of mine about his keyboard. He had decided it was dirty and needed to be cleaned.

The night before, he filled his sink with hot, soapy water and gave the keyboard a good scrub. Realizing it was an electrical device, he hung it up to dry overnight but was concerned when his computer didn't work the following morning.

My colleague had to break the bad news that the reason his keyboard didn't work was because it was built in to the rest of his laptop!

Monitors

Probably the least problematic hardware component associated with your computer is the monitor. If a problem does occur, for example, you do not see the display, the source of the issue is often caused by something easy to fix, such as one of the following:

- The power cable has fallen out of the monitor.
- The video cable is not properly attached to the monitor.
- The monitor has accidentally been switched to a different video input.

> **INSIDE OUT** **Windows 8 and touch screen drivers**
>
> **Windows 8 includes its own touch screen drivers so that you can use touch to install the operating system on a tablet. It is possible, though, that a driver is not compatible with your system or doesn't load correctly. It is always wise to keep a spare USB keyboard and mouse around for a tablet installation of Windows 8.**

Other Devices

You might need to troubleshoot problems with other devices, such as printers, cameras, or scanners, when a specific device malfunctions or when Windows can't see that device. A useful method for troubleshooting such devices is to test the device by plugging it into another port on your computer, such as into a USB port. If that doesn't work, try the device with a different connecting cable.

> **INSIDE OUT** **The Wi-Fi USB dongle doesn't work**
>
> **After moving a computer, some people find that their Wi-Fi USB dongle won't connect them to the Internet. Because of the way Windows loads drivers for hardware, you might find that the lack of connection is just a result of the dongle being plugged into a different USB port from the port it was plugged into previously. Usually, changing to a different USB port on the computer solves the problem.**

Surge Protectors, UPS, and Power Supply

Your computer should always be plugged into a spike or surge protector to prevent any sudden spikes in the power supply from passing through your computer and damaging sensitive components. Some surge protectors also protect computer components such as network and telephone cabling. Most uninterruptable power supplies have this feature built in. These devices can maintain temporary supply of electricity in the event of a power outage or brownout.

I also recommend that you do not plug your computer into the same outlet as any large appliance. Some appliances such as refrigerators can cause spikes in the power supply, which can disrupt other electrical devices. For instance, in an old house, you might notice that the lights flicker when the cooling element in a refrigerator or freezer comes on.

Note

If you live in a rural area or a town or city where the electricity supply is unreliable, investing in an uninterruptable power supply can be a cost-effective way to save data and extend the life of your hardware.

CHAPTER 10

Working in a Virtual Environment

THIS CHAPTER DESCRIBES VIRTUALIZATION and the benefits of working in a virtual environment. It describes how to work with virtual hard disks in Windows 8, including how to create virtual hard disks, use existing ones, and set up a virtual machine by using Microsoft Client Hyper-V. You also learn how to create a virtual switch to ensure that you have network connectivity for your virtual machine.

What Is Virtualization?

Virtualization is an operating system that runs on software-simulated hardware, creating what is known as a *virtual machine*. A virtualized operating system typically shares the same hardware with one or more operating systems. To do this, the host operating system shares the computer's resources among the different virtual machines. This sharing includes isolating areas of memory for each virtual machine, or in the case of a multicore processor, sometimes assigning a specific processor core to each virtual machine. Each virtual machine has its own hardware resources and can operate at close to the full speed of the computer. A virtual machine resides within a file on your hard disk—a bit like a compressed zip folder. The operating system sees this file as a hard disk and operates from within it.

The use of virtualization varies depending on the industry and application, but as portable computers and smartphones become more powerful—now equipped with quad-core processors as a standard—virtualizing operating systems and software will become more and more prevalent. The Windows 7 Professional, Enterprise, and Ultimate editions had a free add-in that you could download called *Windows XP Mode*, which contained a virtualized image of a fully licensed edition of Windows XP Pro. On this edition, you could install your earlier software to maintain compatibility. Windows 8 does not support XP Mode, primarily because *all* support for Windows XP is scheduled to end in April 2014.

Instead, in the 64-bit versions of Windows 8 Pro and Enterprise editions, the powerful Client Hyper-V virtualization software is included. This is a full-featured virtualization package capable of running any operating system; it is very powerful and flexible.

Using virtual machines at home or at work affords you many advantages. For example, you can use a virtual machine copy of Windows 8 if your copy is unresponsive, eliminating the downtime of restoring a backed-up copy. When you run Windows on a virtual machine, you just log on to the desktop operating system and replace the virtual machine file with a clean backup copy. All you are doing is copying or renaming a single file, so you can still be productive on your computer while the virtual machine is being restored.

Another advantage of using virtual machines is that you need only a single computer to run different operating systems and tasks simultaneously. The impact this has on your electricity consumption and your carbon footprint—not to mention your IT costs—can be enormous.

All of this is made possible because modern processors and computers are almost never used to their full potential by everyday computing and server tasks. Why have five computers using only 20 percent of their computing power (but consuming 80 percent of their maximum electricity consumption) when you can have one running at full potential?

INSIDE OUT **Accessing Windows XP programs in Client Hyper-V**

Client Hyper-V in Windows 8 does not support pinning your Windows XP or other virtualized software icons to the Windows 8 desktop taskbar, although you could do this in previous Microsoft virtual PC technology. To access virtualized programs on the Windows 8 desktop in Windows XP Mode, you will need a copy of Microsoft Enterprise Desktop Virtualization (MED-V), which is part of the Microsoft Desktop Optimization Pack (MDOP) suite. This is available to enterprise users through volume licensing and to other businesses through Windows Intune.

Virtualization vs. Multibooting

To multiboot a computer, you need separate operating systems installed on different hard disks or partitions. This is how Boot Camp manages Windows and OS X on an Apple Mac. The disadvantages of multibooting are twofold. First, if the boot sector or boot options menu of the computer changes, you might lose access to one of the operating systems, because Startup Repair might not rebuild entries correctly for non-Windows operating systems, and those operating systems might not be able to write to the Windows boot loader. Second, if you want to switch from one operating system to another, you have to close all your programs, shut down the machine, and then restart it.

Virtualization allows you to run different operating systems side by side on your Windows desktop or full screen and makes it easy to switch between them. Furthermore, you still have only one operating system in your Windows boot loader (unless you choose to start the computer from a virtual hard disk; more on this in the section "Starting the Computer by Using a Virtual Copy of Windows 8" later in this chapter).

Note

You need a separate and valid license for each operating system that you install into a virtual machine. This means you will need a separate and valid product key for each copy of Windows you install into Client Hyper-V.

Also, virtual machines are very easy to back up. As mentioned in the introduction to this chapter, a virtual machine is really just a file, like a really large zip file, that can be copied from one place to another when the virtual machine isn't running. This makes virtual machines considerably simpler to back up and restore than operating systems installed on a separate hard disk or partition.

Although you can multiboot between Windows and other operating systems such as Linux, you are limited regarding the order in which you can install these operating systems for security reasons. Many other operating systems use a different, older style of boot loader, so Windows 8 should always be the last operating system you install. Although the Windows 8 boot loader can incorporate the other operating boot loaders into itself, not all operating systems can incorporate the Windows 8 boot loader. Windows 8 won't be able to start if a non–Windows 8 boot loader has overwritten the Windows 7 boot loader.

Virtualization circumvents this problem by running all of the operating systems from within Windows 8. You can install any other version of Windows or Linux by using Client Hyper-V. Apple Mac OS X isn't supported, but you can get third-party virtualization packages such as VirtualBox and VMWare, which might support a wider range of operating systems.

Benefits of Virtualization

Virtualization offers significant benefits, one of which is starting up a virtual copy of Windows 8 to keep your main copy clean, protected, and running smoothly.

Two other benefits of virtualization are software and hardware compatibility. For instance, perhaps you like to use an older printer or scanner that isn't supported by Windows 7 drivers. If nothing is wrong with the hardware, you could use virtualization to install an earlier operating system with drivers that support the hardware and then install the hardware into that virtualized operating system.

Similarly, you might require the use of software that won't run in Windows 8 or even in Windows XP Mode. You can use virtualization to create safe test computers into which you can install and test new software, software updates, security updates, and hardware. This is becoming common practice in environments in which system administrators want to know what impact an update or new software package will have on the organization's computers.

Virtual Hard Disks and Windows 8

Support for virtual hard disks is built into the Windows 8 operating system. A *virtual hard disk* (abbreviated VHD in the interface) is different from a virtual machine but can be used like a virtual machine. In its basic form, a virtual hard disk is simply a file you can mount in a copy of Windows 8 so that the file appears in File Explorer as another hard disk. You can store any type of file or data on a virtual hard disk just as you can on a regular hard disk.

INSIDE OUT Fixed vs. expandable virtual hard disk files

When you create a virtual hard disk file, you can make it a fixed size or expandable. The latter option creates a small file that the copy of Windows 8 on the virtual hard disk can expand to as needed, up to its maximum size. So what are the pros and cons of fixed and expandable hard disks? If you choose a fixed-size hard disk, you may find that you have inadvertently selected a disk size that's too small to accommodate all the software and the operating system you want to install onto it; or perhaps it will be too large, which wastes hard disk space on your computer. Dynamically expandable disks get around this problem by making the virtual hard disk only the size it needs to be, all of the time. This can be useful when hard disk space is in short supply.

Creating a Virtual Hard Disk in Windows 8

You can create a virtual hard disk in Windows 8 by using a simple wizard interface.

1. Open the WinX menu by pressing Windows logo key+X, and then click Disk Management.
2. In Disk Management, on the Actions menu, click More Actions, and then click Create VHD.
3. In the Create And Attach Virtual Hard Disk dialog box that appears, you must decide where on your hard disk or disks the virtual hard disk file is to reside, what it will be called, and how big it will be. You can choose whether the file will be a Fixed Size or Dynamically Expanding. (See the preceding Inside Out titled "Fixed vs. expandable virtual hard disk files" for information about choosing a fixed size or dynamically expanding file.) It is in this step that you will specify the name for the VHD.

   Click the default, Fixed Sized (Recommended), to create the fixed-size file, as shown in Figure 10-1.

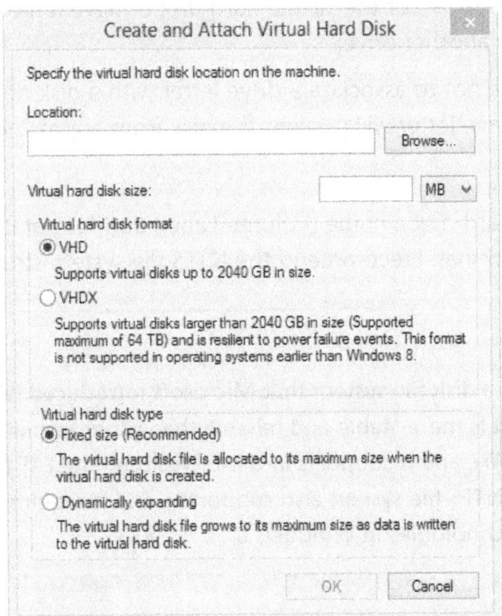

Figure 10-1 When you specify a location for a virtual hard disk, you must also specify its name (which is not immediately apparent in the dialog box), in addition to its size, which you can specify in megabytes, gigabytes, or terabytes.

4. Enter your virtual hard disk attributes and click OK. The new virtual hard disk appears in the list of available disks in Disk Management.
5. Initialize this disk. Right-click in the disk's information pane, and then click Initialize Disk on the shortcut menu. (If you do not see this menu item, you might be right-clicking a volume instead of a disk.)
6. Click a partition style in the Initialize Disk dialog box for the disk and then click OK.

   I recommend multiple bit rate, or MBR, because the initialization dialog box informs you that the GUID partition table (GPT) partition style is not recognized by all previous versions of Windows. If you needed to use the virtual hard disk on another computer, it might not work.
7. Place a partition on the virtual hard disk so that you can write files to it. In Disk Management, right-click the virtual hard disk, and then click New Simple Volume.
8. You are asked to choose a size for the volume. For a virtual hard disk, you should use the default (maximum) size available.
9. Either assign a drive letter for the virtual hard disk or have it mounted automatically as a subfolder onto another drive.

   You can also choose not to associate a drive letter with a disk or partition, although not associating a drive letter will prevent the disk from appearing in File Explorer views.
10. Assign the virtual hard disk a name (Volume Label) and format it by using either a quick or standard format. I recommend the NTFS file system structure.

Note

The NTFS file system is a disk file system that Microsoft introduced with Windows NT and has since refined. It is more stable and reliable than other formats, including the File Allocation Table (FAT), and it supports larger drives than the FAT file system or the FAT32 file system. The NTFS file system also supports—and is required for—the folder and disk encryption technologies in Windows 8.

Reattaching the Virtual Hard Disk

You will probably need to reattach the virtual hard disk you created in the previous section the next time you start Windows. The default behavior for Windows 8 is to always detach virtual hard disks when you turn off the computer. If you want to automatically reattach a virtual hard disk whenever Windows 8 starts, you can set this up as a task in the Task Scheduler. See Chapter 20, "Using Advanced Repair Methods," for details about how to configure this automatic task.

To attach a virtual hard disk, perform the following steps:

1. Press Windows logo key+X and then click Computer Management to access Computer Management.
2. In the left pane of the Computer Management console, click Disk Management.
3. On the Actions menu, click More Actions, and then click Attach VHD.
4. Select the virtual hard disk file from the location where it is stored on your computer. It appears as a drive in File Explorer.

Starting the Computer by Using a Virtual Copy of Windows 8

With the Enterprise and Pro editions of Windows 8, you can install another copy of Windows 7 or Windows 8 inside a virtual hard disk and start the computer from it. You can find an official guide to creating a bootable virtual hard disk by going to *http://www.microsoft.com* and searching for *Demonstration: Windows 8 VHD Boot*, but there is a simpler way to create such a disk, which I explain later in this chapter in the section "Creating a New Virtual Hard Disk."

Creating a bootable virtual hard disk is an excellent way to keep your main copy of Windows 8 clean and problem-free. You'll probably use it only when making backups of the virtual hard disk and restoring the system. You can also take advantage of this bootable virtual hard disk to have a multiboot environment on your computer that's easier to manage than a traditional dual-boot system.

INSIDE OUT **Licensing and starting up Windows from a virtual hard disk**

Remember that if you want to install a copy of Windows 7 or Windows 8 on a virtual hard disk, you will need an additional valid product key for that extra copy of Windows.

Also, you can use only the Pro and Enterprise editions of Windows 8 to start the system from a virtual hard disk. You cannot use this feature to install another, earlier version of Windows (such as Windows XP or Windows Vista) or another edition of Windows 8 (such as RT) on the virtual hard disk.

INSIDE OUT **Breaking the 32-bit barrier with bootable virtual hard disks**

Windows Virtual PC and Windows XP Mode are supported by only the 32-bit (x86) editions of Windows and other operating systems. When you create a bootable virtual hard disk, you can install a 64-bit (x64) version of Windows 7 or Windows 8. This is something to consider doing if your computer has more than 4 gigabytes (GB) of RAM so that Windows will be able to see all of your installed memory.

To install Windows on a virtual hard disk, perform the following steps:

1. Start your computer from your Windows 8 installation DVD.

   If your computer didn't come with a Windows 8 installation DVD, you will need to obtain one. The company you purchased your computer from may charge for a disc (usually around $10.00), but be aware that some will not provide a disc at all. If you have a Microsoft subscription, however, such as MSDN or TechNet, you can download a disc image that you can use.

   Note

   You cannot install Windows this way from within a currently loaded copy of Windows 8. You must start your PC from the installation disc.

2. On the Windows Setup screen, click the installation language, and click Next.

3. On the Install Now screen, press Shift+F10 to open the Windows PE window.

4. Type **diskpart**, and then press Enter.

Using an Existing Virtual Hard Disk

To use an existing virtual hard disk, perform the following steps:

1. Type **Select vdisk file=C:*path1**path2*\disk.vhd**, using the drive letter and paths where the virtual hard disk is stored on your computer.

2. Type **attach vdisk**.

Creating a New Virtual Hard Disk

To create a new virtual hard disk, perform the following steps:

1. Type **Create vdisk file=C:*path1**path2*\disk.vhd maximum=20480 type=fixed**, and then press Enter, where *C:* and the paths indicate the location where you want the virtual hard disk stored on your hard disk.

   20480 is a number in kilobytes (KB) that specifies the size you want the virtual hard disk to be. In the example in this procedure, this size would create a virtual hard disk of 20 GB; for a 15-GB virtual hard disk, for example, you would type **15360**.

2. Type **select vdisk file=C:*path1**path2*\disk.vhd**, and then press Enter.

3. Type **attach vdisk**, and then press Enter.

4. Type **exit**, and then press Enter.

5. Type **exit** again, and then press Enter.

6. On the Windows Setup screen, click Install Now, enter the product key, and then click Next. Accept the license terms, and then click Custom: Install Windows 8 Only (Advanced).

   In the pane where you indicate on which hard disk to install Windows 8, the hard disks in your computer are normally referred to as Disk 0 or Disk 1. The virtual hard disk will have a different disk number and thus will stand out. You will probably find it at the bottom of the list of available drives.

7. Click the virtual hard disk, and then click Drive Options (Advanced).

8. Create a new partition in the space available for the partition by clicking New and selecting its size.

9. Ensure that the virtual hard disk drive is highlighted, and then click Next to install Windows on it.

Windows will install and automatically configure the boot loader; however, you will now have two copies of Windows to choose from when you start your computer. Follow these steps to change the names of the programs after either copy of Windows starts:

1. Press Windows logo key+X to open the WinX menu, and then click Command Prompt (Admin).

2. In the Command Prompt window that appears, type **bcdedit /v**, and then click Enter.

3. Locate the virtual hard disk copy of Windows in the list. It will be associated with a GUID, which is a long string of numbers and letters, as shown in Figure 10-2.

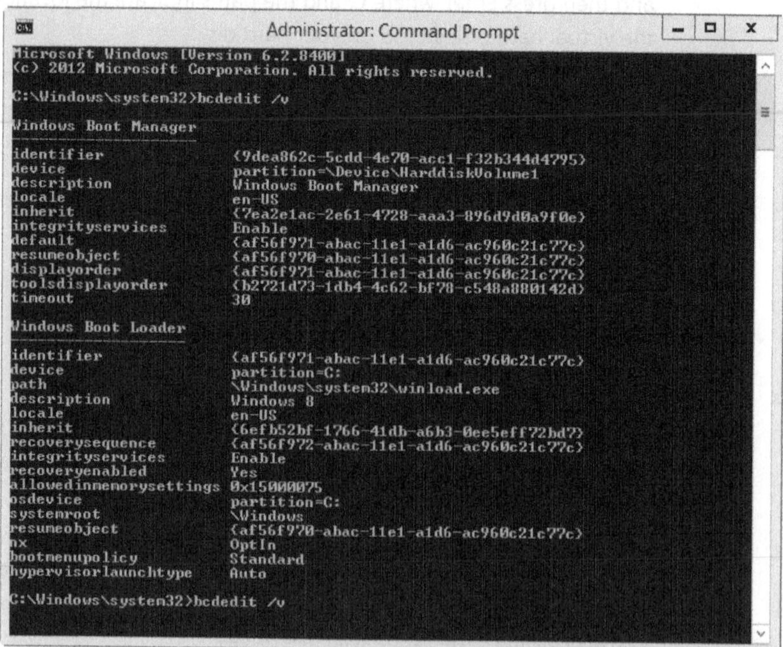

Figure 10-2 You can locate the GUID of an installed operating system by using BCDEdit. When you use BCDEdit to view GUID numbers, those numbers will appear in curly braces ({}) as a long string of letters and numbers.

4. Type **bcdedit /set {GUID} description "OS Name"**, and then press Enter.
5. Optionally, you might want your virtual hard disk copy of Windows to be the operating system that loads by default when you start your computer. To do this with any of the entries listed, type **bcdedit /default {GUID}**, and then press Enter.

INSIDE OUT Cutting and pasting in a Command Prompt window

You can select text in a Command Prompt window by right-clicking anywhere in the window and selecting Edit\Mark from the shortcut menu. Move the insertion point to the beginning of the text you want to select, and then press and hold the Shift key while you select the text. Then, press Ctrl+C to copy the text. To paste this text, right-click in the window, and then click Paste. Cutting and pasting in this way can be very helpful when writing long GUIDs.

INSIDE OUT Why start your computer from a virtual hard disk?

The primary reason to start your computer from a virtual hard disk is to protect your main copy of Windows 8. When you start from a virtual hard disk, you can use the full features of your computer and still be able to restore it if something goes wrong by starting from your original copy of Windows 8 and restoring the virtual hard disk file from a backup. Restoring your operating system takes no longer than the time required to start Windows 8 a couple of times and rename a file.

Your virtual hard disk copy of Windows 8 will be able to see all your hard disks hardware, so running a virtual machine is an invisible process to the user. Using a virtual hard disk copy in this way enables you to get up and running quickly after a crash and prevents inadvertent damage to your desktop copy of Windows 8.

Using Client Hyper-V in Windows 8

If you've used Windows Server in the last few years, you may already be familiar with Hyper-V and setting up virtual machines. The Hyper-V client is new to Windows 8, but this doesn't mean that setting up a virtual machine in the Hyper-V client is confusing, difficult, or in any way overly technical. It really is quite a simple process.

INSIDE OUT Is Client Hyper-V activated on your computer?

Client Hyper-V might not be visible when you search for it on your computer. If this is the case, search for Programs And Features and run it from the search results. In the left pane, click Turn Windows Features On Or Off; you will see Client Hyper-V listed in the Windows Features dialog box that appears. Select its check box to activate it. Remember that Client Hyper-V is supported only in the 64-bit versions of Windows 8 Pro and Enterprise.

To set up a virtual machine in the Hyper-V client, follow these steps:

1. Access Client Hyper-V on the Start screen and type **hyper**.

   You are presented with two options: Client Hyper-V Virtual Machine Connection and Client Hyper-V Manager. Choose Client Hyper-V Virtual Virtual Machine Connection when you want to connect your computer to a virtual machine that is hosted on a Windows server or running quietly in the background on your computer. For this procedure, you will want the second option, Client Hyper-V Manager.

2. Click Client Hyper-V Manager. The main controls are in the Actions pane on the right (see Figure 10-3).

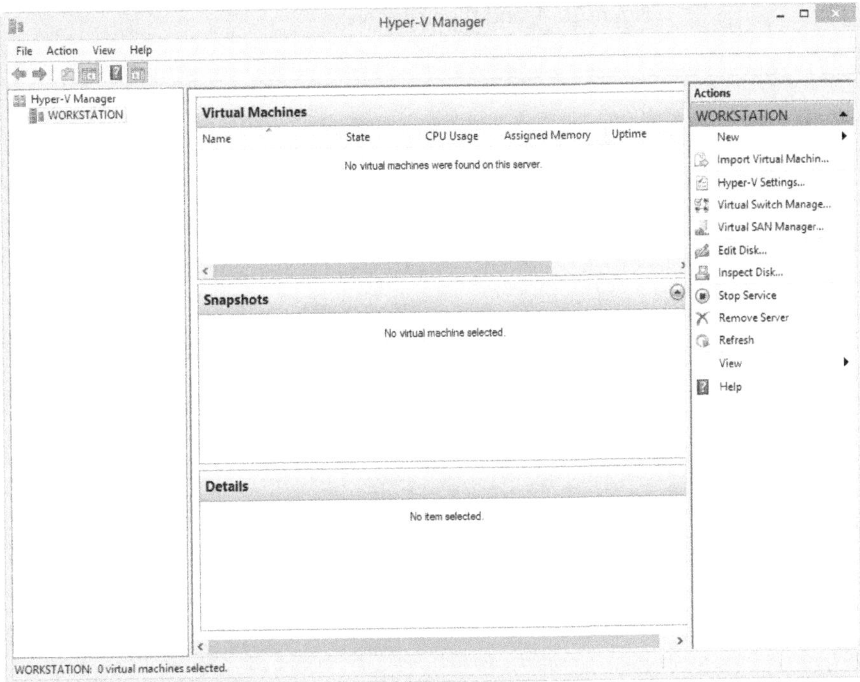

Figure 10-3 The Client Hyper-V Manager resembles many other management windows.

3. In the Actions pane (see Figure 10-3), click New, and then click Virtual Machine to open the New Virtual Machine Wizard.

4. Click through the first page of the wizard. On the second page (the Specify Name And Location page), assign the name of the virtual machine and the hard disk location where you want the virtual hard disk file to be stored, as illustrated in Figure 10-4, and then click Next.

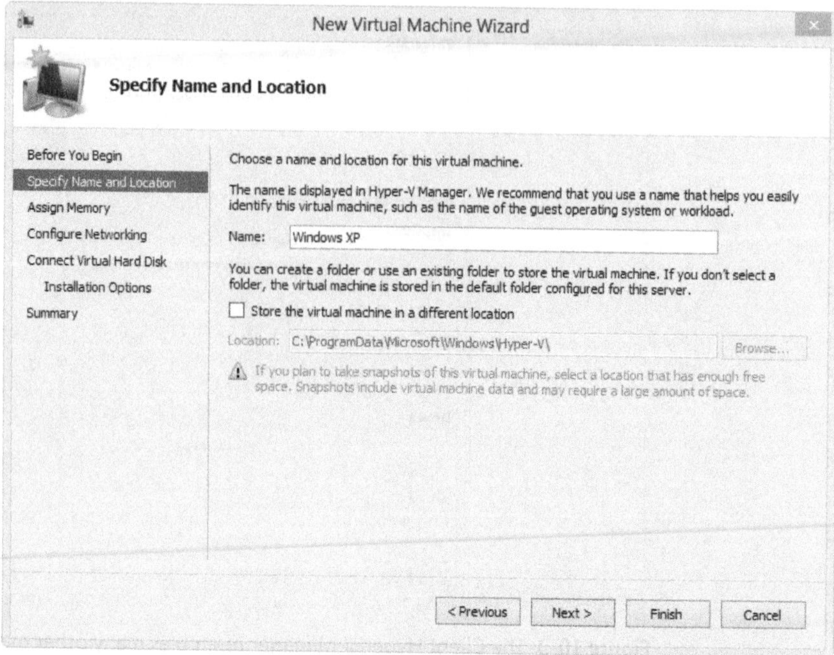

Figure 10-4 The default storage location for the virtual machine is in the C:\ProgramData folder, but you may want to store it elsewhere. Select the Store The Virtual Machine In A Different Location check box to move the virtual hard disk.

5. On the next page (the Assign Memory page), specify how much memory to allocate to the virtual machine, as shown in Figure 10-5, and then click Next.

   If you think you might need more memory for the virtual machine in the future but can't allocate it all at this stage (it can't be changed later), select the Use Dynamic Memory For This Virtual Machine check box. This option allows Client Hyper-V to automatically increase the memory allocation to the virtual hard disk when required.

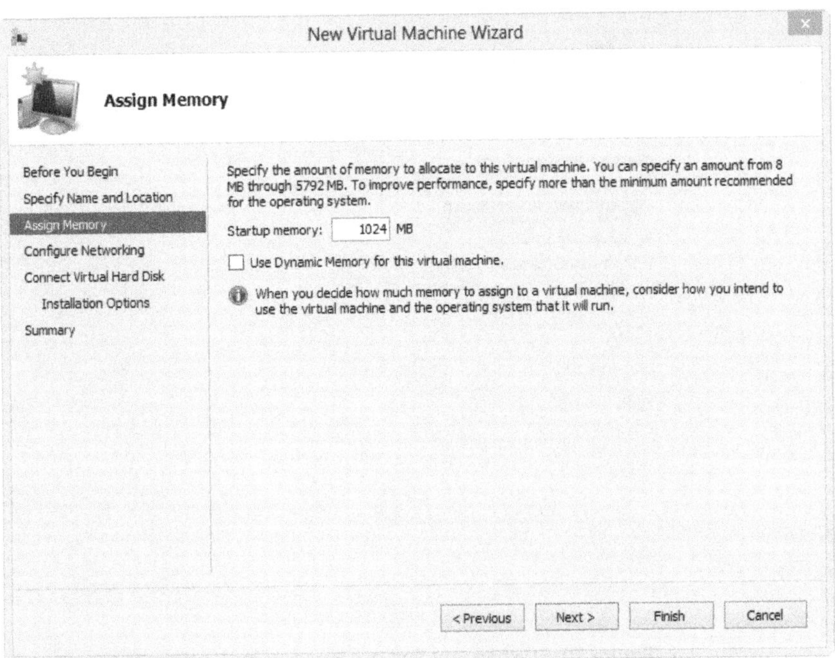

Figure 10-5 You must allocate memory to a virtual hard disk.

6. On the Configure Networking page, specify what network connector you want to attach to the virtual machine, as depicted in Figure 10-6, and then click Next.

   You might find that no available options are listed here; I will show you how to add networking in the section "Creating Virtual Switches in Client Hyper-V" later in this chapter.

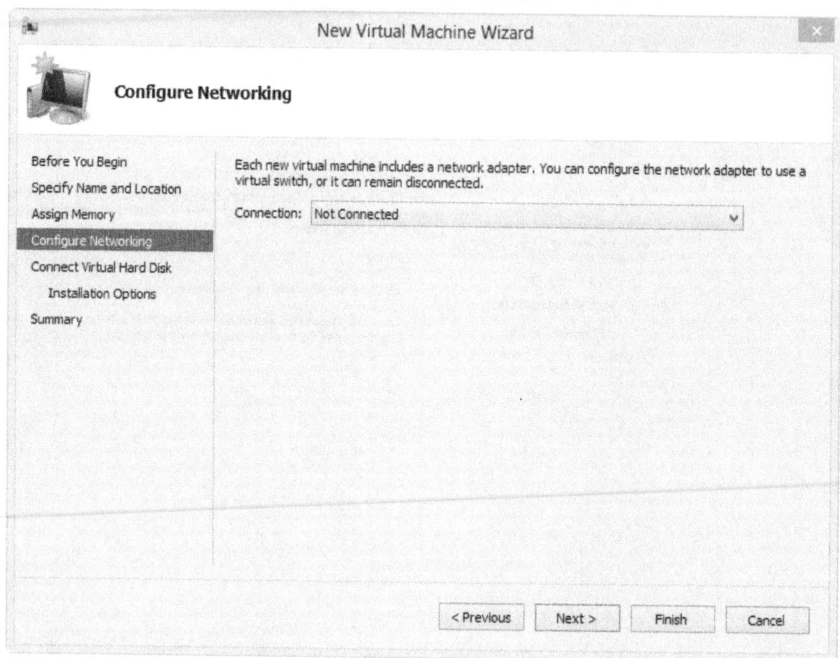

Figure 10-6 When you first use Hyper-V in Windows 8, no networking options will be available, but you can easily configure them afterward.

7. On the Connect Virtual Hard Disk page (see Figure 10-7), the wizard asks you to specify the size of the virtual machine. You can also attach an existing virtual machine at this point. When you are finished entering information on the page, click Next.

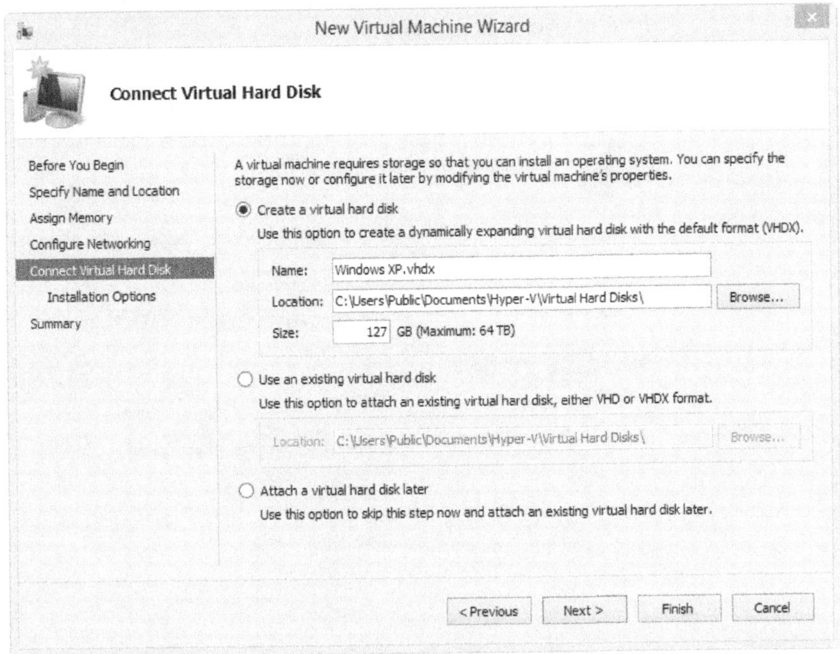

Figure 10-7 When you are asked what size you want the virtual hard disk to be, you might want to check the available space on your hard disk drive, because this wizard doesn't give you feedback about how much space is actually available.

8. On the Installation Options page, decide whether you want to install an operating system into the virtual machine now, later, or not at all, as illustrated in Figure 10-8, and then click Next. Client Hyper-V displays your chosen settings for you to review.

   Note that you can install an operating system from a CD, DVD, ISO file, USB flash drive, or even a floppy disk.

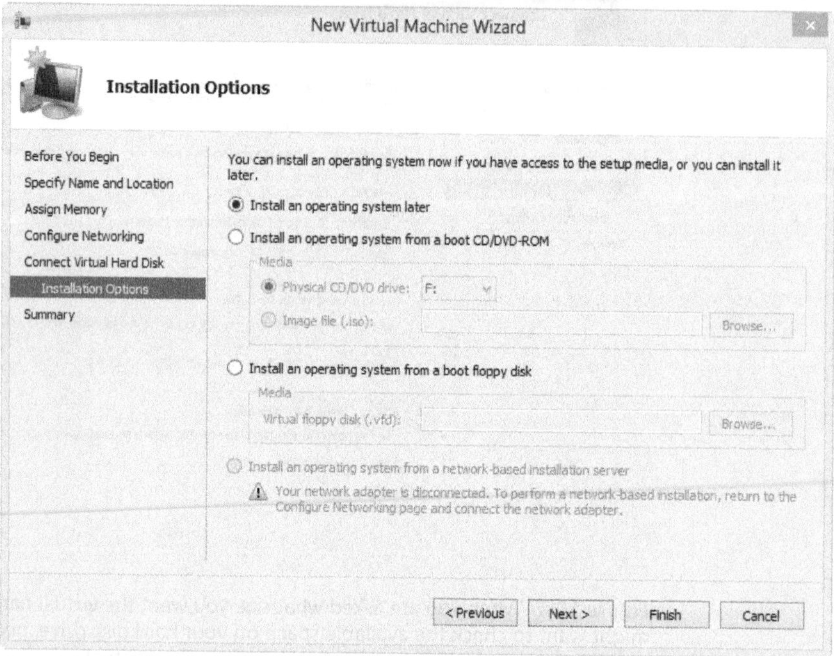

Figure 10-8 The final choice to make when creating a new virtual machine is whether you want to install an operating system now or later.

9. Confirm the setup, and then close the wizard by clicking Finish (see Figure 10-9). Alternately, click Previous if you need to make any changes.

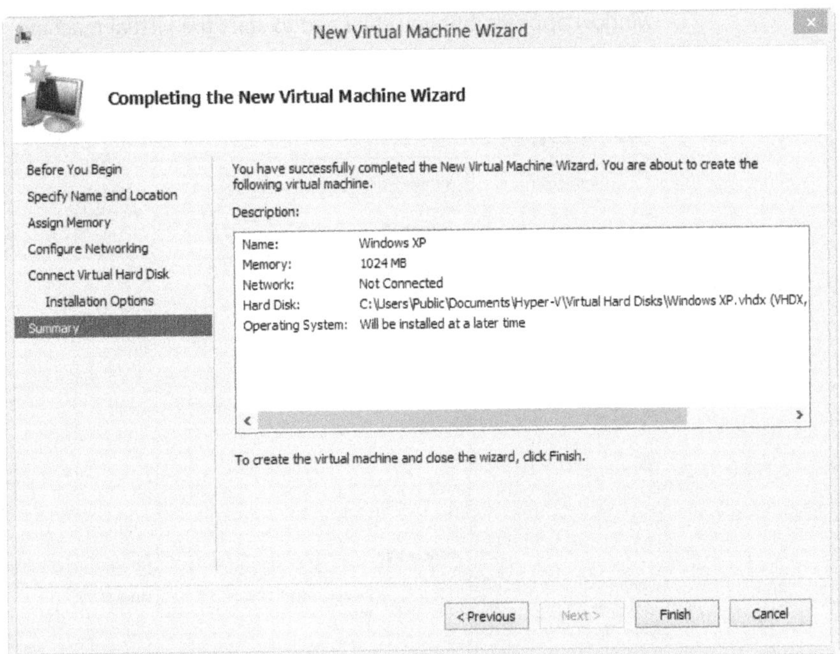

Figure 10-9 Before you close the New Virtual Machine Wizard, you are shown your settings and asked to confirm them. If any are wrong or you would like to change them, you can click the Previous button.

You now need to start the virtual machine so that you can install an operating system in it.

10. In the Client Hyper-V Manager, in the Virtual Machines pane (in the top center of the screen), select your virtual machine (Windows XP), and then in the bottom half of the Actions pane, click Connect, as illustrated in Figure 10-10. A virtual machine window appears, but you still need to start the virtual machine.

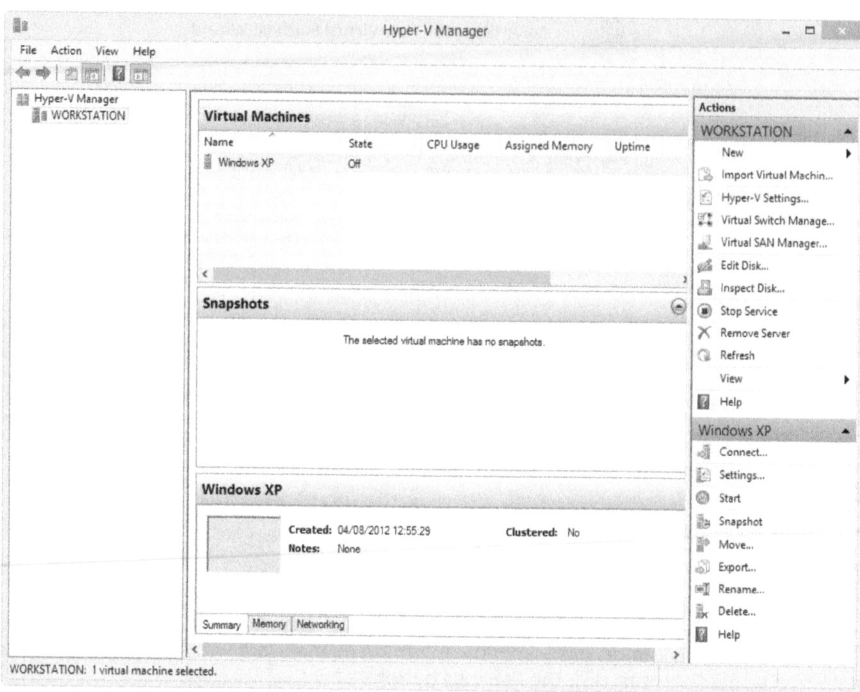

Figure 10-10 Information for the newly created virtual machine appears in the Hyper-V Manager.

11. To start the virtual machine, on the Action menu of the virtual machine window that appears, click Start, as shown in Figure 10-11.

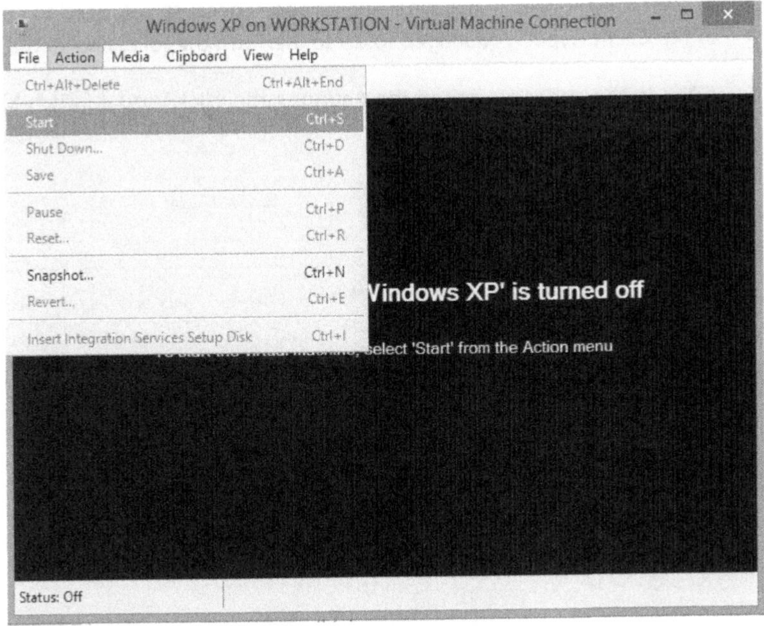

Figure 10-11 When you open a virtual hard disk, it does not start automatically. You need to start it manually from the Action menu across the top of the window.

Your virtual machine is now created and working in Client Hyper-V.

Creating Virtual Switches in Client Hyper-V

I mentioned earlier in this chapter that network connections might not be available when you set up your virtual machine. This happens because you need to create a virtual switch in the Client Hyper-V Manager. To do so, perform the following steps:

1. In the upper portion of the Actions pane, click Virtual Switch Manager (see Figure 10-12).

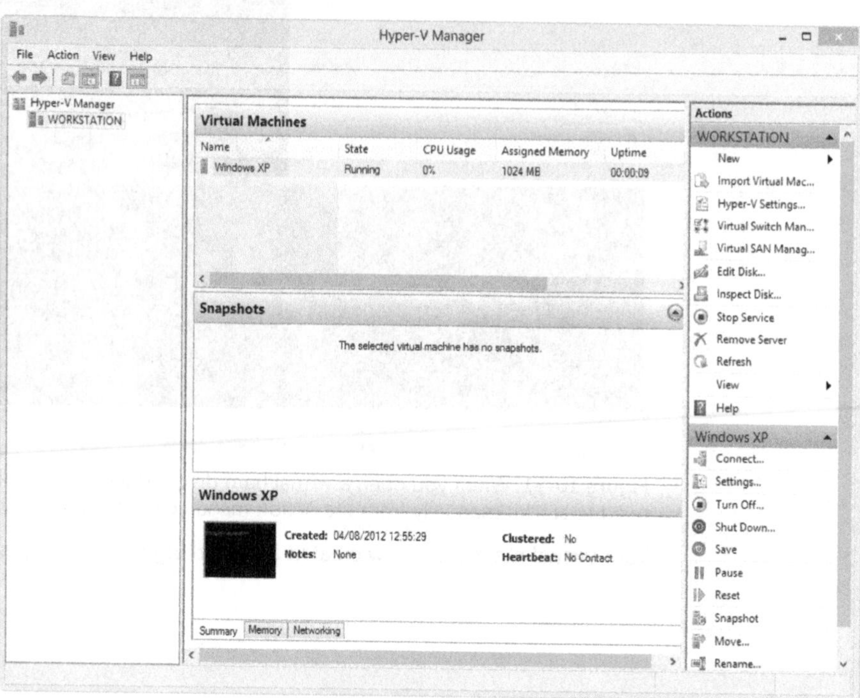

Figure 10-12 Click Virtual Switch Management in Hyper-V Manager to create network connections.

2. In the window that appears, give the virtual switch a name, and then select what type of network connection you want it to have (see Figure 10-13).

   Only external network types can access storage on the host computer, shared storage on the network, and the Internet. Internal and private networks are only for connecting to other virtual machines.

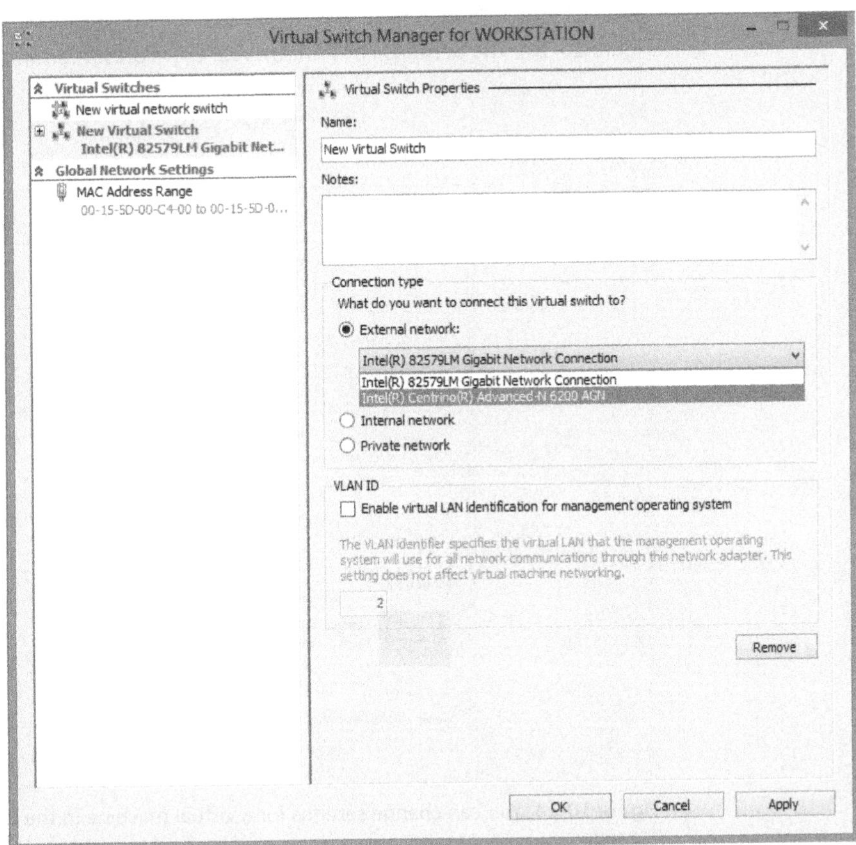

Figure 10-13 When you create a virtual switch, you can choose whether you want the switch to connect you to the Internet or just internally to other Hyper-V virtual machines.

3. If you click External Network, you need to specify which network card in your computer the virtual machine can use.

   To connect the virtual switch to your virtual machine, perform the following steps in the Client Hyper-V Manager console:

4. Select your virtual machine in the Virtual Machines pane (at the top center of the window). Then in the lower area of the Actions pane, click Settings (see Figure 10-14). The Settings For Windows XP On Workstation window appears.

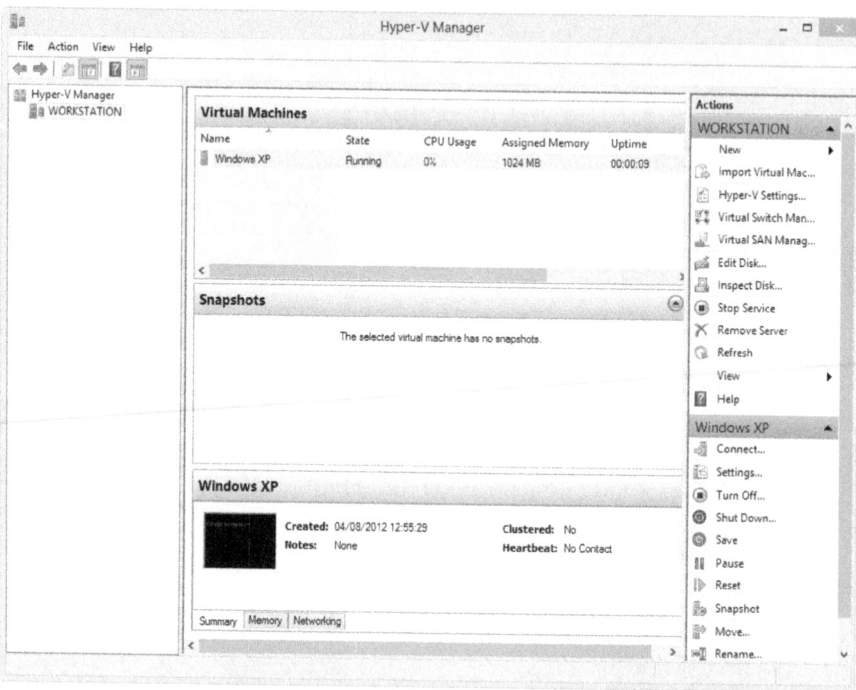

Figure 10-14 You can change settings for a virtual machine in the Client Hyper-V Manager.

5. In the Settings For Windows XP On Workstation window, in the left pane, see whether a Network Adapter is listed (see Figure 10-15). If one is listed, select it, and then change the Virtual Switch option to the switch you created.

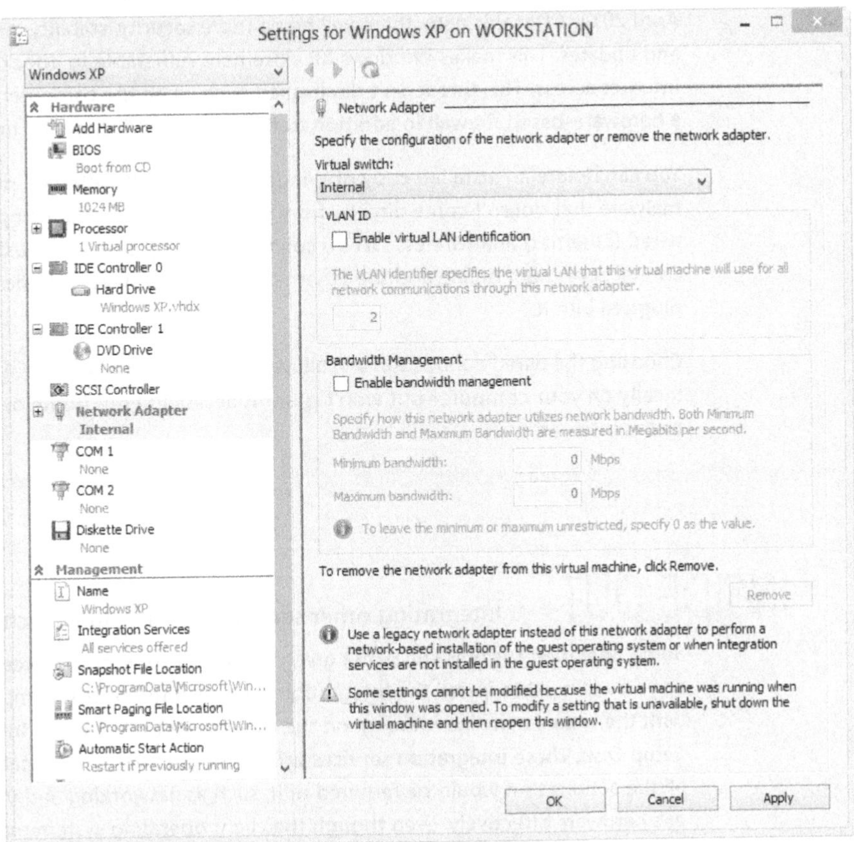

Figure 10-15 You can change the settings for a virtual machine.

6. If you do not have a Network Adapter listed in the Settings For Windows XP On Workstation window, click Add Hardware in the left pane to add one, and then add your virtual switch to it, as described in step 2.

INSIDE OUT Isolating Windows XP from the Internet and why you should do it

As mentioned at the beginning of this chapter, all support for Windows XP ends in April 2014. After this date, there will be no more security, stability, or other patches and updates. This makes Windows XP extremely vulnerable to attacks if it is allowed Internet access. This threat isn't diminished even when the computer is sitting behind a hardware-based firewall in addition to the standard Windows XP firewall.

You can isolate an installed copy of Windows XP from the Internet, protecting it from malware that doesn't come directly from your own files, if your computer has both wired (Ethernet) and wireless (Wi-Fi) connections. However, you must use the Wi-Fi connection to get online and the Ethernet port *cannot* have a physical network cable plugged into it.

Choosing the wired connection will allow the virtual machine access to files stored locally on your computer but won't grant it access to your home or work network, or the Internet.

INSIDE OUT Integrating other services into a virtual machine

Some operating systems still won't give you Internet or network access at this point, so you will need to install the Integration Services into the virtual machine. To do this, with the virtual machine running, on the Action menu, click Insert Integration Service Setup Disk. These integration services will ensure that the virtual machine can perform all the actions that would be required of it, such as networking and using your computer's hardware effectively, even though the client operating system may not know how to perform these tasks natively with your hardware.

PART 2

Applying Easy Technical Fixes

CHAPTER 11

Troubleshooting Windows 8 Issues

WINDOWS HAS SOME BIG CHALLENGES: to be self-managing for end users and flexible for system administrators. It has to support earlier versions of software and hardware and countless combinations of hardware and software. It also needs to be reliable, flexible, and robust in addition to being configurable and customizable to an almost limitless degree—all while maintaining strong security.

Despite these challenges, Microsoft does a remarkable job of ensuring that Windows 8 is stable and secure on nearly every platform, and Windows 8 is by far the most robust and resilient version of the operating system. Windows RT is the first version of the operating system that really can be considered consumer electronics. On devices with ARM processors, Windows RT is preinstalled and is as simple and easy to set up out of the box as a television set.

Common Windows 8 Issues

Users of Windows 8 will encounter some challenges depending on how they use the system. This section covers the most common issues.

Where Is My Windows 8 Installation DVD?

Not receiving an installation DVD with your system can be frustrating. Your computer didn't come with a copy of the Windows 8 installation DVD when you bought it to reduce the potential for piracy. This is an agreement between Microsoft and its OEM partners, who produce and sell computers. You have paid for your copy of Windows, however, so when you are buying a computer, see whether the inclusion of a Windows 8 installation DVD is an option.

If your Windows 8 installation DVD isn't included as an option when you purchase the computer, most OEMs will allow you to order one separately, though there might be a nominal postage charge. If you find yourself negotiating to buy a computer from an OEM who does not have a policy of providing installation discs, you may want to shop around with other companies before committing to buy.

INSIDE OUT Downloading Windows 8 images with software subscriptions

If you have a Microsoft TechNet, MSDN, or Action Pack subscription, you will be able to download ISO disc images of Windows 8 that you can use for repair work. These images, however, will not work with your OEM Windows 8 product key and instead will come with their own. It should be noted that some subscription software from Microsoft such as that coming from TechNet or the Action Pack are not licensed for use other than testing or demonstration.

The Windows 8 Installation DVD is incredibly useful to have for troubleshooting and repairing Windows problems. Regarding the issue of piracy, the OEM installation DVDs are commonly tied to the BIOS or Unified Extensible Firmware Interface (UEFI) system on the motherboard and simply won't install on other computers (so don't try this at home), which pretty much invalidates the piracy counter claim.

As a backup, you can create a System Image Disc, which I explained in Chapter 6, "Optimizing Backup and Restore." I recommend that you do this anyway. However, a Windows 8 installation disc is optimal if you are going to do any serious repair work.

INSIDE OUT Windows installation DVDs and ARM tablets

Windows RT software on ARM architecture is supplied only to OEMs and is not available for purchase via retail outlets. Thus, if you buy a Windows RT–powered tablet, you will not be able to get an installation disc. However, as a result of differences with the way Windows RT works, mainly the fact that it is incompatible with the Intel processors found inside desktop and laptop computers, which I describe in Chapter 15, "Understanding the Windows 8 Folder and File Structure," you will not need the installation disc.

I Want to Change File Associations

Sometimes you might not want the Windows 8 apps opening all your files. By default, Windows 8 opens music, video, pictures, and PDF files (yes, there's a native reader for PDFs now) in Windows 8 apps, but it's a simple matter to change the default program or app that is associated with a file.

To change the default program or app, perform the following steps:

1. On the desktop, open File Explorer.
2. Right-click the file for which you want to choose the default program, and then click Open With\Choose Default Program, as depicted in Figure 11-1.

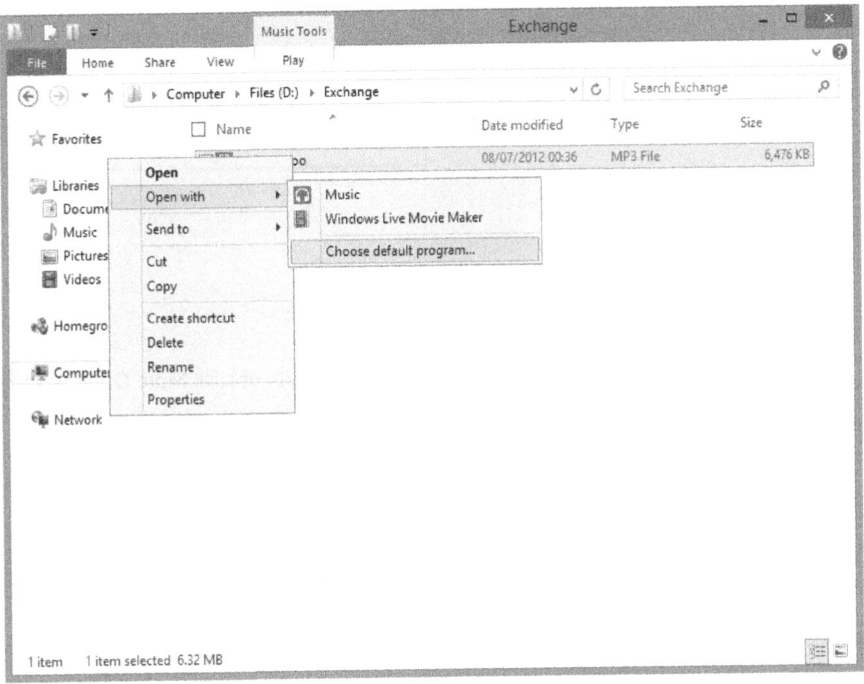

Figure 11-1 You can right-click a program to change the association.

A pop-up dialog box opens, displaying a list of recommended programs, as shown in Figure 11-2.

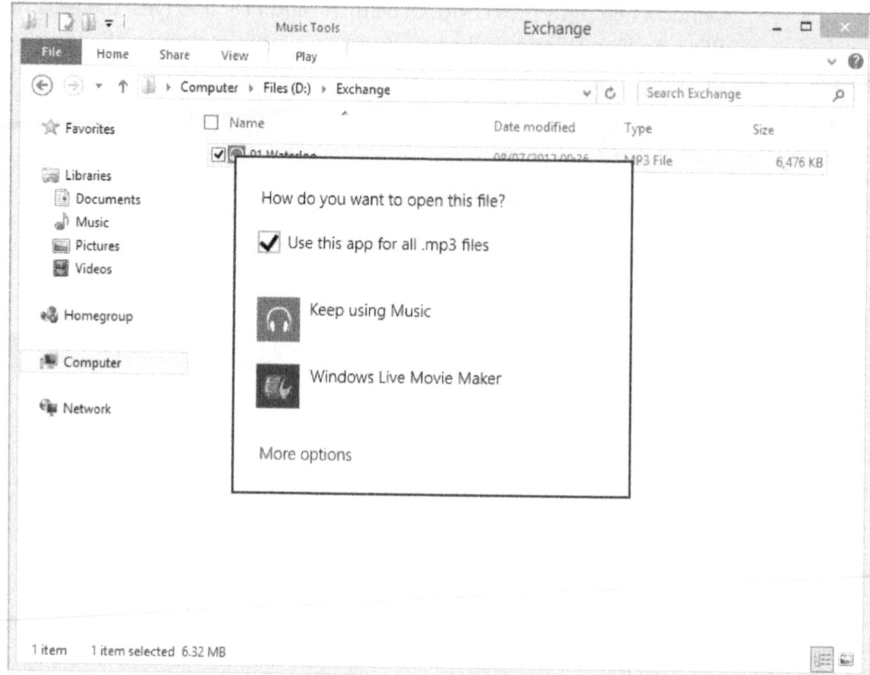

Figure 11-2 You can choose a program, or click More Options if the one you want to use isn't in the list.

3. If the default program or app you want does not appear in the list, click More Options at the bottom of the list.

4. If you still do not see the program or app with which you want to associate a file, you can search for it specifically at the bottom of the list of choices (see Figure 11-3).

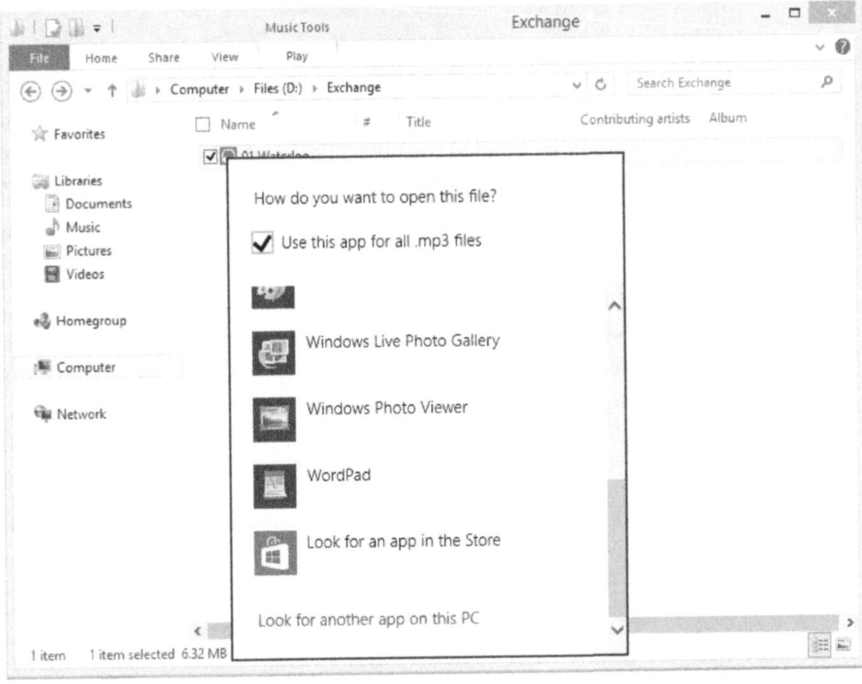

Figure 11-3 You can search for programs and apps by clicking Look For Another App On This PC.

After you choose the desired association, Windows 8 will open that file type with it. If you want Windows 8 to *always* use this program or app to open the file, select the Use This App For All.

I Can't Get Online to Download My Wi-Fi Driver

Sometimes, when you install Windows 8, the operating system hasn't found the driver for your Wi-Fi card, and without that card, you can't get online to download the driver. Windows might have a compatible driver, but you'll need to know a bit about your hardware first, and you might just have to make an educated guess.

> **INSIDE OUT** **Always keep a copy of your hardware drivers**
>
> **You should always keep a full copy of the hardware drivers that came with your computer, either by keeping the original driver discs in a dry, safe place, or by copying them to an internal partition (which is what I do) or to an external USB hard disk.**

If your Wi-Fi is part of your computer's motherboard, and your computer was relatively inexpensive, you can look to the manufacturer of the motherboard for clues. For example, if you have an Intel motherboard, you likely have an Intel Wi-Fi controller. Here's how you can identify the manufacturer of your computer's motherboard:

1. Open the WinX menu by pressing Windows logo key+X.
2. Click Control Panel. Ensure that you are using the Large Icons or Small Icons view, shown in Figure 11-4.

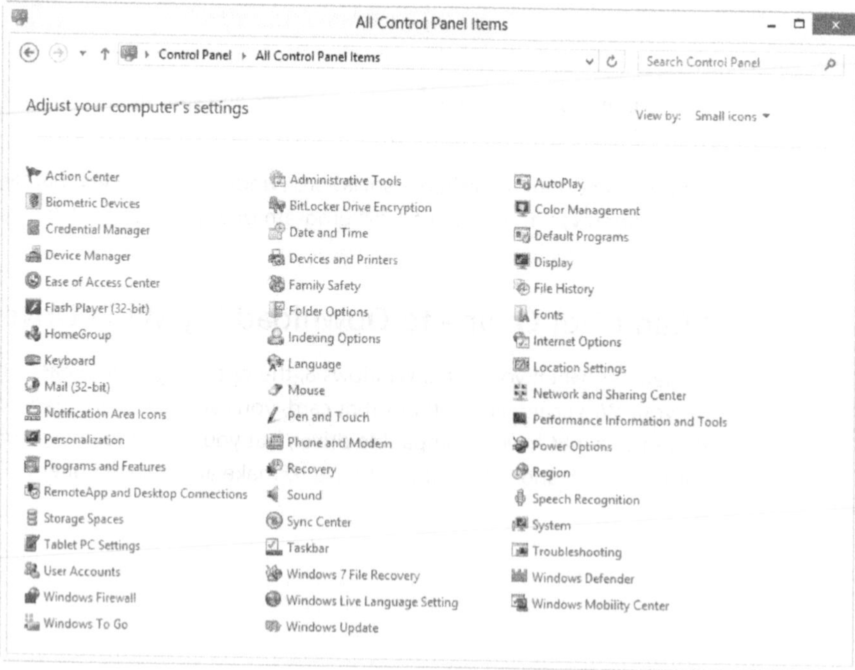

Figure 11-4 All Control Panel Items lists options for discovering information about your system.

3. Click Administrative Tools to display a list of tools, as shown in Figure 11-5.

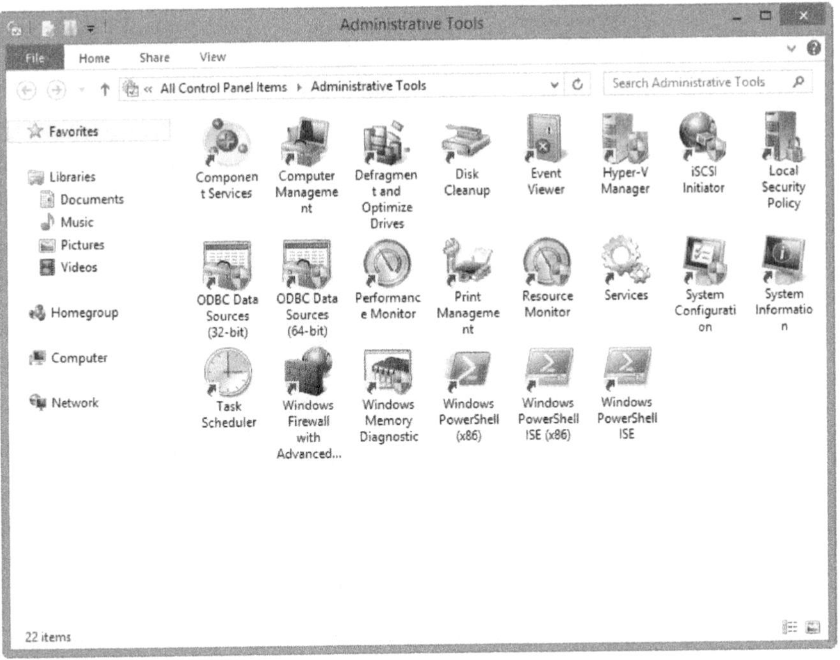

Figure 11-5 The Administrative Tools in Control Panel are clearly labeled with explanatory icons.

4. Double-click System Information to open the System Information window, shown in Figure 11-6.

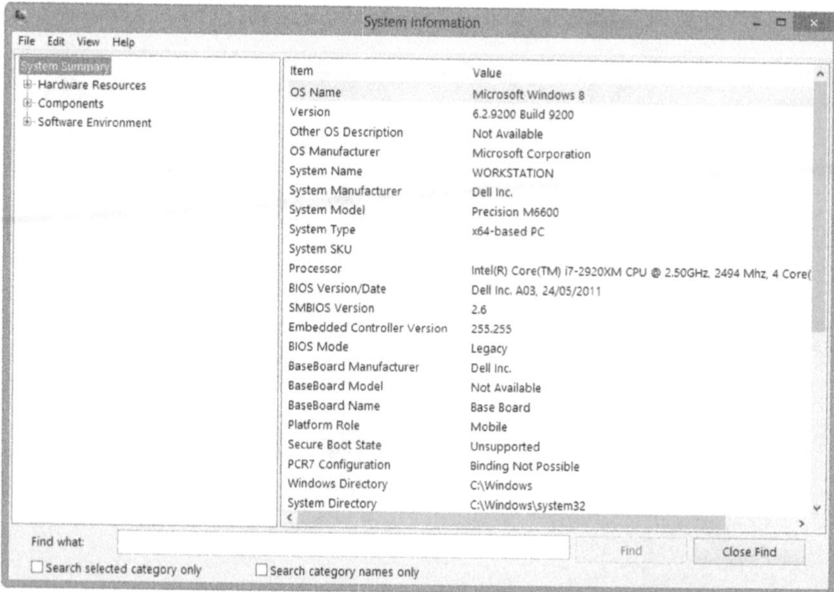

Figure 11-6 System Information displays a great deal of information about your computer. Your wireless driver information will be found in Components\Network\Adapter.

The System Information window might display the name of your motherboard. You will find information about your wireless driver in Components\Network\Adapter. Another place to look for clues is in the Components\Network section, but you are more likely to find clues in Components\Problem Devices.

Note

If you can get online by using your smartphone, you might be able to find the make and model of your Wi-Fi chipset by searching for the specifications of your computer model on the computer manufacturer's website.

Now you want to see whether you can force Windows to install a compatible driver. Follow these steps to do so:

1. Open Device Manager from the Start screen by typing **Device** and then clicking Other Devices.

   Alternately, open Device Manager from Control Panel.

2. Find the nonfunctioning driver by looking for a yellow warning icon. Any driver that isn't working shows this icon.

3. Right-click the desired driver, and then click Update Driver Software, as illustrated in Figure 11-7.

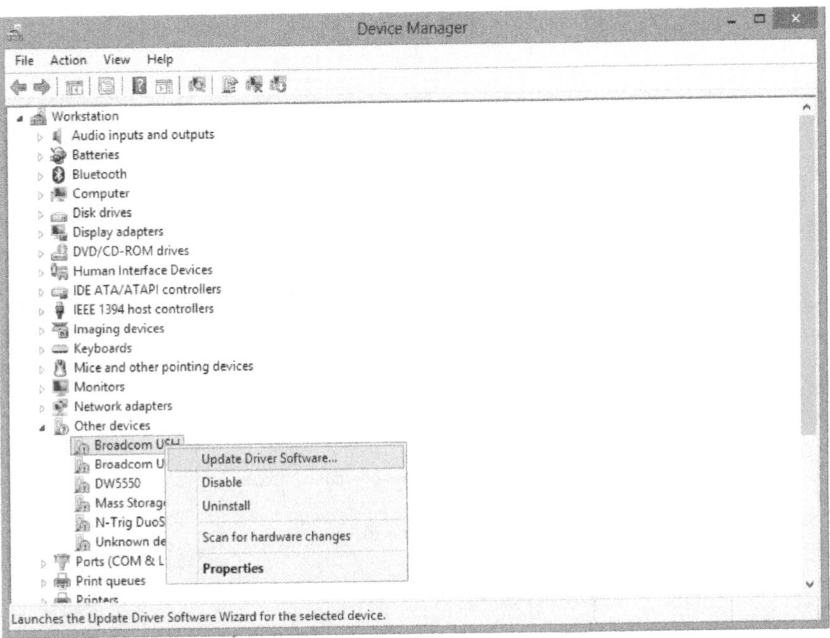

Figure 11-7 Updating a hardware driver can be accomplished in Device Manager.

4. On the How Do You Want To Search For Driver Software page (see Figure 11-8), click Browse My Computer For Driver Software.

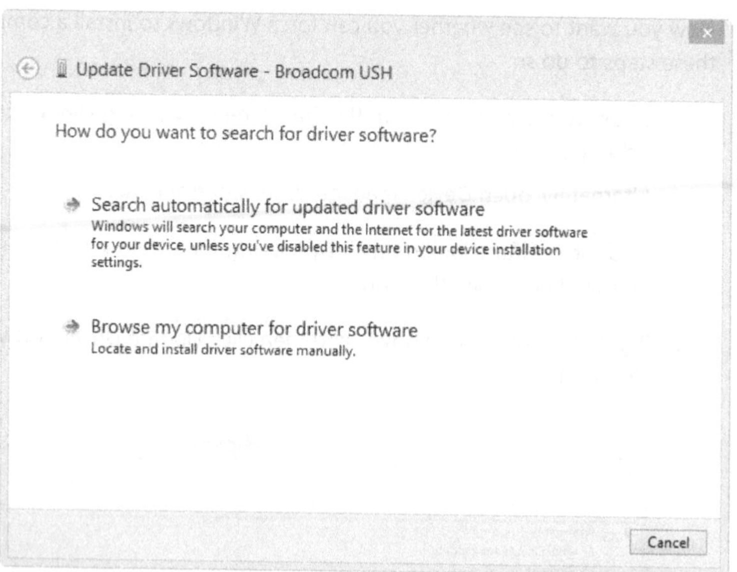

Figure 11-8 Windows 8 will ask you how to want to find an updated driver. You will need an active Internet connection to search for the driver automatically.

5. On the Browse For Driver Software On Your Comupter page (see Figure 11-9), click Let Me Pick From A List Of Device Drivers On My Computer, and then click Next.

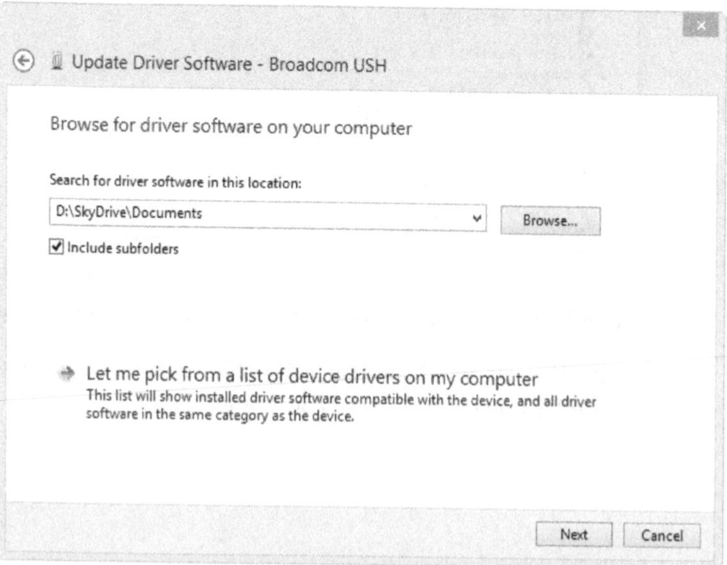

Figure 11-9 You can manually browse for a driver and tell Windows to include all the subfolders in the location you have chosen. When you search manually for a driver, a check box under the address box will allow Windows 8 to automatically search all the subfolders in the selected location.

6. On the Select Network Adapter page, clear the check box for Show Compatible Hardware, shown in Figure 11-10, and then click Next.

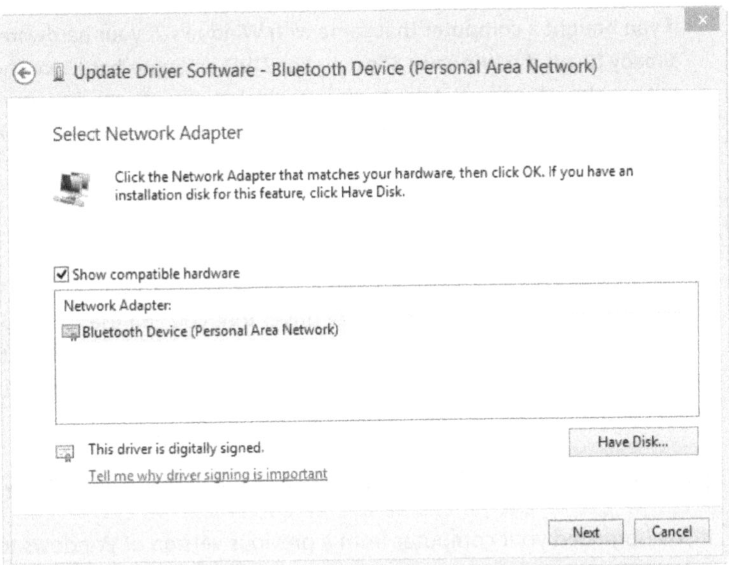

Figure 11-10 By default, Windows will display only the drivers it knows are compatible. It will not include drivers that have not been submitted for certification by Microsoft.

7. In the Manufacturer list, look to see whether a compatible driver for your hardware exists, as illustrated in Figure 11-11.

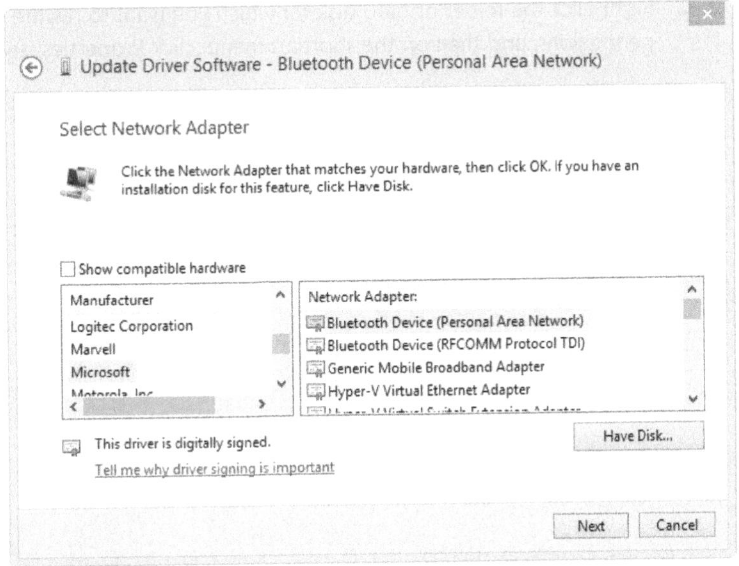

Figure 11-11 When you clear the compatible hardware option, the dialog box displays a list of every driver that comes with Windows 8 for that device type.

INSIDE OUT **Windows 8 and newer hardware**

If you bought a computer that came with Windows 7, your hardware drivers should already be on the Windows 8 installation DVD and your hardware should install without problem. However, if your computer includes hardware that was released after Windows 8, that will not be the case, and you should download a copy from the manufacturer's website.

Although Windows might not contain a compatible hardware driver, it's a good idea to check. You can often find a temporary driver that you can use to get online. However, the best solution is to download the appropriate driver from the manufacturer's website by using another computer. Also, your computer might have a 3G or 4G mobile broadband connection that you can use to download the driver.

I Don't Have Permission to Write Files to a Disk

If you upgraded your computer from a previous version of Windows to Windows 8 by using a clean install, and you stored files on a separate partition on the hard disk or on a USB-attached hard disk, you might find that you don't have permission to access those files any longer. In this case, the Windows user security system locked the permissions to the account that had access to the files previously. You can change these permissions, but you need to be logged in as an administrator to do so. Follow these steps:

1. Right-click the folder or hard disk for which you want to rewrite the security permissions, and then on the shortcut menu, click Properties (see Figure 11-12).

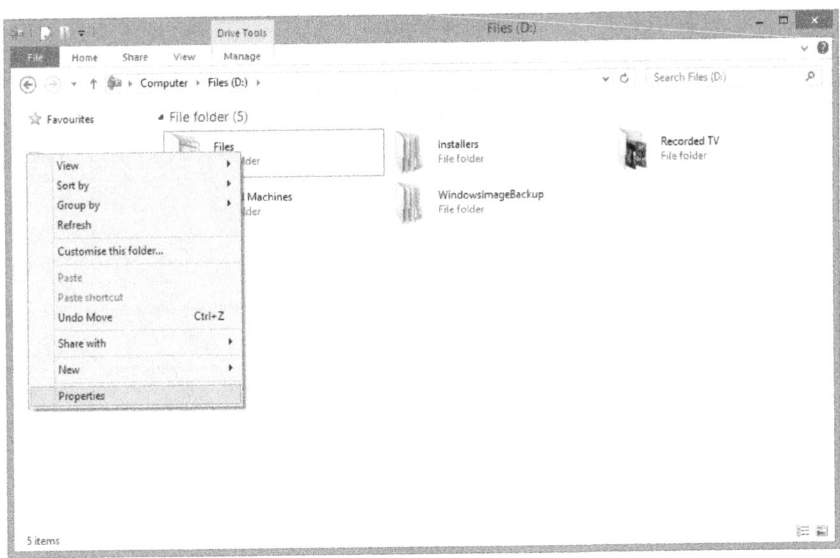

Figure 11-12 Right-click the disk or folder you want to change security permissions for.

2. In the Properties dialog box that appears, click the Security tab, as shown in Figure 11-13.

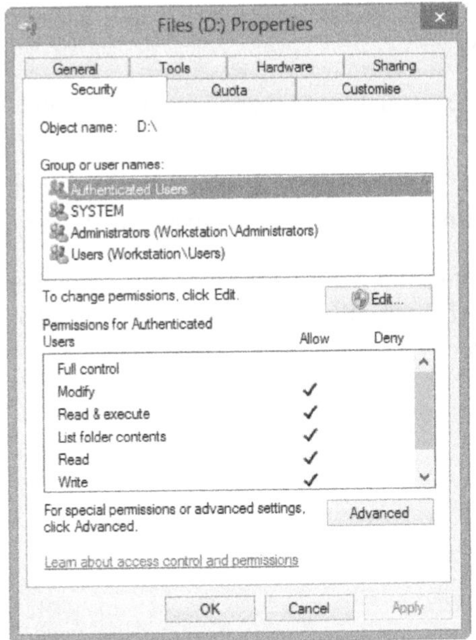

Figure 11-13 You begin the process of changing security permissions on the Security tab.

3. Click the Advanced button.

   The Advanced Security Settings dialog box appears (see Figure 11-14).

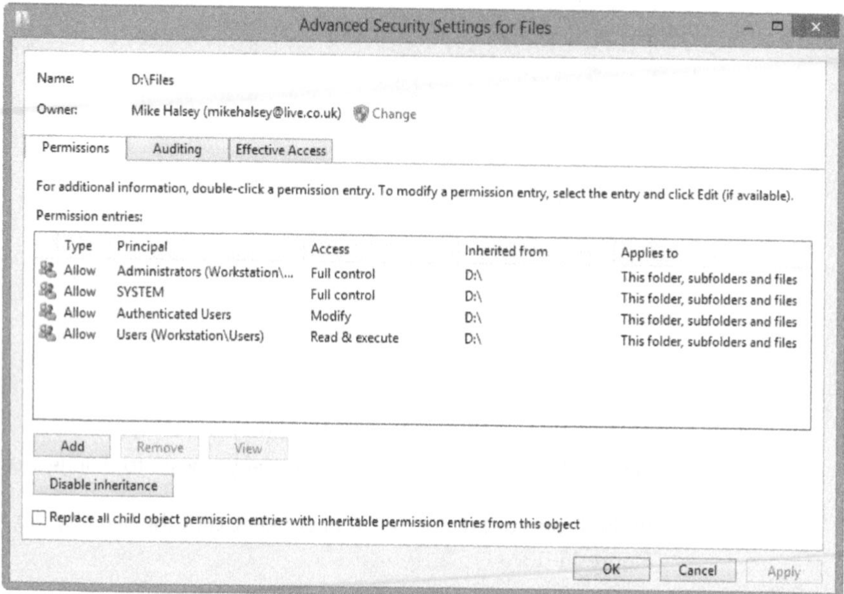

Figure 11-14 The Advanced Security Settings dialog box contains the options you need on the Permissions tab.

4. Select the user for whom you want to change permissions, and then click the Edit button.

   If you don't see an Edit button, click the Disable Inheritance button and then click Convert Inherited Permissions Into Explicit Permissions On This Object.

5. Choose the appropriate permissions for the user. You will probably want to give yourself Full Control of the files and folders, as you can see depicted for some user types in Figure 11-15.

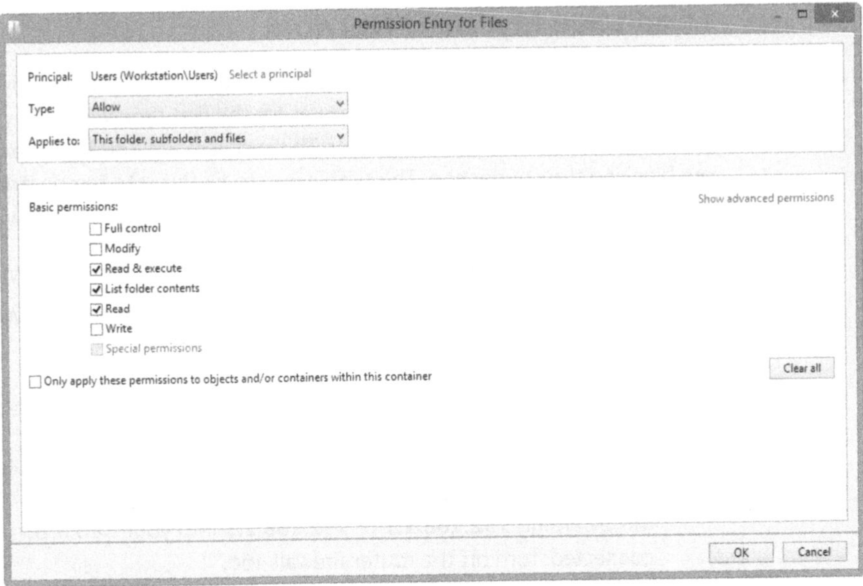

Figure 11-15 You can change specific file permissions and display additional permissions in the Permission Entry dialog box.

Windows 8 will now change the permissions on each individual file, and you should not close the dialog box that sets permissions while security changes are taking place. Keep your computer on during the process, and be aware that it can take a while if you have a lot of files.

I Don't Have Permission to Perform a Task

Anyone who has seen the classic 1968 movie *2001: A Space Odyssey* might remember the haunting line of dialogue, "I'm sorry, Dave, I'm afraid I can't do that," that occurred when the rebellious on-board computer, H.A.L., detects that the humans are trying to shut him down. You might even have wondered if this will ever happen on your own computers! Windows 8 might also occasionally refuse to do something for you, citing that you don't have permission to perform a particular action.

To work around this, exit whatever you're doing, and when you run the program again, right-click it, and then on the shortcut menu (or on the Windows 8 App bar), click Run As Administrator. You will now be able to resume your task. Please bear in mind, though, that doing this will give the program full administrator rights on your computer, so you should not do this with software that you do not know well and trust.

I Can't See My Wi-Fi Network

If you have a new broadband router that's already been configured by using another computer, or if you are connecting to a router for the first time via Wi-Fi, you might find that your computer can't detect the router. This problem is caused by one or two firewalls that are blocking the connection. The simple way to fix this is to temporarily turn off Windows Firewall and, if necessary, the router firewall, by performing the following steps:

1. From Control Panel, click System And Security, and then click Windows Firewall.

   Alternately, on the Start screen, type **firewall**, and then select Windows Firewall from the Settings results that appear.

2. Turn off Windows Firewall, and then try again to connect to the router.

3. If you still can't see your router, plug your computer into the router via a physical network cable so that you can log on to its configuration panel. You normally do this by typing **192.168.1.1** or **192.168.2.1** into your web browser. When you are connected, turn off the router firewall, too.

4. Connect your computer to the router via Wi-Fi. The two devices will be able to see each other.

5. Reenable both firewalls.

   Your computer will continue to connect to your router each time you access it via Wi-Fi after you follow this procedure.

I Can't Activate My Graphics, Sound, Keyboard, or Mouse Drivers

Sometimes, graphics or sound drivers can cause problems with Windows, for example, they don't play sound at all or display an image only in a low quality, low resolution mode. The DirectX Diagnostic Tool can identify these issues.

1. Open the Start screen, search for **dxdiag**, and then click dxdiag.exe when it appears in the Apps search results.

   The DirectX Diagnostic Tool dialog box opens, as shown in Figure 11-16.

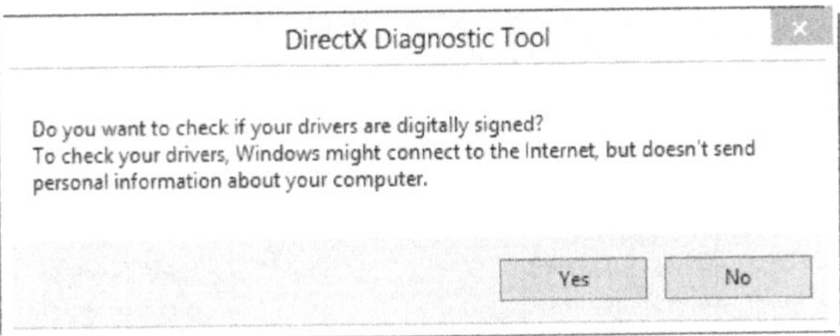

Figure 11-16 The DirectX Diagnostic Tool can help detect some driver problems.

2. The dialog box asks if you want to check whether your hardware drivers are digitally signed. Click Yes to verify that the drivers have been approved by Microsoft for compatibility with Windows 8.

   The DirectX Diagnostic Tool starts (see Figure 11-17), checking your display, sound, and input devices for problems. If DirectX Diagnostic Tool identifies any problems, it displays them.

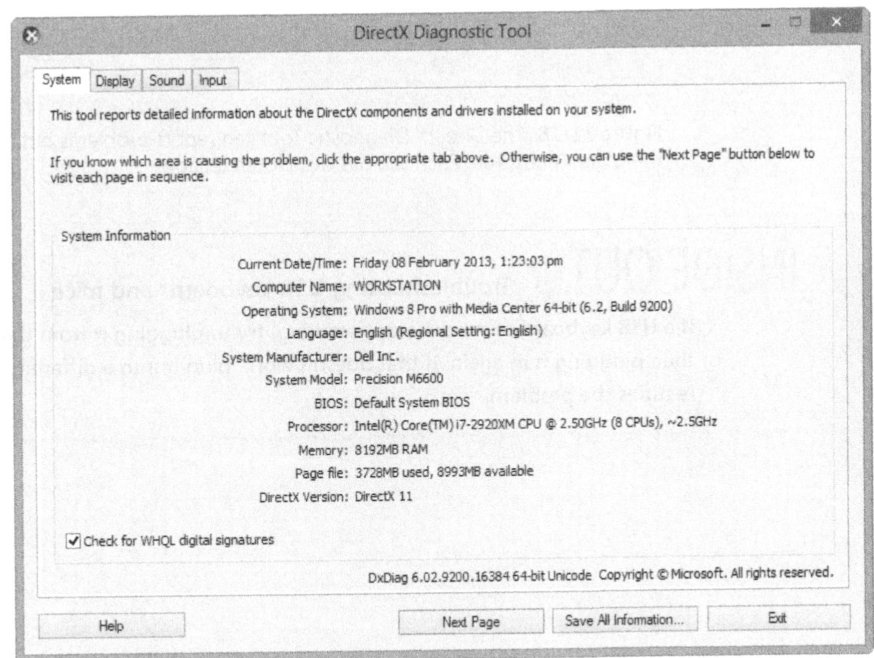

Figure 11-17 The DirectX Diagnostic Tool provides in-depth reporting on your hardware.

3. Click the tabs along the top of the screen to review the reports. You will be alerted in the Notes section as to whether problems are found (see Figure 11-18). If a problem is identified, you can use an appropriate diagnostic tool or method to rectify it.

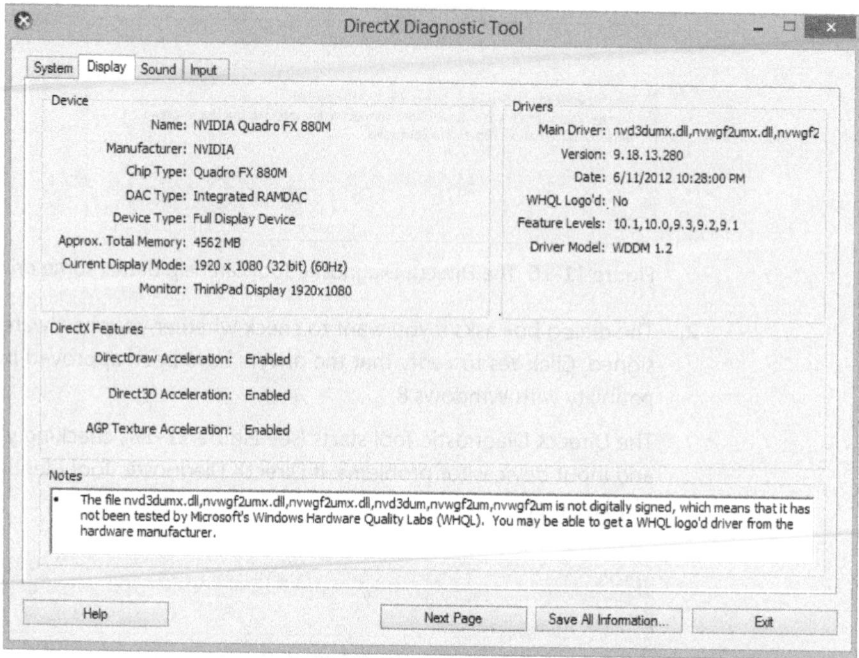

Figure 11-18 The DirectX Diagnostic Tool can report problems but will let you know if there aren't any, too. Each tab has this Notes section.

INSIDE OUT Troubleshooting USB keyboards and mice

If a USB keyboard or mouse stops working, try unplugging it from the USB port and then plugging it in again. If that doesn't work, plug it into a different port. This usually rectifies the problem.

This Copy of Windows 8 Is Not Genuine

Sometimes, even though you have a legitimate, fully activated copy of Windows 8, you see the message "This Copy of Windows is Not Genuine" when you turn on your computer. You receive this message because a file is being read incorrectly at startup. To fix this, you need to turn off the computer normally and then restart it.

Windows Update Won't Install Anything

Windows Update can become stuck and thus unable to install any updates. This happens because the temporary files stored for the program have become corrupt. To fix this problem, go to the *X*:\Windows\Software Distribution folder, where *X* represents the hard disk on which Windows 8 is installed. Delete the contents of this folder to reset Windows Update, which deletes all the temporary files associated with Windows Update. It also resets Windows Update to the default settings, so any updates you've previously hidden will reappear. You will need to hide them again.

Why Am I Not Getting "Optional" Windows Updates?

The new Windows 8 interface for Windows Update in PC Settings automatically downloads all important and critical updates for your computer. What it won't do, however, is install some optional updates for Windows and other Microsoft software that you have installed. If you find this is the case, from the desktop, set up Windows Update (in Control Panel) to manually install updates on regular basis.

Search Isn't Finding My Files

If you have moved your files and folders away from your main Windows 8 partition, or if you have files located on another hard disk or partition, these files might not be indexed automatically and thus might appear in search results right away.

You can add folders and drives to the index by searching for **index** on the Start screen and then clicking Indexing Options in the search results. In the Indexing Options window that appears (see Figure 11-19), you will be shown all the current folders and drives that are automatically indexed by Windows 8. You can click the Modify button to change these locations and add more drives and folders to the index.

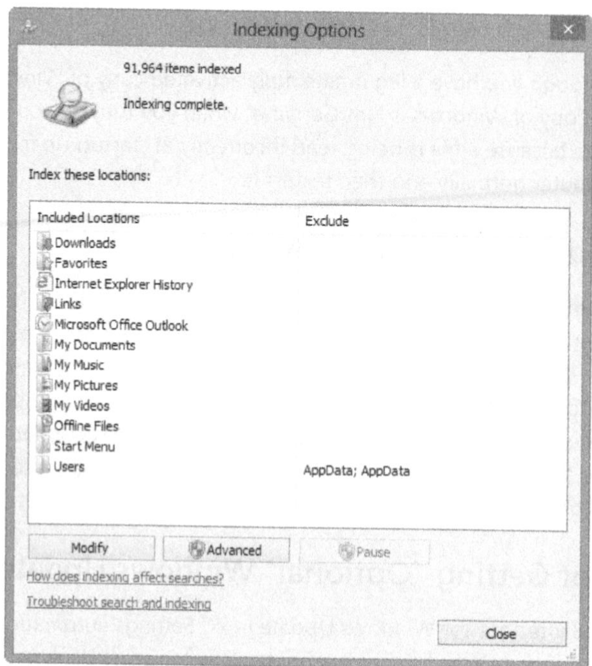

Figure 11-19 You can add or remove items to be indexed in the Indexing Options dialog box by clicking Modify.

INSIDE OUT Indexing options and network storage

The indexing options in Windows 8 do not allow you to add network-attached drives or other external storage, such as USB hard disks, to the index. However, there are two ways to work around this. You can right-click a network drive or folder and select Always Available Offline. After this sets up the sync partnership between your computer and the drive, the external storage will become available for indexing. You can also add networked music, pictures, and video folders to the index in a more friendly manner by adding them to the libraries in Windows Media Center, which is available as an optional update for Windows 8 Pro and can be purchased by clicking Add Features To Windows in the Control Panel.

The Service Pack or Update Install Was Interrupted

Windows recommends that you do not unplug or turn off your computer while it is installing updates and service packs, and it can be very difficult to interrupt the installation of an update. Windows 8 is extremely resilient in the face of power failures during the update process. You can trust me on this one, because it's my job to try to interrupt installation, and believe me, I've tried. So far, I've never actually succeeded in doing so.

There might be times, however, when you do experience a momentary power interruption during an installation—perhaps somebody tripped over the power cord and unplugged it, or perhaps a power cord is inadvertently cut. If Windows 8 does interrupt the installation, you can use System Restore to take the computer back to a point before the update was initiated. Details about how to do this are in Chapter 2, "Repairing Common Issues in Windows 8."

Windows Starts Up Very Slowly

When Windows starts slowly, software that is running in the background might be the cause, and you'll be pleased to hear that Windows 8 is very good at diagnosing slow startup software. The new Task Manager (see Figure 11-20), which you can access by pressing Ctrl+Alt+Del or by right-clicking the taskbar, has a Startup tab where you can view the status of startup items. Just open Task Manager, click the More Options button in the lower-left corner, and then click the Startup tab. Here all startup items will be shown with their impact listed in the Startup Impact column.

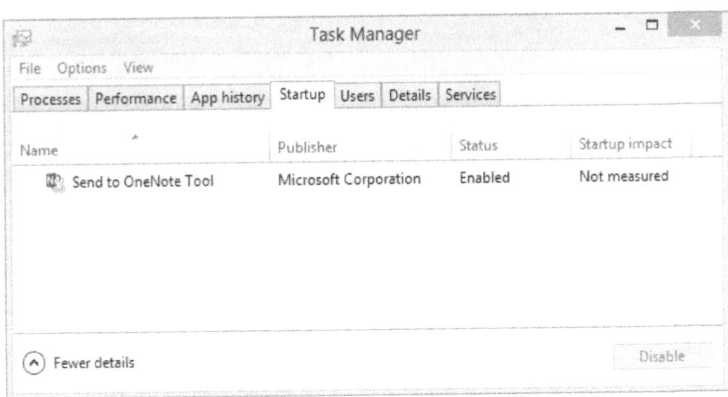

Figure 11-20 In Windows 8, you now manage startup items in Task Manager.

You can also disable startup items. If Windows 8 is reporting that something is slowing down your computer, you can select it and click the Disable button in the lower-right corner of the window.

Note

The free third-party program Soluto is very popular for weeding out slow startup items in Windows. You can download it from *http://www.soluto.com*.

Windows Shuts Down Very Slowly

Changing a registry setting might fix a slow shutdown problem. To access the Registry Editor, on the Start screen search for **regedit**. Click regedit.exe, and in the left pane of the Registry Editor window, click HKEY_LOCAL_MACHINE, click SYSTEM, click CurrentControlSet, and then click Control.

In the right pane, reduce the WaitToKillServiceTimeout setting (the last item in Figure 11-21) to a lower number by right-clicking it and then clicking Modify. The recommended setting is 5000. (This is the number of milliseconds Windows will wait before terminating a program.) Reducing the shutdown timeframe will exit programs more quickly than the Windows standard timing but might also prevent them from saving documents properly if you have any open at the time. Always close your documents first if you need to change this setting.

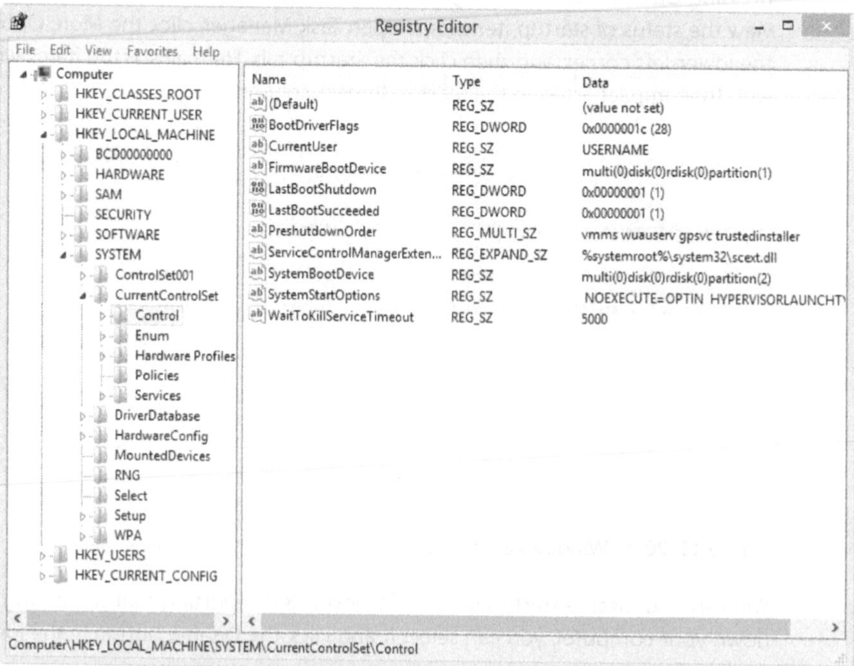

Figure 11-21 You can change the setting that controls how quickly Windows shuts down.

CAUTION!

Changing the WaitToKillServiceTimeout registry key can prevent some software from saving files or shutting down properly. This can cause problems with the software and perhaps make it unstable.

Sleep and Hibernation Problems

Some people experience issues when Windows 8 goes to sleep, ranging from Wi-Fi reconnection problems to the computer not coming out of sleep mode at all. If you have problems with Windows in sleep mode, especially if the computer is not coming out of sleep mode, you can change the default action to either turn the computer off or use hibernate mode instead.

To change the default, on the Start screen, search for **power**, and then click Power Options. (You can also find Power Options in Control Panel.) Next, click Change When The Computer Sleeps, and then click Change Advanced Power Settings.

On the Advanced Settings tab of the Power Options dialog box (see Figure 11-22), in the sleep section, you can change both of the Sleep After numbers settings to zero (0) while perhaps changing the Hibernate After options to the prior sleep setting if you want the computer to hibernate instead of sleep. This option is not available in Windows RT.

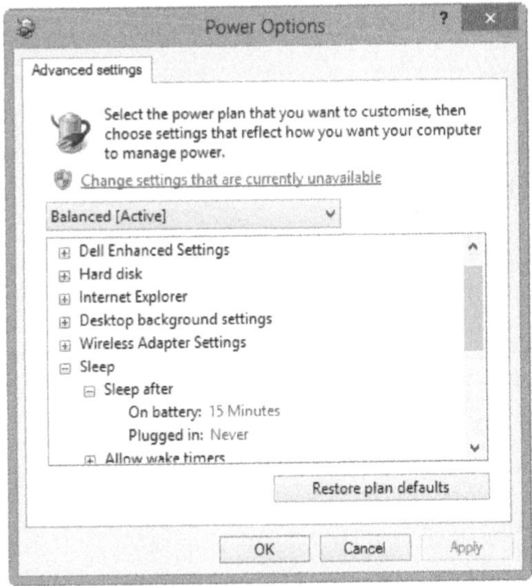

Figure 11-22 You can manually change sleep (if available) or hibernation settings in Advanced Settings.

You can also change what the power and sleep buttons do on your computer. Click the Choose What The Power Buttons Do link in the main Power Options window of Control Panel to access the System Settings screen. Here you have options for choosing actions for physical shutdown, on-screen shutdown, and sleep buttons, as illustrated in Figure 11-23. You might, for example, want to change the When I Press The Sleep Button action to either Do Nothing or Hibernate.

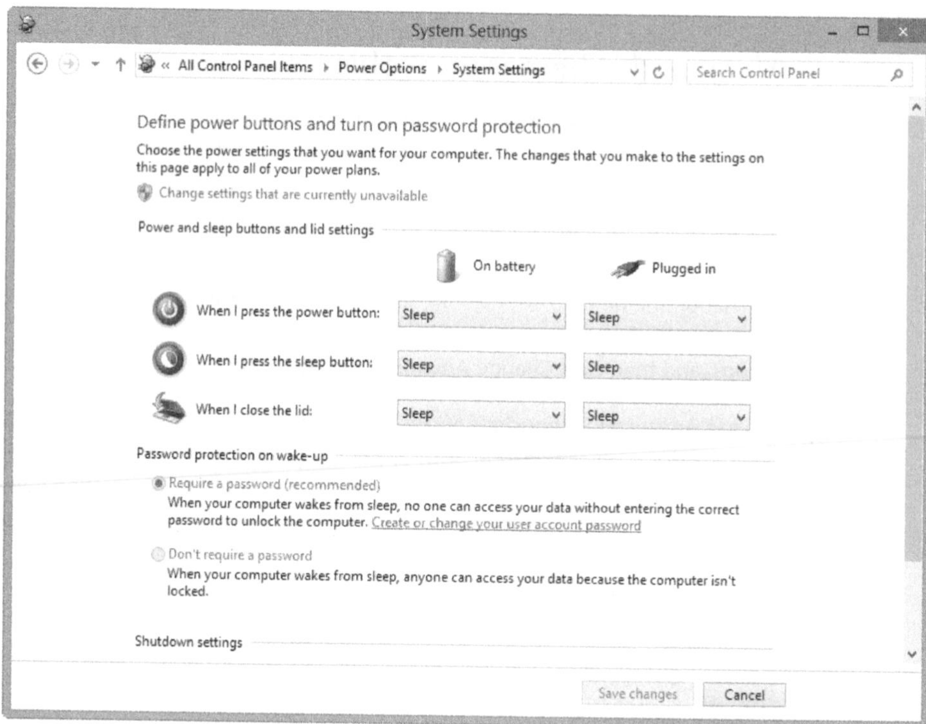

Figure 11-23 You can change the Sleep Button Action setting.

BitLocker Has Locked Me Out of My Computer

If your computer and your copy of Windows 8 are encrypted with Microsoft BitLocker, which is a full-disc encryption technology designed to keep your files safe from theft and prying eyes, it may occasionally get confused and lock you out of your own computer. Your only option is to use a USB flash drive that contains copies of your BitLocker encryption keys to unlock the computer or to manually type in the very long decryption key; inserting the USB flash drive on startup will allow Windows 8 to search it for the correct unlock key. You will see an option to search USB flash drives for the key displayed on your screen.

I strongly recommend you keep a USB flash drive handy, especially when traveling. If you have access to another computer and a USB flash drive, you can store a copy of your encryption keys in a cloud service such as SkyDrive and download them from *https://skydrive.live.com/RecoveryKey*. Note that your key will *not* appear in your regular SkyDrive files list!

BitLocker Doesn't Work in My Multiboot System

BitLocker does not support multiboot systems. If you have created a multiboot system and one operating system is protected by BitLocker, you will be asked for your encryption key every time you start both operating systems. If you do have a multiboot system, my advice is to turn off BitLocker drive encryption for your computer completely.

My Multiboot System Doesn't Work

Many Windows 8 computers, including all computers from OEMs, have a BIOS replacement system called UEFI on the motherboard. Microsoft has dictated that all new computers must come with a feature called Secure Boot, enabled by default.

This system, which is a security feature that is intended to prevent malware from loading on startup, can also interfere with multiboot systems. You can disable Secure Boot in your UEFI system. Its location will vary from system to system, and you should refer to your computer manual for its location.

I Can't Modify the First Partition on My Second Hard Disk

When you install Windows 8, Windows wants to create a small System Reserved partition for storing the startup files. If your computer has two or more hard disks, and those disks already contain partitions, the Windows 8 installer puts those startup files on the first partition of one of those secondary hard disks because the second hard disk has displayed in the Windows Installer as Disk 0, probably because of the socket on your computer's motherboard it's plugged into. Thus, you have Windows 8 installed on one hard disk and the startup files on the first partition of another hard disk. Windows will not allow you to perform any partitioning, resizing, or restructuring on the partition on which the startup system is located.

INSIDE OUT **Keeping Windows 8 and the System Reserved partition together**

You can ensure that the partitions containing the Windows boot information and Windows 8 are on the same physical hard disk (which also helps maintain resiliency) by unplugging all your other hard disks before turning the computer on to install the operating system.

You may not be able to do this on a dual–hard disk laptop, such as a dedicated workstation or gaming laptop, so if Windows 8 uses an existing partition on your hard disk for the System Reserved files, you might need to move them later. I show you how to do this in Chapter 25, "Troubleshooting a Windows 8 Installation."

Items on the Desktop Are Too Small

If you have difficulty reading items on the monitor, you can rescale text and icons on the desktop to a more comfortable size. To do this, on the Start screen, search for **text**, and then click the Make Text And Other Items Larger Or Smaller link in the results. In the Display dialog box that opens (see Figure 11-24), you can increase the size of everything on the screen by up to 150 percent. Note that the Make Everything On Your Screen Bigger option within Ease of Access in PC Settings will scale up only the Windows 8 interface.

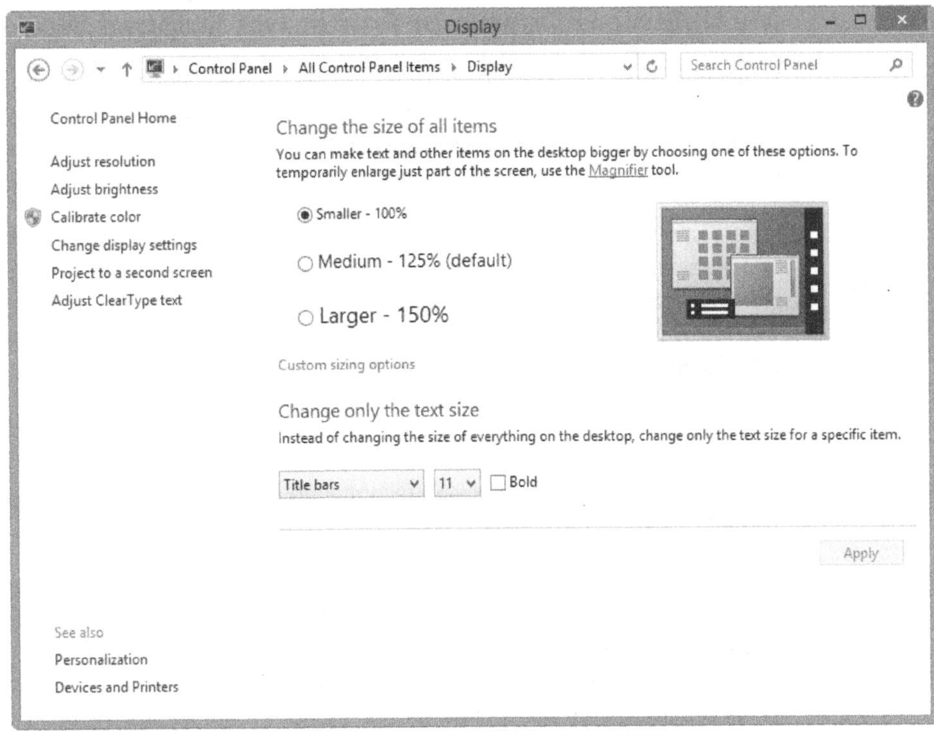

Figure 11-24 You can change the size of text and icons in Windows 8, scaling it without reducing legibility. Additional options are available for people with vision challenges, such as increasing text up to 24 points in size and displaying text in bold by default.

Hardware-Specific Issues

Hardware can sometimes be the cause of issues you experience with Windows 8 such as USB devices causing issues and not working, touchscreens not working, or the computer simply being unable to find an operating system. The following sections describe the most common issues and solutions.

Windows Gets Stuck at Its Loading Screen

On occasion, as Windows loads, it gets as far as its loading screen and then just sits there. It doesn't crash; it doesn't load; it doesn't do anything. And no matter how many times it gets this far, it just flat-out refuses to go any further.

Always check the network cable plugged into your computer. First unplug this cable to allow Windows to successfully start. You can then plug the cable back in. Windows should operate properly after this fix.

My USB Wi-Fi Dongle or Printer Has Stopped Working

Sometimes, especially after you have moved or cleaned your computer, you might find that you can no longer get online with your USB Wi-Fi dongle or other USB device such as a printer. This is caused by a driver problem that can sometimes lock the device to a single USB port.

If you just move the USB device to another port, the device still might not work. This is an odd problem, but you can work around it by moving the dongle between USB ports, or preferably back to the port it was plugged into previously to fix the problem.

My Tablet Touchscreen Isn't Working

If the touchscreen isn't working on your tablet, usually during installation, the issue is caused by a driver problem. (I show you how to fix these in Chapter 14, "Easy Ways to Repair Windows 8.") I would always recommend having a USB keyboard and mouse available, however, if you have a Windows 8 Pro tablet.

No Operating System Found

If you get a message stating "No Operating System Found," you probably have a CD, DVD, Blu-ray disc, or USB flash drive plugged into your computer, and the computer BIOS is set to start up from this device before starting up from your main hard disk. Just unplug or remove the media and restart the computer.

A New Monitor Results in No Picture

If you connect a new monitor but nothing displays on the screen, the maximum resolution of your new monitor is likely less than the Windows 8 setting for your previous monitor. Windows 8 does a good job of automatically detecting screen resolutions, but a quick way around this is to start the computer into Safe Mode (press F8 after the BIOS screen disappears but before you see the Windows loading logo). While in Safe Mode, you can change the resolution to a setting supported by your new monitor.

Alternatively, if you have a secondary graphics card installed, verify that you haven't inadvertently plugged the monitor into the video output on the motherboard instead of into the output of the graphics card. I explain this hardware in Chapter 25.

Lastly, it is possible that your monitor is set to the incorrect input (perhaps it's set to DVI and you've plugged your computer into the HDMI port). You can change the input in the monitor's (or TV's) on-screen menu.

My Thunderbolt Device Doesn't Work

Thunderbolt is an Intel device connection technology designed to offer an alternative to USB 3.0. You may find that you cannot use your Thunderbolt device. Although Windows 8 comes with full support for USB 3.0 devices, it does not support Intel's new Thunderbolt interface. You will encounter Thunderbolt through third-party drivers (at least initially; I anticipate a service pack will be released to fix this). You can find out how to add missing drivers in Chapter 14.

My Headphones or Microphone Won't Work

Sometimes a pair of headphones or a microphone won't work when you plug them in to your computer. To fix this, you need to set the headphones or the microphone as the default device.

In Control Panel, click Hardware And Sound, and then click Sound. In the Sound window that appears, click the appropriate tab, and set the default sound and recording devices, as shown in Figure 11-25.

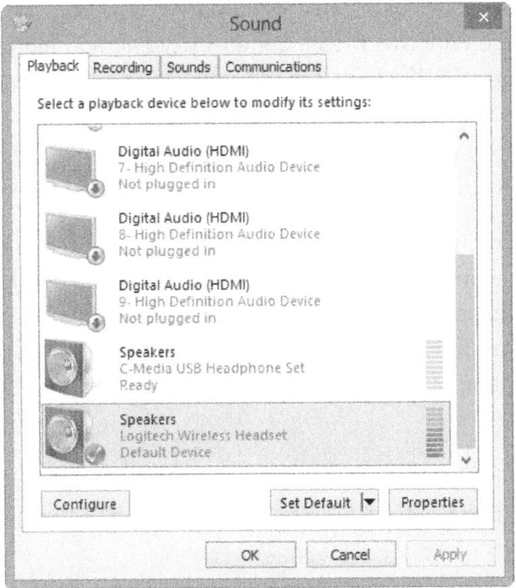

Figure 11-25 Headsets, microphones, and headphones are among the devices listed here. To change the default device, select it and then click the Set Default button (which also includes a drop-down list).

My Computer Has No Sound

After you install headphones, especially when you install Windows 8 with the headphones plugged in, the operating system might set them as the default sound device instead of your speakers. You use the same method as detailed earlier in the section "My Headphones or Microphone Won't Work" to set your speakers as the default sound device.

> **Note**
>
> **For quick access to the Sound dialog box, on the taskbar, right-click the sound icon, and then in the shortcut menu, click Playback Devices.**

My DVD or Blu-Ray Disc Won't Play

Windows 8 does not ship with video codecs that will play DVD movies or Blu-ray discs. You will need a third-party codec to play these movies. Codecs will most commonly be provided with Blu-ray playback software. You can get DVD and Blu-ray codecs by purchasing the Windows 8 Pro Pack upgrade; however, these discs will play only through Windows Media Center. You can purchase Windows Media Center by typing add features on the Start screen and clicking Add Features To Windows. On the How Do You Want To Get Started page, click I Want To Buy A Product Key Online.

The Drive Letter Has Changed on My USB Backup Hard Disk

When you use an external hard disk for backups, depending on the backup software you use, you might find that the second time you try to perform your backup, the software can no longer find the drive. This happens because when you unplug and reattach a USB drive, Windows 8 can reassign its drive letter. A hard disk that was drive G the last time you used it could now be drive H, for example, especially if you also have something such as a flash drive attached to the computer.

You can reassign drive letters in Disk Management. To ensure Windows remembers your preferred USB drives, you can find third-party software online, free of charge. They are useful utilities to have.

To reassign the letter of a drive in Disk Management, perform the following steps:

1. Open the WinX menu by pressing Windows logo key+X.
2. Click Disk Management.

3. In the window that appears, right-click the USB drive, and then click Change Drive Letter And Paths, as depicted in Figure 11-26.

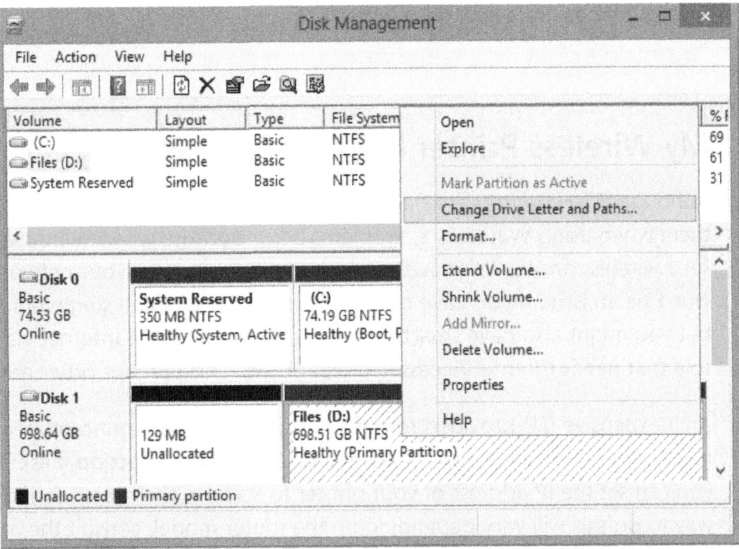

Figure 11-26 You can change a drive letter in Disk Management by right-clicking the visual representation of the partition or its name, and then clicking Change Drive Letter And Paths.

4. In the Change Drive Letter And Paths dialog box (see Figure 11-27), click Change, and then select the correct drive letter.

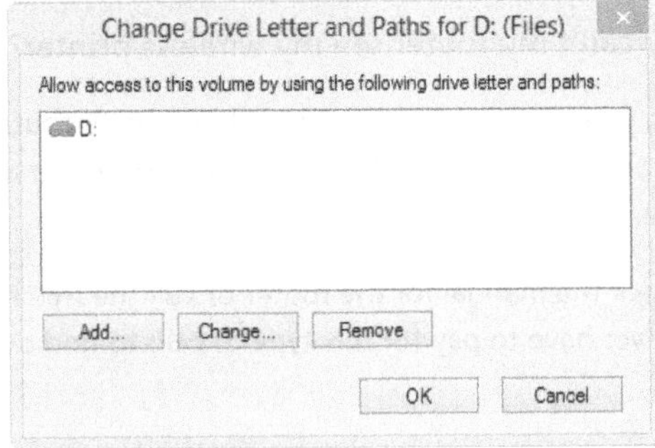

Figure 11-27 You are asked if you want to add, change, or remove a drive letter. Removing a drive letter is useful for hiding system and some backup drives.

Note

If another disk is currently using the drive letter that you want, you will need to reassign that device a new drive letter first.

My Wireless Printer Has Stopped Working

Although Wi-Fi printers are becoming commonplace, you can encounter problems with them when using Windows 8. Problems occur because when Windows 8 installs the driver for a wireless printer, Windows can lock the IP address on your network for the printer. This won't be an issue if you have only a single computer and a single printer at your location, but you might also have smartphones that connect to the Internet via Wi-Fi, a games console that needs Internet Access, a tablet or two, and perhaps other devices.

An inexpensive ISP-provided router can shuffle devices around on IP addresses when the router is reset (which is common when the Internet connection fails). To work around this, you can set the IP address of your printer to Static in the router configuration pane. The way to do this will vary depending on the router model; consult the manual that came with your router.

If the router is reset, the next time you want to print something, the printer will be on a different IP address and Windows 8 won't be able to see it. If this happens, all you can do is uninstall and reinstall the printer driver from Windows.

INSIDE OUT **Why can't my router see my wireless printer?**

Sometimes, just getting your wireless printer connected to your router can be a challenge. To correct the problem, press the WPS button on your router and then on the printer to connect them.

If this doesn't work, check the manual for the router or call the free help number for your ISP (you should never have to pay for this type of call) to find out how to get the printer connected.

My Laptop Battery No Longer Holds a Charge

Modern batteries are much better and more resilient than older battery designs. It is still true, though, that leaving your laptop continually plugged into a power source with the battery still inserted results in a constant trickle-charge that can deplete the battery over time.

Leaving the battery in while the computer is charging sets the battery's memory lower and lower so that eventually it believes that only a small charge is the same as a full charge. With these batteries (and again they tend to be only the older ones), you can sometimes reset this memory by completely draining the battery and charging it fully several times.

I would recommend removing the battery from your laptop if you intend to use the laptop while it's plugged in for a long period of time.

CHAPTER 12
Managing Application Compatibility

ALTHOUGH OPERATING SYSTEMS SEEM TO ADVANCE QUICKLY, our use of software tends to advance not quite as quickly. When you find an application that does a great job for your needs and you really enjoy using it, you want to keep using it. It's as comfortable as an old shoe. I'm a great example of this. I have Microsoft Photodraw 2, which was released in 2000. In Windows 7, I had to run Photodraw 2 in Windows XP Mode because some of the Direct3D capabilities were incompatible with those in Windows Vista and Windows 7.

Windows 8 is compatible with almost every piece of software that runs on Windows 7, but there obviously needs to be a small caveat here, because the amount of software available that it needs to be compatible with is vast. However, Windows XP Mode, which was the software compatibility virtualization package provided as a free extra for Windows 7 Professional and newer versions, is no longer supported and won't install in Windows 8. This makes managing application compatibility for earlier software slightly trickier in Windows 8 than it was in Windows 7. The reason for this is that all support for Windows XP ends in April 2014, which will be during the lifetime of Windows 8. After this time, there will be no more updates for Windows XP. You can still use Windows XP in the new virtualization client provided in the 64-bit versions of the Pro edition and newer versions for Windows 8, and I covered how you can use Client Hyper-V in Chapter 10, "Working in a Virtual Environment."

In this chapter, you learn about how to set up and troubleshoot application compatibility in Windows 8 and troubleshoot issues with Windows XP software compatibility.

Setting Up Application Compatibility in Windows 8

You set up application compatibility via the Start screen. To configure application compatibility, perform the following procedure:

1. Open the Start screen, and right-click the program icon you want to configure compatibility for, to open the App bar (see Figure 12-1).

Figure 12-1 The App bar opens from the bottom of your screen.

2. On the App bar, click Open File Location to open File Explorer, which shows the location of the app files.

3. Right-click the app's icon, and then click Properties, as shown in Figure 12-2.

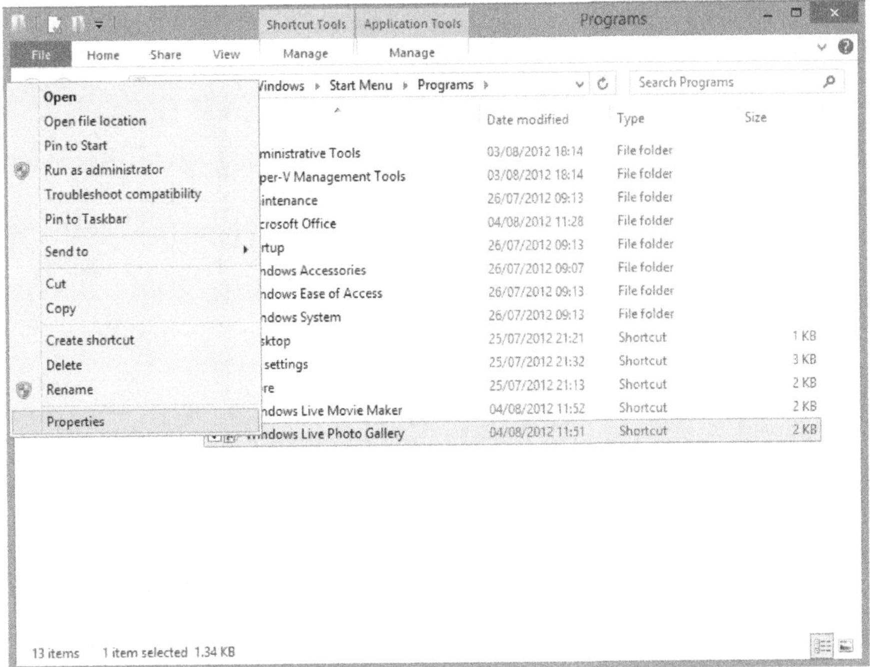

Figure 12-2 An app's Properties menu.

4. In the Properties dialog box, click the Compatibility tab, shown in Figure 12-3.

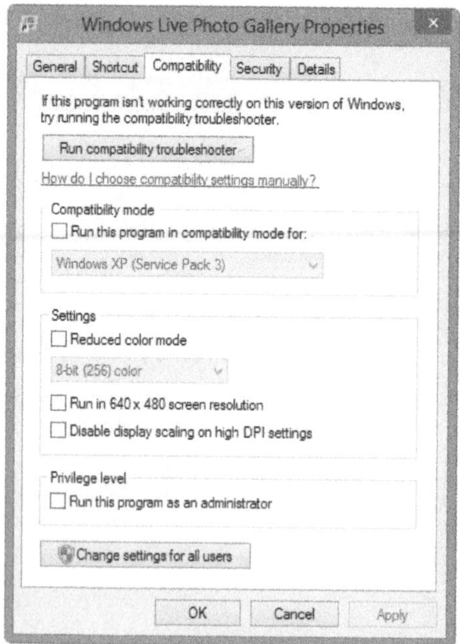

Figure 12-3 The Compatibility tab is available in the program's Properties dialog box.

The Compatibility tab is where you manage the compatibility settings for the operating system. The easiest way to do this is to select the check box in the Compatibility Mode section and then choose a version of Windows in which the software ran flawlessly. You can choose from the following versions:

- Windows 95
- Windows 98/Windows Me
- Windows XP (with Service Pack 2, or SP2)
- Windows XP (with SP3)
- Windows Vista
- Windows Vista (with SP1)
- Windows Vista (with SP2)
- Windows 7

Though Windows 8 can accommodate software through Compatibility Mode, I want to stress that compatibility mode doesn't run the software in an emulator. Compatibility Mode marks the app to let Windows 8 know that it must treat certain aspects of the app—such as *dynamic-link libraries* (*DLLs*), which are small files containing preprogrammed procedures that can be used by multiple software packages—differently from how it would treat a native application.

Because Compatibility Mode isn't emulation, not all the features of the previous operating systems will work with your app. In the example I described in the introduction to the chapter, Photodraw 2 doesn't work with the current version of Direct3D, and you receive an error when you try to do 3-D work.

In the Settings section, options such as Reduced Color Mode are for much earlier software or software that absolutely *must* have administrator rights. You can run much earlier software in an 8-bit or 16-bit color mode to emulate the effects of a CGA or EGA graphics card (remember those?), or you can run it at a maximum resolution of 640 x 480 pixels if it is not displaying correctly. You can also disable the display scaling feature of Windows 8.

You might have detected a hint of caution when I mentioned software that absolutely must have administrator privileges. Running apps as an administrator not only potentially poses an increased security and stability risk (because software can do whatever it wants with your operating system and files), it potentially indicates that code has been written quickly and carelessly, which presents yet more risks. Although you can select the Run This Program As An Administrator check box if you know for certain that administrator elevation is required, I would always advise against it.

INSIDE OUT

Managing application compatibility for all users

You might see an option to change application compatibility only for yourself or to do so for all users. If you are automatically elevating a program to administrator status, I would advise against elevating the privilege for all users unless completely necessary, because you do not know what software those other users might install—they may even install malware that can adversely affect the computer.

Troubleshooting Application Compatibility

You have two ways to troubleshoot compatibility issues in Windows 8. One way is to click the Run Compatibility Troubleshooter button, which is located at the top of the Compatibility tab in the Properties dialog box for any given program. You can also access troubleshooting help by right-clicking the program's icon in the File Explorer folder view and then clicking Troubleshooting Compatibility (see Figure 12-4), or by clicking the program's icon in the File Explorer folder view and then clicking Troubleshooting Compatibility on the Application Tools ribbon.

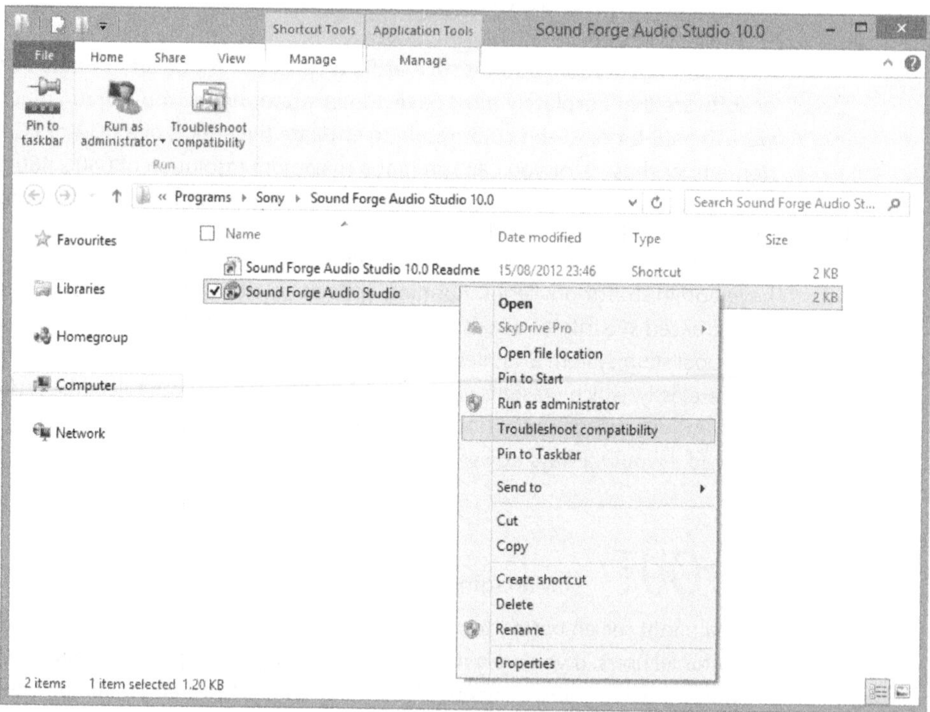

Figure 12-4 You can start the Program Compatibility Troubleshooter by right-clicking an app.

This troubleshooter will attempt to automatically detect the compatibility settings for the program and if it is unable to, it will ask you some questions about the program, as illustrated in Figure 12-5.

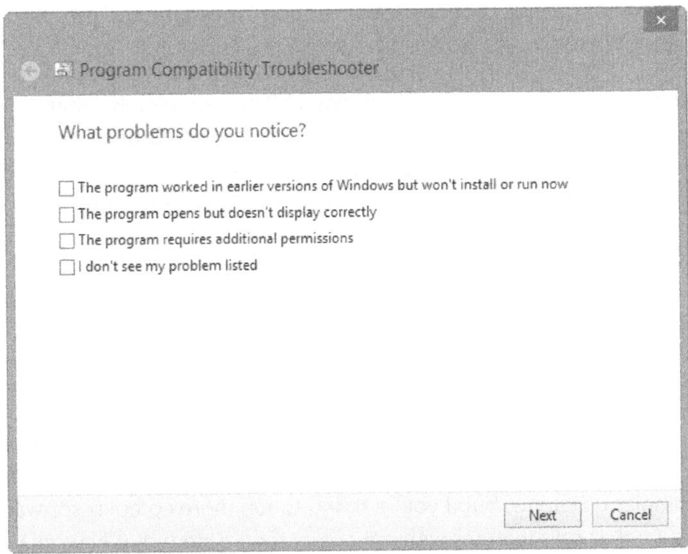

Figure 12-5 The Program Compatibility Troubleshooter wizard guides you through the troubleshooting process.

The wizard interface is a way to troubleshoot the manual settings, and it can be a very useful way to rectify problems with some programs that are causing issues in Windows 8.

INSIDE OUT Automatically detecting compatibility problems

Windows 8 will occasionally (usually upon installation of a program) detect that something isn't quite right with a program, and you will probably need to run the Program Compatibility Troubleshooter. If this is the case, you will be automatically prompted by the operating system.

Issues with Windows XP Software Compatibility

When Microsoft released Windows Vista, it changed the entire core operating system and moved to a new operating system kernel. This shift included changes to hardware drivers and the addition of graphics hardware acceleration for programs. The upshot of this is that some earlier software doesn't work in Windows 8.

As operating systems, Windows 8 and Windows XP are completely different in the way they work, in how they manage programs, and in their underlying technologies. This makes newer Windows software considerably more stable than Windows software running in Windows XP, Windows ME, Windows 98, and Windows 95.

However, suppose you have earlier software that you just don't want to give up. You might be in a business environment where costs, or development or compatibility issues, make adopting newer software prohibitive. Thus, you must use either software that runs only in Windows XP, or even more challenging, a web system that works only in Windows Internet Explorer 6.

The Program Compatibility Troubleshooter will help, but not always. Remember that many operating system features have changed significantly in Windows 8. You'll have the best luck with simpler programs, but if you're trying to run more complex software—for example, a program that calls features within the operating system that have changed in any way—you may experience errors or an unresponsive system. The best advice I can give you in that case is to try to find a newer software alternative.

CHAPTER 13

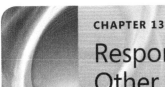

Responding to Viruses, Malware, and Other Threats

Chapter 13

Windows 8 is the first version of a Microsoft operating system to come with built-in antivirus protection: Windows Defender, which is a rebranded version of Microsoft's free Security Essentials antivirus product that is itself based on the scanning engine from the Microsoft Forefront security product for Windows Server. Windows 8 is, thus, also the most secure version of Windows, especially on newer hardware that has Unified Extensible Firmware Interface (UEFI) firmware, which is a replacement for the older basic input/out system (BIOS) motherboard firmware. The new Trusted Boot system can help prevent unauthorized software—namely malware and rootkits—from starting with the computer and infecting it.

Windows 8 is not completely immune to attack, however. The inclusion of Client Hyper-V virtualization software, into which you can install any operating system including, Windows XP, can leave your system vulnerable to malware attack. Also, much of today's malware is designed to trick the user into giving it permission to infect the machine and steal sensitive information, and Windows 8 is not completely immune to this threat, either. However, the excellent tools described in this chapter can help address threats like these. If your system is infected with a virus, this chapter will show you how to manually remove it.

Understanding Threats to You and Your Computer

Today, all viruses and criminal software fall under the umbrella name *malware*. Specific types, however, function differently from one another. In this section, you learn about these types: viruses (including file macro viruses), trojans, keyloggers, bots, rootkits, and spam.

Viruses

A virus is the traditional type of infection on a computer. The first virus to infect my computer was back in 1991. All it did was play "Yankee Doodle Dandy" to me every day at 5:00 P.M. I was lucky that's all it did. Many viruses can be extremely nasty. Ten years later, a much worse threat appeared when several major viruses suddenly attacked computer systems worldwide, causing widespread disruption and data loss. The Kournikova, Sircam, and Code Red viruses are just three of the viruses that everybody in the technology industry was talking about in 2001.

Today, viruses tend to fall into the bot category (more on this in the section titled "Bots" later in the chapter) because of the commercialization of the malware industry, which is, in part, a result of trends such as Internet shopping. Occasional stand-alone viruses do still exist, though, and a common example is the fake antivirus package (see Figure 13-1). These propagate through websites that present pop-up alerts telling you that dozens, if not hundreds, of pieces of malware have been found on your computer. The alerts explain that this malware can be removed if you purchase and download the company's antivirus software. Note that in this scam, *you did not seek out a malware detection program nor give explicit permission for the software to detect the malware*; the virus claims to have found the malware for you on its own. In this scenario, after you unwittingly give the virus permission by purchasing and downloading its removal app, the software claims that the malware miraculously has been removed, but of course at this point you've surrendered all your credit card and personal information, and you've given the company permission to install something potentially even nastier on your computer.

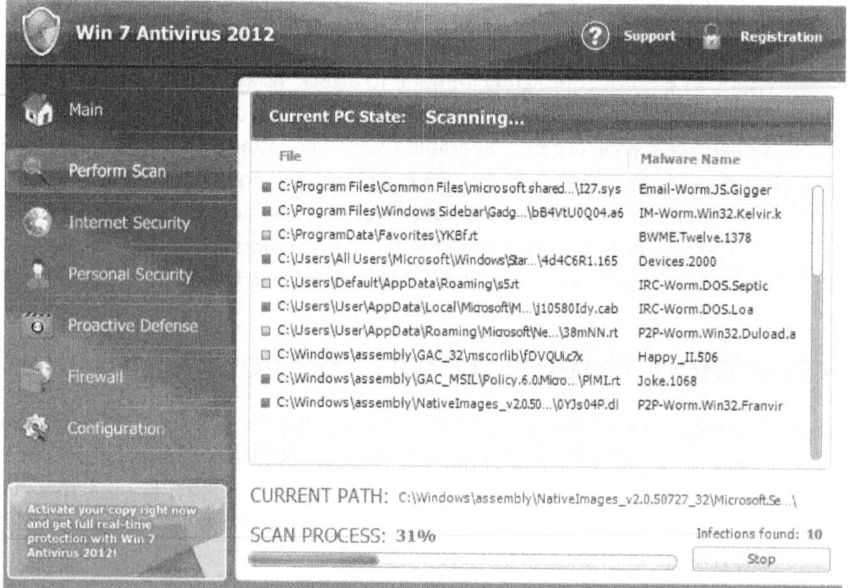

Figure 13-1 A fake antivirus package can look deceivingly legitimate.

The reality is that no virus infection was ever on your computer. It's impossible for any website to detect malware on your computer unless you *explicitly* give the website permission to do so. If any website claims to be able to scan your computer on its own, it's a scam.

Trojans

Trojans are named for the Trojan War legend in which the Greeks left a large wooden horse as a gift to the city of Troy. Waiting inside the horse, however, was a force of soldiers that broke out of the horse at night and ransacked the city. In the same way that the Trojan horse was a disguise, a *trojan* on a computer is malware wrapped in a seemingly innocuous package, such as a codec required to play a video or a game. A good example of a trojan is a YouTube video that requires you to download a codec to play a video. If you have the Adobe Flash player installed on your computer or an HTML5-compatible browser, you should never need to install a codec to view YouTube content.

Trojans are also commonly hidden within Internet browser toolbars and plug-ins. I always advise against installing toolbars onto your web browser, and also advise being vigilant when installing desktop software on your computer by not clicking any Yes or Next button just because it's there, because some of that software will try to install toolbars from Microsoft, Google, Ask, and more. Toolbars are unnecessary because they are redundant and slow down your web browser—you already have a search box. If you want to use Google search by default in Windows Internet Explorer, you can make it the default browser.

Fortunately, the industry is slowly moving away from toolbars. The version of Windows Internet Explorer 10 in Windows 8 doesn't support any toolbars or plug-ins, thus greatly increasing security. If you have a Windows 8 ARM tablet, you won't find toolbars there, either. The widespread adoption of HTML5 also precludes the need for toolbars and plugins.

Macro Viruses

One of the most popular ways to deliver malware is through macro viruses. *Macro viruses* are small snippets of code buried in popular file types, such as Microsoft Word, Microsoft Excel, and Adobe PDF documents that can trigger malware downloads and infections on your computer.

If you are using Microsoft Office 2010 or 2007, the protection against this type of attack is extremely good, which is why Adobe's PDF portable document format is currently a preferred way to deliver viruses. The Adobe Reader software triggers the macro virus, which is commonly written to exploit vulnerabilities in the Adobe Reader program. Fortunately, Windows 8 comes with its own PDF reader, so you don't need to install Adobe's version. If you already have Adobe Reader installed or want it installed on your computer, I recommend that you keep the Adobe updater service running and install all new security and other updates as they are released.

Keyloggers

Keyloggers are programs that record what you type on your computer, including website addresses, user names, passwords, and credit card details. Let me dispel the myth that using an on-screen keyboard defeats keyloggers. This is untrue, because the messages that are sent to the operating system from either a physical or a virtual keyboard are the same. Always run regular virus scans.

INSIDE OUT **Fooling the keyloggers**

Some antivirus packages now come with special virtual keyboards that can be used for logging on to sensitive websites such as banks. Although these keyboards, which scramble the messages that a keylogger can detect, aren't completely foolproof, they do offer an additional and very valuable layer of defense on your computer.

Bots

Bots are probably the most common type of modern malware. *Bots*, which take their name from a truncated version of the word *robots*, are pernicious little programs that sit silently on your computer until activated by an outside party. Bots are connected to networks, which sometimes have hundreds of thousands of computers, all of which are infected and for sale (potentially giving a buyer remote control of your computer).

Bots can be programmed to do many things, including sending spam emails and subjecting companies, organizations, and even governments to cyber-attack. Bots are often used in Distributed Denial of Service Attacks (DDoS), which are used as corporate blackmail and to attack government infrastructures.

Rootkits

Rootkits are by far the nastiest type of malware. The *rootkit* is designed to bury itself deeply within the base (the root) of the operating system to both gain elevated privileges and make their presence extremely difficult to detect. If your antivirus package informs you that your computer is infected with a rootkit, removal is usually quite challenging, and you will sometimes have to reformat the hard disk (possibly all of your hard disks) and reinstall Windows.

Windows 8 includes the Trusted Boot technology, which takes advantage of a feature found in the new UEFI firmware on motherboards. This technology prevents unauthorized code from executing when Windows starts and can prevent rootkits from taking hold. It is a condition of sale for Windows 8 that all OEM computers come with UEFI motherboards that have Trusted Boot enabled.

CAUTION!

Hackers often embed rootkits (and other malware such as bots) into pirated software and operating systems. If you download a pirated copy of Windows 8, Microsoft Office, Adobe Creative Suite, or any other software—especially an operating system—there is a high risk it is infected with a rootkit.

Spam

Probably the most annoying, but also the most harmless, threat on modern computers is spam email. Some *spam* is malicious and is used to trick you into buying what you are led to believe are genuine products. This form of spam extracts personal information from you, such as date of birth, passwords, and credit card details. For those of you unfamiliar with the reference, spam (a shortened form for spiced ham) is a processed meat made from pork, salt, water, and potato starch that was a staple food for the British population during World War II. It was, and still is, much disliked! Thus, when a term needed to be coined to label the ever-increasing volumes of unwanted email, spam became the obvious choice.

INSIDE OUT **Beware of the little phishes**

Phishing emails **are emails that look like they're from a reputable bank or business and attempt to glean information from you by asking you, for example, to log on to your account to confirm your security details. The simple rule here is that *no* reputable bank or business will *ever* email you asking you to log on to your account! If you receive such an email, you should forward it to *http://abuse@companyname.com* (where *companyname* is the name of the organization that the ruse purports to be) to alert the organization that a phishing attack is taking place.**

Malware and Windows RT

Many people have the impression that modern operating systems running on ARM processors are immune to malware attack, but they are not, even though both Apple and Microsoft go through a vetting process. Each requires software developers to pay to become registered developers for the iPhone, iPad, and Windows Phone, and also for apps for the Windows Store. Each app that is submitted is scanned by Apple and Microsoft for malware, and if any malware is found in an app after it is released, the developer is likely to have the registration account revoked and be banned from future distribution. Scanning submitted apps acts as a deterrent to malware writers, and this is mostly responsible for the very low incidence of malware that manages to get on to these platforms. These platforms also don't support plug-ins and toolbars, and although the desktop does still exist on Windows RT tablets, you can't install any Intel-based software onto it.

Google, conversely, does not engage in a vetting process, which is why a flourishing malware problem exists on Android smartphones and tablets. The company does regularly take down malware-laden apps from its store, but it doesn't monitor app submissions in the way that Apple and Microsoft do.

In general, you can consider Windows RT architecture to be secure. Third-party companies release antivirus software for these platforms, though, and both iOS and Windows Phone have some available for purchase. However, take into account that malware isn't an established type of software; it changes in ways that can be difficult to predict. Always be vigilant and install an antimalware app if you find one that's had good reviews.

Repelling an Attack

How can you repel a malware attack in Windows 8? Much of the time, the operating system does it for you automatically: Trusted Boot will help keep rootkits away, User Account Control (UAC) will help prevent malware from running, Internet Explorer 10 in Windows 8 will help prevent trojans from being installed, and so on. There are a few caveats, though, and this is because there is still a vulnerability—the user. Most computer users know somebody who has been the victim of a computer virus, identity theft, suspicious download, or phishing email, but that doesn't stop those users from clicking Yes to things online.

I'm being a bit harsh here, really, because I have already said that malware writers and criminals are getting better all the time at tricking us into believing something is genuine and safe when it's not. As human beings, though, we're all fallible and can be distracted, tired, or any number of things that can cause us to inadvertently click Yes when we meant to click No. Following is a discussion of tools that come with Windows 8 to help you repel attacks.

Windows Defender

As mentioned earlier in this chapter, Windows 8 is the first version of the operating system to come with full antivirus protection built in. I say "now" because although Windows Defender has been a part of Windows since Windows Vista and has also been available for Windows XP for years, that former Windows Defender was just a basic antimalware package. Windows Defender is set up with the default configuration when Windows 8 is first installed, which is to periodically check for updates, all of which come through Windows Update. Don't turn it off! It will scan your computer for threats regularly.

Windows Defender is maintained through a desktop program (see Figure 13-2), but there is no Start screen interface for it. Such a screen isn't necessary, which reduces clutter and keeps the things that people don't want to have to worry about out of the way.

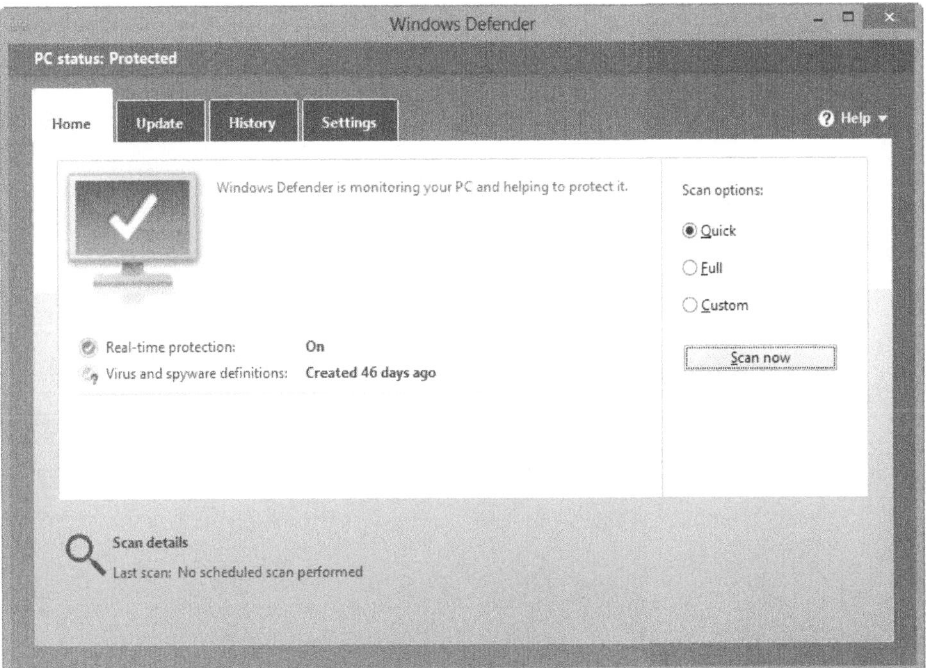

Figure 13-2 Windows Defender in Windows 8 is a full-featured antivirus program, unlike the former Windows Defender.

INSIDE OUT Disabling Windows Defender when you want to use third-party protection

If you prefer to use a third-party antivirus solution, you can turn off Windows Defender. To do so, open Windows Defender, click the Settings tab, and then click Administrator. In the right pane (see Figure 13-3), clear the Turn On Windows Defender check box to disable the program.

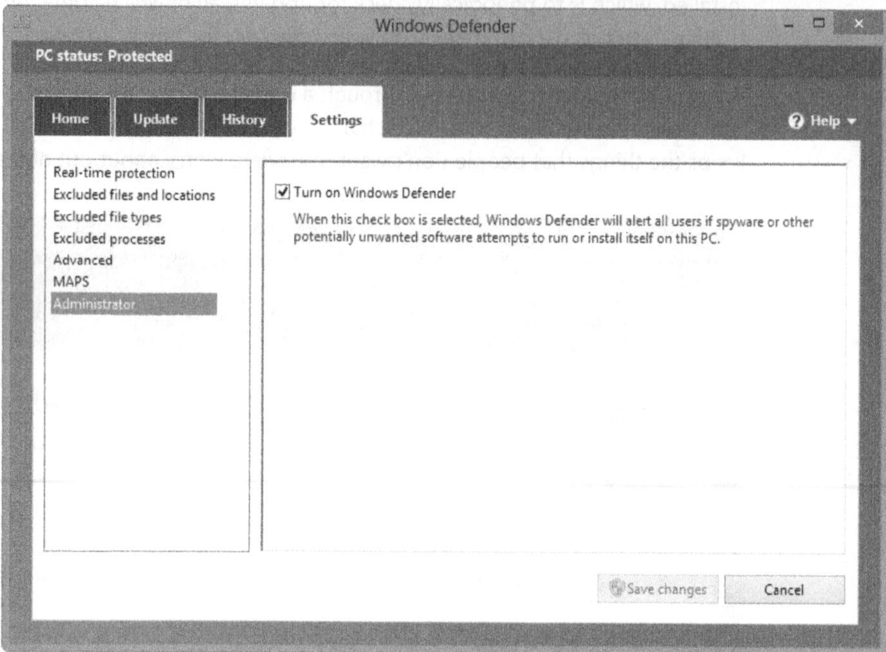

Figure 13-3 Each option in the left pane displays additional settings in the right pane.

INSIDE OUT **Run only one antivirus package and keep it up to date**

Although you aren't limited to running a certain number of antimalware packages on your computer, you should have only a single antivirus package installed and operating at any given time. Antivirus packages can interfere with one another and compromise your computer's security.

Your antivirus and antimalware software packages can keep your computer protected only if you keep them up to date and set them to run regular scans, so make sure you always have current antivirus software installed on your computer.

Windows Malicious Software Removal Tool

Once a month, on what is known as *Patch Tuesday*, Microsoft releases the latest updates for the various versions of Windows and Office. Included in these updates is a program called the Microsoft Windows Malicious Software Removal Tool. This program (see Figure 13-4), which is updated only through Windows Update and not available to run separately from the Start screen, works as additional protection against viruses and malware on your computer. The program is also available to download separately from the Microsoft website at *http://www.microsoft.com/en-us/download/details.aspx?id=16*.

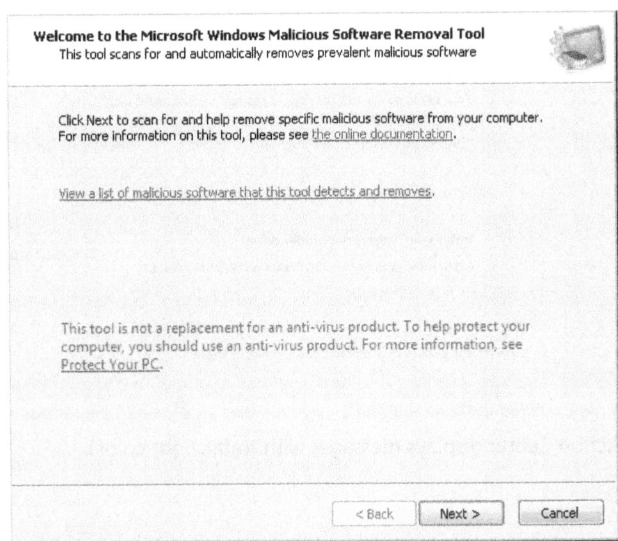

Figure 13-4 The Microsoft Windows Malicious Software Removal Tool normally runs silently in the background.

The Microsoft Windows Malicious Software Removal Tool scans for and removes only a limited number of viruses and malware. It is not a replacement for other antivirus and anti-malware programs.

Action Center

Accessible from the desktop is Action Center, shown in Figure 13-5, which is the central location for all your security, troubleshooting, maintenance, and update messages from Windows 8 and your hardware and software. You can access Action Center by clicking the Action Center icon (signified by a white flag) in the notification area. When you first click the Action Center icon, you are shown only pending messages, which keeps the initial information simple and helpful for you. If you want, you can click the link to open the full Action Center.

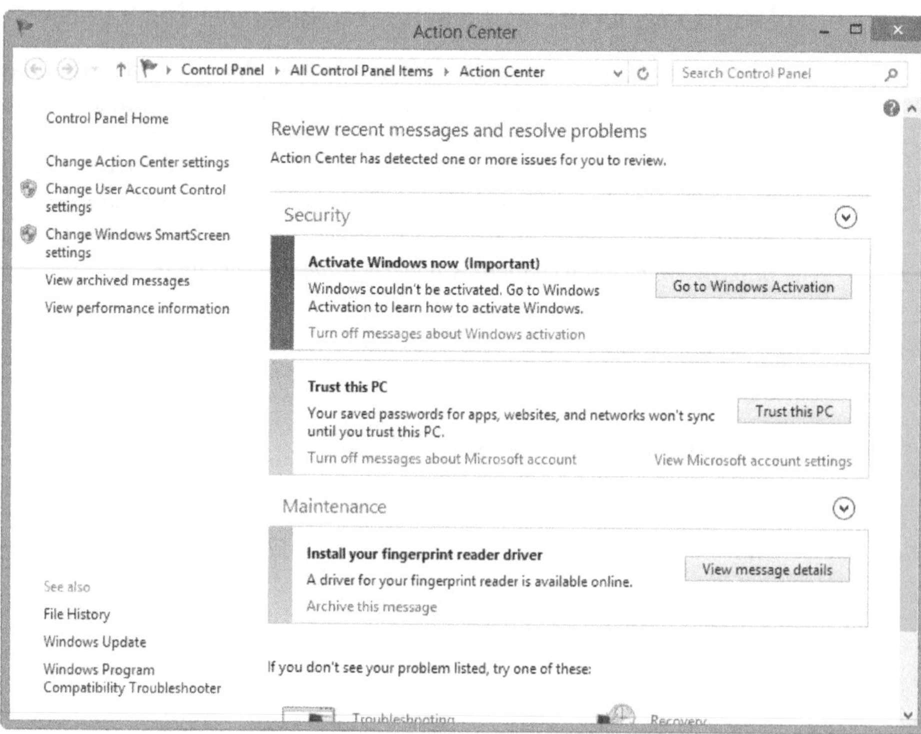

Figure 13-5 The Action Center displays messages with traffic light colors.

Colors indicate the message importance: red for an urgent message, amber for a general message not requiring immediate attention, and green when all is well. People with visual challenges should scan Action Center text carefully because text labels are not always available for critical messages. Each section also comes with a collapsible pane so that you can hide specific messages you don't need to see, whereas critical and important messages are always displayed.

Identifying an Attack

It's almost impossible for a computer to be infected with a virus or trojan without a human at some point permitting access. In this section, I share some guidelines for ensuring your computer is safe from unwanted software.

Most attacks today will come from the Internet. This is probably where you probably spend more time than ever before, shopping, banking, visiting websites, and providing all types of personally and commercially sensitive information. Be careful about what information you give and to whom you give it.

Figures 13-6 and 13-7 show an example of a safe website (from two different vantage points). You know the website is safe because the address bar displays a padlock (in these examples, the padlock is to the right of the website address). Clicking the padlock brings up details about the security certificate associated with the website. In Figures 13-6 and 13-7, the certificate is registered to Paypal, which matches the address of the website in the address bar.

Figure 13-6 The padlock, as seen in the Internet Explorer 10 app.

Figure 13-7 The padlock, as seen in Internet Explorer 10 on the desktop.

INSIDE OUT **Look for the padlock**

You should never submit personal or sensitive information (such as a password) to a website that does not display the padlock. Some pages do not display a padlock because they might consider the information you are entering—your name, for instance—to not need to be encrypted when collected through the website, but any page in which you enter details such as date of birth or credit card numbers should always display the padlock. Note that different web browsers might display the padlock in different locations, at the top or bottom of the browser window.

Modern web browsers highlight the domain you are visiting online, such as *.com* and *.co.uk*. For example, Figures 13-6 and 13-7 show *http://www.paypal.com*. In the case of commerce websites, the address bar will often turn green to signify that the website is known to be safe and secure. If the address bar turns amber or red, the website might be suspicious or known to be used by criminals. If the browser displays a highlighted website domain other than what you are expecting, you have probably been misled.

Creating a Strong Password

Many people use common dictionary words and names as passwords. These are the weakest passwords you can use, and they can be cracked within seconds by any modern computer. To create a strong password, you should use a mixture of uppercase and lowercase letters, numbers, and symbols.

Examine your password to determine where you can substitute letters for other characters. Can you slip a capital letter into the middle, substitute the letters *i* or *L* for a 1, or use a % instead of the letter *o*? For example, you could spell the password *microsoft* as *m1cr%S0ft*. The inclusion of the characters 1, %, capital S, and 0 make the password much more secure.

Note

Avoid using the asterisk symbol (*) and the question mark (?) in passwords. These characters are used to represent wildcards in searches, and many services do not allow their inclusion in passwords.

Table 13-1 shows how long it could take a criminal with an ordinary computer to crack passwords of varying numbers of characters. Where do your passwords fit in the chart? I recommend that any password or passwords you use comprise a minimum of 10 to 14 characters and use the letter combinations in the last two columns of the table.

Table 13-1 Amount of Time a Computer Needs to Crack a Password

Number of Characters	Numbers Only	Upper or Lowercase Letters	Upper or Lowercase Letters Mixed	Numbers, Upper and Lowercase Letters	Numbers, Upper and Lowercase Letters, Symbols
3	Instantly	Instantly	Instantly	Instantly	Instantly
4	Instantly	Instantly	Instantly	Instantly	Instantly
5	Instantly	Instantly	Instantly	3 secs	10 secs
6	Instantly	Instantly	8 secs	3 mins	13 mins
7	Instantly	Instantly	5 mins	3 hours	17 hours
8	Instantly	13 mins	3 hours	10 days	57 days
9	4 secs	6 hours	4 days	1 year	12 years
10	40 secs	6 days	169 days	106 years	928 years
11	6 mins	169 days	16 years	6k years	71k years
12	1 hour	12 years	600 years	108k years	5m years
13	11 hours	314 years	21k years	25m years	423m years
14	4 days	8k years	778k years	1bn years	5bn years
15	46 days	212k years	28m years	97bn years	2tn years
16	1 year	512m years	1bn years	6tn years	193tn years
17	12 years	143m years	36bn years	374tn years	14qd years
18	126 years	3bn years	1tn years	23qd years	1qt years

k = Thousand (1,000 or 10^{-3}); m = Million (1,000,000 or 10^{-6}); bn = Billion (1,000,000,000 or 10^{-9}); tn = Trillion (1,000,000,000,000 or 10^{-12}); qd = Quadrillion (1,000,000,000,000,000 or 10^{-15}); qt = Quintillion (1,000,000,000,000,000,000 or 10^{-18})

One important consideration is Moore's law, which is a rule of thumb in the computer industry that postulates that the number of transistors that can be fitted on an integrated circuit doubles approximately every two years. Thus, the processing power of computers also increases (not quite necessarily at the same rate, but still fast) every few years, so hackers can take advantage of increasing speed to crack passwords.

As an example of this, in the book I wrote titled *Troubleshooting Windows 7 Inside Out* (Microsoft Press, 2010), the most up-to-date figures at the time quoted 2.25 years for decoding an 8-digit password that contained uppercase and lowercase letters, numbers, and symbols. This timeframe is now down to 57 days, as you can see in Table 13-1.

The other consideration is how much computing power is dedicated to the task. Some modern graphics cards are capable of being used for cracking passwords because they are designed to process huge numbers quickly, unlike mainstream processors that have to perform many more functions. If a powerful graphics card, twin graphics card system, or a multicore server is given the task of decoding passwords, the times stated in Table 13-1 will be even less. As this technology becomes less expensive, criminals will be able to crack even complex passwords.

INSIDE OUT **Use an online password checker**

Some excellent online password checkers exist that analyze how secure your current password is and help you to create really strong ones. My two favorites are *http://www.howsecureismypassword.net* **and** *http://www.grc.com/haystack.htm*.

Manually Removing Malware

If your antivirus software cannot remove a virus, you might have to remove it manually. This can be a complex process and usually involves deleting files, removing Windows services, and removing entries from the Windows 8 registry. Modern smartphones all have a web browser, and this can be a good way to search for the removal instructions for a virus if you do not have access to another computer.

The first thing to do—either in Safe Mode with Networking or, preferably, on an uninfected computer—is to search the Internet for instructions about manually removing the particular virus. Use the name of the virus provided by your antivirus software. Figure 13-8 shows an example of the instructions Microsoft provides on its website for manually removing the W32/SirCam@MM virus. This is one of the major viruses from 2001 that I mentioned at the beginning of the chapter.

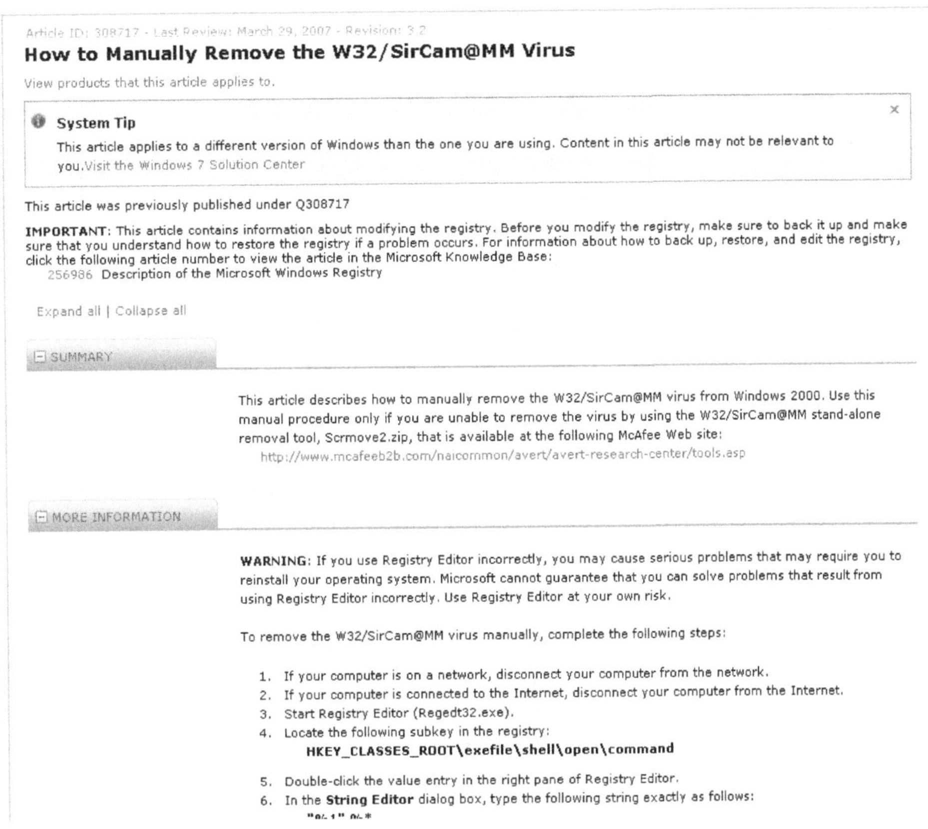

Article ID: 308717 - Last Review: March 29, 2007 - Revision: 3.2

How to Manually Remove the W32/SirCam@MM Virus

View products that this article applies to.

System Tip

This article applies to a different version of Windows than the one you are using. Content in this article may not be relevant to you.Visit the Windows 7 Solution Center

This article was previously published under Q308717

IMPORTANT: This article contains information about modifying the registry. Before you modify the registry, make sure to back it up and make sure that you understand how to restore the registry if a problem occurs. For information about how to back up, restore, and edit the registry, click the following article number to view the article in the Microsoft Knowledge Base:
256986 Description of the Microsoft Windows Registry

Expand all | Collapse all

SUMMARY

This article describes how to manually remove the W32/SirCam@MM virus from Windows 2000. Use this manual procedure only if you are unable to remove the virus by using the W32/SirCam@MM stand-alone removal tool, Scrmove2.zip, that is available at the following McAfee Web site:
http://www.mcafeeb2b.com/naicommon/avert/avert-research-center/tools.asp

MORE INFORMATION

WARNING: If you use Registry Editor incorrectly, you may cause serious problems that may require you to reinstall your operating system. Microsoft cannot guarantee that you can solve problems that result from using Registry Editor incorrectly. Use Registry Editor at your own risk.

To remove the W32/SirCam@MM virus manually, complete the following steps:

1. If your computer is on a network, disconnect your computer from the network.
2. If your computer is connected to the Internet, disconnect your computer from the Internet.
3. Start Registry Editor (Regedt32.exe).
4. Locate the following subkey in the registry:
   HKEY_CLASSES_ROOT\exefile\shell\open\command
5. Double-click the value entry in the right pane of Registry Editor.
6. In the **String Editor** dialog box, type the following string exactly as follows:

Figure 13-8 Instructions for removing a virus manually can be found on the Microsoft website.

The Microsoft website contains thousands of articles related to every aspect of your computing experience. These articles also contain specific security information about how to manually remove some viruses and malware from Windows 8. The instructions provided by Microsoft or other third-party antivirus vendors, such as Symantec and McAfee, are sometimes complicated. The following instructions might help you make sense of a complicated procedure.

1. Note the name of the virus or malware that has infected your computer, as provided by your antivirus or antimalware program.
2. On an uninfected computer, search online for **virusname manual remove**.

3. Print out or write down the instructions so that you have them in hand. You will need access to these Windows features:

   - **File Explorer** You can access this on the Start screen or taskbar.
   - **Services window** You can access this from the Start screen by searching for **services.msc**. The Services window provides a list of all the Windows 8 components, including plug-in and third-party services, that make up the operating system. You can view the components by status, which you might find helpful, because the copy of Windows 8 running on your computer will not need every service that ships with the operating system. Right-click any service and then click Properties. In the Properties dialog box, you can disable the service.
   - **Windows registry** You can access this from the Start screen by searching for **regedit**. This is the database of settings for the operating system and all your software. I cover advanced tasks and the Windows registry in Chapter 20, "Using Advanced Repair Methods."

CAUTION!

You should always exercise caution when disabling a Windows service or changing a registry setting. Changing a setting that is critical to the operation of Windows 8 or a program can cause a malfunction or lead to the entire operating system becoming unresponsive, even after restarting the computer.

Removing Malware by Using Third-Party Startup Tools

Many types of common malware will do just about anything to prevent you from removing them while Windows is running. In this circumstance, you must restart the system from another device. Some valuable third-party and Microsoft tools are available that you can use to start your computer to help with malware removal, such as Windows Defender Offline. When deciding which antivirus package to buy, the inclusion of startup tools should be a factor you consider. Always download the latest version of these products before using them to ensure that their virus definition databases are up to date.

You can burn these tools to a CD or DVD, or use them to create a startup USB flash drive. You will need to ensure that your computer's BIOS or UEFI is set to start from an optical disc and/or a USB drive *before* it starts from the physical hard disk.

Windows Defender Offline

Microsoft has a free tool you can use to start up your computer to remove viruses and malware. Windows Defender Offline can be run from a CD, DVD, or USB flash drive that has at least 250 megabytes (MB) available. You can access this tool at *http://www.windows.microsoft.com/en-US/windows/what-is-windows-defender-offline*.

McAfee Free Tools

McAfee's free online tools have long been a favorite for virus removal, and there are now a great many of them. The most useful for malware removal include the following:

- **GetSusp** For manually removing of viruses and malware.
- **RootkitRemover** For removing rootkit viruses from a computer.
- **Stinger** For removing common fake antivirus software.

You can access McAfee tools at *http://www.mcafee.com/us/downloads/free-tools*.

Removing Malware by Using Another Computer

If Windows 8 cannot even start in Safe Mode because of an infection *and if you can physically remove your hard disk from your computer*, you can still remove the virus, but you will need another computer or laptop to do so. You can physically remove the infected hard disk from your computer by unplugging its power and data cables. (Always ensure that your computer is turned off and is disconnected from the main power source before you do this.) You can connect this hard disk to another computer either by plugging it in inside the case of the alternative desktop computer or by putting it into a USB removable–hard disk caddy (recommended). Before you start this other computer, ensure that its antivirus and antimalware software is up to date. Then run full scans passively on the infected disk. I say *passively* because you don't want to open or run any files on the infected drive during this process; if you do, you run the risk of infecting the second computer with the virus or malware.

Restoring Windows 8 from a Backup

A good way to quickly and easily remove a virus infection is to restore Windows 8 from a clean system image backup. If you created such a backup, you can use it to restore your copy of Windows and all of your software exactly as they existed when the backup was made. This might be inconvenient, especially if the backup was created a long time ago, because there will be many updates and new software to install. However, it can be a quick and easy way to remove a virus infection.

INSIDE OUT **Run a full virus scan after restoring from a backup**

You should always ensure that your antivirus and antimalware packages are fully up to date, and run full scans by using them after restoring Windows 8 from a system image backup, because a virus infection might sit in a file on your hard disk. If this is the case, you could reinfect your computer the next time you open the file.

Virus Corruption of BIOS Firmware

All new Windows 8 computers come with the new UEFI firmware, which is much more resilient to attack than the earlier BIOS motherboard firmware. Most BIOS firmware, however, does come with built-in protection to defend against viruses rewriting or erasing the BIOS code. Its location varies from one BIOS to another. Although this feature can, on rare occasions, interfere with certain hardware, it can also be very useful. You will need to turn off this feature to update the firmware in your BIOS (see Figure 13-9).

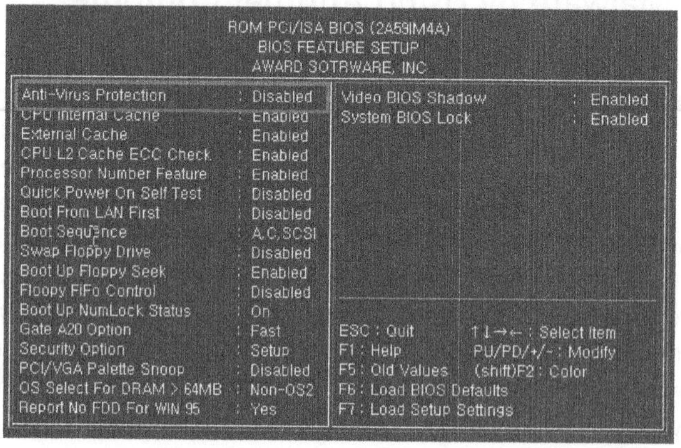

Figure 13-9 BIOS-level virus protection can be found in many computers.

In some extreme cases, viruses have been known to rewrite a computer's BIOS chip on the motherboard. Fortunately, virus attacks on the BIOS are rare, but when they do occur, they can cause devastating damage to your computer. If this happens, your computer will no longer communicate with Windows and won't be able to start until the BIOS is completely reset or reloaded. The message in Figure 13-10 shows a BIOS error.

```
Phoenix-Award BootBlock BIOS v1.0
COPYRIGHT (C) 2000, Phoenix-Award Software.INC.
BIOS ROM Checksum error
Detecting floppy drive A media...

Drive media is : 1.44 MB
```

Figure 13-10 A corrupt BIOS prevents a computer from starting.

In Chapter 9, "Maintaining Hardware," I describe how to reset the computer's BIOS. This should be the first thing you try if your computer does not start after a virus attack. Sometimes, however, resetting the BIOS won't be enough, and you will need to upgrade the firmware in the BIOS by using a utility provided by your motherboard manufacturer. This software is usually on a CD that comes with your motherboard or computer, and you can find the firmware update on the manufacturer's website.

Consult the motherboard manual for instructions on exactly how to update the BIOS firmware, but typically, you need to create a startup CD, USB flash drive, or even a floppy disk on another computer by using the supplied software. You start the infected computer using this disk or drive, and the utility upgrades the BIOS firmware. This usually fixes the problem. If upgrading the firmware for your BIOS does not fix this type of attack, contact an IT professional for further assistance.

CAUTION!

Always be very careful upgrading the firmware for your motherboard's BIOS, because if you do not follow the process exactly as directed in the manual, or if the upgrade is interrupted for some reason, your motherboard can become unusable.

INSIDE OUT Virus infection and UEFI firmware

New UEFI firmware on motherboards, especially those with Trusted Boot enabled, is much more resilient to virus infection than the traditional BIOS, which is over 20 years old. It is possible that in the future, however, some methods of UEFI infection might be created.

Where Can Viruses Hide?

Even if you think you've gotten rid of a virus, a virus might still be somewhere on your system or in your files. Here are some places viruses can hide:

- **Email** A virus or malware can sit in an infected email, usually as an attachment, although it can also sit in the body of an HTML-formatted email and can reinfect your computer the next time you open the email. Delete all infected emails.
- **Files** Files on your computer can contain viruses. Office and PDF files are commonly used to hide viruses. If your antivirus software cannot remove the infection from a file, either delete the file or quarantine it (this choice is usually offered by antivirus software) until it can be repaired in the future.
- **Backups** Have you backed up your files since your computer became infected? You should check the dates of your backed-up files to see whether the virus is there, ready to reinfect your computer if you restore the files. If this is the case, consider deleting and redoing the backup.
- **System Restore** This is a Windows service that can roll back critical operating system files in the event of a failed driver or software install. Open Control Panel, click System And Security, click System, click Advanced System Settings, and then in the System Properties dialog box, click the System Protection tab. Turn off System Restore on all drives and restart your computer. Reactivate System Restore only when the virus is gone. To do this, in the System Properties dialog box, on the System Protection tab, click Configure in the System Restore pane, and then disable protection for all drives. It is worth noting that although it was common for viruses to hide in System Restore in Windows XP, it is very rare for this to happen in newer versions of Windows where UAC is enabled.

CHAPTER 14

Easy Ways to Repair Windows 8

YOU MIGHT BE SURPRISED AT JUST HOW EASILY you can address a range of issues you might face when using Windows 8, from lost or corrupt files to the operating system not starting. This chapter explains which tools you need to address those issues, such as File History and Device Manager. You'll find that handling many problems is almost always a case of the right tool for the right job.

Using File Versioning with File History

Windows 8 is the first version of Microsoft's operating system with a file versioning feature. *File versioning* means that the operating system keeps copies of your files as they change and as you save them. If you make a change to a file that you didn't intend to make, you can restore an older copy of that file.

You can configure the feature in the File History dialog box (see Figure 14-1), which you can access in Control Panel by clicking All Control Panel Items and then clicking File History.

The options pane on the left presents four links that you can click to customize how the system handles file history and the restoration of previously saved files. For example, you can choose where to save previous versions, such as to an internal hard disk, a USB-attached hard disk, or a network location. You can choose to exclude certain folders or even turn File History off altogether if you're running short of hard disk space. When File History is turned on, the main pane shows the status of your file history.

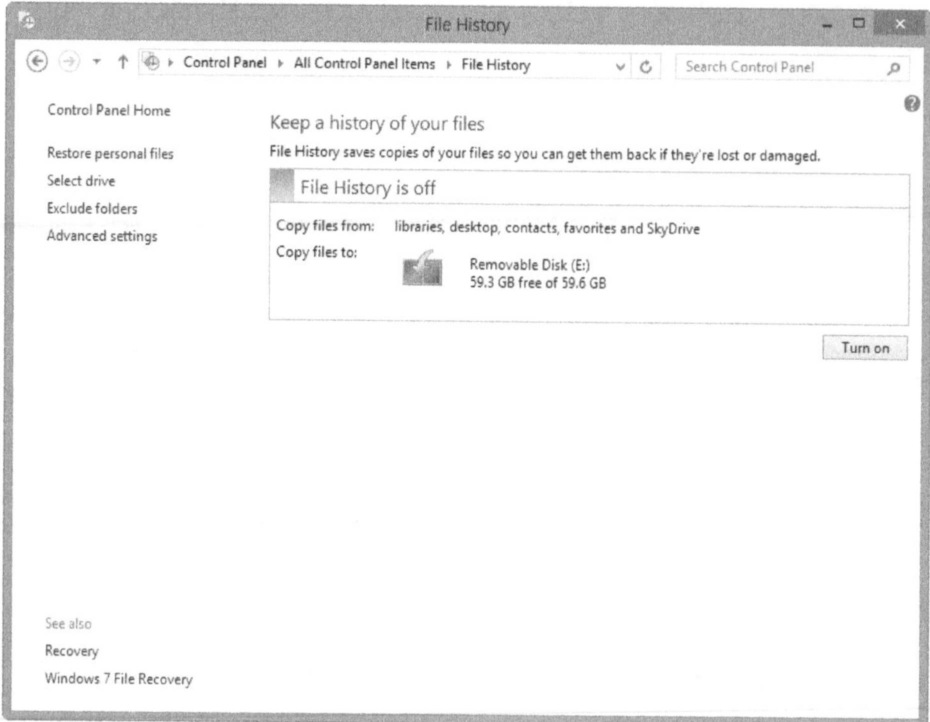

Figure 14-1 The File History window is easy to use.

INSIDE OUT Why should you exclude folders from File History?

When you perform any action on any type of file, even if you're only opening the file and not changing anything, the *last accessed* date of the file is changed and thus the file is also changed slightly. Files that you access regularly, such as picture and music files, can end up having a significant number of changes. Even though you haven't changed these files, the files are marked as changed and the file history stores the last version of the file.

The result of this is that your free space for File History can quickly be filled up with music, pictures, and other files for which the only change is the Date Accessed marker. Thus, you might want to exclude the folders that contain your music, video, and perhaps your picture libraries from File History.

To obtain a more detailed level of control over File History, click Advanced Settings to open the Advanced Settings window (see Figure 14-2).

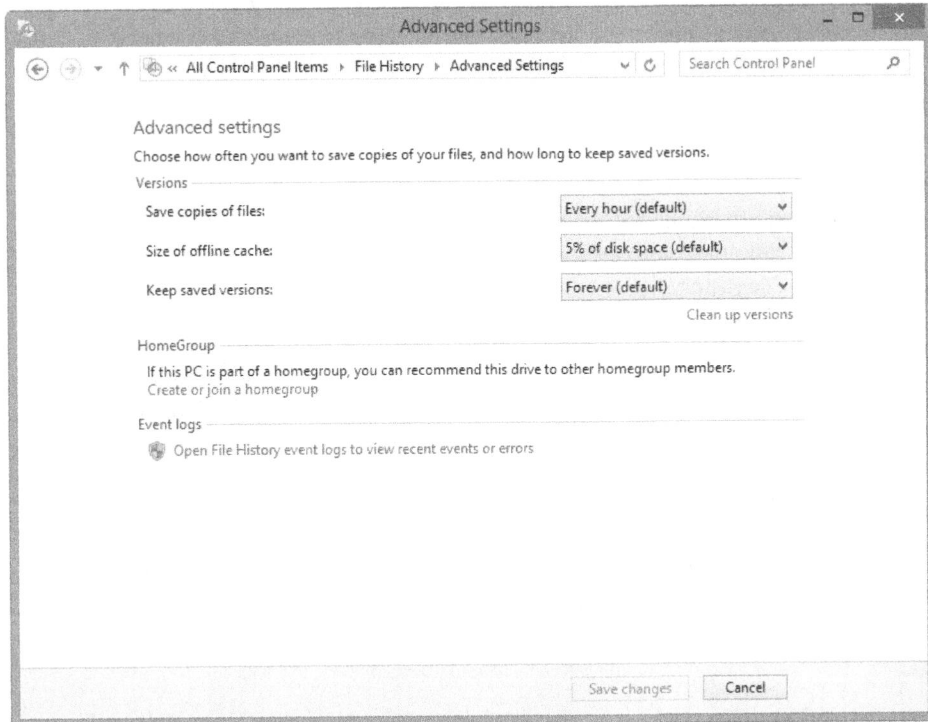

Figure 14-2 The Advanced Settings for File History are straightforward.

The Advanced Settings dialog box offers several options. The way you work will determine how you want them set. For example, for the Save Copies Of Files setting, the default time between Windows automatically saving changed files is one hour. Because I am an author, I work on the same files multiple times and my files are changing constantly, but I tend to work on them only in bursts for a few short days. Thus, a 10-minute period is what I personally prefer. If you do not work on files all that often, however, perhaps once a day is best, because this will help reduce the amount of disk space that is consumed by the File History feature.

CAUTION!

File History will make copies of only those files that have been saved and are closed. If files are open, they won't be copied to File History. This means that if you commonly leave important files open on your desktop, there's no guarantee that older versions will exist in File History if you need them later.

Use the Size Of Offline Cache setting to choose how much of the total available hard disk space is used for File History. The default is just 5 percent. The maximum amount of hard disk space you can use is 20 percent, even if you have an entire spare hard disk set aside for File History.

The Keep Saved Versions setting determines how long you want File History to maintain your copies. You can set it to keep versions of your files forever, although the system won't actually do that, because the total amount of disk space available to the feature is finite, and keeping versions indefinitely will make the feature much less effective over time. I suggest that a period of three months is typically sufficient for you to realize something's gone wrong with a file and you want to restore it.

Lastly, if you would like to do some housekeeping, you can click the Clean Up Versions link, which lets you delete older files if you are indeed running short of disk space.

INSIDE OUT **Can I use File History as an alternative to Windows Backup?**

Because File History saves files individually rather than compressing them into a VHD, it could be argued that this is a great alternative to the Windows Backup feature. However, because File History can use a maximum of only 20 percent of the total disc space on a drive, and because it prioritizes multiple copies of a single changed file, you cannot guarantee that it will have copies of some files at all when you need to restore them. This is because the system has to delete older files when it runs out of space. File History, therefore, should be used only in conjunction with a proper backup solution.

Restoring Files by Using File History

To restore previous versions of your files, in the File History dialog box, click the Restore Personal Files link. In the dialog box that opens, you can view all the saved versions of previous files. It's important to remember, though, the way this feature works: it saves every file (except files in excluded folders that you have set manually) that has been updated in any way, but it has only a finite amount of backup space. When the space allotted for File History is full, the oldest versions of files are deleted. Thus, it's possible that it you are looking for an older version of a particular file, but it is no longer available. It is for this reason that File History should never be considered a viable alternative to a full backup solution.

Using System Restore

System Restore takes snapshots of critical Windows 8 operating system files when changes are made, such as when you install new software or a driver for a new hardware device. Should something go wrong—for instance, the driver causes Windows 8 to misbehave—you can restore all critical Windows operating system files prior to the point at which the driver was installed. System Restore doesn't roll back any changes to your files or documents, nor does it delete any of them. It makes changes only to Windows 8 operating system files. The User Account Control (UAC) security system in Windows 8 restores critical Windows 8 files without the risk of restoring viruses.

Configuring System Restore

To set up System Restore, in Control Panel, click Recovery. In the Advanced Recovery Tools dialog box, click Configure System Restore, click the System Protection tab (see Figure 14-3), and then click Configure.

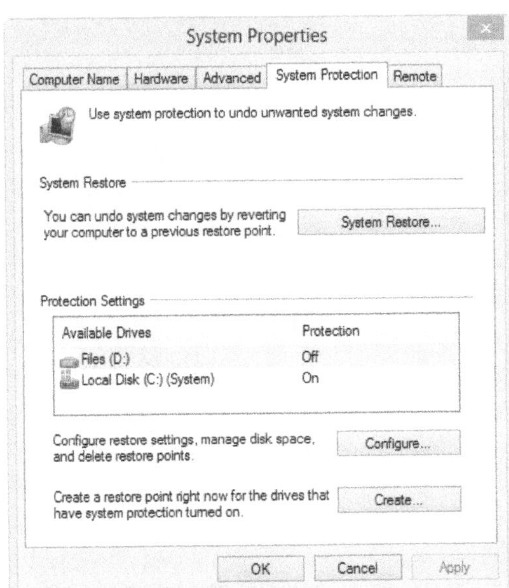

Figure 14-3 System Restore in Windows 8 allows you to configure which hard disks are protected.

INSIDE OUT

Don't deactivate System Restore

System Restore in Windows 8 is an essential tool, and you should leave it on. It is the quickest and easiest to way get Windows 8 backed up and running if you make a change that causes the system to become unstable.

Creating a Restore Point Manually

You can also create your own restore points, which are snapshots of your system and its files at specific moments in time. You might want to do this if you're changing some operating system settings and are not certain what the result will be, or if you're installing some software or a hardware driver that you suspect might cause a problem and you want to ensure that a particular restore point is saved. To set your own restore point, in the System Properties dialog box, on the System Protection tab (see Figure 14-3), click Create.

Restoring Windows 8 by Using System Restore in Windows

You can restore Windows 8 to a specific earlier point. To do so, in Control Panel, open Recovery, open the Advanced Recovery Tools section, and then click Open System Restore. The System Restore window opens, displaying a list of dates and times at which restore points were made along with descriptions of what triggered them, such as a software install (see Figure 14-4).

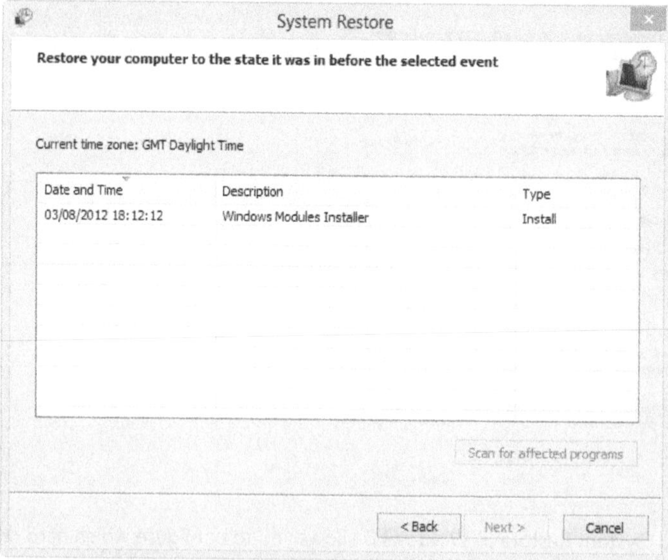

Figure 14-4 Restore Windows 8 files to a specific date and time by using System Restore.

Choose the restore point that best reflects the change you want to undo, such as when you installed a new device driver or application. Click Next to start the process. Keep in mind that your computer needs to restart during this process. If you choose a System Restore point that doesn't go back far enough to undo the changes you made, don't worry; you can just repeat the process, selecting an earlier point.

When your computer restarts and the System Restore has successfully completed, a message is displayed that is similar to the one shown in Figure 14-5. You are also notified when System Restore is unable to restore Windows 8.

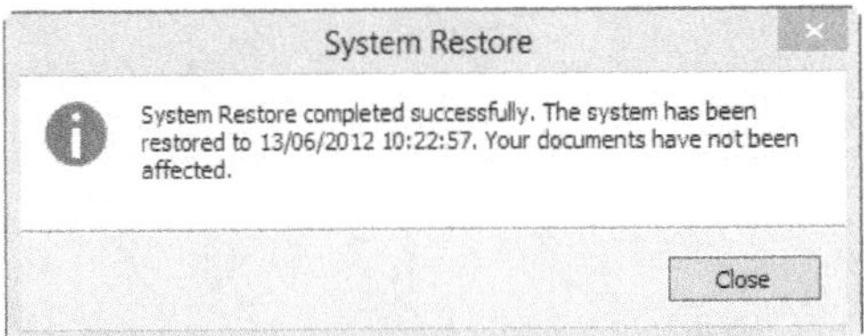

Figure 14-5 A successful System Restore message tells you to what point your system is restored and whether documents are affected.

Restoring Windows 8 by Using System Restore on the Start Screen

You can access System Restore on the Windows 8 Start screen in several different ways:

- Start from your Windows 8 Install DVD and click Repair Your Computer.
- Start from a Windows 8 system repair disc.
- Start from a Windows recovery drive.
- Press F8 when Windows starts, and then in the Startup Options, click Repair Your Computer.

After starting the boot options menu, on the Choose An Option page, click Troubleshoot, click Advanced Options, and then click the System Restore option (see Figure 14-6). In the System Restore dialog box, choose Windows 8, and then restore your computer to a previously created restore point.

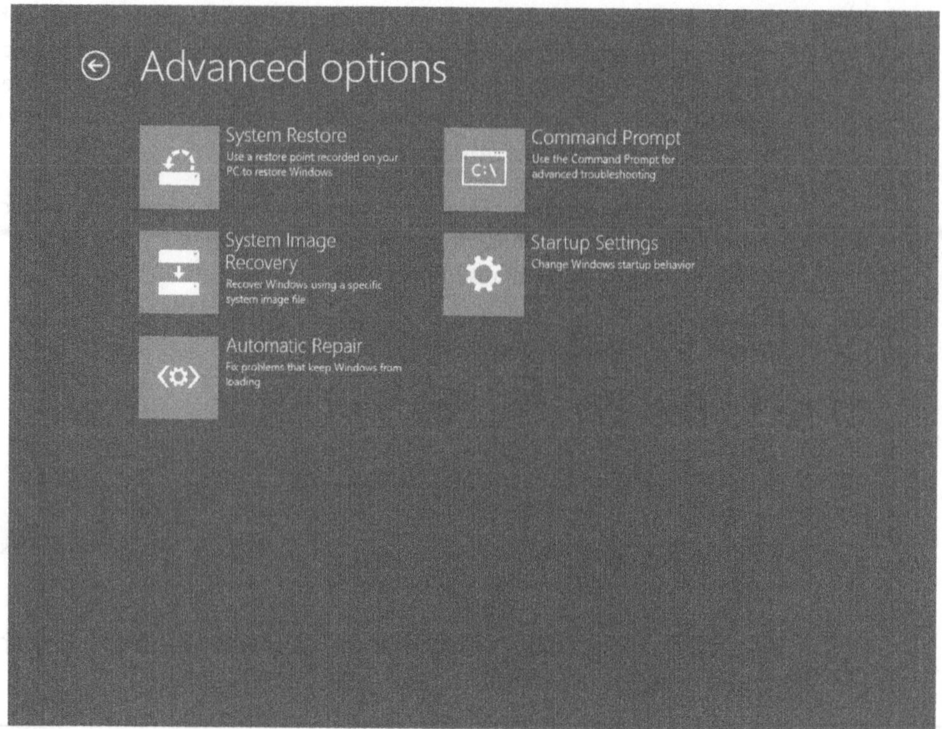

Figure 14-6 Accessing System Restore.

Undoing System Restore Changes

You can undo System Restore changes provided you're not using System Restore in Safe Mode or in Windows Startup Repair (more on this service later in the chapter in the section titled "Running Startup Repair"). Figure 14-7 shows that a new restore point is created just before your changes are rolled back.

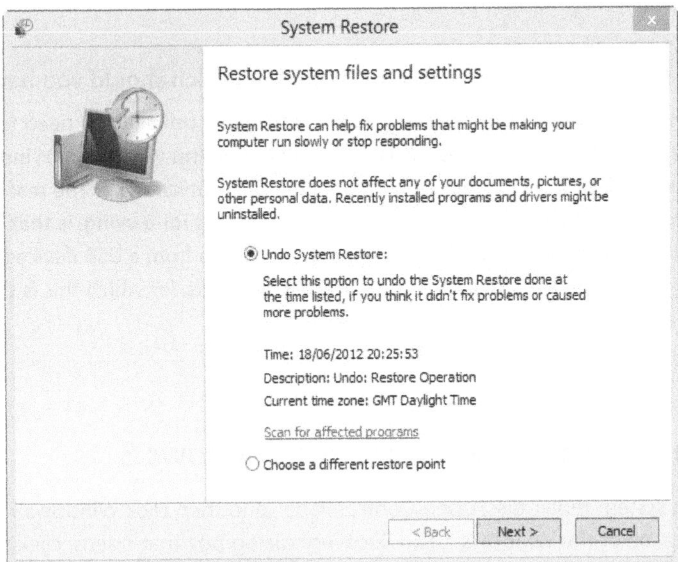

Figure 14-7 You can undo System Restore changes.

When you run System Restore again, the feature gives you an option to undo any changes you've made and restore the system to the state it was in before you used System Restore. You would use this option if, for example, you realized that restoring older files uninstalled a critical program you need, did not fix the problem, or made the problem worse. You can try again with your other restore points until you find one that provides a stable operating system in which you can work.

Understanding System Repair Disc vs. Recovery Drive

In Windows Vista and Windows 7, you were able to create a system repair disc (a startup CD or DVD that contained the Startup Repair files for Windows). This was a very useful system because it allowed you to start the recovery options without carrying your Windows installation DVD with you. However, you had to carry the physical disc with you. Also, increasing numbers of new computers, especially netbooks and Ultrabooks, don't have optical drives, so you'd have to carry an external USB optical drive as well.

In Windows 8, you have another option: a recovery drive. This is essentially the same as a system repair disc, but it can be created only on a USB flash drive, which is much more convenient to store and carry.

> **INSIDE OUT** **Repair disc or recovery drive: which should you have?**
>
> My advice is to create both a repair disc and a recovery drive (you'll need to create both 32-bit and 64-bit versions by using 32-bit and 64-bit versions of Windows 8). Between the two of them, you shouldn't need a USB optical drive. The reason for still requiring repair discs, especially if you repair computers for a living, is that some of the computers you encounter might not support starting up from a USB device (Windows 8 will run on very early hardware), but typically, computers for which this is the case will almost always have a built-in optical drive.

Creating a System Repair Disc in Windows 8

To create a system repair disc, open Control Panel, and then click Windows 7 File Recovery. In the left pane of the Windows 7 File Recovery dialog box that opens, click the option to Create A System Repair Disc (see Figure 14-8).

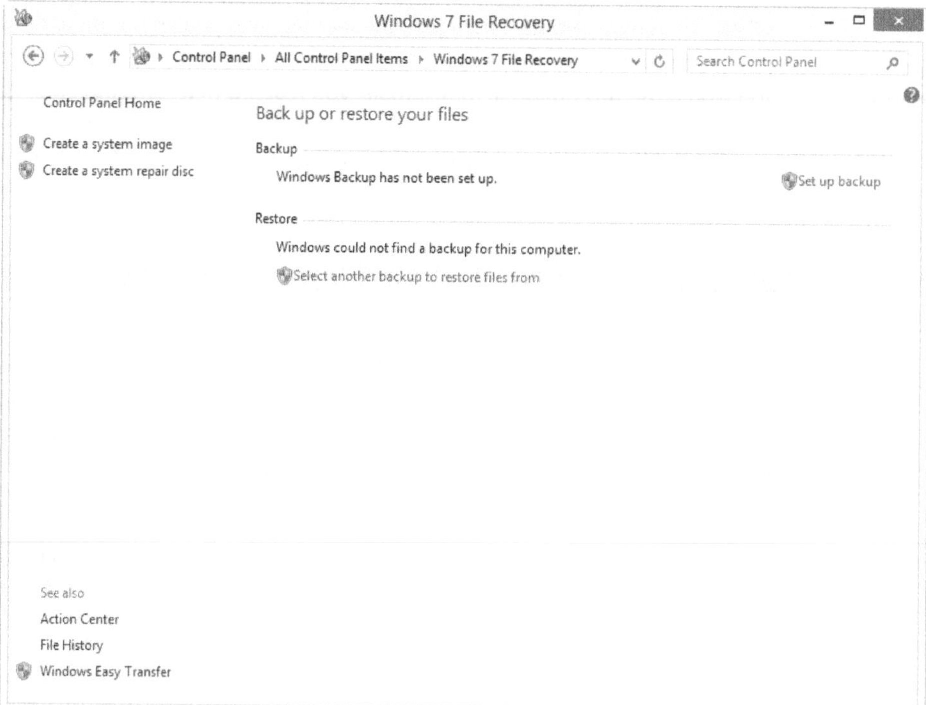

Figure 14-8 You create a system repair disc on a CD or DVD in Windows 7 File Recovery.

This disc can be created on either a blank CD or a blank DVD (Windows 8 can burn to Blu-ray discs, but this is expensive and unnecessary). You will need separate 32-bit and 64-bit discs, which can be created only by those versions of Windows 8. The discs will also not work with Windows 7, and vice versa. For your own computer, you will need only the disc relevant to your specific PC and version of Windows. If you repair computers for a living, however, you may want to carry both 64-bit and 32-bit discs.

Creating a Recovery Drive in Windows 8

To create a Windows 8 recovery drive, in Control Panel, click Recovery. In the Advanced Recovery Tools section, click the Create A Recovery Drive link (see Figure 14-9).

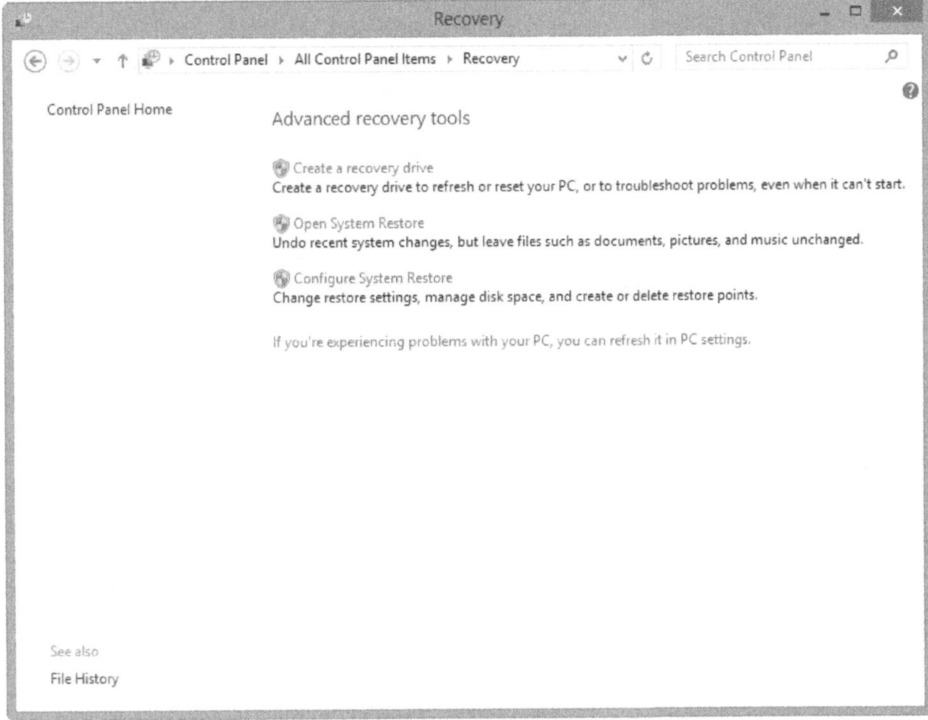

Figure 14-9 You create a recovery drive in the Recovery window.

A recovery drive can be an extremely useful tool for recovering an unresponsive copy of Windows 8. Because it's a USB flash drive, it's very small, easy to carry around, and handy. You need a USB flash drive that you can use for starting the system, so it needs a capacity of at least 256 megabytes (MB). (This is a good use for older USB flash drives that you might have lying around.) If you provide technical support, keep in mind that you will need to have both a 32-bit and a 64-bit version (each created on 32-bit and 64-bit installed versions of Windows 8, respectively; one cannot be used to rescue the other). Also, be aware that you cannot use either version to recover Windows 7.

Troubleshooting Software Compatibility

Software compatibility has always been a major issue for Windows users. When users like a particular application and are used to working with it, they often want to stick with it. Sometimes new features are introduced, or perhaps even an entirely different software package is released, and users are tempted to upgrade. For the most part, though, users continue to use what they know and like. You'll be glad to know that Windows 8 is technically compatible with all software that runs on Windows 7; however, it's not compatible with the same software Windows 7 is incompatible with.

Windows 8 is also quite good at detecting when there is a compatibility problem with a particular software package, and it will alert you if it believes a program needs to be run in a compatibility mode. Occasionally, though, you will need to set this program compatibility manually.

Manually Setting Program Compatibility

Opening the program compatibility options for a program in Windows 8 is slightly more complex than it was in Windows 7 and earlier versions. Let's take a look at how to set compatibility in Windows 8. Note that you can't set compatibility for Windows 8 apps. There are no compatibility options, because these apps are completely new and won't run on any previous versions of Windows. You will be able to set compatibility only for desktop apps.

On the Start screen (or in the All Apps view), right-click the icon of the program for which you need to set the compatibility, and then on the App bar, click Open File Location. In File Explorer, right-click the application icon, click Properties, click the Compatibility tab (see Figure 14-10), and then choose the settings you want to use. Note that some applications, especially those that ship as part of Windows 8, don't have this option available.

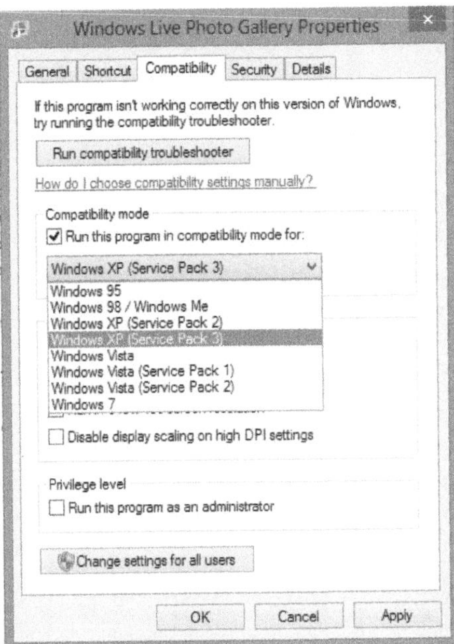

Figure 14-10 Adjust the compatibility settings for a program.

Compatibility mode allows you to emulate every version of Windows going back to Windows 95. You should choose the option for the most recent version of Windows with which the desired software worked properly. If you're not sure which version of Windows to choose, try different settings until you find one that works with the software you want to load.

The app compatibility settings offer more options (see Figure 14-11), the most important of which is the ability to run a program as an administrator. You should always be careful with this option, because it means the app has complete access to and can modify the Windows 8 system files. Some earlier software, however, especially custom business software, requires this level of access to function.

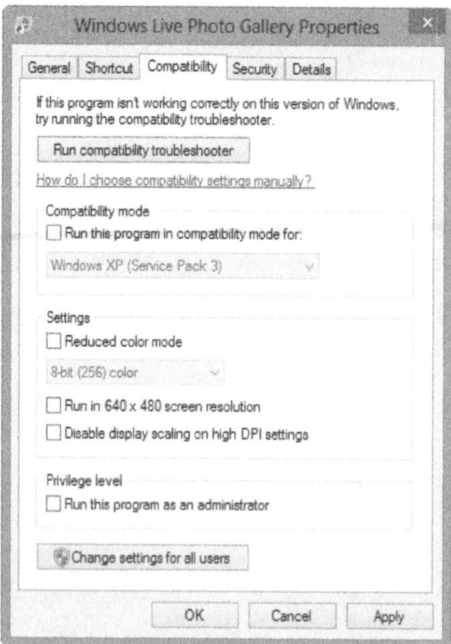

Figure 14-11 Many program compatibility options are available to users.

You will need the remaining options only for much earlier or problematic software, such as a program that causes an error when run or that doesn't function properly on high-resolution screens.

Using the Automatic Program Compatibility Troubleshooter

If you are not sure of the appropriate settings needed for a program to maintain application compatibility, you can run the Program Compatibility Troubleshooter. You access this in the same way as you access the manual compatibility settings, but instead, right-click the program icon in Windows 8, open the file location, right-click the program in File Explorer, and then click Troubleshoot Compatibility.

Figure 14-12 shows the Program Compatibility Troubleshooter, which tries different compatibility settings for the program by asking you questions about how and where the software worked in the past, changing the corresponding settings automatically, and then asking you each time a change is made whether the program is now working properly.

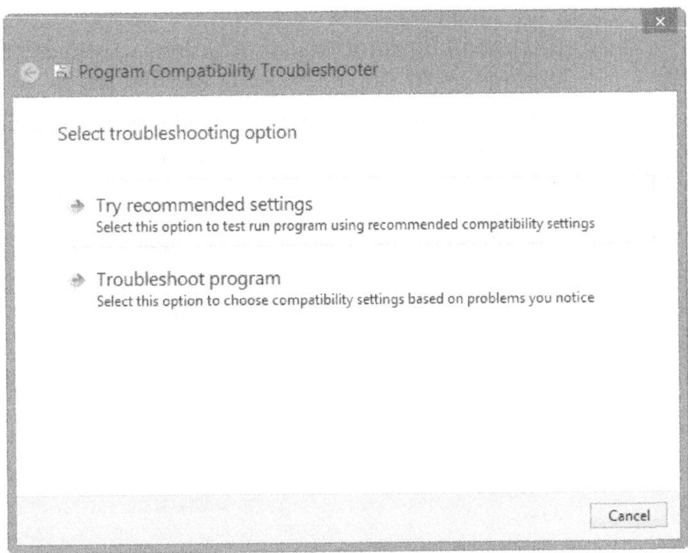

Figure 14-12 The automated Program Compatibility Troubleshooter gives you two options.

This troubleshooter is an automated version of the program compatibility options mentioned earlier, but it isn't as flexible as manual modification of the program compatibility settings.

Program Compatibility Notifications in Action Center

Occasionally, Action Center in Windows 8 alerts you to a potential program compatibility problem. When applications stop responding on your computer, you are asked whether you want to send the error information to Microsoft, which gathers a significant amount of detail about programs that won't work, with the goal of finding a fix.

Note

One of the most significant problems facing computer users is maintaining compatibility with older software that ran perfectly in Windows XP. When Microsoft introduced Windows Vista, it reengineered the operating system in substantial ways. This broke much of the program compatibility that users had enjoyed in the past. In Windows 8 Pro and Enterprise versions, you will find the Hyper-V virtualization client, into which you can install a working copy of Windows XP (you will need a valid product code for it). I discuss Windows XP compatibility using Client Hyper-V in more depth in Chapter 10, "Working in a Virtual Environment."

INSIDE OUT Discontinuing automatic notifications to Microsoft regarding programs that stop responding in Windows 8

You may not want Windows to send any information to Microsoft. The data sent to Microsoft doesn't include any personally identifiable data, but you can opt out of sending any information in Action Center.

In Action Center, in the left pane, select Change Action Center Settings, and then click Customer Experience Improvement Program Settings. In the dialog box that opens, you can opt out of this program by selecting the No, I Don't Want To Participate In The Program option (see Figure 14-13).

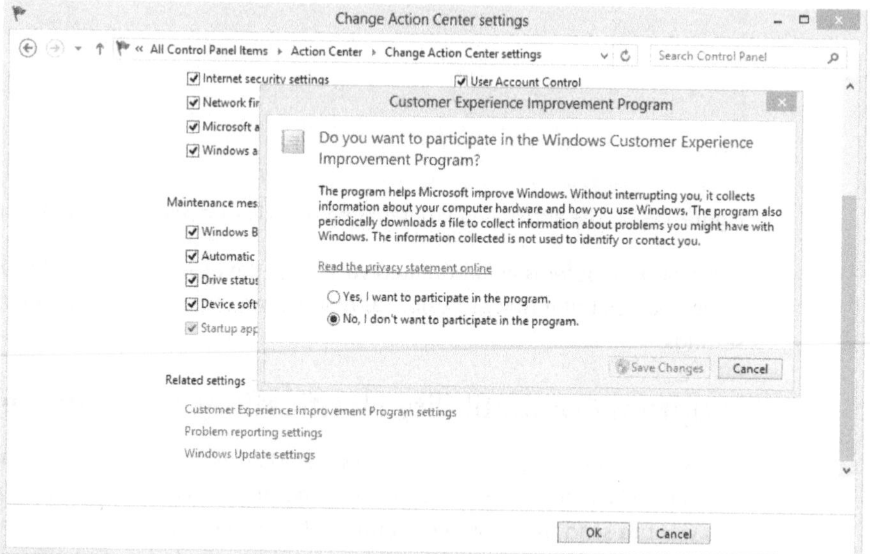

Figure 14-13 You can change the Customer Experience Improvement Program settings in Windows 8.

I recommend that you leave this option enabled. This tool is useful to computer engineers and developers as they continually strive to improve the Windows user experience. Plus, turning it off might mean that you don't automatically receive useful troubleshooting advice about Windows 8 from Microsoft.

Figuring Out Why Windows Won't Start

Occasionally, Windows 8 doesn't start. A configuration file or some other minor issue is usually the cause in such cases. This is a frustrating situation, but sometimes the answer is as simple as turning off your computer and turning it on again. However, sometimes you need to use additional options, some of which can be found in the new Windows 8 boot options menu and some of which you might run from a recovery drive or your Windows 8 installation DVD.

Accessing the Windows Boot Options Menus

Windows 8 includes two boot options menus, which it maintains for compatibility with earlier hardware that can't load graphics support when the system starts. You can access these menus are in slightly different ways.

The new boot options menu (see Figure 14-14) is accessible by pressing F8 on your keyboard when your computer starts (or during some Unified Extensible Firmware Interface, or UEFI, boot loaders run). The boot options menu is a new graphical system that is compatible with touchscreen-enabled devices. It is lacking some features that are available in the classic startup menu, however, including support for Safe Mode.

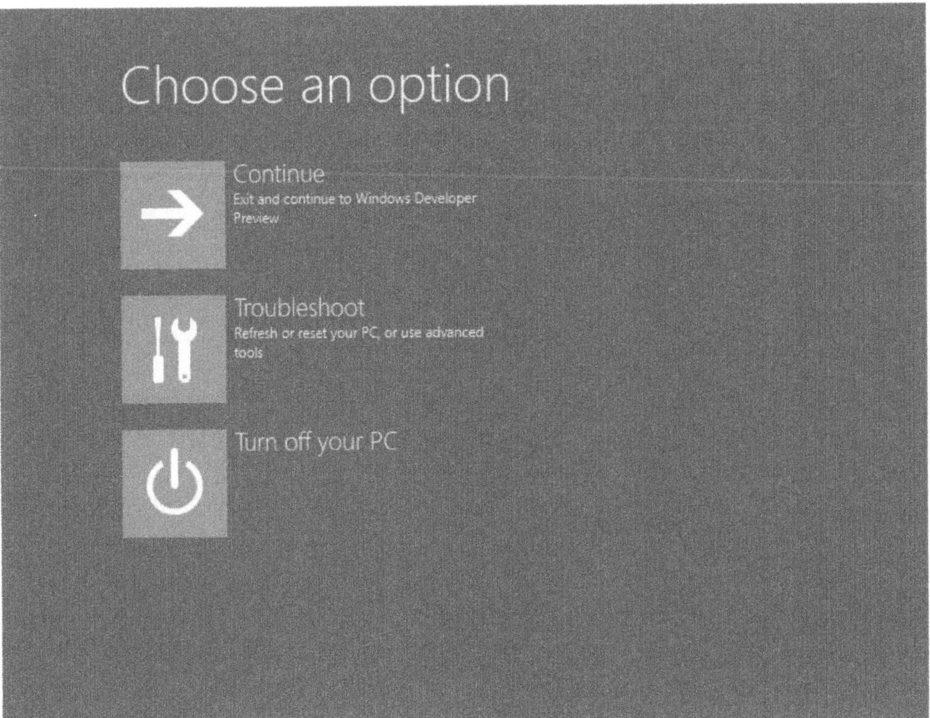

Figure 14-14 The Troubleshoot link provides additional options.

The following process describes the boot loader:

1. After the user presses the power button, the PC's firmware initiates a power-on self test (POST) and loads firmware settings. This preboot process ends when a valid system disk is detected.

2. The firmware reads the master boot record (MBR), and then starts Bootmgr.exe. Bootmgr.exe finds and starts the Windows loader (Winload.exe) on the Windows boot partition.

3. Essential drivers required to start the Windows kernel are loaded and the kernel starts to run, loading into memory the system registry hive and additional drivers that are marked as BOOT_START.

4. The kernel passes control to the session manager process (Smss.exe), which initializes the system session, and loads and starts the devices and drivers that are not marked BOOT_START.

5. Winlogon.exe starts, the user logon screen appears, the service control manager starts services, and any Group Policy scripts are run. When the user logs in, Windows creates a session for that user.

6. Explorer.exe starts, and the system creates the Desktop Window Manager (DWM) process, which initializes the desktop and displays it.

If you want the classic options menu (see Figure 14-15), you need to press Shift+F8 after (or sometimes during) the boot loader. This classic options menu maintains compatibility with earlier hardware and also provides additional options not available in the boot options menu system.

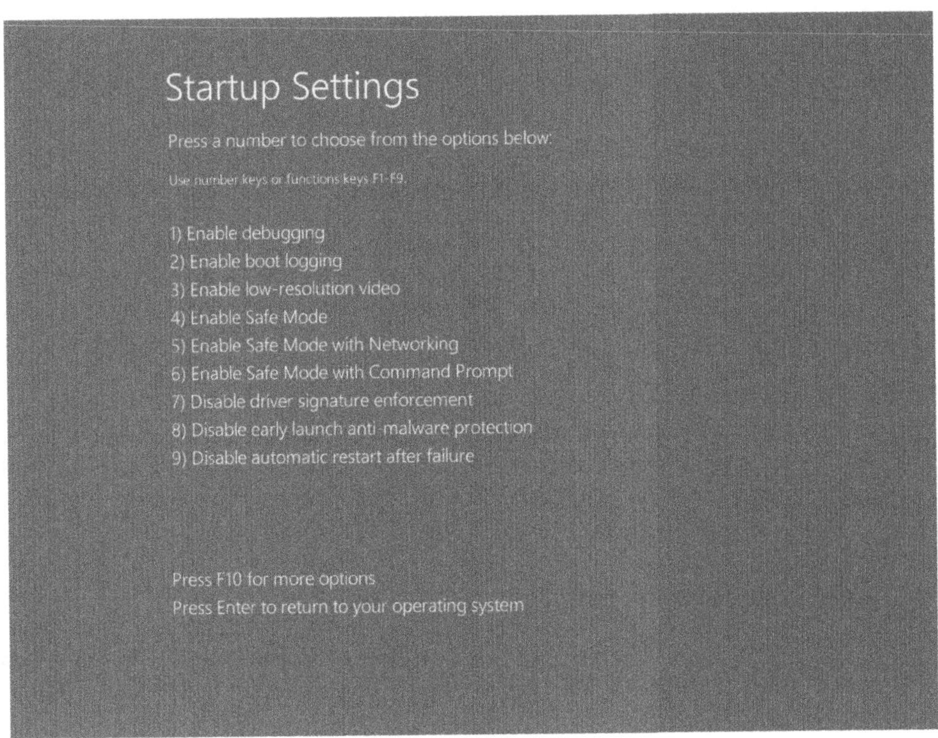

Figure 14-15 The Startup Settings menu offers familiar options for Windows users.

Options When You Can't Access the Boot Options Menu

Occasionally, you can't access either of the startup menus, particularly on newer computers, and no combination of pressing F8 or Shift+F8 before, during, or after the boot loader will display a startup options menu. But don't worry: if this happens, all is not lost! There are two ways to access the features you are most likely to need in Windows 8:

- Start your computer from a system repair disc or recovery drive. This will bring up the system menu that will allow you to perform diagnostic and repair operations such as running the automated startup repair or performing a system restore.
- Use the boot options in the MSConfig window to trigger Safe Mode manually. Full instructions about how to do this are in Chapter 21, "Demystifying Windows 8 Problems."

Using the Last Known Good Configuration

If you install Windows 8 on earlier BIOS PCs, you might still see the black-and-white DOS boot options menu. This menu offers an additional Last Known Good Configuration option, which can start your copy of Windows 8 by using the same settings the system started with properly the last time. You may not see this option in the new Startup Settings menu, however.

When you power on your computer, press the Shift+F8 key just after the BIOS screen has disappeared. If you see the Windows logo, you've gone too far and will have to try again. Pressing Shift+F8 brings up the Windows Recovery options (see Figure 14-16).

From the options presented, click See Advanced Repair Options, and then on the next screen, click Last Known Good Configuration (Advanced) to reset the current Windows 8 instance in favor of the one recorded the last time Windows successfully started. Windows 8 should now start. Note that this option won't change any Windows settings since you last started the operating system, so it's safe to use

Starting in Safe Mode

If Windows 8 still won't start by using the Last Known Good Configuration option, you can choose another option from Advanced Options. Press Shift+F8 when you start your computer, and choose the Safe Mode option.

If Windows 8 loads to the Safe Mode desktop, turn off your computer and restart it. Many startup problems with the operating system are fixed by doing this.

> **INSIDE OUT** **Avoid using the reset button**
>
> **You should avoid restarting your computer by using the reset button, especially if you're restarting only because you haven't pressed F8 in time to show Advanced Boot Options. Pressing your computer's reset button at the wrong time can cause essential Windows 8 startup files to become corrupt. If possible, let Windows load to the desktop and then restart your computer by clicking the Restart charm.**

Running Startup Repair

If Windows 8 does not start after three tries, the boot options menu will appear the next time you attempt to start your computer. The boot options menu is an automated feature in Windows 8 startup. Figure 14-16 shows the dialog box that opens when Windows determines that you need to access the boot options menu. To access the Automatic Repair option, click See Advanced Repair Options. Next, click Troubleshoot, select Advanced Options, and then click Automatic Repair.

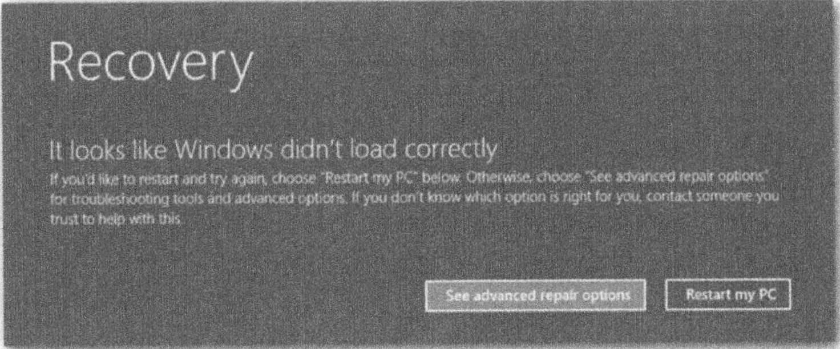

Figure 14-16 The automated Recovery tool in Windows 8 appears if Windows doesn't start.

INSIDE OUT Reverting to the traditional boot options menu by default

You have the option to click Windows Startup Settings to revert to the traditional startup options menu. This returns the system to Safe Mode, but you lose new options such as Refresh and Reset (see Figure 14-17).

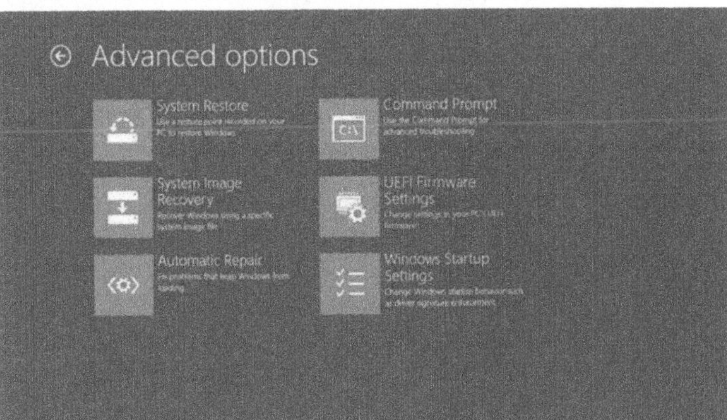

Figure 14-17 Start Automatic Repair from the boot options menu.

This service looks at your Windows 8 installation and tries to identify and fix any problems that are preventing Windows 8 from starting. If the service finds something wrong, it attempts to repair the problem and then prompts you to restart the computer if the problem is fixed.

Figure 14-18 shows the message you receive when Startup Repair is unable to fix the problem. It offers you Advanced Options, which you can use to restore Windows from a System Restore point or restore Windows completely from a backup. A faulty hardware driver and recently installed software are common culprits that prevent Windows 8 from starting.

Figure 14-18 When Startup Repair cannot fix the startup problem, click Advanced Options.

Running Startup Repair from Removable Media

You can also run Startup Repair from your Windows 8 installation DVD, a system repair disc, or a recovery drive. These approaches offer you more options for fixing your computer when it won't start. When starting from your Windows 8 install DVD, on the Install Now screen, click Repair Your Computer (see Figure 14-19).

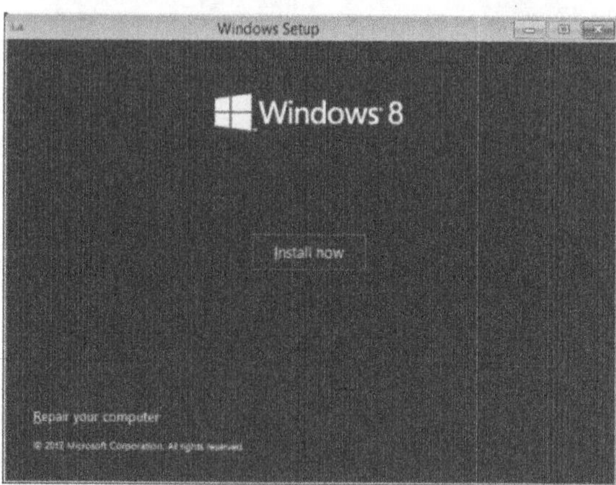

Figure 14-19 Click Repair Your Computer to access repair options.

Using a Backup

If you still can't get Windows 8 to start, on the Advanced Options screen, click System Image Recovery and then restore Windows 8 from a backup. I covered backups in Chapter 3, "Setup and Backup Strategies for Avoiding Major System Issues." Unfortunately, if you don't have a system image of your Windows 8 installation, you will need to reinstall your operating system, including all of your programs and updates.

Working with Device Drivers

There are multitudes of hardware devices for Windows-based computers, ranging from inexpensive components to extremely expensive graphics cards. Microsoft has a certification program for hardware drivers, but it isn't mandatory for the 32-bit versions of Windows 8, and many hardware manufacturers don't want to pay for it.

With the 64-bit editions of Windows 8, driver certification is mandatory, but you can still install drivers that are uncertified. Understand, however, that hardware drivers control your entire experience with Windows, and uncertified device drivers can cause problems with Windows or even prevent the operating system from starting. Device drivers are one of the principle causes of computer problems.

Fortunately, Microsoft has made working with hardware drivers easy in Windows 8, so if you need to remove, reinstall, or update one, you shouldn't encounter any problems. But before explaining how you handle device drivers in Windows 8, let me caution you about some of the issues that can arise with them.

Common Problems with Device Drivers

Device driver problems are at the root of many issues with Windows 8. Here are some of the most common ones:

- Windows doesn't start.
- A device stops working.
- A device doesn't work properly.

A problem can occur for the first time after you perform one of the following actions:

- Install hardware for the first time.
- Update the hardware driver manually.
- Update the driver by using Windows Update.

In Chapter 17, "Environmental Factors Affecting Your Computer," I tackle the topic of diagnosing device problems in more detail. For now, let's deal with troubleshooting techniques for specific types of drivers.

Graphics Driver Problems

Some of the most common driver problems occur with the computer's graphics drivers. The graphics card driver differs from other Windows drivers because it is one of the first drivers to load when Windows starts.

Here are a few common problems caused by graphics drivers.

- Windows loads but does not display an image on the monitor.
- Windows shows the blue screen while loading (see Figure 14-20).

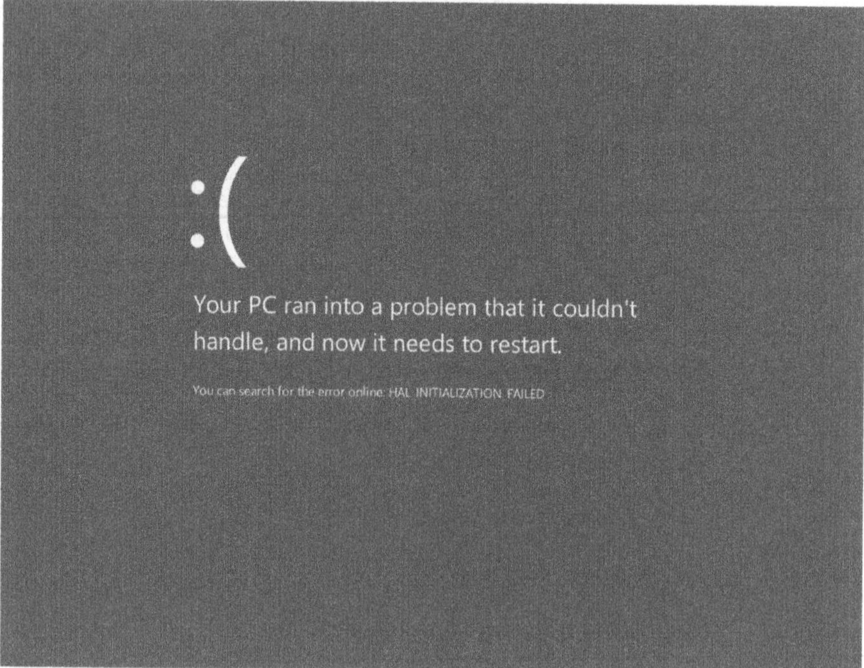

Figure 14-20 The redesigned blue screen in Windows 8 just gives you a simple description of the error.

- Your screen resolution is stuck at its lowest settings.
- Windows 8 stops responding while loading games.

If you encounter one of the preceding problems, it's best to start your computer in Safe Mode. As mentioned earlier in the chapter, you do this by pressing Shift+F8 when Windows starts but before the Starting Windows screen appears. If you see the Windows logo screen, the startup process is too far along and you need to restart the computer again.

Pressing Shift+F8 brings up the Advanced Boot Options screen. From here, choose Safe Mode, and then press Enter. This is a reduced functionality mode in which Windows loads only the minimum required drivers and software. Refer to the section titled "Figuring Out Why Windows Won't Start" earlier in this chapter for more options.

Device Manager

Device Manager (see Figure 14-21) is where you can see and control all the drivers for the hardware installed on your computer. You access Device Manager through Control Panel by clicking Hardware And Sound\Device Manager. Alternatively, on the Start screen, type **device manager**, and then click Device Manager in the Settings results.

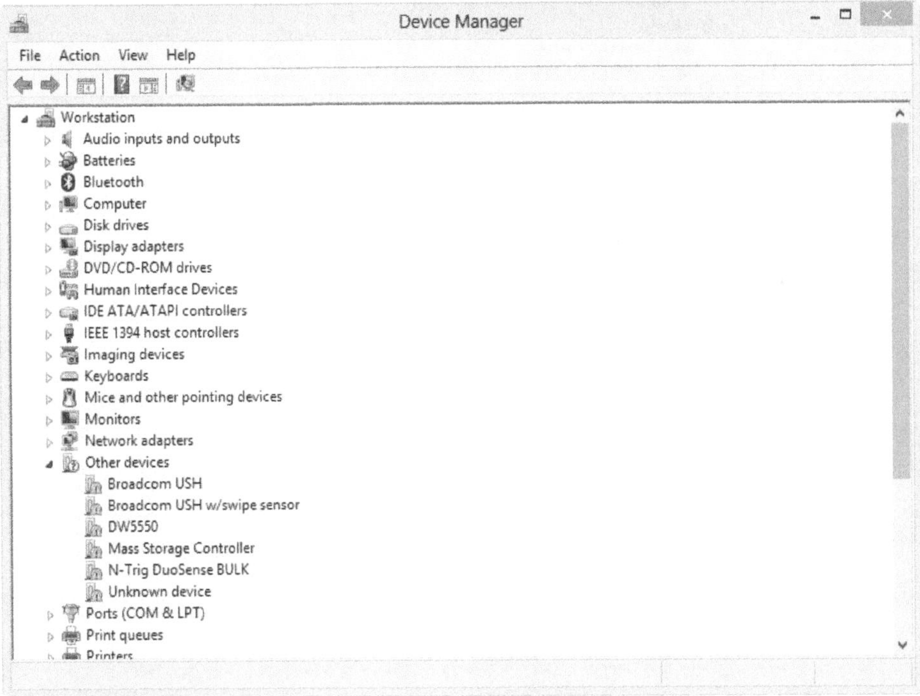

Figure 14-21 Hardware categories.

The hardware is organized into categories, most of which are self-explanatory: disk drives, display adapters, DVD/CD-ROM drives, keyboards, network adapters, and so on. Here are two categories you might not be familiar with:

- Human Interface Devices is where drivers for hardware such as USB input devices (graphics tablets and remote control sensors) are located.
- Sound, Video, And Game Controllers includes everything, from your computer's sound card and gaming joystick to TV tuner cards and webcams.

Figure 14-22 shows expanded categories.

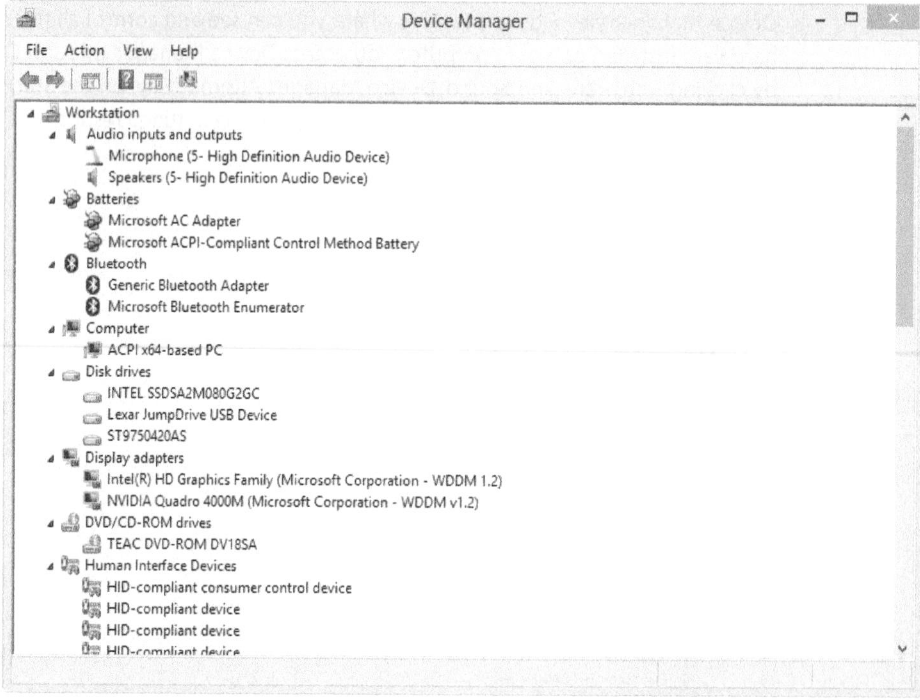

Figure 14-22 You can view specific hardware in Device Manager.

You can also see whether a particular driver is listed. A yellow warning triangle or a red cross next to a device (see Figure 14-23) means that the driver either isn't working properly or is disabled, respectively. If any devices have warning triangles, the device group will expand automatically when Device Manager starts. Any nonfunctioning devices are also listed in the Other Devices category, which can make finding nonfunctioning devices with a screen reader simpler.

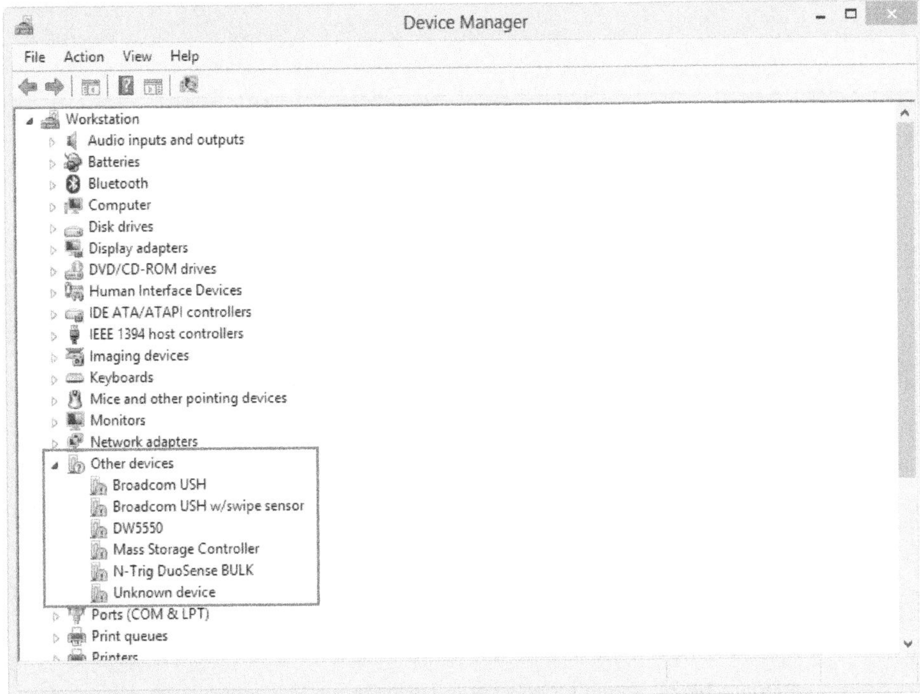

Figure 14-23 Problem hardware is indicated by a warning triangle.

If your hardware isn't listed, on the Action menu, click Scan For Hardware Changes (see Figure 14-24). After the scan, your hardware should appear in the list, and Windows 8 might automatically install the correct driver for that hardware, if for example the driver came with Windows or can be found by Windows Update. Windows will inform you as to whether it was able to find and install the appropriate driver.

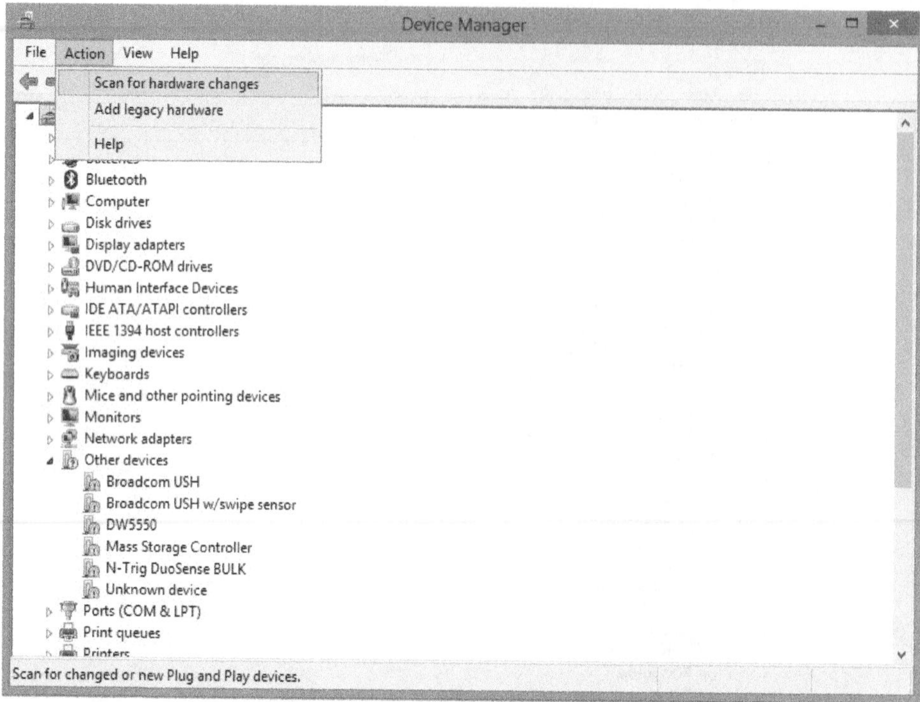

Figure 14-24 Search for new hardware in Device Manager.

If your hardware still doesn't show up, on the View menu (see Figure 14-25), click Show Hidden Devices. Hidden devices are usually hardware drivers for Windows components, but they can also be your computer's hardware.

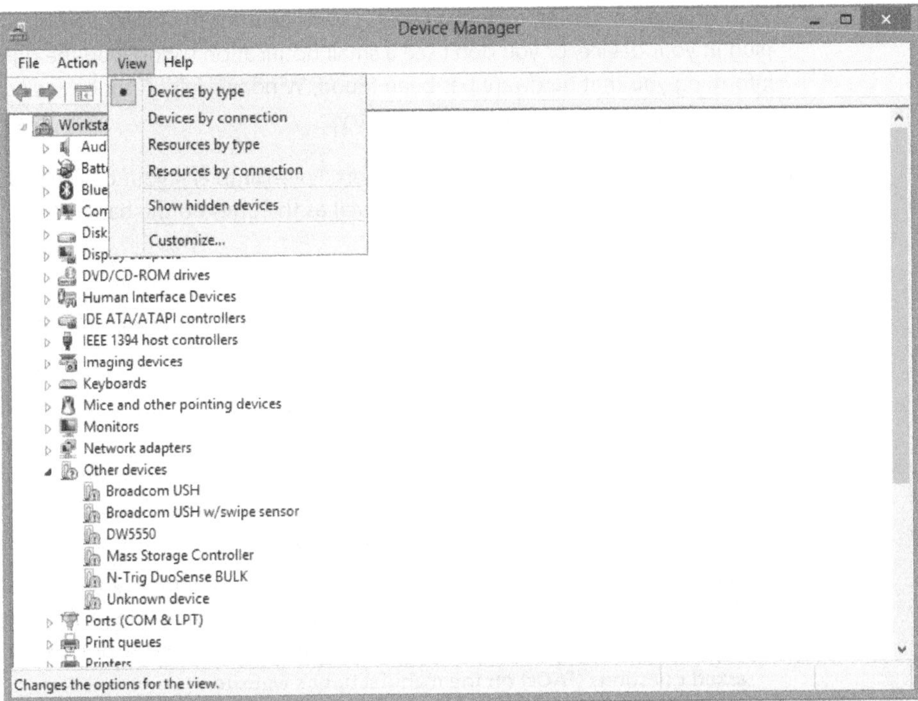

Figure 14-25 View hidden devices in Device Manager.

Troubleshooting Why Hardware Is Not Appearing in Device Manager

In a few situations, your hardware doesn't appear in the device list. At this point, ask the following questions:

- Could the hardware be called something else in Device Manager? Look through the list to see whether your hardware shows up with a name different from the one you're expecting. For example, many devices are just called "Human Interface Device."
- If the device is removable, such as a USB device, does unplugging it cause something to disappear from the device list?
- Is the device firmly plugged in, and are all the relevant power and data cables attached to it? Ensure that your computer is turned off and disconnected from the main electrical supply before checking this.

With USB and other removable devices, if Windows doesn't make any sound when you plug in your device, or you don't see a small notification window on the right of the taskbar informing you that hardware has been found, Windows might not be seeing the device. Following are several strategies you can try:

- Plug your device into a different port. For example, if your device is USB, try the ports on the front of your computer as well as the ones on the back.
- Try a different connecting cable.
- If your device requires its own external power supply, ensure that it is connected, turned on, and receiving power.
- Leave the device plugged in and restart your computer.

INSIDE OUT

Using older USB devices

Some older USB devices (and possibly some new ones) require you to install the device driver from the manufacturer-supplied CD before plugging it in to the computer for the first time. Check the manual that came with your hardware, or look for frequently asked questions (FAQs) on the manufacturer's website.

If you still can't get your device to work, the device might be faulty. If you have the option, try to use the device on another computer. This test will be much easier with a USB or other removable device. If the device is a graphics card, however, you might want to check the manufacturer's website for support and review some help forums before trying to install it in a different computer.

Installing Device Drivers

Windows normally updates the drivers for new hardware automatically. Although Windows 8 comes with more hardware drivers than any earlier version of Windows, Windows 8 still might not be able to find certain drivers or install them automatically. To update a driver manually, perform the following steps:

1. Right-click the desired driver in Device Manager, and then click Update Driver Software (see Figure 14-26).

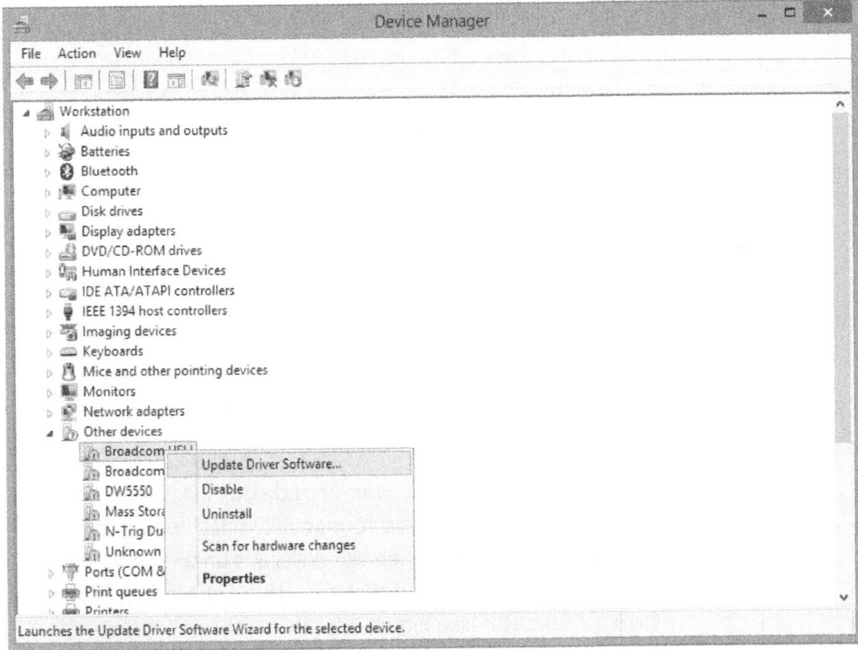

Figure 14-26 You update the driver for a device by right-clicking it.

2. You can choose to have Windows 8 find and install the driver, or you can install it manually from a disk or other location. If you have a copy of the driver on CD or DVD, click Browse My Computer For Driver Software (see Figure 14-27).

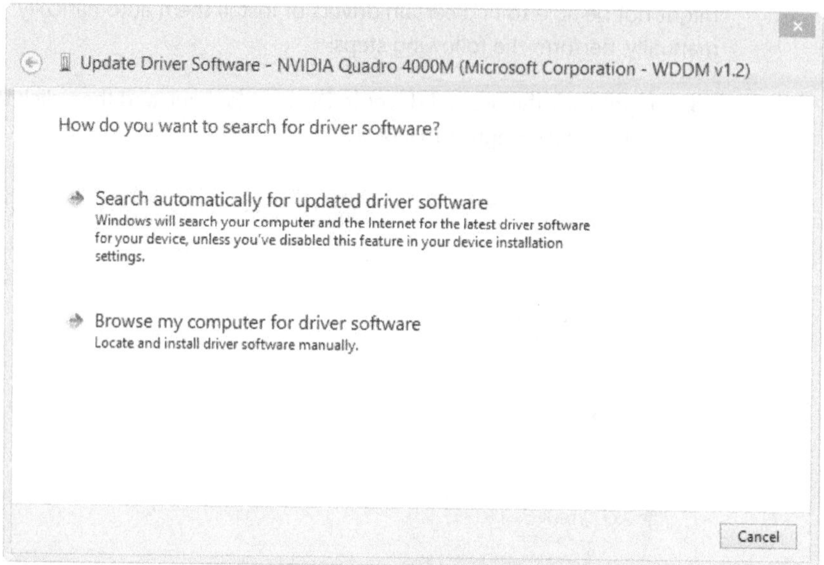

Figure 14-27 If you choose to search automatically for an updated driver, you will need an Internet connection.

3. Browse to the location on your hard disk or CD where the driver is located. Sometimes you might need to manually select which driver you want Windows to install, for example, when Windows 8 is unable to find the exact driver for your hardware automatically. In that case, click Let Me Pick From A List Of Device Drivers On My Computer (see Figure 14-28).

4. Click Have Disk (see Figure 14-29), and then browse to the folder on your hard disk or CD where the driver is located. The folder should be something similar to *Device Name*\Driver\Win8. Only device drivers will appear in this list—no other file types in that location will be visible. Choose the correct driver, and then click OK.

Figure 14-28 Click the link to choose a driver from all of those that have been provided with Windows 8 or later downloaded automatically during a Windows Update.

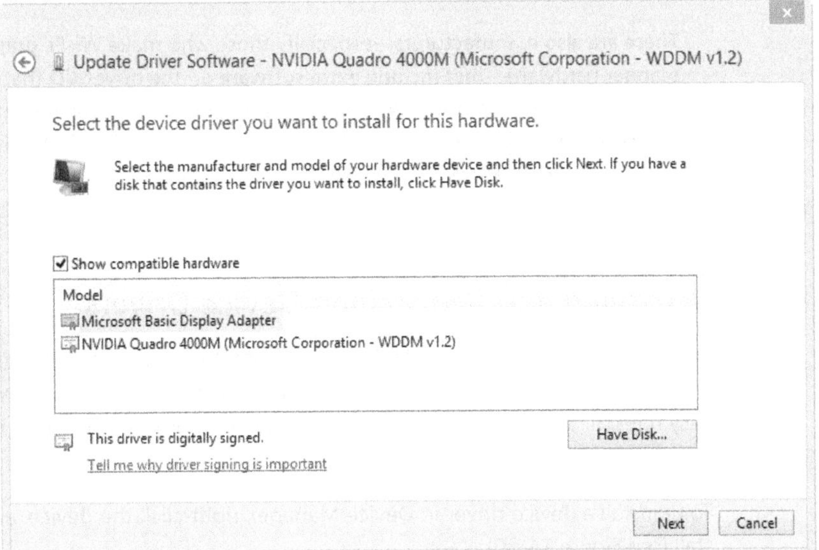

Figure 14-29 When the Show Compatible Hardware check box is cleared, all the drivers in Windows are displayed.

INSIDE OUT **Always ensure that you have a copy of your Network/Wi-Fi driver**

If Windows 8 doesn't come with a suitable driver for your network or Wi-Fi card, you must have a copy on a separate disk ready to install. If you don't, Windows won't be able to search online for a driver for you, and the hardware will not work.

Sometimes, when you're installing a driver manually, the Driver folder will include several driver (.inf) files. You might need to go through the manual driver installation process several times to find the correct file.

INSIDE OUT **Why not just install drivers by using the Setup program on the supplied CD?**

Installing a driver from the manufacturer-supplied CD can be quick and easy. In certain situations, however, you shouldn't install the driver this way. For example, if the hardware is older and the supplied CD doesn't include Windows 8 drivers, don't install the driver via the CD (although most of the time Windows 7 or Windows Vista drivers will still work).

There are also manufacturers—especially those who make Wi-Fi, graphics, and printer/scanner hardware—that include extra software on the driver CD that, by default, is set to load every time you start Windows. This software can often be unnecessary and add unwanted bloat to your computer, perhaps even causing conflicts with other software that can cause problems.

Removing and Reinstalling Device Drivers

You might want to remove a device driver from Windows when you are updating it. One of the reasons for doing this is that when you reinstall the driver, Windows might automatically reinstall the previous version of the driver that doesn't work (the one you were trying to get rid of in the first place).

To uninstall a device driver in Device Manager, right-click the device, and then click Uninstall (see Figure 14-30).

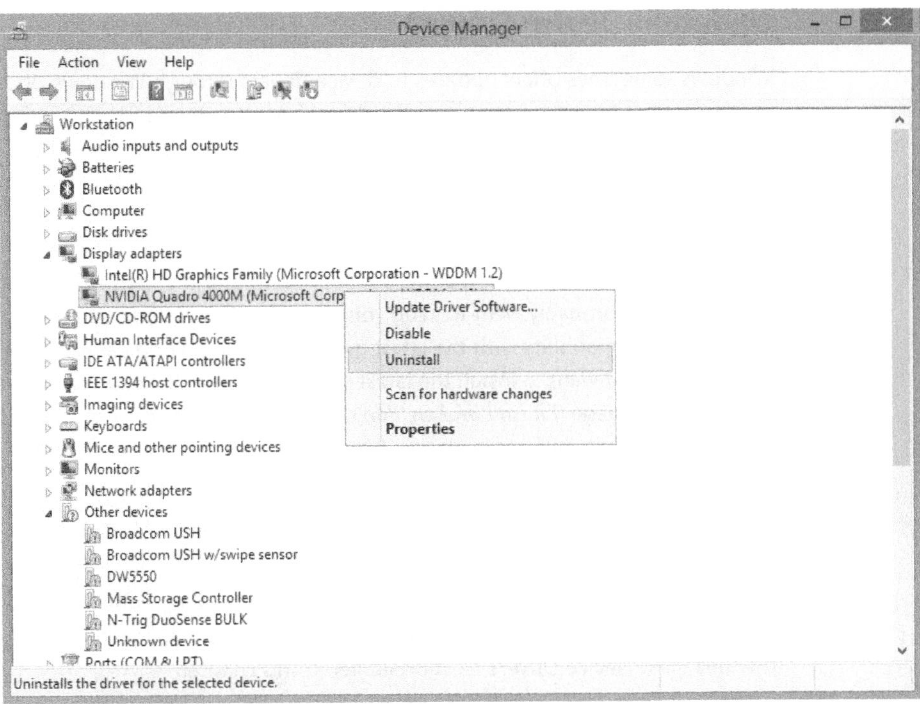

Figure 14-30 You can remove a device driver from Windows by right-clicking it.

For many devices, Windows then asks if you want to delete the driver software for the particular device (see Figure 14-31). You should select this check box if you want to reinstall a specific driver and don't want Windows to reinstall the current one. The installed driver files are then deleted from your hard disk, and you can reinstall the driver.

Figure 14-31 Selecting the check box deletes all the files associated with that driver from your computer, preventing accidental reinstallation.

Updating Device Drivers

Windows sometimes offers updates to device drivers through Windows Update, but at times you might need to download the driver from the manufacturer's website.

> **INSIDE OUT** **If it isn't broken, don't fix it!**
>
> **Do you really need the latest driver for your hardware? If you use your computer for gaming, you probably want to keep your graphics drivers updated for speed and to maintain compatibility with the latest graphics features. For most hardware, however, you might not want to install the latest drivers, because these can cause problems. This follows the adage *if it isn't broken, don't fix it*. Because new drivers, especially *very* new ones, can include unforeseen bugs, if your current driver works perfectly fine, don't change it.**

To update the driver for a specific device, in Device Manager, right-click the device, and then click Update Driver Software (see Figure 14-32). Next, follow the process described in the "Installing Device Drivers" section earlier in this chapter.

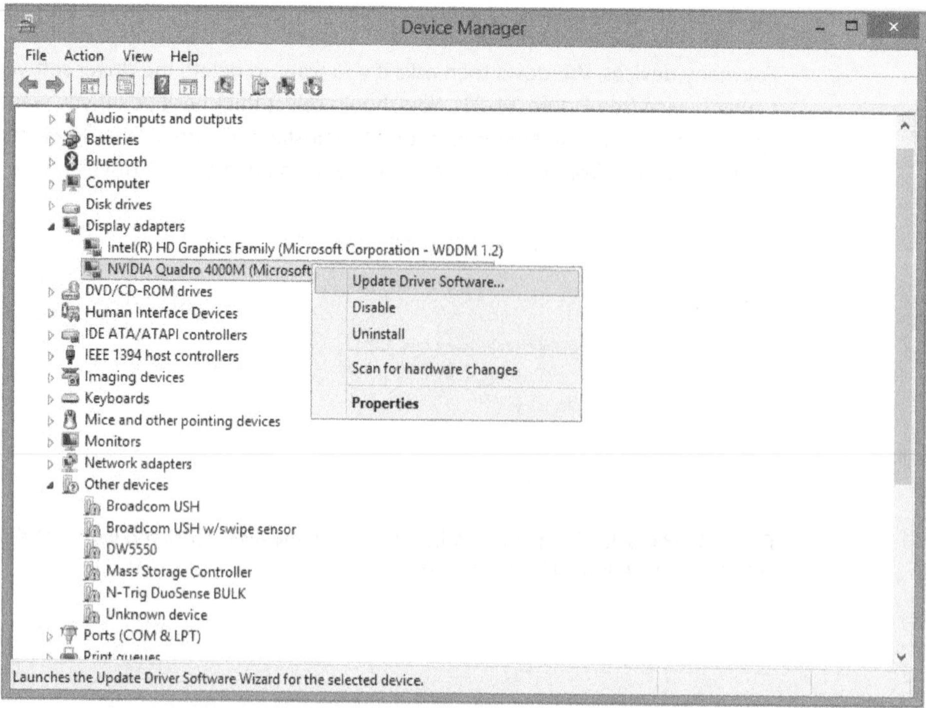

Figure 14-32 You update a driver in Device Manager by right-clicking it.

INSIDE OUT How to back up device drivers in Windows 8

You can back up all of your device drivers if you want—for example, maybe you've lost the original driver CD for a piece of hardware. You can find these device drivers on your Windows drive (usually drive C) in the Windows\System32\DriverStore folder (see Figure 14-33).

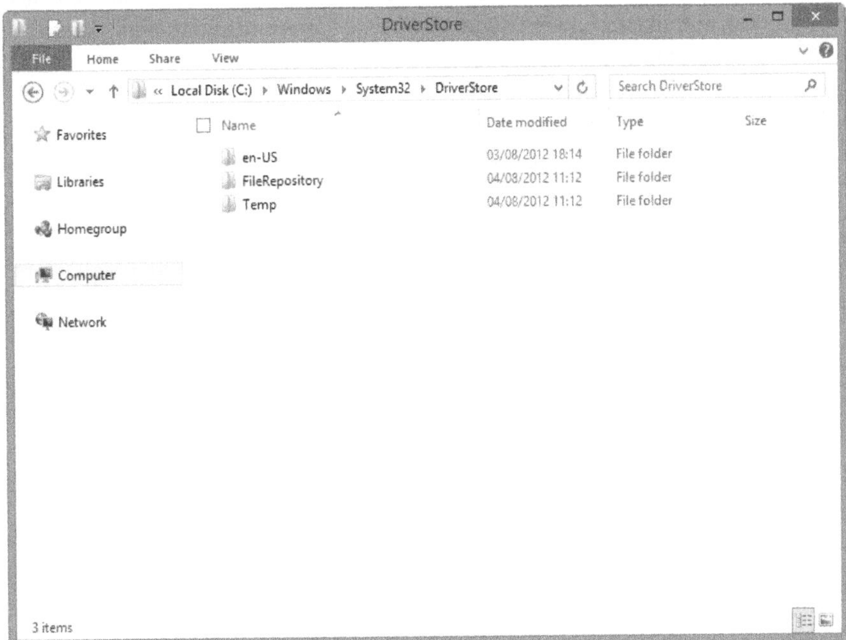

Figure 14-33 You can back up Windows 8 drivers in the DriverStore folder.

You can back up the entire DriverStore folder and copy it back to the hard drive if you need to reinstall Windows. After doing this and restarting the computer, Windows should be able to install the correct drivers for all of your installed hardware.

Rolling Back Device Drivers

Sometimes, when a recently installed driver causes a problem, you will want Windows 8 to reinstall the previous driver—the one that worked. This is easy to do.

In Device Manager, right-click the correct device, and then click Properties. The Properties dialog box for a device appears (see Figure 14-34). Click the Driver tab. On this tab, if there is a previous driver you want Windows 8 to revert, you can click Roll Back Driver. This starts an automated process that removes the current driver and reinstates the previous one. Your computer might need to restart during this process.

Figure 14-34 If your driver software has been updated, the Roll Back Driver button is available.

Using Action Center Troubleshooters

Action Center has an excellent troubleshooting pane that helps you fix common problems in Windows 8. To access it, click the Action Center icon and click Open Action Center. Next, click the Troubleshooting (Find And Fix Problems) link at the bottom of the Action Center window (you might need to scroll down the window to find it) to bring up the troubleshooters (see Figure 14-35).

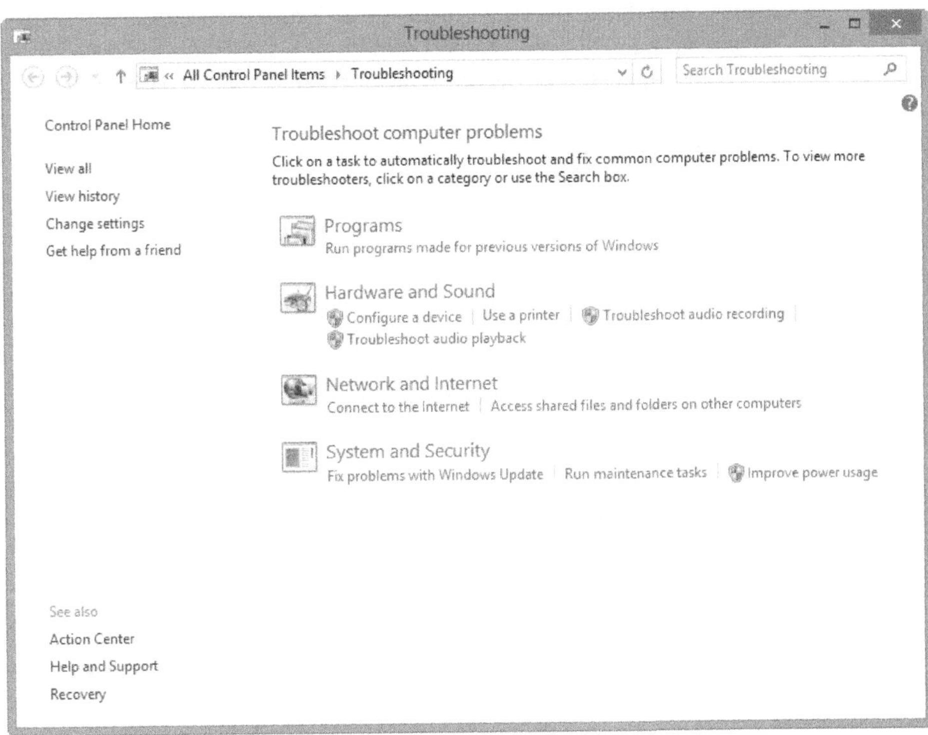

Figure 14-35 Action Center Troubleshooter.

This pane contains many automated Windows 8 troubleshooters that are easy to run. These troubleshooters don't always find and fix the problem with your computer because they work by resetting Windows components to their default state, but this pane is an excellent place to start troubleshooting minor issues.

Using Microsoft Fix It Center

Microsoft provides an automated problem-solving solution for all versions of Windows called Microsoft Fix It Center, which you can download from *http://fixitcenter.support.microsoft.com*. This is an excellent tool you should run periodically to check for solutions to problems on your computer that you might not even be aware of.

Microsoft's Fix It automated solutions help you solve problems with Windows and other Microsoft products. The Fix It process, which is easy and intuitive, automates manual steps commonly found in online support content such as Microsoft Knowledge Base articles. When you search the Knowledge Base for the solution to a problem, you sometimes will see a Fix It button that you can click to run an automated fix for the problem. This button can really take the pain out of fixing problems.

PART 3

Using Advanced Technical Fixes

CHAPTER 15

Understanding the Windows 8 Folder and File Structure

WINDOWS RUNS FROM PARTICULAR FOLDERS AND FILES on your computer's hard disk. The basic folder structure is logical and accessible. In this chapter, you learn about the three core Windows 8 folders and the essential files and subfolders that start your system and keep it running smoothly. You also learn about folders that contain user and configuration data and temporary files.

Important Windows 8 Folders

The three core Windows 8 system folders, Program Files, Users, and Windows, are shown in Figure 15-1. These files store programs, your files, and the operating system, respectively. When Windows 8 is installed, it occupies many folders on the hard disk, including these folders (and the Program Files x86 folder on 64-bit computers).

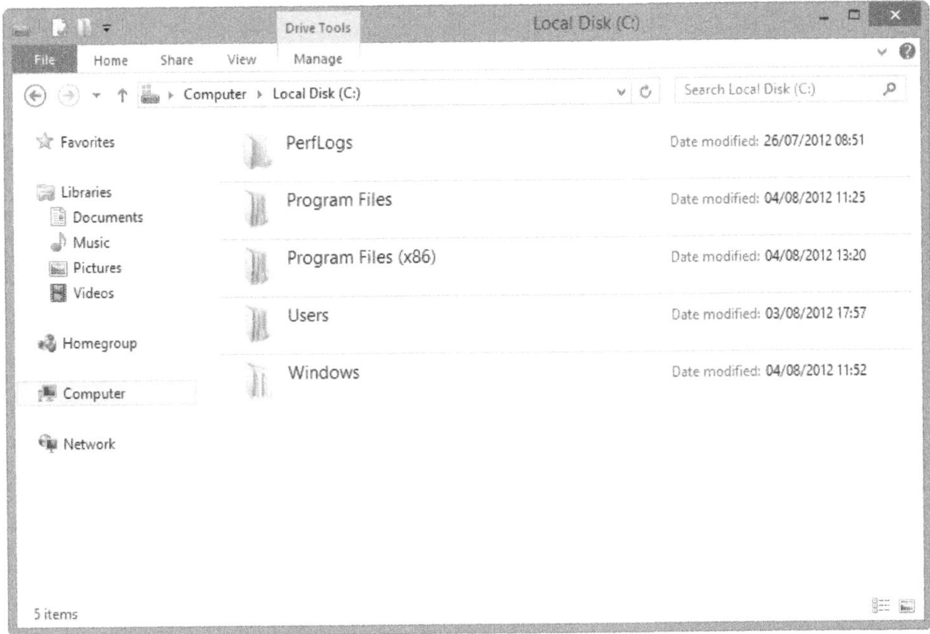

Figure 15-1 The folder structure in a computer running Windows 8, 64-bit.

The following list describes the purpose of the three core folders:

- **Program Files** All the files for any programs and software you install in Windows 8 reside in this folder. In the 64-bit version of Windows 8 are two Program Files folders: Program Files x86 for 32-bit software; and Program Files for newer, 64-bit software. Each program has its own custom folder within one of these folders. Only a Program Files folder exists in the 32-bit version of Windows 8.

- **Users** By default, all of your documents and files reside in this folder. This is also the location of your registry settings, which sit in a hidden Ntuser.dat file, with one registry file for each user. Within the main Users folder is one subfolder for each user and another folder called Public, where shared files and folders are kept. There are also hidden user folders called Default and All Users.

- **Windows** This is the main folder into which the operating system is installed. The main Windows registry files reside in the \Windows\System32\config folder.

Windows also installs hidden system files across the hard disk (shown as slightly dimmed in Figure 15-2).

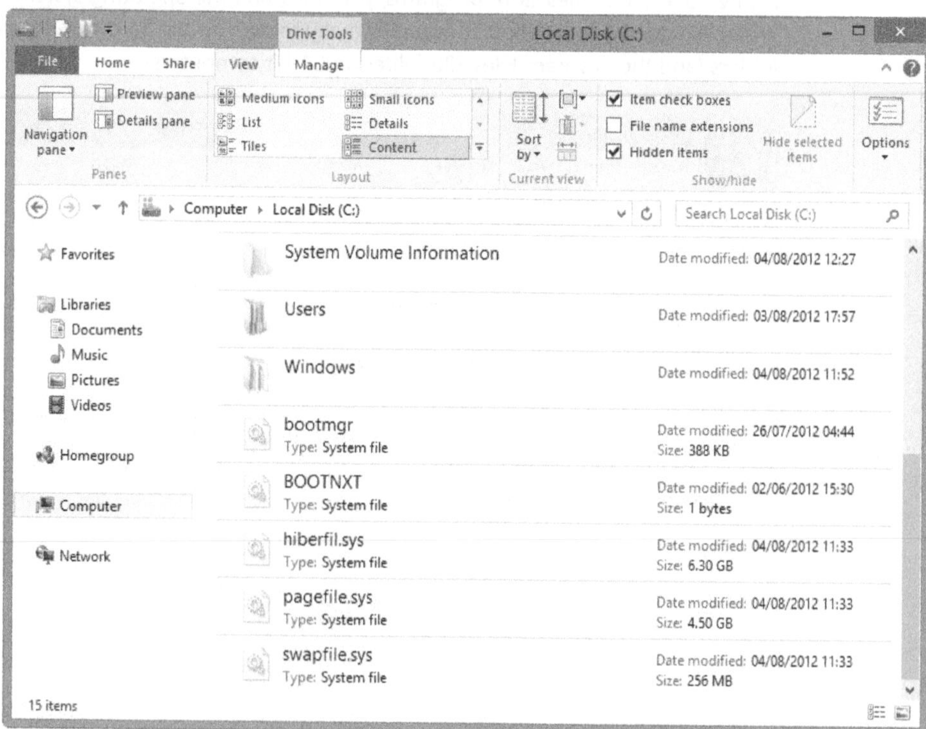

Figure 15-2 When you show hidden Windows 8 system files and folders, many more files will appear in File Explorer. Rarely will you have a reason to display these files.

These hidden files and folders, which you can display by selecting the Hidden Items on the View tab of the File Explorer ribbon, are where Windows stores operating system recovery software and folders to support earlier versions of software, including Documents And Settings, and the hibernation and paging files (virtual memory) for the operating system.

Inside the main Windows folder are many subfolders (see Figure 15-3), some of which exist to maintain compatibility with earlier hardware and software, and some of which service specific features within the current operating system.

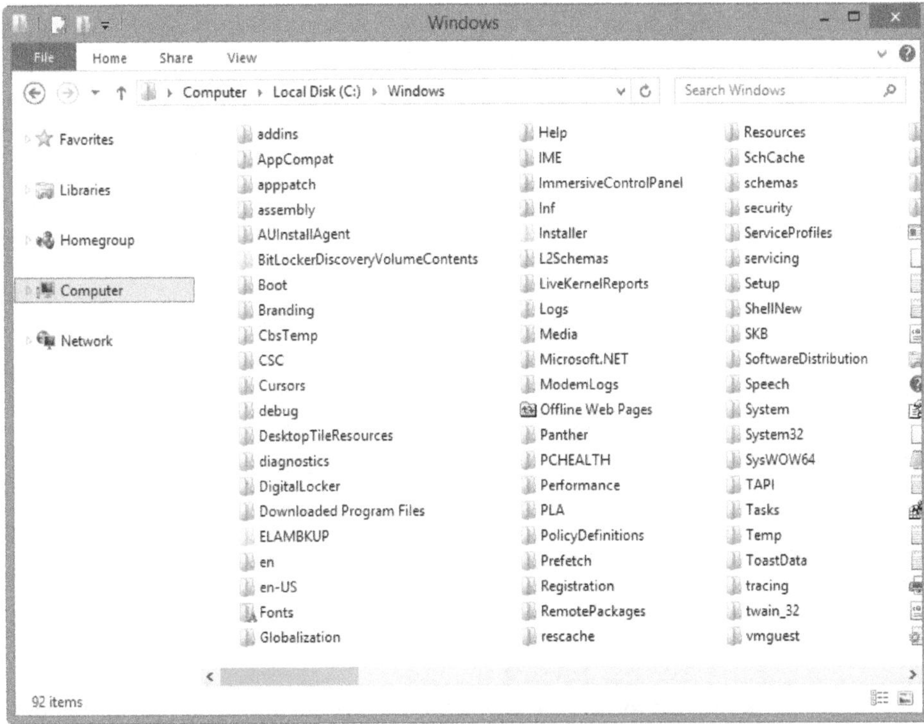

Figure 15-3 The main Windows folder contains the guts of the operating system.

The files and folders in the Windows subfolders are essential to maintain a properly functioning system, and you should not move, rename, or delete any of them. One folder of particular note is System32, which is the main operating system files folder store. All the core Windows files, including hardware device drivers, are located in this folder.

The files in the following folders are responsible for starting Windows, handling your applications, reporting errors, updating the system, storing media, and providing sound, in addition to other tasks:

- **WinSxS** WinSxS stands for *Windows Side By Side*. This folder can grow to many gigabytes in size, and it doesn't appear to contain anything important (see Figure 15-4). However, the WinSxS folder is responsible for Windows 8 working. This folder allows Windows to load different versions of system files simultaneously. Without it, applications may become unresponsive.

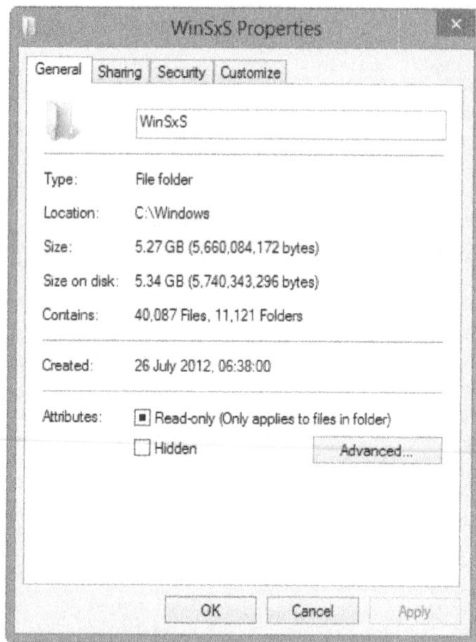

Figure 15-4 The Properties dialog box for the WinSxS folder.

- **64-bit folders** The 64-bit folders include Programs Files and Program Files (x86), with the former including 64-bit programs in the 64-bit version of Windows 8, and the latter including 32-bit software. The SysWOW64 folder, which stands for *Windows on 64-bit Windows*, contains the 32-bit files that are required to maintain full 32-bit compatibility on 64-bit systems.

- **Boot folder** The Boot folder contains files necessary for starting Windows 8.
- **Debug** Debug contains text file error logs that you can open and read.
- **Desktop.ini** Desktop.ini is a file that contains information about folder customization for File Explorer, such as how that folder is displayed.
- **Fonts** The Fonts folder is the main storage folder for Windows fonts.
- **Globalization** The Globalization folder contains the spelling checker and other files related to languages such as language packs for localization.
- **Media** The Media folder contains sound and other files associated with Windows, such as error sounds.
- **Prefetch** Prefetch is the folder that contains preloaded versions of commonly used files. The content of this folder is intended to speed up the loading of some programs and Windows components. If you find that programs you use commonly are not opening or are opening slowly, you can delete the contents of this cache folder; the next time each application starts, the program will rebuild its cache files.
- **Resources** The Resources folder contains desktop and ease-of-access themes for Windows 8.
- **Software Distribution** Software Distribution is the folder used for downloading and storing Windows Updates. If you find that Windows Update isn't working and isn't installing updates, you can delete the contents of this folder to reset the service.
- **System Volume Information** The System Volume Information folder is used by the System Restore feature to store information about changes that have been made to that hard disk. A hidden System Volume Information folder at the root of each disk is monitored by System Restore.
- **System32 \ config** The System32 \ config folder is the main folder for the Windows Registry, the central database for Windows, hardware and software settings, and configuration.
- **Web** Web is the storage location for lock screen and desktop wallpapers.

Location for Windows 8 Apps

If you look in the Program Files folder—or the Program Files (x86) folder, if you are using the 64-bit version of Windows 8—you will see all the folders and files for your installed desktop apps but not your Windows 8 apps! Windows 8 apps are hidden by default in the \Program Files\WindowsApps folder and cannot be opened without changing complex security settings (see Figure 15-5). I do not recommend that you change the security for this folder, because the security is set to prevent malware from tampering with and infecting your apps.

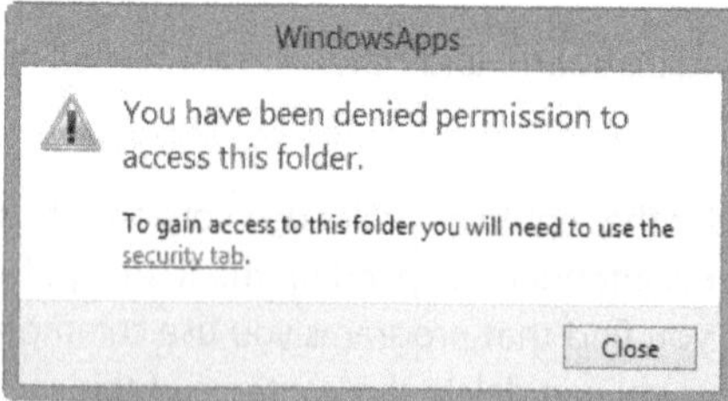

Figure 15-5 Not even an administrator can access the new WindowsApps folder. This is a security measure designed to prevent the spread of malware.

CHAPTER 16

General Windows 8 Troubleshooting Tips

In Sir Arthur Conan Doyle's novel *The Sign of Four*, the second story featuring the world's greatest detective, Sherlock Holmes, the gallant hero makes one of his most famous statements when addressing his loyal friend, Doctor Watson:

> *"When you have eliminated the impossible, whatever remains, however improbable, must be the truth."*

I have always used this theory as the basis for all technical support because it implies that you have to take a methodical, step-by-step approach to diagnosing problems. I find it much easier and quicker to diagnose what isn't causing a problem than to identify what actually is causing it. This is especially true when diagnosing problems with computers, operating systems, and programs, all of which can be extremely complex.

This chapter describes the basics of diagnosing problems you encounter with the Windows operating system. By starting with these methods, you may quickly resolve many problems and issues. Chapter 20, "Using Advanced Repair Methods," through Chapter 25, "Troubleshooting a Windows 8 Installation," provide greater detail on how to diagnose more complex problems with Windows 8 and your computer.

Causes of Common Problems

Windows 8 rarely stops responding unless it experiences a power surge or a sudden reset while Windows is modifying a critical system file. Problems are more commonly caused by something outside of Windows, such as software, updates, and drivers. Physical hardware is also rarely a cause of problems in Windows; the driver usually causes the system to stop responding. (I talk about diagnosing hardware problems in Chapter 24, "Diagnosing Hardware Problems.") The following is a list of common sources of problems:

- Device drivers
- Poorly written software
- Poor security
- BIOS corruption

  For more information about resetting the BIOS, see Chapter 9, "Maintaining Hardware."

The Domino Effect

Some problems can cause a domino effect, whereby one event sets off a string of other events. One unchecked problem leads to others; a malfunctioning process, service, or driver can cause other programs or Windows functions to stop responding, because all these are often shared by several applications or Windows components. So, it's always advisable to diagnose and repair problems as early as you can after they first appear.

For instance, you might have a problem with Windows Internet Explorer not responding. Perhaps a component that Internet Explorer shares with another Windows program (for example, File Explorer) is corrupt. I cover the sometimes complex process of repairing Internet Explorer in Chapter 21, "Demystifying Windows 8 Problems." The source of a problem is not always obvious; a program that is not responding might not be the root cause of the issue. In these cases, you can use more advanced diagnostic methods and tools to diagnose an issue. I cover these in Chapter 20, Chapter 21, and Chapter 23, "Using Remote Help."

Taking a Step-by-Step Approach

Your first step when following the methodical approach to a Windows 8 problem is to perform basic fault isolation by eliminating the impossible. For example, if you suspect Windows on your desktop computer has an instability issue with a hardware device, unplug all the devices that you can (USB flash drives, joysticks, and so on), leaving only the keyboard, the mouse, and the monitor attached. If the problem persists, you have very quickly established that the unplugged devices aren't part of the problem, and you can move on to investigate another cause. But if the problem goes away, you know that one of the unplugged devices is the culprit. Plug in the devices one at a time. When the problem resurfaces, you will have identified which of the devices is at fault.

Similarly, if you suspect that a program is causing a problem, you can exit each program separately. If the problem persists after you exit a particular program, you can eliminate that program as the source of the issue. Likewise, if the problem goes away when all of the programs are exited, you can be reasonably sure that one or more programs are the root of the trouble. This all sounds incredibly simple and straightforward, I know, and I am well aware that there are many occasions when a technique as simple as unplugging hardware and exiting a program doesn't work. However, this process is an essential first step to identifying what really is causing a problem.

At this point in a troubleshooting book, you probably expect to find a large and very complex flowchart to follow: is it A or B? If it's B, go this way and do X, Y, and Z. However, with computers, countless possible issues might cause the problems you encounter, and so any such flowchart would by necessity cover a football field and still might not help you diagnose the problem.

Frequently I encounter a problem that neither I nor my colleagues have ever seen before, even after years of providing IT support. The Microsoft Knowledge Base, which you can access at *http://support.microsoft.com*, contains multitudes of articles about Windows problems and still does not address them all. This is where taking a more structured and step-by-step approach to troubleshooting can help enormously.

Minimizing the Windows Configuration

Sometimes, it's a good idea to begin with the minimum number of programs running and the minimum amount of hardware installed to help diagnose what's causing an issue. The basis of this approach is this statement: reduce your Windows operating system to its minimum configuration to diagnose the problem. You can reduce the number of running programs in several ways. One way is to use the hidden items in the notification area. To access the hidden items in the notification area, click the arrow; this displays some but not all of the programs that are currently running on the computer (see Figure 16-1). To exit a program, right-click it, and then click Exit; or open the program if an exit option doesn't appear so that you can exit the program properly.

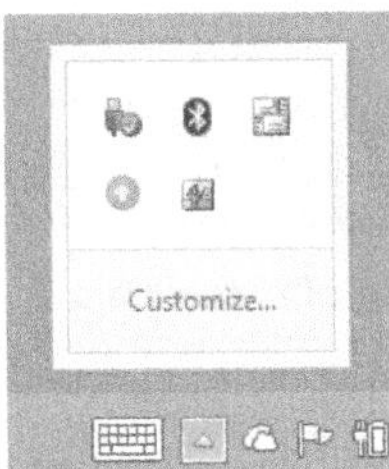

Figure 16-1 You can exit programs from the notification area.

INSIDE OUT How to open Action Center

Sometimes, especially after a new installation of Windows 8, you might not see the Action Center icon in the notification area for a while. To open Action Center without this icon, you can open Control Panel and search for Action Center, or you can search on the Start screen, or you can open the All Icons view.

You also need to exit running apps. The easiest way to do this is on the Start screen. If you point to the upper-left corner of the screen, thumbnail images of any running apps will appear (see Figure 16-2). Right-click each thumbnail, and then click Close to exit the app.

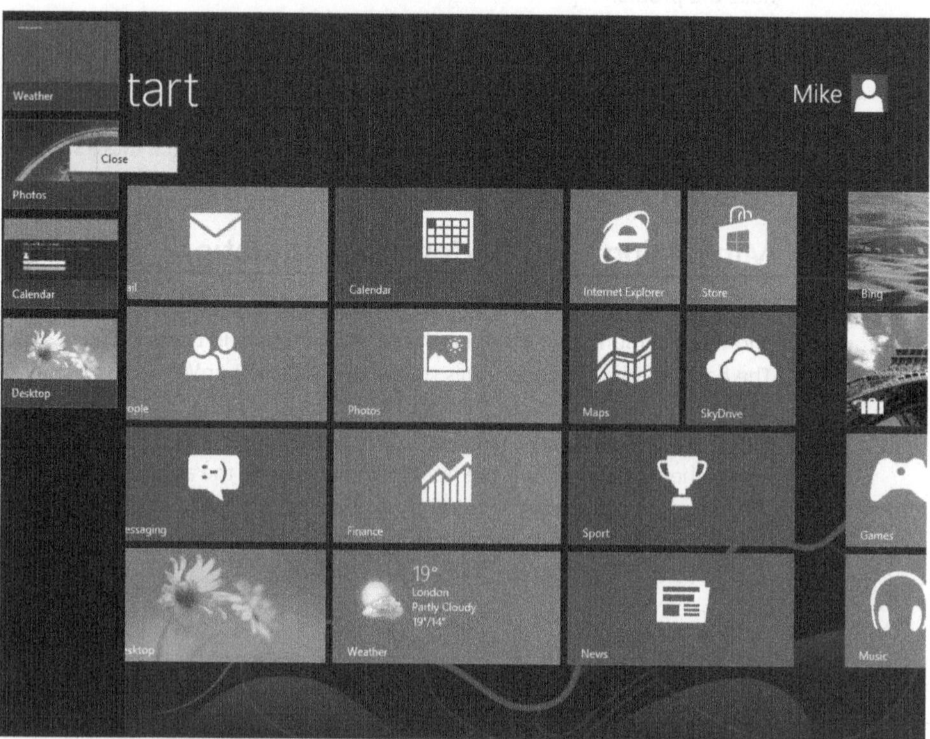

Figure 16-2 You can exit an app by opening the thumbnail list of running apps.

You can also exit programs through Task Manager. To access Task Manager, right-click the taskbar, and then click Task Manager; or press Ctrl+Alt+Del, and then click Task Manager. You can view running applications on the Processes tab. To exit a program, right-click its corresponding process, and then click End Task (see Figure 16-3).

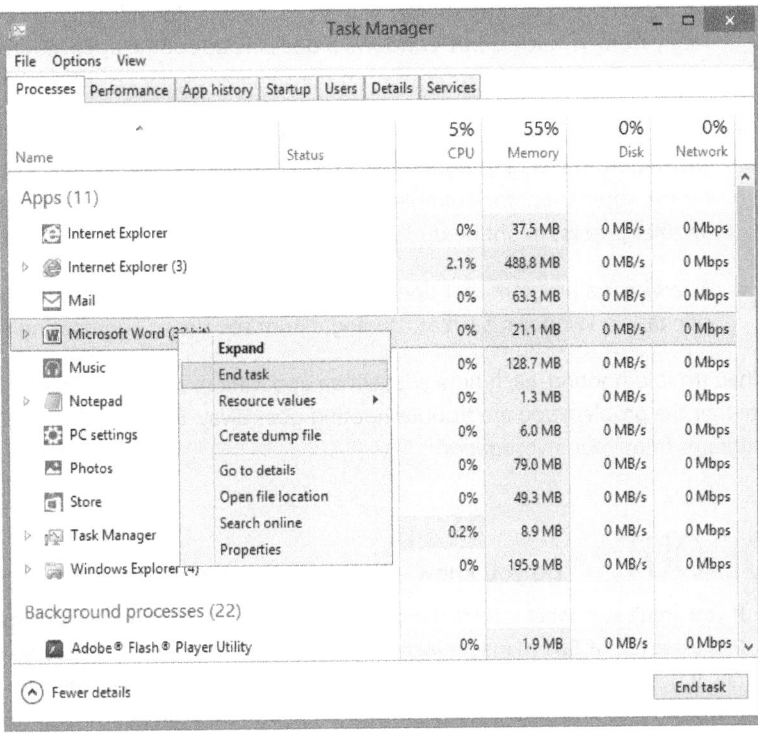

Figure 16-3 Exit programs from Task Manager.

INSIDE OUT Determining what a process does

You can do a quick Internet search using a process name to find out what it is. For example, searching on the process vmusrvc.exe returned the following result: "vmusrvc.exe is a VMUSrvc belonging to Virtual Machine Additions from Microsoft Corporation."

The following list describes how an application, a process, and a service differ. Understanding the differences is important because each performs very different tasks on your computer, and although Windows will happily run with some running, others can cause problems if you exit them:

- An *application* is a program running on your computer. It is typically installed separately from Windows, but Windows 8 does include some applications, including Internet Explorer.
- A *process* is a component for a program or service. Sometimes an application is constructed from several programs that run together, each providing different functions for the application; for example, one process might be running the application, and another process might be updating it.
- A *service* is a program that does not require user interaction and that performs a specific task in Windows, such as running a print spooler or aggregating a media library.

When troubleshooting, each time you exit an application, a process, or a service, determine whether the problem you are troubleshooting goes away. By doing this, you can eliminate programs from your investigation.

INSIDE OUT **Do you know what you're exiting?**

If you aren't sure what a certain process is doing, do not exit it. Each process on the Processes tab of Task Manager includes a description, which is available on the Details tab. If necessary, you can maximize the Task Manager window and adjust the column widths to read the descriptions. However, sometimes, even the descriptions on the Processes tab aren't detailed enough for you to determine what a process is doing. One quick way to establish whether a process is important is to determine where the file that is associated with the process is stored. To do this, right-click the process, and then select Open File Location. If the file is in your Windows folder, you might want to leave the process alone. Exiting the wrong process can cause Windows to become unresponsive or shut down.

CAUTION!

Exiting Windows services is risky. Unless you suspect a specific service is causing your problem, don't exit any Windows service. Doing so can cause Windows 8 to stop responding.

Operating in Safe Mode

Another way to exit all running programs is to restart Windows 8 in Safe Mode. You do this as Windows starts by pressing Shift+F8 on your keyboard after the BIOS screen disappears but before the Starting Windows logo appears.

This method is probably less useful than other methods, because no software will be running (unless it's set as a Windows service, such as antivirus software), and only minimal hardware drivers will be loaded when the computer starts. (*Drivers* are the software interface.) However, if you do restart in Safe Mode and everything is working fine, you can eliminate a problem with your core Windows 8 installation (for example, a corrupt file) as the cause of the problem.

Note

On newer machines, to access Safe Mode, press the Windows Logo key+I, and then click Change PC Settings. In PC Settings, click General and then, in the Advanced Startup area at the bottom right of the screen, click Restart now to force the computer to restart. Nine options appear on the screen that is displayed, including Safe Mode With Networking and Safe Mode With Command Prompt. Pressing F10 is another way to start the recovery environment. Pressing Enter returns to Windows.

Manually Starting Safe Mode

As mentioned in Chapter 14, "Easy Ways to Repair Windows 8," some computers—especially those with Unified Extensible Firmware Interface (UEFI) firmware—won't let you access the boot options menu by pressing F8 or Shift+F8 while the system is starting, so you might need to run Safe Mode manually. (Note that on newer UEFI-enabled computers, the time you have to press F8 is only about 200 milliseconds, so you'll probably still need to run Safe Mode manually). You can even lock the computer in Safe Mode for a period of time.

To start Safe Mode manually, on the Start screen, type **msconfig** to open the System Configuration dialog box. Click the Boot tab (see Figure 16-4), select the Safe Boot check box, and then click the Minimal option (which will become enabled after you select Safe Boot). By default, System Configuration selects a minimal Safe Boot; this is the Safe Mode you may have used in earlier versions of Windows.

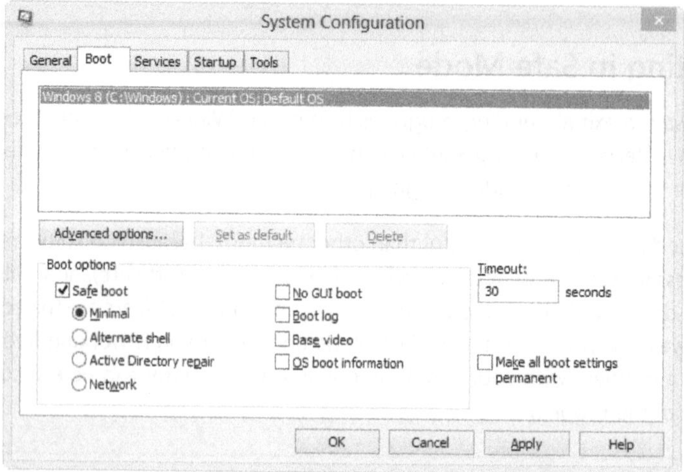

Figure 16-4 Set Safe Mode in MSConfig for the next restart.

The next time you start Windows 8, Windows 8 starts in Safe Mode, and it will continue to do so when you restart it. To revert to starting the system normally, you must open System Configuration again and clear the Safe Boot check box.

Note

If you need to have network access in Safe Mode to help diagnose a problem, in System Configuration, click the Network option under Safe Boot instead of clicking Minimal.

Checking Hardware and Interrupt Requests

Interrupt requests (IRQs) are communications channels that your hardware uses to send and receive data. They're called *interrupts* because it's impossible for every device to talk to the computer's motherboard simultaneously, and communications channels must take turns, with one channel interrupting another to take over. Windows 8 also uses IRQs to manage the power usage on a computer, ensuring that all devices receive the power they require to function. There are 15 IRQ channels in a computer; any additional IRQs are virtual channels for which Windows 8 handles all the communication.

Windows 8 handles interrupt requests very effectively, but in rare cases, an IRQ-related problem may occur, for example, with a poorly written driver. This can cause some hardware to stop responding or seem to malfunction. Conflicts are more likely if you are using earlier hardware (some laptops still ship with serial and parallel ports for this very reason).

Sometimes IRQ conflicts are caused by a device appearing twice in Device Manager. To resolve this issue, right-click one of the duplicate devices, and then click Uninstall.

To check IRQs, in Device Manager, on the View menu, click Resources By Type, and then expand the list of device IRQs by clicking the arrow next to Interrupt Request (IRQ). Right-click the device, and then click Properties to open the Properties dialog box. In the Properties dialog box, click the Resources tab. You will see a list of the IRQ assignments for your hardware (see Figure 16-5).

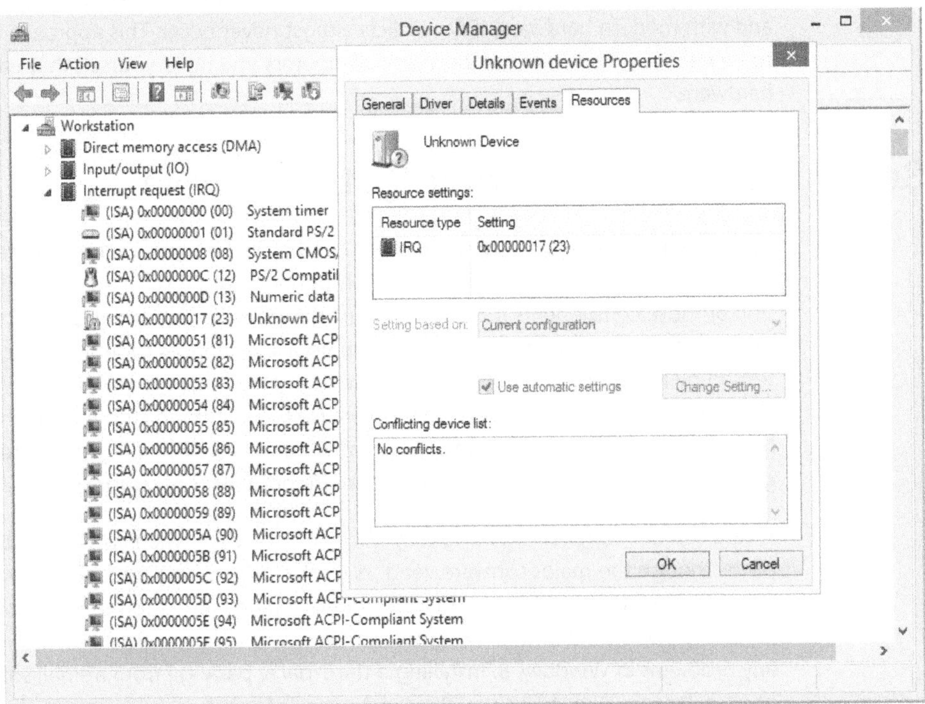

Figure 16-5 You can view devices by IRQ.

The more hardware devices you have plugged into a computer, the more they must share the IRQs. Windows 8 is extremely good at sharing the IRQs, but occasionally two hardware devices sharing the same IRQ causes communication problems. To see whether one or more IRQs are being shared by multiple devices, view Resources By Type in Device Manager, as described earlier in this section. On the Resources tab, the Conflicting Device List box will indicate whether there are any conflicts for this device as a result of IRQ sharing (see Figure 16-5).

In Windows 8, you can't manually change the IRQ of a device. However, you can move the device to a different channel. This might involve moving a peripheral component interconnect (PCI) card inside your computer to a different slot (be sure that your computer is turned off and disconnected from its power source before you do this). Moving the component will force Windows 8 to reassign the device a new IRQ, possibly fixing the problem. With some motherboards, you can manually set IRQs for devices in the BIOS. Windows 8 may, however, ignore this BIOS setting and reassign the IRQ anyway. For a new computer that comes with Windows 8 and that you do not upgrade, you won't need to do this, because OEMs check for potential issues such as IRQ conflicts before shipping machines, and with modern hardware, IRQ conflicts almost never occur. This approach is more likely to be necessary in earlier computers or computers you build yourself that contain earlier hardware.

Best Practice: Keeping Your System Simple

Issues occur with Windows because every computer is unique. Each computer comprises a custom mix of programs and hardware components, and testing every possible combination of those components for stability is just not possible. Although logo certification programs for Windows hardware and software do allow vendors to submit their products for testing by Microsoft, the tests only validate that, on a basic system running Windows, the device or program is stable and does not cause the system to stop responding. What can't be tested is how that same hardware or software will interact with other hardware or programs on your computer, some of which might not have been submitted for certification.

A case can be made for choosing only Microsoft software when you have a choice of suppliers, though the major software vendors work closely with Microsoft to ensure their software works without problems. Microsoft has complete access to the Windows base code, so you can be confident that Microsoft software will almost always operate without causing any problems in Windows 8. Installing a third-party package from a small software vendor or a freelancer will not give you the same peace of mind.

The sheer number of programs you have installed or the number of hardware devices you have plugged in can cause problems on your computer. I always keep my Windows systems uncomplicated. As for hardware, I like multifunctional devices such as printer/scanner combinations, and I avoid unnecessary USB devices, such as USB-attached speakers. Your computer already comes with good audio jacks. Ideally, this won't cause any performance problems with the operating system, but I would recommend that you install only those apps and programs that you actually need and will use regularly.

I also try to avoid installing all the programs that come with a new device. Devices, Wi-Fi adapters, and printers are common culprits because they load your computer with programs that install multiple applications, sometimes referred to as *software bloat*. When you buy a new computer, the OEM might pre-load it with software and utilities they think will be useful for you. You might personally not need some or all of these and in this circumstance you can uninstall them. The programs that come bundled with hardware devices broadly fall into the following categories:

- Software that expires after a certain period of time, typically 30 days. If you do not intend to buy the software after this time, you should uninstall it because it might, especially in the case of trial antivirus software, leave programs and services running that can slow down Windows 8 or cause other problems.
- Programs that duplicate Windows features such as Wi-Fi connection software, media players, or CD/DVD burners.
- Utilities that your computer supplier might have preloaded onto your computer. They are intended to simplify certain tasks, such as writing notes or accessing media files. They always run when Windows starts, even though you will probably never use them.

Finally, avoid installing programs that duplicate features in Windows. The more software you install on your computer, the harder it can become to diagnose the cause of problems. If at all possible, avoid having software packages installed that duplicate functionality already in Windows such as CD/DVD burning software, if for no other reason than you really don't need them anyway.

Note

Occasionally, you will find a useful utility that comes with hardware, for example, printer status (and ink/toner) monitoring, a document scanning utility, or an overclocking utility for your gaming graphics card. (*Overclocking* is the process of making a computer or component operate faster than the clock frequency specified by the manufacturer by modifying system parameters.) These programs are fine to keep on your computer if you use them.

INSIDE OUT **The media player exception**

The only possible exception I would make to the rule about not installing duplicate programs is media player software. If you have an iPhone, iPad, or iPod, you will need to install Apple iTunes software on your computer to synchronize your device. Many people find the iTunes software very good and like shopping in the iTunes store.

Turning the Computer Off and On

When you call an IT support department, the first question a support person is likely to ask you is this: "Have you tried turning the computer off and on again?" You might be amazed by how often it fixes problems! It might not be a permanent fix when something more serious is happening, but on occasion, restarting the computer will fix the problem. Unresponsive software is common, but just because a program doesn't respond once does not mean it will continue to be unresponsive. Unresponsive software can be caused by unlikely conditions that may not recur, such as two programs trying to access the same file simultaneously. Also, restart all external hardware devices attached to your computer when you restart the computer by manually turning them off and on again (if they have on/off switches).

Stopping the Perpetual Restart

Sometimes Windows 8 will automatically restart when it encounters a critical error. This can cause the computer to constantly restart and never start Windows. You can disable automatic restart on the startup menu shown in Figure 16-6. To access this menu, when Windows starts, press Shift+F8 on your keyboard after the BIOS screen disappears but before the Windows logo appears.

To get to this from the standard F8 boot options menu, click Troubleshoot, click Advanced Options, and then click Startup Settings.

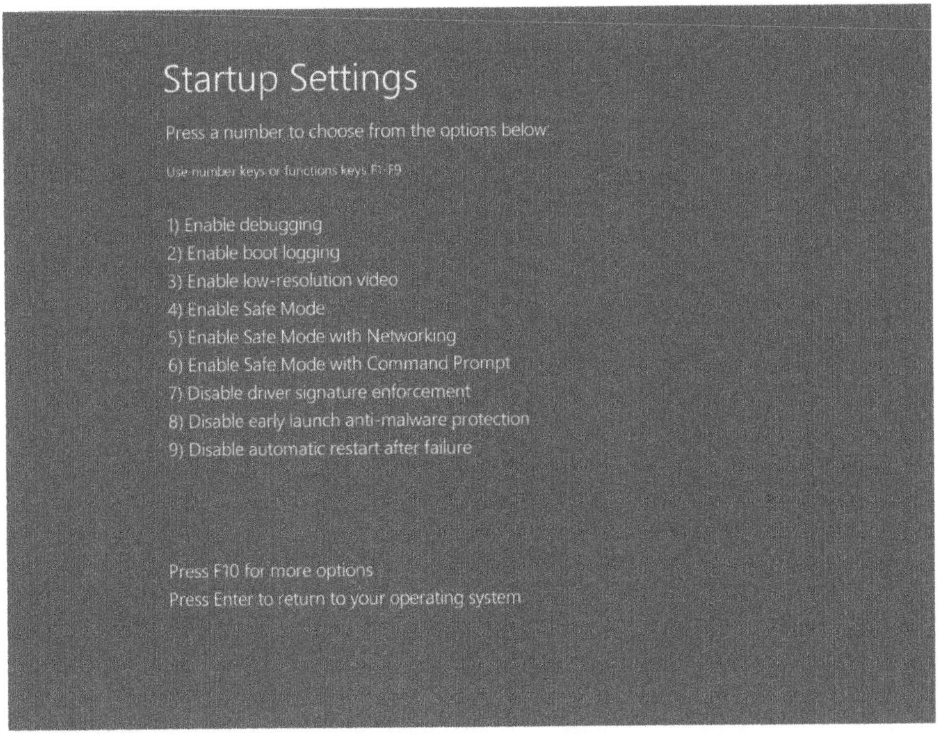

Startup Settings

Press a number to choose from the options below:

Use number keys or functions keys F1-F9.

1) Enable debugging
2) Enable boot logging
3) Enable low-resolution video
4) Enable Safe Mode
5) Enable Safe Mode with Networking
6) Enable Safe Mode with Command Prompt
7) Disable driver signature enforcement
8) Disable early launch anti-malware protection
9) Disable automatic restart after failure

Press F10 for more options

Press Enter to return to your operating system

Figure 16-6 You can disable Windows automatic restart when the system stops responding.

INSIDE OUT You can't open the Windows startup menu

Earlier in this chapter, in the section "Manually Starting Safe Mode," I mentioned that on modern UEFI systems, the time you have to press the F8 or Shift+F8 key is just *200 milliseconds*. On BIOS systems, you also have a short timeframe in which you can press this key combination.

If you can't prevent a perpetual restart, you will need to start your computer from a rescue disc, a restore drive, or your Windows 8 installation DVD, and then run System Restore or Refresh to reset the system to a stable condition.

On the Startup Settings screen, click Disable Automatic Restart On System Failure from the options (see Figure 16-6). At the next unrecoverable hardware or software problem, Windows will display the error message on the blue screen instead of automatically restarting. You might discover that after making a note of the stop error code, you can start your computer in Safe Mode.

CHAPTER 17

Environmental Factors Affecting Your Computer

An important consideration when troubleshooting issues with a computer running Windows 8 is the influence of factors external to your computer. These factors can be increasingly problematic the more you are connected to devices such as tablets, smartphones, game consoles, and Network Access Storage (NAS) drives: the more those devices are connected to each other, the more the people you live and work with are connected to those devices, too. For this reason, I always encourage people to look at troubleshooting in a holistic way and to consider how factors in the environment might be influencing or directly causing problems. This chapter helps you determine which factors might be causing your problems.

Look around a typical home, and you will find a number of devices that attach to a broadband router and home network. These can include several different smartphones, running a variety of operating systems; tablets, for which the variety in operating systems can be even more diverse; game consoles, with operating system diversity; USB-attached hard disks plugged into the router or NAS; Voice over Internet Protocol (VoIP) telephones, which are increasingly popular with the move to fiber-optic broadband lines; and, of course, the devices that nearly every home has—laptops and desktop computers. Even the kitchen and bathroom are wired for Internet-connected fridges, microwave ovens, and intelligent bathroom mirrors. The household that once had 2 or 3 devices with their own IP addresses now has 20.

The workplace can be even more complicated than the home. A network that is based on IPv4, for which the maximum number of available IP addresses that can be allocated by your router is 256, will reach its ceiling fairly quickly when workers start connecting their smartphones and tablets, especially if you already have many computers and laptops in the office.

Offices commonly reduce costs by using central servers, accessed via a secure Internet connection, and have only some network storage and a network switch box to manage computers, printers, and other devices internally. A server system in an office has software managing and regulating the allocation and distribution of IP addresses for hardware. Take away the server, and the workplace environment can become much less manageable.

Your IT infrastructure doesn't end at your front door, whether you're in the office or at home. You are connected to your broadband network either through your local telephone exchange or through a dedicated server data center. Cables are laid under pathways and roads and run around and through buildings and maintenance sites; other external hardware over which you have no direct control is, too.

Any fault somewhere in a data center you use or at your Internet Service Provider (ISP) will have a ripple effect. These are usually easy faults to spot because they affect all computers simultaneously. You might have a file server in your office, however, that is not responding, because it alone connects to a virtual private network (VPN). And perhaps that VPN is inaccessible and is trying to perform an action that is causing it to time out or seem frozen as a result of data traffic not getting through.

Although many factors, both inside and outside your home or office, can affect your computers and your network, you will rarely find external factors affecting just a single computer. This can make those factors simple to diagnose. It is the internal hardware and factors that can cause problems more directly for individual computers. This chapter helps you determine which factors might be causing your problems.

Diagnosing and Repairing Network Issues

Some of the most common problems associated with external factors are related to the network. These same problems can also be caused by issues on your own computer, however, so you need to determine whether the issue is external or internal. This section discusses how to diagnose and repair problems on your own computer when the network is involved.

Two types of Wi-Fi connection issues exist: issues related to connecting to a public network, including mobile broadband; and issues related to connecting to your own network.

The first question to ask regarding a public Wi-Fi, 3G, or 4G network connection is how many people are using it. If you suspect that many people are connected or that your issue is occurring during a busy period for the network, such as during a festival or civil emergency, when mobile networks typically become clogged with traffic, you might find that waiting for a few minutes and trying again permits a connection.

With mobile broadband, and indeed on your smartphone, the display of four signal bars doesn't necessarily guarantee a connection. Even though the signal might be strong, only so much bandwidth is available to go around, and the network is configured to reject phone calls and broadband connections when not enough bandwidth is available on a given cell tower to support them.

The same might be the case with public networks in coffee shops or other hot spots. A connection at that time might not be possible because a router failure or similar technical error is occurring. The best way to diagnose a problem is to determine whether any other computer users are also having difficulty. Remember, though, that someone using a computer or tablet might not necessarily be connected to the same network you're trying to access.

Internet Connections

One of the most significant improvements to Windows 8, at least when it comes to diagnosing network problems, is the improved Task Manager. You can access this either by pressing Ctrl+Alt+Del or by right-clicking the taskbar.

On the Performance tab in Task Manager, you can see each of your network connections, including your Wi-Fi, LAN, and Mobile Broadband, with live data about upload and download activity displayed in graphs, as illustrated in Figure 17-1. When you're experiencing a problem, check this first so that you can determine whether you have any live network activity.

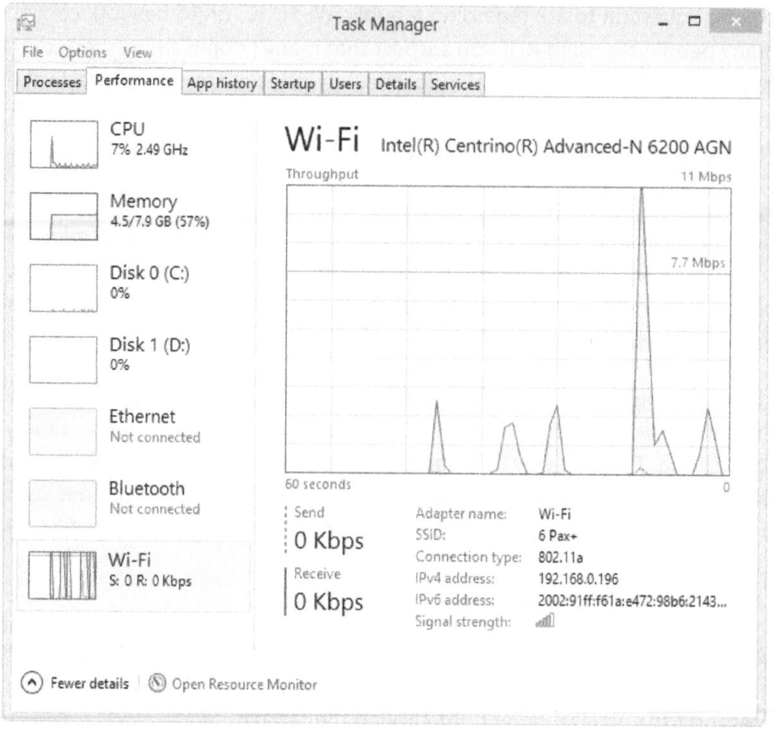

Figure 17-1 The Performance tab in Task Manager.

You can click any of the connections to display additional information, such as numeric details of the current upload and download speeds, your IPv4 and IPv6 addresses, and signal strength, if applicable.

At the bottom of this window is the Open Resource Monitor link. Click this to open Resource Monitor, which displays activity for all processes, services, and programs that are running Windows for the current live network (see Figure 17-2).

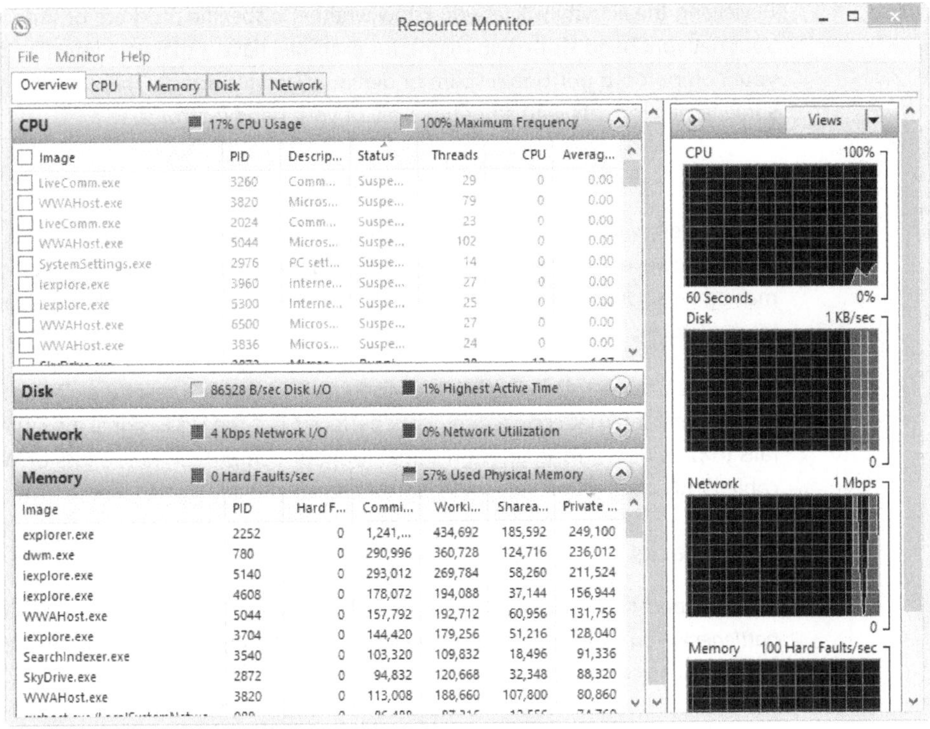

Figure 17-2 The Windows 8 Resource Monitor.

> **INSIDE OUT** **Resetting TCP/IP in your computer**
>
> Sometimes, network problems in your computer are caused by the TCP/IP stack becoming corrupt. You can easily reset the TCP/IP stack in Windows 8 by opening a Command Prompt (Admin) window, typing the command **netsh int ip reset resetlog.txt**, and then pressing Enter.

Reviewing the activity will let you know whether a specific program or service is using all your network bandwidth. You might, for example, have a malware infection that is using your computer to perform a spam or denial-of-service attack. These attacks typically consume large amounts, and sometimes all, of your bandwidth.

Routers

The simplest way to fix a problem with a router is to turn it off and on again. Before you do this, however, you should check whether anyone is successfully connected to it and is making a call on a VoIP system. Resetting the router will temporarily cut people off from Internet access.

Sometimes, routers drop the Internet connection and need resetting. Other times, wired network and Internet connections work perfectly, but the Wi-Fi signal from the same router fails to provide a strong enough signal for your computer. Thus, a loss of Wi-Fi when a cabled LAN connection still works doesn't mean you shouldn't reset the router.

Bottlenecks

If you suspect that a program or service is using up all your network bandwidth, creating a *bottleneck*, you can exit it. To do this, go to Task Manager and click the Processes tab. Right-click the suspicious program or service, and then click End Task.

If you can't diagnose and repair the problem from Task Manager, open the Network And Sharing Center (see Figure 17-3) to display information pertaining to your network connection. To do this, right-click the Network icon on the taskbar, and then click Open Network And Sharing Center.

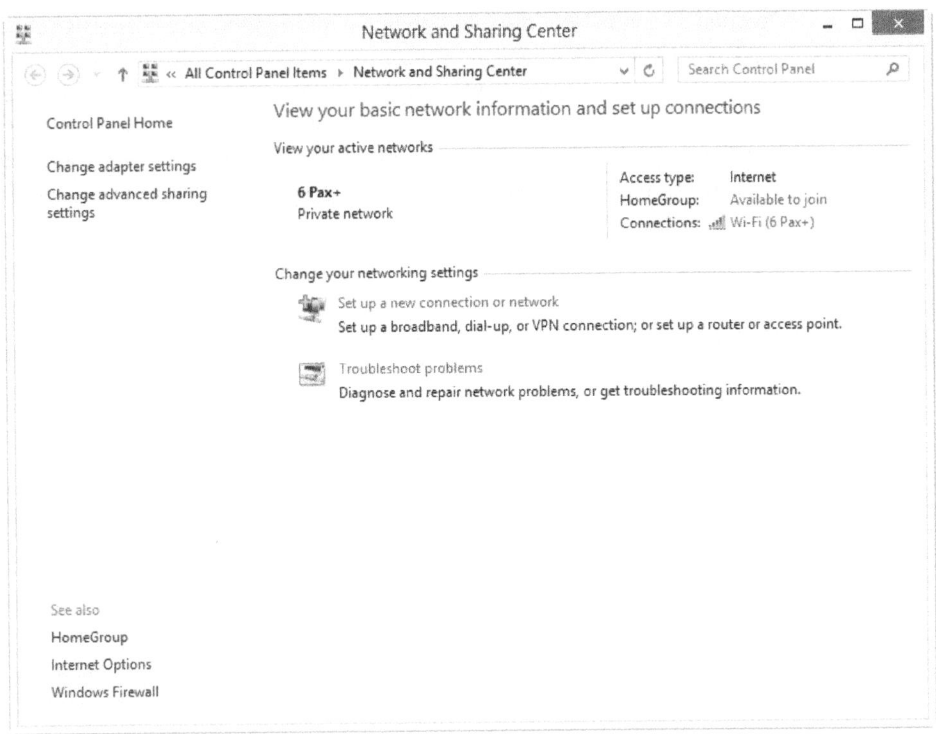

Figure 17-3 The Network And Sharing Center provides tools to help you diagnose and repair network problems.

You can perform automatic troubleshooting in the Network And Sharing Center, too. Start the automated troubleshooter by clicking the Troubleshoot Problems link (or right-click the Network icon on the taskbar and then click Troubleshoot Problems). The automated troubleshooters of Windows 8 reset components to their default configurations, but in the context of network problems, that might be exactly what you need, especially if a problem such as configuration files becoming corrupt occurs.

To open a window that displays additional information and properties about your network connection, click the connection's name. Windows informs you whether it detects Internet connectivity and shows statistics on precisely how much data has been sent and received since you connected, including the amount of time you have been connected (see Figure 17-4). You might, for example, find that Windows keeps dropping your connection, in which case the connection time shown for Duration will be short.

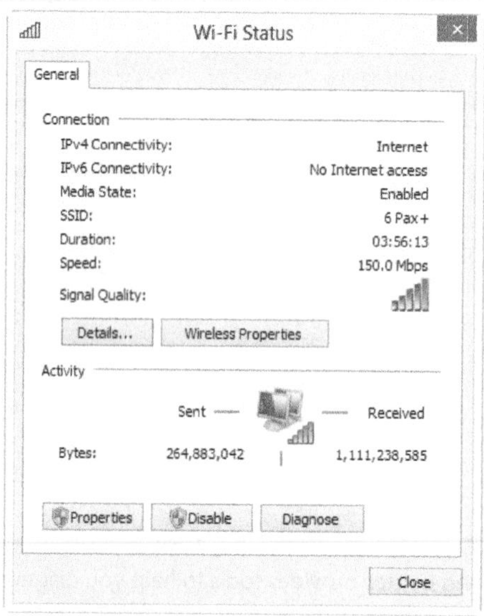

Figure 17-4 You can find out about signal quality, speed, and the duration of your connection to help you troubleshoot issues.

To display the network properties for a connection, click the Properties button. In the Properties dialog box that opens (see Figure 17-5), you can see the services that are running for the network connection, such as IPv6 and IPv4. These services could potentially cause problems on some networks if they are incorrectly configured for IPv6, and almost certainly if you have accidentally disabled IPv4 on your computer's network connection protocol in the networking settings.

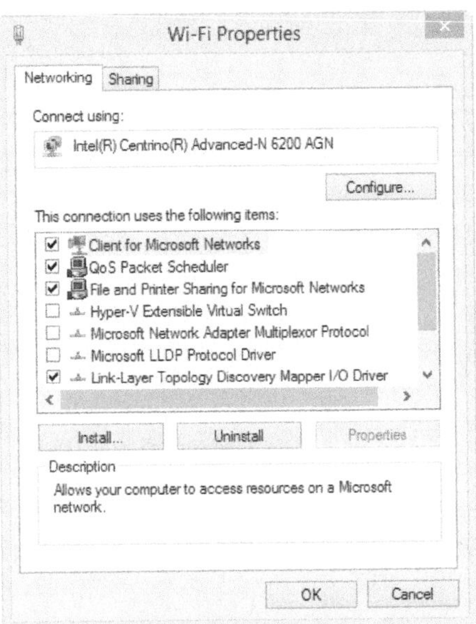

Figure 17-5 Change the settings for a property by selecting it and clicking Properties.

Click the Configure button to open the adapter's Properties dialog box, in which you can check the status of the hardware driver. Click the Events tab to obtain information about the connections that a particular network adapter has made.

I mentioned earlier the possible incompatibilities with the relatively new IPv6 standard. If you have earlier network hardware or are perhaps using your computer in a place where IPv6 has become the norm and IPv4 services might be switched off, you can select or clear the check boxes for these services as needed to turn them on or off, respectively.

With Internet Protocol Version 4 (TCP/IPv4) highlighted, click the Properties button in the This Connection Uses The Following Items section to open the Internet Protocol Version 4 (TCP/IPv4) Properties window (see Figure 17-6).

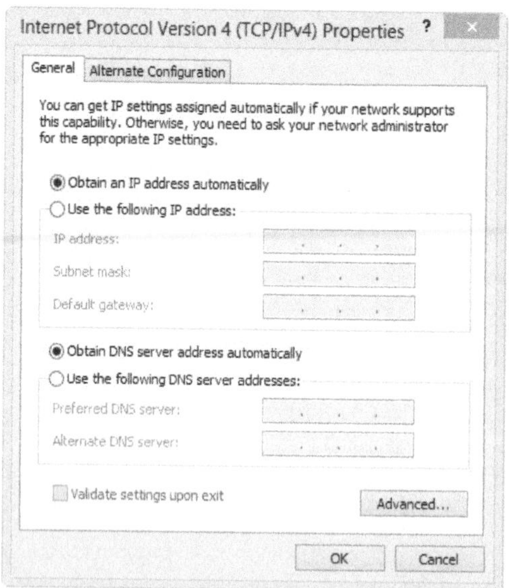

Figure 17-6 When you change the settings for a network protocol, the information you can change in the dialog box will vary. For example, you can change the IPv4 settings by manually setting an IP address and DNS server address.

You can set static IP and DNS server addresses for the network if the connection requires them. For example, you might be having trouble connecting to a business network; this could indicate that you're on the wrong workgroup (more on this shortly) or that the network requires you to enter specific IP and DNS address information. Click the Advanced button to display additional options you can set if you are connecting to a dial-up network.

INSIDE OUT Changing the Windows 8 workgroup or domain

You can change workgroup and domain settings in the System tool in Control Panel if your computer is connected to the wrong workgroup or domain (which is more likely to occur in a work environment). To do this, on the Start screen, search for system in Settings results. When the System tool opens, click Change Settings to open the System Properties dialog box.

Wi-Fi Passwords

Occasionally, you might try to connect to a Wi-Fi network, but the password stored on your computer isn't the one the router is expecting, and Windows won't prompt you to re-enter the password. In this case, go to Network And Sharing Center, click the name of the network to open the network status, and then click Wireless Properties. On the Security tab (see Figure 17-7), you can change the security type and password for that particular wireless network. Click Advanced Settings for an extra setting that might be required when connecting to certain government-related or other secure networks.

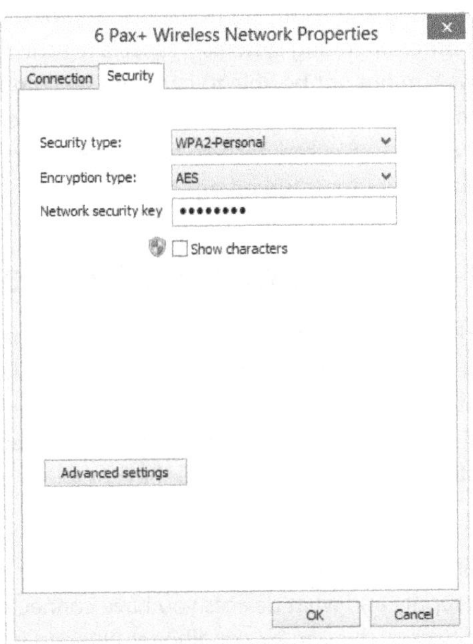

Figure 17-7 When changing the settings for a wireless network, you can change the logon security type, the encryption type, and the network security key.

Network Equipment

How do you diagnose issues with hardware? If you are in an office, for example, and have multiple computers at your disposal, you can first determine whether the problem exists for computers besides yours. Suppose that some computers have a good network connection but yours does not. Could the connection be faulty?

To check out this situation, on the network switch panel, find the plug for the faulty computer and find another for a computer that's working properly. Swap the plugs to see if the other computer experiences the same problem.

If you are using a hardware appliance designed to block certain traffic types, you can temporarily disconnect and bypass the device. Be aware that some corporate networks are designed to not operate at all if appliances such as SonicWalls and firewalls can't be detected by a remote server.

Determine whether you have an IP address conflict that is causing problems. Windows 8 is generally very good at both detecting and rectifying problems caused by IP address conflicts, but computers running other operating systems—especially earlier ones—might cause conflicts for which Windows 8 might not be able to compensate completely. In this case, you can try turning off all the other computers and network devices temporarily—you will probably want to restart the Windows 8 computer also to determine whether the problem remains when only a particular computer is turned on.

Managing Peripherals and Equipment on a Network

Whether you are at home or working in an office, security is a critical part of maintaining a healthy and trouble-free network. Without the correct security in place, malware can easily move from one device or computer to another. You shouldn't consider different operating systems as being immune to this. A specific piece of malware might not infect a computer running a different operating system, but files transferred to that computer and then onto others can still result in infection.

Many factors can affect the stability and reliability of devices on your home or work network, for example, the electricity supply and what devices you have connected to which socket. If you have a high-draw device such as an air-conditioner plugged into the same circuit as a computer, the sudden drop or spike that results from this device when it turns on and off, respectively, could be enough to cause a power interruption that can cause Windows to stop responding. When this happens, operating system files or files associated with your software can stop responding. And, of course, you can lose documents that were open at the time.

INSIDE OUT **Always use a surge protector**

You should always ensure that computer equipment is plugged into a spike/surge protector on your electricity supply. The components inside modern electronics work on micro-voltages, and spikes and surges, especially in areas with unreliable electricity service, can be enough to destroy sensitive modern electronics.

Turning off equipment when you don't need it is also important. If you leave many devices plugged into your computer for extended periods of time, you are possibly inviting problems. At the very least, you could slow down the operating system, because it occasionally starts a USB hard disk for defragmentation, backup, or other automated functions. Poorly written drivers can create incompatibilities with your currently running software and other hardware, although this scenario is rare. The cost-saving benefits alone is usually reason enough to turn devices off when they're not in use.

The same advice applies for equipment attached to your network. Avoid network slowdowns caused by computers constantly contacting a file server or the NAS drive that is left on, including during nights and weekends. The longer amount of time that computers are left on, the shorter their lifespan will be, and this also applies to computers running Windows 8 and the hardware attached to them, such as monitors.

INSIDE OUT **The heating and cooling of microelectronics**

Modern electronics are commonly made of metals. As you heat up a metal, it expands. When the metal cools, it contracts. In a computer, the process of general use will cause the components within it to heat up, and consequently expand. Over a long period of time, this creates stress on the metal and can result in it fracturing. Thus, some argue that you can improve the longevity of these devices by leaving them turned on, but modern electronics are fairly resilient, and I would personally prefer to turn devices off, but this is a personal decision.

Similarly—and this was once explained to me in detail by a physicist who was very excited talking about it—in devices that are moved around a lot, such as a smartphone, tablet, or radio, the constant movement of the device places additional stresses on the electronics, exacerbating the effect of heating and cooling the metals.

Educating Employees About the Use of Personal Devices

Should staff be allowed to use their own computing devices in the workplace for business tasks, or use their own computers when working from home? Many IT professionals are concerned about the practice of staff members using their own devices for work on secure business networks. Indeed, there is good reason for being concerned. IT departments do not have control over the security on personal devices, and they also have no control over who uses them.

If you are an IT administrator, assume that it is inevitable that people will use their own laptops, tablets, and smartphones more and more frequently in the business space in the coming years. Education about how to keep these devices secure will be important.

If you are a worker who wants to use your own computing device in the workplace and can see no reason why this shouldn't be allowed, but the IT department says you can't, assume there is a good reason. However, if you ensure that your computer is regularly updated with security and other patches, run active and regularly updated antivirus software, don't install every piece of software that comes along, and know how to keep yourself and your computer safe online, you have a reasonable argument for using your own computer. Keeping the children away from the device would also be a very good idea.

Although computers are flexible devices with many uses, business has for many years struck the right balance by using different disk images for a single computer so that you can have a computer for sales or accounting or management, but not a computer for everything at the same time.

It's a good idea to have a specific computer dedicated for a specific task. In my own home/work environment, I have a laptop that I use exclusively for work. I also have a tablet that I use exclusively for light web browsing, email, and games. This way, I can keep things neat and separated.

If you have a laptop that you use for work, it's wise not to let the children (or anybody else) use it. You might expose yourself to data protection and legal issues as a result of such use; downtime is very costly for a business and frustrating for the user.

Although IT departments don't like staff members running Windows Update on their own computers—we prefer a centralized management system—it is good to show users how they can do this in case they need to.

If you are on the IT staff, explain to employees the context for these policies and explain the threats. Chapter 13, "Responding to Viruses, Malware, and Other Threats," is a good resource that can help in this regard. Tell employees how to ensure that they stay safe online and what to look for. You could point out that the way an IT department manages computers is very much the way families with young children manage their computers. Parents don't want their kids to install just any program, make critical changes to a computer, or look at inappropriate web content. By doing this, you are not only helping yourself, you are helping them, too, and they will be grateful for having learned something that will be genuinely valuable to them and their families (what they learn for their work devices extends to personal devices).

Managing the Family on Your Computers

How do you, as a computer user, manage your own home devices that are running Windows 8? This section describes the best way to keep your family and children safe and how you can ensure that visitors to your home use your devices responsibly.

Best Practice for Managing User Accounts in Windows 8

In the same way that you have your own carefully managed logon with strict permissions in the workplace, you should have logons with strict permissions at home. Never allow children to have an administrator account. Administrators can make any changes they want to Windows 8, including installing new software, changing critical operating system settings, or even deleting parts of the operating system.

You can create new user accounts in PC Settings, and by default Windows 8 will prompt you to make all new accounts standard users, and this is what I would recommend. To access Windows 8 Family Safety, on the Start screen, search for **family** in Settings search results.

Using Family Safety in Windows 8

The Family Safety options in Windows 8 (see Figure 17-8) are excellent. They include the ability to control what times and on what days the computer can be used by a specific user, the games that user is allowed to play according to particular ratings (though bear in mind that this is by no means a catch all), what programs the user is allowed to use (though this control is fiddly), and most important, what types of websites the user is allowed to visit.

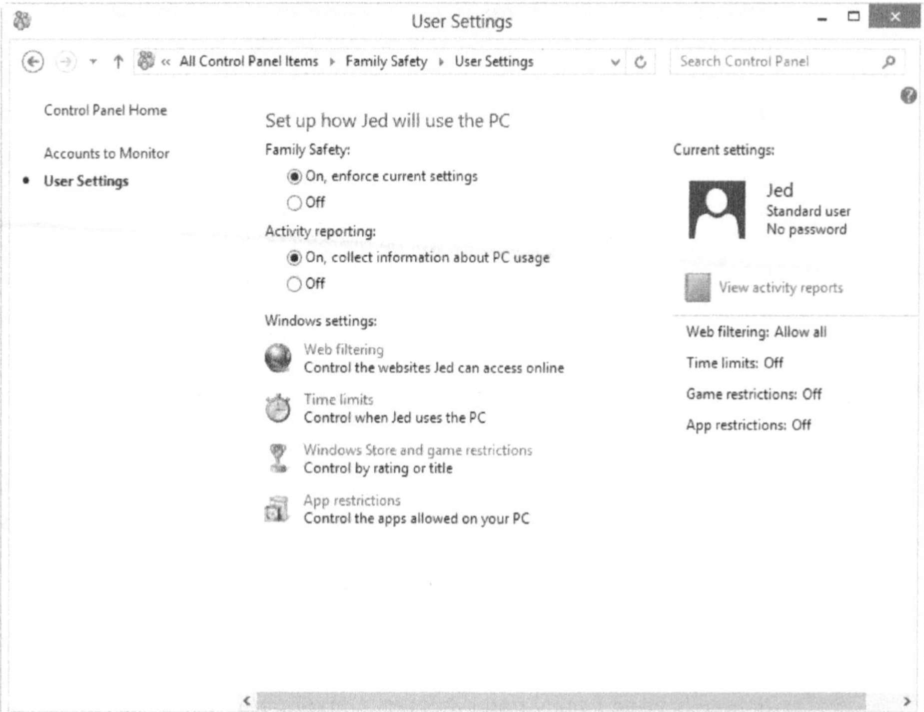

Figure 17-8 You can use family safety settings to set limits for children and also work staff.

Settings include blocking certain websites, such as social networks, and blocking the playing of games on the computer. For small organizations, this can be a cost-effective alternative to dedicated business server tools.

These controls are simple to set up and use, and Windows prompts you if you have not performed an important task such as set a password on your Administrator account before configuring Family Safety.

Family Safety can help considerably toward maintaining a healthy Windows 8 system, as can having separate standard user accounts. These users cannot make any changes to Windows that will affect any other user, significantly reducing the chance of accidental changes that could cause the computer to perform in an unexpected way.

Using the Windows 8 Guest Account

Another feature for which you need to go to the desktop is the Windows 8 guest account. You can access this in the Users section of Control Panel, or by opening the Start screen and searching for **guest** in Settings.

Figure 17-9 shows the Manage Accounts dialog box, in which you can turn the guest account on and off. The Guest account has minimal permissions, but to ensure that you maintain the maximum security, you should have a password on your own account. This password prevents a guest user from passing through User Account Control (UAC) controls and changing critical Windows settings or installing software.

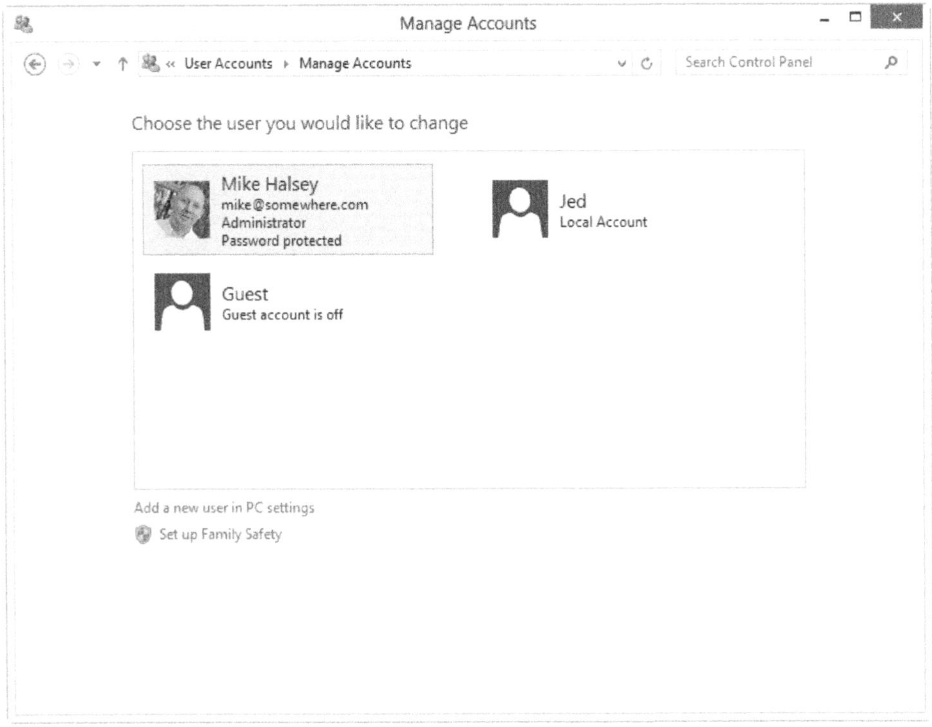

Figure 17-9 You can switch user accounts by using the Windows 8 guest account feature.

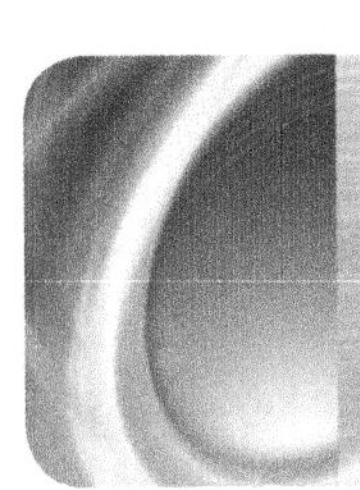

CHAPTER 18

Troubleshooting Windows 8 Startup Issues

THE QUESTION I AM ASKED MOST OFTEN IS HOW TO FIX A PROBLEM involving the Windows startup process. Your computer isn't much use to you if you can't start it and get to the logon screen. The startup system for Windows changed significantly in Windows Vista, and it has changed again in Windows 8. Windows 8 provides a Start screen and supports new features such as the Trusted Boot. This chapter explores how to address issues when Windows won't start.

Using Windows Startup Repair

The easiest way to repair a faulty Windows 8 startup process is by using Startup Repair. Startup Repair runs automatically when the computer does not start after three attempts, but you can also run it manually in one of the following four ways:

- Press F8 on your keyboard when Windows starts, click Troubleshoot, and then on the Troubleshoot page, click Advanced Options.
- Press Shift+F8 when Windows starts, and then click Repair Your Computer.
- Press Shift while restarting your computer.
- In PC Settings, click General, and then in the Advanced Startup section, click Restart Now.

On the Advanced Options page, which you access from the Windows boot options menu (also referred to as the Windows Recovery Environment, Windows RE, or WinRE menu in earlier versions of Windows), you can use System Restore to roll back your system if you suspect that a recent update, hardware, or software installation has caused your computer to become unstable.

Note

Windows 8 starts so quickly that you might not have enough time to press a key to display the startup menu, especially on computers with Unified Extensible Firmware Interface (UEFI) firmware. If you can't start Windows to activate the boot options menu, start your computer from a system repair disc, restore drive, or your Windows 8 installation media. When the Install screen appears, click Repair Your Computer.

You can restore from a system image if you have made one, or you can run the Automatic Repair tool (see Figure 18-1).

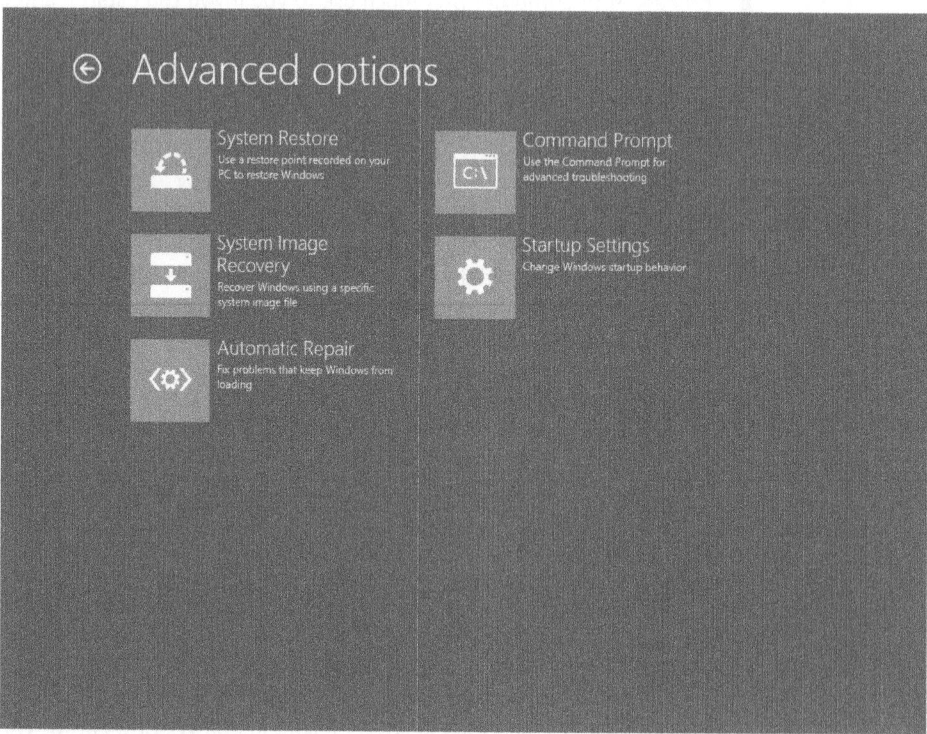

Figure 18-1 The boot options menu offers tools for repairing and resetting Windows 8 in a wide variety of ways. This screen is not compatible with screen readers.

The Automatic Repair option resets the Windows startup system to its default configuration, so it is worth a try in many circumstances. However, sometimes you cannot use this option. For example, Automatic Repair cannot fix a corrupt boot partition. If Automatic Repair is unable to fix the problem, it will create a log file (see Figure 18-2) that you can read (perhaps on another computer), containing information about the error.

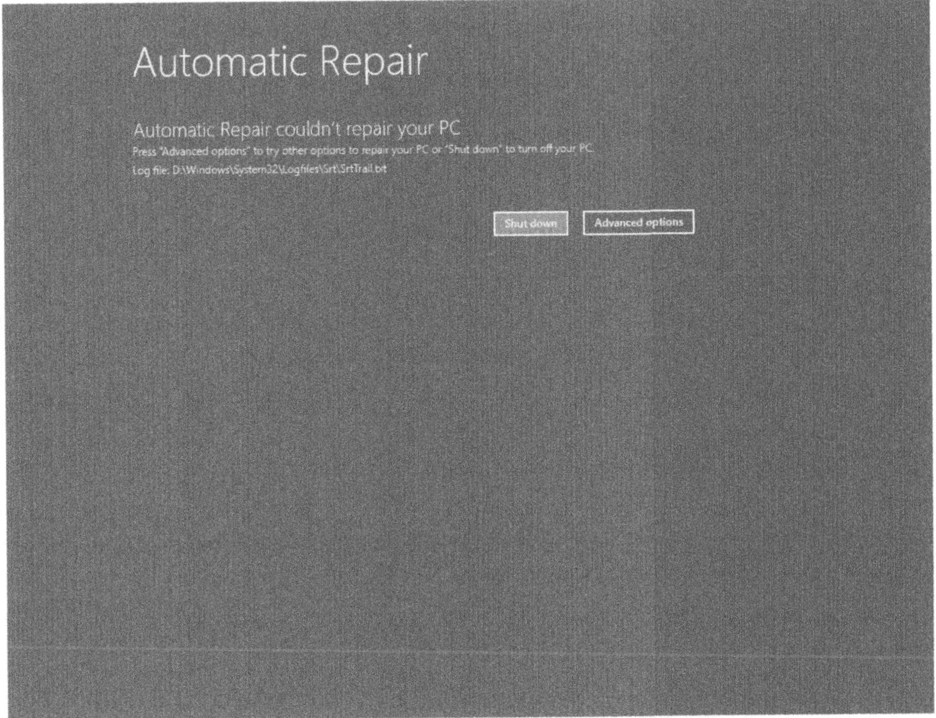

Figure 18-2 Automatic Repair creates a log file if it can't fix the problem. This screen is not compatible with screen readers.

Manually Repairing Corrupt Startup Files

Occasionally, you will need to manually repair the startup files on your computer. To do this, start the system in the operating system selection menu, as described previously, and click Troubleshoot\Advanced Options\Command Prompt.

To manually repair the boot options menu for a BIOS-based computer in Windows 8, perform the following procedure (for UEFI firmware computers, additional notes follow):

1. Type **BcdEdit /export C:\BCD_Backup** (where *BCD_Backup* is the location in which you want the backup to reside), and then press Enter. This creates a backup of the boot options menu options so that it can be restored if needed.
2. Type **C:**, and then press Enter.
3. Type **cd Boot**, and then press Enter. This takes you to the Windows 8 startup options.
4. Type **attrib bcd -s -h -r**, and then press Enter. This allows you to modify and overwrite the startup options.
5. Type **ren C:\Boot\bcd C:\Boot\bcd.old**, and then press Enter. This renames the current startup file.
6. Type **Bootrec /RebuildBCD**, and then press Enter to force Windows 8 to rebuild the boot options menu from scratch.

Note

If you have a multiboot system, repairing the startup menu in this way might restore Windows 8 only to the boot options menu. To restore other operating systems afterward, see the instructions in the section "Editing the Boot Options Menu by Using BCDEdit" later in this chapter.

In a computer with UEFI firmware, the Boot Confirmation Data (BCD) registry file is located instead in the Extensible Firmware Interface (EFI) system partition. This partition doesn't have a drive letter associated with it. You can still use the BootRec command, but you should skip steps 2 through 5 in the preceding procedure. If you need to reimport the backed-up BCD file, use step 1 with the **/import** switch.

The following are switches you can use with the Bootrec command to perform other actions on the boot options menu:

- **FixMbr** This creates a new Master Boot Record file for the disk and can be used if the Master Boot Record (MBR) is corrupt.
- **FixBoot** This switch writes a new boot sector to the disk. Use this if the boot sector has been replaced with a non–Windows 8 sector or is corrupt.
- **ScanOS** This scans your hard disks for compatible operating systems and reports the relevant details so that you can manually add them to the boot options menu.

INSIDE OUT **What if Windows 8 still won't start?**

Sometimes Windows 8 won't start even after repairing the startup system. There is little else you can do at this point except reinstall the operating system. I always recommend, therefore, that you keep a system image backup copy of Windows that can be restored in the event of this type of disaster.

Windows 8 and Multiboot Systems

Some of the most complex startup problems associated with Windows involve dual or multi-boot systems on your computer. You might, for example, run a copy of GNU/Linux or an earlier version of Windows (perhaps Windows 7) on your computer.

Because of modifications that Microsoft has made to its startup system, if you install a multi-boot system, ensure that you install operating systems on your computer in the following order:

1. GNU/Linux, Windows XP, or earlier versions of Windows
2. Windows 7
3. Windows 8

Trusted Boot

Windows 8 introduced a new feature called Trusted Boot. This is a UEFI feature by which the firmware can validate the authenticity of software at startup. It is intended to prevent the execution of malware and other malicious code such as rootkits when the computer starts up. Trusted Boot isn't restricted to computers running Windows 8; you can also find it on computers running Windows RT and on Windows Phone 8 handsets.

BitLocker and Multiboot Systems

If you use Microsoft BitLocker encryption on your computer and want to create a multiboot system, you will run into issues with Windows 8 locking you out of your computer almost every time you try to start the system.

BitLocker doesn't support multiboot systems, and although some people on the Internet claim to have workarounds, even they will admit that those workarounds are not guaranteed. If you do need (or simply want) to create a multiboot system, you must turn BitLocker off on your computer.

INSIDE OUT **Trusted Boot is tied to UEFI**

Trusted Boot is a feature only of computers equipped with UEFI firmware; it is not functional on computers with BIOS firmware. However, Microsoft has mandated to all OEM partners that *all* computers they sell that are running Windows 8 *must* have UEFI firmware and *must* have Trusted Boot turned on.

Trusted Boot can prevent some operating systems from starting, including GNU/Linux. You will find that in many UEFI systems, especially on more expensive computers and laptops, Trusted Boot can be turned off completely. If you are buying a new computer on which you plan to run multiboot operating systems, it is a good idea to check the UEFI system first to see whether this feature can be turned off. You can normally access the UEFI menus on a computer by pressing the Esc key when the system starts.

Editing the Boot Options Menu by Using BCDEdit

Sometimes, you will need to manually edit the boot options menu and add missing operating systems to it. To do this, you need to gain access to the Windows 8 command line by using the method I described earlier in the chapter, or by starting your computer from your Windows 8 installation DVD and selecting Repair Your Computer on the Install screen.

BCDEdit follows the structure *BCDEdit /Command [Argument1] [Argument2]*. Useful commands you will need to add in an operating system are as follows:

- **/?** Displays a full list of BCD commands.
- **/default {GUID}** Sets the default entry on the boot menu on the computer.
- **/enum all** Displays your current disk structure. You should run this to make a note of the globally unique identifier (GUID) for the operating system or systems you want to add to the boot options menu.
- **/export** and **/import** Backs up and reimports the boot options menu.
- **/timeout [num]** Changes the length of time for which Windows waits at the operating system selection menu; for example, */timeout 10* instructs Windows to pause for 10 seconds.

To use BCDEdit, perform the following steps:

1. Open a Command Prompt window, as described at the beginning of this section.
2. Type **bcdedit /enum all**, and then press Enter to show all the data for each installed operating system on your computer. You will see Windows 8 listed as {current}, and a different entry (or more) for an earlier operating system listed as {legacy}. Sometimes the operating system might be displayed as {ntldr}.

To change the name of an operating system that already appears in BCDEdit, perform the following steps:

1. Create a backup of the BCD file in case something goes wrong. Type **bcdedit /export "C:\BCD_Backup"** (where *BCD_Backup* is the location at which you want the backup to reside), and then press Enter.
2. Type **bcdedit /set {legacy} Description "OS Name"** (where *OS Name* is the name of the operating system), and then press Enter. You can also use {current} to change the name of the main Windows 8 installation.

> **Note**
>
> To set the entry for a second Windows 8 installation, type **bcdedit /set {GUID} Description "Windows 8 Alternate"**, where *GUID* is the long string of numbers and letters.

3. To change the default operating system in BCD, type **bcdedit /default {current}** to set the Windows 8 boot loader as the default. You can also use {legacy}, {ntldr}, or a {GUID}.

When an operating system is showing with an incorrect partition, you can change this by using the command **bcdedit /set {GUID} device partition=X:**, where *X:* is the correct partition. You *must* also then use the command **bcdedit /set {GUID} osdevice partition=X:**.

However, sometimes an operating system simply won't show up. In this case, you will need to add it to the boot options menu manually. To manually add an operating system to the boot options menu, perform the following steps:

1. Type **bcdedit /create {legacy} /d "Windows XP"**, and then press Enter to create a new boot entry for the operating system.
2. Type **bcdedit /set {legacy} device partition=D:** (where *D:* is the drive on which the operating system is installed), and then press Enter.
3. Type **bcdedit /set {legacy} path /ntldr**, and then press Enter. Note that if your Linux installation is already showing in *bcdedit /enuml*, all you can change is the path to **/linux.bin**.
4. Type **bcdedit /displayorder {legacy} /addlast**, and then press Enter to add Windows XP to the end of the current boot options menu.

Manually Setting Dual Booting for Windows 8 and Linux

If multibooting both a GNU/Linux installation and Windows 8 doesn't work by using the simple commands described in the preceding section, you will need to follow a slightly more complex process. Run the following commands in Linux before installing Windows 8:

1. Boot into Linux and launch a terminal with root privileges.
2. Determine on which partition Linux is installed by typing **fdisk -l** and then pressing Enter. The Linux operating system will be on a partition such as /dev/sda1 or /dev/hda1.
3. Install the GRUB boot manager by typing **grub-install /dev/sda1** and then pressing Enter.
4. Copy the Linux boot sector by typing **dd if=/dev/sda1 of /tmp/linux.bin bs=512 count=1** and then pressing Enter.
5. Copy *linux.bin* to a different partition or USB flash drive as a backup.
6. Install Windows 8.

7. In Windows 8, press Windows logo key+X to start Command Prompt (Admin).
8. Copy your *Linux.bin* backup file to the root (active) partition on your hard disk, which is the partition containing bootmgr. If you do not know which /partition this is, type **diskpart**, and then **diskmgmt.msc** to determine it. Type **exit** to leave the diskpart tool.
9. Create a GRUB entry by typing **bcdedit /create /d "GRUB" /application BOOTSECTOR**, and then pressing Enter.

   BCDEdit will return a {GUID} for this entry. You should make a note of this. For this exercise, call it {LinuxGUID}.
10. Type **bcdedit /set {LinuxGUID} device boot**, and then press Enter to specify which device hosts the Linux boot sector.
11. Type **bcdedit /set {LinuxGUID} PATH /Linux.bin**, and then press Enter to specify the path of the Linux boot sector.
12. Type **bcdedit /displayorder {LinuxGUID} /addlast**, and then press Enter to add Linux to the end of the boot order.

INSIDE OUT **Software alternatives to BCDEdit**

The methods for editing the boot options menu and manually setting dual booting, which are quite complex, should be implemented only when the system won't start at all. You can also use software such as EasyBCD (*http://www.neosmart.net/EasyBCD*) to manage and edit BCD entries.

Backing Up the Windows 8 Boot Partitions

I've talked a lot about GNU/Linux in this chapter primarily because when multibooting Windows is desired, GNU/Linux is the operating system that enthusiasts most seem to want as the secondary system. Linux can perform one task that Windows cannot: Linux can allow you to create full backups of the Windows System Reserved partition and other boot partitions.

To create a full backup of the Windows System Reserved partition, you need to download a Linux ISO file and burn it to a CD or DVD. You can then start your system from the disc (don't install Linux), and you will be able to see—and most importantly, access—all the partitions on your computer's hard disk (see Figure 18-3).

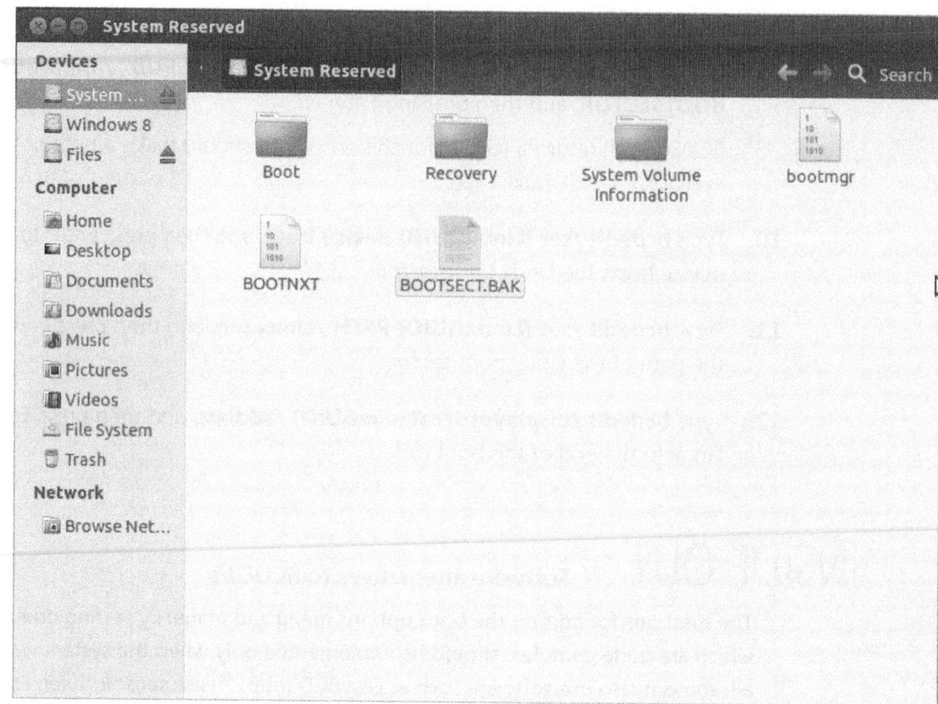

Figure 18-3 Use GNU/Linux to back up the Windows boot partitions.

After you start your computer from the Linux disc and you're looking at the computer's hard disk in its own File Explorer, you can make copies of the partitions in two ways. You can copy the files into backup folders (note the partition types and sizes so that you can re-create them later). Or, if you have an imaging tool, you can create an ISO file of each image that you can later copy back, again by starting from your Linux disc.

You can get the full details of a partition by using the Disk Utility in Linux (see Figure 18-4), which will give you valuable information, including data about the following:

- Partition type
- Label
- Capacity

You will need all this information to rebuild the partition if it becomes completely corrupt.

Figure 18-4 The Disk Utility includes tools that provide detailed information about the structure and format of hard disk partitions. This is something that even Windows 8 is unable to do without the use of third-party software.

Normally, however, just copying the contents of the boot partitions (including System Reserved, which is the most important) means that you can then use a Linux startup disc to copy the contents back afterward if a disaster occurs.

CHAPTER 19

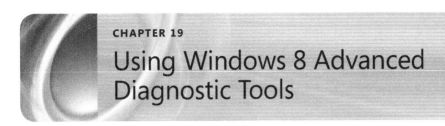

Using Windows 8 Advanced Diagnostic Tools

SO FAR IN THIS BOOK, you've seen how to use the basic tools that come as part of Windows 8—or perhaps more accurately, the simple-to-use tools—that you can use to help you diagnose and repair problems. You've learned that problems on your computer can be caused not only by a wide variety of local factors, including your software and drivers, but also by a wide variety of external factors. To diagnose more complex problems in Windows 8, you can employ a battery of more advanced tools. In this chapter, I show you what those tools are and how you can use them.

Performance Information And Tools

Performance Information And Tools (see Figure 19-1) is a central location for many types of information about your computer, such as what hardware is installed and how it is performing. The easiest way to access Performance Information And Tools is to open the Start screen, type **performance**, and search in Settings results. You can access components separately in Control Panel by clicking System And Security\Administrative Tools.

The basic function of Performance Information And Tools is to provide an interface to features such as the Windows Experience Index and options for adjusting the visual effects, power settings, and indexing options of your copy of Windows. To access the Advanced Tools dialog box, in the Performance Information And Tools window, click Advanced Tools (see Figure 19-2).

These advanced tools are very useful for diagnosing performance problems with Windows 8 and your software and hardware drivers. I don't provide details for every tool in this chapter, but I do cover what I consider to be the vital tools: Event Log, Performance Monitor, Resource Monitor, Task Manager, System Information, System Health Report, and the Computer Management console.

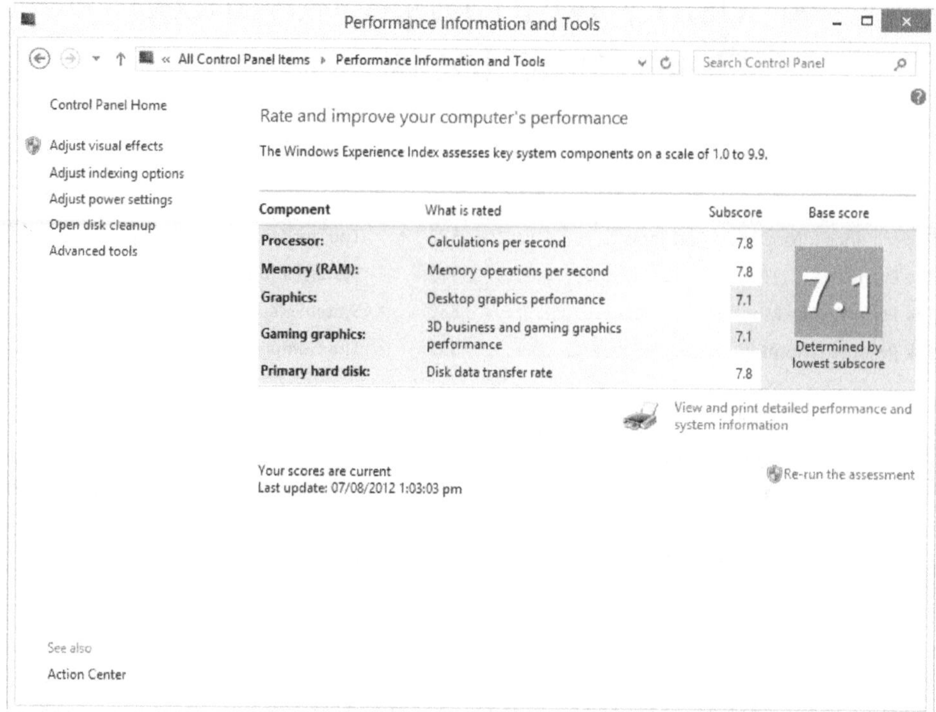

Figure 19-1 The Performance Information And Tools window.

At the top of the Advanced Tools dialog box, in Performance Issues, Windows 8 alerts you to any problems it has detected. Links are provided to direct you to fixes, if Microsoft knows of any, or to give you more information so that you can rectify the problem yourself.

The performance tools in Windows 8 offer some advanced information that might be used primarily by IT professionals, either remotely or when working on the computer directly, but these tools can be helpful to anyone responsible for diagnosing and repairing problems on a computer. These tools quickly display a large amount of real-time data about your computer, your copy of Windows 8, and your hardware, and you have some flexibility regarding formatting and level of detail in data presentation, depending on your requirements. For most of your troubleshooting needs, the Event Log will suffice. If you're going to a third party for additional guidance, or if you're helping someone else, a System Health Report might be required.

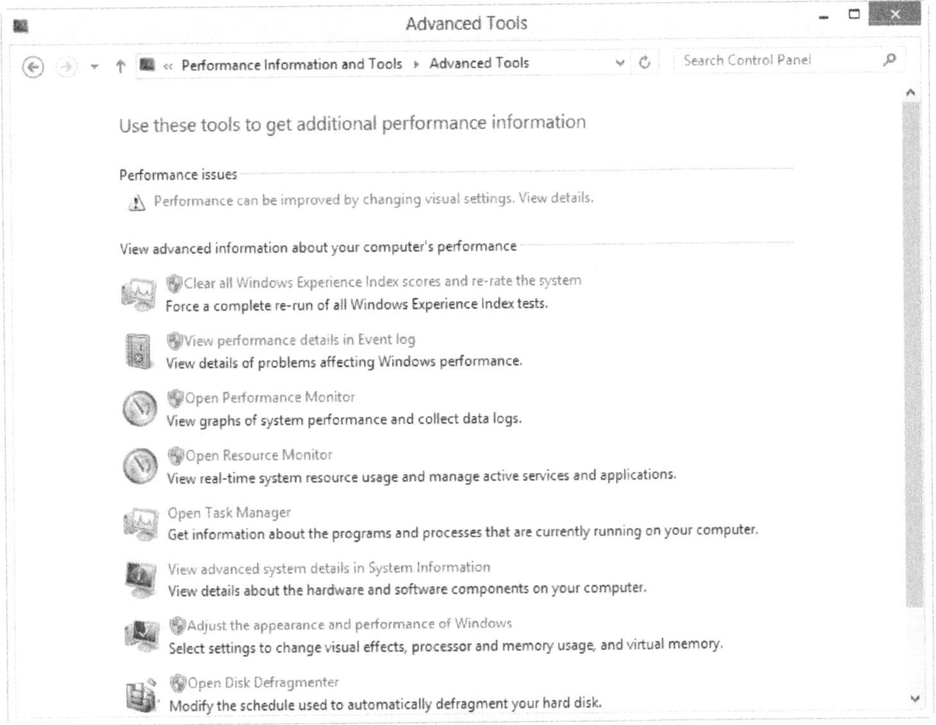

Figure 19-2 Advanced Tools in Performance Information And Tools gives you information for addressing system issues.

The Event Log

The Event Log is probably the single most useful feature in Windows 8 when it comes to troubleshooting problems. Everything that happens in Windows 8, from user logons to unresponsive program components that users never even know about, is logged and recorded. The amount of helpful information it provides, which you can see in the Event Viewer, is far greater than the information provided by other Windows utilities. The two most important views provide you with information about most of the errors recorded by Windows 8.

To find all events, which are specified actions, and errors that Windows 8 has recorded on your computer, in Advanced Tools, click View Performance Details In Event Log. In the Event Viewer, click Event Viewer (Local), click Windows Logs, and then click System. Warnings are highlighted with yellow triangles; errors are indicated by a red icon (Figure 19-3).

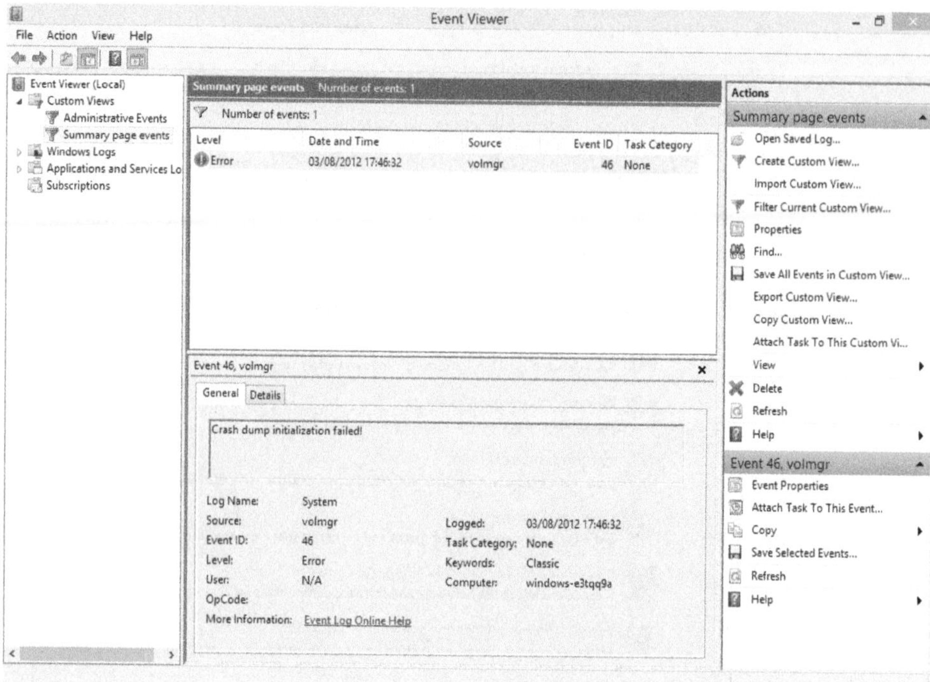

Figure 19-3 The Event Viewer shows system activity and errors.

Under Custom Views\Administrative Events (see Figures 19-4 and 19-5), notice the error highlighted in the Administrative Events pane. In a separate pane below the highlighted error list is a description of the error, such as the name of the offending file or service, and other information to help you track down the source of the problem and address it.

In the bottom pane of the Event Viewer are two tabs: General and Details. The General tab (see Figure 19-4), which is selected by default, contains general information about errors and events in an easy-to-read format. Although the General tab can exclude some relevant details, it presents the most essential information. Select an error in the list to display information in the center pane at the bottom of the screen.

You can get many more details by clicking the Details tab (see Figure 19-5), which you can expand upward to see more information. Details are displayed in an XML-type manner, which simplifies the exporting and reading process in dedicated error reporting and logging tools and databases.

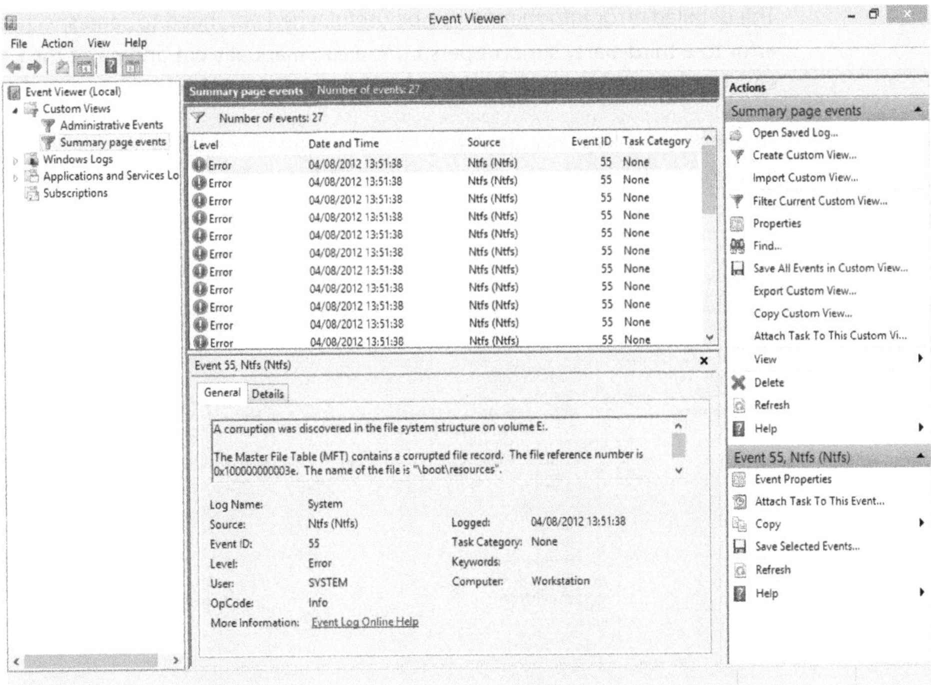

Figure 19-4 Administrative errors are displayed in the Event Log.

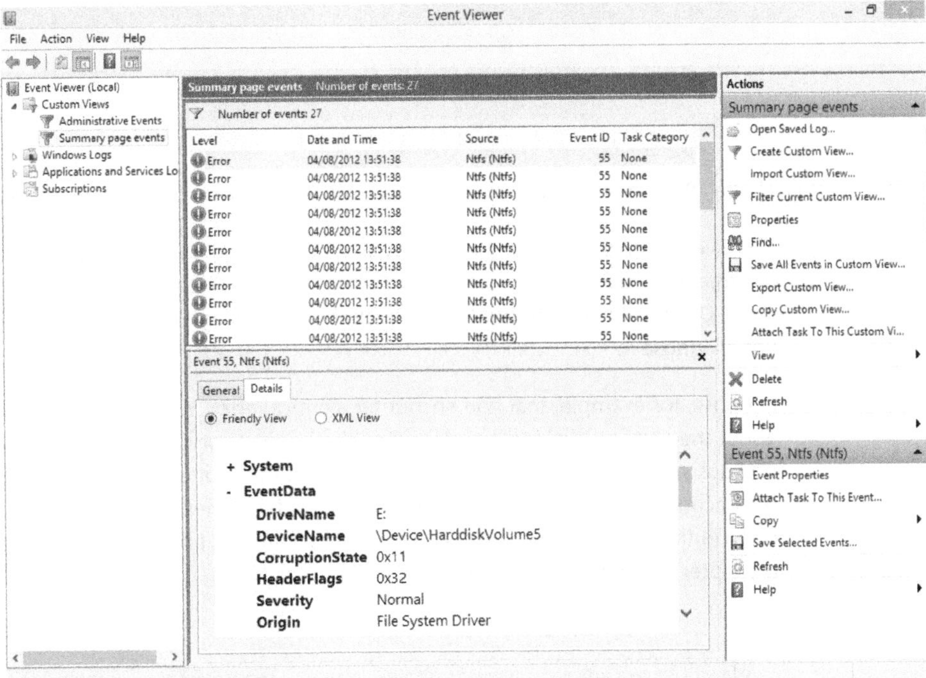

Figure 19-5 You can send formatted error information to third parties.

The detailed error information can be useful when you need to send specific data about an error to a third-party support person. You can manually cut and paste the details into an email, or automate this process by clicking Save Selected Events in the Actions pane.

To gauge the overall health of your computer, go to the Event Viewer and click Event Viewer (Local) to open the window shown in Figure 19-6.

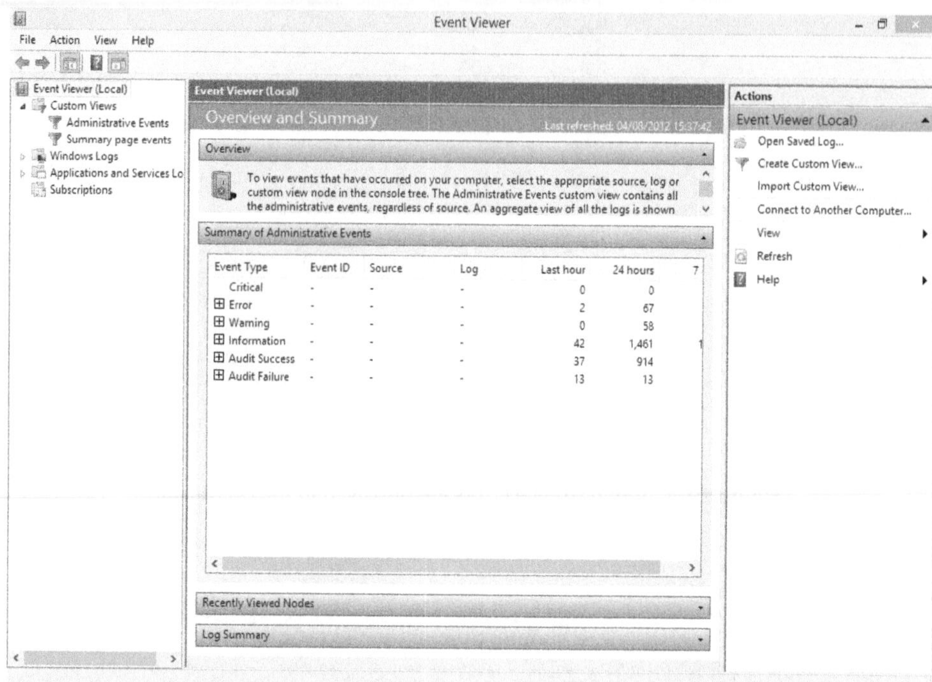

Figure 19-6 The Event Viewer can give you a good overview of a computer's health.

The Overview And Summary view shows you clearly the number of Critical, Error, Warning, Information, Audit Success, and Audit Failure messages generated in the last hour, day, and week. Use this timing information to track the general age of a problem, which will help you diagnose it.

Suppose, for example, that you encounter a critical error. You look up specific information about the error by clicking it and reading the information provided in the Event Viewer, but perhaps you don't find a definitive answer about the root cause. If you see that the error has occurred a couple of times in the last hour, a few times in the last day, but not any more often in the last seven days, you can isolate the cause to an issue that has changed on the computer within the last 24 hours (or thereabouts).

Here is where your detective skills come into play, as you determine what has changed during that time. Was an update, a new driver, or new software installed? Has a new user been on the computer, perhaps as a new role? This information can significantly help in diagnosing errors.

You might find the information provided by the Event Viewer pretty technical. How can you draw details from it that will be meaningful for you, even if you have the name of the offending file or service, or an error code that you can look up online to get further information?

In the Event Properties dialog box (see Figure 19-7), the complicated-looking numerical or hexadecimal codes often provide the most useful clues when troubleshooting.

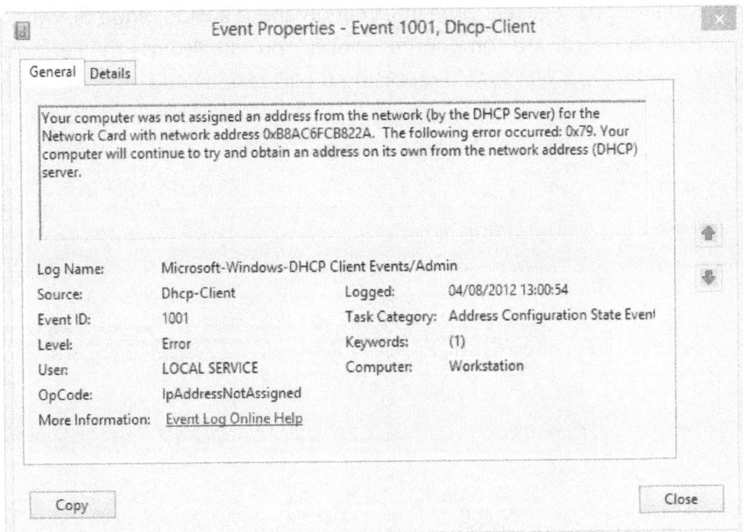

Figure 19-7 You can draw meaningful data from the Event Viewer.

> ## Note
> **Double-click an event or error in Event Viewer to display details about it in the Event Properties dialog box. The information displayed in this dialog box is the same information you see in the center pane of the Event Viewer when you click an event. However, having this information displayed in a secondary window might provide you with more space or better manageability of the information if you are using a small screen or a screen reader.**

You can look up the codes, file names, and other information about the error online. The More Information field provides a link to a forum in which people who have encountered the same error post knowledge about the error; many of these posts provide solutions. You can use the Event ID in an online search to find information about the specific event and possible solutions.

The Performance Monitor

You access the Performance Monitor (see Figure 19-8) through the Performance Information And Tools screen or by searching directly from the Start screen. Although many users find the information provided by the Performance Monitor a little difficult to interpret, this information can be extremely useful in monitoring your system performance. The Performance Monitor provides real-time information about a wide range of Windows 8 performance data and hardware components events. You can also use the Performance Monitor to check whether the Windows 8 reporting tools are activated.

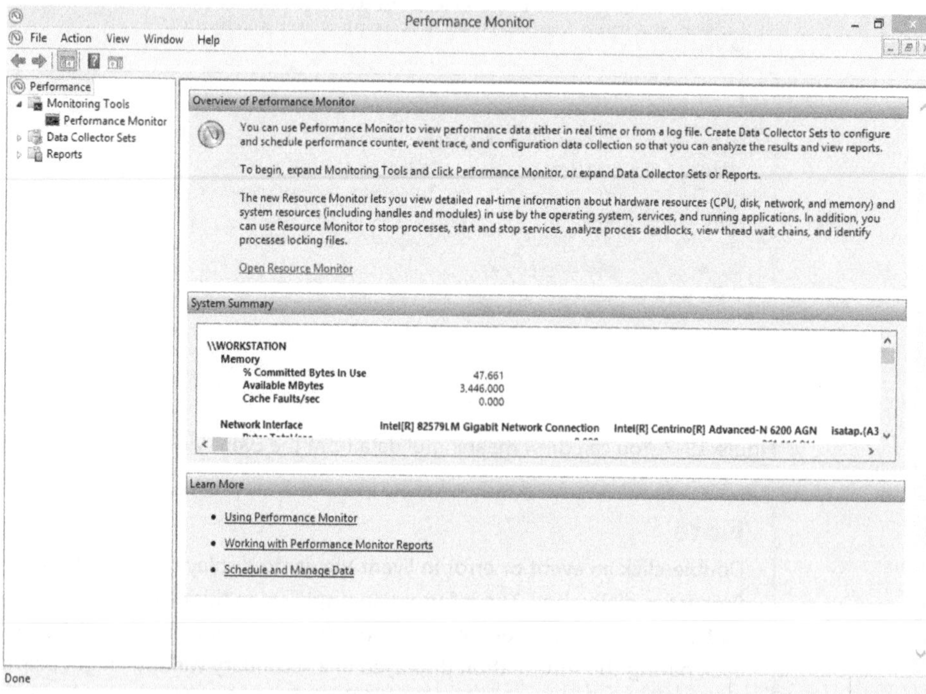

Figure 19-8 The Performance Monitor in Windows 8.

You can use the real-time monitoring options in the Performance Monitor to add information about specific criteria such as the read/write data for your hard disk or the power distribution to individual components. In Chapter 33, "Using Advanced Windows 8 Diagnostic Tools," I talk about these tools in much greater detail.

To view information about specific Windows components, such as the networking, memory, or processor components, in the left pane, click Monitoring Tools, and then click Performance Monitor. This brings up a graph view showing (by default) the processor usage on your computer. For example, perhaps you suspect that the ReadyBoost cache isn't working properly. (ReadyBoost cache is additional cache memory you can add to a PC to speed up the starting of applications and operating system performance by plugging in a compatible USB flash drive.) You can monitor this component in real time via the Performance Monitor.

You can add data lines (called counters) to this graph by clicking the green plus icon (+) on the toolbar; potentially hundreds of additional options will appear, all in collapsible panes (see Figure 19-9).

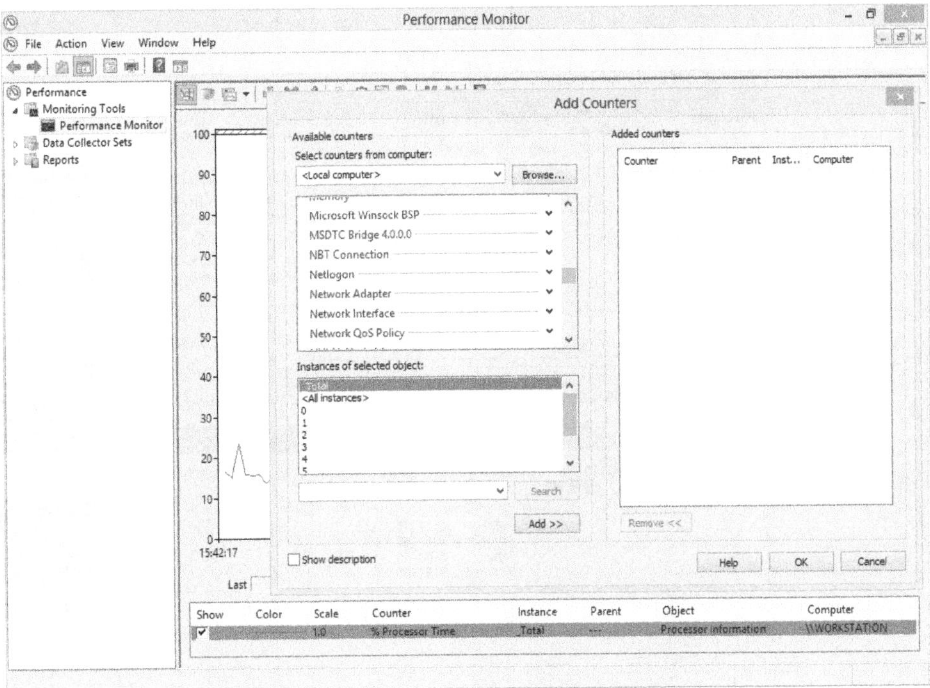

Figure 19-9 You can add custom counters to the Performance Monitor.

Below the graph view, all the currently selected options are displayed with their line color so that you can identify individual lines if you have several active at any one time. After you add lines to the graph, you can remove them at any time by clearing their check boxes below the graph view.

The Resource Monitor

Whereas the Performance Monitor helps you diagnose problems with Windows 8 services and components and can give you a real-time graph showing overall performance for individual Windows 8 components, the Resource Monitor gives you extensive real-time information about every process and service running on your computer (see Figure 19-10). Each tab indicates exactly what's going on at a given moment in different parts of your system, from the status of processes and services running (or not running) on your CPU to the current activity on your network. The Memory tab, for example, would show whether one of your applications is consuming vast amounts of memory.

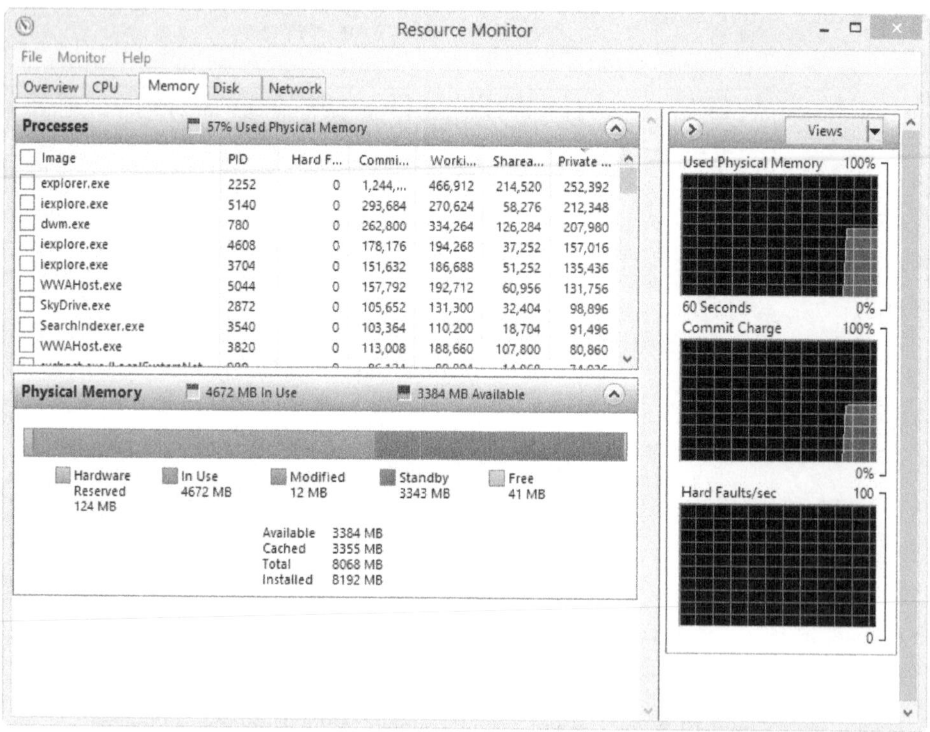

Figure 19-10 The Resource Monitor in Windows 8.

The Resource Monitor provides information similar to that provided by Task Manager but supplies many more details, which can be useful when you're diagnosing more complex problems in Windows 8 or in your applications.

Click the Overview tab to display collapsible panes showing summary information about processes that are running, disk activity, and network traffic. The other four tabs provide more detail. The Network tab (see Figure 19-11) can give you specific information about the network activity for particular programs and apps, for example, whether Microsoft Outlook is actually connecting to the email server. You can also see specific information about TCP/IP traffic for programs and services, so you can examine whether a program—or Windows 8—is dropping data packets (small blocks of data that are sent together to maximize network throughput) or suffering from high latency. If you need to monitor many different functions in real time, such as various network connections or processors, you can click Views above the graphs to reduce the size of each graph so that more information can fit in the window.

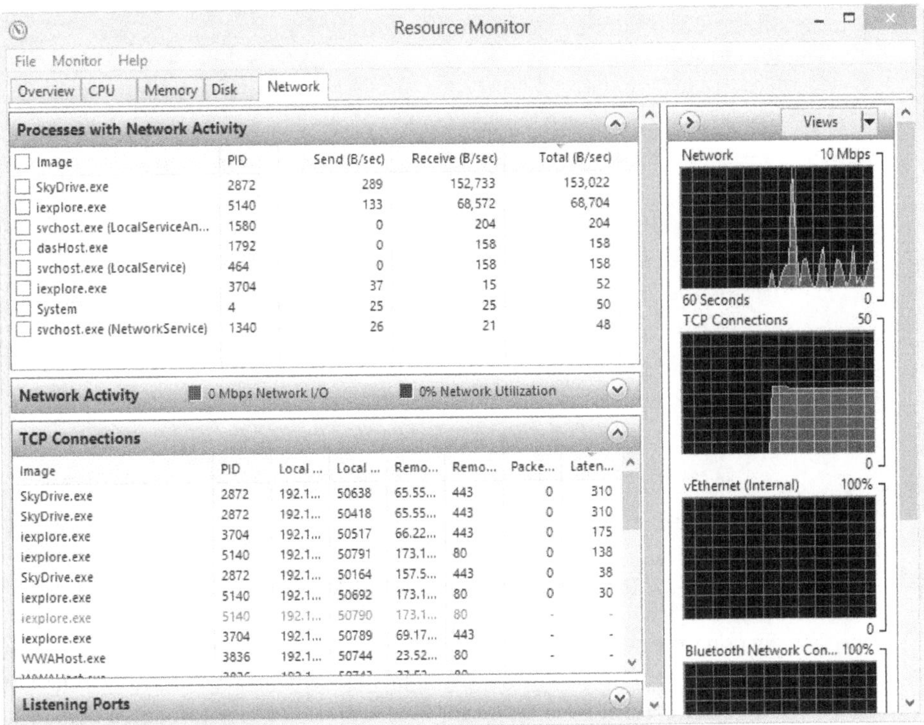

Figure 19-11 You can get a great deal of Network information from Resource Monitor.

The Improved Task Manager

The Task Manager has remained relatively unchanged since its introduction with Windows NT 4.0 in 1996, until Windows 8. It has been given a significant overhaul, but you'll likely find it simple and intuitive to use.

By default, the Task Manager displays only a list of current running programs, but you can click the More Details link in the lower-left corner to display more information. The Processes tab (see Figure 19-12) provides a heat-mapped chart showing the current processor, memory, disk, and network usage for every running program and Windows 8 component.

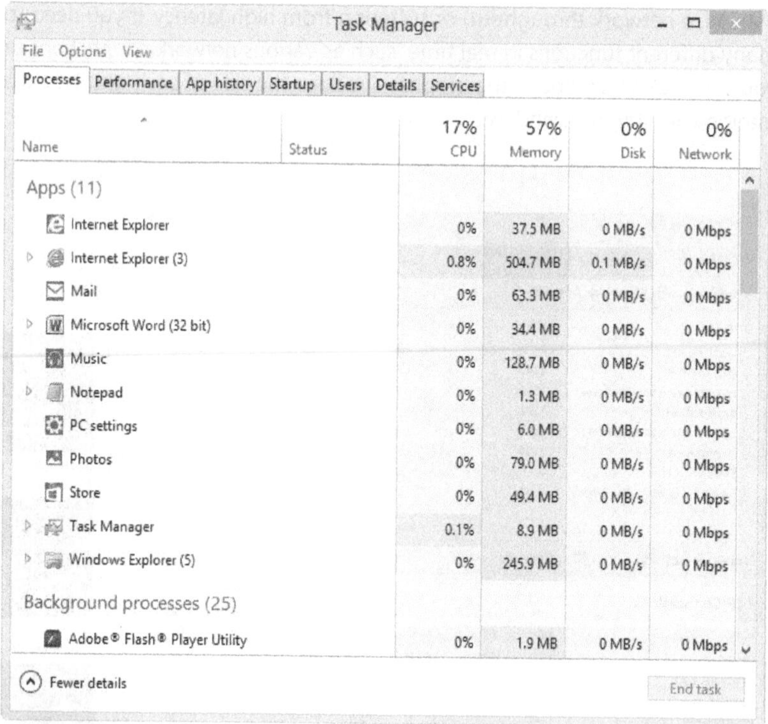

Figure 19-12 The improved Windows 8 Task Manager.

By using the heat-mapped data in Task Manager, you can quickly identify the cause of a problem, because Windows 8 highlights the item in red. Previously in Task Manager, to see what was using all your processor time, you had to look through a numerical list.

INSIDE OUT Ending process trees

On the Processes tab in the Task Manager, you can end the currently selected task by right-clicking it and then clicking End Task. However, on the Details tab, you can exit a task and all other tasks, processes, and services associated with it by clicking End Process Tree. You might want to do this if a complex application has several subprograms running at the same time to support it, such as its own database manager or updater.

The Performance tab (see Figure 19-13) provides real-time graphs that display what is happening on your computer with respect to individual hardware components, such as processor, memory, hard disk(s), and network connections.

This is a slimmed-down version of the information provided in the Performance and Resource Monitors, but it can still be helpful, especially if you want to keep an eye on a particular component.

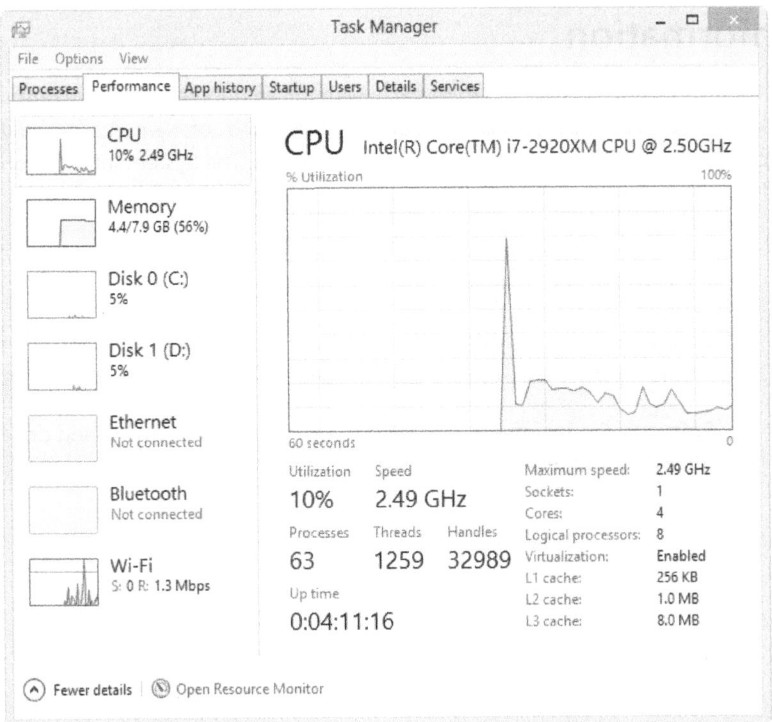

Figure 19-13 Task Manager can provide live information to help you diagnose problems.

> **Note**
>
> **Right-clicking the graphs on the Performance tab displays a Summary View. The Summary View minimizes the Task Manager to show only the graphs (or just numerical data if you prefer) so that you can keep an eye on what's happening with your computer while you continue working.**

Use the App History tab to help you determine what is malfunctioning on a computer that has a large number of installed Windows 8 apps. This tab shows a heat map of all resources used by an app over a period of time. You can use this view to see, for example, whether a particular app is using too much memory or processor time—even when it isn't running—so that you can consider whether to uninstall or review it.

The Details tab is where you find full descriptions of running programs, apps, processes, and services—useful when you are unsure about what something is. The Details tab is more like the traditional Task Manager view and operates in much the same way.

System Information

When you need to provide a third party with information about your computer, including data on Windows 8, your hardware, and your installed software, the System Information tool is the place to find that data (see Figure 19-14). The System Information window is divided into three sections that provide the following information:

- **Hardware Resources** Hardware conflicts, interrupt requests (IRQs), memory allocations, and so on.
- **Components** Hardware attached to your computer, with a separate section called Problem Devices for devices that Windows 8 has identified as problematic.
- **Software Environment** Everything from installed software and drivers to startup programs and recent Windows 8 error reporting.

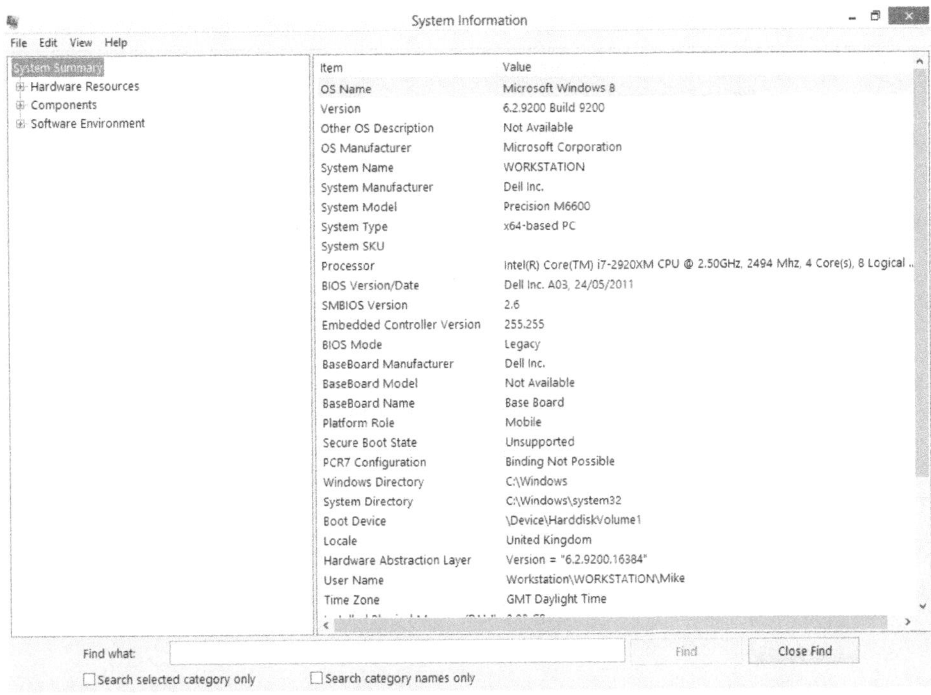

Figure 19-14 The System Information tool.

Each category can be expanded by clicking its plus sign. Anything in the left pane can be selected to display more detailed information in the main pane.

To export any or all data from the System Summary as a text file that can be read on any computer, click File\Export, name the text file, and then save the file to any location on your hard disk or to removable storage.

System Health Report

One of the most useful automatic diagnostic features in Windows 8 is the System Health Report tool. This tool produces detailed reports of the current status of your computer, including every part of Windows 8, your hardware, and your installed software. Problems that are found are highlighted. To access this tool, in the Performance Information And Tools window, in the Advanced Tools section, click Generate A System Health Report (see Figure 19-15). It takes about 60 seconds to collect the data, and it captures a snapshot of everything to do with your computer, including how it's running at that time, in a report file.

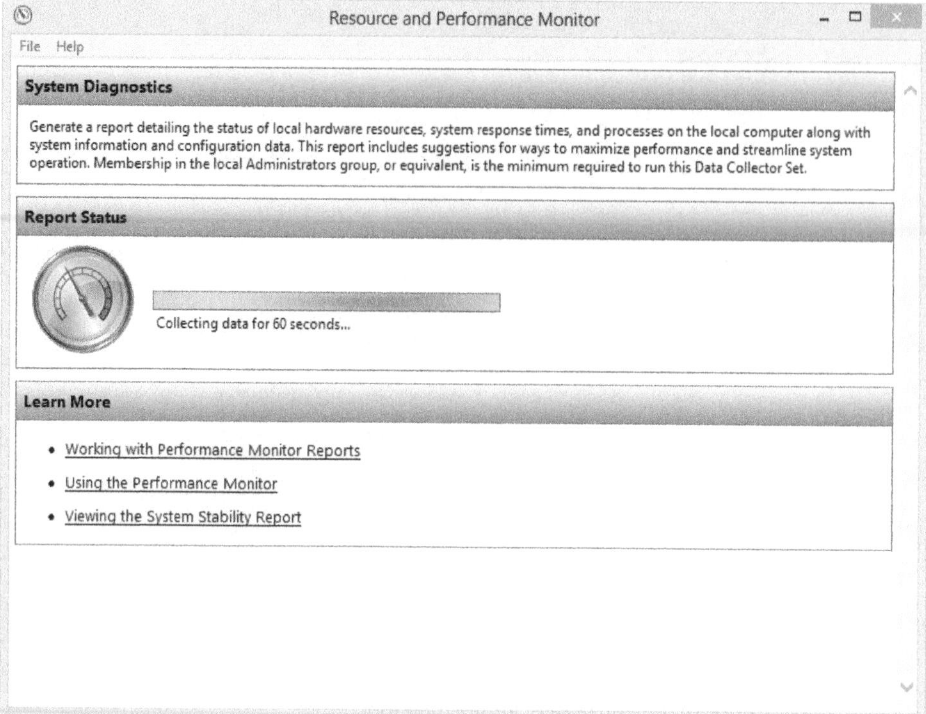

Figure 19-15 The System Health Report tool for generating detailed reports in Windows 8.

The File menu in this window includes options to send the report to the email client configured on your computer, or to save the report as a file that you can then send via your email software or a web mail application. (You would in this case attach the file manually to an email in the same way you would any other attachment.) This method will vary depending on your email provider.

Before you dive into the details of the System Health Report, you should read the information that appears in the Diagnostic Results pane (see Figure 19-16). The Diagnostic Results pane shows information about currently detected problems in addition to links to the Microsoft website, which contains helpful articles about these problems.

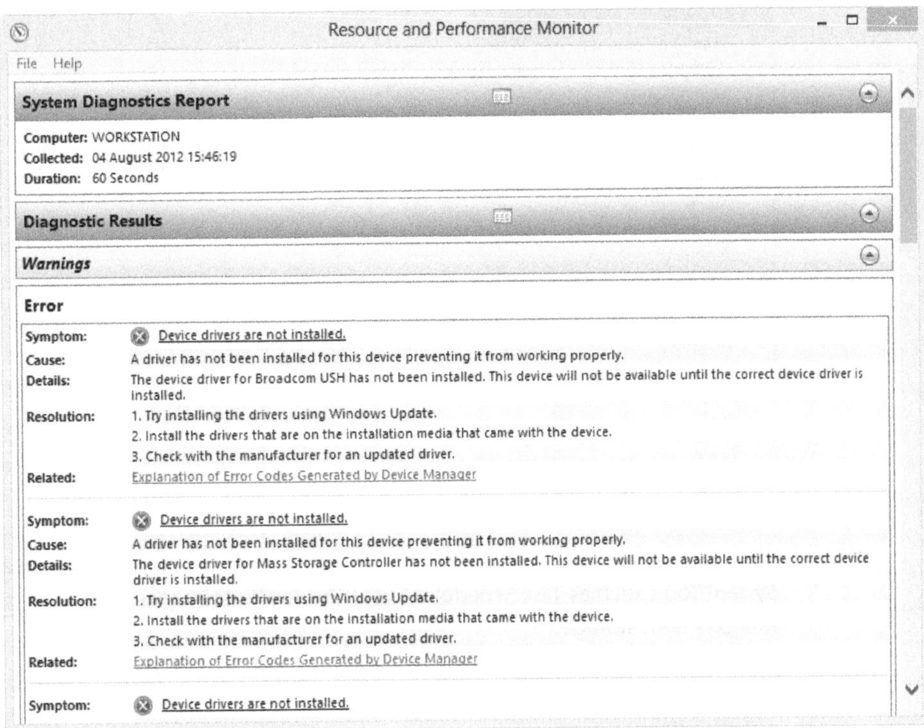

Figure 19-16 A sample System Health Report.

The Computer Management Console

The Computer Management console is where you can access the Performance Monitor in addition to other management features in Windows 8. To easily access this console, open either the desktop or the Start screen (it doesn't matter which), press Windows logo key+X to open the WinX menu (see Figure 19-17), and then click Computer Management.

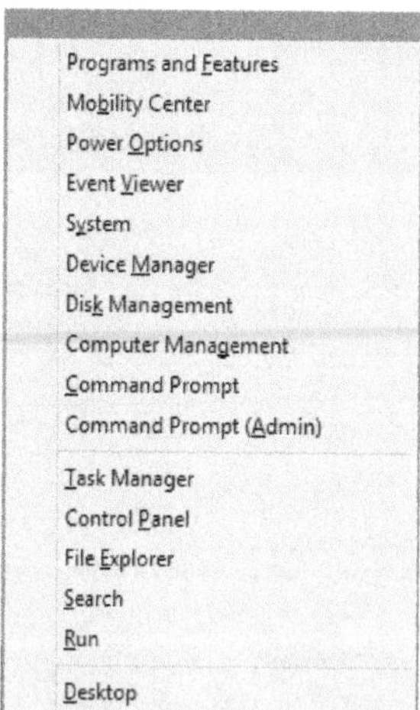

Figure 19-17 The new WinX menu.

From the Computer Management console (see Figure 19-18), you can view and control System Tools such as Task Scheduler, Event Viewer, Performance, Device Manager, and Disk Management storage.

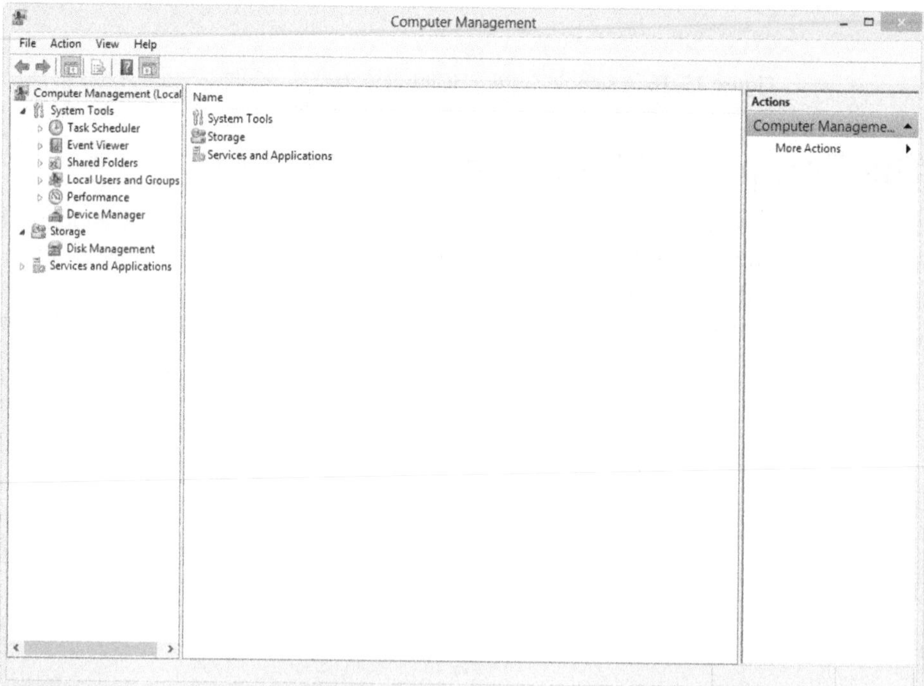

Figure 19-18 The Computer Management console.

Click Disk Management to open the Disk Management console, in which you can view and find problems with all the fixed and removable drives in your computer (see Figure 19-19). For example, you might see that a disk isn't being recognized or is being reported as unformatted. (When you access the console through Computer Management, the console looks different versus when you open it directly from the WinX menu. The former approach adds to the window the familiar categories in the left pane and context options in the right pane. You might find some of these additional options useful.)

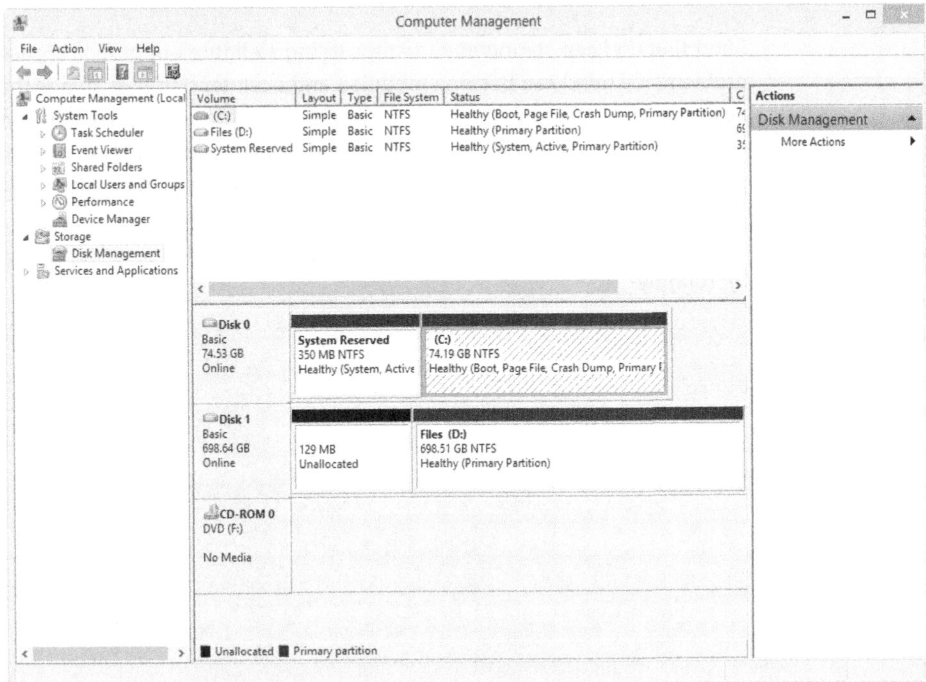

Figure 19-19 The Disk Management console.

INSIDE OUT Be careful when working with suspected faulty disks

Just because Windows 8 is reporting a disk as "unformatted" or "not initialized" in the Disk Management console doesn't mean that the disk is really faulty. If the disk has been working fine until now, the problem is more likely to be the result of a driver or a corrupt BIOS. Thus, reformatting or reinitializing the disk might not fix the problem.

INSIDE OUT Are you too close to the problem?

Sometimes the best troubleshooting tool isn't built into the system. If you're stuck on a problem that you just can't figure out, I advise you to step away from your computer. Take a break, maybe even a day, and come back to the problem with a clear mind. The old adage that one sometimes can't see the forest for the trees can apply when diagnosing computers; a person can be too close to a problem to see it clearly.

I find that if I keep staring at a monitor trying to figure out or fix a challenging problem, my mind can become muddled and I can tend to miss things that I would normally catch. If you (or your company) can't justify such a respite, try reading some of the reports you generated with the Performance Information And Management tools offline. The reports that the Advanced Performance Information And Tools utilities can provide are good to read when you're away from your computer and can't be tempted to try quick fixes. It can give you time to digest a problem and read the logs thoroughly.

CHAPTER 20

Using Advanced Repair Methods

You might face a situation in which you need to completely reset a Windows component, identify and repair specific Windows 8 files, or perform actions that are not covered by the tools included in Windows 8. In this chapter, I describe the commands and utilities you need to handle these scenarios and show you how you can quickly get up and running.

Repairing Internet Explorer 10

Windows Internet Explorer 10 shares many components with Windows 8, such as File Explorer. Internet Explorer is one of the most heavily used apps in the operating system, and one of the biggest targets of attack. As such, issues can occur. However, because it is an integrated Windows component, Internet Explorer 10 can be challenging to fix. Also, because Windows 8 includes Internet Explorer 10 as both a desktop application and an app, users sometimes don't know where to turn for answers, because the two versions of Internet Explorer can appear to be completely separate programs. What are your best strategies for addressing issues in Internet Explorer 10?

Disabling Internet Explorer 10 Add-ons and Toolbars

The root of many problems with Internet Explorer—or any web browser, for that matter—is caused by add-ons and toolbars. The system starting very slowly is one such issue. Fortunately, you can easily turn off problematic add-ons and toolbars from within the browser. Although the Windows 8 app version of Internet Explorer 10 doesn't support any add-ons or toolbars, the desktop version of the software does. From time to time, you will want to disable some of these.

To disable add-ons and toolbars on the desktop version, with Internet Explorer open, in the upper-right corner of the toolbar, click the cog icon to open the Tools (Alt+X) menu, and then click Manage Add-Ons (see Figure 20-1).

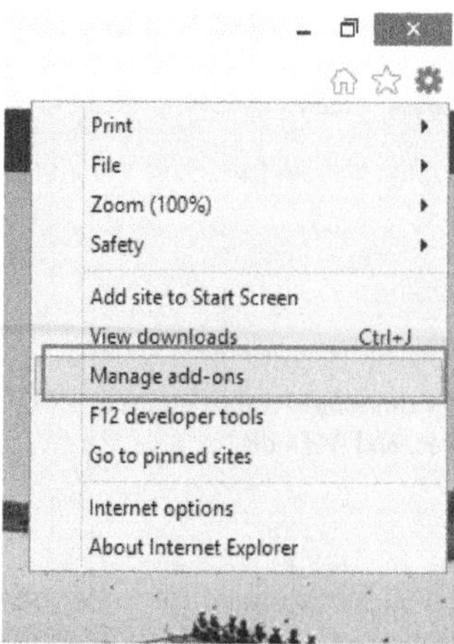

Figure 20-1 Managing add-ons in Internet Explorer.

In the Manage Add-Ons dialog box are details about your add-ons and toolbars (see Figure 20-2). When you click a type in the left pane, the add-ons that are installed in Internet Explorer for that type appear in the right pane. When an add-in is highlighted, a disable (enable) button appears in the bottom-right corner of the window. Disable each suspicious add-on, one at a time, and restart Internet Explorer each time to see whether the problem persists.

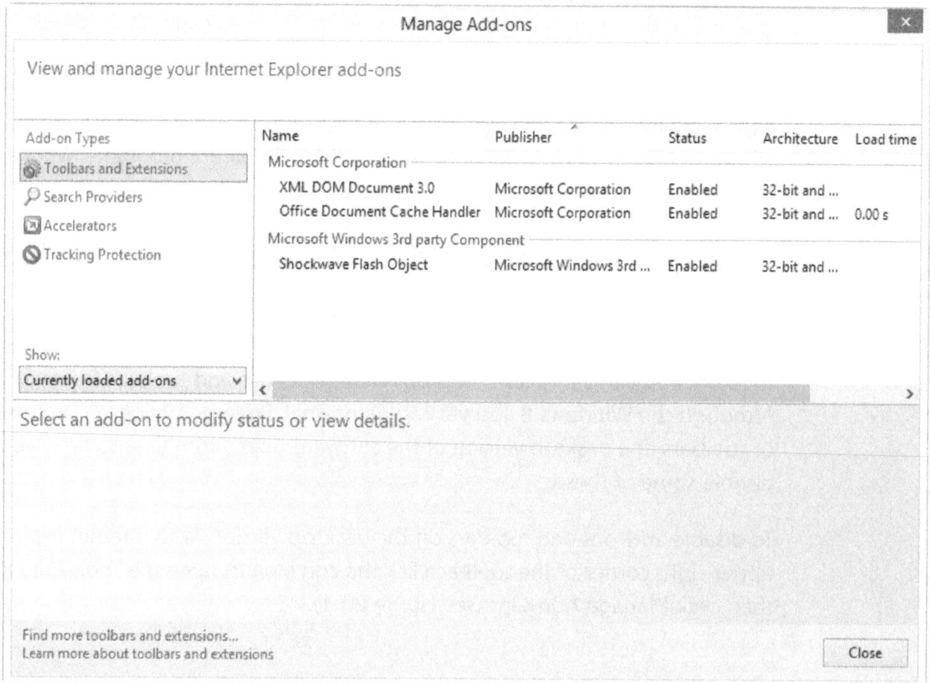

Figure 20-2 You can disable problematic add-ons in Internet Explorer.

INSIDE OUT

Keep add-ons and toolbars to a minimum

Add-ons can very quickly slow down any Internet browser you use. I recommend keeping installed add-ons and toolbars to a minimum to help with speed and efficiency and to minimize problems and errors. The reason for this is that add-ons can significantly slow down your web browser and also interfere with some basic functions such as search, even going so far as to hijack your favorite search engine in favor of their own.

Managing Add-ons from the Control Panel

Another way to manage add-ons in Internet Explorer 10 is through Control Panel. To access add-on settings, click Network And Internet, and then click Manage Browser Add-ons, as shown in Figure 20-3. In the dialog box that opens, click Manage Add-ons.

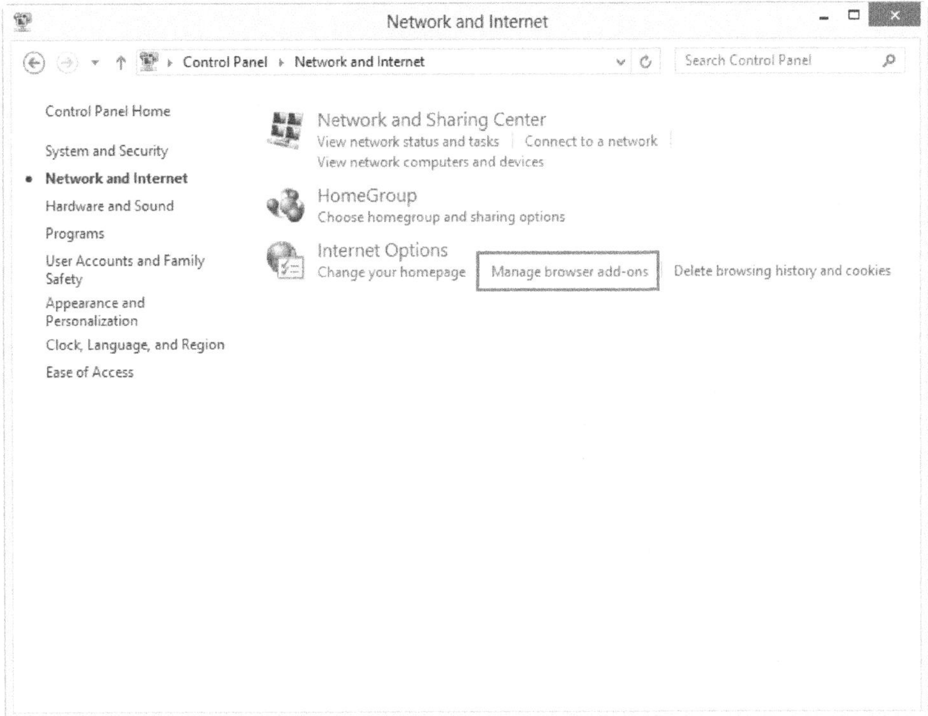

Figure 20-3 Manage Internet Explorer add-ons via the Control Panel.

Resetting Internet Explorer 10 to Factory Defaults

If the problem with Internet Explorer is not caused by add-ons or toolbars, you can use a Windows 8 option to revert Internet Explorer to its default settings, restoring the browser to the state it was in when you first ran it.

> **Note**
>
> **Resetting the desktop version of Internet Explorer will also reset the Windows 8 app version. This is the only way to reset the app version if it has problems or stops responding.**

To reset Internet Explorer to its default settings, perform the following steps:

1. In the upper right of the Internet Explorer toolbar, click the Cog icon, and then click Internet Options (see Figure 20-4).

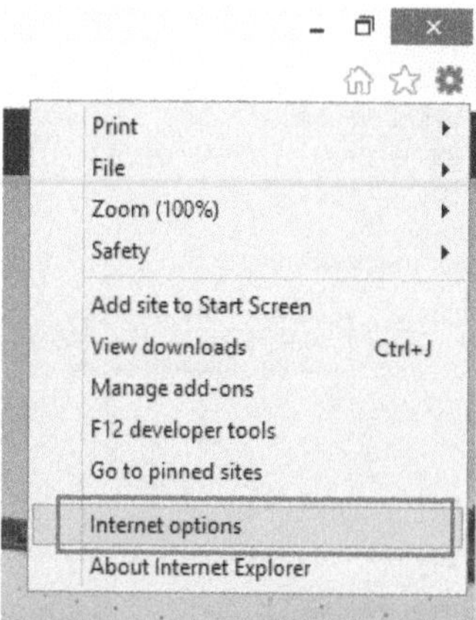

Figure 20-4 Opening the Settings menu in Internet Explorer on the desktop.

2. In the Internet Options dialog box, click the Advanced tab, and then in the Reset Internet Explorer Settings pane (see Figure 20-5), click the Reset button.

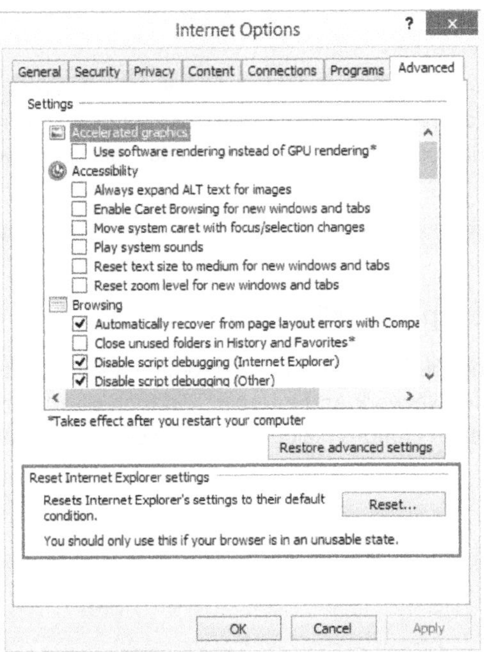

Figure 20-5 The Reset button is on the Advanced tab.

3. In the alert window that opens (see Figure 20-6), which asks if you really want to reset all Internet Explorer settings, and optionally, your personal settings, review the information, and then click Reset. This is a safeguard against pressing the button accidentally, because resetting Internet Explorer will remove all your add-ins and toolbars and can delete all your settings for the program.

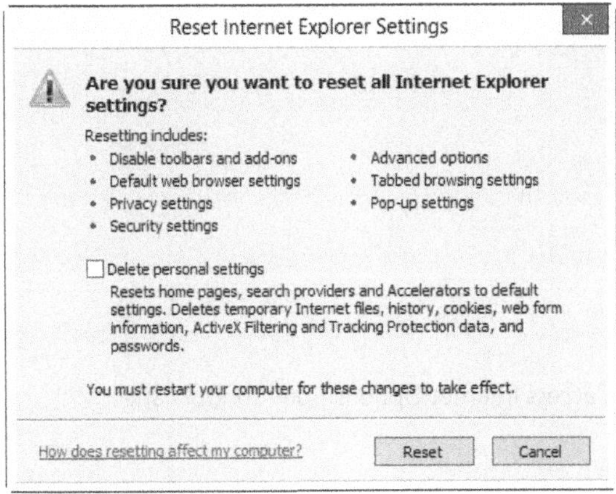

Figure 20-6 Windows informs you as to what will be reset.

> **Note**
>
> **Because your favorite websites are stored in your Windows Users folder and are not a part of Internet Explorer, resetting the browser does not delete Internet Favorites. You can perform this action comfortable in the knowledge that your favorites and bookmarks are safe.**

Resetting Internet Explorer When It Won't Start

When you can't start Internet Explorer, you need to reset it from Control Panel. To do this, open Control Panel, click Network And Internet, and then click Internet Options (see Figure 20-7). In the Internet Options dialog box that appears, click the Advanced tab, and then click Reset.

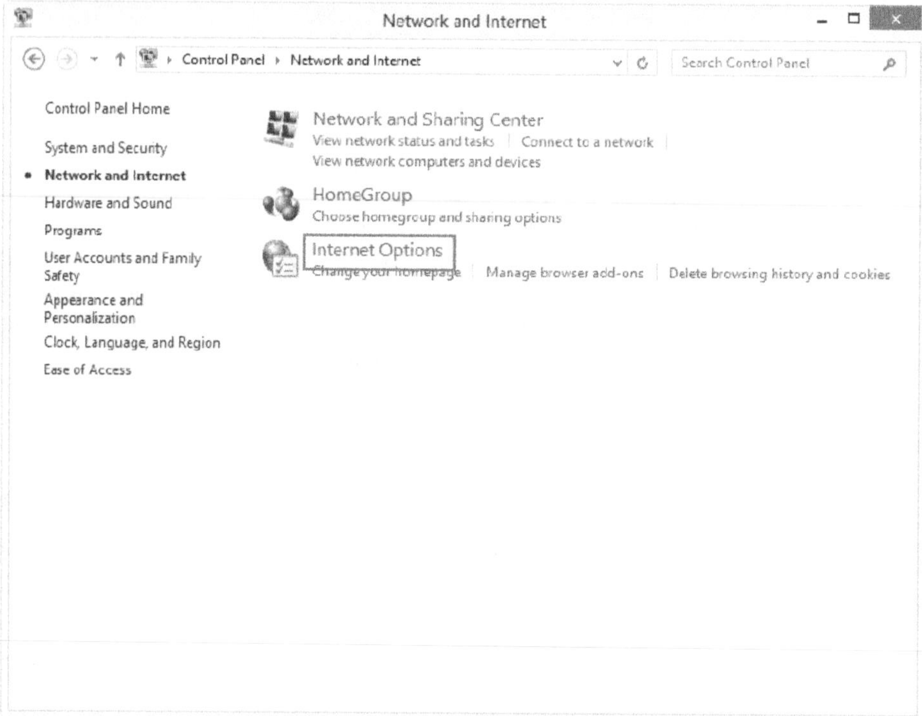

Figure 20-7 You can access Internet Options from Control Panel.

Resetting Internet Explorer 10

You can't actually reinstall Internet Explorer 10 for either the desktop or Windows 8 version of Internet Explorer 10 because Microsoft does not provide downloadable software to support them. If you try to download the Internet Explorer versions for Windows 8, you will be notified that they are not compatible with Windows 8.

You can, however, reset Internet Explorer by running the System File Checker, which replaces any corrupt files in the program. (See the section "Using the System File Checker" later in this chapter for more information.) If Internet Explorer still malfunctions after you run the System File Checker, and you are unable to restore Windows 8 from a backup made at a time when the browser was working properly, you might need to turn Internet Explorer off and use a different web browser. To turn off Internet Explorer, in Control Panel, click Programs, click Programs And Features, and then click Turn Windows Features On Or Off.

Updating Internet Explorer via Windows Update

In other chapters of this book, I stress the importance of turning Windows Update on. Windows Update might provide an update that can fix browser problems you are experiencing. Performing a manual update is also worth a try to check whether any new updates for the browser are available, and you do this by running Windows Update from Control Panel.

Alternatives to Internet Explorer

Internet Explorer 10 is one of the safest, fastest, and most compatible web browsers available. Although I regularly advise against installing any software in Windows that duplicates features that are already part of the operating system, I would say that sticking with Internet Explorer 10 is fine. However, some people still might not want to use Internet Explorer, and so here are my suggestions for alternatives:

- **Google Chrome** As a rival and mainstream alternative to Internet Explorer, the Google Chrome browser is really the only one I can recommend. It is quick, stable, and very secure, and it has been designed with speed in mind. You can download it from *http://chrome.google.com*.

- **Mozilla Firefox** Some people like feature-packed web browsers, and the move away from supporting add-ins might be one step too far. In this case, then, the only browser to consider is Mozilla Firefox, because it has the best and biggest ecosystem of third-party add-ins of all the web browsers. Please keep in mind, however, that add-ins will not only make the browser slow but also pose serious risks to your security and the reliability of your computer. You can download Firefox from *http://www.firefox.com*.

Using the System File Checker

The System File Checker has for a long time been the hidden gem in Windows. It checks the integrity of each file that makes up Windows 8 and replaces any that are corrupt, have been tampered with (perhaps by malware), or have been accidentally deleted with a copy from the original installation DVD or installation flash drive.

To open the System File Checker, perform the following steps:

1. From the desktop or on the Start screen, press Windows logo key+X.
2. Click Command Prompt (Admin) (see Figure 20-8). You need to run this option because the System File Checker needs administrator privileges to overwrite Windows operating system files.

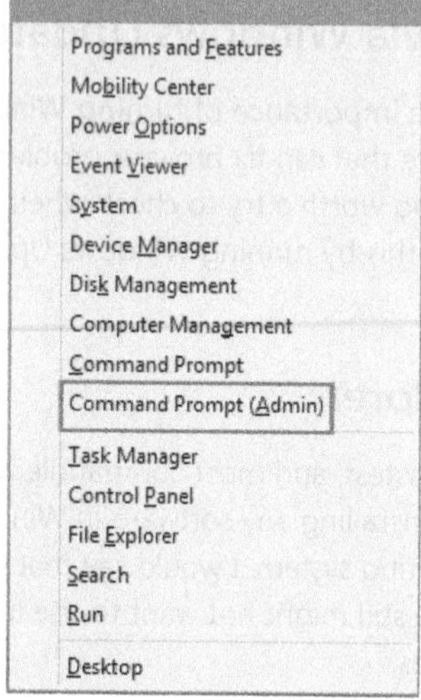

Figure 20-8 The WinX menu.

3. In the dialog box that appears, type **SFC /SCANNOW**, and then press Enter to start the System File Checker.

> **NOTE**
>
> **The System File Checker can verify the integrity of your system files at any time, but if you need to repair any, you will need a copy of your Windows 8 installation media with any additionally released service packs.**

The following are switches that you can use with the System File Checker in Windows 8:

- **/SCANNOW** Scans all the operating system files and repairs any that are corrupt or missing.
- **/VERIFYONLY** Reports any corrupt or missing files but does not attempt to repair them. This can be run without requiring the Windows 8 installation media.
- **/SCANFILE** Scans and, if necessary, attempts to repair a specific Windows file. It is used in the format **/SCANFILE=*c:*\Windows\system32\file.dll**, where *c:* represents the hard disk on which Windows 8 is installed.
- **/VERIFYFILE** The same as SCANFILE but scans only to verify the integrity of a specific file.
- **/OFFBOOTDIR** Can be used in offline mode to verify the boot files for Windows 8, perhaps if you have a multiboot Windows 8 system or are starting your computer from a Windows To Go USB flash drive. It is used in the format **/OFFBOOTDIR=d:**.
- **/OFFWINDIR** The same as **OFFBOOTDIR**, but performs an offline scan of a Windows folder. It is used in the following format: **/OFFWINDIR=d:\windows**.

INSIDE OUT

System File Checker and Windows 8 service packs

To run System File Checker in repair mode, you must have an installation DVD or an installation USB flash drive containing the service pack that's currently installed in your copy of Windows 8. This might mean that you need to create new installation media. See Chapter 21, "Demystifying Windows 8 Problems," for instructions about how to do this.

Using System Configuration for Diagnostic Startup

You can use MSConfig to start your computer into several different diagnostic startup modes. To access MSConfig, on the Start screen, search for **msconfig**. On the Boot tab of the System Configuration dialog box are several options that you might find useful.

Select the Safe Boot check box to start the computer in Safe Mode the next time you start it. You might want to do this if you have a keyboard error or you keep missing the chance to press Shift+F8 when starting the system.

> **NOTE**
>
> **As useful as the System File Checker is, the question I am asked about it more than any other is whether it can be run from Safe Mode, Diagnostic Startup Mode, or from a system repair disc or recovery drive. The answer to this is No, it will run only from within a startup copy of Windows.**

Select Boot Log (see Figure 20-9) to create a text file called Ntblog.txt. When you start the system next, that file will report on everything that worked (and didn't work). This can be an invaluable tool for diagnosing drivers or services that are unresponsive when Windows loads. You can find this boot log on your Windows drive in the root folder (see Figure 20-10). Note that sometimes the extension might be hidden.

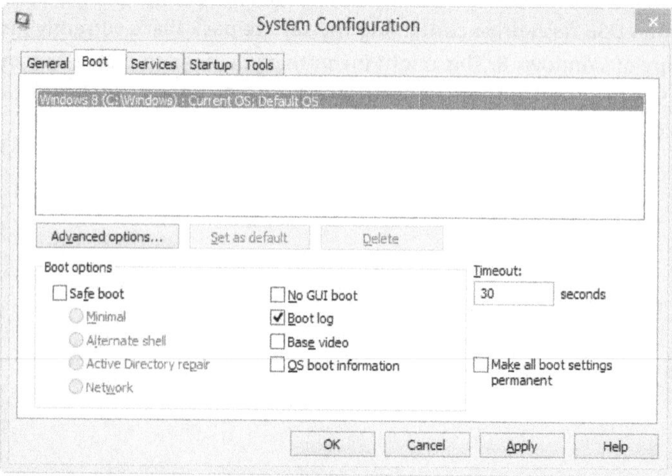

Figure 20-9 Diagnostic startups in MSConfig.

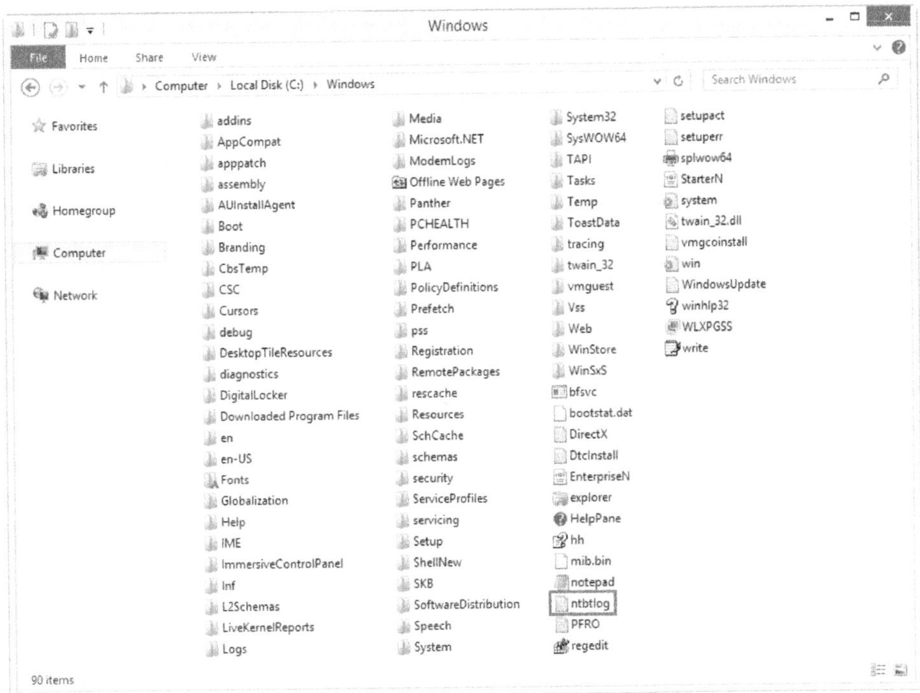

Figure 20-10 The boot log file in Windows.

Double-click the boot log to open it in Notepad. A complete list of every system service, driver, and program that loaded—or did not load—when Windows last started is displayed (see Figure 20-11). You can use this information to diagnose problematic services or drivers.

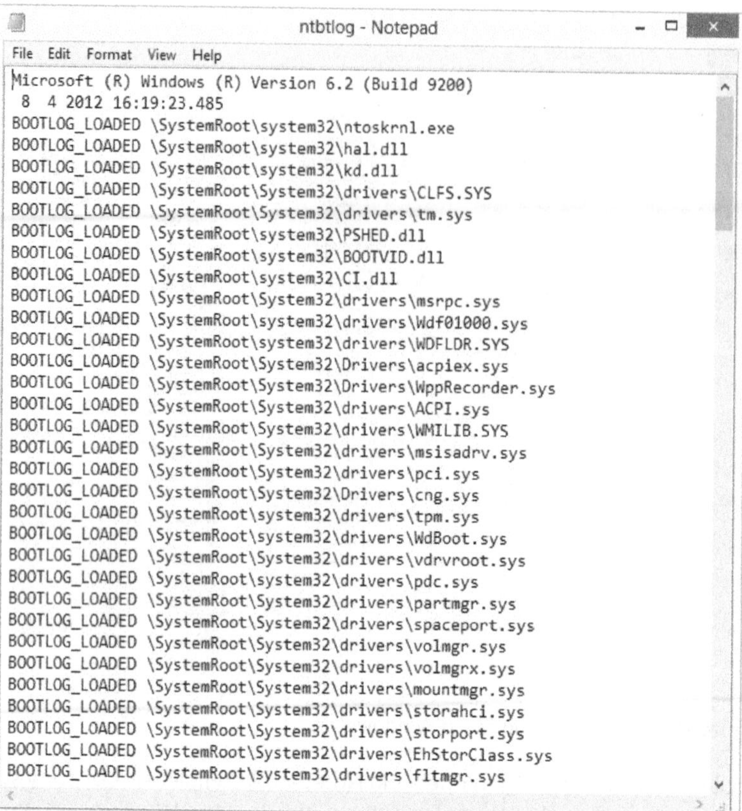

Figure 20-11 The boot log as viewed in Notepad.

You can find additional (and arguably the most useful) startup options on the General tab of the System Configuration dialog box (see Figure 20-12). Here you can disable startup programs and some services to start Windows 8 in a Diagnostic Startup mode, which offers more functionality than Safe Mode. This diagnostic mode is a simplified version of Windows 8 that you can use to troubleshoot problems.

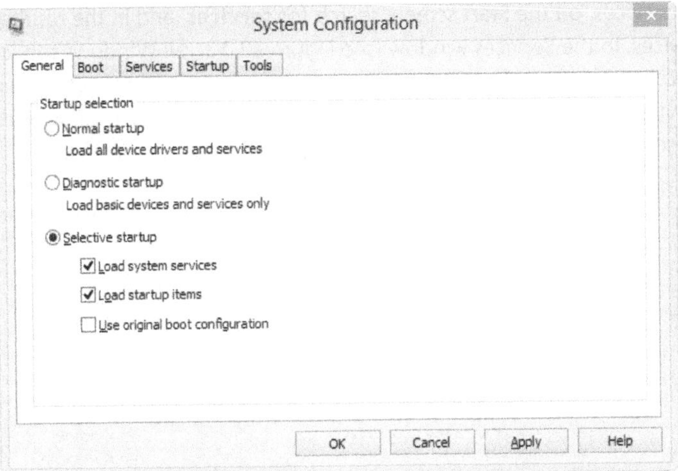

Figure 20-12 System Configuration offers an additional Diagnostic Startup mode.

> **NOTE**
>
> **Remember that the System File Checker cannot be run in Safe Mode or in Diagnostic Startup mode.**

Managing Windows Services

Services are operating system components that start when Windows loads or when you perform an action that requires a specific feature within the operating system. These services include managing the desktop interface, the firewall, and printer spooling.

> **CAUTION!**
>
> **You should always be very careful when working with services in Windows 8, because disabling the wrong one can make Windows stop responding.**

To access services, on the Start screen, search for **services**, and in the results, click View Local Services. In the Services window (see Figure 20-13), all Windows services are listed alphabetically by default. The Status column is the most useful to sort by because it shows which services are running. You can make columns wider to more easily read the content. Read the service descriptions to ensure you disable the correct service.

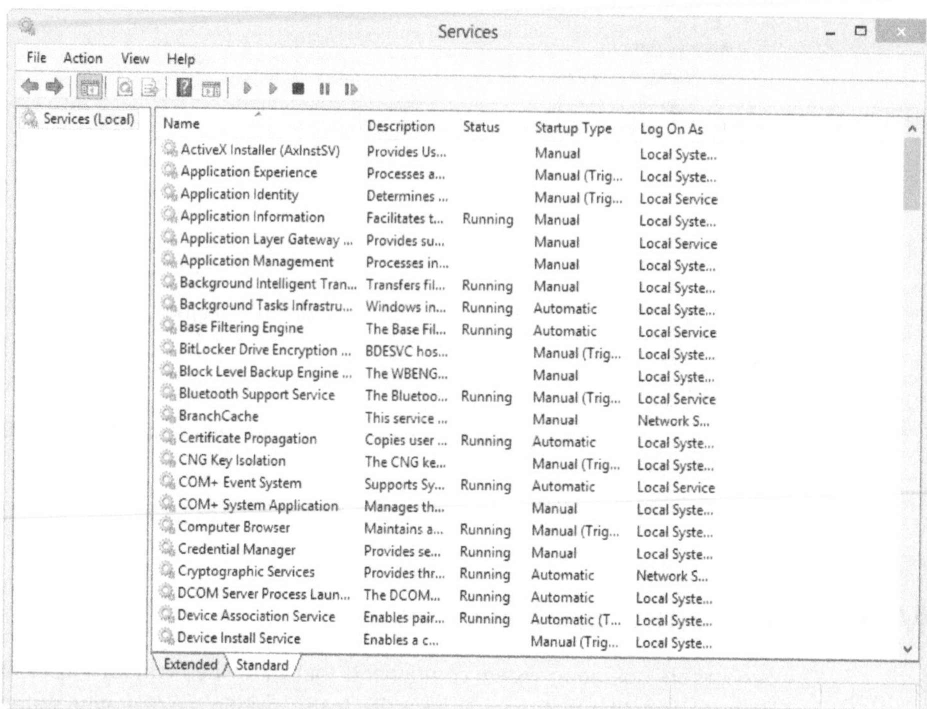

Figure 20-13 The Services window.

INSIDE OUT

When would you want to disable a service?

I would not recommend disabling any services that are a part of Windows, but you might want to disable third-party software services (such as trialware antivirus software) that are causing slowdowns or other problems. In the Services dialog box, you can stop these services from running or change the startup type to manual (so that they start only when needed).

Right-click a service, and then click Properties. In the dialog box that appears, click the General tab. On the General tab, you can disable the service if required (see Figure 20-14). On the Recovery tab, you can choose which actions Windows should take if the particular service stops working for any reason.

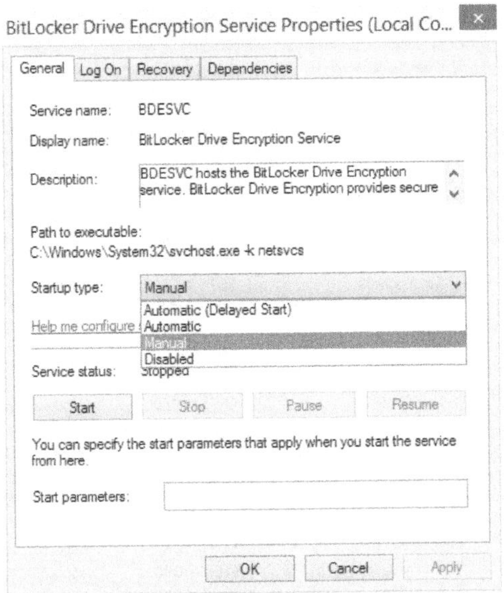

Figure 20-14 You can set the properties for a service.

On the Dependencies tab, you can check whether the service cannot run without other services being active. This can help you to determine whether exiting a service will cause another service to stop responding.

Working with the Windows Registry

The *registry* is a database in which the settings for Windows and all of your installed software are kept. One copy of the registry is maintained for each user, in hidden files called Ntuser.dat files. These files contain individual settings and preferences for each user. They are located in the root of each user account folder on your Windows drive; the main registry files are located in the \Windows\System32\Config folder.

The Windows registry can be manually edited by using the Registry Editor (see Figure 20-15). To access the Registry Editor, open the Start screen, and then search for **regedit**.

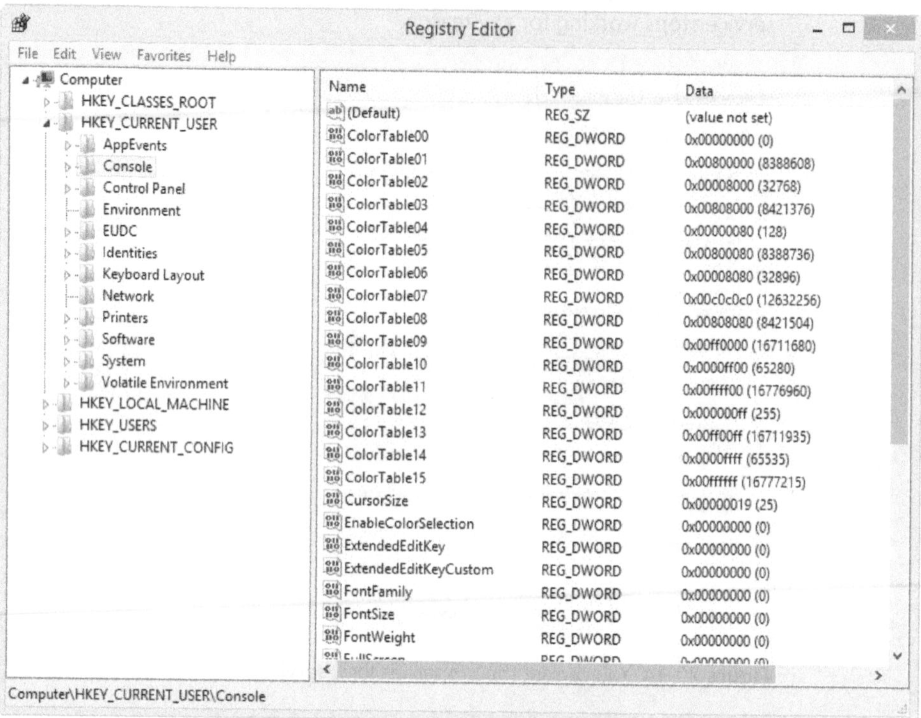

Figure 20-15 The Windows registry.

Occasionally, you might need to change or remove a setting in the Windows registry, for example, if a Microsoft Knowledge Base (KB) article advises a change to fix a problem. Do this with great care, however, because changing the wrong setting in the registry can cause Windows 8 to stop responding. Thus, when you're looking for information, always be wary of random search engine results or blogs that suggest changes.

The registry is separated into the following five different sections. (I cover how to use the registry in depth in Chapter 35, "Working with the Registry.")

- **HKEY_CLASSES_ROOT** You should not change these settings. They include essential Windows system settings along with other elements such as file associations.
- **HKEY_CURRENT_USER** These are the custom settings for the currently logged-on user and are the most commonly changed. These will include settings for Windows and installed software.
- **HKEY_LOCAL_MACHINE** This section is for general Windows and software settings. You might need to make changes in this section.
- **HKEY_USERS** This section is for general controls for user accounts; you will not need to change these settings.
- **HKEY_CURRENT_CONFIG** These are additional settings related to your current configuration; you will not need to change these settings.

In only two situations will you really need to change or remove settings in the Windows registry:

- When you are following specific written instructions about how to deal with a problem or are tweaking advanced (hidden) settings in Windows 8.
- When you are removing settings left behind by an uninstalled program that are causing problems with Windows 8 or other programs.

The most common tasks you will need to preform are creating a new setting or changing an existing one. To do these tasks, go to the correct location in the registry (you might be following specific instructions from a website or manual, which will guide you to exactly the right place in the registry), and then right-click either a blank space to create a new setting, or an existing setting to change the setting (see Figure 20-16).

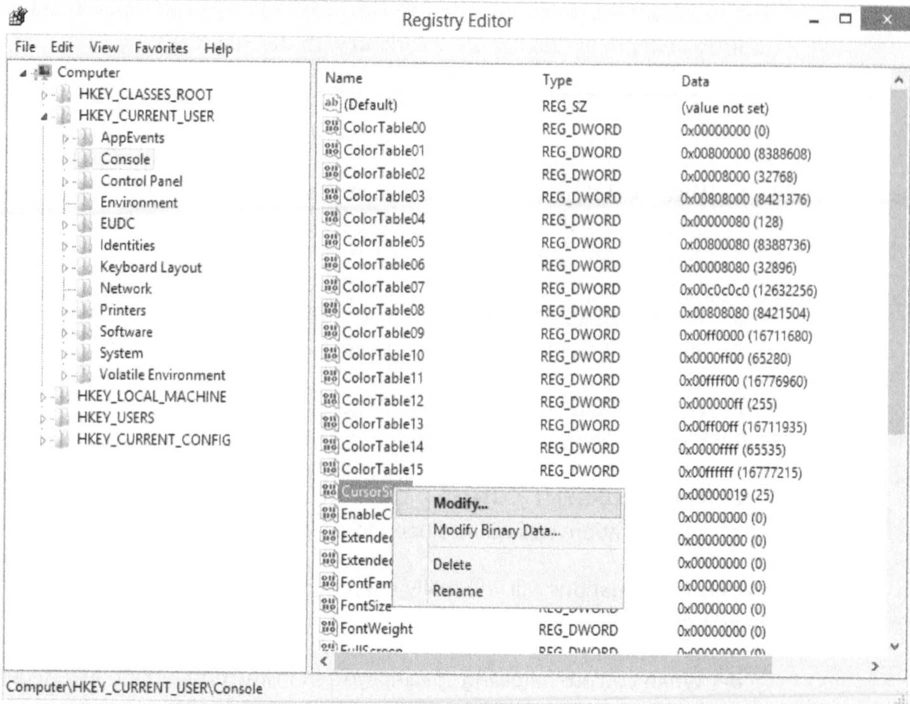

Figure 20-16 Changing a setting in the Windows registry.

Removing the Registry Settings for an Uninstalled Program

You can find settings left behind by an improperly uninstalled program in two ways. The simplest way is to use the Find and Find Next commands on the Edit menu in the Registry Editor. These commands are also available by pressing Ctrl+F (Find) or Ctrl+F3 (Find Next).

You can also search for the settings manually. You will find them in the following two locations:

- HKEY_CURRENT_USER/Software
- HKEY_LOCAL_MACHINE/SOFTWARE

To remove a setting for a specific program from the registry, right-click the setting, and then click Delete (see Figure 20-17). You should always be careful when you do this and back up the registry before you make any changes.

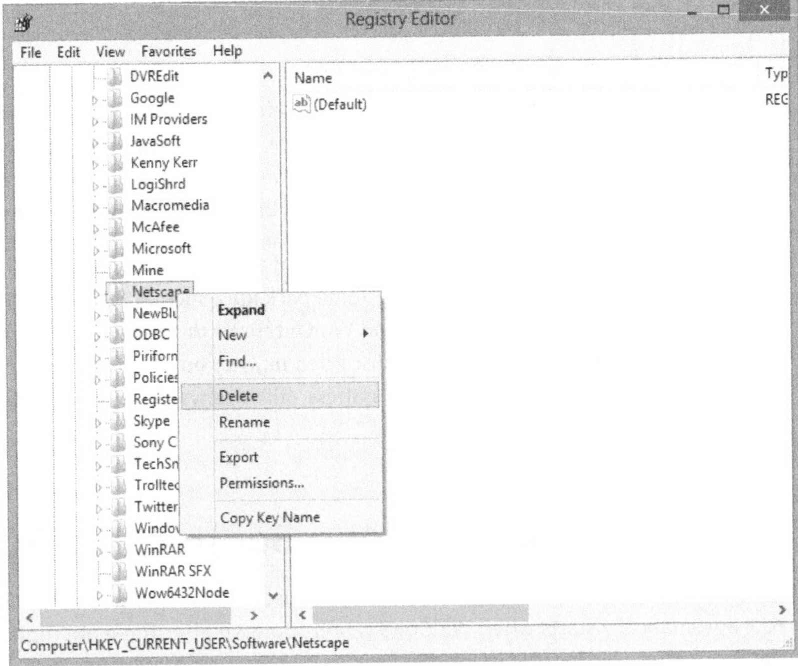

Figure 20-17 You can remove unwanted software settings in the Windows registry.

INSIDE OUT Back up the registry before making changes

Always create a backup copy of the registry before making any changes to the registry. To do so, on the File menu, click Export. To restore this backup, on the File menu, click Import. (Note that you might need to do this in Safe Mode if the changes you have made render Windows 8 unstable.)

INSIDE OUT **Using registry optimizers**

Opinion is generally divided regarding the benefits of registry optimization software. Certainly, on computers running earlier software, for which both memory and hard disk space were at a premium and very expensive, anything you could do to reduce the overall memory and disk footprint of Windows brought noticeable benefits.

Now, however, optimizing the registry is less of an issue, and a messy registry is unlikely to slow down your computer. Some packages, such as the excellent CCleaner (*http://www.piriform.com/ccleaner*) and WinOptimizer (*http://www.ashampoo.com*), do a great job of removing unused and discarded registry entries. The choice of whether to do this is entirely yours, but I do run these utilities myself once in a while.

Using Command Prompt Options, Bootrec, and BCDedit

Chapter 14, "Easy Ways to Repair Windows 8," discussed Windows Startup Repair. This tool automatically starts when Windows is unresponsive after three attempts, but you can get more repair options for diagnosing and troubleshooting problems that occur when Windows 8 starts by starting your computer from your Windows 8 installation DVD or by creating a system repair disc or recovery drive.

INSIDE OUT **Accessing the boot options menu from the hard disk**

You can access the boot options menu (formerly the Windows Recovery Environment, or WinRE), if it has not been disabled, by pressing F8 on your keyboard after the basic input/output system (BIOS) screen disappears but before you see the Starting Windows logo. In the boot options menu that appears, click Repair Your Computer. Note that the boot options menu might not function properly, however, if there is a problem with Windows or your hard disk.

> **NOTE**
>
> **Even though you might have a USB3 flash drive, your computer might not recognize it as a boot device in a USB3 port. If this happens, plug it into a USB2 port, and it should work as a boot device.**

To access some very useful options for repairing your computer, click Troubleshoot, click Advanced Options, and then click Command Prompt (see Figure 20-18). You might be pleased to learn that Chkdsk (Chkdsk.exe) is still available at the command prompt in Windows 8. You can use it with the following command-line switches:

- **/F** To fix errors on the disk
- **/R** To locate and attempt repairs on bad disk sectors
- **/X** To force, if necessary, the disk to dismount before checking

Other options are available by typing **chkdsk /?** and you can find a complete list with details at *http://technet.microsoft.com/en-us/library/cc730714(v=WS.10).aspx.*

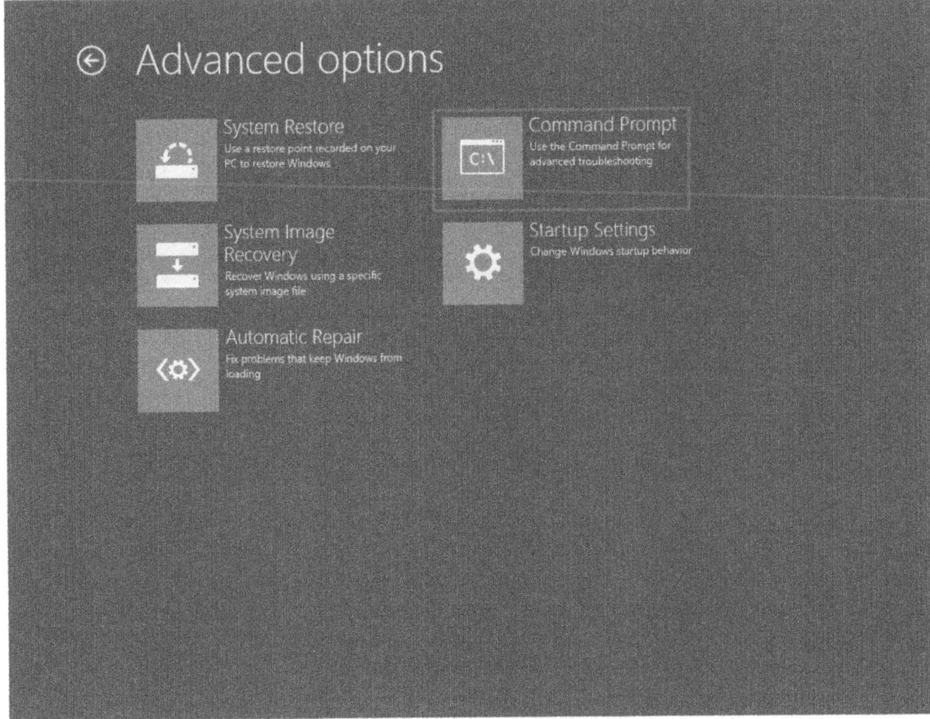

Figure 20-18 The Advanced Options in the startup menu.

Using Bootrec.exe

If you miss the Recovery Console, fear not; it's still in Windows 8, but in a different form. You use it by adding command-line switches to perform various actions. You can access the new Bootrec.exe command from the command prompt in the boot options menu.

Repairing the Boot Options Menu by Using BootRec

The boot options menu is the list of installed operating systems on your computer that appears when Windows starts. You will not see this menu if you have only one operating system installed. This menu can become corrupt, however, and if it does, you will need to rebuild it. You can do this by typing the following in a Command Prompt window (see Figure 20-19): **bootrec /RebuildBcd**. (The Command Prompt window is compatible with screen readers. By right-clicking the bar at the top of the window, you can change its properties, for example, the font size and the background color to make the window more legible).

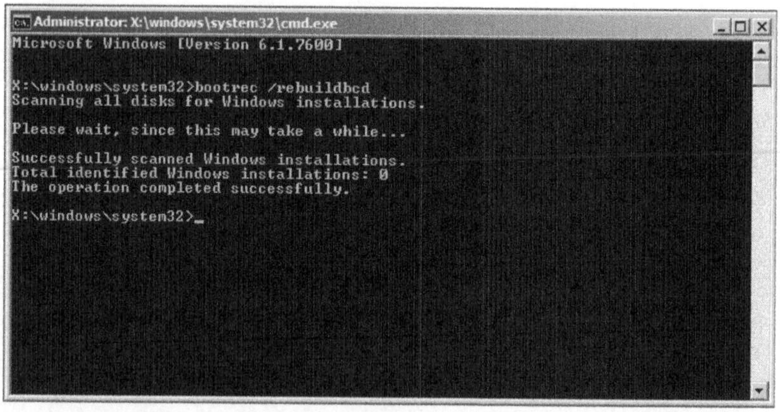

```
Administrator: X:\windows\system32\cmd.exe
Microsoft Windows [Version 6.1.7600]

X:\windows\system32>bootrec /rebuildbcd
Scanning all disks for Windows installations.

Please wait, since this may take a while...

Successfully scanned Windows installations.
Total identified Windows installations: 0
The operation completed successfully.

X:\windows\system32>_
```

Figure 20-19 You can rebuild the boot options menu.

Sometimes, this command won't work, and you will need to delete the boot options menu and rebuild it from scratch. To do this, in the Command Prompt window, type the following commands:

```
Bcdedit /export c:BCD_Backup
c:
cd boot
attrib bcd -s -h -r
ren c:\boot\bcd bcd.old
bootrec /RebuildBcd
```

Here are other switches you can use with the BootRec command:

- **/FixMbr** This switch repairs the master boot record (MBR) in Windows 8.
- **/FixBoot** This option writes a new boot sector to the system disk. This can be useful if the boot sector has become corrupt or damaged, perhaps by trying to install an earlier version of Windows on the hard disk.
- **/ScanOS** This option scans your hard disks for any compatible operating systems that might not be viewable on the boot options menu.

Using BCDEdit

BCDEdit is a program used for maintaining, changing, and rebuilding the boot options menu in Windows 8. You should not need to use BCDEdit to repair your copy of Windows 8, because the tools I have mentioned in this chapter should repair any problems. (For instructions about how to use it, see Chapter 18, "Troubleshooting Windows 8 Startup Issues.") When you are finished using the Command Prompt window, type **exit** to close it.

Other DOS Commands in the Command Prompt Window

Other DOS commands are available in the Command Prompt window:

- **Copy** Copies files from one location to another
- **Move** Moves files from one location to another
- **Rd** Removes an empty directory
- **Ren** Renames a file or directory
- **More** Shows the contents of a file, one page at a time
- **Type** Shows all the contents of a file without pausing the screen
- **Xcopy** Copies a folder and all its content to another location
- **Mkdir** Makes a new directory
- **Diskpart** Loads the Windows disk management program
- **Dir** Displays a list of files and folders
- **Cd** Moves you to a different folder
- **Attrib** Changes the attributes of the file (such as read-only)
- **Del** Deletes a file

The switch options for each command are available by typing the ***/?*** switch after the command, where *?* is the specific switch.

INSIDE OUT Starting in Safe Mode

You might also want to start your computer in Safe Mode. To do so, press Shift+F8 while Windows is starting to open the boot options menu. On this menu, you'll see a stripped-down diagnostic mode of Windows in which you can run tests and check to see whether the operating system is functioning correctly.

CHAPTER 21

Demystifying Windows 8 Problems

The core structure of Windows 8 is enormous, with tens of thousands of files containing millions of lines of programming code, a huge and complex folder structure, and additional files required for 64-bit operating system. Sometimes you have to work with this file and folder structure when you are troubleshooting problems or optimizing the operating system before you back up a clean installation. In this chapter, I explain the purpose of certain files and folders and their significance. You want to make sure you do not remove an element that could compromise your system.

Understanding the Core Operating System Files in Windows 8

Figure 21-1 shows the Windows 8 folder structure. Some of these folders contain files for specific functions. For example, the \Windows\ehome folder includes Windows Media Center files, and the \Windows\fonts folder stores Windows fonts.

A few of these folders contain core operating system files, described in the following list. I focus on these because file corruptions are most likely to occur in them.

- **C:\Windows\Boot** This folder contains files necessary for starting Windows 8.
- **C:\Windows\Help** The Windows 8 Help files are located in the Help folder. If you cannot start Help, these files might be corrupt or missing.
- **C:\Windows\Inf** Windows uses the INF files in this folder when installing hardware and software drivers.
- **C:\Windows\System32** This folder contains the guts of Windows 8. All the main Windows components are located here. A problematic Windows file is likely located here.

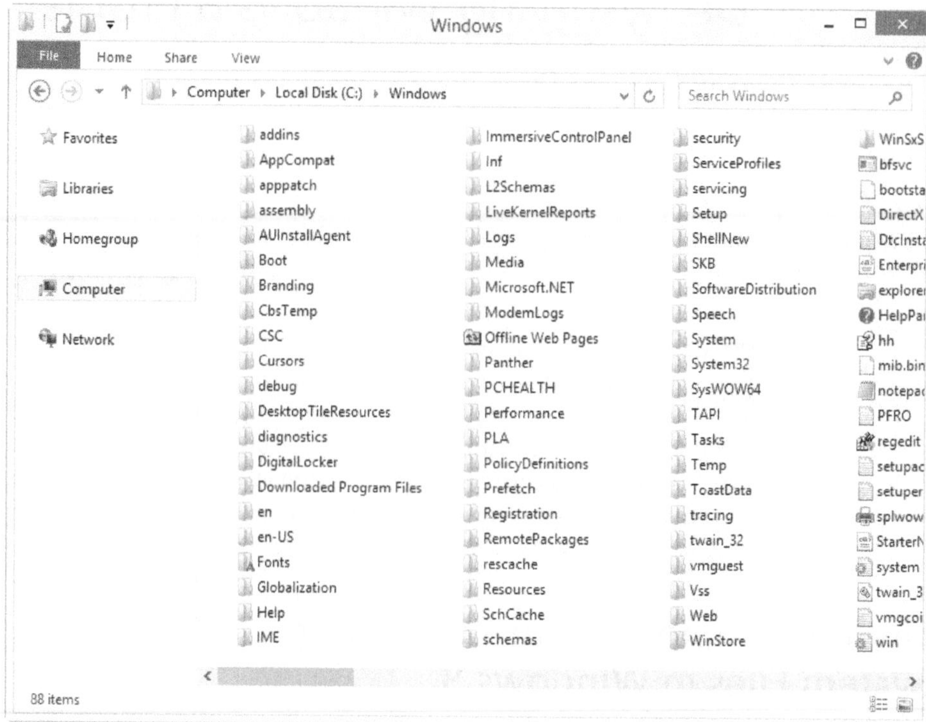

Figure 21-1 The folder structure for Windows 8.

The following files are commonly located within the C:\Windows\System32 folder structure. Note that you will need to change the default setting to show hidden files to see the contents of hidden folders. See the Inside Out sidebar "Show hidden system files and file extensions in File Explorer" in this chapter for more information.

- **ActiveX Files (*.ocx)** Microsoft ActiveX is a programming framework that software authors use to design reusable components to be shared across applications. Sometimes, these controls are shared across programs from different software houses, and in earlier software, incompatibilities with various versions of the .ocx files might exist. For example, two programs might require different versions of the file. Windows 8 is very good at handling these conflicts and more successful than in previous versions of Windows; however, conflicts can still occur.

- **Applications** *Applications* are the main programs that constitute Windows 8. If you are trying to start a built-in Windows feature and it cannot be found, the associated application file might be missing from the Applications folder.

- **Dynamic-Link library (.dll)** Dynamic-link library files are shared library files. Like .ocx files, .dll files are program and Windows components that can be shared across software applications. Occasionally, Windows becomes unresponsive because a .dll file is corrupt, or because the .dll file is an incorrect version that is not supported by the program or feature trying to access it.

  As with .ocx files, Windows 8 is very good at handling .dll file conflicts, but issues with these files can still occur. Windows 8 includes more .dll files than any other type of file.

- **Control Panel Item (*.cpl)** Windows 8 starts .cpl files when you access features in Control Panel. If an item cannot be found, the associated .cpl file might be missing or corrupt.

- **Microsoft Common Console Document (*.msc)** The Microsoft Management Console (MMC) programs are stored in various folders in the main \Windows folder. If you cannot start an MMC item, the program file might be corrupt. Bear in mind, though, that to maintain backward compatibility, multiple versioned copies of the appropriate MMC file in the WinSxS folder might exist.

- **VBScript Script File (*.vbs)** Scripts produced in Visual Basic Scripting (VBScript) can be a target for virus writers. Some VBScript scripts are stored in the main Windows 8 folders.

- **C:\Windows\System 32\Drivers and C:\Windows\System 32\DriverStore** These folders contain all the hardware and software drivers for your hardware. You can back up these folders and restore them manually if an event such as a driver malfunction or faulty driver upgrade causes problems with Windows 8.

- **C:\Windows\WinSxS** Windows stores and organizes compatible duplicate versions of files in the WinSxS folder. This folder is usually very large, even bigger than the System32 folder.

CAUTION!

Although it can be tempting to look at the C:\Windows\WinSXS folder and ask why you need a 7-gigabyte (GB) folder, never delete the folder. This folder contains files that are critical for the operation of Windows 8 and your software.

- **C:\Users\%username%\AppData** In each user's folder is a subfolder named AppData (see Figure 21-2), which is hidden by default. Application-specific files and settings, which are stored in this folder, are used by desktop software on your computer to store settings and other relevant files associated with program operation.

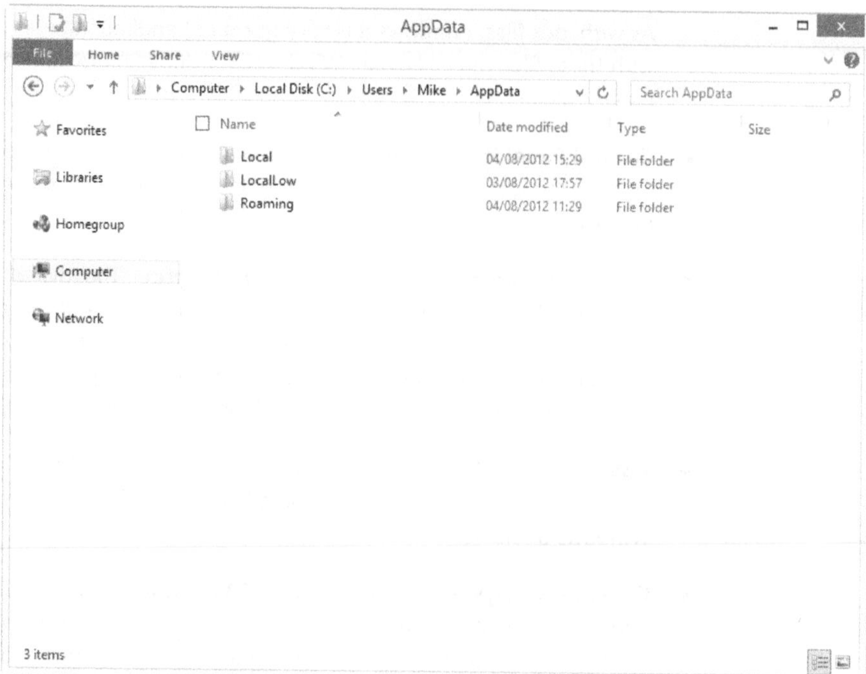

Figure 21-2 The AppData subfolders.

- **C:\Windows\System32\Config** The main operating system registry files are located separately from the user registry files; thus, they can be backed up (and restored) independently.

- **C:\Program Files and C:\Program Files (x86)** These are the two folders for programs and software in Windows 8. If you are running the 32-bit version of the operating system or Windows RT, you will see only a \Program Files folder.

- **C:\Program Files\WindowsApps** This is a hidden folder that contains the program files associated with any installed Windows 8 apps.

INSIDE OUT **Show hidden system files and file extensions in File Explorer**

By default, Windows 8 hides certain system files and file extensions so that you can't see them when you explore files and folders on your computer. To view these hidden files and extensions, on the View tab, click Options. In the Folder Options dialog box that appears, click the View tab, and then select the following: Show Hidden Files and Folders And Drives. Clear the check boxes for Hide Extensions For Known File Types and Hide Protected Operating System Files (Recommended).

Windows 8 Security and Policy Folders

Windows security and other policies that control logon, software, and user behavior and permissions are stored in the following folders:

- C:\Windows\Security
- C:\Windows\ServiceProfiles

The Windows 8 Registry

The *registry* is a database that contains configuration options and settings for Windows and your installed programs. Each user has one registry file, named Ntuser.dat (see Figure 21-3), and you can display it by showing hidden and operating system files. (See the Inside Out sidebar "Show hidden system files and file extensions in File Explorer" in this chapter for details.) You can back up registry files, but do not delete or modify them outside of the Windows Registry Editor.

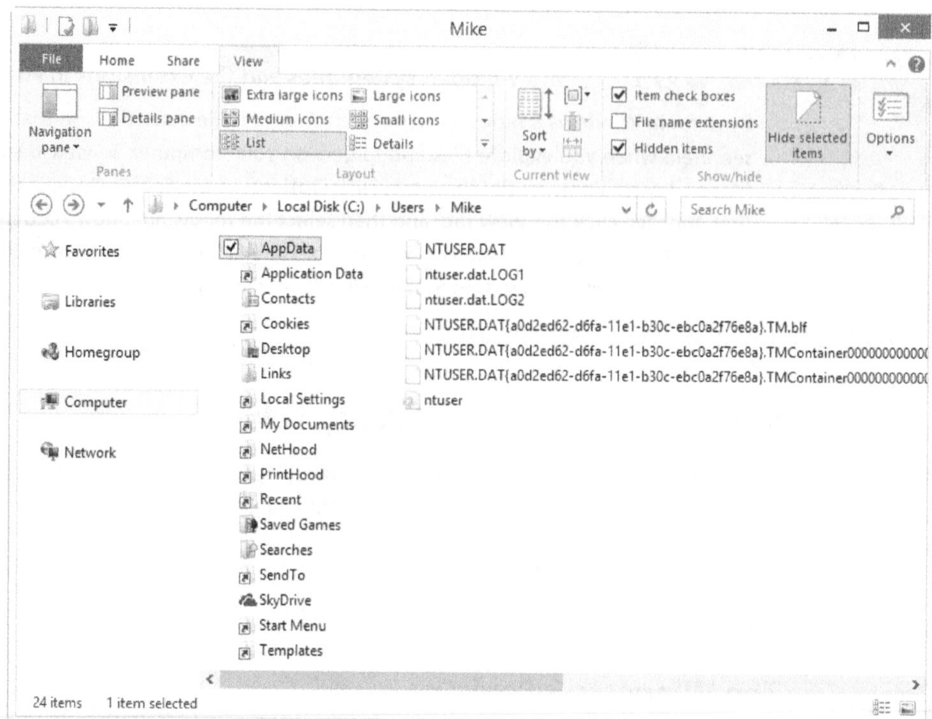

Figure 21-3 The registry files are hidden in user folders.

Personalization Folders

The main folders containing wallpapers and other personalization options are as follows:

- C:\Windows\Globalization
- C:\Windows\Media
- C:\Windows\Resources
- C:\Windows\Web

Windows 8 Logs

Several folders contain Windows 8 logs, including everything from startup information to error records. You can normally access these logs via Control Panel and MMC. You can also access the logs manually if you can't get Windows 8 to start. You can find the logs in the following folders:

- C:\Windows\Debug
- C:\Windows\Diagnostics
- C:\Windows\LiveKernelReports
- C:\Windows\Logs
- C:\Windows\ModemLogs

Temporary Files Stores

You can delete all the contents in the following Windows 8 folders if you suspect the files within them have become corrupt and are causing problems:

- **C:\Windows\Downloaded Program Files** Windows does not usually use this folder, so it will normally be empty. It contains functionality that enables you to easily uninstall ActiveX controls.
- **C:\Windows\Prefetch** Windows tracks the programs and files you frequently use and stores this information in the Prefetch folder so that it can preload them when appropriate (for instance, when starting a program that you run often). Sometimes the prefetch files can become corrupt. If you suspect this has happened, you can safely delete the contents of this folder. Windows will then rebuild the prefetch database.
- **C:\Windows\SoftwareDistribution** This folder contains Windows Update configuration options and downloaded files. If Windows Update will not install updates, you can delete the contents of this folder to try to fix the problem. However, doing this will also reset Windows Update, revealing any hidden updates (which you may have hidden because they cause incompatibilities or problems), and changing other Windows Update settings to their defaults. You will need to change these settings back in Windows Update after deleting the contents of this folder.
- **C:\Windows\Temp** This folder is the temporary files store. Its contents can be deleted at any time if you suspect any temporary files are causing a problem, for example, if your downloads are unable to run, open, or install.

Using Advanced File Restore

I could write an entire book on the Windows 8 file and folder structure. But the information presented in the previous section will help you restore Windows 8 files and folders on a file-by-file, folder-by-folder basis. You do not need to restore folders that contain temporary files; temporary files are unnecessary when restoring Windows to working order, and you could run the risk of restoring a corrupt file. You can also use the preceding descriptions to decide which folders containing personalization options to include or ignore in a restore.

The most important folders—the ones you are most likely to restore—are the Boot, Inf, System32, and WinSxS folders. These folders contain the essential parts of the operating system. Most likely, problems are caused by corrupt or missing files in these critical folders.

CAUTION!

If you restore the folders containing security or other computer policies, be certain that no changes were made since the backup was created. If changes were made, you could encounter additional problems, such as a faulty smart card or fingerprint reader.

Creating a Slipstreamed Install DVD

Slipstreaming is the process of integrating a service pack into the original installation media. You might want to do this for a couple of reasons. First, a slipstreamed installation DVD is useful when you need to reinstall Windows or install it on a new computer. A slipstreamed version of the software is much more up-to-date than the original install. You might also want to create a slipstreamed installation DVD if you want to use System File Checker, as mentioned in the preceding section. The installation DVD you use with System File Checker must include the service pack that matches the one installed on your computer; if it doesn't, some operating system files will not match, and System File Checker will abort with an error.

Creating a slipstreamed service pack installation DVD image for Windows 8 isn't as simple as it was for Windows XP. In the following section, I describe how to do it step by step. The System File Checker quickly repairs problems with Windows 8, but if you have a service pack installed on your computer, you will also need to slipstream the service pack onto the installation media before running System File Checker. The following section details how to create a slipstreamed DVD.

What You Will Need

Before beginning the slipstream procedure, gather the following items:

- A spare hard disk or partition on which you can install a fresh copy of Windows 8.
- The Windows Assessment and Deployment Kit (Windows ADK), which you can download for free by searching the Microsoft website for **Windows 8 ADK**. You will need approximately 4.2 GB of free disk space to install the Windows ADK on your computer.
- A blank CD or DVD.
- Software for creating an ISO image, such as UltraISO (available from *http://www.ezbsystems.com/ultraiso*) or WinISO (available from *http://www.winiso.com*). You might be able to download a free trial version of the software, which will be fine for a quick job.

Step 1: Create a Windows Preinstallation Environment Startup Disc

You first need to create a startup disc for the Windows Preinstallation Environment (WinPE). To do this, perform the following steps:

1. Run the Windows 8 ADK installer, and then click Windows ADK Setup.
2. After the Windows 8 ADK is installed, open the Start screen, right-click Deployment And Imaging Tools Environment, and then click Run As Administrator.
3. In the Command Prompt window that appears, type **C:**, and then press Enter to access the ADK folder. Type **cd C:\Program Files (x86)\Windows Kits\8.0\Assessment and Deployment Kit\Windows Preinstallation Environment**, and then press Enter again.
4. Use the C:\Program Files (x86)\Windows Kits\8.0\Assessment and Deployment Kit\Windows Preinstallation Environment\Copype.cmd script to change the arguments as necessary to match the locations for your WinPE files and the desired destination folder. Valid versions include 32-bit (x86) or 64-bit (x64). Other supported types are amd64 and ia64. Type **copype.cmd x86 C:\winpe_x86** or **copype.cmd x64 C:\winpe_x64**, and then press Enter to create a folder structure in a new folder. (For the purposes of this tutorial, assume this is C:\winpe_x86.)
5. Copy the base WinPE image to this folder structure by typing **copy C:\winpe_x86\winpe.wim C:\winpe_x86\ISO\sources\boot.wim**, and then pressing Enter.

6. Add disk boot files to the files you created in steps 4 and 5 and prepare to burn them to a CD or DVD. Type the following commands, in the following order, pressing Enter after each one:

   a. **dism /Mount-wim /Winfile:C:\winpe_x86\ISO\sources\boot.wim /index:1 /MountDir:C:\winpe_x86\mount**

   b. **copy C:\winpe_x86\ISO\bootmgr C:\winpe_x86\mount**

   c. **mkdir C:\winpe_x86\mount\boot**

   d. **xcopy /cherky C:\winpe_x86\ISO\boot C:\winpe_x86\mount\boot**

7. Add the ImageX disc image creation program to the folder. Type **copy "C:\Program Files\Windows AIK\Tools\x86\ImageX.exe" C:\winpe_x86\mount**, and then press Enter.

8. Create the Boot Configuration Data (BCD) file for the disc. Type the following commands, pressing Enter after each one:

   a. **Del c:\winpe_x86\mount\boot\BCD**

   b. **Bcdedit /createstore c:\winpe_x86\mount\boot\BCD**

   c. **Bcdedit /store c:\winpe_x86\mount\boot\BCD -create {bootmgr} /d "Boot Manager"**

   d. **Bcdedit /store c:\winpe_x86\mount\boot\BCD -set {bootmgr} device boot**

   e. **Bcdedit /store c:\winpe_x86\mount\boot\BCD -create /d "WINPE" -application osloader**

9. The command in step 8e returns a GUID value. Type the following commands, substituting the GUID value returned by step 8e for *{GUID}*. The GUID should look similar to *{21EC2020-3AEA-1069-A2DD-08002B30309D}* but will contain different numbers and letters. Press Enter after each step.

   a. **Bcdedit /store c:\winpe_x86\mount\boot\BCD -set *{GUID}* osdevice boot**

   b. **Bcdedit /store c:\winpe_x86\mount\boot\BCD -set *{GUID}* device boot**

   c. **Bcdedit /store c:\winpe_x86\mount\boot\BCD -set *{GUID}* path \windows\system32\winload.exe**

   d. **Bcdedit /store c:\winpe_x86\mount\boot\BCD -set *{GUID}* systemroot \windows**

   e. **Bcdedit /store c:\winpe_x86\mount\boot\BCD -set *{GUID}* winpe yes**

   f. **Bcdedit /store c:\winpe_x86\mount\boot\BCD -displayorder *{GUID}* -addlast**

10. Create an ISO disc image that you can burn to a CD or DVD. Type **oscdimg –n –m –o –bC:\winpe_x86\etfsboot.com C:\winpe_x86\mount C:\winpe_x86\winpe_x86.iso**, and then press Enter.

    If you are instead building an ISO to an Advanced Micro Devices, Inc. (AMD) Extensible Firmware Interface (EFI) ISO, instead type **oscdimg.eXE –bC:\winpe-x64-efi\efisys.bin–pEF –u1 –udfver102 C:\winpe-x64-efi\ISO x64-efi-winpe.iso**, and then press Enter.

    For Intel Itanium–based architecture, replace *efisys.bin* with **etfsboot.com**.

11. You now have an ISO file in the C:\winpe_x86 folder. Double-click the file to start the Windows Disc Image Burner (see Figure 21-4). Note that not all computers come with DVD burning drives; you might need to obtain a USB-attached disc burner. I always recommend you select the Verify Disk After Burning check box.

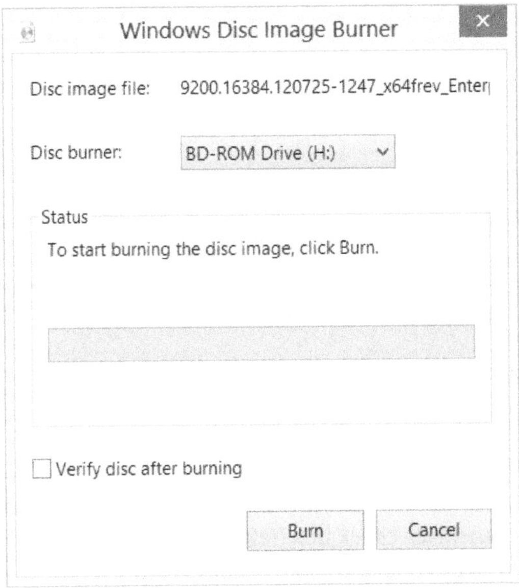

Figure 21-4 Burning a disc image in Windows 8.

Chapter 21

> **Note**
>
> You need to create only a single WinPE startup disc (and disc image). You can use the same disc to install a slipstreamed version of Windows 8 on any computer.

Step 2: Install a Fresh Copy of Windows 8

1. Using your Windows 8 installation DVD, install a fresh copy of Windows 8 onto a spare hard disk or partition. Use the version for which you want to create the slipstreamed disc, that is, Professional, Enterprise, and so on.
2. After Windows 8 is installed, and the dialog box asking for your user name and password appears, press Ctrl+Shift+F3. The system restarts in audit mode. Do not close the System Preparation Tool dialog box that appears (see Figure 21-5); you will need it later.

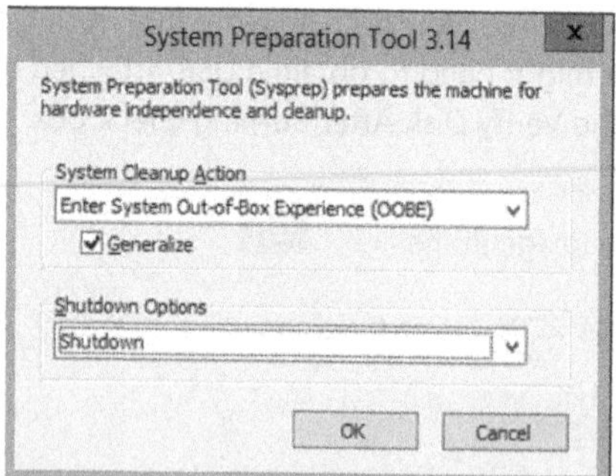

Figure 21-5 The System Preparation Tool in Windows 8.

3. Install the appropriate service pack. You can either download the service pack or install it from a CD, network, or USB flash drive.
4. Windows might restart during the service pack installation. If the Windows 8 password screen appears again, press Ctrl+Shift+F3 again to reenter Audit Mode.
5. In the System Preparation Tool dialog box, on the System Cleanup Action page, in the System Cleanup Action list, click Enter System Out-Of-Box Experience (OOBE), and then select the Generalize check box (refer to Figure 21-5), which makes changes for all user accounts created by using the custom image.

   Place the WinPE startup disc in the CD/DVD drive. In the System Preparation Tool dialog box, in the Shutdown Options list, click Restart, and then click OK when you are ready to create the new Windows image.

INSIDE OUT **Performing other actions in Audit Mode**

You can also perform other actions in Audit Mode, such as installing software, changing Windows settings, or installing device drivers. Be careful when installing drivers if you intend to use this new install image to install Windows on a different computer from the one on which you are creating the image, because the hardware will likely be different. Also take care when installing software; you must leave enough space for the final disc image to fit on a single blank DVD or USB flash drive.

Step 3: Create a New Windows Image File

After you follow the previous procedure, the system starts in the WinPE environment, and a Command Prompt window appears.

Noting the following substitution guidelines, type **E:\imagex /compress fast /check /flags "Pro" /capture D: E:\install.wim "Windows 8 Pro" "Windows 8 Pro Custom"** at the command prompt:

- If necessary, substitute the name of your Windows 8 edition for *Pro* in the command.
- Substitute the drive letters of the disks on which you have the second copy of Windows 8 installed and the disk where you want WinPE to store the new Windows 8 Image file. The file will be approximately 2 to 2.5 GB.

Step 4: Create a New Windows 8 Installation DVD

1. Use ISO creation software to make an ISO file from your original Windows 8 installation DVD. (See the Inside Out sidebar titled "Extracting a Windows 8 DVD to your hard disk" for more information about where you can get this.)
2. Using the same ISO creation software, locate the newly created Install.wim file you created in the previous procedure, and add it to the disc image file, overwriting the one that exists there in the \sources\ folder. Double-click the image to burn it to the DVD by using the Windows Disc Image Burner.

INSIDE OUT Extracting a Windows 8 DVD to your hard disk

Depending on what ISO creation software you are using, you might need to extract the contents of the installation DVD to your hard disk and then add the new Install.wim file to the installation contents there. To reburn your image to a disc, you might need a Microsoft bootable disc image.

To mount a disk image in Windows 8, double-click or right-click it, and then click Mount. Here you can view the contents of the disk image in File Explorer (see Figure 21-6).

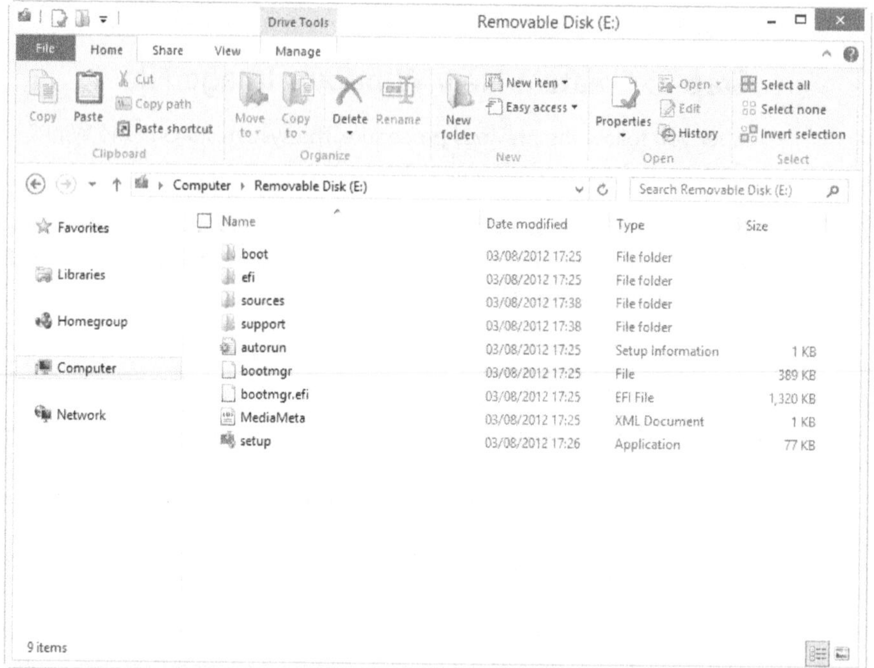

Figure 21-6 Extracting a Windows 8 Image in Windows 8.

You will also need DVD-burning software such as Nero (*http://www.nero.com*) or Roxio (*http://www.roxio.com*) to burn this new replacement Windows 8 install disc. In Nero, use options for No Emulation; Load segment of Sectors as "07C0"; and Number of Loaded sectors as "4".

Note

You can delete the second copy of Windows 8 after you finish the procedures, although I always recommend testing the install disc before deleting anything that's taken a long time to install and configure.

Third-Party Slipstreaming Software

Third-party solutions are available for slipstreaming Windows service packs, such as RT7Lite for Windows 8, which can be updated to support Windows 8. These third-party programs can simplify the Windows 8 service pack slipstreaming process and can also offer support for creating discs that will install into any edition of Windows 8. When software becomes available to make slipstreaming Windows 8 service packs simple, I will announce it on my website *http://www.thelongclimb.com*.

CHAPTER 22

Finding Help on the Internet

Windows is used around the world, and unless you're an early adopter of technology or are using newly released software, you can be reasonably certain you aren't the first person to encounter your problem.

Windows 8 is similar to Windows Vista, Windows 7, and Windows Server, and these operating systems share many features, components, and error codes. Lots of information about the operating systems is available; an enormous ecosystem of help and support for Windows 8 has been building since 2012, with technical community leaders, Microsoft Most Valuable Professional (MVP) awardees (including myself), enthusiasts, and bloggers all asking and answering questions online, so you're never alone as long as you have an Internet connection. Many websites exist to help with computer problems, and technical experts can be very generous about sharing solutions to problems they've encountered. An Internet search should always be your first step toward addressing a problem. It is for me. In this chapter, I explain how to query effectively and where you can find quality information online.

Optimizing Your Searches

The major search engines, including Bing, Google, and Yahoo, are good at recognizing search queries and providing relevant results. When I search on the phrase **network driver for dell laptop**, for instance, I see an entire page of results, all offering appropriate drivers to download. Use precise search entries to avoid returning too many results. Here are some simple search techniques you can use in all major search engines to improve the returned results:

- **Quotation marks** Place text in double quotation marks (for example, **"dynamode BT878a"**) to ensure the search engine treats the text inside the quotation marks as a phrase, or *string*, and not as separate words.

- **Plus (+) or minus (–) sign** Adding a plus or minus sign before a word or phrase ensures that term either definitely is, or is not, in the search results, respectively. For instance, if you are searching for a driver for specific hardware, but you don't want search results that advertise the item, adding **–shop** could help filter consumer sites from the search results.

- **AND, OR, and NOT** Use terms in search entries to further tailor your results (although I find the plus and minus signs easier to use). For example, if you are looking for a driver and know the name of your hardware but not the name of the generic driver you need, you might search for **connexant OR dynamode BT878a driver** (where *BT878a* is the name of your hardware). Linking the qualifiers with OR narrows the search more than just searching for *BT878a*.

Of course, you first need to know what to search for when trying to find a solution to a problem. Try to pick up clues from the information provided by antivirus or antimalware software, the Windows event log, or a Windows or other software error message. If you notice a code or the name of a program, virus, or service, write it down right away. You never know when that on-screen message might disappear.

Try not to use irrelevant words in your search terms; keep the information short and to the point. Combine strategies. If your search item includes characters such as periods or forward slashes (common in virus names), enclose the term in quotation marks, for example, **"Win32.Gattman.A"**.

Microsoft Support Sites

Plenty of websites provide excellent help and support, including Microsoft sites, and you might be surprised at just how quickly people can answer your questions.

Microsoft's main support website (*http://support.microsoft.com*) features a huge amount of help and support in an easy-to-browse interface (see Figure 22-1). The Microsoft Support site is written mostly by Microsoft staff, so you might not see tips and guides that aren't officially endorsed. You do occasionally have Microsoft Most Valued Professionals (MVPs) contribute, and indeed some of my own videos have appeared on this site, but the information here can be fairly technical for the lay person.

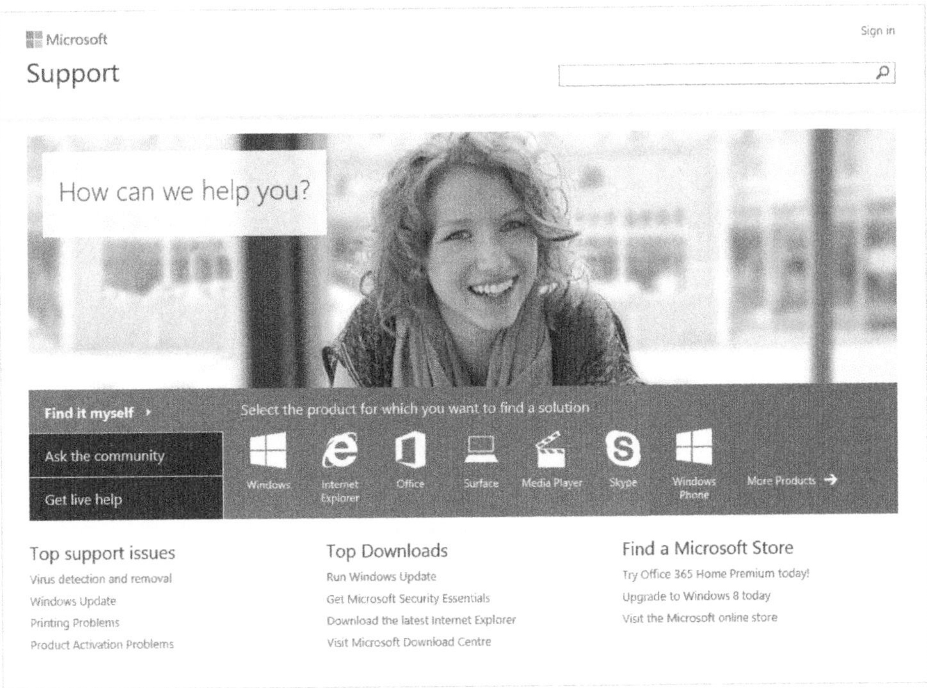

Figure 22-1 The Microsoft Support website.

You can customize the Microsoft support center depending on whether you are a home user, an IT professional, or a developer. You can also find advanced search tools.

You can easily access the Windows 8 Product Solution Center (see Figure 22-2) by clicking the Windows link on the Microsoft Support website. The site contains a whole host of Windows 8 problems and solutions, all categorized and written to be easily consumable.

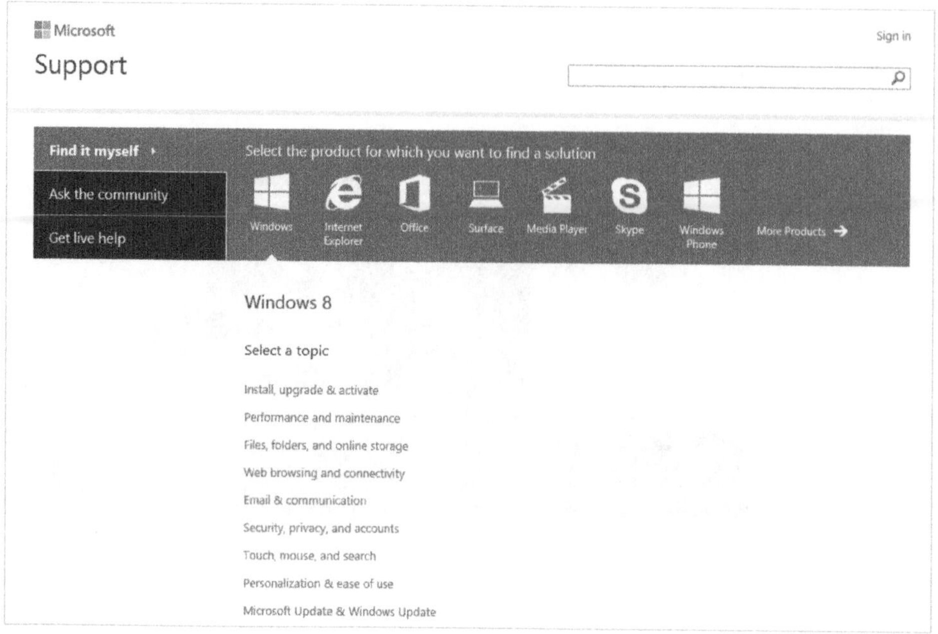

Figure 22-2 The Windows 8 Product Solution Center.

Also available through the Microsoft Support website is Microsoft Answers (see Figure 22-3). This is an advanced forums tool where experts help you find the answers to the problems you have. This site will grow over time, and already contains a vast array of knowledge, all presented in a helpful and friendly way. One of its best features is that you can choose from many different languages, and although the volume of support can change from language to language, this accessibility can be a great help for non-English speakers. You can access Microsoft Answers directly at *http://answers.microsoft.com*.

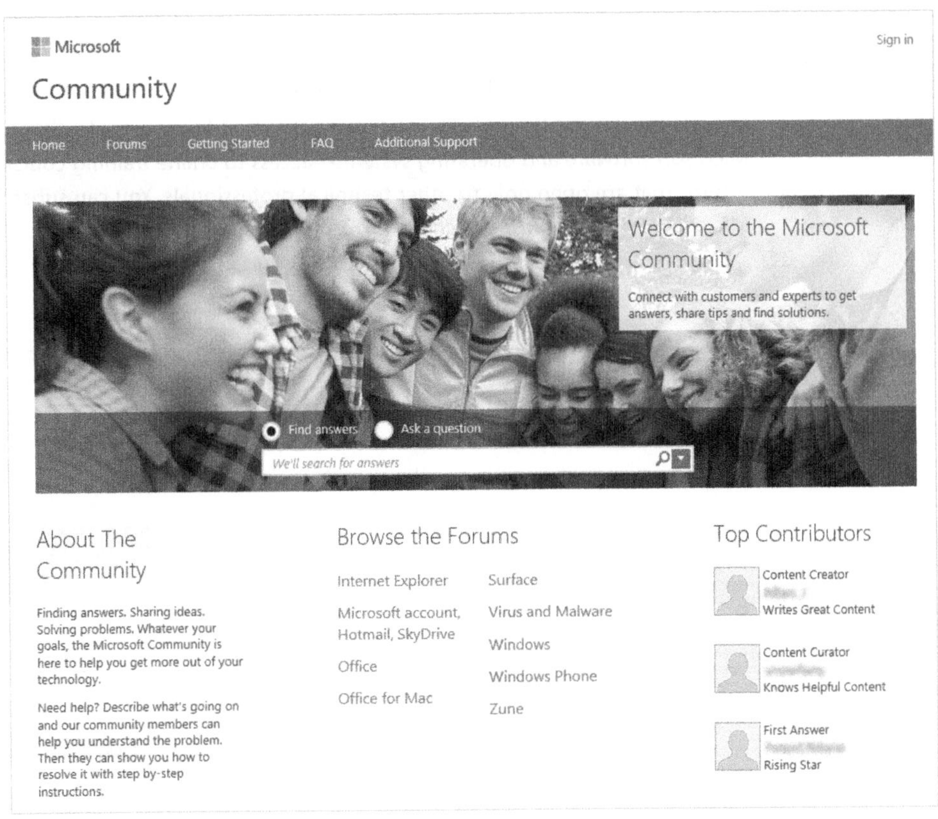

Figure 22-3 The Microsoft Answers website.

Advanced users and IT professionals might want to use Microsoft TechNet, at *http://technet.microsoft.com* (see Figure 22-4). Here you can get advanced help in real time from experts and other users on all aspects of every Microsoft product, and you can post answers. If you have more technical questions about deployment, Microsoft AppLocker, Group Policy, and other subjects more commonly found in enterprise environments, TechNet is a great place to check. You don't need to be a TechNet subscriber to use the forums and the knowledge base.

> **INSIDE OUT**
> ### Subscribing to Microsoft TechNet
> **If you subscribe to Microsoft TechNet, you get—in addition to evaluation copies of Microsoft software and operating systems—access to online training courses and forums that are open only to other technical professionals. You can subscribe to Microsoft TechNet at *http://technet.microsoft.com/en-us/subscriptions*.**

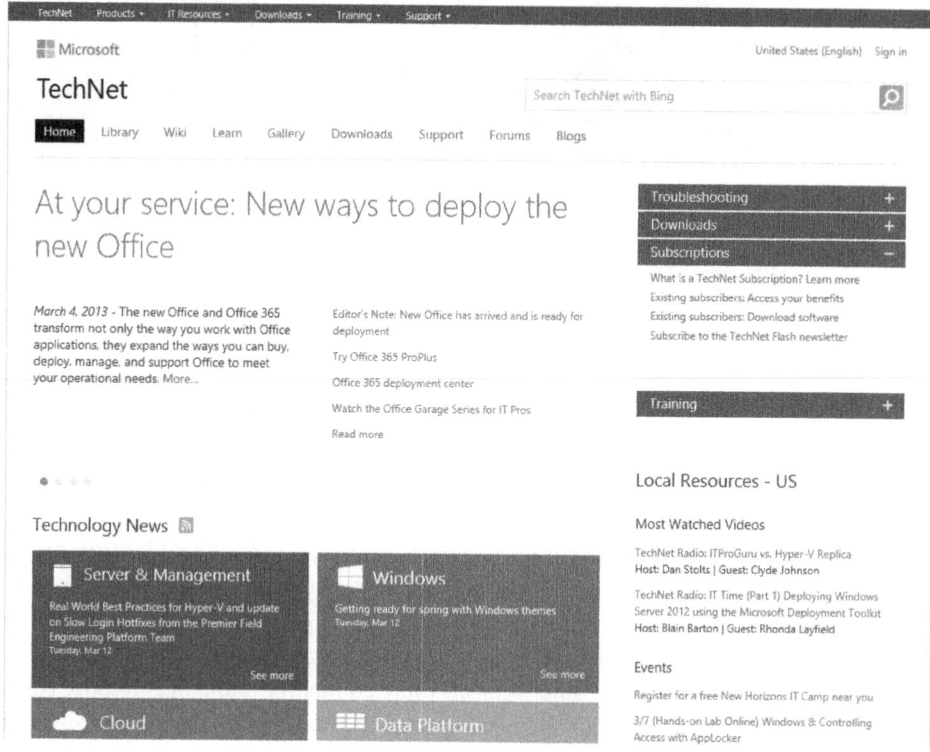

Figure 22-4 Microsoft TechNet.

Third-party hardware and software manufacturers almost always host help forums on their own websites. These sites are a good way to reduce a company's support costs by helping customers help one another. These manufacturers also have their own experts available to help with problems, and many companies offer email and technical support, too.

You can find other online forums and articles containing help and advice. The best ones are always free; I don't suggest that you pay to join a help forum. You will need to decide for yourself how valuable a particular website or service is.

Other Helpful Sites

Following is a list of additional online sites I think are helpful:

- **Bing (*http://www.bing.com*) and Google (*http://www.google.com*)** Search engines are possibly the best troubleshooting tool at your disposal. A search online for the problem or error can reveal the answer many more times than you might expect.
- **Tom's Hardware (*http://www.tomshardware.com*)** Tom's Hardware is a long-standing website devoted to hardware and hardware problems. This site includes extensive forums containing a wealth of information, and experts are available to help diagnose and fix difficult problems. Tom's Hardware tests all new hardware in an impartial and unbiased way.
- **Computing.net (*http://www.computing.net*)** This site is run by the people who run Tom's Hardware. Computing.net is an excellent resource for help with some of the more complex computer problems you might encounter.
- **How-To Geek (*http://www.howtogeek.com*)** How-To Geek helps you perform a wide variety of tasks in Windows and other operating systems and software packages, such as use automated utilities to resolve computer issues.
- **Gibson Research (*http://www.grc.com*)** Steve Gibson is a well-respected IT security expert. On the Gibson Research website, Gibson provides many tools to help diagnose and repair security flaws in your installation of Windows.
- **ATI Support (*http://support.amd.com*)** Graphics card problems are common with Windows. Fortunately, only two major manufacturers provide the core hardware for graphics card technology, so help is centralized. You can find support for an ATI-based graphics card at the ATI support website.
- **NVIDIA Support (*http://www.nvidia.com/page/support.html*)** Similar to the ATI support page, the NVIDIA support website is the place to visit if you have an NVIDIA-based graphics card in your computer.
- **MSDN Diagnostics (*http://msdn.microsoft.com/en-us/library/ee663269(v=VS.85).aspx*)** The Microsoft MSDN site offers an extensive section for diagnosing and troubleshooting Windows 8. This includes the Windows Troubleshooting Platform that system administrators can use to write custom troubleshooting packs.

Windows Help

You can access Windows Help at any time by pressing F1 on your keyboard (only from the desktop, however; this doesn't work in the Windows 8 interface). You might be wondering why I haven't mentioned Windows Help before this chapter. The reason is that the Help system in Windows is more of a basic manual than anything else. It can be useful for guiding you through unfamiliar features, but it is not exhaustive. The other resources covered in this chapter might provide more assistance.

Third-Party Software

You can download many different utilities, some free of charge and others for a fee, that can help solve problems on your computer. Some of these are more helpful than others. You will need to decide about the value of individual software packages, but I recommend the following programs:

- **SiSoftware Sandra Utilities (*http://www.sisoftware.net*)** SiSoftware Sandra is an excellent information and diagnostic tool. This package produces detailed reports about every aspect of your computer, including hardware, drivers, and installed software, which can help enormously when diagnosing computer-related problems. You can also use SiSoftware Sandra tools to create diagnostic reports on the current health and status of your computer. These can be very useful if you need to send reports to third parties for diagnosis.
- **AIDA 64 (*http://www.aida64.com*)** An alternative to Sandra is the excellent Aida64. Using this program, you can benchmark your computer, monitor its health, and perform diagnostics. As with SiSoftware Sandra tools, you can create diagnostic reports of your computer simply and easily with Aida64.
- **Windows Sysinternals (*http://technet.microsoft.com/en-US/sysinternals/*)** Windows Sysinternals is a suite of tools and applications from Microsoft that help you manage, troubleshoot, and diagnose your Windows systems and applications. These extensive tools provide a tremendous amount of detailed data about your computer when troubleshooting problems. However, some of these tools are quite complex and are designed for experienced computer users.
- **GoToAssist (*http://www.gotoassist.com*)** GoToAssist is software that performs the same functions as Windows Remote Desktop and Windows Remote Assistance but offers a few more technical functions. Most notably, you can use it to restart the remote computer (which can be essential when performing some support functions), and it runs on and from Apple Mac computers, too.

- **SpinRite (*http://www.grc.com*)** Another program that is held in extremely high regard by many computer professionals is SpinRite from computer-security specialist Steve Gibson. This tool runs from a disk or USB flash drive and checks your hard disk for errors, physical or otherwise, that are causing malfunctions and/or data loss and then helps to repair the problems. I describe SpinRite in more detail in Chapter 30, "Third-Party Rescue Tools and Services."
- **Symantec Ghost (*http://www.symantec.com/themes/theme.jsp?themeid=ghost*)** Symantec Ghost is one of two packages on this list that create system images of Windows. Although this functionality is already built in to Windows 8, these programs offer additional backup and restore functionality for people who work in a corporate environment.
- **Acronis True Image (*http://www.acronis.com*)** Acronis True Image is another system image backup-and-restore application. This package is useful for business scenarios in which you need more control over Windows 8 system images than is available through the Microsoft Windows Image Backup that ships as part of Windows 7.
- **Paragon Partition Manager (*http://www.paragon-software.com*)** Sometimes, you need a tool to manage the partitions on your hard disks. Windows 8 includes a partitioning tool, but it's not especially powerful. Paragon Partition Manager can make working with partitions much simpler.
- **Acronis Disk Director Suite (*http://www.acronis.com*)** Acronis Disk Director is another partitioning management package that makes working with and managing partitions on your hard disks much simpler.

CHAPTER 23

Using Remote Help

SOMETIMES, YOU JUST CAN'T TROUBLESHOOT the solution to a system issue by yourself, and you need help that isn't located in your area. Perhaps you need technical support from a corporate IT center, for example. Windows 8 provides Remote Desktop and Windows Remote Assistance so that you can safely and securely enlist remote help, whether you are an employee or a home user. This chapter discusses how to use these technologies to allow others access to your system, and how to record your actions on the computer, which you can then share with the individuals trying to help you.

Remote Desktop

If your computer is in a corporate environment, your IT help desk might be able to use Windows Remote Desktop (see Figure 23-1) or a similar system to gain access to your computer. You might consider it slightly disconcerting to see your computer being remotely manipulated, but this is a good way for an organization to provide support and reduce overall costs, because support personnel don't need to be on site. Before beginning a remote help session, ensure that your computer is turned on. If you want to set up a remote desktop connection to another computer, on the Start screen, search for **remote**.

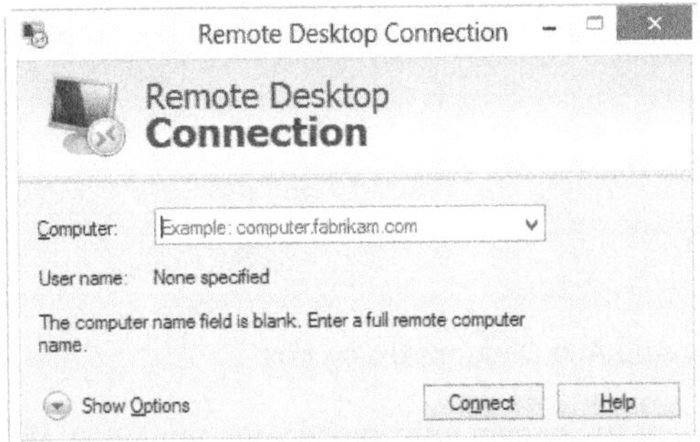

Figure 23-1 The new Remote Desktop Connection dialog box.

INSIDE OUT Third-party firewalls and remote help

Third-party firewalls, and even a badly configured Windows Firewall, can block Remote Desktop or Windows Remote Assistance attempts to connect to your computer. You can temporarily disable the firewall to allow a connection, if required, by opening Firewall in the Control Panel and disabling it (remember that you will need to turn it on again). If you are using the Windows 8 built-in firewall, it is already correctly configured for remote help, and you won't need to do anything at all.

You might want to connect to software that's stored and run from a local or remote server. To do this, on the Start screen, search for **remoteapp**, and then in the Settings results, click Access RemoteApp And Desktops to open the Access RemoteApp And Desktops dialog box (see Figure 23-2).

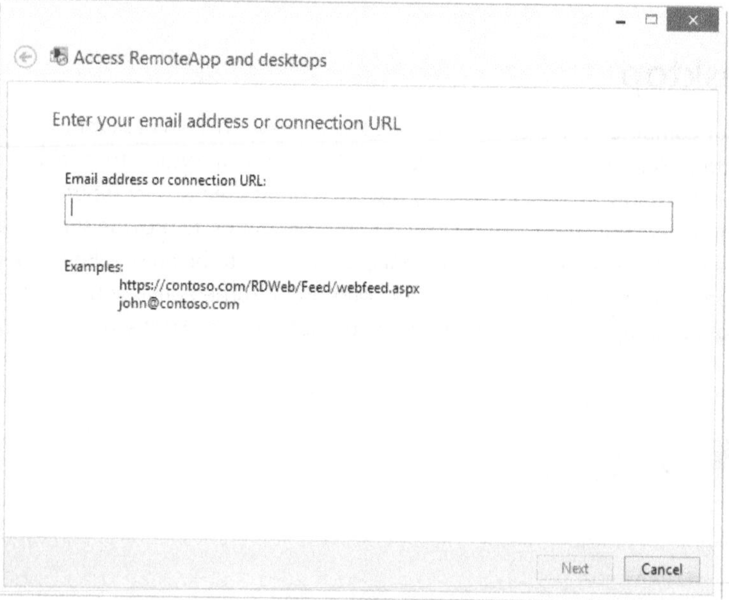

Figure 23-2 The Access RemoteApp And Desktops dialog box.

The computer to which you want to connect must be on your network or virtual private network (VPN), and you will need to know its name on the system to connect. Some organizations use Remote Desktop across the Internet to provide support for customers, whereas others might use Remote Assistance (see the section "Using Windows Remote Assistance" later in this chapter).

The target computer also needs to be configured to receive Remote Desktop connections. To access these settings, in Control Panel, click System And Security\System\Advanced System Settings. In the System Properties dialog box that opens, open the Remote tab, where you can set the options to allow remote connections (see Figure 23-3). Select the Allow Connections Only From Computers Running Remote Desktop With Network Level Authentication (Recommended) check box for added security.

Figure 23-3 Advanced system settings for remote connections.

You might need to allow Remote Desktop through your firewall; however, if you are using the default Windows Firewall, Windows 8 will normally take care of this for you. To access Windows Firewall settings, in Control Panel, click System And Security, and then click Windows Firewall. Click Allow An App Or Feature Through Windows Firewall to allow Remote Desktop (see Figure 23-4). The Details and Remove buttons appear for some, but not all, of the selected options. If the desired app doesn't appear in the list, you can click the Allow Another App button.

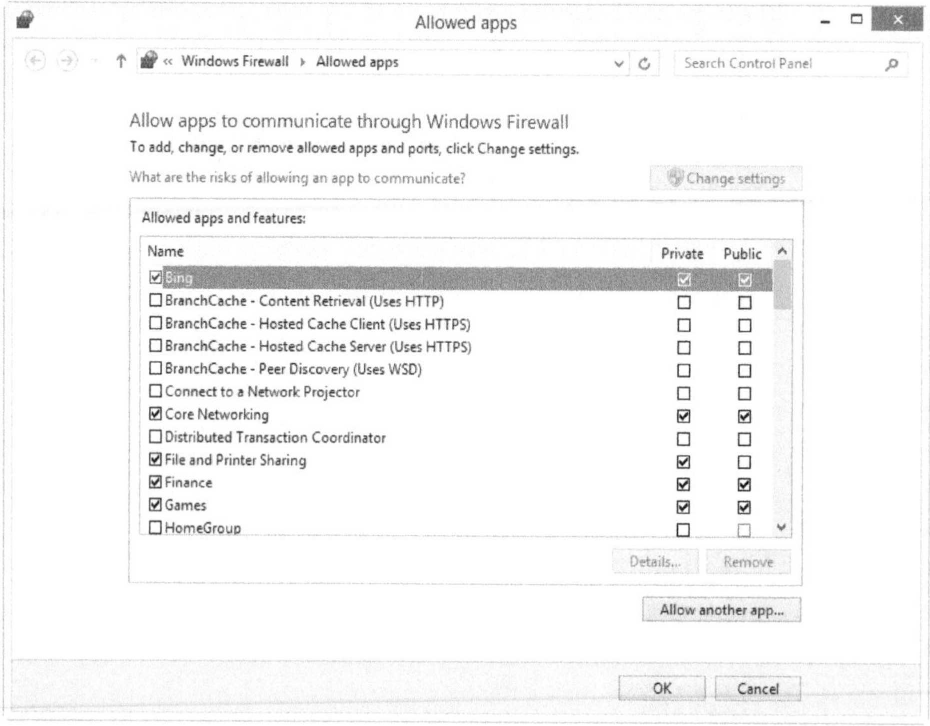

Figure 23-4 Allow Remote Desktop through Windows Firewall.

If Remote Desktop is unable to verify the identity of the computer when you try to connect to a remote computer, and Windows suspects that connecting to this device could pose a security risk to your system, a warning will appear (see Figure 23-5).

Figure 23-5 Windows displays an alert to potential security threats when you use Remote Desktop.

After you are connected to Remote Desktop, the person who initiated the Remote Desktop connection has access to your computer to remotely diagnose any problems, but different levels of access might be required to perform some specific tasks.

INSIDE OUT **Configuring Network Address Translation in your router**

By default, most routers allow a Remote Desktop connection across the Internet, but you might also need to configure your router's network address translation (NAT) settings when using Remote Desktop on internal networks. If you cannot connect, however, you might need to log on to your router and change certain router settings, for example, to open a connection port or permit Remote Desktop. You should consult your router manual or Help document for details about how to do this.

Windows Remote Assistance

Although Remote Desktop is helpful and common in organizations in which the computers are owned by the employer and people do not keep personal files and data on them, home users need something that can provide more control over what a remote user can access. Windows Remote Assistance addresses this issue by enabling the user who is receiving the support to monitor exactly what's being performed throughout the remote help session. Remote Assistance also provides controls that let a user regain full control of the computer and exit the remote connection at any time.

Remote Assistance is intended for use over the Internet; you will need a broadband connection that's not busy with other activities (such as downloading files).

Note

The computer offering the remote assistance does not need to be running Windows 8. It can be running an earlier version of Windows that supports this feature.

INSIDE OUT **Remote Assistance via Easy Connect**

When you use Remote Assistance, you can use Easy Connect to connect two computers running Windows 8 in a straightforward manner, without you needing to send an invitation file. Easy Connect uses a secure peer-to-peer network managed by Microsoft to handle the connection. For this to work, your router must support the Peer Name Resolution Protocol.

To use Remote Assistance, follow these steps:

1. To access Remote Assistance, on the Start screen, search for **remote**, and in the Settings results, click Invite Someone To Connect To Your PC And Help, Or Offer To Help Someone Else.
2. When Windows Remote Assistance opens, you can either invite someone to help you, or help someone else (see Figure 23-6). Click Help Someone Who Has Invited You to help someone if you received an invitation through Easy Connect.

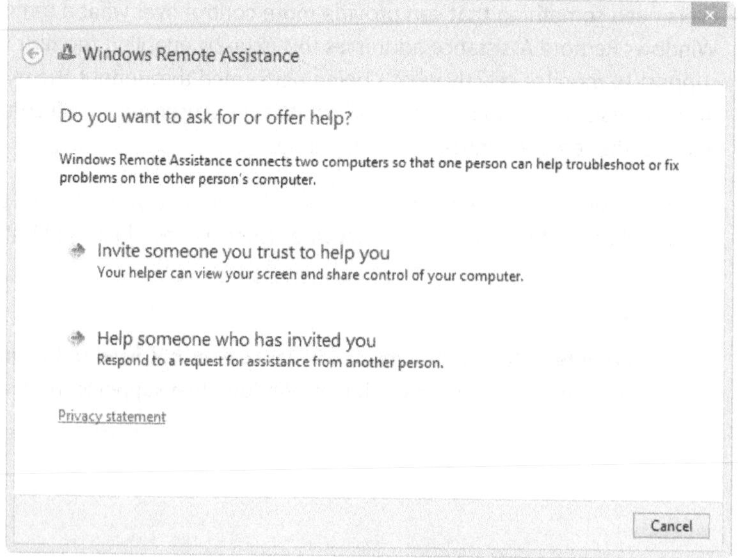

Figure 23-6 The main Windows Remote Assistance screen.

3. If you are requesting assistance, you will need to indicate how to send a remote assistance invitation (see Figure 23-7). These invitations are typically sent via email. If you have an email program installed on your computer, such as an email app or Microsoft Outlook, click Use Email To Send An Invitation. Otherwise, click Save This Invitation As A File, and then send the file via webmail. Alternatively, you can click Use Easy Connect. (See the preceding Inside Out sidebar "Remote Assistance via Easy Connect.")

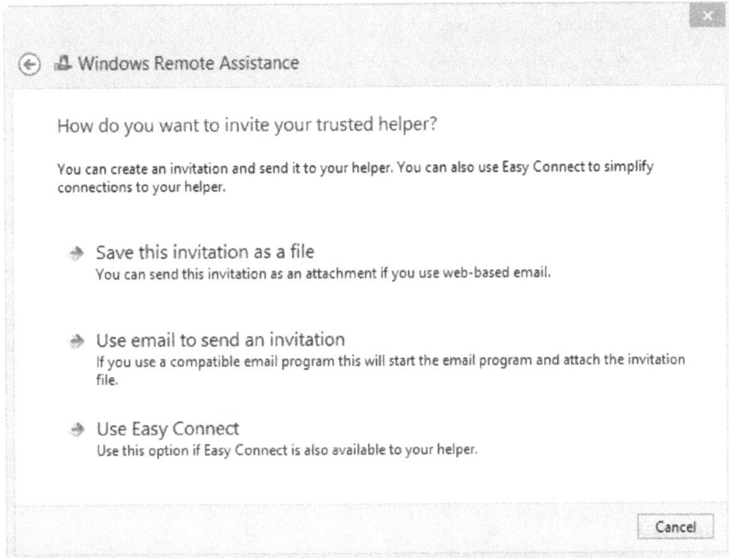

Figure 23-7 The invitation options in Remote Assistance.

4. You are given a password. If you are using Easy Connect, give the password to the person providing the support (see Figure 23-8). Otherwise, email the invitation file that was saved to your computer. Never include this password in the same email as the support invitation to help maintain your security.

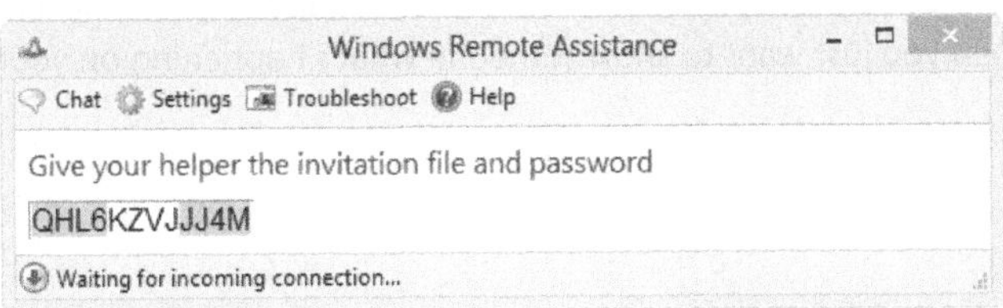

Figure 23-8 The Remote Assistance Password dialog box.

5. If you are the person providing the support, either enter the password in the Remote Assistance dialog box that appears on your screen, or enter it after you open the invitation file you received (see Figure 23-9). The individual who is providing the assistance does not need to be using Windows 8; he or she can be using Windows 7 or Windows Vista.

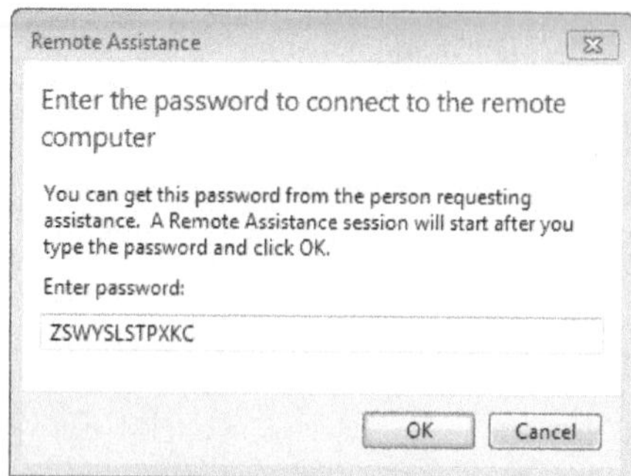

Figure 23-9 Enter a password to gain remote access.

6. If you are the person receiving the support, in the dialog box that appears (see Figure 23-10), allow the person providing the support access to your computer by clicking Yes.

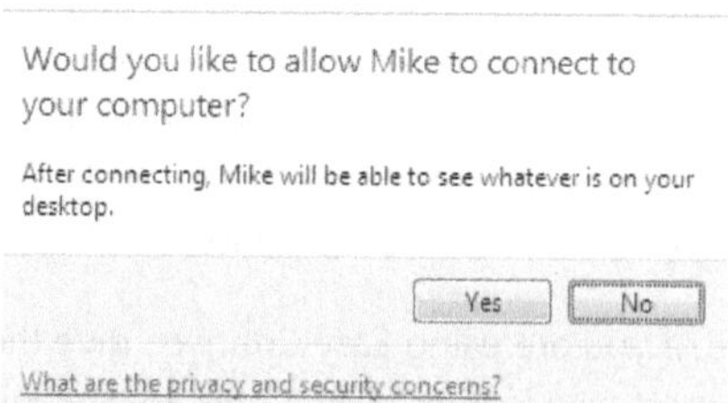

Figure 23-10 The person receiving the request must grant permission.

At this point, the person providing the support can look at what's happening on the other computer but cannot control it by default. This can be a handy security feature when you just want to show someone what's happening on your computer.

7. If you are providing support, in the Windows Remote Assistance console, click Request Control, as shown in Figure 23-11.

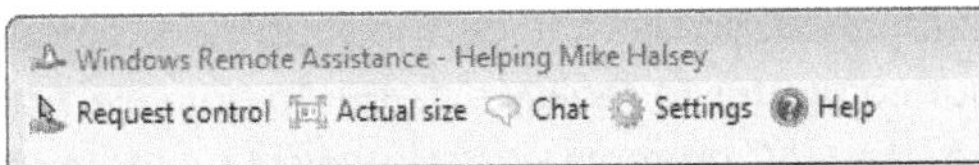

Figure 23-11 The Windows Remote Assistance control toolbar appears on the screen of the person who is providing support.

If you are receiving support, do not be too alarmed about someone taking control of your computer, because you will be able to see what is going on at every stage. Figure 23-12 shows the settings available in Remote Assistance, including a helpful ESC key, which you can use to stop sharing control.

> **Note**
>
> **In the Remote Desktop settings, you can also set the software to break the connection instantly when you press the Esc key on your keyboard.**

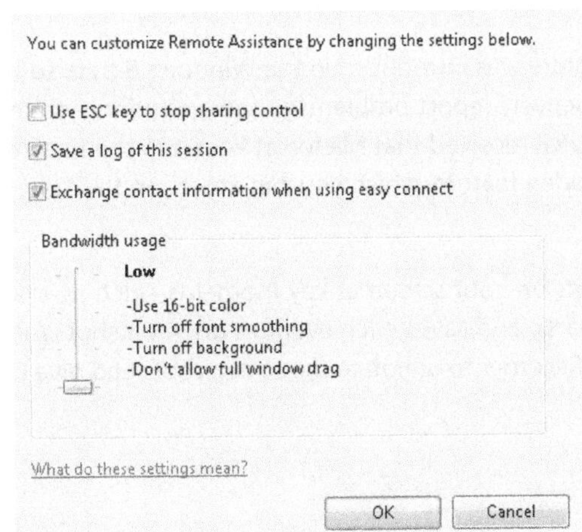

Figure 23-12 Modify transmission settings to reduce bandwidth.

When someone requests control of a remote computer, a dialog box appears requesting confirmation that you're allowing this. If you allow the access, select the check box allowing the help provider to respond to User Account Control (UAC) security prompts (see Figure 23-13) so that the person supplying remote support will have full control of your computer to repair it. If you do not select this option, you will need to respond to the UAC prompts yourself, which is a more secure approach and can be used if you do not completely trust the person providing the support. However, it can also slow down the process, and you will need to remain at your computer throughout the entire session.

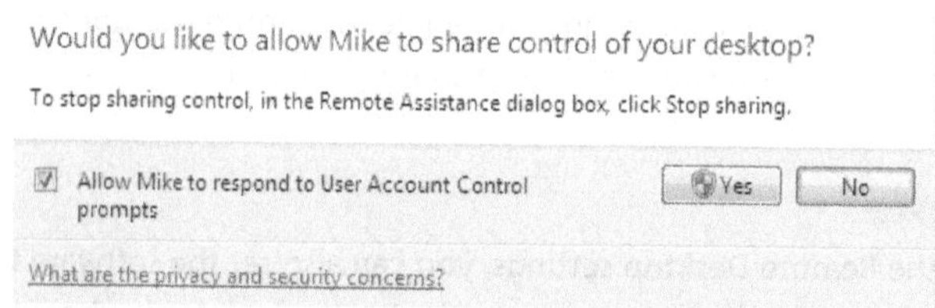

Figure 23-13 Granting permission for a remote person to control your computer.

The Steps Recorder

The Steps Recorder feature was introduced in the Windows 8 beta so that technical beta testers could more effectively report problems to the operating system development team at Microsoft. It was so well received that Microsoft kept it in the final release of the operating system. This is a hidden feature, which you can access on the Start screen by searching for **PSR**.

This tool records actions on your screen at key moments (such as when you click something or an error appears), and saves each event as a screen shot. You can click Add Comment in the Steps Recorder to annotate the screen shots and give more information (see Figure 23-14).

Figure 23-14 The Steps Recorder.

When you stop the recording, the Steps Recorder saves all the information it captured, complete with additional details about your computer and what software was running at the time, as a zip file that can be sent via email to a support person. This zip file contains a document that is viewable in any web browser (see Figures 23-15 through 23-17).

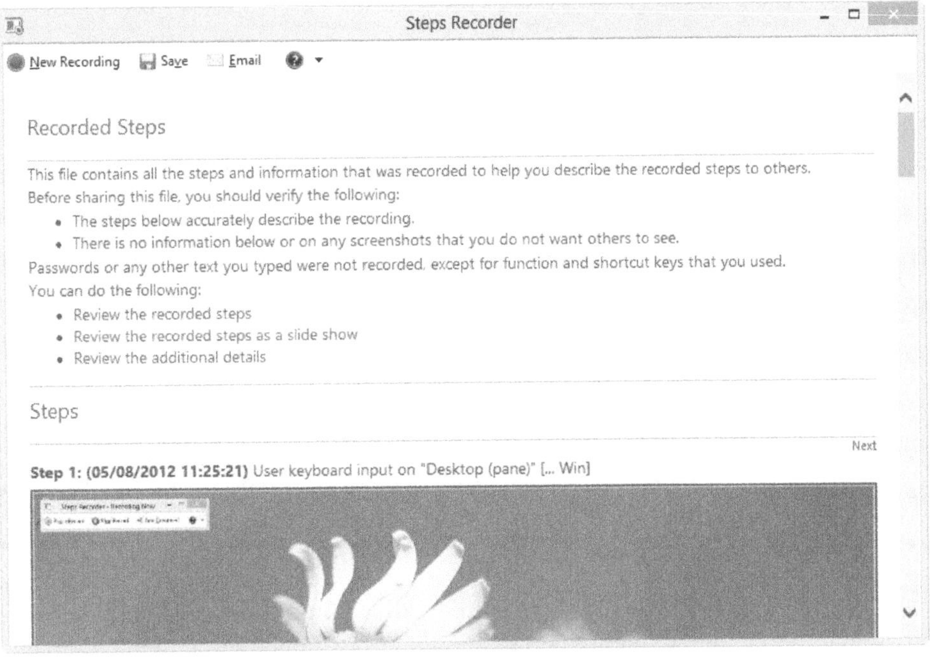

Figure 23-15 The Steps Recorder information file (1 of 3).

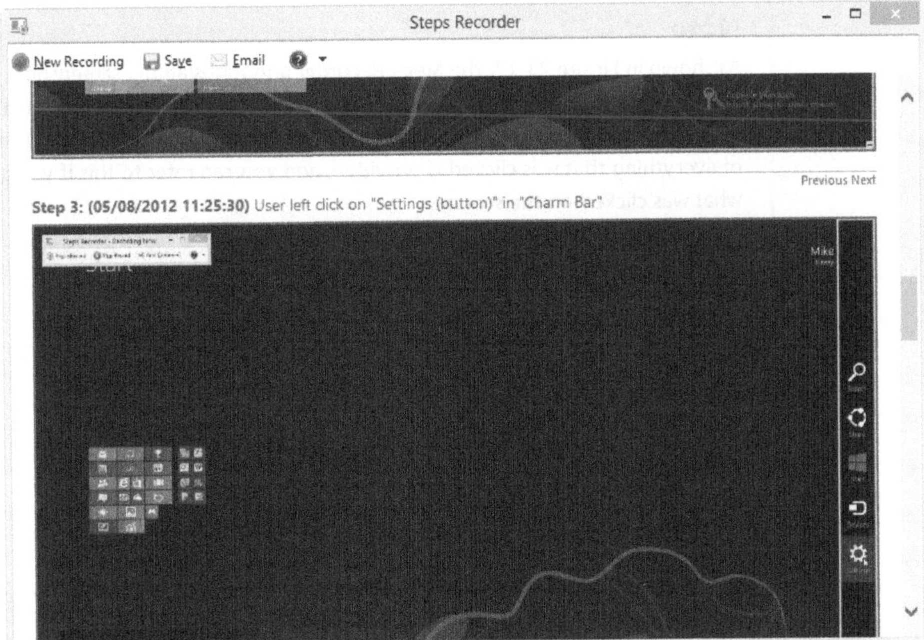

Figure 23-16 The Steps Recorder information file (2 of 3).

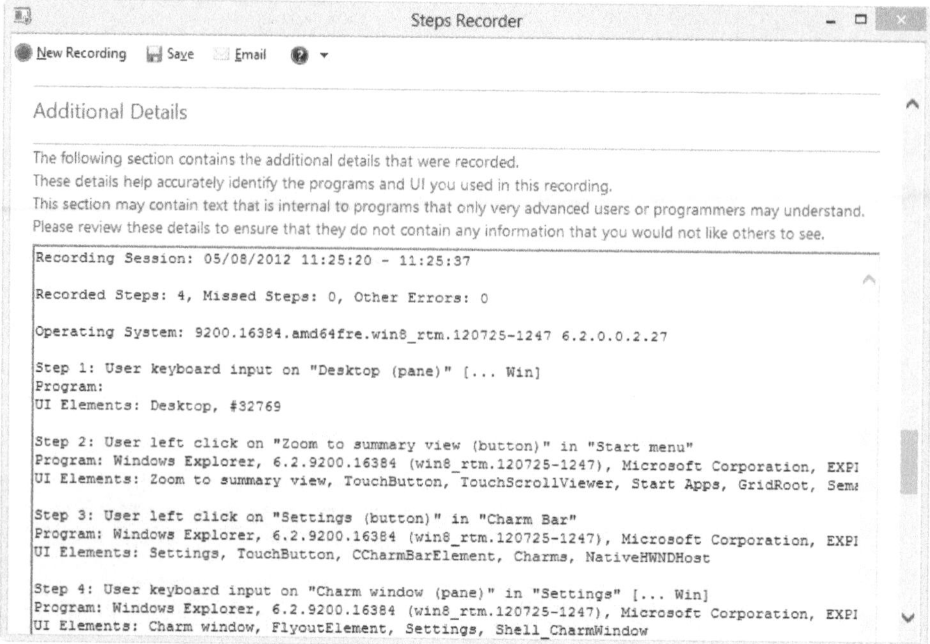

Figure 23-17 The Steps Recorder information file (3 of 3).

> ### Note
> **As shown in Figure 23-17, the Steps Recorder annotates all the screenshots to show what you were clicking when an event occurred, but it does not annotate individual screen items in the Windows 8 interface. At the bottom of the report, a text description of everything that was clicked is provided, and you can refer to this if you are not sure what was clicked on the screen.**

CHAPTER 24

Diagnosing Hardware Problems

SOFTWARE AND DRIVERS AREN'T THE ONLY COMPONENTS of your computer that can cause problems. Your hardware can cause issues, too. In this chapter, I describe the different components of computer hardware and show you how you can diagnose and repair problems with them.

Knowing Your Computer Hardware

A computer is a collection of many assorted parts that work interdependently. Each of these parts, including hardware components, has its own vulnerabilities and characteristics.

CAUTION!

Always ensure that your computer is disconnected from the electrical outlet before you work inside the case. This will avoid risk of electrical shock to yourself and avoid electrical damage to the components, many of which are fragile.

Desktop Computer Case

The base unit on a computer is the main case that contains all the parts that make a computer work. In a laptop, notebook, or all-in-one desktop, all these parts are inside the same case that the monitor is in, because the computer is only a single unit. With a standard desktop computer, however, the base unit is the large case that sometimes rests on your desk, or more commonly, on the floor. Figure 24-1 shows the front and back of the desktop case.

Figure 24-1 A typical desktop computer case layout.

Power Supply

The power supply is probably the part of the computer most prone to failure. The *power supply* is where you plug your computer in to the main electrical supply (see Figure 24-1). It regulates and distributes the power going into the computer and extra components, and it is one of only a few components inside the computer to have a fan to keep it cool. Fortunately, the power supply is very simple to replace if it does fail.

Motherboard

The *motherboard* is the substrate of the computer. This is the board to which all other components are plugged in or attached (see Figure 24-2).

Figure 24-2 A typical computer motherboard.

The motherboard is the component located on the bottom or side of your computer and is the most difficult to remove if something goes wrong with it.

The back panel connectors on the motherboard are where you plug in additional accessories, such as your keyboard and mouse, speakers, and any USB accessories (see Figure 24-3).

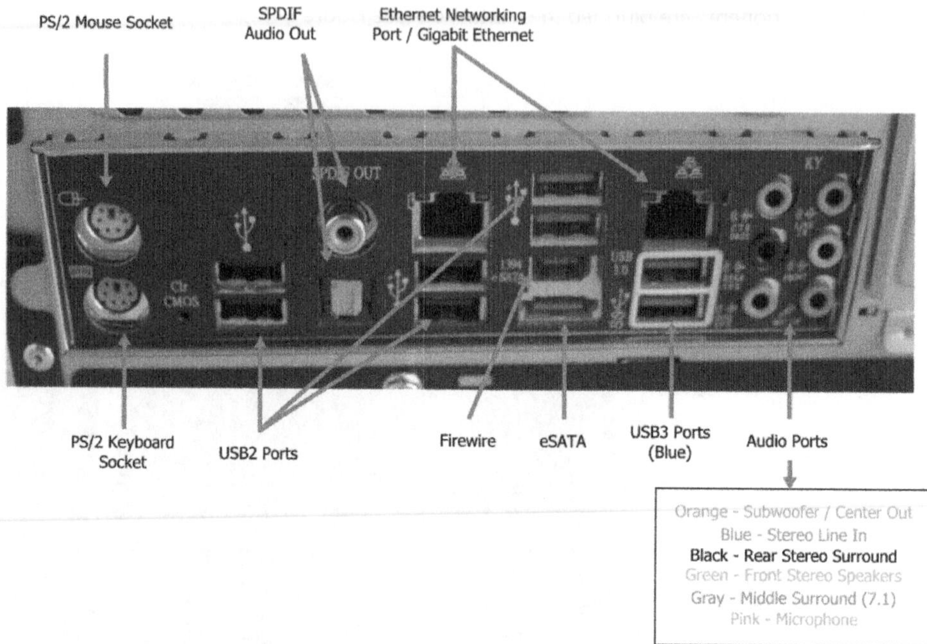

Figure 24-3 The back panel connectors on a motherboard.

Processor

The processor (also known as the central processor unit, or CPU) is the brain of the computer; it's the chip that does all the computational work (see Figure 24-4). The processor is quite fragile and needs to be handled with care.

Figure 24-4 A typical CPU without its heat sink.

The processor fits into a socket on the motherboard and requires a heat sink; in current models, it needs a fan to keep it cool. When installing a processor, ensure that you use plenty of silicon paste between it and the heat sink to prevent overheating and cracking.

Memory

Memory in your computer (not to be confused with the hard disk) is where Windows loads files while it works with them (see Figure 24-5). It's a temporary storage, and files are wiped from memory when the device is turned off.

Figure 24-5 The computer memory, removed from the motherboard.

Hard Disk

The *hard disk* (or disks) in your computer is the physical storage device on which Windows 8 and your files reside. Different types of hard disks have different connectors. Figure 24-6 shows a small, 2.5-inch hard disk (which is the smallest of the three types in the figure, on the left side of the image) and two standard 3.5-inch hard disks. All three have Serial ATA (SATA) connectors. Earlier integrated device electronics (IDE) drives have a long connector with many pins for data, and a smaller connector with large pins for power.

Figure 24-6 Hard disk and optical disk connectors.

Optical Drive

The *optical drive* (refer to Figure 24-1) is the CD/DVD or Blu-ray drive on your computer. An optical drive connects to the motherboard by using either the SATA or IDE connectors, as described for hard disks.

Graphics Card

Your computer probably does not include a separate graphics card if the graphics technology is built in to the motherboard or, as is the case with the newest processors, built in to the processor itself. If you do have a separate graphics card, it might look similar to the one shown in Figure 24-7. This component connects to the monitor and manages what is displayed on the screen.

Figure 24-7 A graphics card is plugged into a motherboard expansion slot and protrudes outward from the motherboard.

Expansion Cards

Expansion cards plug into your computer like graphics cards but likely use a different socket (refer to Figure 24-2). Expansion cards can do anything from connecting to the Internet, to providing more USB ports, to acting as a television tuner.

Fans

Your computer has several fans to keep it cool: one or more in the power supply, one on the processor, one on the graphics card, perhaps one on the motherboard, and one or more in the case itself. Fans are important for keeping the components at acceptable temperature levels, because some components can heat up to temperatures near 100 degrees

Celsius (212 degrees Fahrenheit). It's a good idea to ensure that these fans are clean and operational. If any are rattling, they might need to be replaced.

Keyboards and Mice

Keyboards and mice don't normally malfunction, but the keyboard will occasionally need to be cleaned, especially if you eat or drink around your computer (which I strongly discourage). I don't recommend washing a keyboard, however. Normally, light vacuuming (on a low setting) and a wipe will do the job.

If you have a ball-mouse, the rollers that the ball runs up against can become clogged with dust and debris from your desk. You can remove the ball by removing a small panel on the underside of the mouse and then cleaning the rollers.

Laptops, Netbooks, and All-in-One Devices

As mentioned earlier in this chapter, in a laptop, netbook, or all-in-one device, the arrangement of components is slightly different from a standard computer, because all the components and hardware are integrated into a single, compact case that has removable panels on the underside (see Figure 24-8).

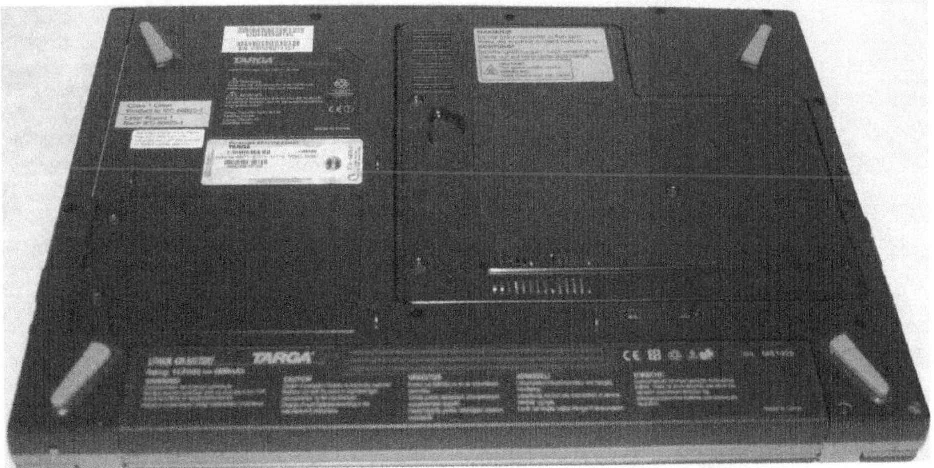

Figure 24-8 You can remove the underside of a laptop for maintenance and cleaning.

Although the user can't service many of the components inside a laptop, those that can be serviced can usually be detached by removing a few screws. In a laptop, the optical drive, hard disk, and memory, respectively, can be replaced after unscrewing the removable panels on the underside of the case (see Figures 24-9, 24-10, and 24-11).

Figure 24-9 You can remove the optical drive from a laptop computer.

Figure 24-10 You can remove the hard disk from a laptop computer.

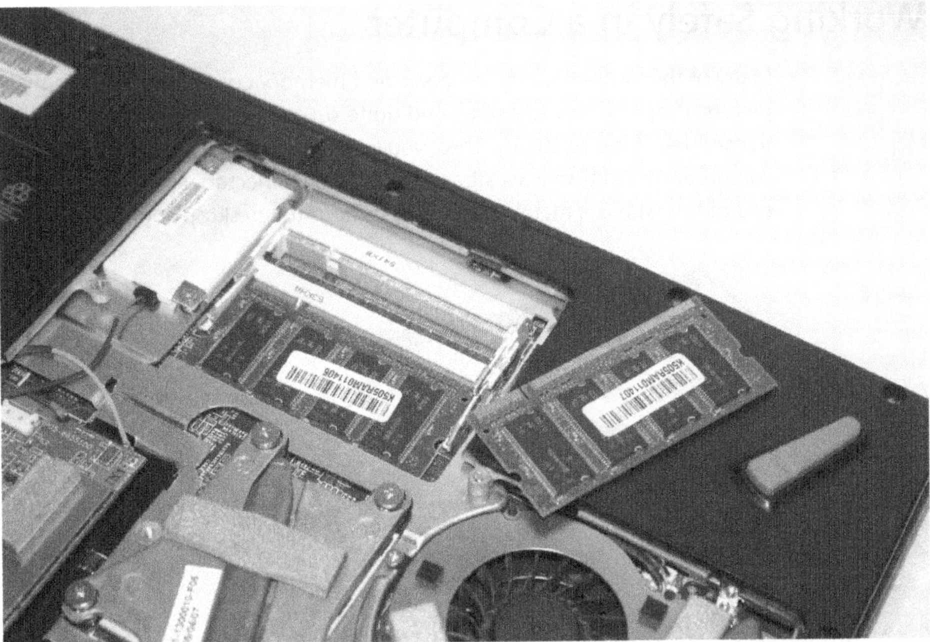

Figure 24-11 You can change the memory cards in a laptop computer.

Tablets and Ultrabooks

Consider Windows 8 tablets and Ultrabooks to be non-serviceable by the user. Both are very thin and light computers, and all their internal components—memory, storage, motherboard, and so on—are usually custom-fit items. This means that even if you want to swap in a different or upgraded component, chances are good that component simply won't fit.

The cases for these computers are also designed to be disassembled only by authorized service personnel, and because the components inside a tablet or an Ultrabook are very tightly squeezed into the case, you face the risk of not being able to close it after you open it. All you can really do with a tablet or an Ultrabook is, as with an all-in-one device, put a vacuum to the exhaust vents and clean out any residual dust that could cause the computer to overheat.

Working Safely in a Computer

Many of the motherboard, processor, and memory components can be measured in nanometers; they're extremely small and quite susceptible to even tiny voltages of human-transmitted static electricity. Thus, you'll need an antistatic wristband to work inside a computer. The antistatic wristband contains a connected wire (see Figure 24-12). On the end of this wire is a metal clip for fastening to the desktop computer's case.

Figure 24-12 An antistatic wristband.

> INSIDE OUT **What to be careful of when working with a computer**
>
> **Try to avoid working on a computer in a room with thick or nylon carpet, because these materials can cause electrostatic charges to build up. Also, always place the device on a flat and stable surface.**
>
> **Skin is a natural insulator, if it is dry, so your fingers can accumulate and store an electrostatic charge. Thus, it is very important to discharge this charge from your fingers while wearing an antistatic wristband before picking up delicate components.**

To work safely with a computer, follow these guidelines:

1. Turn the computer off and unplug it from the electrical outlet.
2. If the computer is a laptop or netbook, remove the battery.
3. Put on an antistatic wristband. Remove the side or back panel of the computer, and then attach the clip on the wristband to the metal frame of the case. This can be difficult to do with a laptop, so be absolutely sure that you do not clip the wristband to any operational components.
4. While touching unpainted metal inside the case, pull the power lead out of the back.

CAUTION!

> **For a desktop computer, touch only unpainted metal inside the case with your finger.**

You can now work safely with your computer.

Checking That Everything Is Plugged In

It's not uncommon for a connector in a computer to come loose. If you find, for instance, that the power button has stopped working, check to see whether the front panel connectors have come off their mountings. The lower-right area of Figure 24-13 shows the front panel connectors and connecting wires. Next to the front panel connectors are other connectors for USB and SATA devices. If you are experiencing issues, you can check this area to ensure that all of the cables are properly and securely plugged in.

Figure 24-13 The front panel motherboard connectors are in the lower left of the image.

Performing a Minimal-Hardware Boot

There are so many components inside a computer that it can sometimes be difficult to determine which one is causing a problem. If your computer won't start or is regularly unresponsive, the problem could be a hardware fault.

The best way to determine whether you have a hardware fault is to perform a minimal-hardware boot. To do this, first remove all external devices from your computer, except for the mouse and keyboard. This includes USB-attached devices except a USB mouse and keyboard.

If your computer is still malfunctioning after you disconnect all the external hardware, open the case and remove the following components:

- Optical drive
- Any hard disks except the one on which Windows 8 is installed
- All but one of the memory cards
- Any expansion cards except the graphics card (if present)

By removing these components, you can start your computer with the minimum number of hardware components. If the computer is still malfunctioning, you can conclude that no external devices are causing the problem. Conversely, if the computer works properly, you can begin adding the components back one at a time, restarting and testing every time you reattach a component until the computer again stops responding. This process of elimination can help you diagnose and isolate the hardware component that is at fault.

If you perform a minimal boot and the computer still doesn't work, your task is harder, because you cannot remove anything else except the graphics card, and you can do that only if your motherboard has onboard graphics. In this case, try each memory card in turn, turning off the computer to change the card and then restarting the computer. This will establish whether you have a faulty memory card.

INSIDE OUT **When changing your graphics card, check your resolution**

Changing graphics cards can sometimes result in a blank display if the resolution of the replacement card is set to be higher than your screen can support. When you are changing a graphics card or removing one for testing purposes, so that you can use the motherboard graphics chip instead, it's a good idea to first lower your screen resolution to 800 x 600 or 1024 x 768. To do this, right-click any blank area of the Windows 8 desktop, and then click Screen Resolution.

If the problem persists, the problem can be caused only by one of four components: the power supply, the primary hard disk, the motherboard, or the processor. I cover how to turn on your computer in the next section, which can help determine whether you have a faulty power supply, but let's discuss how to check the other components.

You can check the hard disk by plugging it into another computer as an extra drive and determining whether the problem persists. Don't try to use the hard disk as the boot drive on this second device, because the installed copy of Windows 8 won't have compatible hardware for the new computer, and Windows might deactivate when it detects the hardware has changed.

If you determine that the hard disk is not the problem, the processor or the motherboard might be the culprit. Because you can't start the computer without either of these, you can attempt a few other tricks, and if these don't work, you might consider consulting a technical professional.

Resetting the BIOS

Sometimes the computer's basic input/output system (BIOS) can become corrupt. When the operating system cannot properly communicate with your hardware, it might malfunction or not start. On these occasions, you can reset the BIOS to its default configuration.

The easiest way to reset the computer's BIOS is first to access it by pressing Delete or F2 on your keyboard while the computer is starting up, and then restore the default BIOS settings.

Your motherboard, on which the BIOS chip resides, has a complementary metal oxide semiconductor (CMOS) battery and a BIOS/CMOS reset button, or jumper. You can remove the battery for between 20 seconds and 2 minutes to reset the clear CMOS. To do so, follow these steps:

1. Place the computer on a level, firm surface, and ensure that it is turned off and disconnected from the electrical outlet. Ground yourself by touching an unpainted area on the case, and use an antistatic wristband (if possible). Open the side of the computer to expose the motherboard.

2. Locate the battery on the motherboard (see Figure 24-14). It looks like a large watch battery (and, indeed, it is one). Unclip the battery to remove it from the motherboard.

Figure 24-14 A clear CMOS motherboard jumper and battery.

Also, in Figure 24-15, you can see a clear CMOS jumper on the motherboard, close by to the battery (check the motherboard manual for the exact location for your computer). The jumper comprises three pins, with a small connector covering two of them.

3. Remove the connector and move it to cover the center pin and the uncovered pin. You can use a small pair of tweezers to do this.

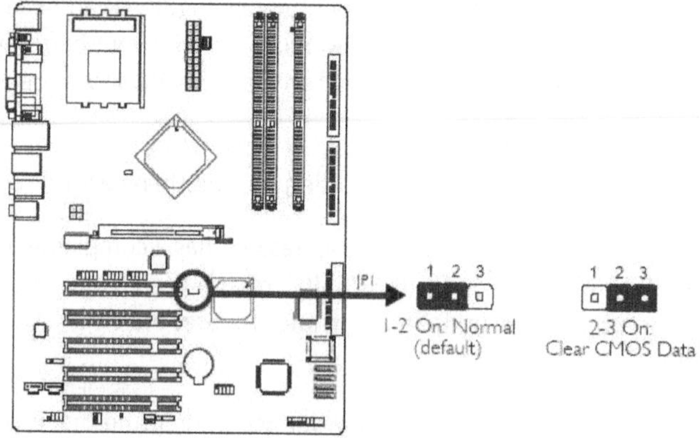

Figure 24-15 The clear CMOS jumper location on a typical motherboard.

4. Leave the jumper as described in step 3 for 10 seconds, and then move it back to its original position.
5. Replace the motherboard battery.
6. Reassemble the computer case and reconnect it to the main power supply.

On some motherboards, instead of a clear CMOS jumper, there is a small reset button on the back of the panel (see Figure 24-16). This button, which you can normally press with a paperclip, makes resetting the BIOS a much simpler task.

Figure 24-16 Some computers, though not many, include a clear CMOS button.

> **NOTE**
>
> **If you find that you can't use new hardware with your computer, you might need to update your computer's BIOS to a newer version. To do this, check your motherboard manual or the support section of the manufacturer's website.**

Checking the Power Supply

If you suspect that the power supply has failed on your desktop computer, you can try to start the computer if you have another computer available. To do this, remove the two power connectors from the motherboard in both computers. Place the computers side by side and plug the power connectors from the working power supply into the motherboard in the nonworking device. (If the cables aren't long enough, unscrew the working power supply, supporting it carefully, and place it in a secure position closer to the other computer.)

Next, try to start the nonworking computer. If lights and fans activate on the motherboard, the computer is drawing power normally, and you can be certain that the power supply in your computer is the issue.

CHAPTER 25

Troubleshooting a Windows 8 Installation

A COMMON ASSUMPTION IS THAT ISSUES WITH WINDOWS 8 on desktop computers start only after you've installed the operating system and are using it with multiple users, complex software packages, and excessive amounts of hardware. However, you may also face an issue after you first install it. Problems can be caused by anything from an incompatibility with the operating systems that you're trying to upgrade from, to the Windows Installer.

In this chapter, I show you how to install Windows 8 on your own desktop PC and create custom install images in a way that avoids problems. I'm not going to focus on deployment from a Windows Server, because System Center 2012 Configuration Manager is a substantial subject in its own right, for which separate books exist.

Troubleshooting Stand-Alone Installation Problems

When you're installing Windows 8 on your own computer for home or work use, you don't want things going wrong. Whether you're performing a clean install of an operating system (for which you need to spend time reinstalling and reconfiguring your software), or you're performing an upgrade (which still takes time), the installation process can be stressful, especially for less technical users. In this section, I examine specific installation scenarios and installation options.

INSIDE OUT Unplug all but your main hard disk when installing Windows 8

When Windows 8 is installed (and this also applies equally to Windows Vista and Windows 7), it creates a separate boot partition called *System Reserved* on the primary hard disk in your computer. The location of this System Reserved partition isn't determined by which hard disk you want to install Windows on to, but rather by the socket on your motherboard to which the hard disk is connected.

If you have the System Reserved and Windows partitions on separate hard disks, you will never be able to remove the hard disk containing the System Reserved partition without preventing Windows 8 from starting. To guarantee that the Windows 8 installer places the System Reserved partition on the same physical hard disk that your copy of Windows is on, either physically unplug all your other hard disks before installing the operating system, or for an all-in-one computer or workstation laptop, install Windows 8 onto Disc 0 (zero).

Upgrading from 32-Bit to 64-Bit

As has been the case with all 64-bit versions of Windows in the past, there's no in-place upgrade path from a 32-bit (x86) version of the operating system to the 64-bit (x64) version of Windows 8, and attempting to upgrade a 32-bit version of Windows to a 64-bit version of Windows 8 returns an error (see Figure 25-1).

If you want to upgrade from a 32-bit operating system to the 64-bit version of Windows 8, ask yourself the following two questions first:

- **Will I benefit from installing it?** If you do not have more than 4 gigabytes (GB) of RAM (including your graphics memory) in your computer, you will not realize a benefit.
- **Can I get 64-bit drivers for all my hardware?** It is best to check the manufacturer's websites before making the move.

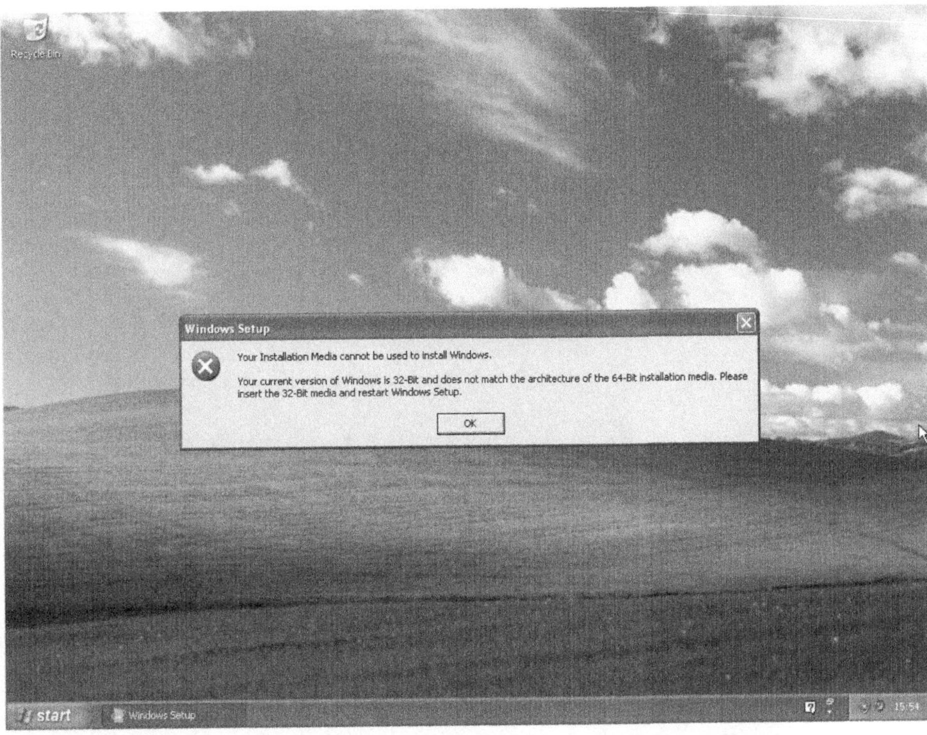

Figure 25-1 Installing a 64-bit operating system over a 32-bit version returns an error.

On this second point, you might think that the Windows 8 Upgrade Assistant can inform you about whether 64-bit drivers are available, but not necessarily. The reason for this is that 64-bit drivers and 32-bit drivers are completely different and can even be called by different names. Just because the Windows 8 Upgrade Assistant can check for new 32-bit drivers for your hardware does not guarantee it will be able to find updated 64-bit drivers if they exist.

Upgrading Windows XP to Windows 8

There is no upgrade path from Windows XP to Windows 8, however, the Windows 8 Installer allows you to keep your personal files and documents intact, and it will ask you if you want to do so early in the installation process (see Figure 25-2).

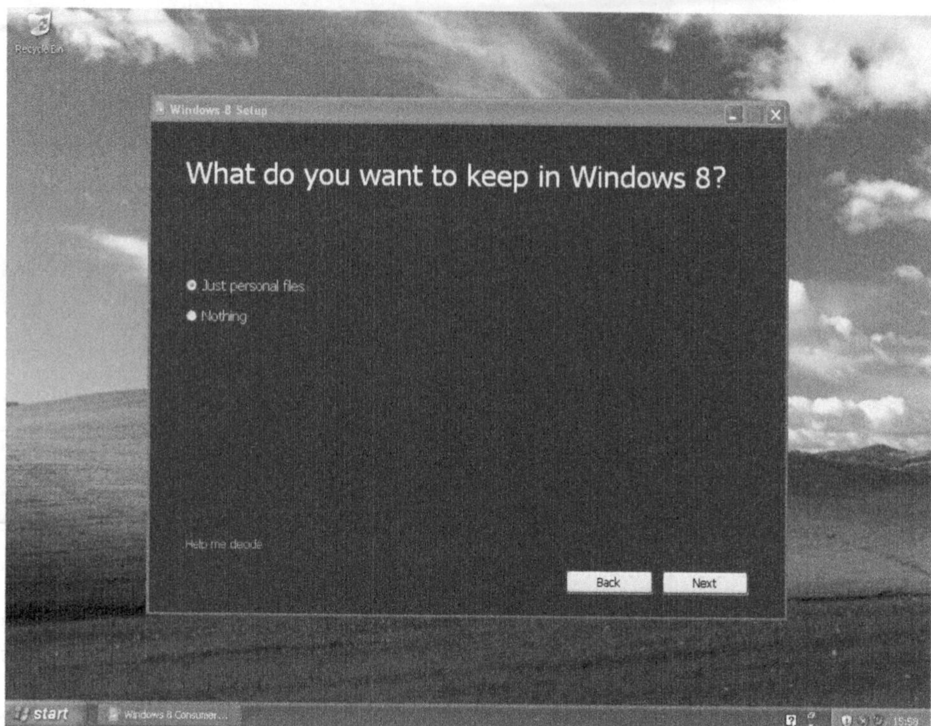

Figure 25-2 Upgrading from Windows XP.

The reason you cannot upgrade anything except your personal files, such as your software from Windows XP, is because Microsoft changed the underlying code of Windows, and as a result, the programs run differently. This is the primary reason for software incompatibilities with XP software.

Because the changes are so pronounced, you will have to reinstall all your software after performing an upgrade to Windows 8. On the upside, because nothing is kept from your previous copy of Windows except your files, no problems can be carried forward to Windows 8.

Upgrading Windows Vista and Windows 7 to Windows 8

Microsoft changed the underlying Windows code base in Windows Vista. Although you might think you can upgrade a Windows Vista installation directly to Windows 8 with everything in place, unfortunately, you can't (see Figure 25-3). The underlying kernel was refined further in Windows 7 and has now been refined even more. Whereas you could perform a Windows 7 upgrade in place from Windows Vista, the differences between Windows Vista and Windows 8 are simply too great to allow the upgrade.

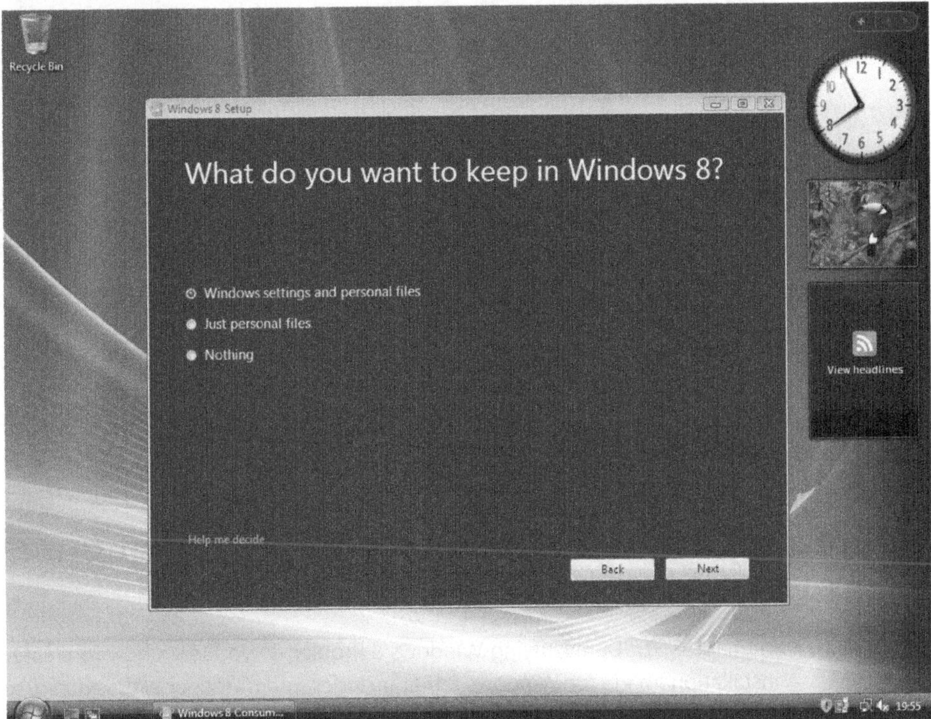

Figure 25-3 Upgrading to Windows 8 from Vista.

Your options for upgrading from Windows Vista to Windows 8 are that you can keep your Windows settings, user accounts, and files, but not your installed programs. Personally, in this circumstance, I think it's far better to perform a clean install (if you have your files backed up somewhere safe, of course). If you have to reinstall your software from scratch, consider the risk of the Windows Installer carrying over problems from your former copy of Windows Vista; it's much safer to format the hard disk and start again.

If you have Windows 7, you can perform a full in-place upgrade of all your programs, Windows settings, and files (see Figure 25-4).

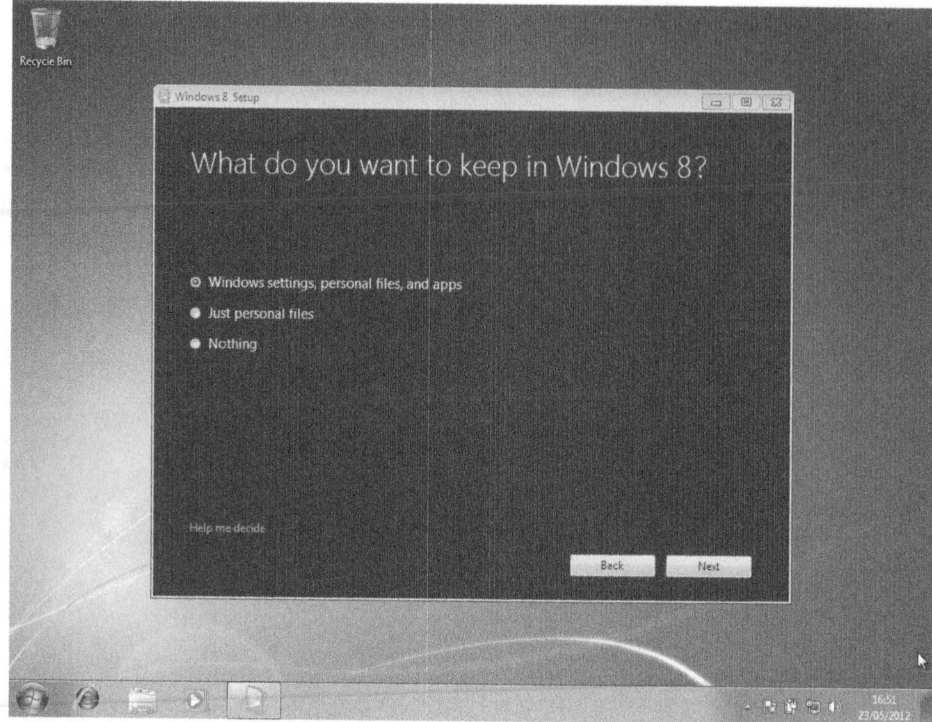

Figure 25-4 Upgrading from Windows 7.

Optimizing a System Image for Deployment on a Small Scale

In Chapter 21, "Demystifying Windows 8 Problems," you learn how to create a custom installation image for Windows 8 that includes integrated, or *slipstreamed*, service packs. You can also use this technique to build custom install images. Let's look at why you might want to do this.

Suppose, for example, that you always put a copy of Microsoft Office in your computer, along with the Adobe Flash Player, CCleaner, and other standard software—the sort of software that's commonly found on computers. You can integrate all of these into an installation image, and even change some system settings such as the virtual memory, so that after the install, you don't have to change the settings on each computer that uses the new installation image.

What are the disadvantages of creating a custom installation image? One disadvantage is that you can't change settings that are specific to user accounts, because you won't have any users configured in Windows 8 when you first install it, and any that you create afterward will always be configured with the default settings. Also, new versions of software

are released, and although some have updaters in Windows, such as Adobe Flash, Acrobat Reader, and Java, others are manual downloads. You can change these settings and create a custom Windows 8 installer, however, by following the instructions in the section "Creating a Slipstreamed Install DVD" in Chapter 21.

Changing the Computer Name After Deployment

Suppose you need to image multiple computers. Either you created a custom Windows 8 Installer for your computers, or your computers are identical, in which case you created a system image backup of the computer that you then intend to roll out to all the other computers in your office. After all, if all of the hardware is the same, you won't have any driver issues, and this is a very common way for system administrators to image multiple computers. You need to change the computer name on each machine that's been reimaged from the same file, because having multiple computers with the same name accessing network and server resources can cause issues. The server can get confused and then can't deliver anything to the computer.

To change the computer name after deployment, you first need to change the computer name, especially if you are sharing files between computers on a network, but especially if the computer is part of a Windows Server network. To do this, on the Start screen, search for **system**, and then click the system in the Settings results. In the System Properties dialog box that appears, in the left pane, click Advanced System Settings, and then in the next System Properties dialog box that appears, click the Computer Name tab. To change the computer name, click the Change button (see Figure 25-5), and then edit the name of the computer.

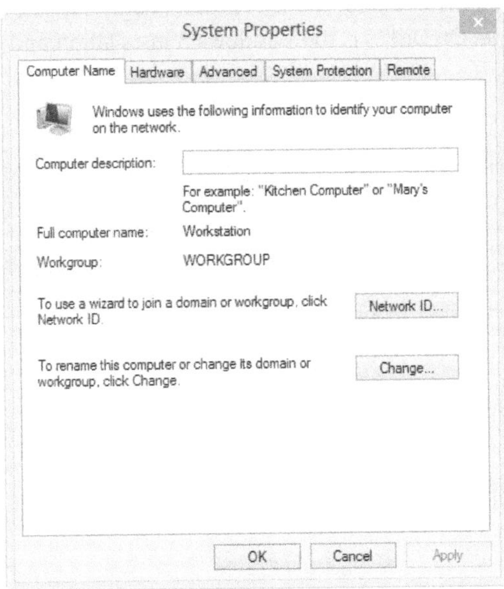

Figure 25-5 You can change the computer name or the Network ID, if you are a member of a specific workgroup or domain.

INSIDE OUT **What should you change the computer name to?**

You will want to be able to clearly identify each computer on a network, and you might consider using the asset tags provided with the computers when you bought them. If you do not use asset tags, find a unique identifier (desk numbers aren't reliable because computers tend to be moved around from time to time), for example, a code based on the department to which the computer belongs and a number that's assigned to a specific user or location.

Moving the System Reserved Partition

One of the biggest problems with installing Windows is that the System Reserved partition can end up on the wrong physical hard disk. I mentioned at the beginning of this chapter that the System Reserved partition is created by Windows 8 during installation and that this partition contains the boot, rescue, and restore options for the operating system.

By default, Windows 8 always puts the System Reserved partition on Disc 0, even if a partition already exists there. This means that sometimes the System Reserved partition can end up either on the wrong physical hard disk or on a partition that's already being used for something else, such as your files. Figure 25-6 illustrates a fairly typical twin hard-disk structure. Disk 0 contains a partition for files and another for a Windows 8 files backup. Disk 1 contains separate partitions so that both the files and image stay safe in the event of a Windows 8 hard disk failure. On Disk 0 is the Windows 8 installation and a local backup of your files.

Figure 25-6 A twin hard-disk system.

Consider an example scenario, which illustrates the importance of moving the System Reserved partition properly. Suppose your computer previously had Windows XP installed, and the operating system was on Disk 0, but before wiping your Windows partition to perform a clean installation, you took the computer apart to give it a good cleaning, and good for you for doing that.

Unfortunately, you didn't pay too much attention to which hard disk plugged into what Serial ATA (SATA) port on the motherboard. As a result, the Disk 0 assignment is now on the wrong drive, because you swapped the disk cables for the two hard disks' data leads in the motherboard sockets. You don't worry about this too much, however, and you install Windows 8 anyway on what in still the old Windows partition. However, that old partition is still seen by the computer as Disk 1 because of the cable swap.

You create a system image backup, but Windows informs you that you can't do this for two reasons: first, because you *must* include your Files partition (where the System Reserved files now reside); and second, because your system image backup hard disk is not recognized as big enough. When you installed Windows 8, a System Reserved partition had to be created at the beginning of Disk 0. It's *always* placed at the beginning of Disk 0. If the System Reserved partition where Windows 8 was to be installed had been an empty partition, the installer would have resized the Windows partition slightly to create a small amount of free space before it for the System Reserved files. However, because Disk 0 already has partitions filling the hard disk, the Windows 8 installer can't do this. Instead, it places the System Reserved files on the first partition on Disk 0, which in this example contains all your files. Now you can't back up Windows without also being forced to back up your files, because the system image backup system must also back up the System Reserved partition. You don't want to do this, because when you restore a backup, you'll also restore earlier versions of all your files as well, plus you'll end up with an enormous image that will take a couple of hours to create and restore.

To remedy this situation, move the System Reserved files to a new location. This is a fairly straightforward process. Because *you're* doing it, you can put this replacement System Reserved partition back on the same disk that Windows 8 is installed on, and wherever on that hard disk you choose (because the only available space might be at the end of the disk), and you can force Windows 8 to accept the change. In following this process, you don't need to reinstall everything (if you swapped the SATA cables over at this point to make the Windows drive Disk 0, Windows wouldn't start anyway), and thus can create a new System Reserved partition at the end of Disk 1.

To move your System Reserved partition files, perform the following steps:

1. Press Windows logo key+X to open the WinX menu, and then click Disk Management.
2. Right-click any partition on Disk 0, and then click Shrink Volume.
3. Shrink the volume by 400 megabytes (MB) by entering **400** in the Enter The Amount Of Space To Shrink In MB box, and then click Shrink.
4. Right-click in the new unallocated space you have created, create a new Simple Volume, assign this drive a drive letter (this is important), and format it as NTFS.
5. Press Windows logo key+X again, but this time click Command Prompt (Admin).
6. Type **bcdboot C:\Windows /s F:**, where *C* is the location of your Windows installation and *F* is the location of your new System Reserved partition, and then press Enter.
7. Type **DISKPART**, and then press Enter.
8. Type **select volume F**, and then press Enter.
9. Type **active**, and then press Enter.
10. In the Disk Management console, right-click the new System Reserved partition, select Change Drive Letter And Paths, and then remove the partition's drive letter.

The next time you start your computer, the System Reserved files will be located on the new volume, and you will be able to create a system image backup.

PART 4

Disaster Recovery

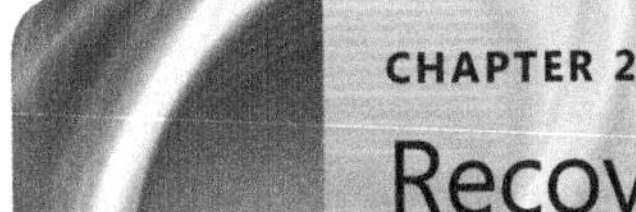

CHAPTER 26

Recovering Encrypted Data

EVEN THOUGH YOU ENCRYPT YOUR FILES, FOLDERS, AND DATA, a time may come when you cannot recover them, for example, when decryption software is either not available or just too expensive to purchase. Thus, I recommend you always keep a backup of your encryption keys, and I show you how in this chapter. Be aware, however, that under certain circumstances, data and files will continue to be encrypted or won't be encrypted after you copy or move them off your computer.

Understanding Encryption

You may have used a cipher to break secret codes in comic books when you were young, where all the letters were shifted a certain number of characters to the left or right. This is a technique that Julius Caesar used and thus is known as the *Caesar cipher*. Here's an example of how an original sequence is encrypted by using the Caesar cipher:

Plain: *ABCDEFGHIJKLMNOPQRSTUVWXYZ*

Cipher: *DEFGHIJKLMNOPQRSTUVWXYZABC*

To decrypt this cypher, you would use simple letter substitution:

Ciphertext: *WKH TXLFN EURZQ IRA MXPSV RYHU WKH ODCB GRJ*

Plaintext: *the quick brown fox jumps over the lazy dog*

Modern ciphers don't work on individual characters; instead they operate on blocks of text. A *block cipher* splits data into data blocks (that is, 128 bits) and encrypts each block separately.

The same key is used to encrypt and decrypt the data; in decryption, the key is used in reverse. Think of it as changing the subject of an equation:

$M=2P$ so $P=M/2$

By making all the text fixed-block sizes, the encryption is strengthened, because the person decrypting the data does not know how long the original block is. Consider the following data examples:

- **The word Dog** This is an easy code to break, because there are not many permutations to decipher: 263.
- **The word Dog with fixed-length encrypted code of 64 characters** This code is more challenging to break, because you have 2664 permutations.

In the two preceding examples, the last 61 characters would all be the same. To further encrypt the blocks, the encryption takes each block through a series of encryption cycles, or *rounds*. Each round uses a slight variation of the encryption algorithm, which randomizes all the remaining characters and produces a code with 2664*x* permutations, where *x* represents the number of rounds.

The block cipher may convert your plain text into blocks of either binary code [number base 2] (0s and 1s) or Hexadecimal code [number base 16] (0, 1, 2, 3, 4, 5, 6, 7, 8, 9, A, B, C, D, E, F). Think of a block key this way: if a block and block key are 64 bits long, you will have a key made up of 64 random characters. Such a key is much harder to figure out than one made up of just 16 characters, because the sheer number of permutations you must go through to decrypt the data is considerably greater.

Encryption Types

The Data Encryption Standard (DES) is a block cipher based on a 56-bit key (a fixed block of 56 characters). It was introduced in the 1970s but is now considered too insecure for modern usage. In 1999, the Electronic Frontier Foundation demonstrated this by cracking a DES key in less than a day.

Triple DES (3DES) is a cipher that applies the DES encryption algorithm to each data block three times. This option is more secure than DES and is backward-compatible with it. It is commonly used in banking. Because it uses 3 DES keys (each of 56 bits), the encryption key for 3DES is 168 bits long.

Advanced Encryption Standard (AES) is a modern standard often used by governments and that is now becoming more common in business. It uses block sizes of 128 bits, and it uses key sizes of 128, 192, or 256 bits. AES uses 10 rounds of encryption for 128-bit keys, 12 rounds for 192-bit keys, and 14 rounds for 256-bit keys.

AES encryption operates on array blocks of 4x4 bytes. The cipher will perform a series of actions on these blocks, including swapping, shifting, and mixing blocks, rows, or columns.

RSA is an algorithm used for public-key cryptography, for example, the Pretty Good Privacy (PGP) Software. This is commonly used for e-commerce. The two keys, public and private, are linked mathematically, but the private key is always kept secret.

Data is encrypted by using the public key but can be decrypted only with the private key. This means that you can, for instance, send sensitive personal information across the Internet in your web browser, and if intercepted, that information cannot be decrypted. The website contains the public key used to encrypt the information, and the web server holds the private key. This process also enables users to send information (such as email) with a digital signature. Anybody with access to the sender's public key can confirm the email was indeed sent from the legitimate sender.

So how do these public/private key systems work? The public key takes your chosen password and runs it through a mathematical equation to produce the custom encryption. The private key also takes the password and uses this, with a different equation, to decrypt the data. Your password is the unique cipher for that data. The stronger the password is, the stronger the cipher.

Internet security certificates are based on public/private key cryptography. Digital certificates are verified by using a chain of trust, the root of this being the certificate authority (CA) such as VeriSign Authentication Services. Your web browser, for instance, will check the public key on a website against the certificate held by the issuer to confirm its authenticity. That key will be locked to a specific domain address.

Secure Sockets Layer (SSL) and its more secure version Transport Layer Security (TLS) are protocols based on RSA security that provide end-to-end encryption on the Internet. They use a public/private key system. The encryption has ciphers with 1024-bit or 2048-bit keys, which are used to determine the server's authenticity, and the client remains anonymous.

The Cryptographic Hash Function is a well-known technique for taking plain text of any length and translating it into a hexadecimal code of a fixed length. Hash codes are commonly used as checksums. What this means is that they take any piece of data and convert it into a fixed-length code. This code can best be compared to the tamper seal on a CD or DVD case.

When decrypting the data, if the contents don't match the hash code, the contents have been tampered with or corrupted. Anyone who's been kicked from an online game because of an MD5 Tool error has fallen foul of data corruption that didn't match the hash (checksum) code.

Hashing can be used so that you don't have to store passwords that can later be hacked. Instead of storing the actual password, you store its hash code, which is unique. Thus the password can be verified without needing to be stored locally. The actual password is kept in a separate *password store*, and the two hash codes compared. The password is never exposed, and it cannot be intercepted by a hacker.

Windows 8 Encryption Types

Windows 8 comes with two types of encryption built in: Encrypting File System (EFS) and Microsoft BitLocker. EFS is a file and folder encryption system; BitLocker encrypts entire hard disks and partitions. EFS was first introduced with Windows 2000, so it's well established but not quite as popular as Bitlocker (you'll see why shortly). The longevity of EFS means that encrypted files will be backward-compatible with other versions of Windows as long as you import the encryption key to the computers running those earlier versions.

You can use other types of encryptions with Windows 8, such as PGP and TrueCrypt, which are widely supported across operating systems, including the Apple OS X and GNU/Linux. Like EFS and BitLocker, these are file and folder encryption methods, but I would argue that the future of encryption is full-disk encryption, such as that provided by BitLocker, and that from a troubleshooting perspective, you shouldn't be using file/folder encryption except on very small scales.

File Encryption After Copy/Move

You will want to perform file encryption after copying or moving data. To understand why, consider how BitLocker works. BitLocker encrypts an entire hard disk or partition. Any files or folders created on or copied to that drive will be automatically encrypted. Because the hard disk, rather than individual files and folders, is encrypted, when you copy any content from the protected hard disk to a nonencrypted storage device, such as a network-attached storage (NAS) unit or USB flash drive, the resulting copied files and folders are not encrypted. Thus, the main reason to perform file encryption after copying or moving data is because you are moving encrypted files onto a medium where the files' encryption is no longer supported.

This loss of encryption after a copy or move operation could be considered an issue when using Bitlocker, but BitLocker does allow you to encrypt removable devices, including USB hard disks and USB flash drives. What it doesn't allow you to do, however, is encrypt network shares such as NAS drives (although Windows Server allows encryption on drives that it manages).

Some context will help illustrate my point. Suppose you have a laptop that is fully protected, and you copy files to an NAS drive, or burn your files to a CD or DVD. Your files on the new medium will not be encrypted, and anybody will be able read them. Also, with EFS, your chances of data loss are greater when copying and moving files between your Windows PC and third-party storage devices, because those third-party devices may have an incompatible disk format or their own proprietary disk format. For these reasons, consider carefully whether EFS is the most appropriate solution for your needs. Instead, consider using TrueCrypt and PGP because of how they work, and because they are so widely supported. You might have less chance of losing your data.

Unlike BitLocker, EFS works only on hard disks formatted with Microsoft's NTFS file system. If you copy an EFS-encrypted file to a drive that is formatted any other way—such as using FAT or exFAT file systems on a USB flash drive, the hierarchical file system plus (HFS+) used on the Apple Mac, or the variety of formatting approaches used by Linux-based NAS drives for disks and RAID arrays—you run the risk of files becoming corrupt, because different disk formats can be incompatible with EFS-encrypted files. I have seen several examples over the last few years of EFS-encrypted files that were copied to NAS drives being completely unreadable when copied back to the host computer, even with the correct decryption key installed. (I have encountered a third-party disk format on an NAS drive that scrambled my EFS-encrypted files.)

Files and folders encrypted by using PGP and TrueCrypt don't have this problem because they are platform-agnostic and can operate on any file system.

Working with EFS Keys to Recover Data

You can use the Manage File Encryption Certificates wizard to export and import EFS encryption keys in Windows 8 (see Figure 26-1). To access the wizard, on the Start screen, search for **encrypt**, and in the Settings results, click Manage File Encryption Certificates.

Figure 26-1 Export and import EFS keys via a wizard.

> **Note**
>
> **To import a previously saved EFS by using the wizard, click the option to Create A New Certificate.**

When you first encrypt files by using EFS, you are prompted with alerts in the desktop notification area to back up your EFS key. You don't need multiple keys for different files and folders that are encrypted. There is always just one key that is locked to your user account.

It is critical that you not only keep a backup of this key, but also that you keep backups (preferably two) in very safe locations where the keys won't be accidentally lost or deleted.

If you have a valid EFS key on your computer, you can decrypt EFS-encrypted files and folders by performing the following steps:

1. Right-click the files or folders you want to decrypt, and then click Properties.
2. Click Advanced to open the Advanced Attributes dialog box.
3. In the Advanced Attributes dialog box, clear the Encrypt Contents To Secure Data check box (see Figure 26-2), and then click OK. A dialog box appears for each file being decrypted, one at a time. Do not close this dialog box; if you do, you will also cancel the decryption.

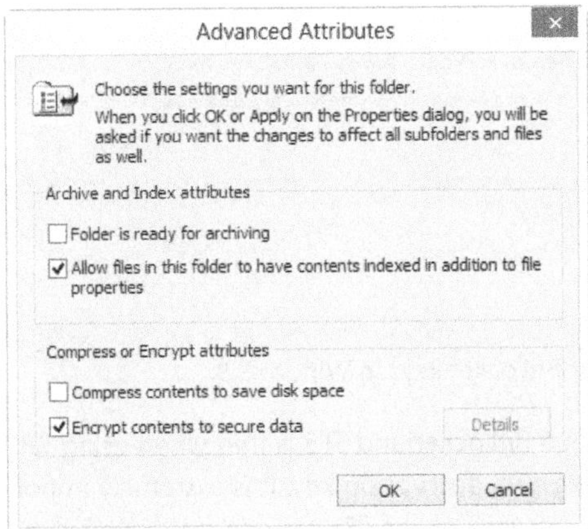

Figure 26-2 Decrypting EFS-encrypted files and folders.

Working with BitLocker to Recover Data

BitLocker is managed through the BitLocker section of Control Panel (see Figure 26-3). BitLocker recovery applies to your internal hard disks and partitions, and any encrypted external hard disks and USB flash drives.

> **Note**
>
> **For you to manage any encrypted external storage in Windows 8, the USB flash drive or other device will need to be plugged into the computer; otherwise, it will not appear in the BitLocker Control Panel.**

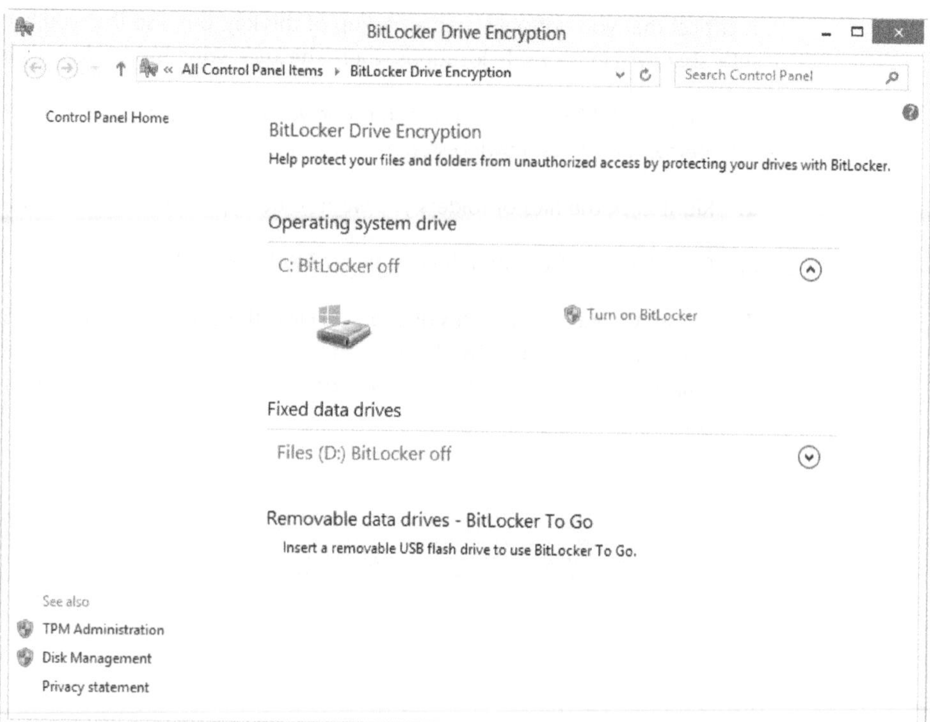

Figure 26-3 Managing your BitLocker keys in Windows 8.

The main difference between BitLocker and EFS is that when using BitLocker, each individual storage device has its own decryption key. It is extremely important that you back up each device separately, because unlike EFS, you do not have just have one key locked to your user account.

In the list of hard disks in the main BitLocker Control Panel, you will see a link to back up the encryption key for each encrypted drive.

CAUTION!

Never store your backup key for a BitLocker-encrypted drive on a disk that is encrypted with BitLocker. If you encounter a problem with the encryption, such as a disk error that triggers your Bitlocker protection and locks you out of your computer, you will probably not be able to restore the key.

As mentioned before, always store a couple of backup copies of the keys in a secure place. Because you are likely to use BitLocker to encrypt an entire laptop or workstation-grade tablet, I recommend a cloud storage location such as Microsoft SkyDrive.

Note

If you are traveling with a BitLocker-encrypted laptop or tablet, carry an unencrypted USB flash drive with a backup copy of your BitLocker encryption key or keys so that you can restore the keys if you find yourself locked out of your computer. Do not keep your laptop and the USB flash drive in the same bag. They should be kept separately so that if one is stolen, the other is safe.

You can decrypt BitLocker-encrypted drives from the BitLocker Control Panel, too, by clicking the decrypt drive option, which turns BitLocker off on that drive.

INSIDE OUT **Saving BitLocker-encrypted data by copying**

When you copy files and folders from a BitLocker-encrypted hard disk, the copies are decrypted on the target volume (if that location is not itself BitLocker-encrypted). This can be a good way to access a decrypted copy of data.

Automatic vs. Manual Unlocking

Sometimes, you can get locked out of your computer when using BitLocker; I've had that happen to me. You might be experimenting with a multiboot system, which BitLocker doesn't support; or there might have been some minor disk, BIOS, or Unified Extensible Firmware Interface (UEFI) error, perhaps caused by a power spike.

In this circumstance, you have two options. You can either plug in a USB flash drive containing the BitLocker key to have the computer unlock the drives for you automatically, or you can manually type in the key. If you decide you prefer to manually type in the key, store the key as a text file on a smartphone and protect that smartphone with its own password. This is in many ways much more secure than keeping a USB drive handy, but I personally still prefer the USB drive option for convenience.

INSIDE OUT **BitLocker and Microsoft Surface**

Microsoft Surface tablets support BitLocker by default and include a Trusted Platform Module (TPM) hardware. In fact, the Full Device Encryption feature in Microsoft Surface RT tablets is indeed BitLocker and can be trusted to safely guard your files.

Using BitLocker To Go to Decrypt Data

For the decryption methods explained in this chapter to work, you must be able to start a working copy of Windows on the computer on which you initiated the encryption. If you have a full hard disk or partition encrypted by using BitLocker, but a TPM chip wasn't used to secure the encryption key, restoration will be possible only if you have access to the USB flash drive or other device used to store the key.

Microsoft BitLocker To Go is designed to permit encrypted drives created on one computer to be readable on another, and so it is a straightforward way to decrypt the data on another computer. All you do is plug in the encrypted disk; Windows and the host computer will prompt you for the unlock password.

By using BitLocker To Go on removable storage and with EFS, decryption can be accomplished on any computer running Windows 8, Windows 7 (if the computer has BitLocker), and versions of the operating system as early as Windows XP with EFS. Because you can import EFS encryption keys into other copies and versions of Windows, you will be able to decrypt files by using the method described in this chapter on just about any other computer running the Windows operating system.

Note

If you are using Windows XP and Windows Vista, you will see the BitLocker To Go Reader software on the USB flash drive or USB hard disk. You will need to run this software to unlock the drive, after which the drive will be read-only. Windows XP and Windows Vista cannot write to drives encrypted with BitLocker To Go in Windows 7 and Windows 8. You can find out more about the Bitlocker To Go Reader software at *http://support.microsoft.com/kb/970401*.

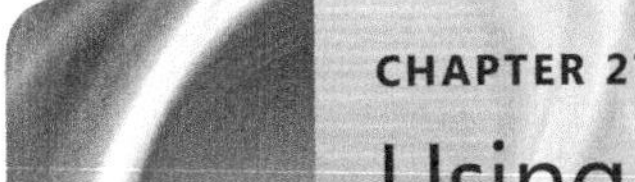

CHAPTER 27

Using Windows Data Recovery Tools

YOUR FILES AND DATA ARE VERY IMPORTANT TO YOU. Even though you might be able to download all your music again after your hard disk fails, lost digital photos and videos represent treasured memories that simply cannot be replaced. I want to stress how important it is to keep backups of all of your files and documents. The three most important rules for using computers are backup, backup, and backup!

If a computer issue prevents you from starting Windows, you will be locked out of using your software, and you won't be able to access your files and data. This kind of challenge seems to happen at the worst time, such as when you're working against a deadline or planning a vacation. However, you might be surprised at just how much you can do to rescue your system and get it working again.

Restoring Windows from a Backup

If your system stops responding, the easiest and quickest way to get up and running can be to restore your operating system or files from a backup. Although restoring from a backup can be much faster than diagnosing and addressing the underlying issue, you should be wary about restoring your files from a backup if the backup isn't recent and might overwrite newer files that you need to keep with the much older versions.

If you cannot repair Windows 8 by using the conventional tools such as System Restore, be prepared to rely on your most recent image backup. Reimaging a computer has long been a favorite repair tool of system administrators, and Windows 8 includes three different ways to reimage your computer. Microsoft has gone to great lengths to ensure that the process is so simple to use that the typical user, whether at home or in the workplace, can do it without assistance. These methods are Windows system image backup, Refresh Your PC, and Reset Your PC.

Windows System Image Backup

If you've used the image backup tool in Windows 7 or Windows Vista, you will be familiar with the Windows system image backup feature in Windows 8, because Control Panel options for creating a backup operate in the same way. (I show you how to create one of these backups in Chapter 6, "Optimizing Backup and Restore.")

The main advantage of a Windows system image backup is that you can install and configure all your updates and software. You can add user accounts to your email software, set your ribbon and other preferences in Microsoft Office, customize all your other desktop software, download your desktop apps, add users, customize your default storage folders for libraries, and much more.

INSIDE OUT **Storing your backups on the same hard disk as Windows**

Windows system image backup warns you if you try to store a Windows system image on the same physical hard disk as your copy of Windows (although on a laptop, this is often unavoidable).

The problem is that if the disk becomes damaged or malfunctions, you could lose your image backup. If you do not have another hard disk in your computer, back up your copy of Windows 8 to a USB-attached external hard disk instead.

When you restore from a Windows system image backup, all you likely need to do is download your email again in Microsoft Outlook (because your user accounts and all their settings from when the backup image was taken will still be in place) and hide some Windows Updates that you'd previously hidden.

After you create a Windows system image backup in Windows, how do you restore it? You can start your computer from your Windows 8 installation DVD, from a system repair disc created by using the Create A System Image wizard, or from a recovery drive created in the Windows 7 File Recovery section of Control Panel. See Chapter 6 for more details about how to create these.

All three methods take you to the same place: the Windows 8 boot options menu. From this menu, click Troubleshoot\Advanced Options\System Image Recovery (see Figure 27-1). Windows 8 searches for and restores the Windows system image backup you created.

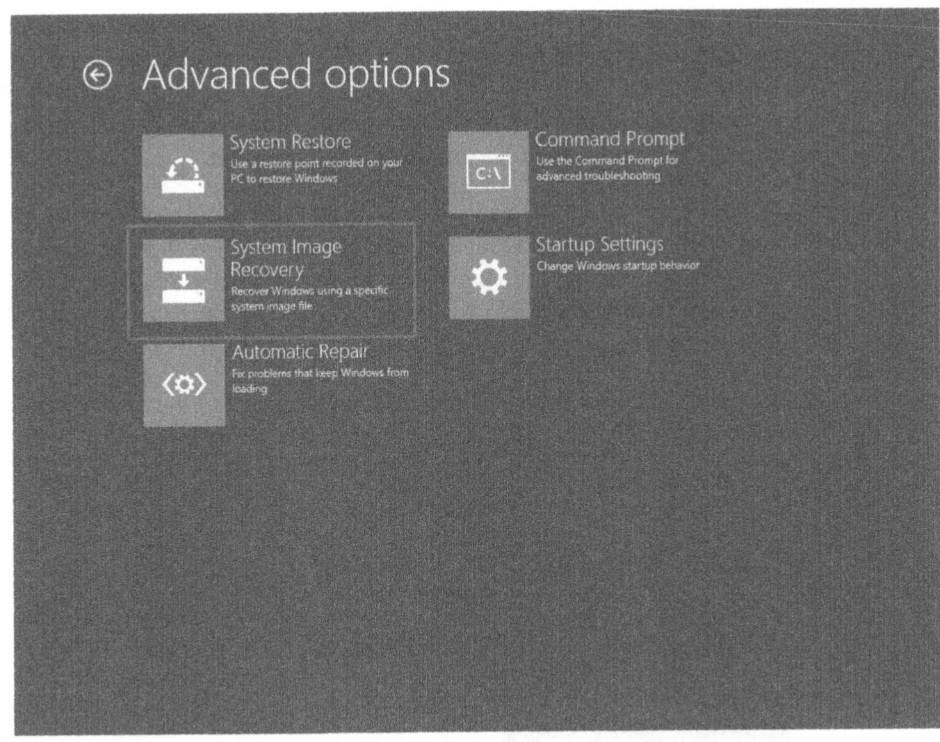

Figure 27-1 Restoring a Windows system image backup. This menu isn't compatible with screen readers.

Using Refresh Your PC

Refresh Your PC is commonly mistaken for Windows system image backup. However, instead of taking a snapshot of your entire Windows drive in the way Windows system image backup does, Refresh Your PC by default keeps only a snapshot of your default Windows files, to which it adds your installed Windows 8 apps. Even though all your desktop software will be installed, none of it will be configured, because your user preferences aren't included in the custom refresh image.

You can quickly and simply create a custom refresh image. Running as an administrator, in the Command Prompt window, type the following command, where *C:\Folder* is the location where you want your image to be stored, and this can be on any hard disk:

recimg -CreateImage C:\Folder

Refresh Your PC looks like a great option for system administrators who want to encourage users to reimage their own computers. However, it works well only if the user is using Windows 8 apps exclusively. After a refresh, starting all desktop software results in a clean installation of that software. For example, starting Outlook after a refresh results in no email accounts being present and no options being configured.

Thus, Refresh Your PC isn't a suitable option for most people who want to reimage their computers and get up and running again quickly. However, if you are providing remote support to a home user who is unlikely to be using desktop software, or who will at least limit usage to Microsoft Word, Microsoft Excel, and perhaps a photo editor, the refresh option is fine to use.

To refresh Windows 8, open PC Settings, click General, and then under Refresh Your PC Without Affecting Your Files, click Get Started (see Figure 27-2).

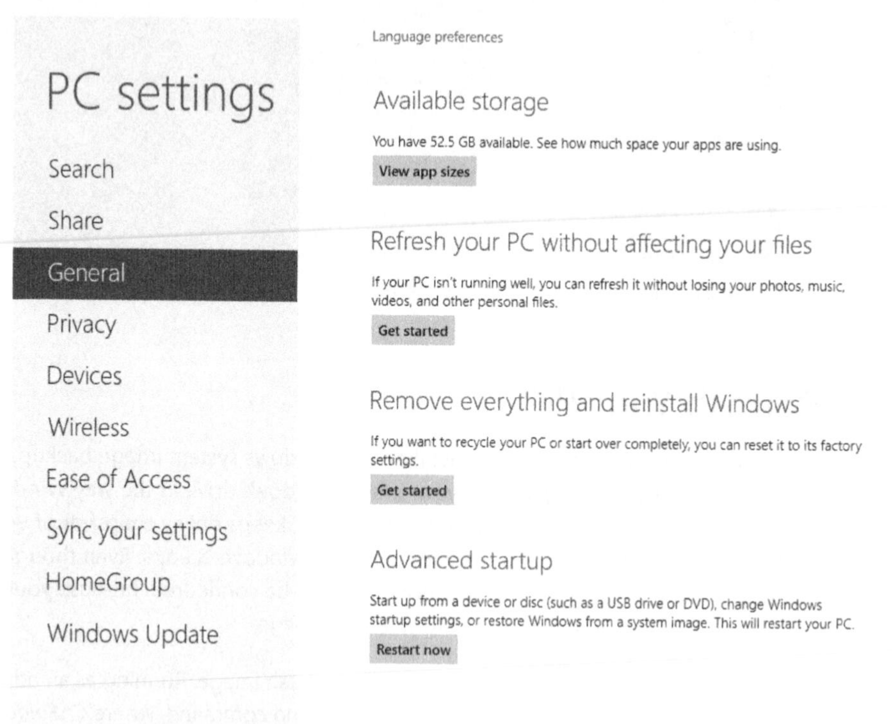

Figure 27-2 Refreshing your computer.

Reset Your PC

Reset Your PC completely resets your computer to its factory state, deleting all your user files (if they are stored in the C:\Users*folder*) and removing your all user accounts, installed Windows 8 apps, and desktop software. To use this option, open PC Settings, click General, and then click Remove Everything And Reinstall Windows. The system carefully warns you of exactly what it will do, but sometimes users do not read the small print. Be aware of what you're clicking!

You can find both the refresh and reset options by starting the computer from your Windows 8 installation DVD, a system repair disc, or a recovery drive, and then clicking Troubleshoot on the boot options menu, which opens the Troubleshoot screen (see Figure 27-3).

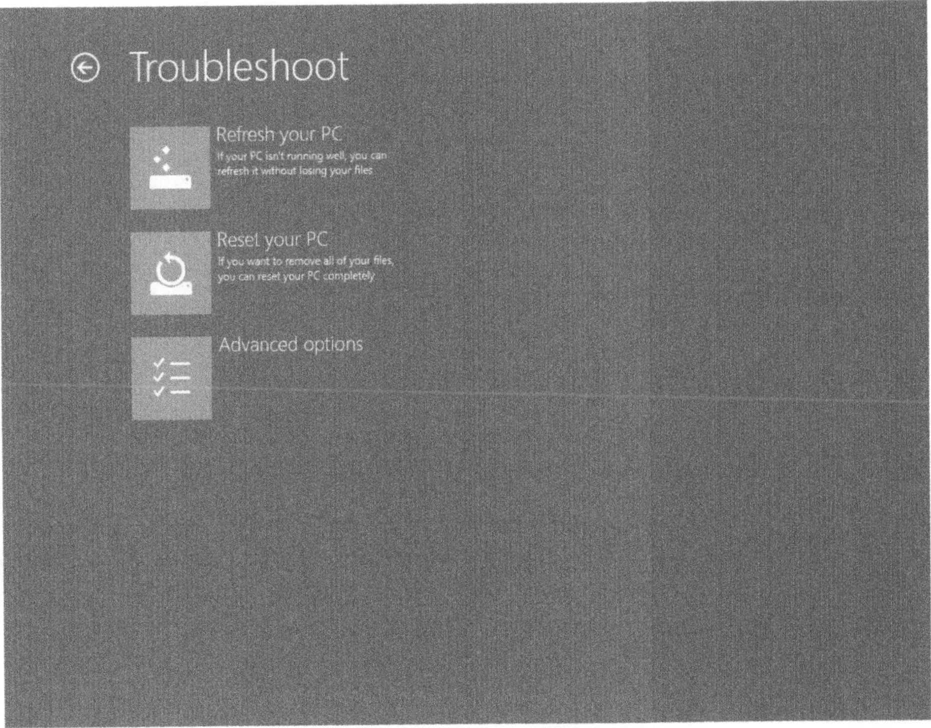

Figure 27-3 Accessing Windows 8 refresh and reset options. This screen isn't compatible with screen readers.

INSIDE OUT Blocking Reset Your PC

In Windows 8 Pro and Enterprise editions, you can block the Windows 8 reset option by using Local Group Policy Editor. To do this, on the Start screen, search for **gpedit.msc**. Next, go to Computer Configuration\Administrative Templates\System\Recovery (see Figure 27-4).

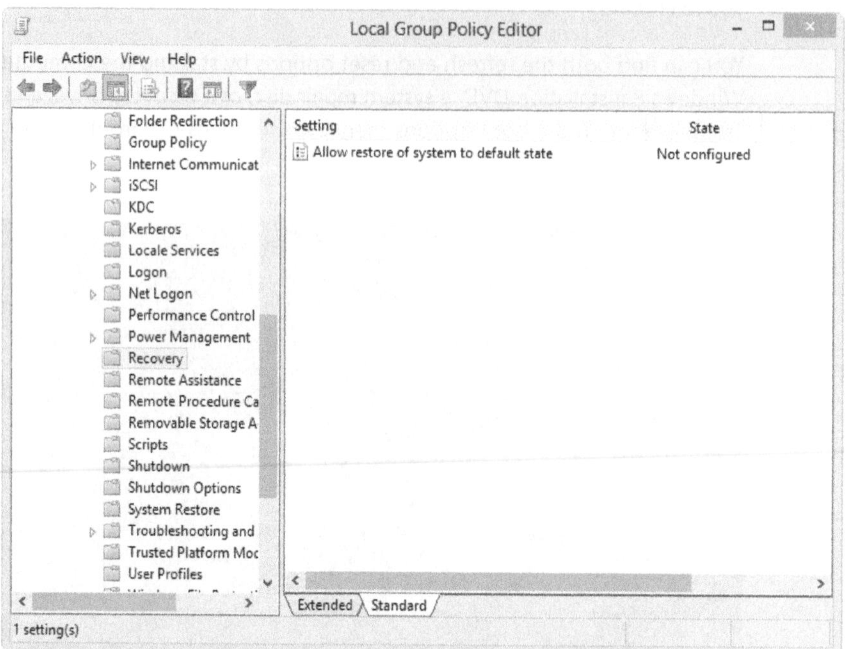

Figure 27-4 Disabling Windows Reset by using Group Policy.

In the Local Group Policy Editor, under the Recovery node, you can block access to the reset option by changing the Allow Restore Of System To Default State setting to Disabled. To do this, right-click the option, and then click Edit.

Restoring Data from a Backup

The method you use to restore your data will vary depending on what file backup software you use. By default, the Windows 8 backup option compresses all your files into a virtual hard disk file. This allows you to open the backup and pull files out of it, but a standard file-by-file backup option can sometimes be easier to work with.

You can find the file backup options in Control Panel, in the Windows 7 File Recovery section (see Figure 27-5). (I cover file backup options in more detail in Chapter 6).

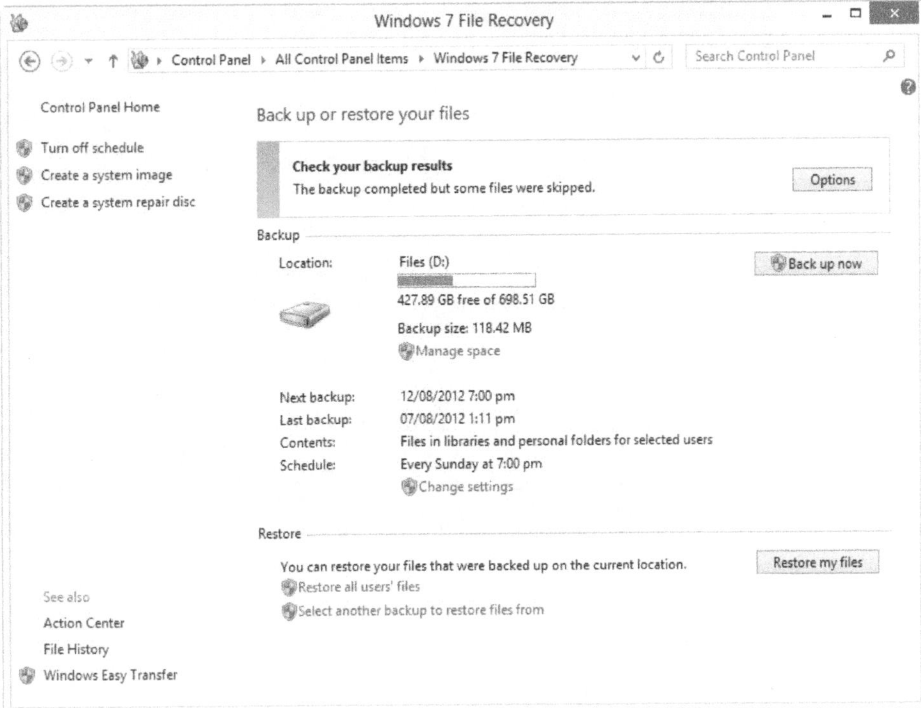

Figure 27-5 Restoring files from a backup by using Windows 8 Backup And Restore.

INSIDE OUT **Always maintain at least two backup copies of files**

If your only backup copy of your files is on a hard disk inside your computer, you could lose your files if disaster strikes. You should always keep at least two copies of your backups—one copy in your home or office for quick restore, perhaps on a network-attached storage (NAS) drive or an external hard disk, and another copy off site.

Saving Personal Files Before a Reinstall

Even if all of your files and data are on the same partition as Windows 8, and you must reinstall the operating system, you can still save the files from deletion. To do this, start your computer from the Windows 8 installation media. You have the option to keep Windows settings, personal files, and apps; personal files only; or nothing at all (see Figure 27-6). Choose the second option, Just Personal Files.

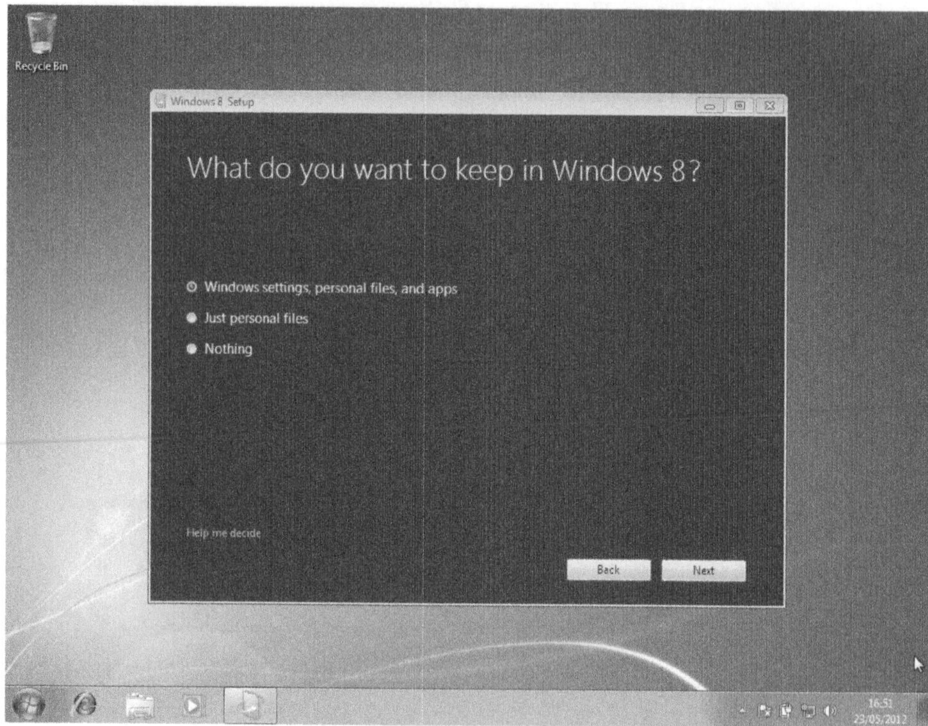

Figure 27-6 Restoring Windows 8 over a previous installation.

Why choose Just Personal Files? If you are recovering Windows 8 because the operating system is unresponsive, you might have no idea what is causing the issue. It could be that some Windows setting, perhaps in the registry or in the AppData folder, which stores settings for your installed desktop software, is the culprit. Because you want to avoid possibly restoring the settings issue, but you want to safeguard the files, you can use the Just Personal Files option.

You can use the first option to maintain your Windows settings and apps if you are confident that the problem is not being caused by a Windows setting, desktop program (remember that these and Windows settings are linked), or an app. Note, however, that the first option wipes out all your installed desktop software. You can always try installation by using the second option if the first option doesn't work.

Hardware RAID

Hard disks can be connected by using a system called *redundant array of independent disks*, or RAID. The RAID system can help ensure that you don't lose files or data in the event that one of the disks fails, and it can also span your files across several disks.

Sometimes, one drive does not appear when the system starts, and you can't access your files and data. This is not necessarily a crisis, however. In this situation, turn off your computer and unplug it from the electrical outlet. Remove the side panel and carefully remove and reseat all the data and power cables to the hard disks that are part of the RAID array. This process will also involve reseating the cables in their sockets on the motherboard or RAID card. You should be careful to keep plugs in their current sockets.

After doing this, a RAID array will often appear online again. If you still encounter problems, you should attempt a repair in the diagnostic console for your RAID hardware. Consult your RAID card or motherboard manual for details about how to access the diagnostic panel and perform a repair, because the procedure will vary from one computer to the next.

Managing Software RAID Arrays

You might have a RAID array on your computer that is managed by Windows 8 rather than by a hardware solution on your motherboard or add-in card. When you reinstall Windows 8, this array might not be recognized. In this circumstance, it is absolutely essential to have a backup of all the files and data on the array itself.

To manage the array, press Windows logo key+X, and then on the WinX menu that appears, click Disk Management. In the main list of your hard disks, right-click one of the disks in your array, and then click either New Striped Volume or New Mirrored Volume, depending on the array type you had before. The following list describes some basic array types::

- **Striped array** Also known as RAID 0, a *striped array* groups all the hard disks in the array together so that they appear as a single large disk. The disadvantage of this strategy is that one disk failing can occasionally lead to the data on the other disks also being unrecoverable.

- **Mirrored array** Also known as RAID 1, a *mirrored array* uses half of the included hard disks—for example, two disks instead of four disks, or one disk instead of two disks—to create an automatic duplicate of the first hard disk. When something changes on the main hard disk, such as a file save, that change is automatically duplicated on the mirrored hard drive.

Add your other array drives to the array in the Computer Management console but *do not* format the array when prompted. There is no guarantee that your data will be recoverable after this, but there is a reasonable chance that the array will function properly.

Repairing Storage Spaces After a Reinstall of Windows 8

Perhaps a better option than RAID if you are using Windows 8 Pro or Enterprise is the new Storage Spaces feature (see Figure 27-7). This is a RAID-type feature that you can use to *aggregate* (or pool) the storage of several different hard disks (drives) in your computer. The hard disks do not need to be the same size, and you can dynamically add hard disks to the pooled storage at a later date. You access Storage Spaces through Control Panel.

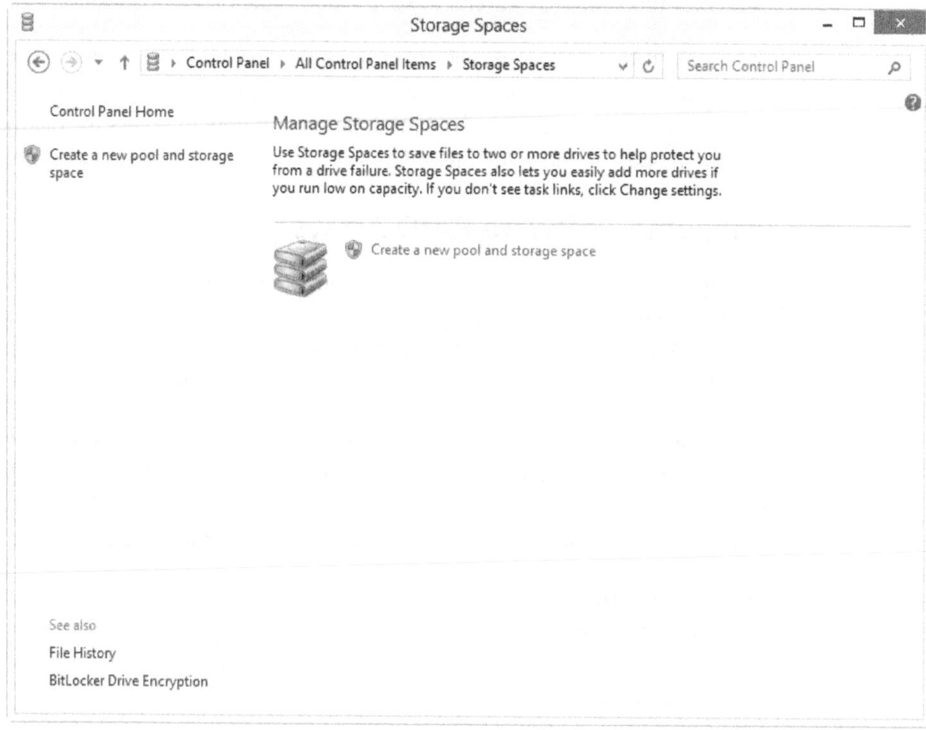

Figure 27-7 The Storage Spaces window in Windows 8.

One advantage of Storage Spaces is that the data residing on Storage Spaces hard disks will remain intact even when you have to completely reinstall Windows 8. After a reinstall, opening the Storage Spaces option should automatically display your existing array, because Windows 8 will search for it and identify it. If Windows 8 does not identify it, you can click Create A New Pool And Storage Space and rebuild the array. All of your files should remain intact.

Storage Spaces is designed to be extremely robust. After reinstalling or reimaging your computer, however, your Storage Space might not be displayed. If this happens, re-creating the Storage Space will almost always force Windows 8 to recognize the pre-existing configuration and get everything working again automatically.

In the very unlikely event, however, that Windows 8 does not recognize your pre-existing Storage Spaces configuration and data, Windows 8 will ask you to reformat all of the drives for the storage space when you rebuild it. In this case, it is vitally important that you already have a full backup of all data and files, because troubleshooting and repair tools are not included with Storage Spaces.

CHAPTER 28

Restoring Windows from Another PC

If your own computer is unresponsive, and you need to access the files and programs stored on it, you can unplug the physical hard disk from the computer and connect that hard disk to another computer. You can connect the hard disk to another computer by either connecting it inside the new host computer as the main or secondary hard disk, or putting the hard disk in a USB hard disk caddy. In this chapter, I explain how to restore Windows by using another PC.

Migrating Your Copy of Windows 8 to a New Computer

When your computer is unresponsive, do you need to go without your copy of Windows and all your software? Is it *really* necessary to reinstall everything on a new computer? Can you just copy a system image in Windows that you've made on one computer over to another and continue working? Depending on the computer hardware you are migrating from and to, copying the system image to a different computer can be challenging, but it's not always impossible. The main problem is the underlying hardware of the motherboard and processor on the two computers.

In a corporate environment—especially where a single image is deployed across dozens, and maybe even hundreds, of computers—you will probably be able to find a few computers that are either identical or very similar. In a home or small office environment, however, finding compatible hardware can be more challenging, because you'll probably buy a new replacement computer only after your old one stops working. Technology changes at a rapid pace, and it's highly likely the new computer's architecture will be very different from the architecture of the computer you are replacing.

However, in a home or small office environment, finding compatible hardware might be more difficult, because you probably buy a new replacement computer only after your old one stops working. Technology changes at a rapid pace, and the new computer's architecture might be very different from the architecture of the computer you are replacing. In this case, you would need to manually inject the drivers for the new computer into the disk image from the old computer. To do this, you need another computer that has a clean, preinstalled version of Windows 8. You will need to create a new partition, or have a second hard disk to which you will copy the system image you created on the older computer. You can, for example, plug in the new hard disk, or put that hard disk in a dock or caddy and access the hard disk or system image from there. It's possible to open this system image file, because it's just a virtual hard disk. Windows 8 will alert you with User Account Control (UAC) prompts that you probably won't want to do, but click OK anyway at each of these UAC prompts.

Drill down through folders to access the system image. The path might be something like the following: X:\WindowsImageBackup\$*MachineName*$\Backup $*dateofbackup*$, where *MachineName* is the name of the computer that's been backed up, and Backup *[date of backup]* indicates the date of the backup. After you go to this location, you are presented with a list of files (see Figure 28-1).

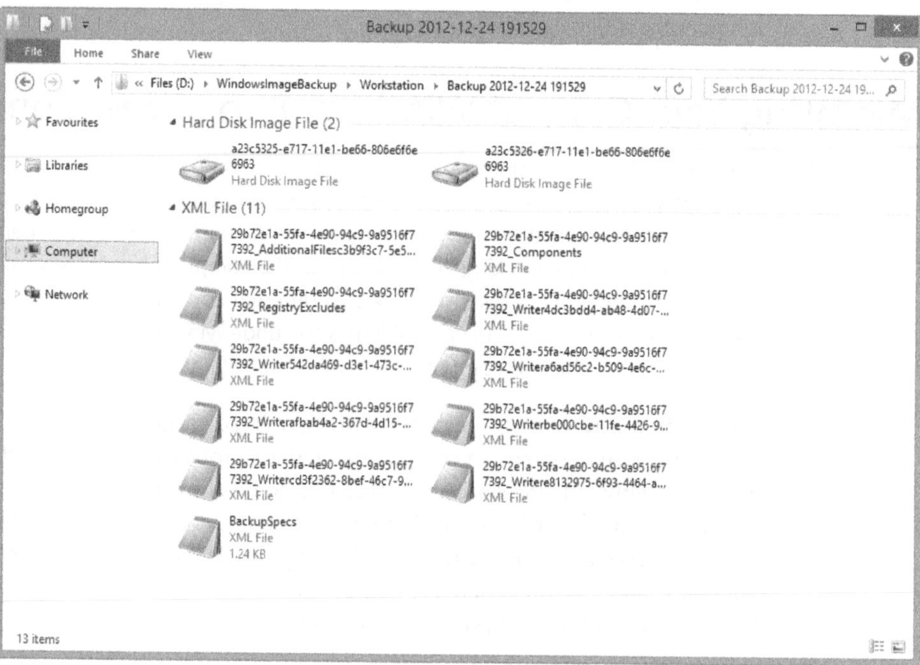

Figure 28-1 Opening a Windows system image backup file.

The file you want is the main hard disk image, which is the big one—it will be many gigabytes in size. You need to mount this image as a drive so that you can work with it. To do this, right-click it, and then click Mount (see Figure 28-2).

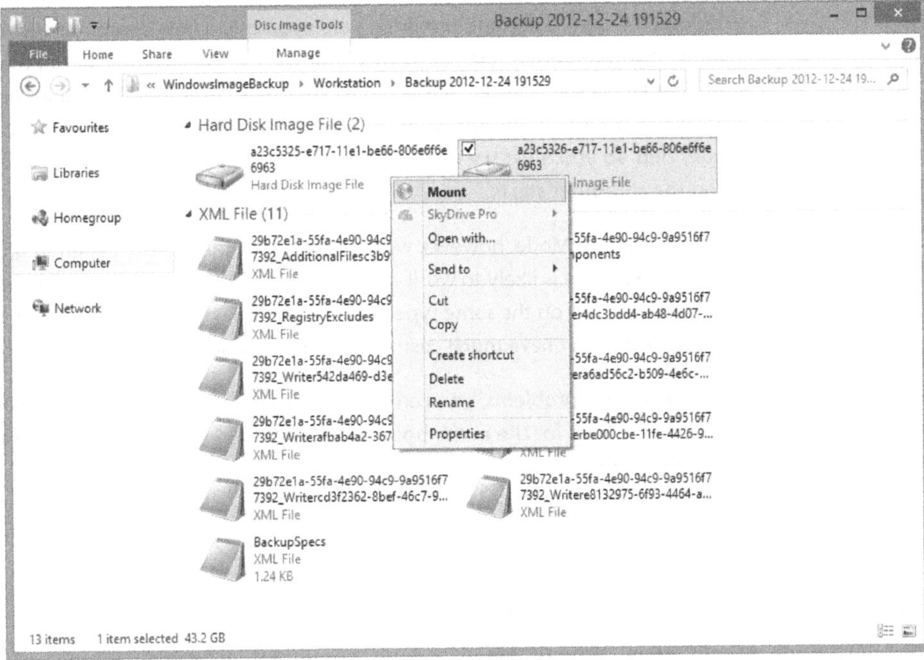

Figure 28-2 Mounting a system image file as a hard disk.

The full Windows hard disk appears inside that system image. You want to change the driver folders. Go to the \Windows\System32\ folder and then look for the Drivers and DriverStore folders. Rename these two folders **Drivers-old** and **DriverStore-Old**, respectively, and then copy the equivalent folders from your new computer's Windows 8 installation to inject them into the backup image. It should be noted that this is not a supported action by Microsoft, but if you do it carefully, it can be an effective method of installing drivers.

You now have a backup that can then be restored to the new computer and that will operate in a trouble-free manner. You might find that drivers are not installed for every hardware device you have. Typically, these are USB and other attached devices such as smartphones, tablets, and webcams, but all the critical drivers required for Windows to start should be in place.

CAUTION!

If you migrate your copy of Windows to a new computer, you might need to purchase an additional license or product key. The license that comes with an OEM copy of Windows 8—that is, the one provided when you buy a new computer—is not transferable. If you bought a retail copy of Windows 8, however, you can call the clearing house and have the license transferred to your new computer. Also, the Windows registry, which points to the correct drivers to load, will try to load drivers that it can no longer find, so you must try to start Windows 8 in Safe Mode by pressing Shift+F8 when the computer starts.

Operating in Safe Mode, however, won't always load the drivers, depending on your computer. This strategy is likely to work only on computers that are broadly similar, meaning that they both run on the same type of motherboard (standard Intel with an Intel chipset), and they don't have much custom hardware installed, such as graphics cards.

If you encounter problems, you can sometimes circumvent them by removing the customized hardware for the initial boot and reinstalling them after you have a stable copy of Windows up and running.

Creating a Custom Windows 8 Installer by Using Refresh Your PC

Chapter 21, "Demystifying Windows 8 Problems," describes how to inject a service pack into Windows 8 and create a new Windows 8 installer. As a part of this process, you must create a custom Install.wim file. This is the same file used by the Windows 8 Refresh Your PC and Reset Your PC features.

As mentioned in Chapter 2, "Repairing Common Issues in Windows 8," you can create a custom refresh image by using the following command (elevated with administrator privileges), where *D:\Folder* is the location where you want your image stored:

recimg -CreateImage *D:\Folder*

You can use the method described in Chapter 21 to inject this custom Install.wim file into a standard Windows 8 installer image. This file is unlikely to fit on a DVD, but you can burn it to a bootable Blu-ray disc or a USB flash drive. The advantage of using this custom Install.wim file is that you can create a custom Windows Installer for your computer that contains all of your software and drivers, which means you will get up and running again very quickly.

Restoring a Windows Image by Using a Surrogate Computer

If you need to restore an image of Windows 8 from a backup, you can plug the hard disk or disks containing the corrupt Windows 8 installation, and the complete system image in Windows, into a working computer. You should probably unplug the host computer's hard disks at this point to prevent accidental damage to or deletion of its files.

Start the computer from the Windows 8 install media, a system repair disc, or a recovery drive. Next, on the boot options menu, click Troubleshoot, click Advanced Options, and then click System Image Recovery (see Figure 28-3).

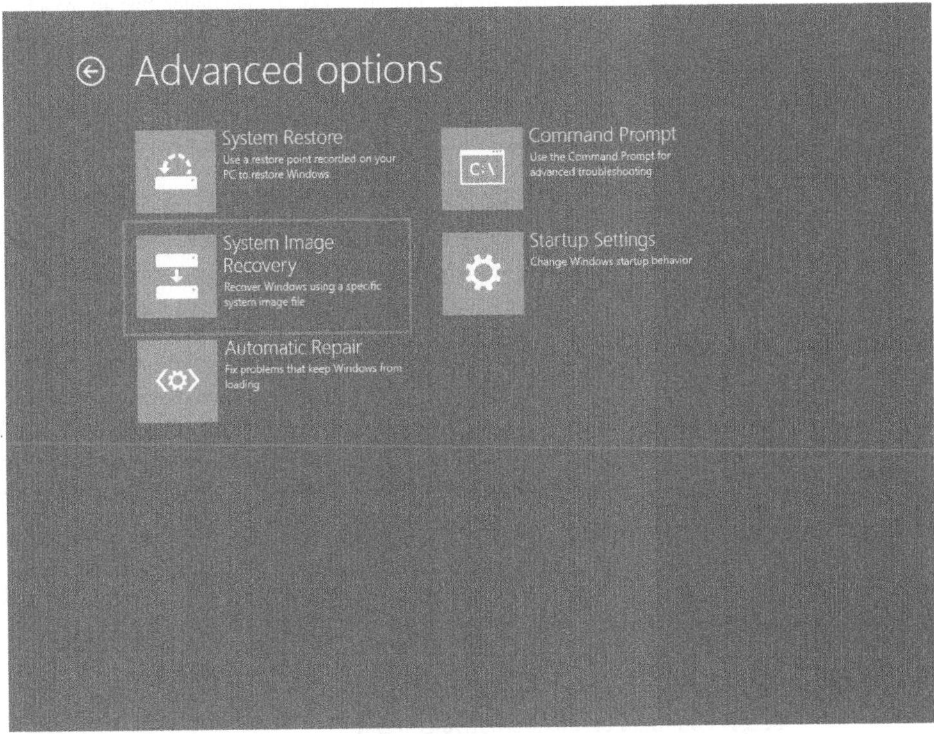

Figure 28-3 Restoring a system image in Windows. Screen readers are not supported by the boot options menu.

After you restore the image, you can reinsert the hard disk in the original computer, which presumably is being repaired, and the computer should work again normally.

Restoring Windows 8 File by File

In Chapter 6, "Optimizing Backup and Restore," you learned about how Windows Backup compresses files into virtual hard drive files so that the files can't be easily opened and read unless you restore them. This discourages some people from using this feature.

Some people prefer to boot into another operating system such as Linux (see Chapter 29, "Restoring Windows by Using a Portable Operating System"), and then create a file-by-file backup copy of Windows on another hard disk or partition. This approach has many advantages when restoring a malfunctioning operating system. For instance, you can copy back only the driver store folders or the registry files, if only they need updating, and in this way, you restore all of your critical operating system files, leaving settings and programs intact. Or, you could replace only the files for a faulty program. However, this approach is not supported by Microsoft, and you need to be careful if you do this. (For more information about the purpose of particular files in Windows, see Chapter 21.

INSIDE OUT To copy the Windows registry or not to copy?

You can choose to copy every file from your file-by-file Windows 8 backup to its original location. Doing so restores Windows, but software or settings might not work because you will have also copied back old Windows registry files.

You can get around this by leaving the existing registry files on the original hard disk. There is one registry file in each user folder called Ntuser.dat. This is a hidden file, so you might need to set your computer to show hidden files before restoring your backup to the original computer. It is sometimes easier to not copy the C:\Windows\Users folder at all, because the only Windows system files it contains are registry files.

Restoring Your Data by Using Another Computer

Although a copy of Windows 8 from one computer won't work on another, you are able to access your data on an alternative computer.

CAUTION!

When attaching hardware to a computer, always make sure the power is turned off and the computer is disconnected from the electrical outlet. Discharge any electrostatic build up by touching an unpainted section of the computer case, and use an antistatic wristband when installing an extra hard disk into a computer, if possible. (For more information about working with computer hardware, see Chapter 24, "Diagnosing Hardware Problems.")

By plugging the hard disk from your nonworking computer into a host computer, you can have access to your files and folders. The hard disk and any partitions from the defunct computer will appear in Computer on the host device. You will be able to recover lost files, but sometimes you won't be able to write data back to that hard disk. This is because Windows 8 on the original computer has set access permissions for the drive's files and folders, and the new computer doesn't have permission to write to them. This is simple to fix, however. In File Explorer, right-click the relevant drive or folder, and then click Properties to open the Properties dialog box. On the Security tab, choose the appropriate user or users for whom you want to set permissions (see Figure 28-4.)

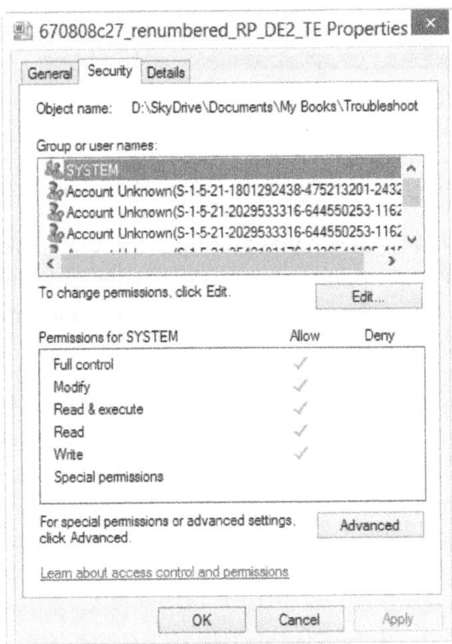

Figure 28-4 Taking ownership of files and folders.

INSIDE OUT Your disk isn't appearing in File Explorer

Sometimes, new hard disks or partitions won't appear immediately in File Explorer on a host computer because they are sharing a drive letter (for example, drive D) with another drive or partition. This is simple to rectify.

Press Windows logo key+X to open the WinX menu, and then click Disk Management to open the Disk Management console (see Figure 28-5).

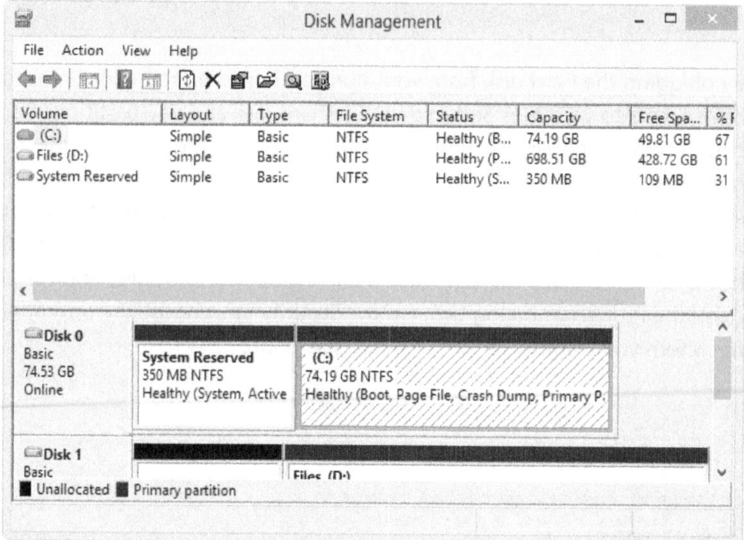

Figure 28-5 Changing and assigning drive letters in the Disk Management console.

Right-click any hard disk or partition that is not appearing in File Explorer, and then select Change Drive Letter And Paths. Designate a new drive letter (only unused drive letters appear in the choice list), or set the hard disk or partition to appear as a folder on another hard disk.

Unless you store your files and data on a separate partition (which I definitely recommend; see Chapter 3, "Setup and Backup Strategies for Avoiding Major System Issues" and Chapter 6), your files and data are stored in the Users folder on the hard disk or partition that contains your Windows 8 installation (see Figure 28-6).

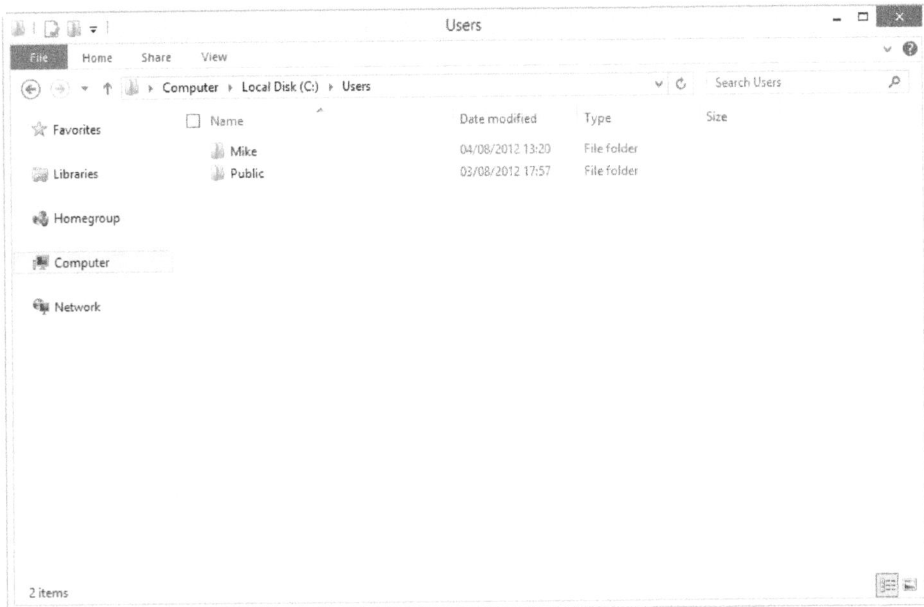

Figure 28-6 The Users folder in Windows 8.

CHAPTER 29

Restoring Windows by Using a Portable Operating System

ONE OF THE BEST WAYS TO RESCUE YOUR DATA or an unresponsive machine might be a GNU/Linux distribution, or version (commonly known as a *distro*). Using Linux in this way has several advantages; most importantly, this approach is nonintrusive, so it won't change or overwrite any files or settings in your Windows installation.

INSIDE OUT **Can You Restore by Using Windows To Go?**

You might be wondering if Windows To Go can be used to restore a nonfunctioning copy of Windows 8. The security in Windows To Go works differently from an open Linux disc in that it won't allow you to see the contents of the hard disks on the host computer. This is a security feature, and a welcome one in my opinion, but it does make Windows To Go unsuitable for this type of restore situation.

Creating a Portable Windows 8 Drive

The introduction of Windows To Go in Windows 8 Enterprise has been widely welcomed by the industry, but users of Windows 8 and Windows 8 Pro still need a feature that will restore a nonfunctioning copy of Windows 8. In many scenarios, having a bootable Windows 8 USB flash drive can be very useful.

Fortunately, you can create such a drive in any version of Windows 8 (and Windows 7, too), which offers an advantage over Windows To Go: because it does not block access to the hard disks on the host computer, you can use it to make file-level repairs to a malfunctioning copy of Windows 8.

To create a portable Windows 8 drive, you need a USB flash drive of at least 16 gigabytes (GB)—32 GB or more is better—plugged into your computer, and a Windows 8 install DVD or ISO disk image file.

Note

Because you are installing a new copy of Windows 8 to the USB flash drive, you will need a spare and valid product key for Windows 8 and any software you install to the drive.

1. Press Windows logo key+X on your keyboard, and then open Command Prompt (Admin).
2. Type **diskpart**, and then press Enter.
3. Type **list disk**, and then press Enter to display a list of available disks in your computer as Disk 0, Disk 1, and so on. Make a note of the disk number for your USB flash drive.
4. Type **select disk 2**, where *2* represents the disk number for your USB flash drive, to indicate to the diskpart tool that the following commands will relate to that disk.
5. Type **clean**, and then press Enter to prepare the drive for formatting.
6. Type **create partition primary**, and then press Enter.
7. Type **format fs=ntfs quick**, and then press Enter to format the drive.
8. Type **active**, and then press Enter.
9. Type **assign letter=e** to give the newly formatted flash drive a letter, where *e* indicates any available drive letter.
10. Type **Exit** to exit the diskpart tool.
11. Either place the Windows 8 installation DVD in your optical drive, or mount your Windows 8 Image ISO file by right-clicking it and then selecting *mount* from the options that appear. Make a note of its drive letter.

12. At the command prompt, type **dism /apply-image /imagefile=f:\sources\install.wim /index:1 /applydir:e:**, where *e:* is your USB flash drive, and *f:* is your Windows 8 DVD or mounted ISO file. The Windows Installer image from your DVD or ISO file will now be copied to your USB flash drive. This process normally takes around 8 GB of space on the drive. Note that this copying process can take some time.

13. Type **bcdboot.exe e:\windows /s e: /f ALL** to set the USB flash drive as bootable.

Now you can start your computer from the USB flash drive, usually by pressing F12 (or sometimes Esc) when the computer starts. The initial startup process takes some time, because Windows installs its hardware drivers, so it's a good idea to run this first startup process on the computer that you intend to use the USB flash drive with, perhaps a work PC or your own PC in your home or home office for repair purposes. I suggest this strategy because, as this is not a dedicated Windows To Go drive, the drive may boot perfectly on some computers and be unresponsive on others.

Note

I tried a Windows 8 USB flash drive with four computers, a Unified Extensible Firmware Interface (UEFI) laptop on which it first installed its drivers, a UEFI desktop where the system became unresponsive and did not start, and two basic input/out system (BIOS) laptops on which the system started fine and identified itself as Windows To Go, circumventing any problems that can occur with Windows 8 thinking its license has been moved to a different computer and requiring reactivation or a new product key.

CAUTION!

Microsoft does not support this method of creating a portable Windows 8 drive. Because the portable drive might behave unpredictably (or be unresponsive) on the computers you want to use it with, use only a Windows 8 product key that is available and currently unused by another computer, and that can be locked to the first computer you will use the drive on, just in case the installation does not recognize itself as Windows To Go on other computers.

Restoring Your System or Data by Using Linux

Many Linux distributions can run from a CD or DVD. Figure 29-1 shows the popular Ubuntu Linux, started from the installation DVD.

Figure 29-1 The Ubuntu desktop.

When you start a copy of Linux that can run from a DVD, you are asked whether you want to install the operating system on the hard disk or run it from the DVD to test it. You should choose the second option if your intention is to use Linux to rescue a problematic copy of Windows or your files.

> **Note**
>
> **Because you likely cannot anticipate when you will need to restore your system, I recommend downloading a Linux disc ISO image file and burning it to a CD or DVD to keep on standby. You can find download links at the end of this chapter.**
>
> **Be aware that Linux distributions vary, and the locations of the specific items I cover in this chapter might differ depending on the Linux version you are using. Also, some of the tools mentioned in this chapter might not be available in your particular copy of Linux.**

One of the big advantages of Linux is that it's free to individual users; the distributors make money by charging for optional support contracts. One disadvantage is that many people do not find Linux as user-friendly as Windows, although variants such as Ubuntu have made great strides toward better usability.

Another disadvantage is that the software you usually use in Windows isn't available in Linux. However, most Linux distributions come bundled with some software already installed, including a web browser, a graphics package, and an office productivity package such as Open Office, which is an open source product licensed by GNU. This software will normally open your files, even the newer Microsoft Office file formats, so you can keep working until your own computer or copy of Windows can be repaired.

INSIDE OUT Linux on a USB flash drive

Some Linux versions include a tool that you can use to start the operating system from a USB flash drive. The name and function of this tool can vary from distro to distro, however, so you might find it worthwhile to check online to determine whether it is available and how it works. As long as your computer's BIOS permits booting from a USB device, this tool can be a useful addition to your Windows troubleshooting toolset.

You can access the Ubuntu computer browser at the top of the desktop, on the Places menu (see Figure 29-2).

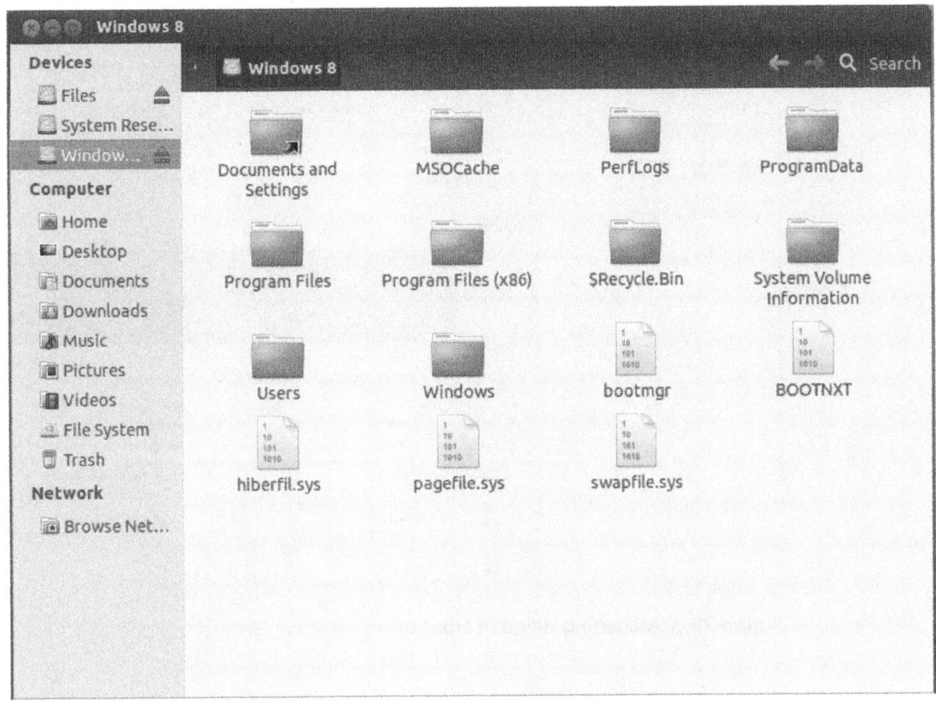

Figure 29-2 You can see every file on your Windows drive in Ubuntu, including hidden files.

You can see all your unencrypted hard disks and files from within Linux, so you can access your files through Linux and back them up to a DVD or to another location, such as a network hard disk or external USB hard disk. You can also use a Linux installation to restore Windows 8 on a file-by-file basis.

> **Note**
>
> **If any of your disks or partitions are encrypted by Windows Encrypted File System (EFS) or Microsoft BitLocker, they will not be readable from within Linux.**

Some Linux distributions can include advanced disk management and diagnostic tools. For example, in Ubuntu, you can edit and work with drives, sometimes on a far more advanced level than Windows 8 allows. You can access the disk management console by opening the System menu at the top of the Ubuntu desktop and then clicking Administration\Disk Utility (see Figure 29-3). (The names of these commands and utilities will vary from one Linux distribution to another.)

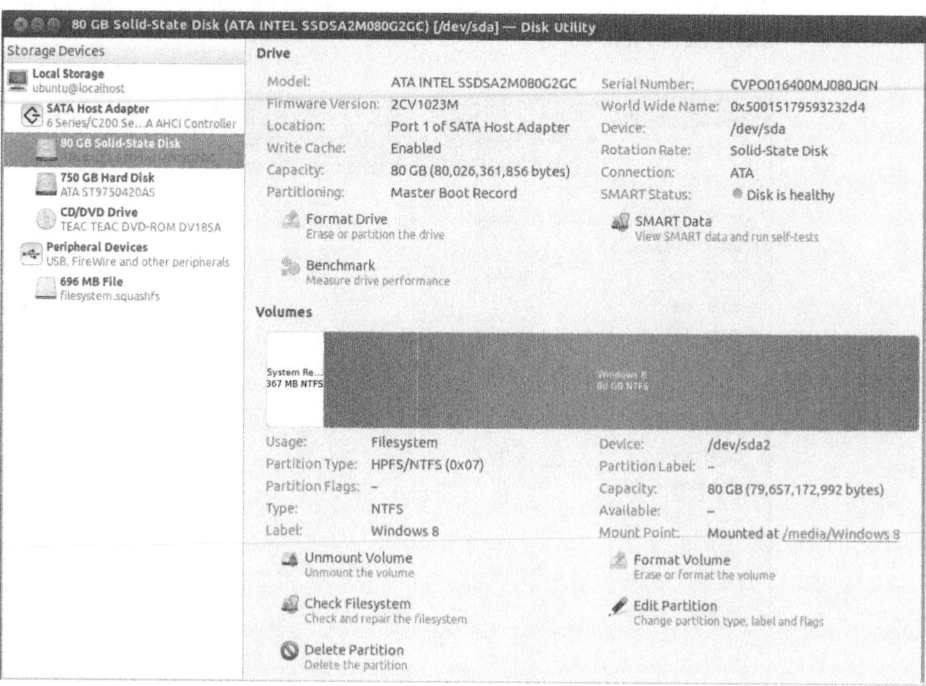

Figure 29-3 Managing drives in Ubuntu.

You can commonly find some useful tools in the Storage Devices pane, including some that Windows doesn't support (but note that the availability of these tools will vary from one Linux distro to another). For example, you can use these tools to check the self-monitoring, analysis, and reporting technology (SMART) data for a hard disk, which can determine whether the drive is faulty; and you can make low-level changes to the partitions and file system—unless the drive is still in warranty and you can get it replaced instead!

> **Note**
>
> **Because many hardware manufacturers do not support Linux, you might be unable to print any documents you need, such as copies of software, or Windows product codes if printer drivers for Linux aren't available.**

To access the Ubuntu partitioning utility (see Figure 29-4), at the top of the desktop, click the System menu, click Administration, and then click GParted. (Again, these menu items vary depending on what Linux distribution you use.)

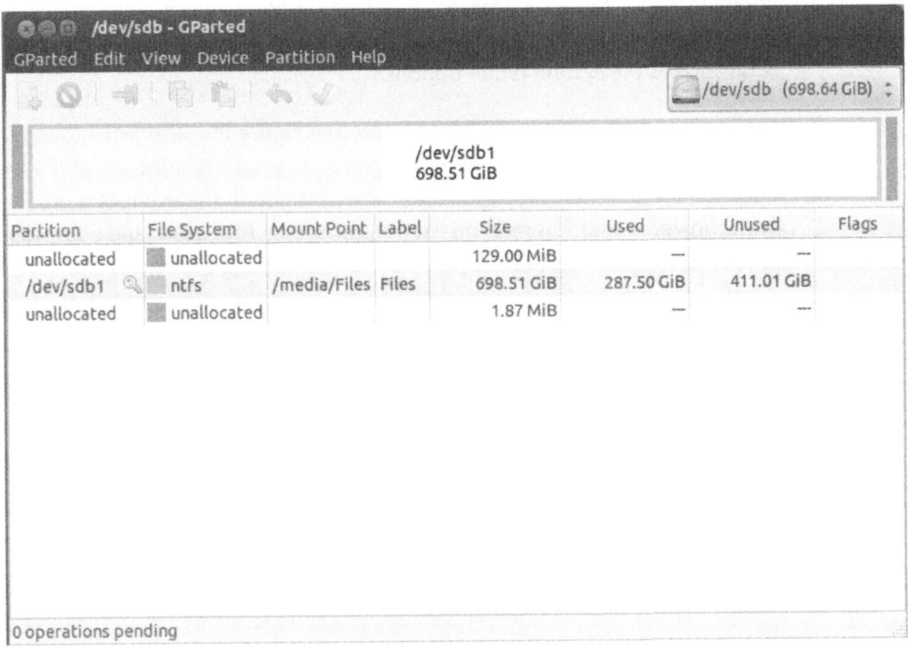

Figure 29-4 Managing partitions in Ubuntu.

Many Linux distributions contain a disk partitioning tool. Sometimes, Windows 8 is unresponsive because the partition on which it resides has become corrupt. You might be able to repair the partition by using a Linux disk partitioning tool, or if you have a system image in Windows, you can use Linux to delete the corrupt partition and create a new one in its place. You can then restore Windows 8 by starting from the Windows 8 installation DVD and restoring from an image backup by using System Image Restore.

CAUTION!

When you start your computer from a Linux CD or DVD, you have full administrator access to Windows and data drives in your computer. Always be careful not to delete critical system files or data that is not backed up or that cannot be replaced.

Restoring the System Reserved Partition by Using Linux

One task you can perform with Linux that you cannot perform with Windows is viewing the contents of the Windows 8 System Reserved partition. This is a hidden partition, which the Windows 8 Installer creates just before installation. It stores the system boot files and other tools such as the system repair options.

You can view this entire partition in Linux (see Figure 29-5), which allows you to perform special operations on it. For example, you can make a backup copy of the healthy copy. You can then use this intact copy to restore the partition in the event of a problem or an error. Note, however, that this method isn't supported by Microsoft, and you should be careful when restoring the partition in this manner.

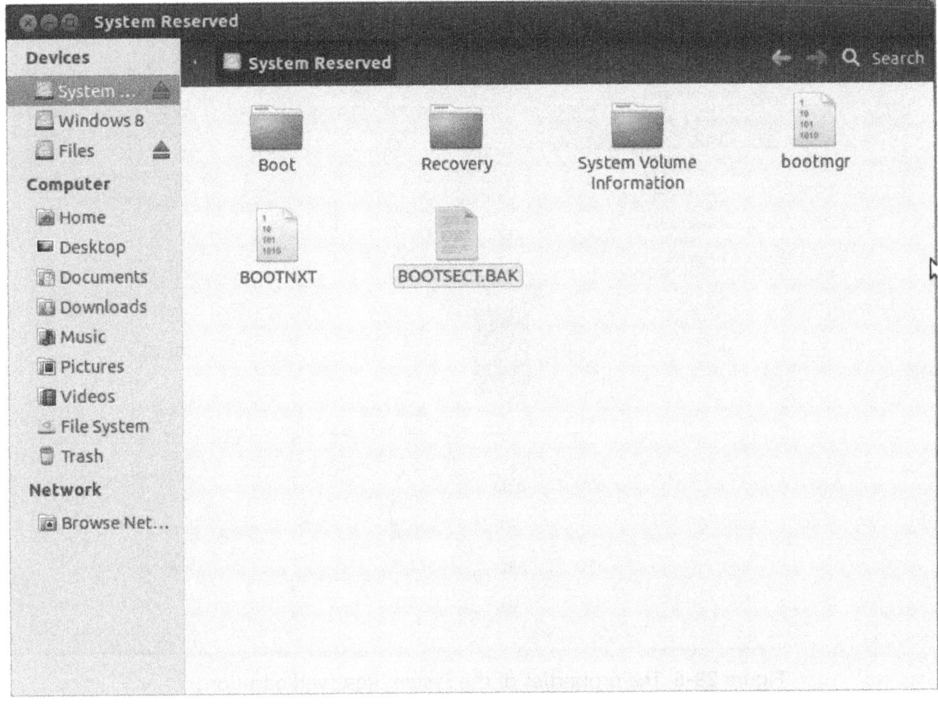

Figure 29-5 Working with the System Reserved partition.

If you need to delete and rebuild the System Reserved partition, ensure that it is created with the correct attributes, which include the following (see Figure 29-6):

- Partition Type: HPFS/NTFS (0x07)
- Partition Flags: Bootable
- Type: NTFS

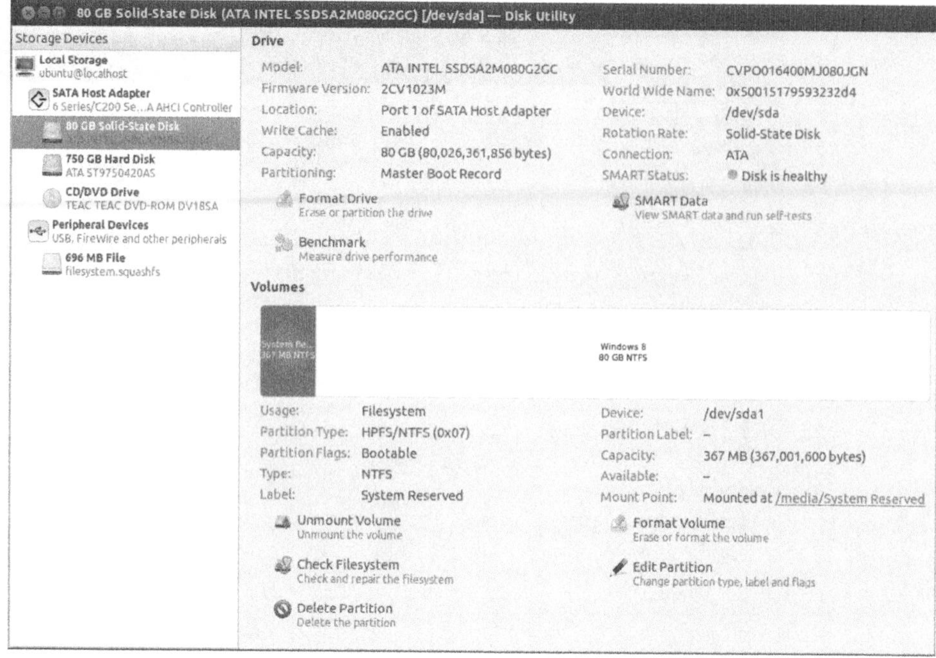

Figure 29-6 The properties of the System Reserved partition.

INSIDE OUT

Backing up the System Reserved partition

You might think that only someone in an advanced state of paranoia would back up the Windows 8 System Reserved partition. But backing up this partition is wise, because if this partition fails, it's possible that only a clean reinstallation of Windows 8 will fix the problem. Starting from a Linux DVD and re-creating the partition from a backup is much quicker than reinstalling Windows from scratch.

Using Helpful Software in Linux

The software packages covered in this section are very useful in the operating system if you have access to them. They vary in name, location, and availability depending on the distro of Linux you are using (Ubuntu, Debian, SuSe, Knoppix, and so on).

Remote Desktop

Some Linux packages include remote access software similar to Remote Desktop in Windows (see Figure 29-7). You can use the Linux version of the remote desktop software to allow a remote support person to access your computer to help diagnose and repair problems with Windows 8. The remote support person might need to be running the same version of Linux that you are, but other operating systems and some third-party remote desktop packages are compatible.

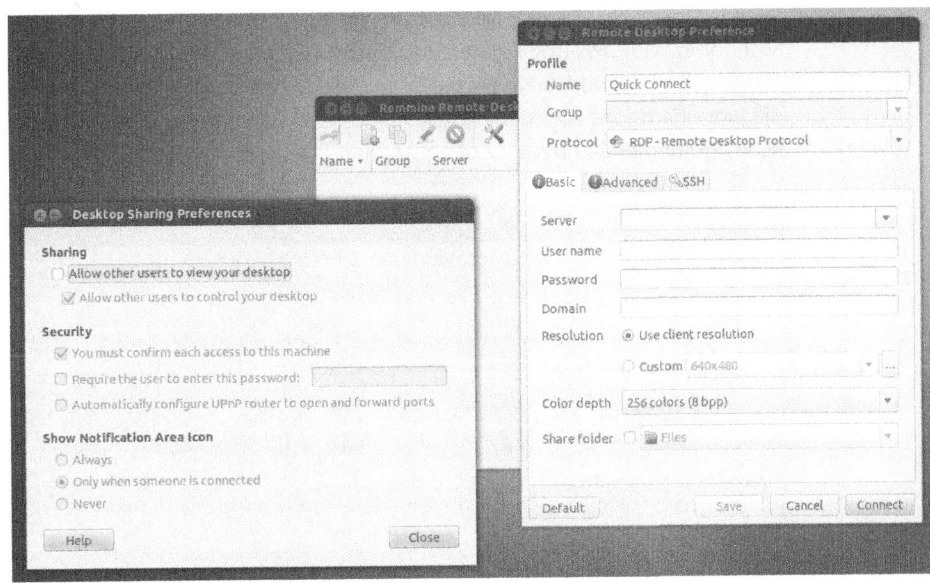

Figure 29-7 The Remote Desktop feature in Ubuntu.

INSIDE OUT Connecting to the Internet with Linux

Hardware driver support for Linux is not as widespread as it is with Windows. You might be unable to get online if you use Wi-Fi on your computer, especially if you connect through a USB dongle. If you intend to use a USB dongle with Linux, using a working computer with Internet access, first visit the manufacturer's website for the USB dongle to see whether it supplies a Linux driver that you can install from a CD or USB flash drive. The best way to get online when using a Linux disc is via a physical network cable.

System Monitor

System Monitor in Ubuntu, as in many Linux distributions, is very similar to the System Monitor in Windows (see Figure 29-8). System Monitor provides real-time details of CPU, memory, and network activity on a computer. This information can be useful for helping to diagnose hardware errors; for instance, it can help determine whether you are having difficulty getting online because of networking problems.

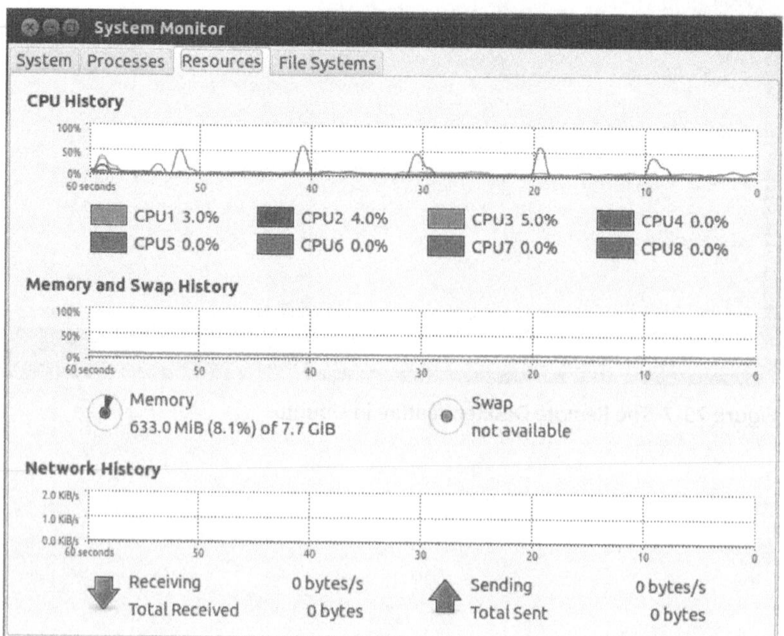

Figure 29-8 The System Monitor in Ubuntu.

System Testing

Some Linux distributions come with advanced system testers (see Figure 29-9), which test many aspects of computer hardware to find and diagnose problems. The system tester in Ubuntu is an excellent example. It tests every aspect of the hardware and guides you through automated diagnostics by using a helpful wizard.

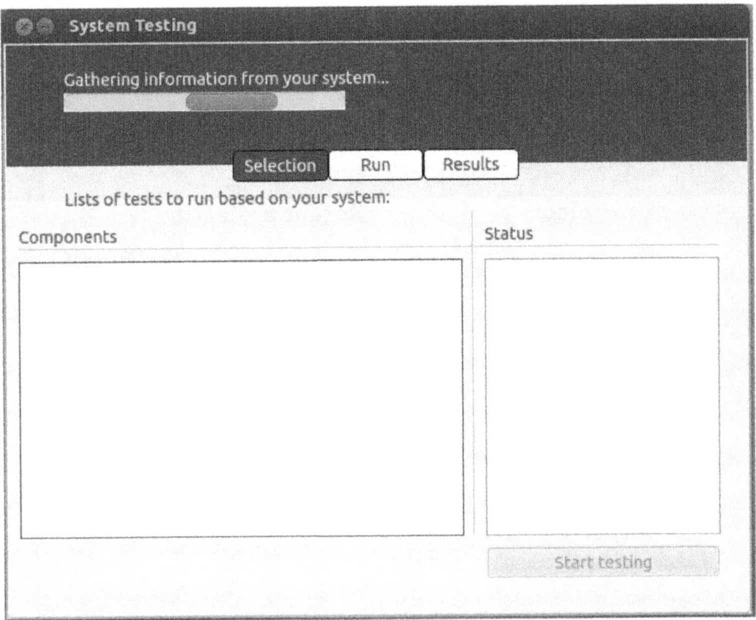

Figure 29-9 The system tester in Ubuntu.

Burning CDs and DVDs in Linux

All Linux distributions come with standard CD and DVD burning software. If you've lost your Windows 8 installation DVD but still have an image of the disc (or of your System Repair Disc), you can use Linux burning software to make another copy of it (see Figure 29-10).

INSIDE OUT Keep an ISO copy of your Windows installation DVD

It is an excellent idea to keep a backup ISO image file (disk image) of your Windows installation DVD in case you damage or lose your original DVD. A quick online search will yield many software packages (some free) that you can use to create a backup ISO.

You can also burn new Windows installation discs from ISO image files in Windows 8 by double-clicking the ISO file to open the ISO Image Burner.

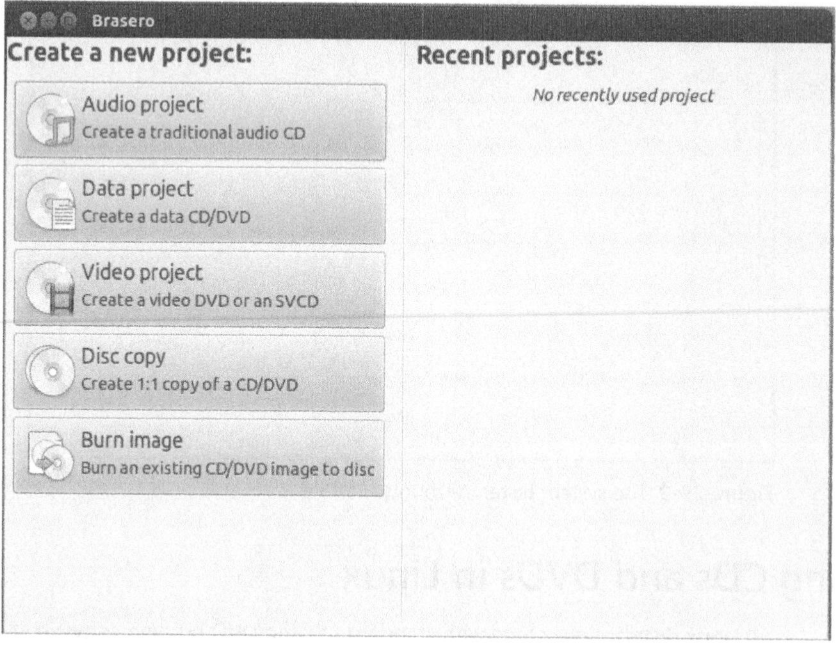

Figure 29-10 Burning a CD or DVD in Linux is pretty easy.

Finding Compatible Linux Operating Systems to Run from a Disc

You can find a list of the best and most popular Linux distributions at *http://www.linux.org*. Ubuntu (*http://www.ubuntu.com*) is the Linux variant that I have used to discuss Linux throughout this chapter (see Figures 29-1 and 29-10). I used Ubuntu because it's widely considered to be one of the most user-friendly Linux variants and is shipped with some new computers by companies such as Dell. Other variants of Linux include the following:

- **Debian** *http://www.debian.org*
- **SuSe** *http://en.opensuse.org*
- **Fedora** *http://www.fedoraproject.org*
- **Knoppix** *http://www.knoppix.net*

Creating a Linux Installation Disc or USB Flash Drive

All downloadable Linux variants are available as ISO image files. Windows 8 now supports these natively, which means that you can burn them to a CD or DVD. To burn an ISO image file to a CD or DVD in Windows, right-click the file, click Burn Disk Image, select the appropriate disc burner, and then click Burn. Note that not all computers come with disc burners these days, such as Ultrabooks and tablets, so you might need to obtain a USB-attached disc burner. If your computer does not have a disc burner, you are notified (see Figure 29-11).

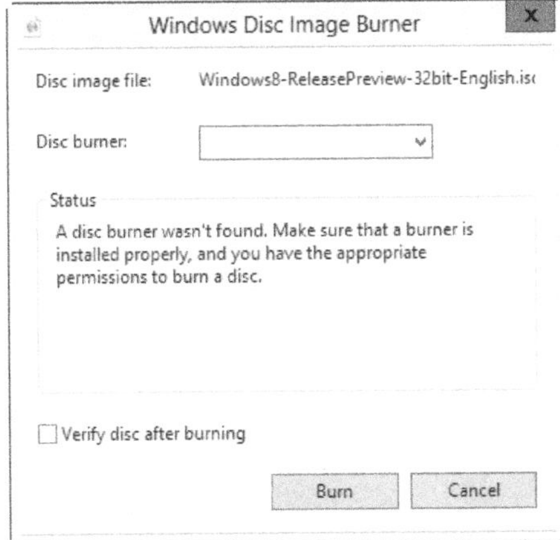

Figure 29-11 Burning a disc image file to CD or DVD in Windows 8.

You should check online for the latest utility to write a bootable ISO image file to a USB flash drive. Note that if you want to start your copy of Linux from a USB flash drive, you should check that the computer's BIOS or UEFI firmware supports starting from a USB device and that this is set in the boot order (see Figure 29-12).

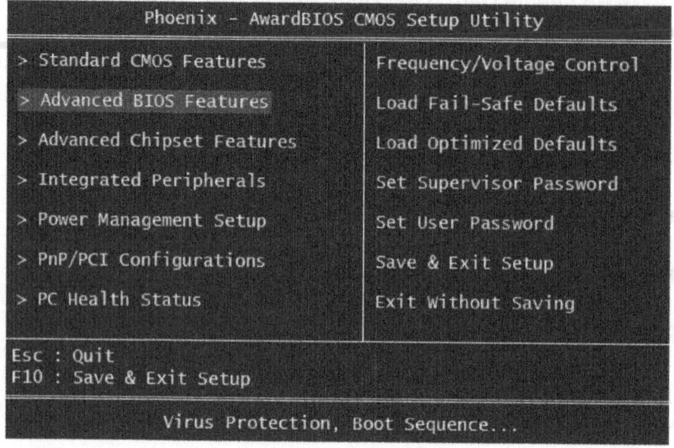

Figure 29-12 Setting the boot options in the BIOS.

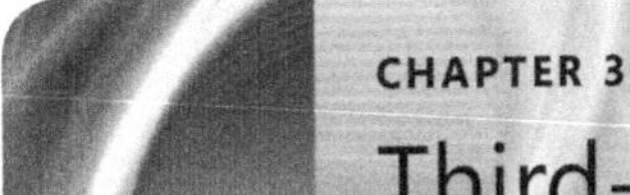

CHAPTER 30

Third-Party Rescue Tools and Services

MANY THIRD-PARTY RESCUE AND RECOVERY TOOLS are available for Windows 8. These tools vary considerably in price, from free to hundreds of dollars. They can also vary considerably in quality and functionality, so it can be challenging to choose the best recovery and rescue option for you. In this chapter, I highlight some of my favorite software and software packages.

The SysInternals Suite

The SysInternals (*http://technet.microsoft.com/en-US/sysinternals*) suite of programs is so good that Microsoft bought it from the originating company and adopted it as an official tool. There are dozens of high-quality tools in the suite, but some are so good that I'm highlighting them in the following list:

- **AccessEnum** Use this tool to find out what access users on a computer have to directories, files, and registry keys. This tool is very useful if you're troubleshooting file access.
- **Autoruns** With Autoruns, you can see what programs are set to run on your computer automatically when the computer starts. Autoruns provides detailed information about the programs, including registry key locations and file locations.
- **BgInfo** You can automatically add information to your Windows desktop app, such as your computer's IP address, name, and details about network adapters.
- **Desktops** This utility provides virtual desktops in Windows like the ones provided in GNU/Linux operating systems, wherein you can switch between different desktops, each displaying their own programs.
- **Disk2vhd** This tool can assist you in turning physical disks in virtual machines.
- **DiskMon** A disk activity monitor that captures and reports on all disk activity, this tool is useful when you suspect there is a problem with a hard disk or solid-state drive.

- **EFSDump** This tool can display information about Encrypting File System (EFS) files on a computer.
- **ListDLLs** This tool displays information about every dynamic-link library (DLL) file running on your computer, including their version numbers.
- **LoadOrder** Use this tool to see in which order Windows loads device drivers.
- **MoveFile** This is a tool you can use to schedule file move and delete commands until the next time the computer restarts, which can help remove malware.
- **Process Explorer** Use this tool to see which files, registry keys, and programs have processes open, what DLLs they are using, and more.
- **Process Monitor** With this tool, you can keep an eye on file system, registry, process, and other activity on your computer in real time. This can help you find the cause of a complex problem.
- **RAMMap** This is a memory usage analysis tool that can display data in several different ways for diagnosis and reporting.
- **RootkitRevealer** You can use this to scan your computer for rootkit viruses.
- **SDelete** Securely delete files and folders, and clean free space on your hard disk by using this tool.

GRC SpinRite Features

For some years, GRC SpinRite (*http://www.grc.com*) has been widely considered one of the best hard disk rescue and maintenance tools available, and is held in high regard within the technical community. It is invaluable for diagnosing and repairing errors on physical hard disks. SpinRite is a DOS program that runs from a bootable CD, DVD, or other device such as a floppy disk or USB flash drive. Because you start your computer into SpinRite, the software has full low-level administrator access to the hard disks on your computer.

In addition to providing an extensive range of drive formatting options, SpinRite can perform a broad range of checks on your hard disks and includes the following features:

- **Real-time graphical status display** This display shows the health and status of your hard disk (see Figure 30-1). This graph displays data and disk recovery and repair as it happens. All events are also logged so that you can review them later.

Drive: C, Level: 4
Graphic Status Display
work — remaining — done
sector: 37,924 2,160
%: 96.3% 3.7%
tests:
cluster status key
•oO analyze / move
· perfect & empty
perfect w/data
R recovered data
B defective region
U unrecovered data

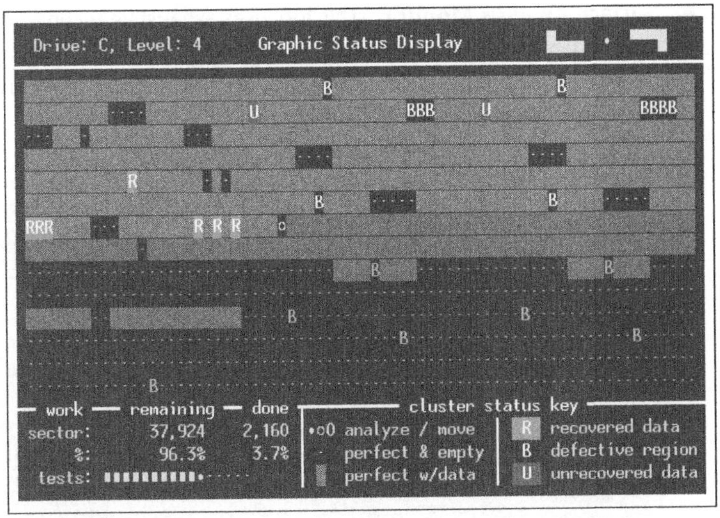

Figure 30-1 A graphical log of the state of a hard disk in SpinRite.

- **Detailed technical logs of the hard disk** The error information provided by these logs includes clear descriptions that can help you determine exactly where errors are located and what they are (see Figure 30-2). GRC boasts about the clarity of the language used when providing reports on your hard disks, and I can confirm that the quality of the information its SpinRite tool delivers is excellent.

Drive: C, Level: 4
Detailed Technical Log
Event | Cyl/Hd/Sec | Dos Sector | Cluster
This root directory sector was completely unreadable, however DynaStat recovery has minimized the loss of data. Most of the sector is now readable. | 24/ 6/28 | 2,543 | 643
Sector tests perfect, returned to full use | 64/15/ 2 | 4,432 | 1,554
There is nothing wrong with this sector which was previously marked bad. It is being returned to the full use of the system. | 75/ 8/ 3 | 6,321 | 2,323
Data in this sector could not be recovered Sector belongs to file C:\dos\fdisk.exe. Data error begins at byte 25,432 in the file and extends for 37 bits. | 223/ 4/12 | 124,564 | 31,324
An unused sector is being marked defective | 514/ 1/ 3 | 257,411 | 62,315
Cursor pad functions may be used to review this log

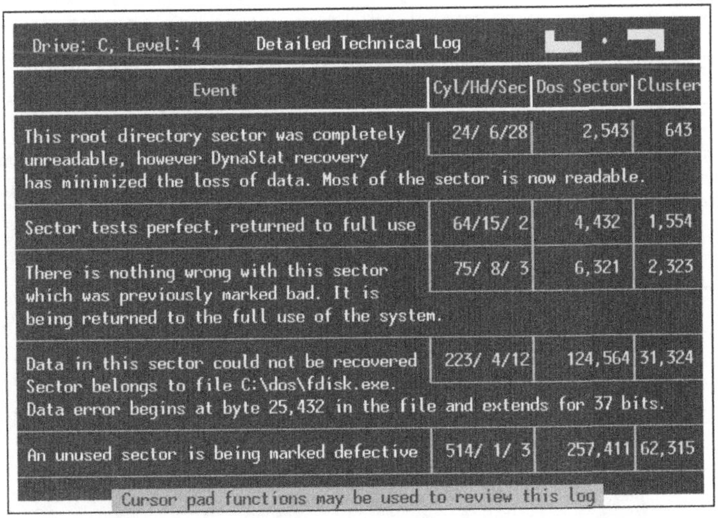

Figure 30-2 The SpinRite tool.

- **Surface Analysis Monitor** This tool uses exhaustive techniques to detect defects on the hard disk (see Figure 30-3). It deliberately creates scenarios on your hard disk to try to replicate the worst types of failure that can occur. This is an extremely thorough way to check for defects.

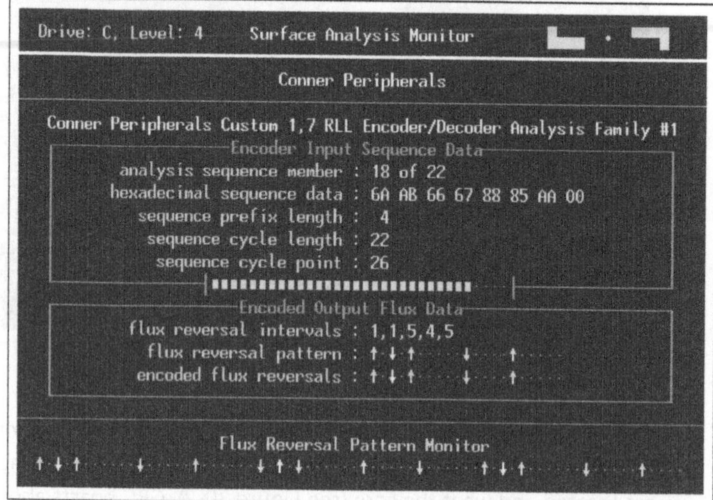

Figure 30-3 The scanning of a hard disk by using SpinRite can take some considerable time, maybe even a few days for a huge drive with a lot of data.

- **Extensive data recovery tools** These data recovery tools work tirelessly to recover your data. A special tool called Dynastat appears if SpinRite has trouble reading data on a faulty hard disk. Dynastat provides more detailed information in real time about the software's attempts to recover your files and data (see Figure 30-4).

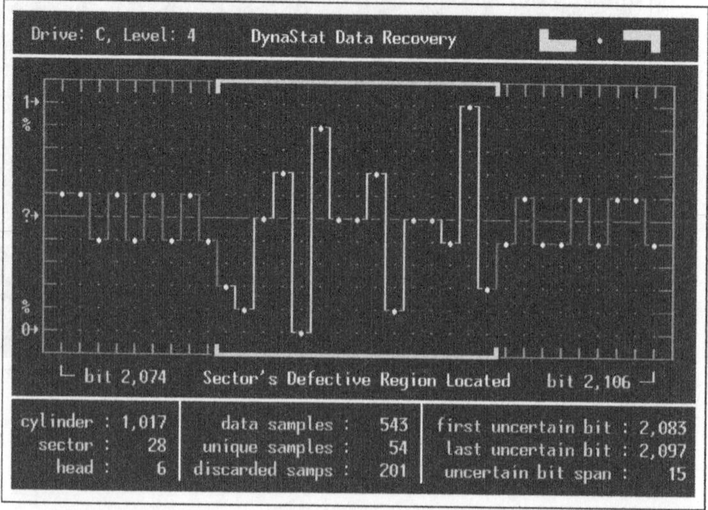

Figure 30-4 SpinRite gives up trying to recover your data only when you do.

- **Detailed information about the existing partition structure on hard disks** In addition to providing information about partition structure, SpinRite checks partitions for errors (see Figure 30-5).

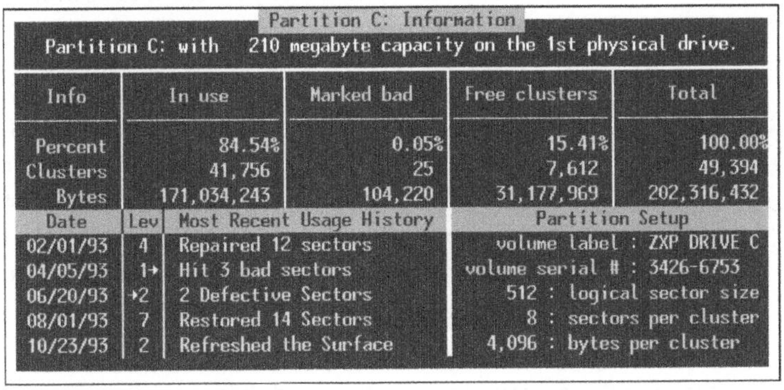

Partition C: Information

Partition C: with 210 megabyte capacity on the 1st physical drive.

Info	In use	Marked bad	Free clusters	Total
Percent	84.54%	0.05%	15.41%	100.00%
Clusters	41,756	25	7,612	49,394
Bytes	171,034,243	104,220	31,177,969	202,316,432

Date	Lev	Most Recent Usage History	Partition Setup
02/01/93	4	Repaired 12 sectors	volume label : ZXP DRIVE C
04/05/93	1→	Hit 3 bad sectors	volume serial # : 3426-6753
06/20/93	→2	2 Defective Sectors	512 : logical sector size
08/01/93	7	Restored 14 Sectors	8 : sectors per cluster
10/23/93	2	Refreshed the Surface	4,096 : bytes per cluster

Figure 30-5 SpinRite checks existing partitions on a disk for errors.

INSIDE OUT **SpinRite and solid-state drives**

Solid-state disk drives operate differently from mechanical hard disks in that there are no moving parts; solid-state disk drives store all of your data on silicon chips, not on a spinning disk. Therefore, SpinRite is not the best tool for diagnosing errors on solid-state disk drives.

Additional Third-Party Rescue Tools

Many companies provide specialist software for rescuing data or hard disks, and you should try the forums mentioned in Chapter 23, "Finding Help on the Internet," for recommendations. Here are details about software packages that I recommend:

- **Ashampoo WinOptimizer (*http://www.ashampoo.com*)** Although Ashampoo WinOptimizer traditionally has not been used as a tool for rescuing a hard disk or data, it now incorporates a small tool that can help you to do just that. This tool analyzes your hard disks, looking for defective areas or problems. It provides tools that can then be used to apply automatic repairs and fix some of the more common problems that you might encounter.

- **CCleaner (*http://www.piriform.com/ccleaner*)** What would a list of recommended third-party tools be without CCleaner? This is the disk cleanup tool for professional computer users. In all my experience, I've never seen another disk and registry cleanup program as highly regarded as this one.

- **Disk Digger (*www.hiren.info/downloads/freeware-tools/diskdigger*)** Disk Digger is a useful file and data recovery tool that can scan any kind of storage media, from hard disks to USB flash drives and digital memory cards, to recover lost and deleted files. Hiren and Pankaj have many excellent tools available on their home page, including the BootCD.
- **O&O Disk Recovery (*http://www.oo-software.com*)** O&O Disk Recovery is a comprehensive package that performs several useful functions. The most commonly used of these is an unerase program to help recover files and folders that have been accidentally deleted. There are also other functions within the software that can provide recovery in scenarios such as the accidental formatting of a hard disk. These functions are useful because accidentally formatting of Windows 8 disks does happen.

  You can also use this software to rescue data or a faulty hard disk in your computer. You can even remove a hard disk from your computer, plug it into another computer, and then run these rescue tools on that hard disk.
- **Toolwiz Care (*http://www.toolwiz.com*)** This is an all-in-one computer optimizer that is, according to its makers, the "ultimate speedup solution." This is a highly regarded and recommended free download to help optimize your computer quickly and simply with just a single click.
- **Ultimate Boot CD (*http://www.ultimatebootcd.com*)** This is an excellent tool that combines many diagnostic, repair, and data recovery tools into a single bootable disc image. A large number of tools come in this disc image and include some of the best and most useful utilities available.
- **WhoCrashed (*http://www.resplendence.com/whocrashed)*** When you get a blue screen indicating an unresponsive system, you will want to know what crashed and why, and sometimes the standard event logging and code displayed on the blue screen don't help you figure it out. This is where WhoCrashed comes in handy. This program examines the crash logs for your computer in detail and can pull out much more meaningful information about the problem than you can find yourself.

> **Note**
>
> **At some point, you might reach the stage where there's nothing more you can do with your hard disk. If it includes critical data that you must recover, you will need to go to a professional data-recovery specialist. These companies offer extremely comprehensive services, and they can be hugely successful at recovering data from damaged hard disks, but they are not inexpensive. You can find data recovery specialists in your area by searching in your local telephone directory online or through a search engine.**

CHAPTER 31

Working Safely with Windows 8 Encryption

SOMETIMES, YOU MIGHT ENCOUNTER A SITUATION in which the files and data you are trying to recover are encrypted. Windows provides some tools to aid in unlocking data, but you will need access to the recovery keys specific to the locked data. Windows 8 offers several methods for encrypting files, data, and entire hard disks, and you examine these methods in this chapter: Encrypting File System (EFS), Microsoft BitLocker, BitLocker To Go, and creating a copy of the encrypted data.

Using the Encrypted File System

EFS, which has been around for more than a decade, is used to provide file and folder encryption for individual users. Suppose two people share a computer and store their files on a hard disk or partition that is different from the location of their Windows installation, however, they want to keep their files private from each other. Encryption can be the best way to achieve this.

EFS employs a public/private key encryption method similar to that used by the popular Pretty Good Privacy (PGP) encryption software. It also uses methods used by digital certificates to send and receive personal information over the Internet. This public/private key encryption technique uses two keys: a copy of the encryption key stored on the computer, and another to which the user has access. You need to carefully configure EFS to avoid losing access to your files.

INSIDE OUT **EFS and removable drives**

EFS encryption works only on drives formatted with New Technology File System (NTFS) file system. This means that if you copy any encrypted files to a non–NTFS-formatted device, such as a FAT32–formatted external hard disk or an exFat-formatted USB flash drive, the encryption on those files will be removed when the files are copied.

Setting Up EFS

To configure EFS, perform the following steps:

1. Right-click the files or folders you want to encrypt, and then click Properties.
2. On the General tab, click Advanced.
3. In the Advanced Attributes dialog box, select the Encrypt Contents To Secure Data check box, and then click OK.

   When prompted, ensure that you apply the action to the folder and all files and subfolders (see Figure 31-1).

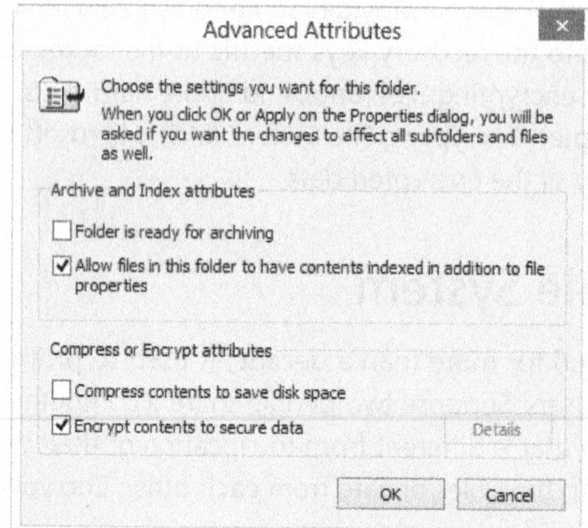

Figure 31-1 Encrypting files and folders by using EFS is handled on a folder level.

The files and folders will be automatically encrypted. When this process is complete, a message in the notification area prompts you to back up your file encryption key (see Figure 31-2).

CAUTION!

If you do not back up your file encryption key to a safe location such as an external hard disk or the cloud, you might never be able to access your files again if you need to reinstall Windows 8.

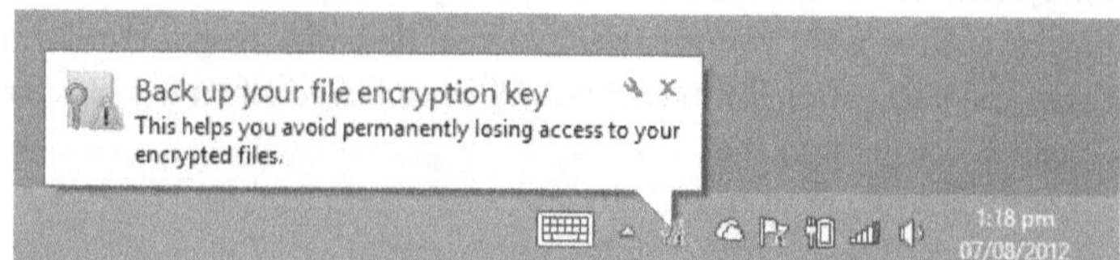

Figure 31-2 Windows alerts you to back up your encryption key.

You can choose to back up your key immediately, or Windows can remind you to do so the next time you log on. I recommend you make a backup immediately.

4. Click Back Up Now (Recommended) (see Figure 31-3).

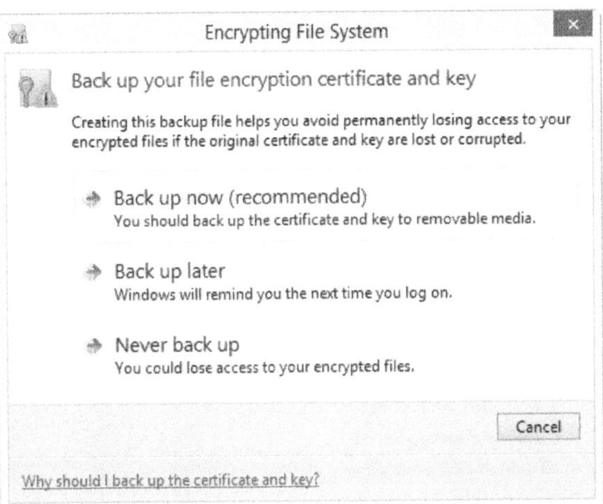

Figure 31-3 You should back up an EFS key immediately.

5. On the Welcome To The Certificate Export Wizard page, click Next (see Figure 31-4).

Figure 31-4 The Certificate Export Wizard.

6. On the Export File Format page (see Figure 31-5), select the preferred file format for your backup file, and then click Next.

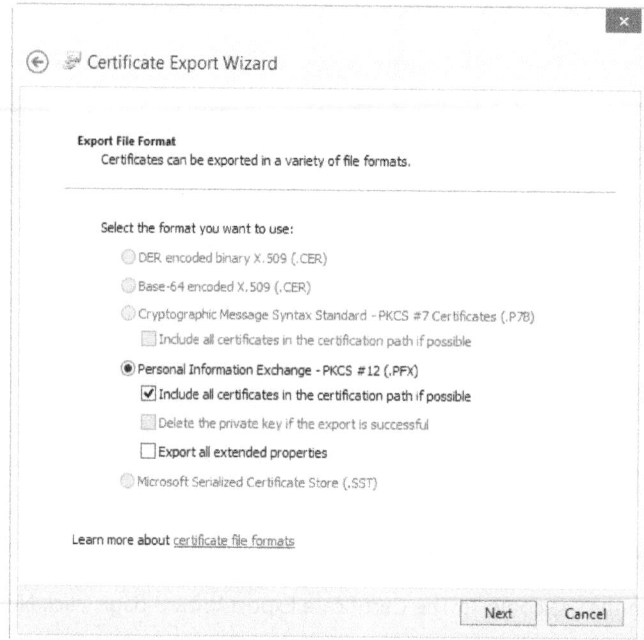

Figure 31-5 Choose what to back up by using EFS.

The standard options will almost always serve your needs, but Windows 8 does offer additional options for the backup copy of your file encryption key. Some of these options might be unavailable because they won't apply to your current export, but you can choose what aspects of your security key you want to back up.

7. On the Security page of the wizard, set a password for your backup (see Figure 31-6), and then click Next.

   You won't need to enter this password to read encrypted files, but you will need it if you must restore the file encryption key. You should not lose a record of or forget this password.

8. Enter a file name and specify where to store your backed-up file encryption key (see Figure 31-7). Ensure that the backup is kept in a safe location and that you have more than one copy.

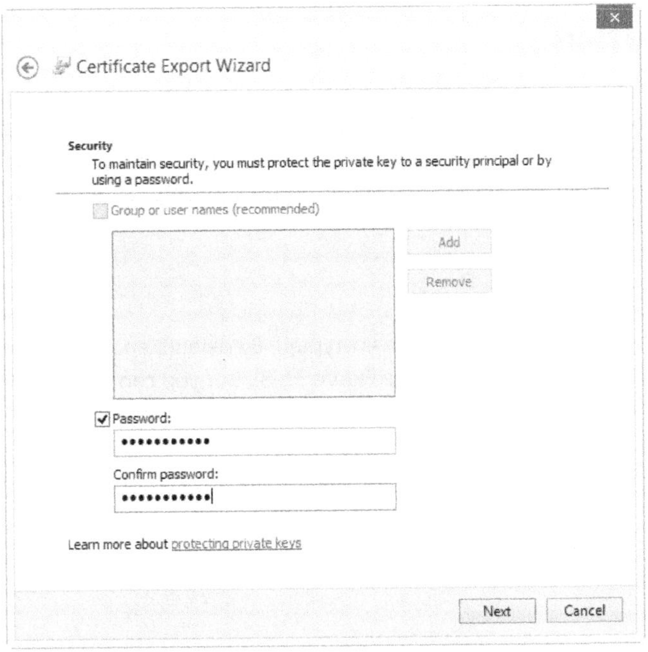

Certificate Export Wizard
Security
To maintain security, you must protect the private key to a security principal or by using a password.
Group or user names (recommended)
Add
Remove
Password:
Confirm password:
Learn more about protecting private keys
Next
Cancel

Figure 31-6 Protect your EFS key with a password.

Certificate Export Wizard
File to Export
Specify the name of the file you want to export
File name:
Browse...
Next
Cancel

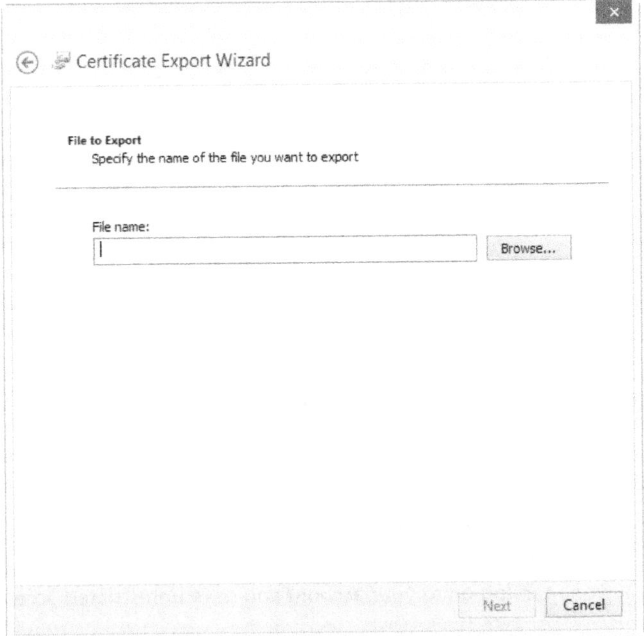

Figure 31-7 Store your backed-up EFS key in a safe place.

CAUTION!

Once, many years ago, while performing the last step of the preceding procedure, I mistakenly backed up my file encryption key to a folder that was encrypted by using EFS. Windows won't prevent you from doing this, so be careful. Any key backed up to an encrypted drive will not be accessible if your computer encounters a problem or you have to reinstall Windows.

Your files and folders will now be encrypted. By default, encrypted files are displayed in a green color in File Explorer (see Figure 31-8), but you can turn the color change off in Control Panel\Folder Options by clicking the View tab and clearing the Show Encrypted Or Compressed NTFS Files In Color option.

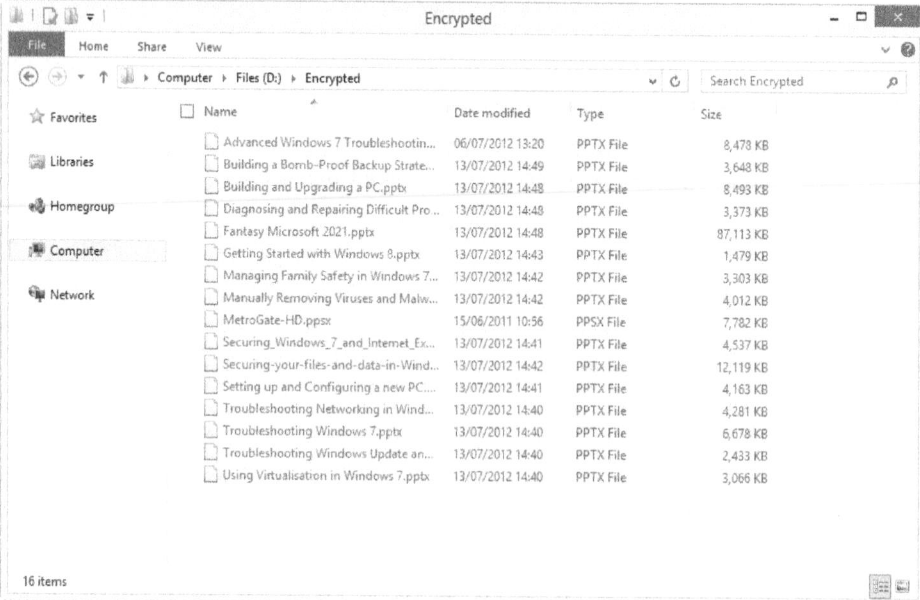

Figure 31-8 Encrypted files appear in a different color in File Explorer.

NOTE

EFS does not require that a user password be set up on your Windows account. However, it does not provide protection if your user account is not password-protected. Thus, anyone can log on to your account and have unrestricted access to the files.

Restoring an EFS Key

If you have to reinstall Windows 8, perhaps because of a critical error, your EFS-encrypted files are unreadable until you restore your EFS encryption key. To restore your EFS encryption key, perform the following steps:

1. Double-click the backup EFS encryption key to open the Certificate Import Wizard, which asks you if you want to import this key for the current user or for the entire computer, and then click Next (see Figure 31-9).

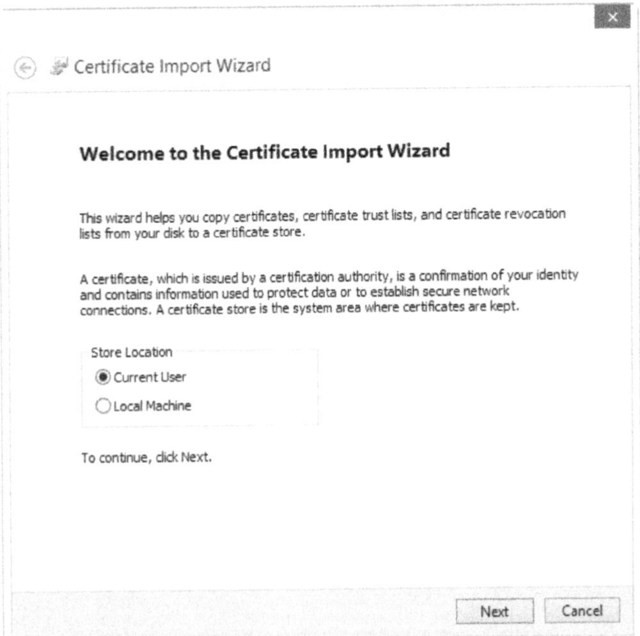

Figure 31-9 The Certificate Import Wizard.

2. Confirm the location of the EFS encryption key, click Next, enter the password you set when you created the EFS encryption key, and then click Next again (see Figure 31-10).

3. Restore the certificate to the default store in Windows 8 (see Figure 31-11) or to a different location if your network requires this.

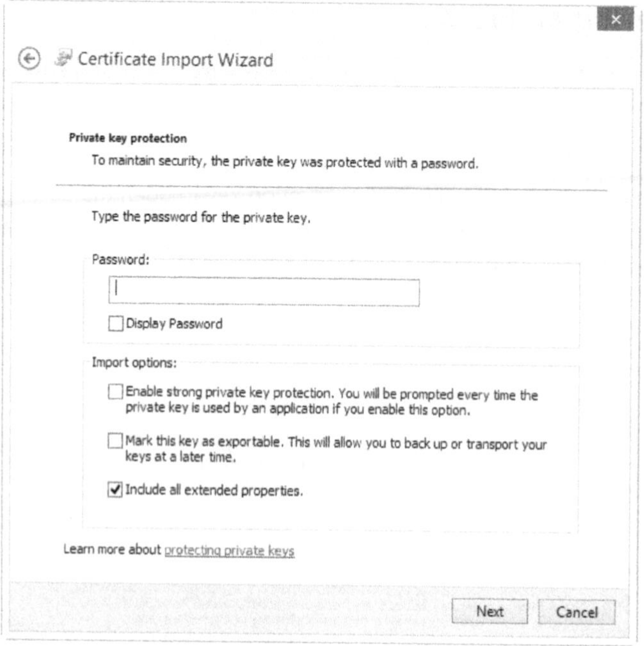

Certificate Import Wizard

Private key protection

To maintain security, the private key was protected with a password.

Type the password for the private key.

Password:

Display Password

Import options:

Enable strong private key protection. You will be prompted every time the private key is used by an application if you enable this option.

Mark this key as exportable. This will allow you to back up or transport your keys at a later time.

Include all extended properties.

Learn more about protecting private keys

Next Cancel

Figure 31-10 Importing an EFS key.

Figure 31-11 The default certificate store is best for a stand-alone computer. If your keys are stored in a central server location, click the second option.

The EFS encryption certificate is restored, and you will again have access to your files and data. If the Windows default password store becomes corrupt, you will need to restore your EFS key. Or, if someone tries to forcibly reset your password to access your files and folders, the system will protect the EFS-encrypted files until you can restore the correct key.

Turning EFS Off

You might want to turn off EFS encryption for files or folders after it has been set up, perhaps to disable it on files that are commonly shared with other people. To do this, you use almost the same procedure you used to set up the encryption:

1. Right-click the files and folders you want to decrypt, and then click Properties.
2. On the General tab, click Advanced.
3. In the Advanced Attributes dialog box, clear the Encrypt Contents To Secure Data check box, and then click OK twice. When prompted, ensure that you apply the action to the folder and all files and subfolders.

Creating and Restoring an EFS Certificate

If your encryption key is damaged or lost, you might be able to recover your files and folders by using an encryption key certificate. You can create one of these when you encrypt your files or at any time thereafter by performing the following steps:

1. Press Windows logo key+X to open the WinX menu, and then click Command Prompt (Admin).
2. Find the folder on a spare hard disk or removable storage device where you want to store your EFS certificate.

   To do this, type the drive letter followed by a colon. For example, type **E:** to move to drive E, and then type the **CD** command to move to the correct folder. To move to the Backups folder in the Files folder, for example, you would type **CD Files/Backups**.
3. Type **cipher /r: *file name***, where *file name* is the name you want to assign to the backed-up EFS certificate, and then press Enter. Windows creates a backup of the EFS certificate.

To restore the EFS certification, perform the following steps:

1. On the Start screen, search for **secpol.msc**, and then run the secpol (Security Policies) program when it appears.
2. In the left pane of the Local Security Policy window that appears, expand the Public Key Policies node, right-click Encrypting File System, and then click Add Data Recovery Agent (see Figure 31-12). Use the wizard that opens to select and install the EFS certificate.

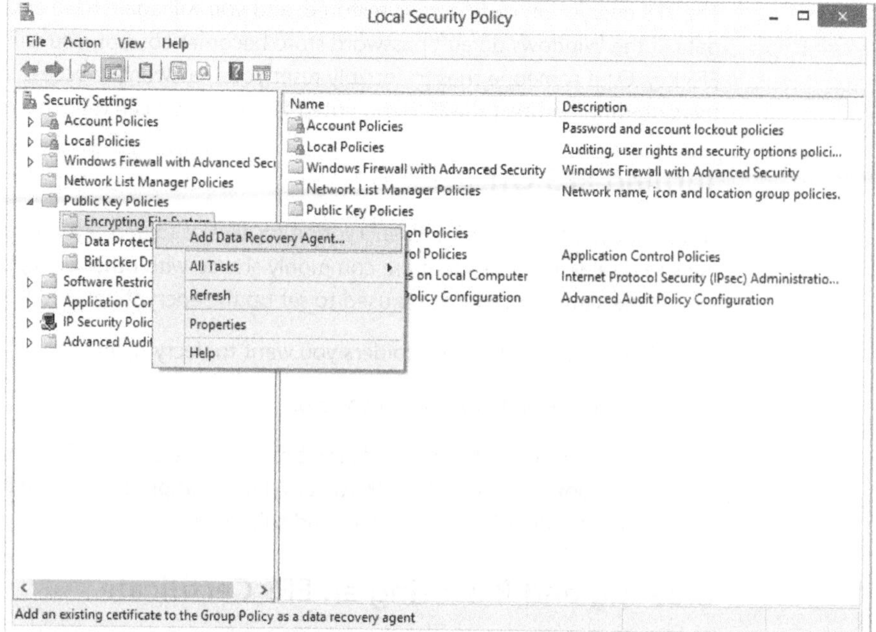

Figure 31-12 The Local Security Policy window.

3. Press Windows logo key+X to open the WinX menu, and then click Command Prompt.

4. Type **gpupdate**, and then press Enter to update the current Group Policies.

Backing Up an EFS Certificate for a Smart Card

If you use a smart card with EFS to access your data, you will need to back up the certificate for your smart card. To do this, perform the following procedure:

1. On the Start screen, search for **mmc**. In the search results, click Mmc.exe to open the Console1- [Console Root] window.

2. On the File menu, click Add/Remove Snap-In (see Figure 31-13).

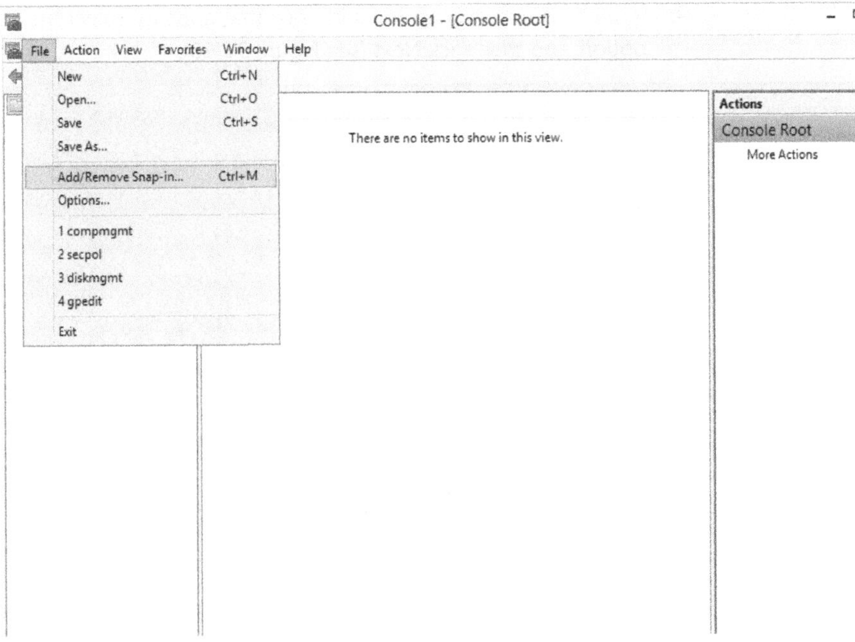

Figure 31-13 The Microsoft Management Console.

3. In the Add Or Remove Snap-ins window that appears, in the left pane, click Certificates, click Add, and then click OK (see Figure 31-14).

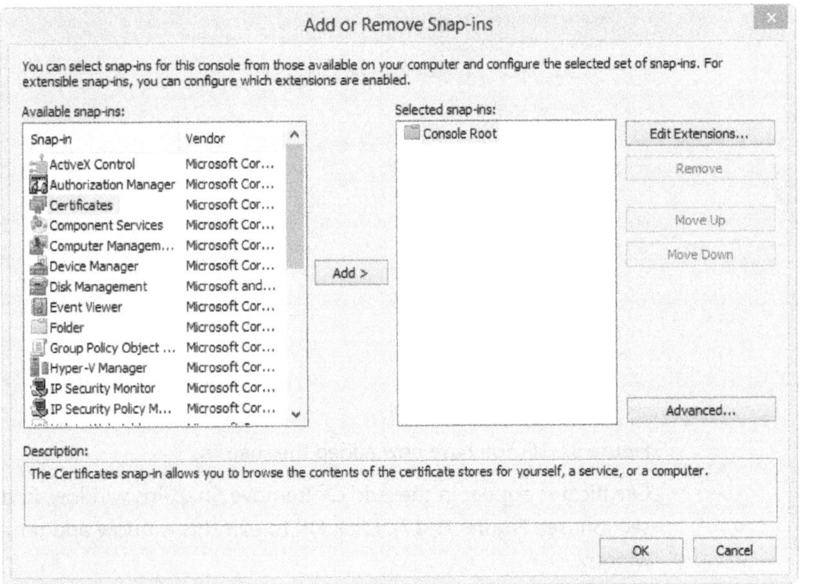

Figure 31-14 Adding a snap-in to the MMC.

4. In the Certificates Snap-In dialog box that appears, select the Computer Account option, and then click Next (see Figure 31-15).

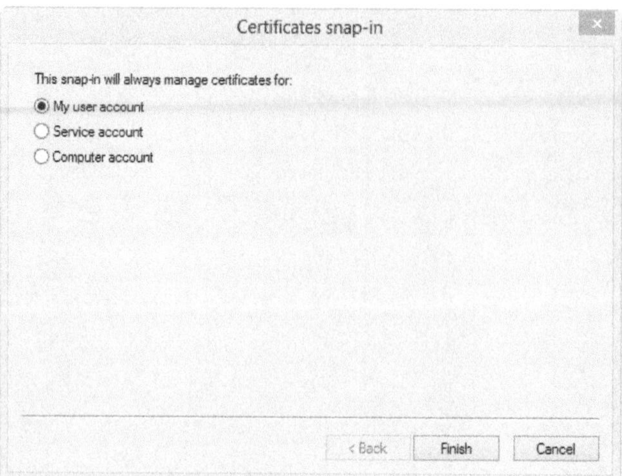

Figure 31-15 Select Computer Account in the Certificates Snap-In dialog box.

5. In the Select Computer dialog box that appears, ensure that the Local Computer option is selected, and then click Finish (see Figure 31-16).

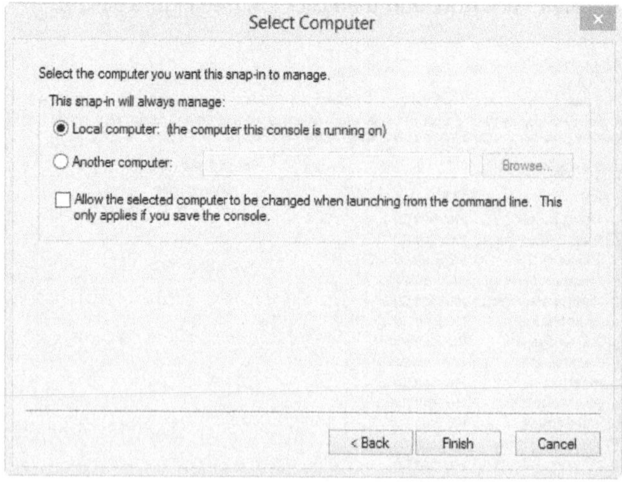

Figure 31-16 You have now added the snap-in.

Certificates appear in the Add Or Remove Snap-Ins window, in the Selected Snap-Ins section (see Figure 31-17). Click OK to exit this window and return to the main MMC window.

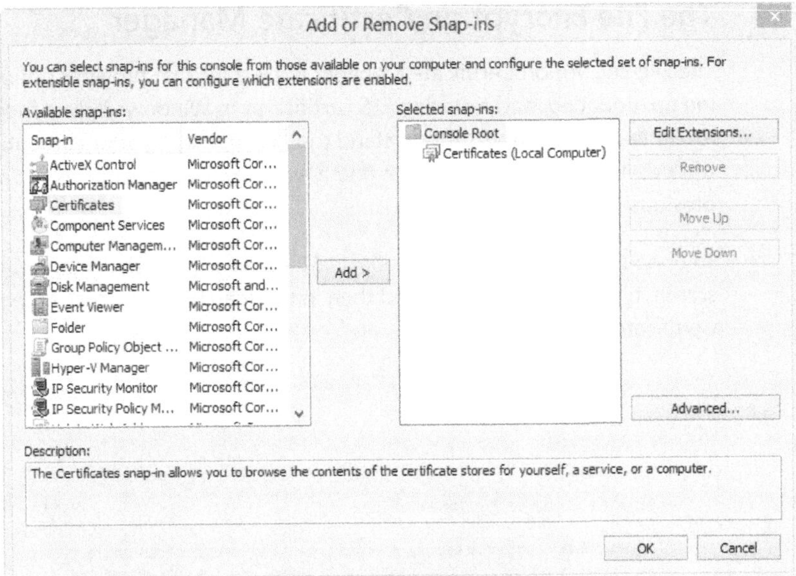

Figure 31-17 Viewing the installed MMC snap-ins.

6. In the main MMC window, click Certificates.
7. On the Action menu, click All Tasks, and then click Export.
8. In the Certificate Export Wizard that opens, click Yes, Export The Private Key.
9. Click Personal Information Exchange, and then click Next.
10. Assign a password for this file—*don't forget this password*. A prompt appears, asking you where you want to save your backed-up security certificate.
11. Specify the location to which you want to back up your security certificate, and then click Finish.

To restore your security certificate, follow steps 1 through 6 in the preceding procedure, and then perform the following steps:

1. On the Action menu, click All Tasks, click Import, and then click Next.
2. Find the location of your backed-up security certificate. In the File Name box, go to the certificate's location, and then select Personal Information Exchange.
3. Type the password you set when creating the certificate, and then click Finish to close the wizard.

The File Encryption Certificate Manager

The File Encryption Certificate Manager is a wizard that provides options for viewing, backing up, updating, and restoring EFS certificates in Windows 8 via a friendly interface. It is a very useful and easy-to-understand tool for managing your computer's encryption certificates. However, you might not find it as powerful or flexible as the methods described previously in this chapter.

To open the File Encryption Certificate Manager wizard (see Figure 31-18), on the Start screen, type **file encryption**, and then in the search results, click Manage File Encryption Certificates.

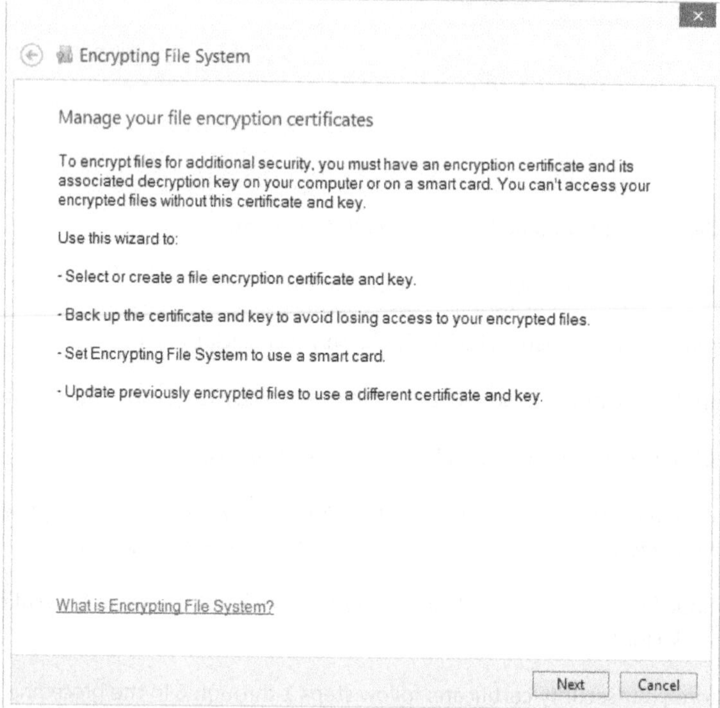

Figure 31-18 Manage your file encryption certificates in Windows 8.

Recovering EFS-Encrypted Files

Always keep a copy of your EFS encryption key and your password safe. If you lose the backed-up copy of your key, you won't be able to gain access to your files, and if you lose your password, you won't be able to restore the key.

Although EFS is very secure—it employs a 256-bit Elliptic Curve Cryptographic (ECC) algorithm cipher to secure your data—it might still be possible to recover your password by purchasing special software or by taking your computer to a computer security specialist. The following are two types of software that you can use to recover a password:

- **Advanced EFS Data Recovery (*http://www.elcomsoft.com/aefsdr.html*)** Advanced EFS Data Recovery is sophisticated software for deciphering EFS passwords. The company claims that even when data is damaged or someone has attempted to tamper with the encryption key, it can still recover data.
- **EnCase Forensic (*http://www.guidancesoftware.com/computer-forensics-ediscovery-software-digital-evidence.htm*)** EnCase Forensic is password-deciphering software for EFS drives and much more. EnCase Forensic includes a full suite of analysis, bookmarking, and reporting features.

Using Cipher.exe

Cipher.exe is a powerful command-line tool for managing encryption and decryption in Windows 8. You access it on the Start screen by typing **CMD** or **command**. To access a list of switches that you can use with the program, type **cipher /?** in the Command Prompt window (see Figure 31-19).

One of the most useful features of Cipher in Windows 8 is the ability to completely and securely wipe data from a hard disk. This is a very powerful capability and must be used with caution, because you cannot later recover those wiped files.

```
Microsoft Windows [Version 6.1.7600]
Copyright (c) 2009 Microsoft Corporation.  All rights reserved.

C:\Users\Mike>cipher /?
Displays or alters the encryption of directories [files] on NTFS partitions.

  CIPHER [/E | /D | /C]
         [/S:directory] [/B] [/H] [pathname [...]]

  CIPHER /K [/ECC:256|384|521]

  CIPHER /R:filename [/SMARTCARD] [/ECC:256|384|521]

  CIPHER /U [/N]

  CIPHER /W:directory

  CIPHER /X[:efsfile] [filename]

  CIPHER /Y

  CIPHER /ADDUSER [/CERTHASH:hash | /CERTFILE:filename | /USER:username]
         [/S:directory] [/B] [/H] [pathname [...]]

  CIPHER /FLUSHCACHE [/SERVER:servername]

  CIPHER /REMOVEUSER /CERTHASH:hash
         [/S:directory] [/B] [/H] [pathname [...]]

  CIPHER /REKEY [pathname [...]]
```

Figure 31-19 The Cipher.exe console.

To wipe a hard disk, type **cipher /w *x:\folder***, where *x:\folder* indicates what you want to wipe. For example, if you want to wipe drive D, type **cipher /w D:**. If you want to wipe a folder named Personal in your Users folder on drive C, type **cipher /w C:\Users\Mike Halsey\Personal**.

Using BitLocker and BitLocker To Go

As explained in Chapter 5, "Optimizing Windows 8 Security," BitLocker is a full-disk encryption method introduced with Windows Vista. It encrypts data by using a 128-bit Advanced Encryption Standard (AES) key. BitLocker is most secure when your computer's motherboard incorporates a Trusted Platform Module (TPM) chip. BitLocker is more flexible than EFS for encrypting drives because you can easily carry a BitLocker drive from one computer to another without having to use complex management consoles to export and import security keys and certificates.

BitLocker works in the following three modes when authenticating the user:

- **Transparent Operation mode** This is used when you have a TPM chip on your motherboard; the encryption key is stored on the chip.
- **User Authentication mode** To provide authentication, this mode requires the user to type a password before the operating system starts.
- **USB Key mode** In this mode, the user must insert a USB flash drive containing the encryption key.

You can use BitLocker in Windows 8 to encrypt internal partitions, hard disks, external hard disks, or USB flash drives. These drives can be encrypted only in the Enterprise or Pro editions of Windows 8, but the drives can then be used in any other Windows 8 version and on any other computer running Windows 8 by entering a password or by using a smart card or USB flash drive containing the decryption key. (See the Inside Out sidebar titled "Reading BitLocker-encrypted hard disks on another computer.")

INSIDE OUT Reading BitLocker-encrypted hard disks on another computer

You can read a BitLocker-encrypted disk on another computer running Windows 8 unless you encrypted the disk by using a TPM chip. This chip locks that hard disk to that specific motherboard, rendering it unreadable on any other computer. If the drive was on locked with a TPM chip, you will be asked for the password to unlock the drive when you plug it into another computer. Then if desired, you can change its status to automatically unlock in the BitLocker management window.

You can read (but not write to) Windows XP drives protected by BitLocker To Go by downloading the BitLocker To Go Reader from the Microsoft website at *http://www.microsoft.com/en-us/download/details.aspx?id=24303*.

> **NOTE**
>
> **If you do not have a TPM chip on your motherboard, you can find out how to use BitLocker with your computer at *http://technet.microsoft.com/en-us/library/ee424319(v=ws.10).aspx.***

Setting up BitLocker on your computer is straightforward. Pages guide you through each step of the process:

1. You can access BitLocker in two ways: on the Start screen, type **bitlocker**, and then click BitLocker Drive Encryption in Settings results; or in Control Panel, click System And Security, and then click BitLocker Drive Encryption.
2. In the BitLocker Drive Encryption window, you can manage the BitLocker-encrypted drives. In the lower-left corner of the window, click the TPM Administration link (see Figure 31-20) to manage a TPM chip on your motherboard, if you have one.

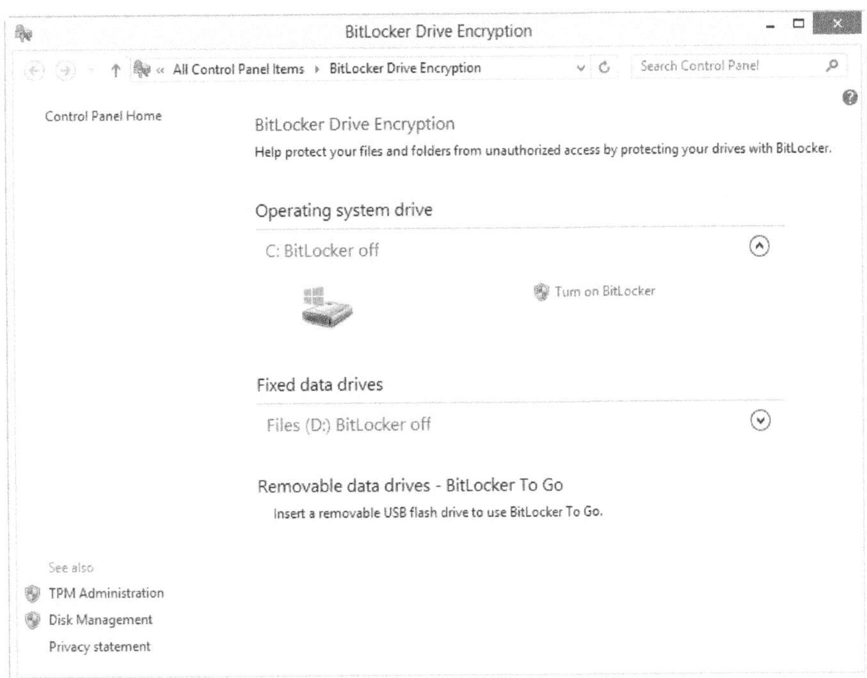

Figure 31-20 Managing BitLocker-encrypted drives in Control Panel.

When you encrypt a drive, you can choose one of two options to access the drive on another computer (see Figure 31-21): setting a password or using a smart card.

Select Automatically Unlock This Drive On This Computer if you intend to use the drive only on the computer where the drive was encrypted (such as a laptop). For this option to work, the copy of Windows 8 on that computer must also be encrypted with BitLocker. Note that this is not always available for all disks and USB flash drives and thus doesn't always appear. (It's not a visible option in Figure 31-21.)

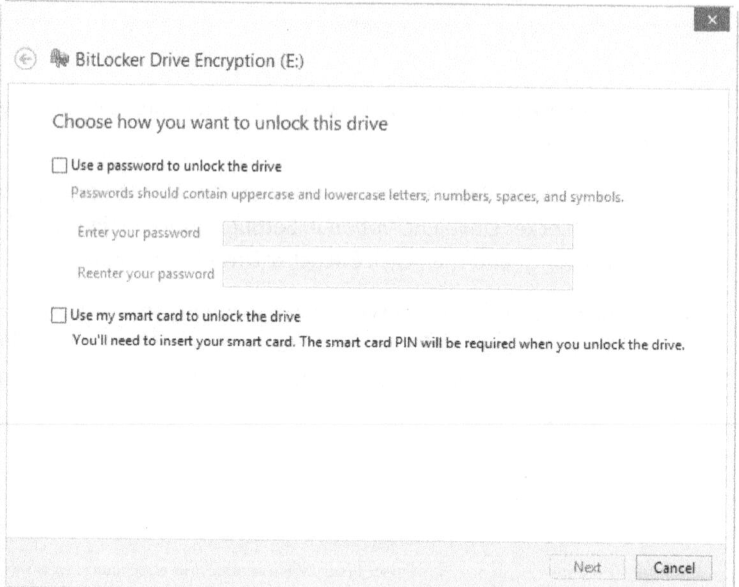

Figure 31-21 Select how you want Windows to unlock the drive. Sometimes, Auto Unlock The Drive is available.

From the BitLocker Management Console, you can change your password, disable BitLocker for a drive, or temporarily suspend BitLocker encryption.

CAUTION!

Unlike EFS, which encrypts specific files and folders, BitLocker encrypts entire disks or partitions and is extremely secure. A hard disk encrypted by using BitLocker will be completely inaccessible on another computer without the password, correct smart card, or USB flash drive access.

Some security and data recovery companies offer professional services to recover lost BitLocker encryption keys. Commercial software is also available, such as the Passware Kit Forensic program (available at *http://www.lostpassword.com*). This product can quickly recover encryption keys for hard disks protected by BitLocker. Passware also offers other security software that can, for example, recover lost Windows user passwords.

Creating a Copy of Encrypted Data

Sometimes it can be difficult to determine whether data you encrypt will still be encrypted when you make a copy of it. Table 31-1 presents different scenarios that determine whether encryption will still be enabled for each.

Table 31-1 **Scenarios in Which Data Will or Will Not Remain Encrypted When You Copy It**

	EFS-Encrypted Folder	BitLocker-Encrypted Drive	Unencrypted Folder or Drive	CD/DVD
FAT32-Formatted	Not supported	Yes	No	Not supported
exFat-Formatted	Not supported	Yes	No	Not supported
CDFS-Formatted	Not supported	Not supported	Not supported	No
NTFS-Formatted	Yes	Yes	No	Not supported

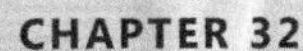

CHAPTER 32

Best Practices for Using Windows 8

THROUGHOUT THIS BOOK, you've seen how to repair, optimize, and configure many aspects of the Windows 8 operating system so that you can have the best possible experience. You've also learned how to back up your data and your copy of Windows 8 to make restoration trouble-free. You might have noticed that you can perform many of these tasks in myriad ways. Consider image backup, for example—you can do this in two ways. Sometimes you may not know which strategy to use for a particular task. This chapter summarizes best practices described throughout the book to help you decide.

Best Practice for Configuration

The Windows XP operating system needed some tweaking and customizing to get it working. In Windows 7, you needed to change very little. In Windows 8, even fewer options need your input, but there are ways that you can tweak the operating system after it is installed to enhance your experience.

Optimizing the Virtual Memory

When your computer starts, all the relevant parts of the operating system and your programs and apps are loaded into your computer's physical memory, or random access memory (RAM). This memory is significantly faster than memory that reads files from a mechanical hard disk, which is why adding more memory to an older computer is the cheapest and quickest way to get a performance boost. In modern computers for which 4 gigabytes (GB), 6 GB, and 8 GB of memory (or perhaps even more) are the norm, you have plenty of space for those files, but Windows 8 still uses a page file (virtual memory) on your hard disk for some commonly accessed files and data.

Because the page file is permitted to expand and contract over time, fragmentation will inevitably occur on your hard disk. Because hard disks are becoming much larger, Windows 8 is less likely to split a large file over several small chunks of space spread across the hard disk. Typically, the operating system saves a file in the most convenient location at the time, which won't necessarily keep the file segments contiguous. Why should you be concerned about this? By default, the Disk Defragmenter in Windows 8 is set to automatically defragment every hard disk, including new disks that you add later on, on a schedule. The problem with defragmenting is that it puts tremendous physical strain on the hard disk.

Once, when I was beta-testing Windows 7, a hard disk I was defragmenting physically exploded in the middle of the process. I could hear the shattered platters rattling around inside the casing. Because this happened when using the Windows 7 beta, the Windows chief at the time, Steven Sinofsky, became personally involved because he wanted reassurance that it wasn't caused by a problem with the defragmenter tool itself. Fortunately, it was just a faulty hard disk, but the fact that it shattered during defragmentation didn't surprise anyone.

Managing the virtual memory is still important, but you might be asking why you need this page file at all. If you have a modern computer with large volumes of RAM, you don't need the page file, but I would still advise against turning it off or even changing it to the minimum size. One reason I recommend this is that some earlier software, even programs written by Microsoft, rely on the page file being available, and some programs will not function if they can't find it. Also, if you are doing very memory-intensive work, such as editing high-definition video or encoding, the page file can be very useful.

To configure the virtual memory to a specific size on your hard disk, perform the following steps:

1. Open Control Panel.
2. Click System to open the System window.
3. In the pane on the left, click Advanced System Settings.
4. In the System Properties dialog box, click the Advanced tab, and then in the Performance section, click Settings.
5. In the Performance Options dialog box that opens, click the Advanced tab.
6. In the Virtual Memory section, click Change.

7. Clear the Automatically Manage Paging File Size For All Drives check box.

8. Select the Custom Size check box.

9. In the Initial Size and Maximum Size text boxes, enter the Recommended value under Total Paging File Size For All Drives (see Figure 32-1). (These values must be the same for both sizes to avoid fragmentation.)

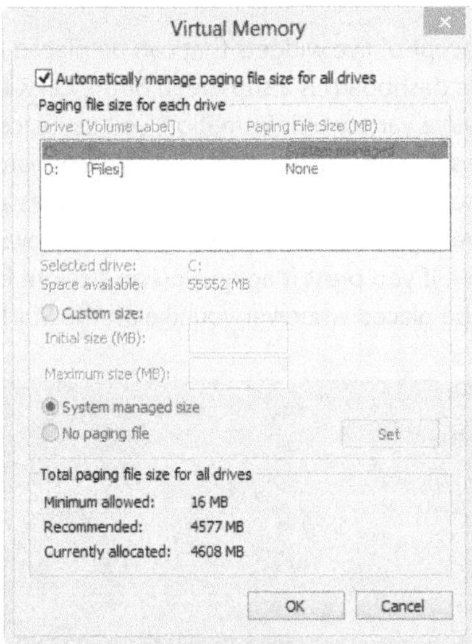

Figure 32-1 Changing the virtual memory allotment.

INSIDE OUT **Virtual memory and solid-state drives**

If you are running Windows 8 from a solid-state drive, keep the virtual memory file but set it to the Minimum Allowed size, (usually 16 MB), because read speeds from the memory chips inside a solid-state drive are quick enough to not require general use of the page file.

Optimizing the Start Screen

The Windows 8 Start screen is the default interface for daily use, and you can configure a lot of it.

Optimizing the Start Screen for Work/Life Balance

The Start screen and Windows 8 apps are a good way to separate your personal and work lives if you use your computer for both. You can strip all desktop software icons from the Start screen and instead pin them all to the desktop taskbar to create two completely separate working environments, each of which can be completely different from the other.

Using the Start Screen As a Widget Dashboard

Windows 7 introduced the concept of live widgets that can be placed anywhere on the desktop. In the Apple OS X, the dashboard is a subscreen of the OS X desktop on which you can see live widgets that contain a variety of information; you can access these with a single click. You can turn the Windows 8 Start screen into a widget dashboard by prioritizing Live Tiles that display information such as email, the calendar, instant messaging, social networking, news, and finance (see Figure 32-2). By pressing the Windows logo key, you can see the latest news and updates. If you press it again, you go straight back to the desktop (your actual desktop icon can be placed wherever you like on the Start screen).

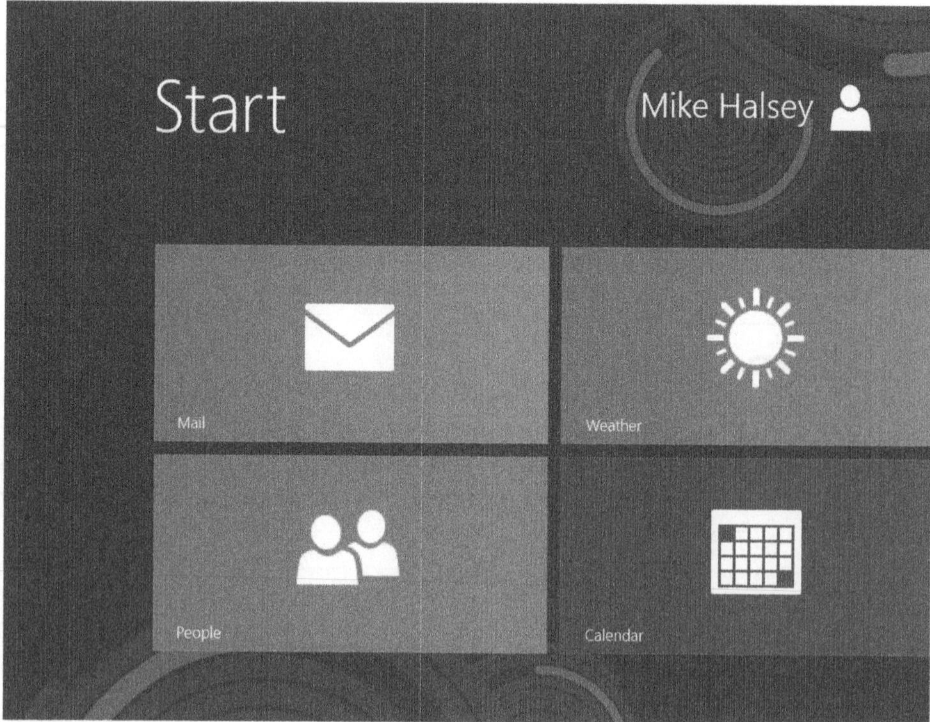

Figure 32-2 The Start screen as a widget dashboard. Larger displays of Tiles make live information easier to read.

You use the Ease of Access features in Windows 8 to scale up everything without affecting the desktop. To do this, perform the following procedure:

1. On the Start screen, press Windows key+C.
2. Click the Settings charm.
3. At the bottom right of your screen, click Change PC Settings.
4. In the PC Settings dialog box, click Ease of Access.
5. Click Make Everything On Your Screen Bigger to turn the feature on (see Figure 32-3). This is a toggle option.

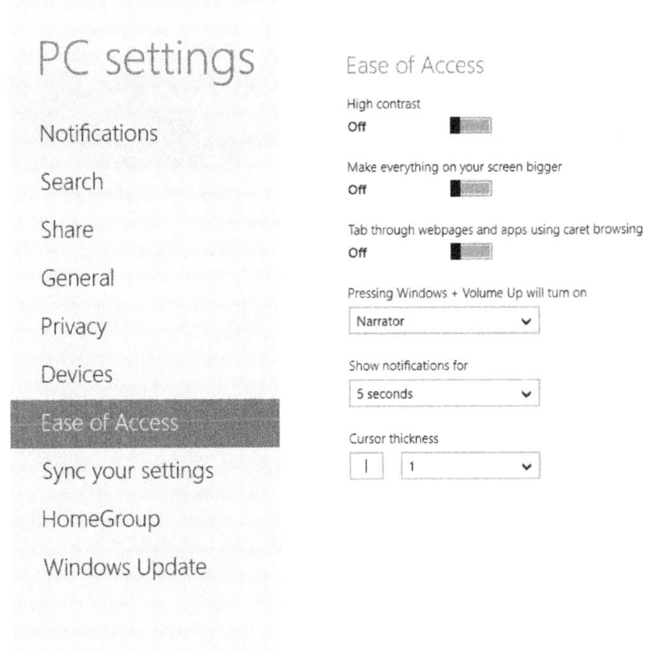

Figure 32-3 Making objects bigger in the Windows 8 user interface.

Avoiding Conflicts Between Windows Defender and Third-Party Tools

By default, Windows 8 is configured extremely well for security—most users will never need to change a single setting in the Windows Firewall, User Account Control (UAC) doesn't pop up whenever you want to change something such as the time or date, and the built-in antivirus protection of Windows Defender provides excellent protection. However, you might want to use a third-party antivirus product if you want features in addition to those offered by Windows Defender. If you do, you'll need to turn Windows Defender off to avoid conflicts between the antivirus packages, as explained in Chapter 13, "Responding to Viruses, Malware, and other Threats." To do this, open Windows Defender, click the Settings tab, and then clear the Turn On Windows Defender check box (see Figure 32-4). Note that this option is not available in Windows RT.

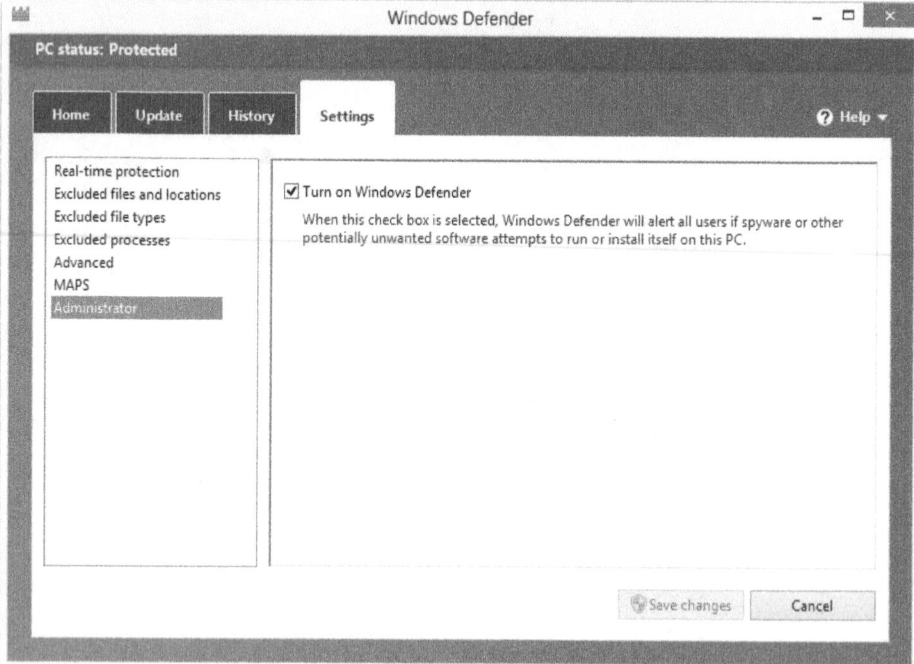

Figure 32-4 Turning off Windows Defender.

Blocking Access to Removable Storage on Business-Use Computers

If you are using Windows 8 in a business environment, you can take additional measures to help maintain excellent security. I would suggest that you deactivate access to USB-attached storage and disc burning, which you can do in Windows 8 Pro and Enterprise by using the Group Policy editor. Doing this can prevent data theft, but it can also help protect the computer from virus and malware. To deactivate access, perform the following steps:

1. On the Start screen, search for **gpedit.msc**, and then open the Local Group Policy Editor.
2. Click Computer Configuration\Administrative Templates\System\Removable Storage Access. In the Local Group Policy Editor dialog box (see Figure 32-5), you can deny access to and use of removable storage media.

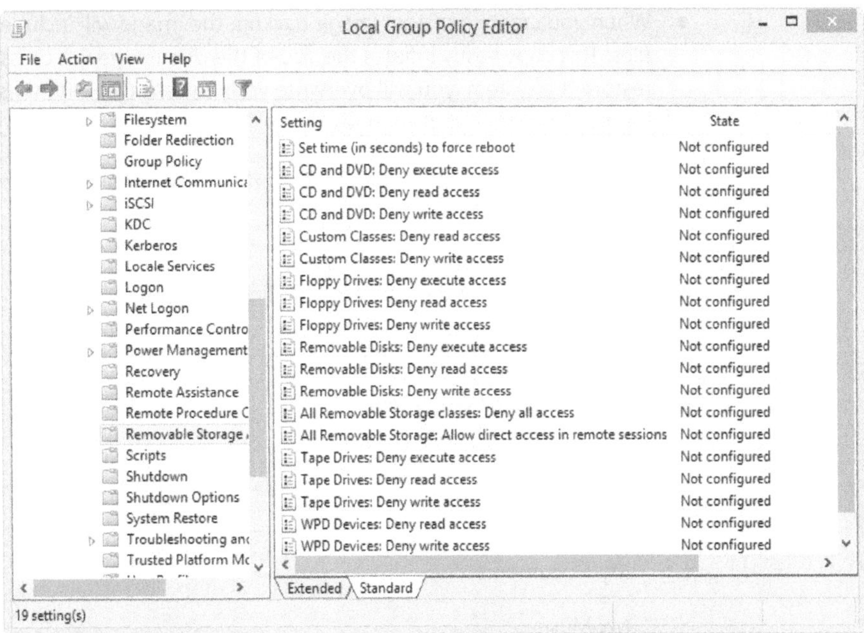

Figure 32-5 Managing removable storage in the Local Group Policy Editor.

Downloading a Copy of CCleaner

The one single piece of software I install on all of my computers is CCleaner, which you can download for free from *http://www.piriform.com/ccleaner*. This is an excellent tool for cleaning temporary files and clutter out of Windows 8 and for helping to keep the system running smoothly and speedily. Run this program every month to help maintain your computer.

Best Practice for File Storage

Don't keep your files and documents in the Users folder on your Windows hard disk; they should always be moved for the following two reasons:

- If Windows 8 becomes unresponsive and you are forced to reformat your hard disk, you will lose your files.
- When you create a system image backup, the image will include a copy of all your files. This copy vastly inflates the size of the disc image unnecessarily, and when you restore the system, you will overwrite your current files with these earlier versions, losing all new files and changes.

To move your files away from Windows 8, perform the following procedure:

1. Open File Explorer.
2. On the left edge of the Address bar, click the arrow.
3. From the locations displayed, click your user name (see Figure 32-6).
4. Select the following folders:

   Downloads

   Favorites

   My Documents

   My Music

   My Pictures

   My Videos

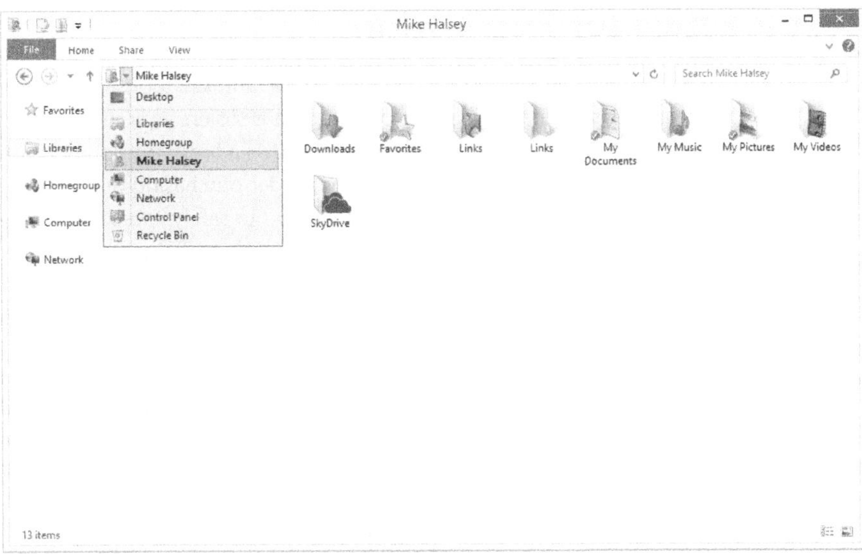

Figure 32-6 Navigating to your user folder.

5. Right-click the selected folders, and then click Cut. *It is very important you do not select Copy.*

6. Go to the spare hard disk or partition where you want to store the files.

7. Right-click in a blank space, and then select Paste.

INSIDE OUT Shrinking your windows partition to create a new drive

If you have only one partition on one physical hard disk in your computer, you will need to shrink it and create a new data partition. To do this, press Windows logo key+X to open the WinX menu, and then click Disk Management. Next, right-click the Windows drive, and then click Shrink Volume. After shrinking the drive, right-click in the blank space and create a New Simple Volume. Make it the maximum size available.

You will need to format the drive (use NTFS file system formatting) and assign it a drive letter. You now have a dedicated partition for your files.

Best Practice for Encryption

BitLocker and Microsoft BitLocker To Go are fantastic tools for encrypting data while on the move to ensure that if your laptop or tablet is stolen, your information cannot be accessed by anyone. BitLocker, if it is available to you, is a preferred solution over Encrypting File System (EFS). If you are buying a laptop, consider purchasing one with an integrated Trusted Platform Module (TPM) chip. This allows you to safely and securely use BitLocker to encrypt your entire hard disks and partitions.

CAUTION!

BitLocker has in the past been susceptible to hacking by which the encryption key was pulled from the sleep or hibernation file on a computer. This does not affect the Windows 8 Fast Start feature, which hibernates only the kernel. To be completely safe, shut your laptop or tablet down when you are not using it instead of putting it to sleep.

Always keep a backup copy of your BitLocker encryption keys in a cloud service, such as Microsoft SkyDrive, so that the keys are available to you at all times. If you are traveling and can't be certain when you will have Internet access, carrying the BitLocker keys on a USB flash drive is also a good idea. Always store them separately from the laptop so that the keys and laptop cannot be lost or stolen together.

Best Practice for Image Backup

As explained in preceding chapters, Windows 8 offers two different methods for imaging your disk: Windows system image backup and Refresh Your PC. These two features appear similar, but they are not. The critical difference is that the Windows system image backup performs a file-level backup of almost every file and folder on the computer (some folders, such as downloaded email in Microsoft Outlook, aren't backed up), and the backup image contains all your settings for every piece of installed software. The advantage here is that you don't have to reconfigure your settings in software such as Outlook, Microsoft Word, or Adobe Photoshop.

The Refresh Your PC option backs up all of your installed software, but only if you create a custom image; it does *not* back up any of your settings for your desktop programs. This means that when you refresh your computer from a custom image, you have to set up all your email accounts and software preferences from scratch.

The Refresh Your PC option does offer a few advantages, however. It's simple for a non-technical user to work with and good for a user who uses the computer primarily for Windows 8 apps. This is an excellent option for friends, family, and businesses using custom Windows 8 apps for work. Refresh Your PC also has the advantage of creating an Install.wim file as the backup image. You can copy this file onto a Windows 8 installer disc image to create a custom installer for the operating system with all your software preinstalled.

Table 32-1 describes best-case scenarios for using Windows system image backup and Refresh Your PC.

Table 32-1 **Best-Case Scenarios for Using Image Backup Methods**

Windows 8 User	Scenario	Image Backup Strategy
Power user	User has a lot of preconfigured software	Windows system image backup
Gamer	User is likely to have Xbox Live, Steam, Origin, or another gaming service that can resync the correct game updates and settings	Custom refresh image
Desktop business user	User has software such as Microsoft Office	Windows system image backup
Casual home user	User can refresh the computer and is more likely to be using apps where none or very little configuration is needed	Custom refresh image

Best Practice for Data Backup

It doesn't matter how you choose to back up your files (see Figure 32-7): a cloud service (such as SkyDrive, Mozy, Amazon S3, or Carbonite), a USB-attached hard disk, or network-attached storage (NAS). Just make sure you *do* back things up and that files are set to be backed up on a regular schedule.

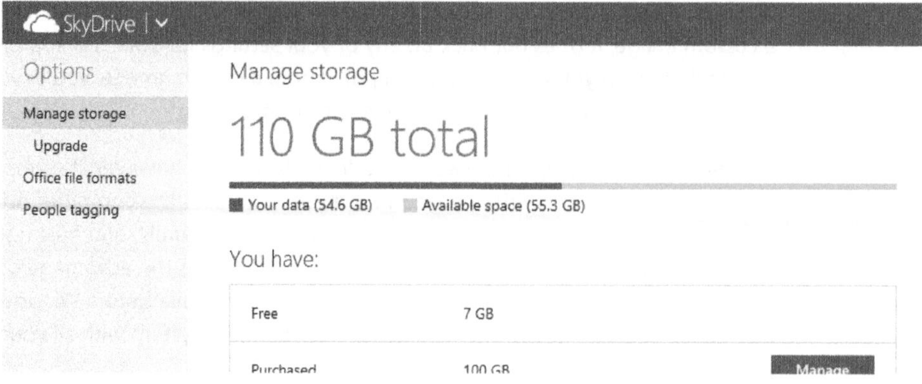

Figure 32-7 Backing up files to SkyDrive.

It also doesn't matter what backup software you use. Windows 8 provides a good backup program, but it creates a virtual hard disk that contains all the files and folders. Although you can open this file and read its contents, this strategy in my opinion is not as good as a basic file-by-file backup solution (which is what I use).

Not only set up an automated backup job—ideally once a month or more often—but check your backups regularly, about once a month, to ensure they are intact. A misconfigured or corrupt backup job can quickly wipe out your only extra copy of vital and irreplaceable files. Many backup packages, especially cloud backup solutions, back up files as those files change.

Optimizing Windows 8 File History

Windows 8 File History is a useful feature, but you should never rely on it as a backup solution for the following two very good reasons:

- By default, it stores its copies of files on your Windows drive, and if you need to reformat the drive, you will lose the files.
- The feature has a finite amount of storage space and will store only the most recently changed files. Every time you open a file (such as when you view a photo or play an MP3 music track), the file is changed as a result of a modification to the last accessed data. This qualifies as a file change. Thus, your File History has the potential to fill up with multiple copies of MP3s, and when it runs out of room, other files will not be stored.

INSIDE OUT

Excluding file locations from File History

In File History (accessible from Control Panel), in the pane on the left side, you can click the Exclude Folders link to prevent the feature from filling up with multiple copies of music, video, and other files that change every time you play them, and that you likely have backed up elsewhere (see Figure 32-8).

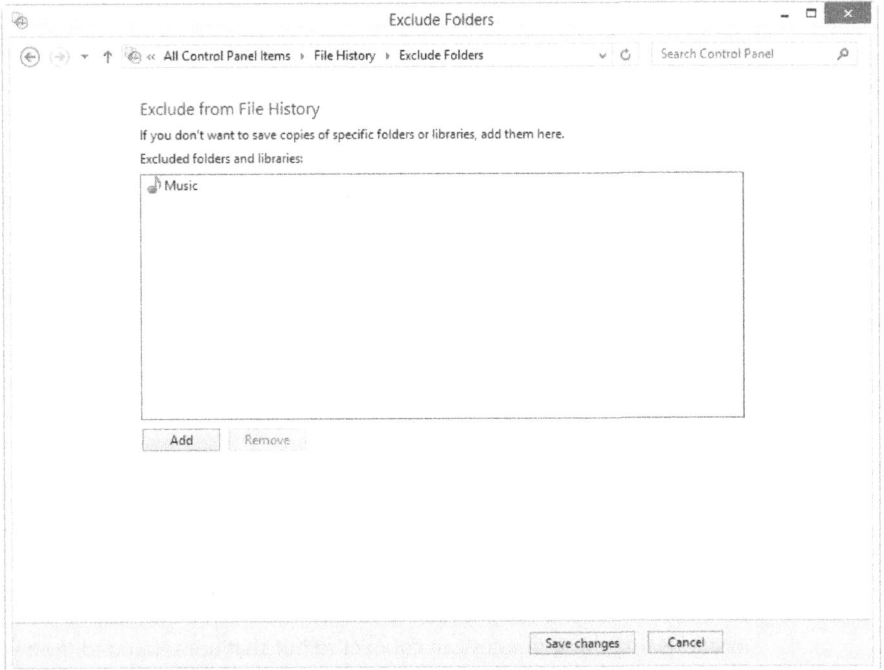

Figure 32-8 Excluding items from Windows 8 File History.

Best Practice for Laptops and Tablets

Every day, many thousands of laptops and tablets are lost or stolen worldwide. If you are using a laptop for work, and you carry with you personal information about colleagues, business associates, and customers, it is essential that you encrypt data on the hard disk. Even the data you carry in email contacts, such as addresses and phone numbers, is covered by data protection legislation.

If you can afford it, buy a laptop with a TPM chip and use BitLocker to encrypt the disk or disks for additional security. If your laptop or tablet doesn't contain a TPM chip, is there anything you can do to minimize the impact of theft? Enforcing strong passwords is a start but doesn't protect against someone physically removing the hard disk. If you can, store sensitive data elsewhere and have the laptop connect to it remotely via the Internet or a virtual private network (VPN) when that data needed. This requires an active Internet connection, but it is much more secure than having unencrypted data sitting around. Also buy a Kensington lock to secure the laptop or tablet in place when you are using it at a desk.

Laptop bags are highly recognizable. When choosing a bag, select a backpack or all-purpose bag that has a special storage compartment for a laptop. A less obvious bag is a less obvious opportunity for theft.

Best Practice for Using Personal Devices at Work

Many people want to use personal devices at work, such as smartphones, laptops, and tablet PCs. If you are a systems administrator with tight controls on security and updates, the presence of unmanaged computers can cause challenges. With Windows RT tablets, you can at least use Microsoft AppLocker and Windows Server to provide access to dedicated business apps over which you have control, but the lack of Group Policy management on these devices can be a worry.

If your company insists on encouraging using personal devices at work—perhaps to help keep IT costs down (or maybe because one of the nontechnically-minded directors is convinced it's a good idea), create a separate wireless network to which these devices can connect. You can isolate this network from your main business network, helping to minimize problems and security breaches. Additionally, you can create separate NAS or other storage locations that these devices can connect to but that are separated from your main company storage.

Best Practice for International Data Protection

If you use a computer for work, you will be bound by the data protection and privacy regulations for every country in which you operate (including those countries to which you travel for business). These laws and regulations vary from country to country but are standardized across groups of countries such as the European Union. Normally, such legislation requires you to take all reasonable steps to ensure that the data of customers and individuals is protected by using encryption, firewalls, and so on. You can normally find information about data protection legislation on your national governmental website. It is critically important that you familiarize yourself with the regulations in the countries in which you operate because the penalties for breaching them can include hefty fines and possibly imprisonment.

Best Practice for Passwords

Passwords are always important, and as computers become more advanced, it becomes much more important to choose strong passwords. I always recommend your passwords conform to the following rules:

- Have one main strong password.
- Append a few characters to this standard password that identify a website or service to make it unique for each use. You can add these characters at the beginning, at the end, or in the middle, but stick with a pattern to help you remember them.
- Use a *minimum* of 10 characters in your main password.
- Use a mixture of uppercase and lowercase letters, numbers, and symbols.
- Use numbers and symbols in the place of letters. For example, use the numeral 1 instead of a lowercase i or l, 5 instead of S, 0 instead of o, 3 instead of e, & instead of a, or ^ instead of v.
- Avoid using characters that are commonly not allowed, such as the asterisk (*), question mark (?), and the at sign (@).

Table 32-2 (which also appears in Chapter 13) shows how long it could take a criminal with an ordinary computer to decipher passwords of various lengths and complexity. I am repeating this table here because I feel that using strong passwords is extremely important. I recommend that any password you use be a minimum of 10 to 14 characters and use the character combinations highlighted with bold in Table 32-2.

Table 32-2 **Amount of Time a Computer Needs to Decipher a Password**

Number of Characters	Numbers Only	Upper or Lowercase Letters	Upper or Lowercase Letters Mixed	Numbers, Upper and Lowercase Letters	Numbers, Upper and Lowercase Letters, Symbols
3	Instantly	Instantly	Instantly	Instantly	Instantly
4	Instantly	Instantly	Instantly	Instantly	Instantly
5	Instantly	Instantly	Instantly	3 secs	10 secs
6	Instantly	Instantly	8 secs	3 mins	13 mins
7	Instantly	Instantly	5 mins	3 hours	17 hours
8	Instantly	13 mins	3 hours	10 days	57 days
9	4 secs	6 hours	4 days	1 year	12 years
10	40 secs	6 days	169 days	**106 years**	**928 years**
11	6 mins	169 days	16 years	**6k years**	**71k years**
12	1 hour	12 years	600 years	**108k years**	**5m years**
13	11 hours	314 years	21k years	**25m years**	**423m years**
14	4 days	8k years	778k years	**1bn years**	**5bn years**
15	46 days	212k years	28m years	97bn years	2tn years
16	1 year	512m years	1bn years	6tn years	193tn years
17	12 years	143m years	36bn years	374tn years	14qd years
18	126 years	3bn years	1tn years	23qd years	1qt years

k = Thousand (1,000 or 10^{-3}); m = Million (1,000,000 or 10^{-6}); bn = Billion (1,000,000,000 or 10^{-9}); tn = Trillion (1,000,000,000,000 or 10^{-12}); qd = Quadrillion (1,000,000,000,000,000 or 10^{-15}); qt = Quintillion (1,000,000,000,000,000,000 or 10^{-18})

Enforcing Password Policies by Using Local Group Policy

In Windows 8 Pro and Enterprise editions, you can use the Local Group Policy Editor to enforce password policies for all users on a computer. To do so, perform the following steps:

1. On the Start screen, search for **gpedit.msc**, and when it appears in the search results, click it to open the Local Group Policy Editor.
2. Click Local Computer Policy\Computer Configuration\Windows Settings\Security Settings\Account Policies\Password Policy.

Figure 32-9 shows how you can use the Local Group Policy Editor to enforce the use of strong passwords on the computer as well as force people to change their passwords on a regular schedule. You can also force Windows to use stronger encryption when using passwords.

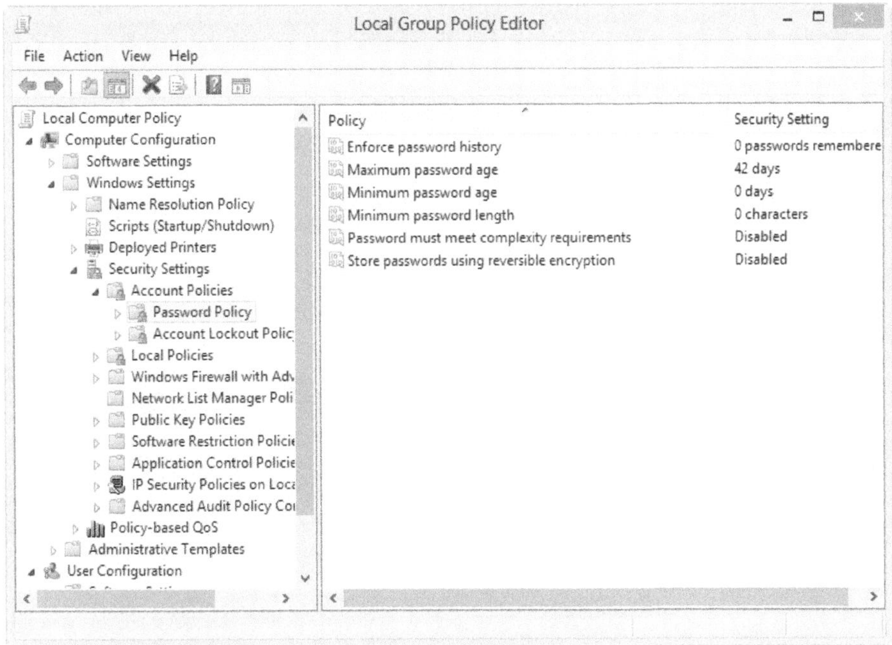

Figure 32-9 Enforcing password policy via the Local Group Policy Editor.

PART 5

Using Advanced Utilities

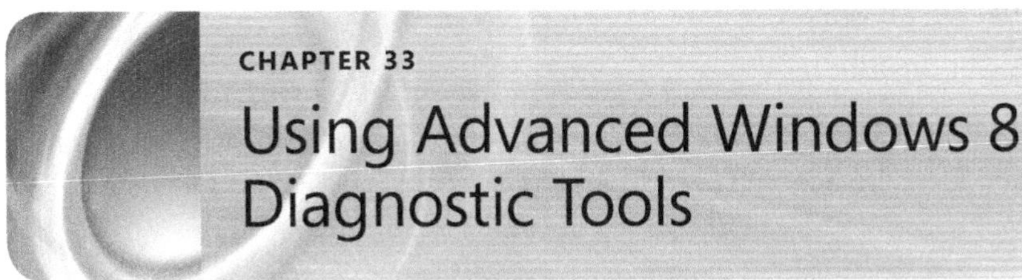

CHAPTER 33

Using Advanced Windows 8 Diagnostic Tools

THROUGHOUT THIS BOOK, YOU'VE LEARNED about some of the more advanced diagnostic and maintenance tools available in Windows 8. In this chapter, you look again in more detail at some of these tools and utilities so that you can get the most out of them.

The Computer Management Console

The Computer Management console is the central location for managing and monitoring Windows 8. To access the Computer Management console, press Windows logo key+X, and then in the WinX menu (see Figure 33-1), click Computer Management.

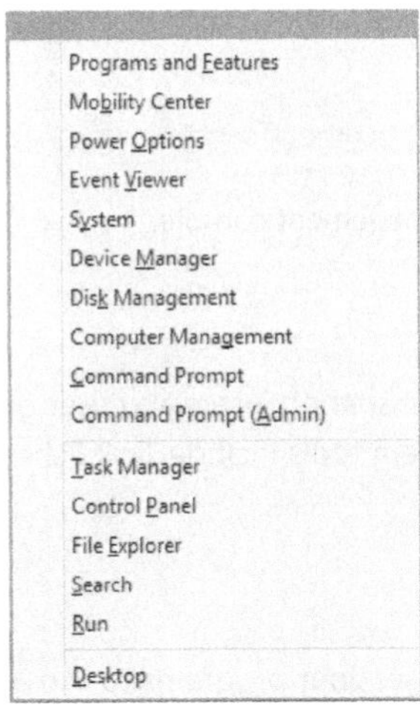

Figure 33-1 Accessing the Computer Management console from the WinX menu.

In the main Computer Management console window, the tools are divided into three categories: System Tools, Storage, and Services And Applications (see Figure 33-2).

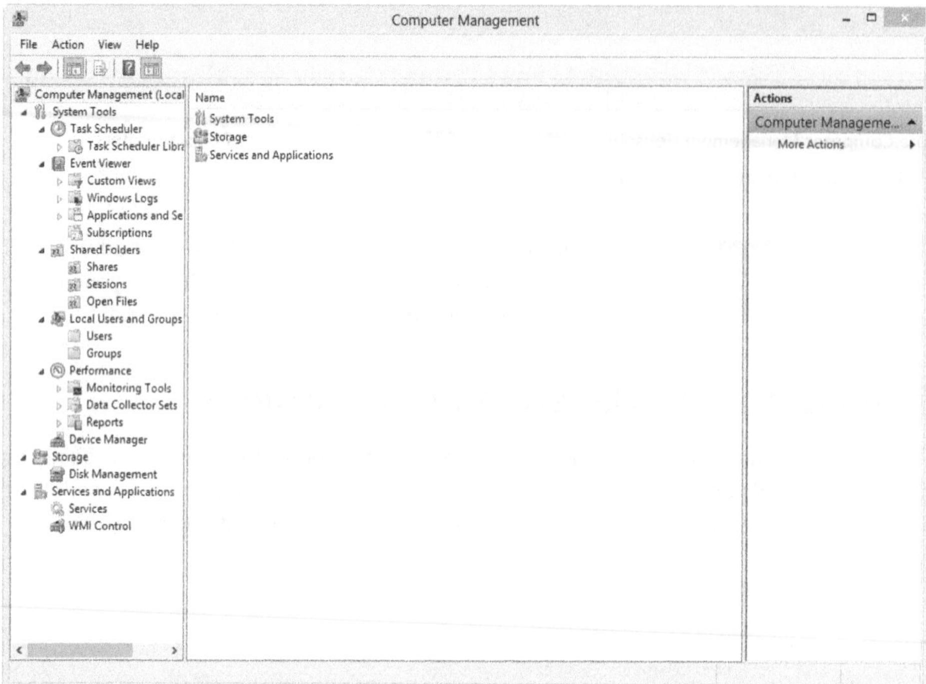

Figure 33-2 The main window of the Computer Management console.

System Tools

System Tools manages events, tasks, file and folder sharing, users and user groups, and monitors the performance of your computer. System tools include Task Scheduler, Event Viewer, and Device Manager.

Task Scheduler

By using the Task Scheduler in Windows, you can set your programs to run automatically at startup or on a schedule. Many Windows components also use this feature.

In the Computer Management console, under Task Scheduler, you can expand any Windows component to see that component's scheduled tasks (see Figure 33-3). In the lower center pane, you can use the tabs, described in the following list, to set up and modify tasks.

- **General** This tab summarizes information about the task and also contains some basic security options for it. A useful feature on this tab is the option to run a task in compatibility mode for Windows Server 2008 or Windows Vista.
- **Triggers** On this tab, you can specify what (if appropriate) triggers the task.
- **Actions** This tab indicates what happens when the task activates. You can set programs to start and commands to run.
- **Conditions** The settings on this tab give you more control over a task; for instance, you can specify to run the task only when the computer is idle or plugged into an electrical outlet.
- **Settings** This tab includes additional settings associated with the task, such as the task's schedule, and what happens if the task does not complete or the task is not scheduled to run again.
- **History** Any events associated with the task appear on this tab.

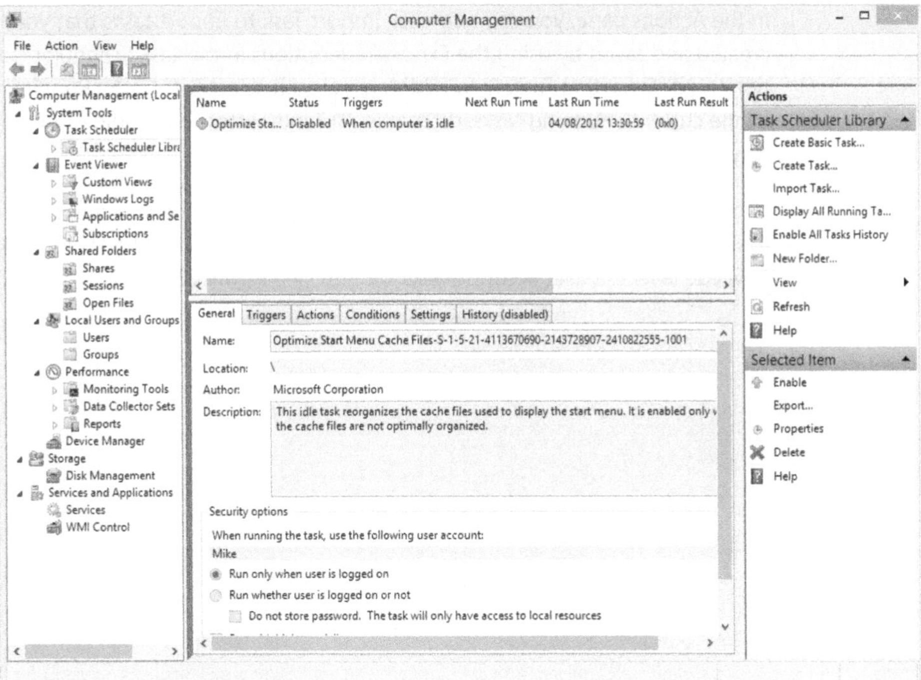

Figure 33-3 The Task Scheduler.

Adding Tasks To add a new task, follow these steps:

1. In the Computer Management console, in the left pane, click Task Scheduler. In the Actions pane in the right pane, click Create Basic Task or Create Task to start the Create Basic Task Wizard.
2. Enter a description and name, and then click Next.
3. On the Task Trigger page, choose when you want the task to start, and then click Next.
4. Depending on what you choose on the Task Trigger page, configure the additional options, and then click Next.
5. On the Action page, choose what action you would like the task to perform, and then click Next.
6. Configure the additional options on the next page, and then click Next.
7. Click Finish.

In the Actions pane, you can also click Import Task to import tasks that you have previously created and saved by using the Export Task options in the Task Scheduler (see the next section titled "Exporting Tasks"). In addition, you can select Display All Running Tasks to display all the currently running tasks, or Enable All Tasks History to enable or disable the event history recording for tasks.

In business or corporate environments where tasks have been created by using the AT.exe tool, it might be necessary to click the AT Service Account Configuration link to set at which privilege level the user account tasks will run (see Figure 33-4).

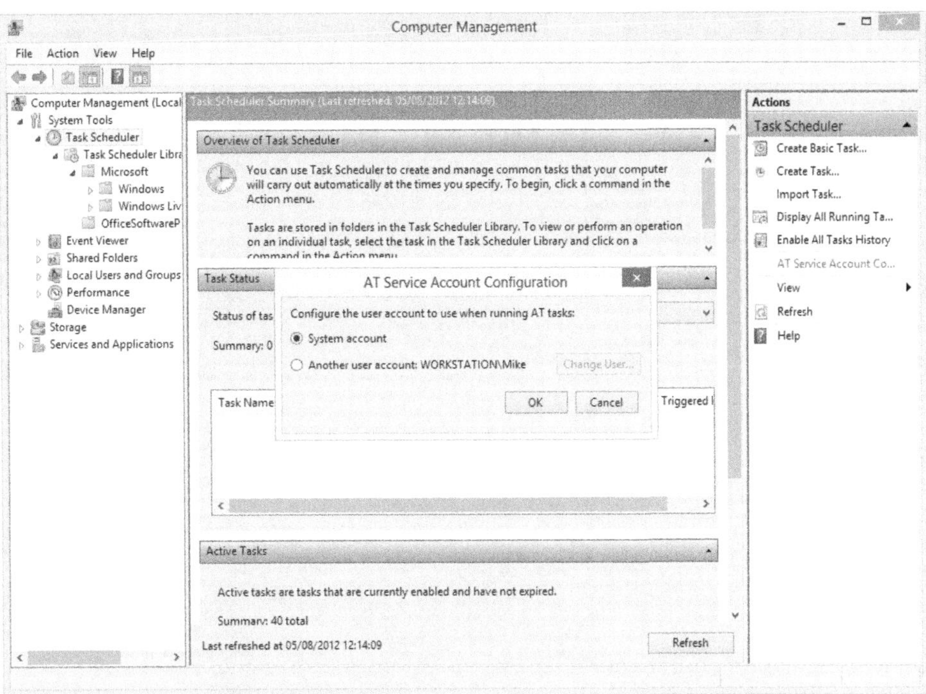

Figure 33-4 Some dialog boxes in Task Scheduler appear as pop-up dialog boxes.

Exporting Tasks You can right-click any task and click Export to export the task to a file (see Figure 33-5). You might want to export a task to a file when you want to use a particular task on different computers, or you want to keep a backup of the task in case it becomes necessary to reinstall Windows 8.

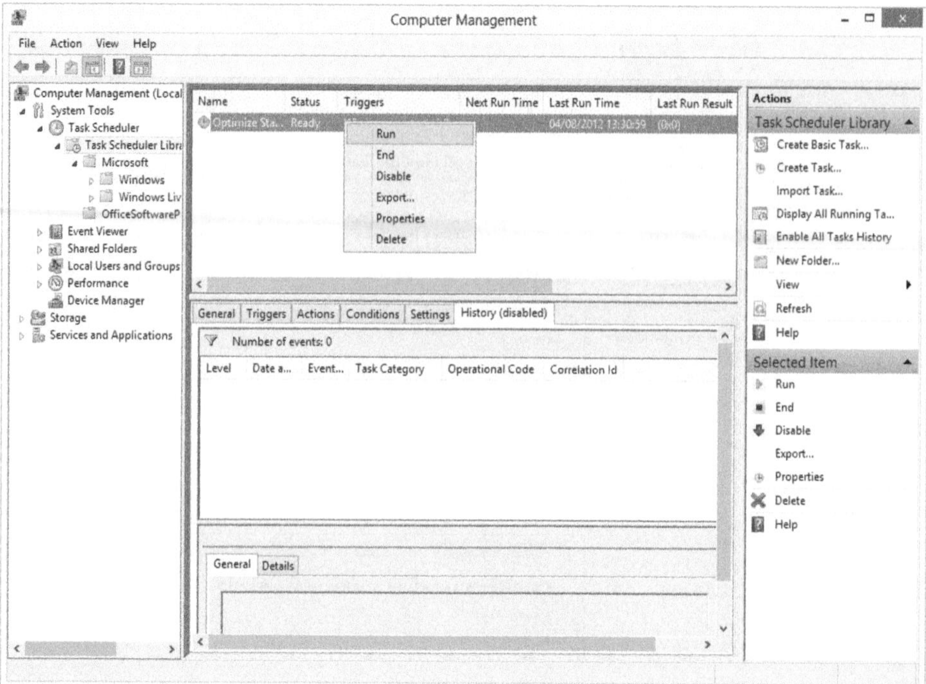

Figure 33-5 Exporting tasks.

To see more detail and have more control over the task, right-click the task and then click Properties.

Event Viewer

The Event Viewer is probably the most useful and configurable troubleshooting component in Windows 8. In the Actions pane of the Computer Management console are options to save and reopen event logs and to search for specific events, such as problems and errors (see Figure 33-6).

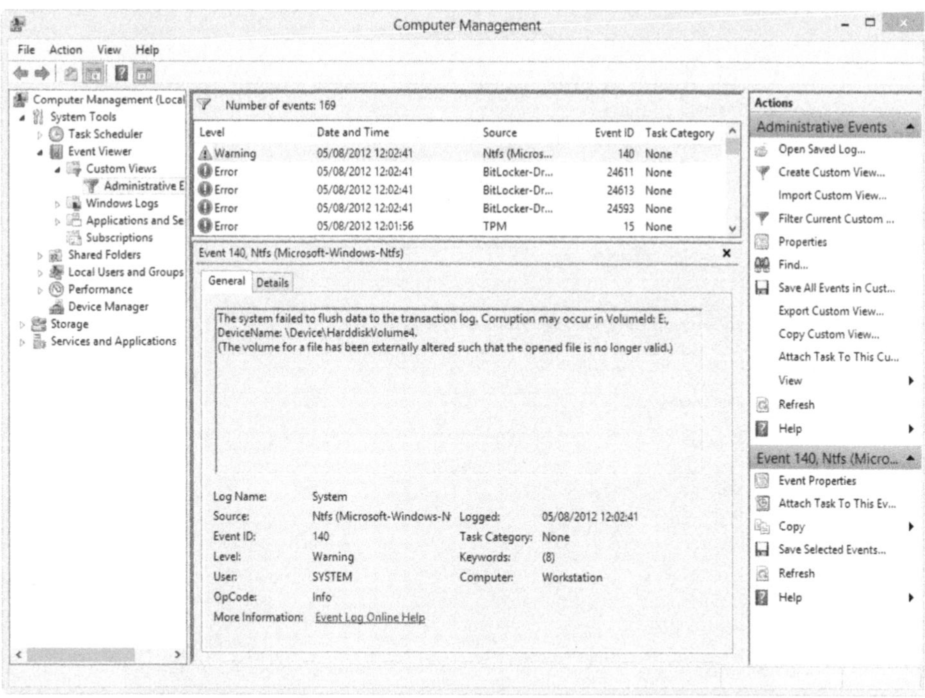

Figure 33-6 The Event Viewer in the Actions pane.

Filtering Event Logs Windows 8 stores a great deal of information in its event logs; being able to filter event log information can be a real time-saver when you're troubleshooting problems. In the Actions pane of the Computer Management console, you can click the Filter Current Custom option to open the Filter Current Custom View dialog box (see Figure 33-7). You can also filter by the event source, namely by Windows component and by user.

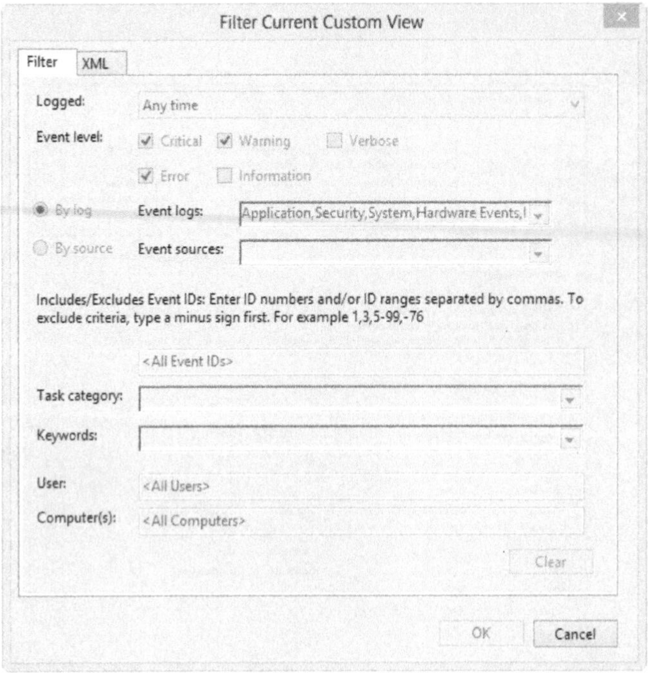

Figure 33-7 Filtering events.

Attaching a Task to an Event You can attach tasks to specific events so that those tasks execute automatically when the event occurs, which is useful for problems that occur only occasionally and are therefore difficult to diagnose. Examples of tasks include automatically running the Problem Steps Recorder to alert you that something you want to see is happening, or sending an email to a support person, letting him or her know that a specific error or event has recurred.

You can also trigger an on-screen message when an event occurs (see Figure 33-8) by right-clicking the event and clicking Attach Task To Event, and then on the Action page of the Create Basic Task Wizard that appears, clicking Display A Message. You might want to use this message as an alert that something has happened (remember, not all errors are immediately obvious), and include instructions about what the user should do when it does happen. For instance, this displayed message could direct a user to send an email to a support person, detailing exactly what software was running, what was happening when the error occurred, what hardware was plugged into the computer, and what user account was being used.

To trigger an on-screen event, in the Actions pane, highlight an event, and then click Attach Task To This Event.

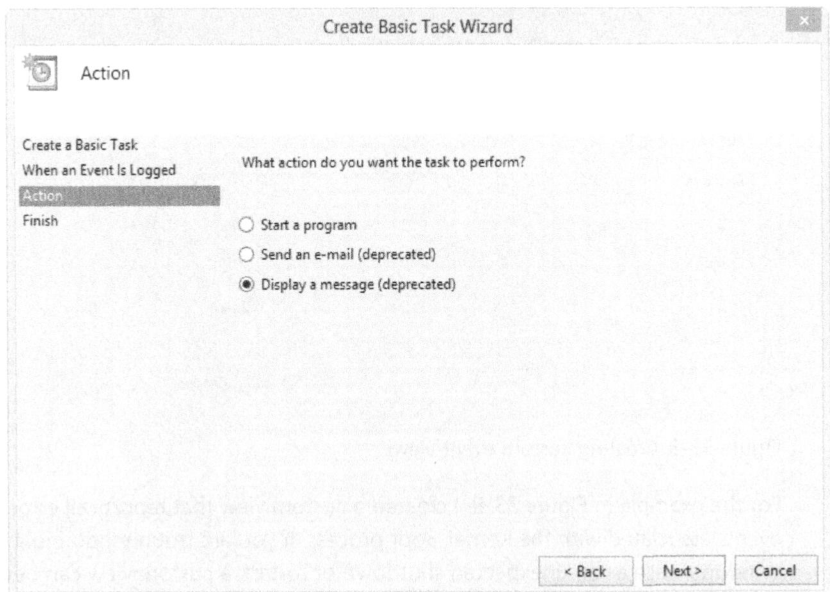

Figure 33-8 Setting up a task to display a message for an event.

Creating Custom Views In the Create Custom View dialog box, on the Filter tab, you can create new views in Event Viewer (see Figure 33-9). To do this, in Computer Management, right-click Custom Views, or on the Actions menu, click Create Custom View.

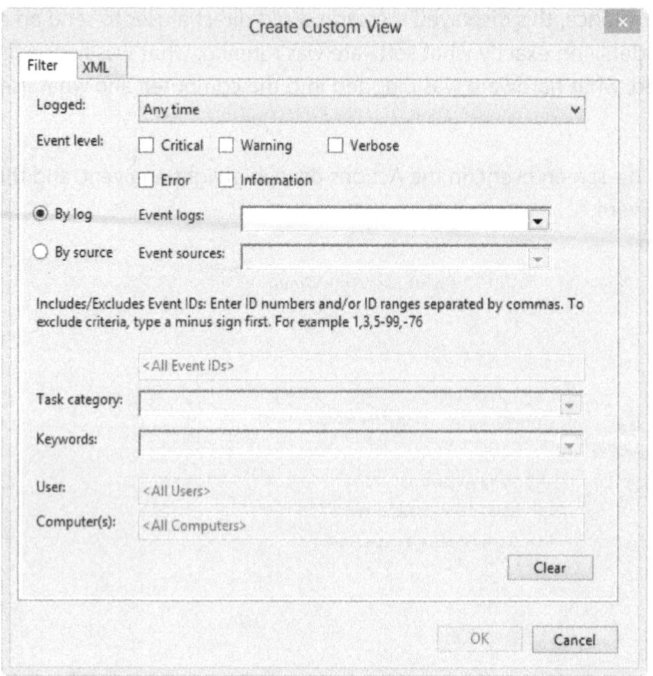

Figure 33-9 Creating custom event views.

For the example in Figure 33-9, I created a custom view that reports all errors and critical events associated with the Kernel-Boot process. If you are troubleshooting a specific part of Windows, such as an unexpected shutdown or restart, a custom view can be an invaluable time saver, because you can create a very detailed and concise error log that can then be exported and emailed to a support person.

Shared Folders and Local Users And Groups

The Shared Folders and Local Users And Groups nodes are similar. Both, which you access in the left pane of the Computer Management console, give you control over file and folder shares, and any users or groups of users on the computer. You can right-click any item in the center pane of this window to review the item's properties. The Shared Folders and Local Users And Groups nodes are useful, for instance, in the following scenarios:

- Shared files are not showing on another computer.
- A file is being reported as open by Windows but does not appear to be open.
- You want to set specific security or other policies for a user or a group of users.

Device Manager

Device Manager is a quick and easy way to gain access to the hardware drivers in Windows 8 (see Figure 33-10).

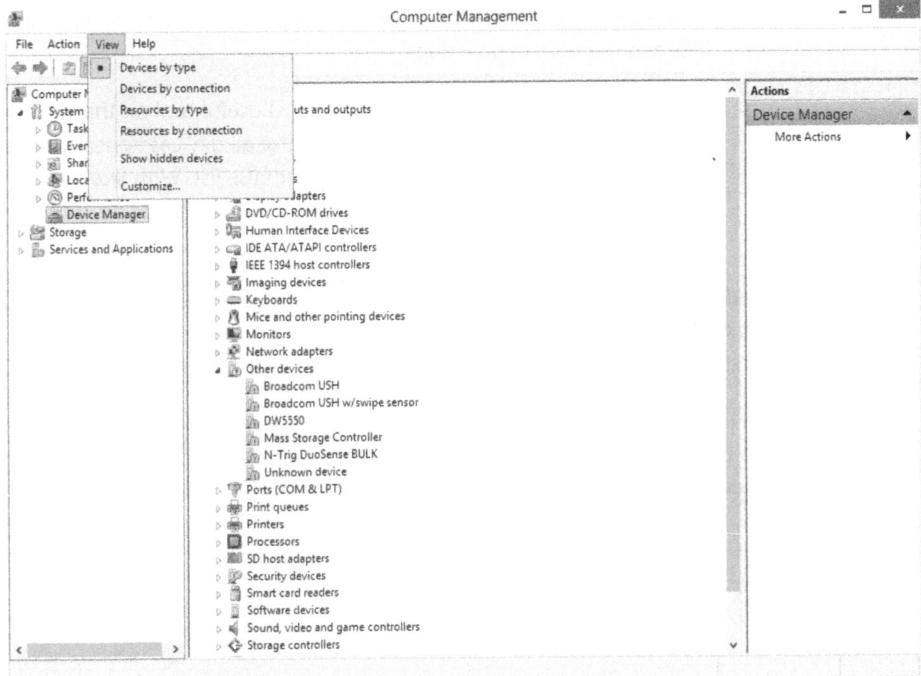

Figure 33-10 Device Manager in Computer Management.

On the View menu are the following options:

- **Devices By Type** This is the default Device Manager view, showing your hardware devices grouped by their device type.
- **Devices By Connection** This view shows core Windows hardware devices for your computer.
- **Resources By Type** This can be an extremely useful view, showing you, for instance, what devices are sharing interrupt requests (IRQs), memory segments, and input/output (I/O) connections with your motherboard. Some hardware problems are caused by IRQ conflicts, and you can determine this in the Resources By Type view.
- **Resources By Connection** This view shows core Windows hardware devices by I/O, IRQ, and memory connections.
- **Show Hidden Devices** Probably the most useful tool on the View menu, this option shows hidden devices. By default, not all devices appear in Device Manager, and sometimes a device can disappear from the list. With Show Hidden Devices, you can enable Device Manager to display all the devices that are attached to or are a part of your computer.

Working with Driver Properties On the tabs in the Properties window for a device, you can find a lot of useful information for troubleshooting hardware and driver problems. To access the Properties window, right-click a device, and then click Properties.

On the Driver tab for the device Properties, you can see the name of the driver provider, the date the driver was written, and its version number (see Figure 33-11). You can also see whether the driver has passed Microsoft Hardware Compatibility Testing.

Figure 33-11 The Properties dialog box for a device may offer custom tabs, but the default tabs are General, Driver, Details, Events, and Resources.

Obtaining driver details can help you troubleshoot issues. For example, suppose you installed a driver from a specific hardware manufacturer because you know it to be stable, but later find that the driver listed in Device Manager shows the driver was written by Microsoft, indicating the driver was updated through Windows Update. If that driver is causing problems, you can click the Roll Back Driver button to restore the previous driver.

INSIDE OUT Hiding driver updates in Windows Update

If you find that a driver delivered through Windows Update is causing problems, and you don't want it to be reinstalled automatically, roll back the driver and then run Windows Update manually. When the driver reappears in the available updates list, right-click it, and then select Hide.

The Driver tab might also show you that a driver is quite old and needs updating. Windows might be unable to find a new driver automatically because the manufacturer hasn't submitted its drivers for official testing. In this circumstance, you would need to visit the driver manufacturer's website and obtain the driver manually.

Backing Up an Individual Driver Sometimes you may want to back up an individual driver. Some hardware—especially earlier hardware that can be problematic to install, or hardware that is used across multiple computers—is easier to install when you have all the relevant driver files. This is especially true of some custom and security hardware.

By clicking the Driver Details button on the Driver tab, you can see exactly what files constitute a particular hardware driver. This is important, because as discussed in Chapter 14, "Easy Ways to Repair Windows 8," you can back up hardware drivers by making copies of the \Windows\System32\DRIVERS and \DriverStore folders. However, you can see in Figure 33-12 that some hardware requires files to be stored elsewhere within the Windows folder structure.

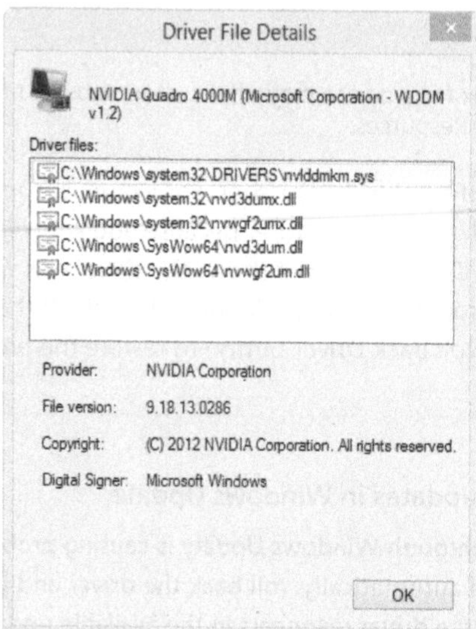

Figure 33-12 Finding the files for a specific driver.

INSIDE OUT **Does a driver require additional software?**

Many hardware drivers require additional software to work properly (or at all). Biometric devices and sensors are good examples; dynamic-link library (DLL) files can be required to plug the sensor controls into Windows Control Panel.

Commonly used hardware such as webcams and printers have additional software installed by default that add plugins to Devices And Printers. These pieces of hardware are unlikely to stop working if this software is missing, but functionality can be reduced.

Note

I cover the Disk Management feature for managing storage and hard disks in Chapter 20, "Using Advanced Repair Methods." You use Disk Management to see all fixed and removable hard disks that are attached to your computer and to partition, format, and initialize new ones.

Services and Applications

Services are programs that require no interaction from the user and that perform specific tasks in Windows, such as searching for Windows updates or print spooling. In the Computer Management console, in the Services And Applications node, click Services to see, in the central pane, what services are installed in Windows 8 and which are running. You can also perform actions on these services. Click the Status column heading to sort the services by status to easily see which are currently started (see Figure 33-13).

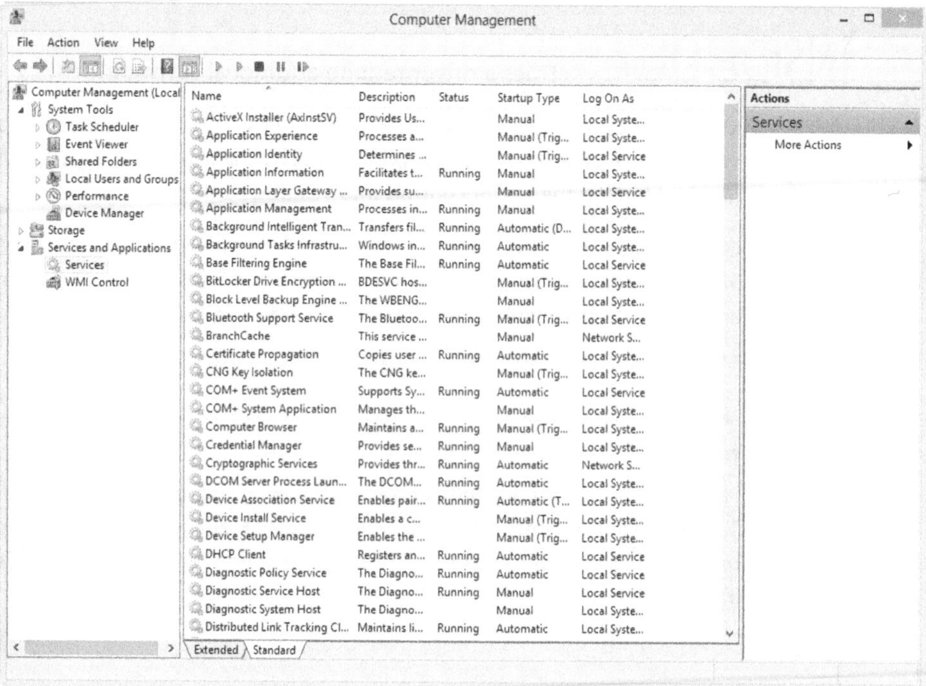

Figure 33-13 Windows services.

Service descriptions can help you determine what the services are and what they do. To view a service's settings, right-click the service, and then click Properties. In the Properties dialog box, you can set the service's status and disable the service if necessary.

On the Recovery tab in the Properties dialog box for a service (see Figure 33-14), you can set what Windows should do when a service causes a problem and stops responding. One option is to Run A Program; for instance, you could run the Steps Recorder.

> **Note**
>
> **You can also start the Steps Recorder from the Start screen by searching for psr. The program is listed on your Windows drive as \Windows\System32\psr.exe.**

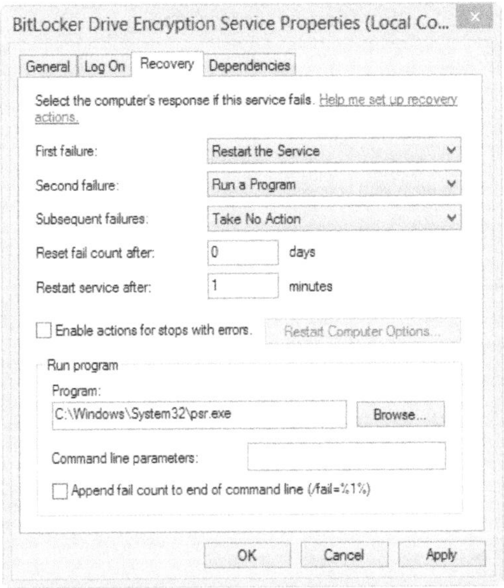

Figure 33-14 The Recovery tab in the Properties dialog box of a service.

WMI Control

Windows Management Instrumentation (WMI) is a way for your computer to access and share management information over an enterprise network. It is used by management tools such as Windows System Center Configuration Manager. WMI Control is listed under the Services And Applications node. (Clicking WMI Control in the Computer Management console will probably not display anything on your computer.)

Performance Information And Tools

Performance Information And Tools, which you access from Control Panel and learned about briefly in Chapter 19, "Using Windows 8 Advanced Diagnostic Tools," offers a large number of powerful diagnostic tools that you can use to repair issues with Windows 8, for example, you can adjust power settings, indexing options, and disk cleanup. Gamers and computer enthusiasts can use it to rate their computers so that they can compare their Windows Experience Index scores to their friends' scores (see Figure 33-15).

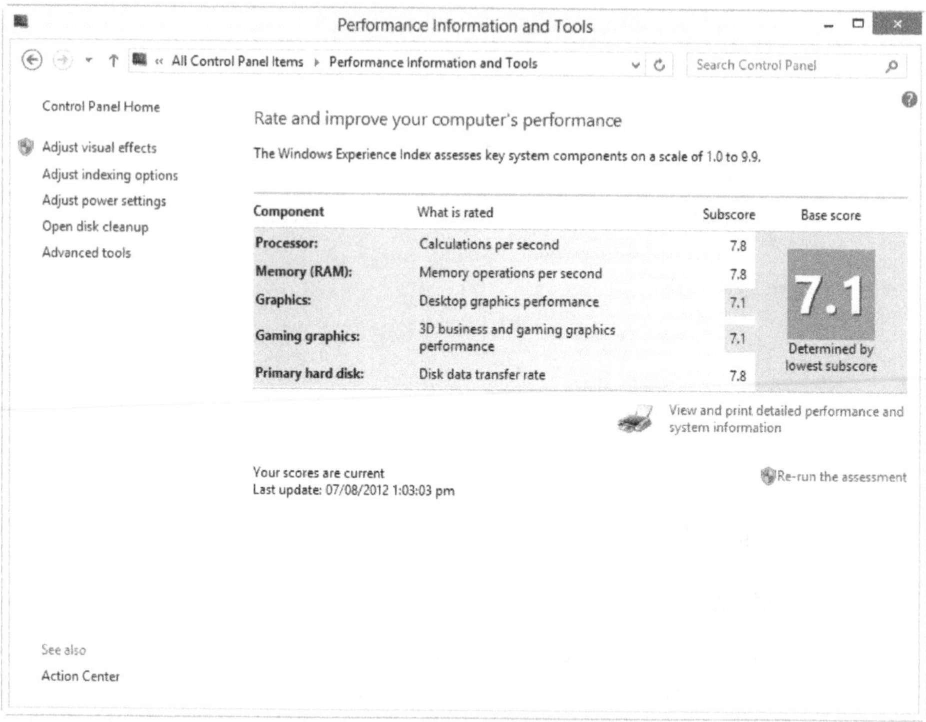

Figure 33-15 The Performance Information And Tools window.

Visual Effects

The visual effects tools control how windows appear on your desktop, and they control features such as animations and shadows. To access the Visual Effects options, in the pane on the left side of Performance Information And Tools, click the Adjust Visual Effects link to show options that you can use to do much more than just change the way some Windows components appear (see Figure 33-16).

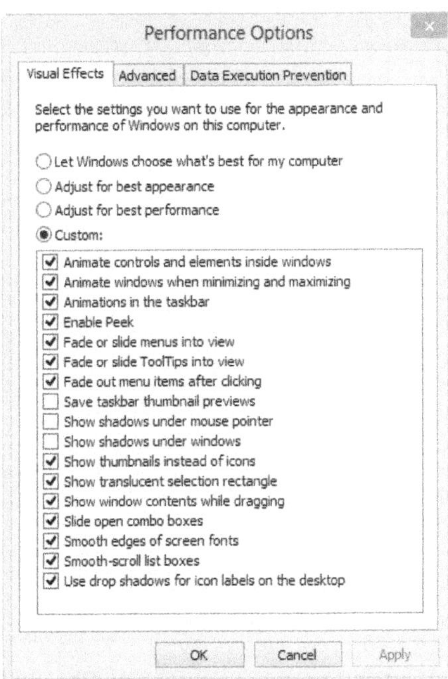

Figure 33-16 Adjusting the visual effects.

On the Visual Effects tab, you can turn off settings that are causing Windows to behave sluggishly, such as animation settings. On some computers, particularly earlier computers or low-power computers such as netbooks and tablets, changing some of these settings improves the performance of the operating system. The Visual Effects tab also includes default settings for running Windows 8 so that it is optimized for best appearance and best performance.

On the Advanced tab (see Figure 33-17), you can adjust the performance of Windows for the benefit of either programs or background services. You should select the Programs option unless you are running a dedicated device for a specific task, such as a file or print server.

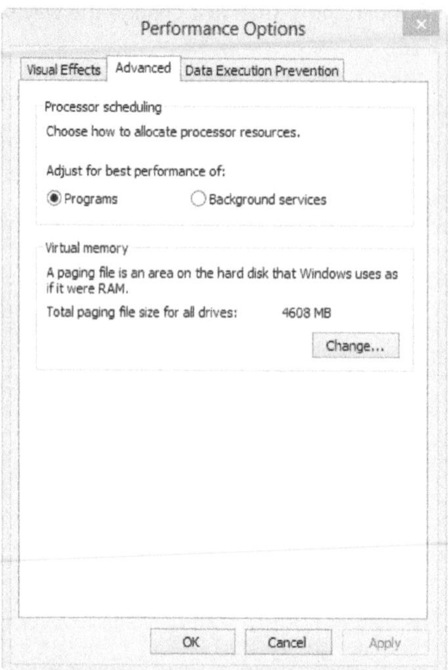

Figure 33-17 Virtual memory and processor scheduling settings.

Data Execution Prevention (DEP) is a system to prevent viruses and other malware from running code from nonexecutable memory. Running code from nonexecutable memory can cause a buffer overflow in the memory stack and cause the operating system to become unresponsive. A *buffer overflow* occurs when a program writes data to memory that is reserved and/or being used by another program or service. On the Data Execution Prevention tab, you can configure the settings for DEP, as depicted in Figure 33-18. These settings are related directly to visual settings.

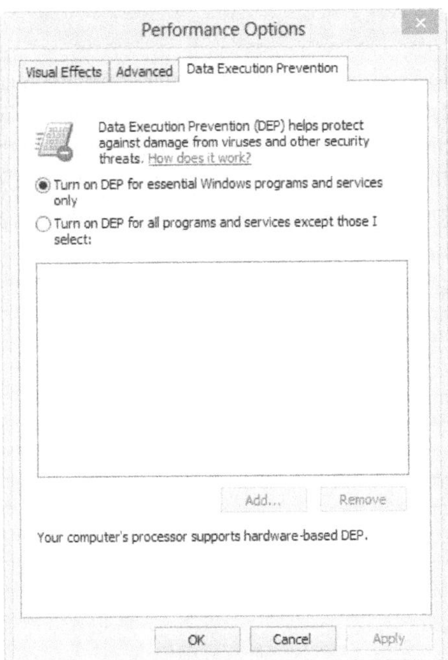

Figure 33-18 DEP settings.

Unfortunately, some software will be blocked by DEP, for example, certain games. If you are having a problem with a program or game, try allowing it through DEP. To do this, perform the following steps:

1. On the Data Execution Prevention tab, click the Turn On DEP For All Programs And Services Except Those I Select option.
2. Click Add, and then go to the folder where the program is located. This location is commonly in the Program Files folder on drive C.
3. Select the program you want to allow through DEP, and then click Open.
4. Add any other related programs (multiplayer mode, for example) the same way. When you are finished, click OK.

Indexing Options

The Windows 8 Index is a database of all of your files and their contents. A corrupted database can prevent the search facility in Windows 8 from operating correctly. To access the Indexing Options dialog box, on the Start screen, search for **indexing**, and then click Indexing Options. You can reset the index by clicking Advanced in the Indexing Options dialog box and then clicking Rebuild in the Advanced Options dialog box (see Figure 33-19).

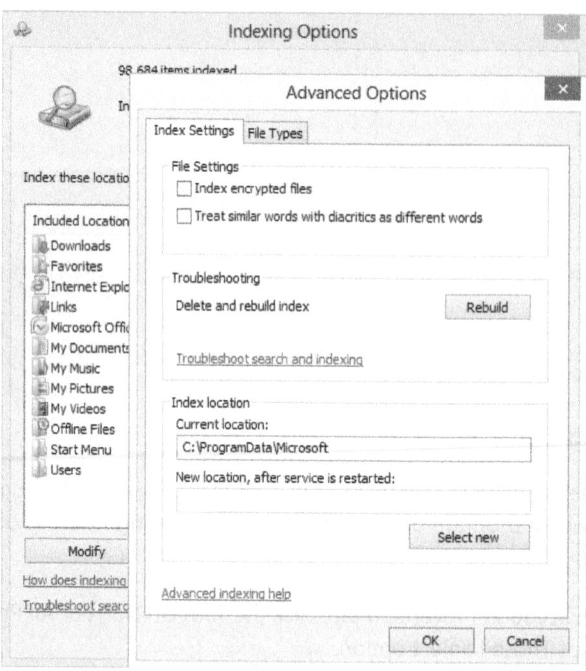

Figure 33-19 Rebuilding the index.

Power Settings

I had a problem on a computer I built myself that caused the computer to go to sleep every few seconds. The only way around this was to keep wiggling the mouse and pressing a key on the keyboard until I could access the power options and disable the Sleep function. This was an annoying first step each time I reinstalled Windows 8.

In the Power Options window (see Figure 33-20), you can change settings for Windows 8 that go far beyond choosing power options for running a laptop or changing the default action of the power button.

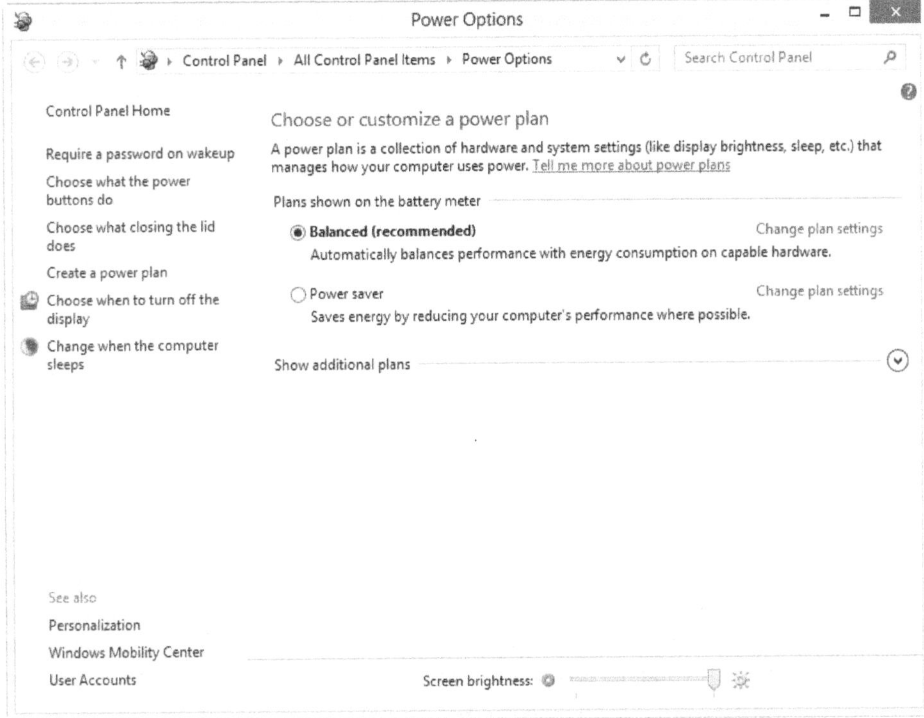

Figure 33-20 The Windows 8 Power Options dialog box.

To open the Advanced Settings dialog box, in the left pane of the Power Options dialog box, click Choose When To Turn Off The Display, and then click Change Advanced Power Settings (see Figure 33-21). In Advanced Settings, you can change the power settings for a wide variety of Windows components. Note that on a portable computer, the Power Options dialog box displays additional options by default, giving you much more control over power consumption and battery life.

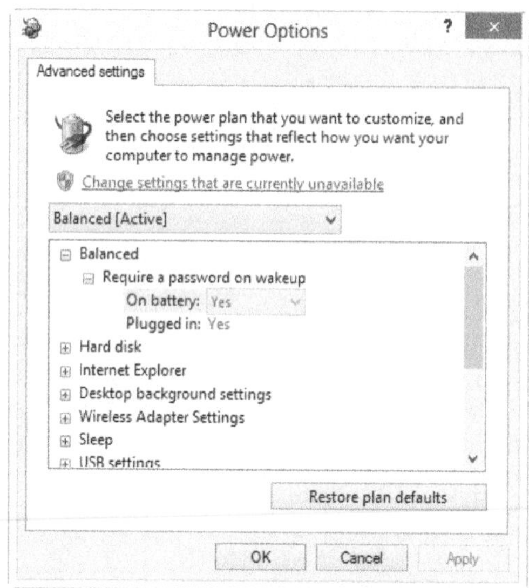

Figure 33-21 Advanced power management options.

Sometimes a hard disk or network adapter doesn't function properly after a computer is brought out of sleep mode. In the Power Options dialog box, you can disable settings such as those for Sleep and Hibernate. Near the top of the Power Options dialog box is the Change Settings That Are Currently Unavailable link, which you can click to access additional power settings in Windows that are not typically available to modify, such as requiring that Windows ask for a password upon wakeup. (This option is typically assumed to be a security setting and not a power setting.)

Advanced Tools

This section describes the major tools in Advanced Tools (Performance Monitor, Resource Monitor, Task Manager, and System Health Report) and shows you shows you how to use them to troubleshoot problems with your computer. Advanced Tools (see Figure 33-22) are also discussed in detail in Chapter 19.

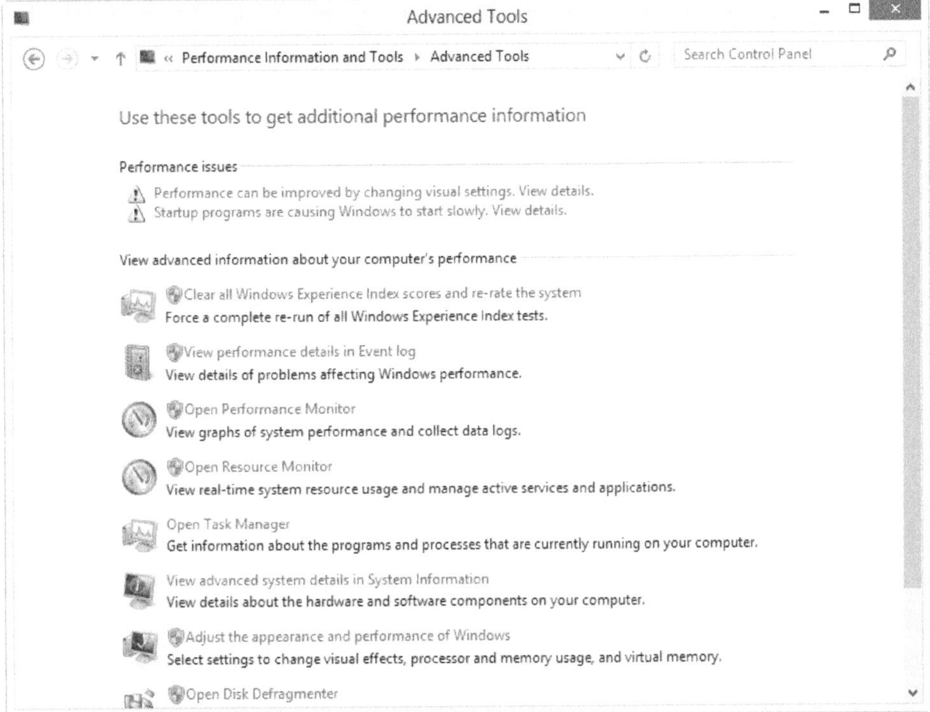

Figure 33-22 The Advanced Tools dialog box.

Performance Monitor

By default, the Windows 8 Performance Monitor shows you only the current processor usage on your computer (see Figure 33-23). You can customize it and add all sorts of other tools and features to it. To access it, from Advanced Tools, click Open Performance Monitor, and then in the left pane, click Performance Monitor. You can read more about the Performance Monitor in Chapter 19.

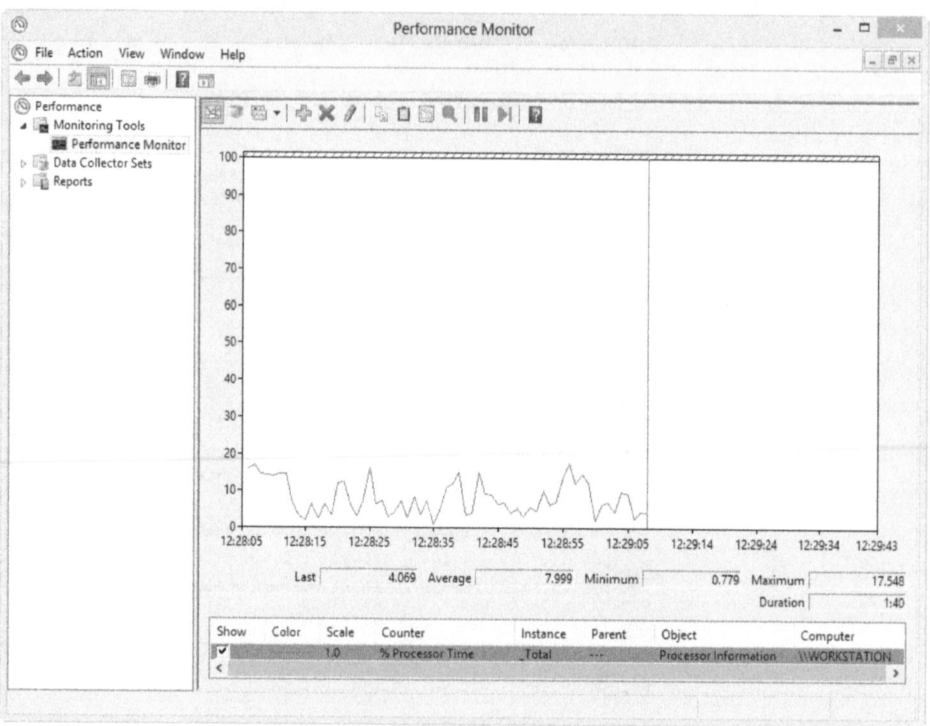

Figure 33-23 The Performance Monitor in action.

A *counter* is a live report for one aspect of your computer's hardware or software performance, such as outgoing network traffic or the data throughput for a Windows service. You can add counters to the Performance Monitor, and there are many to choose from (see Figure 33-24). To add a counter, on the top toolbar, click the plus sign (+), which you can see in Figure 33-23.

Some of the most useful counters you can add are for the network interface. Although the Network Monitor can tell you how much data is being sent and received, the network traffic monitor in Task Manager, which presents the information as a graph, doesn't show Internet traffic. By adding counters to some of the network interface tools in Performance Monitor, you can see a better real-time interpretation of what is going on. This graph view can be more useful than a numeric counter because you can more easily determine what effect particular devices or software are having on your Internet connection.

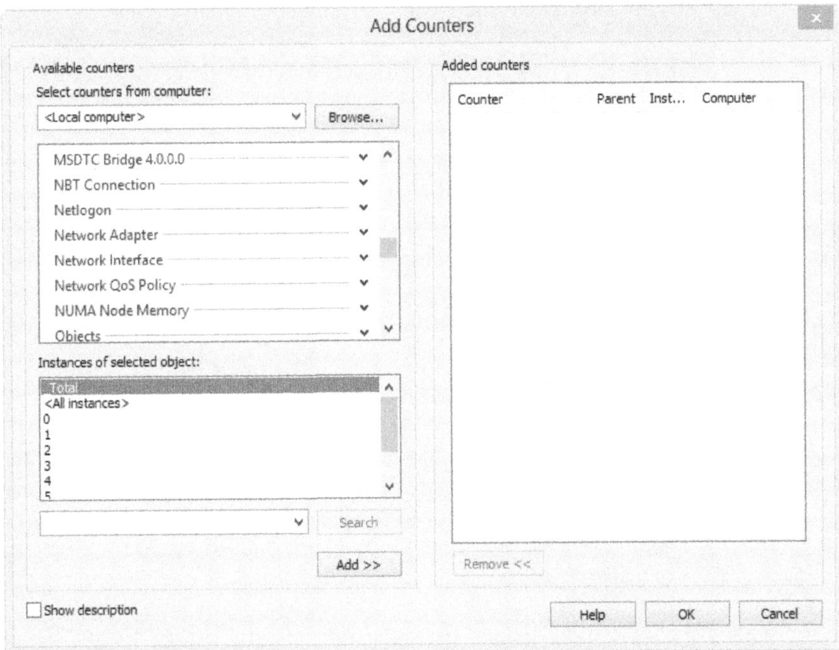

Figure 33-24 Adding counters to Performance Monitor.

You can use the pen icon in the toolbar above the graph in the Performance Monitor window to highlight one or more indicators on the graph to make them stand out. You can also clear any additional indicators in the bottom of the Window to disable them temporarily or permanently.

Creating Data Collector Sets *Data Collector Sets* are invaluable because they provide details about parts of Windows 8 that are causing issues. You can save data from the Performance Monitor as Data Collector Sets and include predefined system and user-configurable options. You access Data Collector Sets in the left pane in the Performance Monitor dialog box.

You can export Data Collector Sets so that they can be viewed on another computer by a support technician, or imported and viewed in Performance Monitor on your own computer. To create a Data Collector Set, perform the following steps:

1. In Performance Monitor, in the left pane, click Data Collector Sets, and then click User Defined.

2. Right-click anywhere in the main pane, click New, and then click Data Collector Set (see Figure 33-25).

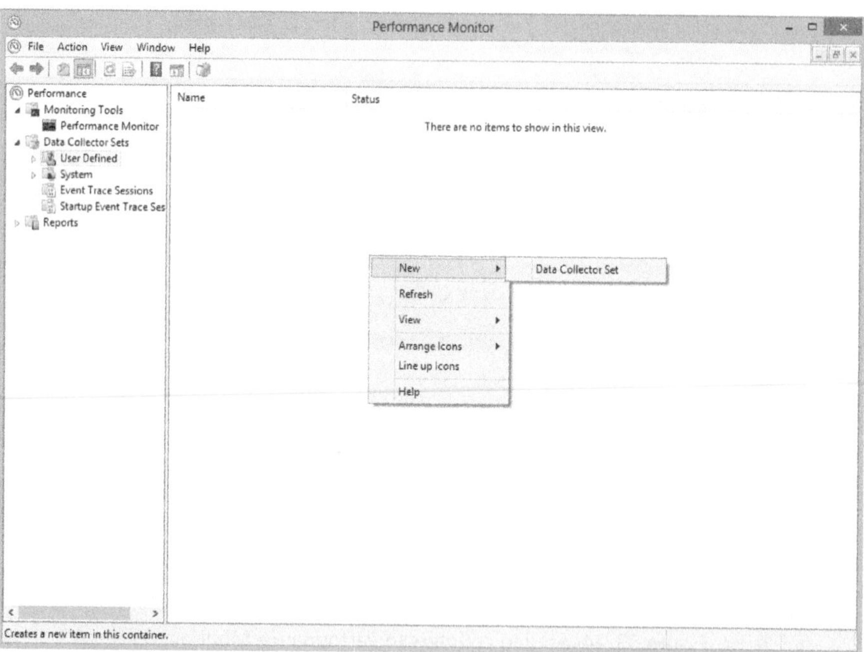

Figure 33-25 Creating a new Data Collector Set.

3. In the Create New Data Collector Set wizard (see Figure 33-26), select either the option to create your Data Collector Set from a template or the option to exercise more control by creating it manually, and then click Next.

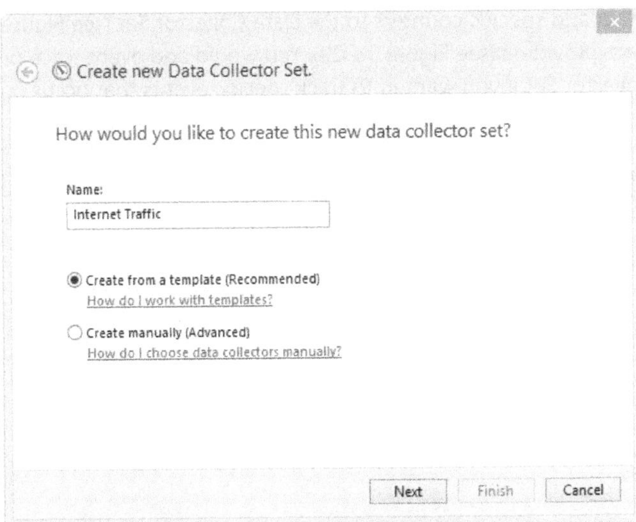

Figure 33-26 Naming your Data Collector Set.

4. If you are creating a Data Collector Set manually, choose the type of information you want collected, and then click Next (see Figure 33-27).

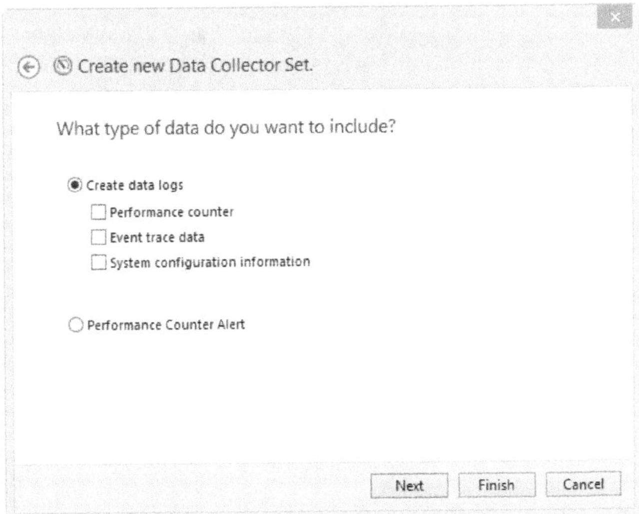

Figure 33-27 Choosing what to include in the Data Collector Set.

5. Either add specific counters to the Data Collector Set (see Figure 33-28) or add event trace providers (see Figure 33-29). You would add event trace providers to the Data Collector Set if you wanted to track specific events that occur on the computer.

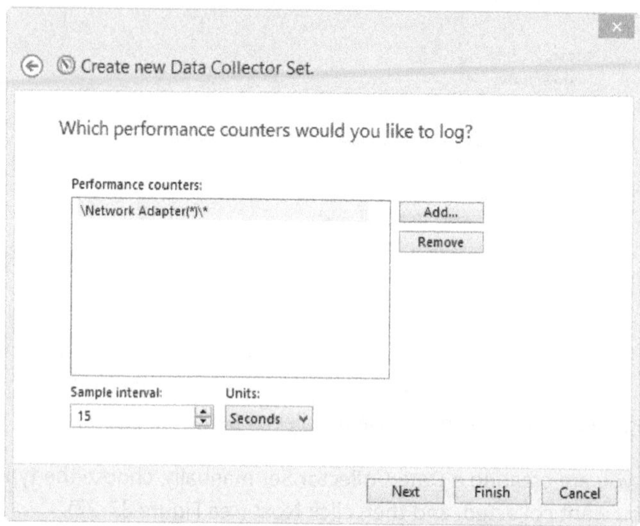

Figure 33-28 Adding counters to the Data Collector Set.

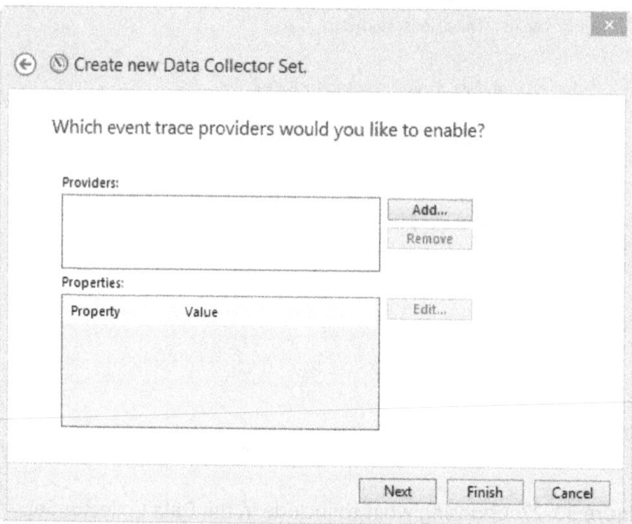

Figure 33-29 Adding an event trace provider to a Data Collector Set. You can customize properties for events by clicking the Edit button.

6. Choose a file name and storage location for the logs. And then click Next. For a stand-alone computer, this location should be the default location, but if you collect logs on a Windows server, you might want to choose a different location. This can be on your computer or on a network location, as illustrated in Figure 33-30.

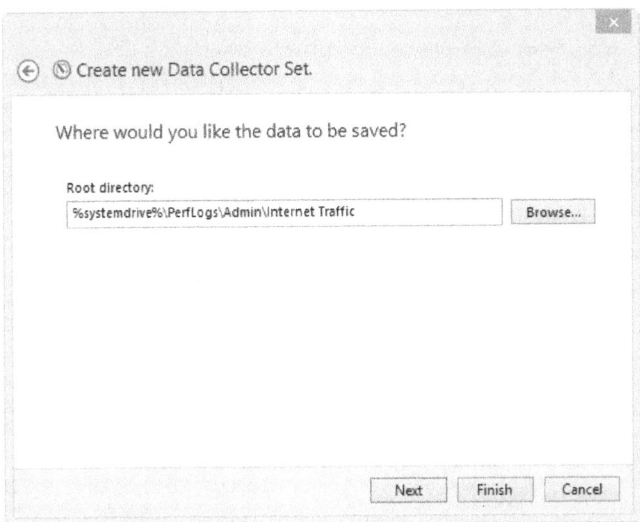

Figure 33-30 Saving the Data Collector Set.

7. Choose a user for which the Data Collector Set should run, or use the default (current) user (see Figure 33-31), and then click Finish.

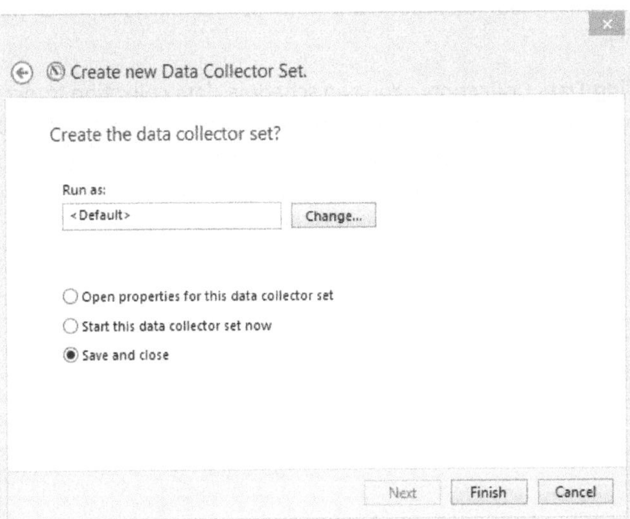

Figure 33-31 Choosing how a Data Collector Set runs.

Viewing Data Collector Sets The performance logs for Windows 8 are kept by default on drive C in the PerfLogs\System\Diagnostics*your computer name* (see Figure 33-32). In this folder, you can either open the files to read them or email them to a support person.

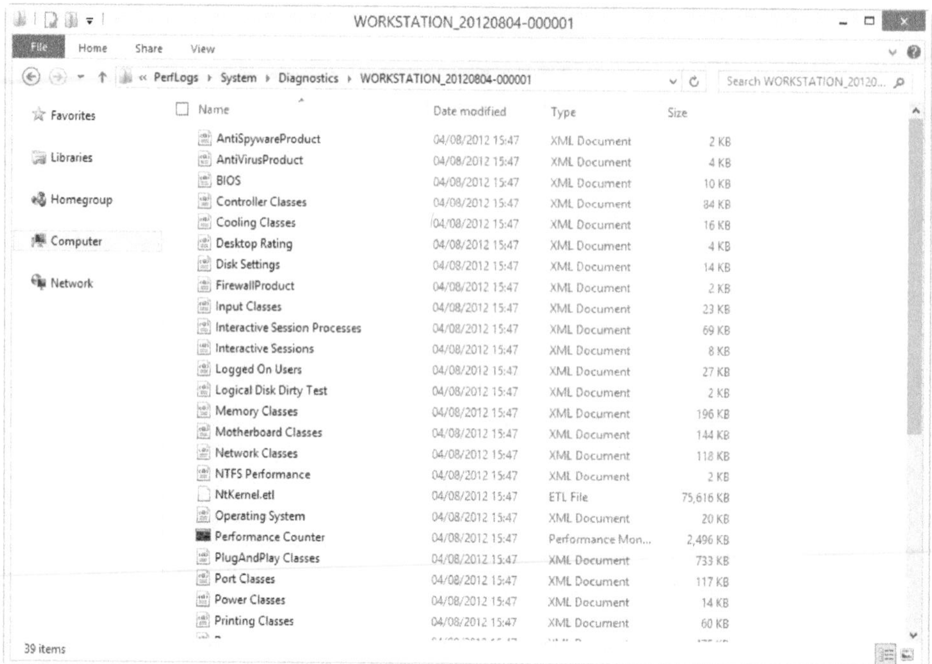

Figure 33-32 The custom performance logs sit in the root of the hard disk or partition on which Windows 8 is installed. You need to drill down several folders to see all your logs and Data Collector Sets.

Scheduling Data Collection You can schedule data collection to occur at certain times and on certain days. You might, for instance, note that a particular problem tends to occur only on Mondays (when, perhaps, the payroll is processed), so you can set the collection to run only on that day. Alternatively, if you are prone to leaving your computer on overnight, you might want to collect data only during working hours.

To schedule data collection, right-click your custom Data Collector Set, and then click Properties. In the Properties dialog box that opens, on the Schedule tab (see Figure 33-33), identify when you want data collected by clicking Add.

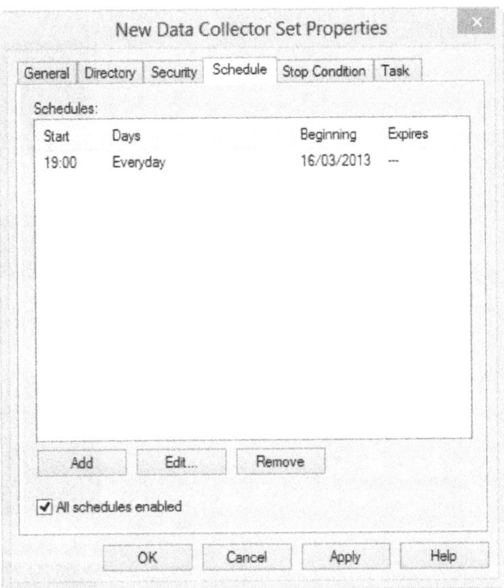

Figure 33-33 Scheduling Data Collector Sets.

Resource Monitor

As you learned in Chapter 19, you use the Resource Monitor to view information about how your hardware and software are operating in real time. You can view data about specific Windows 8 processes or more general information.

Figure 33-34 shows five tabs across the top of the Resource Monitor: Overview, CPU, Memory, Disk, and Network. Each of these tabs provides general or specific information about every piece of hardware, software, and Windows component that is using a resource, complete with the details of how much of the resource each item is consuming.

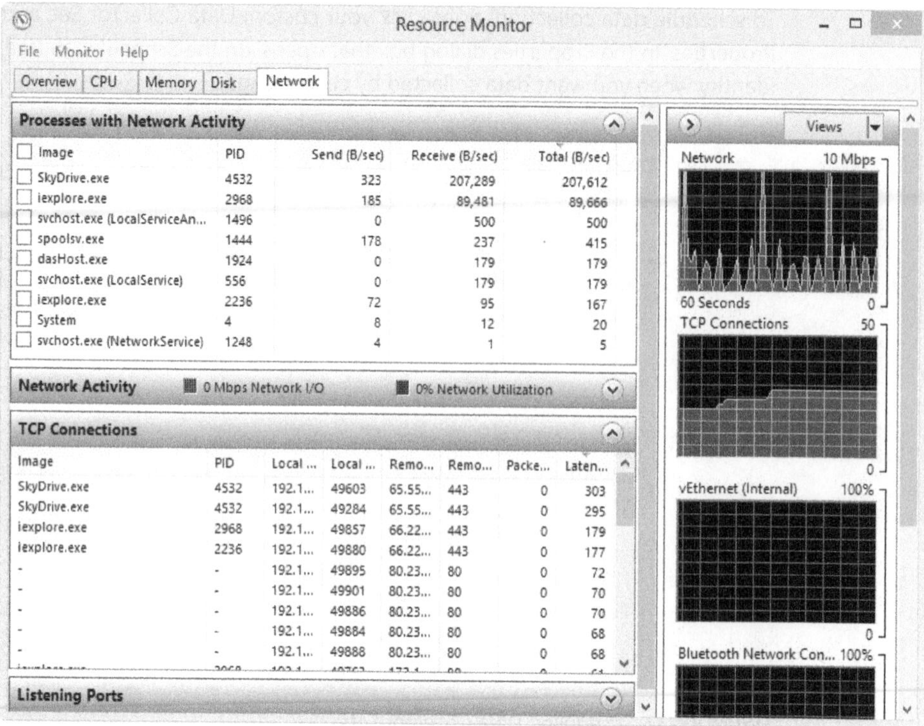

Figure 33-34 The Windows 8 Resource Monitor.

Figure 33-35 shows an active Memory tab. You can see exactly which programs and Windows components are using the memory on the computer and identify whether any are consuming unnecessary resources. The columns can be sorted and filtered by clicking them.

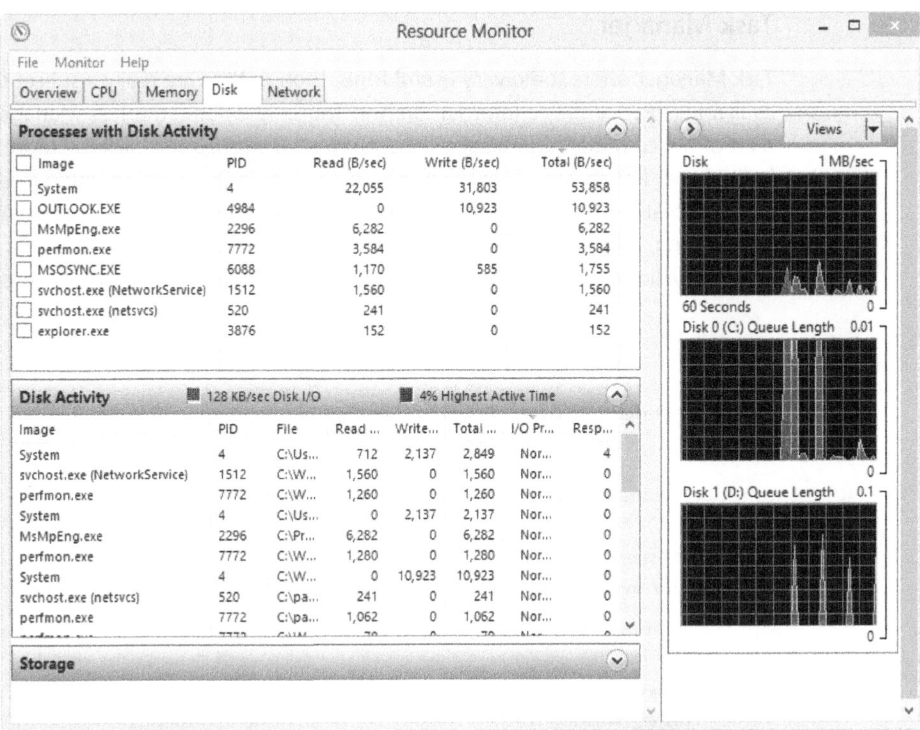

Figure 33-35 You can use the Resource Monitor to find resource-hungry processes.

The Resource Monitor is especially useful for monitoring disk and network activity. On the Disk tab and the Memory tab, not only can you view programs and services that are using those resources, but you can see the throughput of data.

The Resource Monitor offers additional functionality over the Performance Monitor because if there is a problem, you can easily see what specific disk, program, network device, or process is causing the issue.

In the main pane, at the top of the Resource Monitor window, are check boxes adjacent to running programs and processes. If you need to monitor specific programs and processes, you can select their check boxes; all the information in the other graphs and panels will change to show information about these selected items exclusively.

Task Manager

Task Manager offers some very useful tools, though they are really a subset of the tools available in Performance Information And Tools. By default, the Task Manager shows only a list of the currently running apps and programs, but you can click the More Details button in the lower-left corner of the window to display much more information (see Figure 33-36). The information provided, such as the amount of CPU time and memory that a program or app is using, is heat mapped, meaning that greater resource consumption is highlighted in stronger yellows and reds. This makes identifying troublesome programs easy.

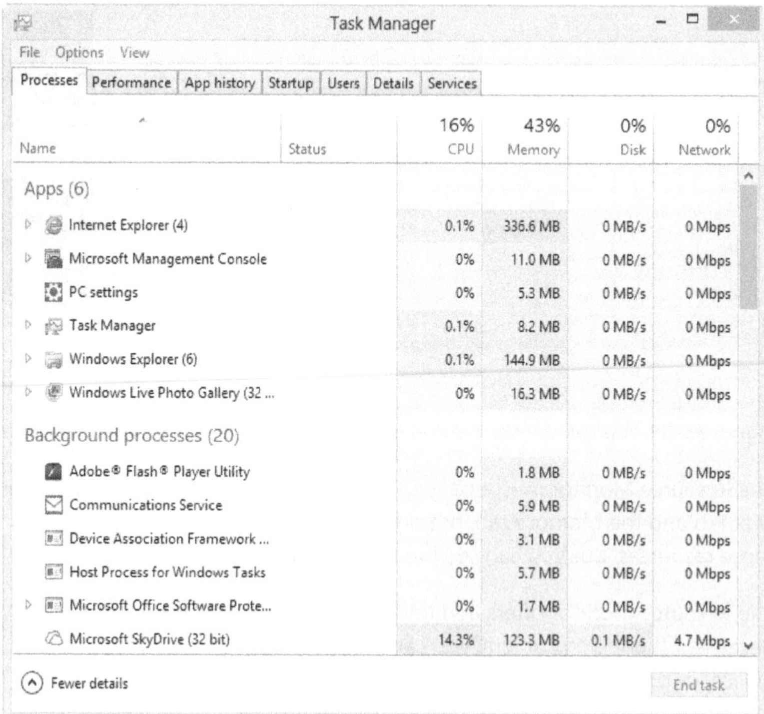

Figure 33-36 The Windows 8 Task Manager.

The Performance tab provides helpful graphs for CPU, Memory, Disk, and Network activity that can give you, on the desktop, a quick overview of the status of your computer. If you want the running software on your computer to inform you of its CPU, memory, and Internet network usage, right-click the graphs, and then click Summary View, which shrinks the Task Manager to a much smaller window (see Figure 33-37). This window can then sit on the desktop as a live monitor for your computer's performance.

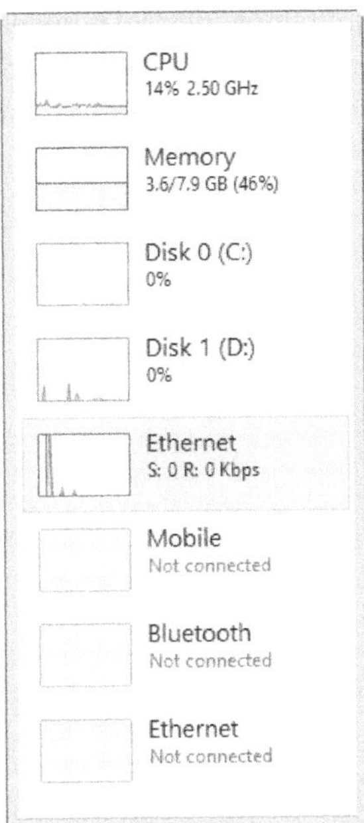

Figure 33-37 The Summary View in Task Manager. You can collapse the graphs in the Performance tab to a smaller window that shows either graphical or text-based information.

You can also right-click the main large graph and click Graph Summary View to view only this single graph on the desktop (see Figure 33-38). You can switch between graphs by right-clicking the graph and selecting another metric from the View options.

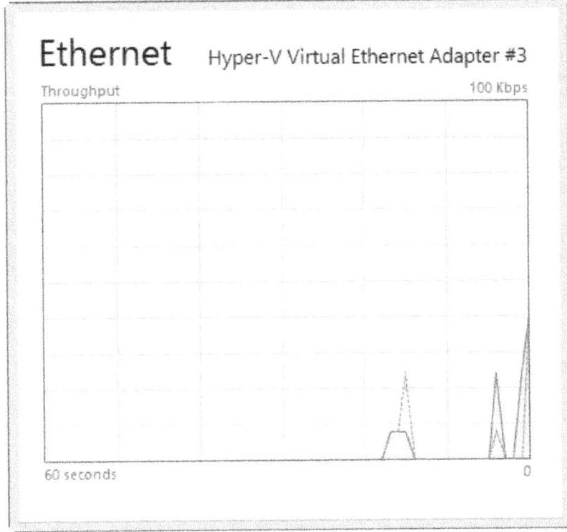

Figure 33-38 A minimized graph view.

Some of these graphs, such as Network and CPU, also offer additional views and information. For example, you can view all the processors in your computer individually (see Figure 33-39), or see full and detailed live information about all your network connections (see Figure 33-40).

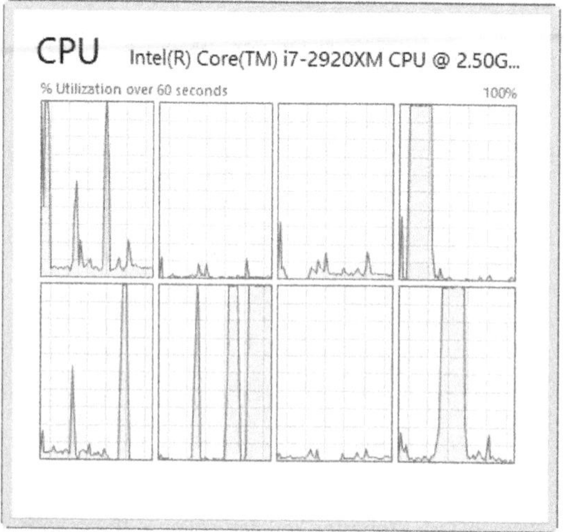

Figure 33-39 Viewing individual processors. This view can be useful for monitoring virtual machines, which can use their own processors.

Network Details

Property	Ethernet	Bluetooth	Wi-Fi
Network utilization	0%	0%	0.04%
Link speed	10 Gbps	3 Mbps	150 Mbps
State	Disconnected	Disconnected	Connected
Bytes sent throughput	0%	0%	0%
Bytes received throughput	0%	0%	0.03%
Bytes throughput	0%	0%	0.04%
Bytes sent	0	0	3,528,423
Bytes received	0	0	18,832,776
Bytes	0	0	22,361,199
Bytes sent per interval	0	0	310
Bytes received per interval	0	0	7,320
Bytes per interval	0	0	7,630
Unicasts sent	0	0	13,964
Unicasts received	0	0	7,938
Unicasts	0	0	21,902
Unicasts sent per interval	0	0	5
Unicasts received per interval	0	0	7
Unicasts per interval	0	0	12
Nonunicasts sent	0	0	32
Nonunicasts received	0	0	7
Nonunicasts	0	0	39
Nonunicasts sent per interval	0	0	0
Nonunicasts received per inter...	0	0	1
Nonunicasts per interval	0	0	1

Figure 33-40 Viewing detailed network information.

On the App History tab, you can see historical information about Windows 8 apps, such as the total network bandwidth they have consumed while in in use, and probably more helpful, how much network bandwidth their Tile Updates or Live Tiles on the Start screen use (see Figure 33-41). You can use this consumption information to monitor 3G or 4G mobile broadband when you do not have an unlimited data plan. This information is heat-mapped, too.

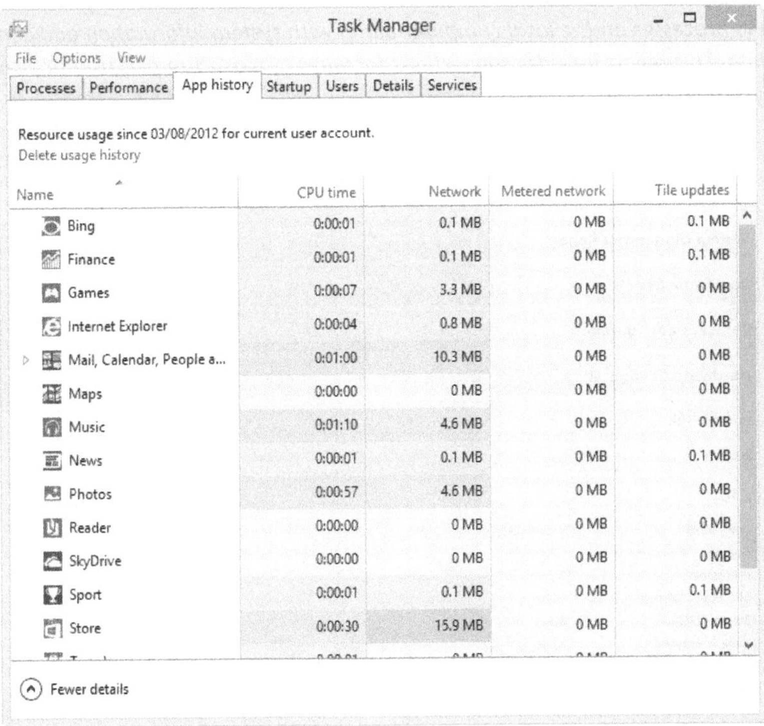

Figure 33-41 Monitoring Live Tile data usage.

On the Details tab, you find the more traditional Task Manager view and information.

System Health Report

As you learned in Chapter 19, a *System Health Report* (see Figure 33-42), sometimes known as a *system diagnostics report*, brings together all of the information from Performance Information And Tools. Windows 8 describes it as a tool that will:

Generate a report detailing the status of local hardware resources, system response times, and processes on the local computer along with system information and configuration data. This report includes suggestions for ways to maximize performance and streamline system operation.

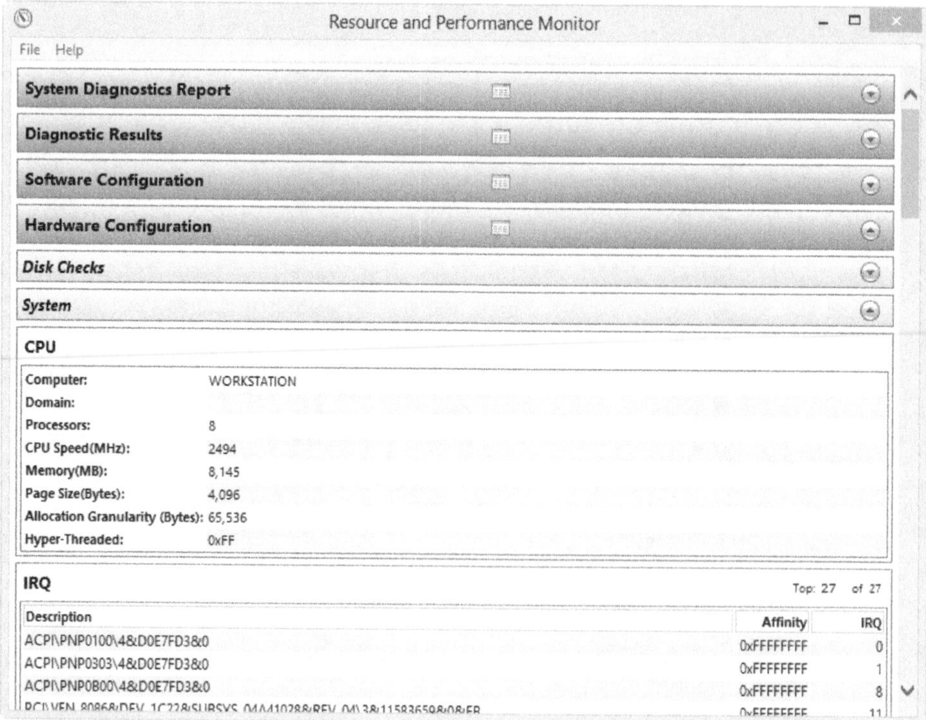

Figure 33-42 A System Health Report. It is fully compatible with screen readers.

It takes a minute for Windows 8 to collect all of its data for the report. Though the report can be long and complex, it is divided into collapsible panes, each detailing a specific part of the computer's hardware or software system, so that you can more easily find the information you require. Some panes, such as CPU, Memory, Network, and Disk, have their own collapsible panes. The available categories of information are as follows:

- **System Diagnostics Report** Provides a general overview of the whole computer system
- **Diagnostic Results** Details any issues or problems that have been found
- **Software Configuration** Reports on the computer's software and apps
- **Hardware Configuration** Reports on the hardware and drivers in your computer
- **CPU, Network, Disk, and Memory** Provides collapsible report sections
- **Report Statistics** Provides an overview of the whole report, with details about the types and number of each issue found

Note

In the System Health Report dialog box, on the File menu, you can choose to either save the report as a file or to automatically send it via email if you have email client software (such as Microsoft Outlook) installed on your computer.

Control Panel Troubleshooters

Windows 8 has built-in troubleshooters that can automatically detect and repair some common problems and issues with the operating system, your software, and your hardware (see Figure 33-43). To access the troubleshooters, on the Start screen, search for **troubleshooting**, and then click Troubleshooting in the search results. You can also access troubleshooters by clicking Troubleshooting in Action Center, or by clicking Troubleshooting when the Control Panel view is set to show all items (Large Icons or Small Icons views).

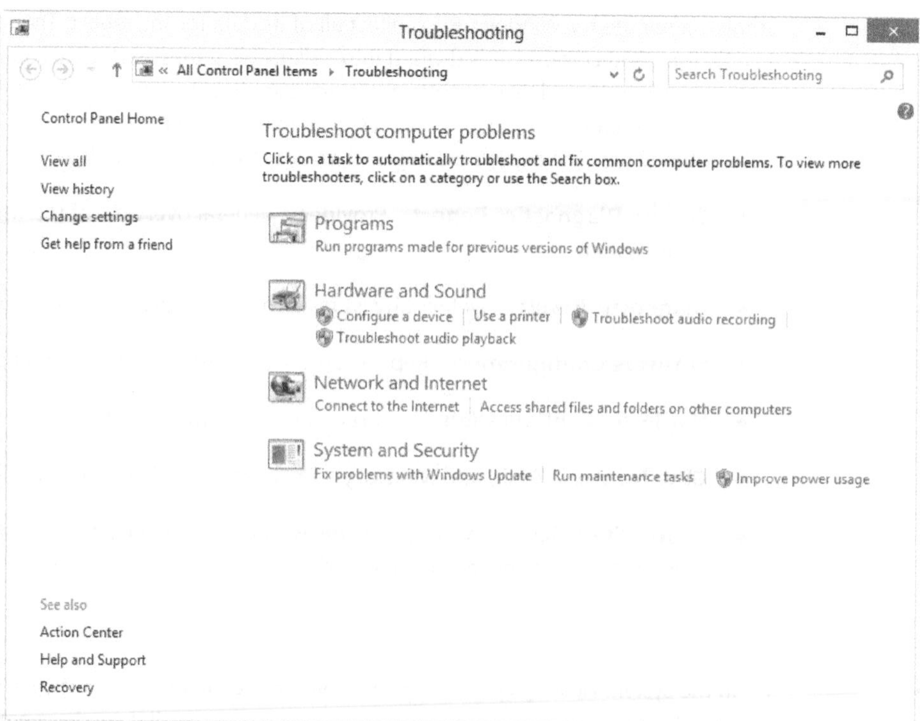

Figure 33-43 The Windows 8 Troubleshooting window.

The Windows 8 troubleshooters provide diagnostics that are extensible in two important ways: you can automatically update the built-in features when newer versions are available to enhance fixes and add functionality (see Figure 33-43), and corporate and business users can write their own troubleshooting add-ins.

The troubleshooters are organized into easy-to-use categories and are also searchable by using the search box in the upper-right corner of the window (see Figure 33-44, in which I have searched for Internet-related troubleshooters).

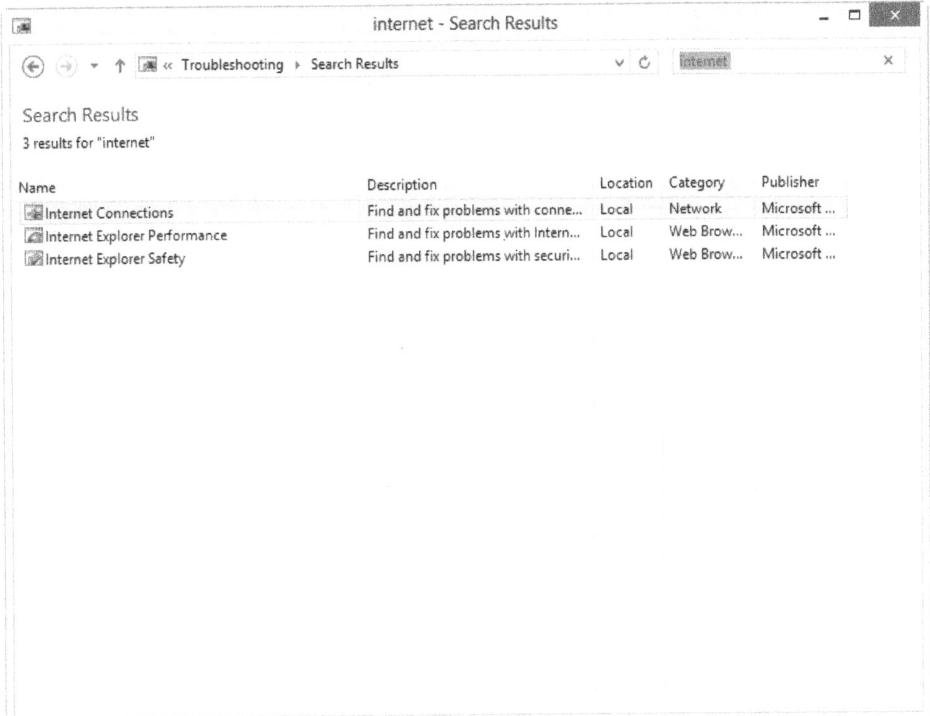

Figure 33-44 Searching for Internet-related troubleshooters.

You have the option to review any potential updates to troubleshooters before Windows 8 applies them. To do this, when you run a troubleshooter, select the Advanced Options check box that appears in the lower left of the Troubleshooter dialog box. You can also optionally run the troubleshooter as an administrator.

If the troubleshooter cannot find a problem or a solution, you can click Explore Additional Options to have the troubleshooter guide you to sources for help and support online (see Figure 33-45).

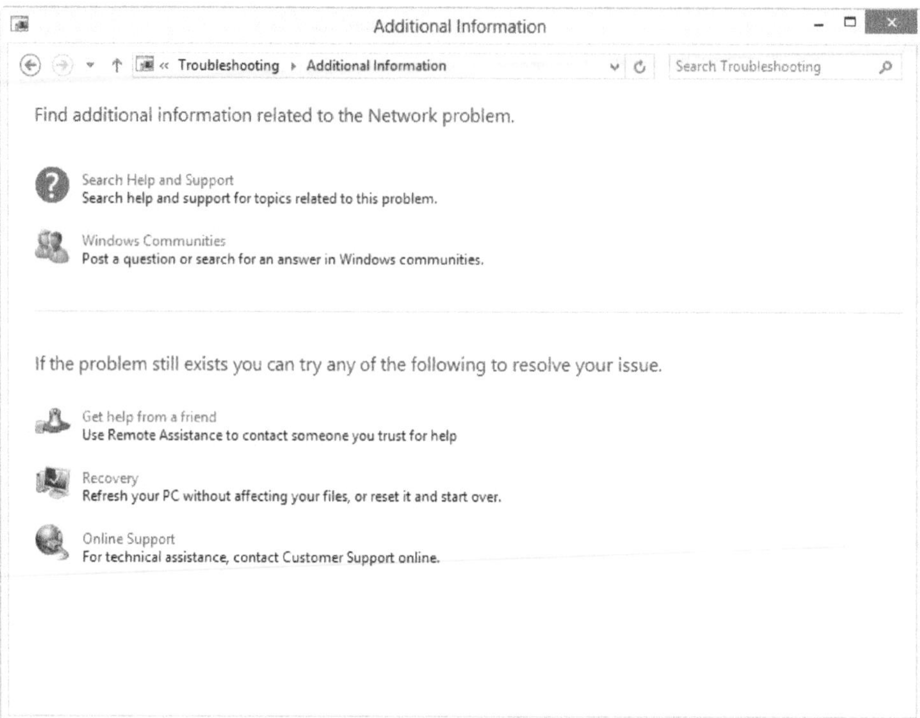

Figure 33-45 The Windows 8 troubleshooters can help you find advice elsewhere.

It's worth noting that not all of the automated troubleshooters fix problems with Windows 8. Some, depending on the troubleshooter, simply reset a Windows component to its default state.

CHAPTER 34

Exploring Windows 8 Firewall

IN CHAPTER 13, "RESPONDING TO VIRUSES, MALWARE, AND OTHER THREATS," you learned about online threats, how to identify and avoid them, and how to repair any harm done by them. I stress that the biggest part of maintaining security on any computer is ensuring that you are properly educated and informed about the threats and problems associated with clicking links or opening files that could contain malicious software. Viruses, malware, and hackers can't gain access to a computer without your intervention. You need to be careful about what you click online and which websites you visit, and about maintaining antivirus and antimalware protection.

As you learned in Chapter 4, "Using the Basic Windows Utilities," you do not have to have third-party antivirus, antimalware, and firewall software in Windows, because all versions of Windows 8 include a competent firewall. In this chapter, I describe how you can use it to great effect to secure your computer.

Assessing Your Firewall

A *firewall* is a gatekeeper that prevents software on your computer from communicating with the outside world and vice versa. A good firewall protects your computer from being detected at all.

You can perform an excellent assessment of your firewall with ShieldsUP!, which you can find online at *http://www.grc.com*. Figure 34-1 shows the results of a test performed on my computer that is running only the standard Windows 8 firewall in the standard configuration. You can see that the firewall successfully blocks some ports but not all. The firewall in my Internet router provides an additional layer of support that hides the computer completely.

TruStealth Analysis

Solicited TCP Packets: RECEIVED (FAILED) — As detailed in the port report below, one or more of your system's ports actively responded to our deliberate attempts to establish a connection. It is generally possible to increase your system's security by hiding it from the probes of potentially hostile hackers. Please see the details presented by the specific port links below, as well as the various resources on this site, and in our extremely helpful and active user community.

Unsolicited Packets: PASSED — No Internet packets of any sort were received from your system as a side-effect of our attempts to elicit some response from any of the ports listed above. Some questionable personal security systems expose their users by attempting to "counter-probe the prober", thus revealing themselves. But your system remained wisely silent. (Except for the fact that not all of its ports are completely stealthed as shown below.)

Ping Reply: RECEIVED (FAILED) — Your system REPLIED to our Ping (ICMP Echo) requests, making it visible on the Internet. Most personal firewalls can be configured to block, drop, and ignore such ping requests in order to better hide systems from hackers. This is highly recommended since "Ping" is among the oldest and most common methods used to locate systems prior to further exploitation.

Port	Service	Status	Security Implications
0	<nil>	Closed	Your computer has responded that this port exists but is currently closed to connections.
21	FTP	OPEN!	FTP servers have many known security vulnerabilities and the payoff from exploiting an insecure FTP server can be significant. This system's open FTP port is inviting intruders to examine your system more closely.
22	SSH	OPEN!	Secure Shell provides a secure-connection version of the Telnet remote console service with additional features. Unfortunately, the SSH services and their security add-on packages have a long history of many widely exploited buffer overflow vulnerabilities. If your system has this port exposed to the outside world you should be vigilant in keeping your SSH service updated.
23	Telnet	OPEN!	Telnet provides a remote command prompt window which allows remote systems to be configured and controlled. Any system that appears to be offering a Telnet connection — like yours is right now — is offering the potential for total command-level access. Since a surprising number of Telnet servers are known to have no password, this open Telnet port will be attracting a LOT of the wrong kind of attention. If your network contains a residential NAT or DSL router, it may be that its "WAN-side" management interface is open and accepting connections. No matter what the cause, you should immediately attend to this open Telnet port.
25	SMTP	Closed	Your computer has responded that this port exists but is currently closed to connections.
79	Finger	Closed	Your computer has responded that this port exists but is currently closed to connections.
80	HTTP	OPEN!	The web is so insecure these days that new security "exploits" are being discovered almost daily. There are many known problems with Microsoft's Personal Web Server (PWS) and its Frontpage Extensions that many people run on their personal machines. So having port 80 "open" as it is here causes

Figure 34-1 A firewall test performed at *http://www.grc.com* by using only the standard Windows 8 firewall provides feedback.

INSIDE OUT How much extra protection is provided by your router?

If you conduct a firewall test at a website such as *http://www.grc.com*, you might be lulled into a false sense of security because of the additional protection offered by modern routers, which can hide computers on the network automatically.

To get a true picture of your firewall's quality, I recommend running the firewall test on a public network or on mobile broadband. By doing so, you will see only the protection offered by Windows 8.

To access Windows Firewall settings (see Figure 34-2), go to the Security section of Action Center, or go to Control Panel\System And Security\Windows Firewall.

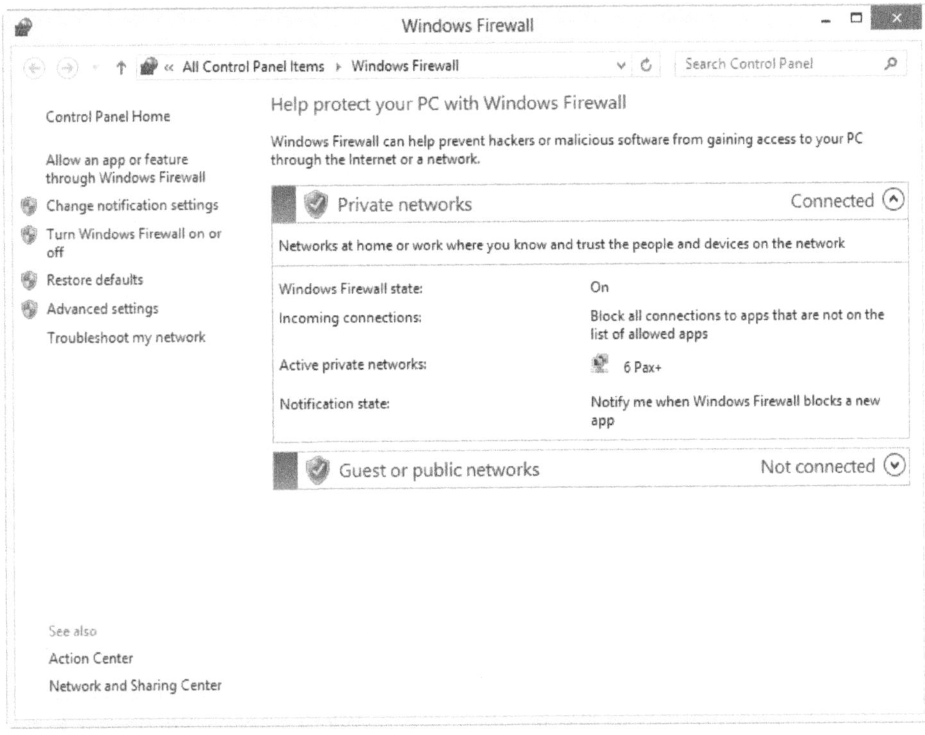

Figure 34-2 Windows Firewall in Control Panel. If appropriate, a collapsible pane for corporate networks also appears.

Windows Firewall with Advanced Security

The basic Windows Firewall settings include turning the firewall on and off and allowing a program through it. To increase the level of security, in the pane on the left of Windows Firewall, click Advanced Settings to open the Windows Firewall With Advanced Security management console (see Figure 34-3).

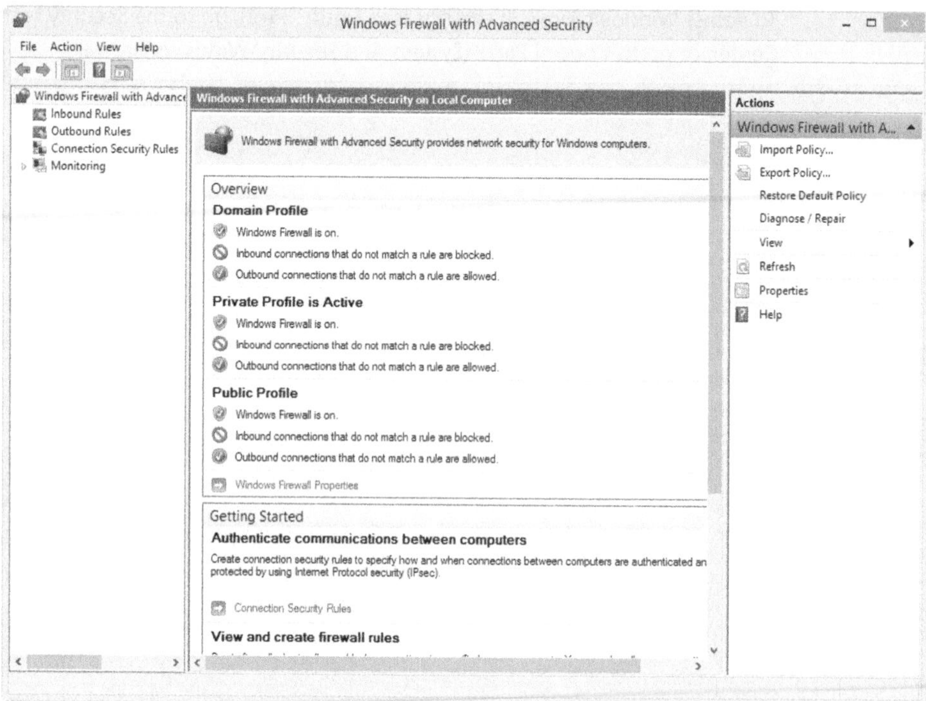

Figure 34-3 The Windows Firewall With Advanced Security management console.

By default, the advanced firewall settings window includes three panes of information and controls, just like any other management console in Windows 8. In the center pane is status information about the firewall. Below that are some quick links to help you set up advanced rules.

In the Actions pane on the right side of the window are links for working with advanced firewall policies after you've set them up. You can import and export firewall policies or reset the firewall to its default state if something has gone wrong or become corrupt. You can also use options in the Actions pane to launch the Windows 8 troubleshooters that are relevant to the Windows Firewall.

INSIDE OUT How to reset Windows Firewall

If something goes wrong with your firewall or the firewall settings become corrupt, you can reset the firewall to its default state by clicking Restore Default Policy, which is located in the Actions pane on the right side of the Windows Firewall With Advanced Security management console.

Managing Firewall Rules

In the left pane of the Windows Firewall With Advanced Security management console, you can manage inbound and outbound rules via links. *Inbound rules* cover connections that are made to your computer from your network or the Internet. *Outbound rules* affect Windows software and installed applications that might want to communicate with your network, the Internet, or other devices. Click these links to open a list of existing rules. Quite a few of these rules deal with individual Windows components that need to communicate with the outside world, such as Windows Update.

The currently enabled rules are identified by a green check mark. If you want to turn a rule on or off, right-click the rule, and then click either Enable or Disable, respectively. To modify a rule, right-click it and then click Properties to open the Properties dialog box (see Figure 34-4).

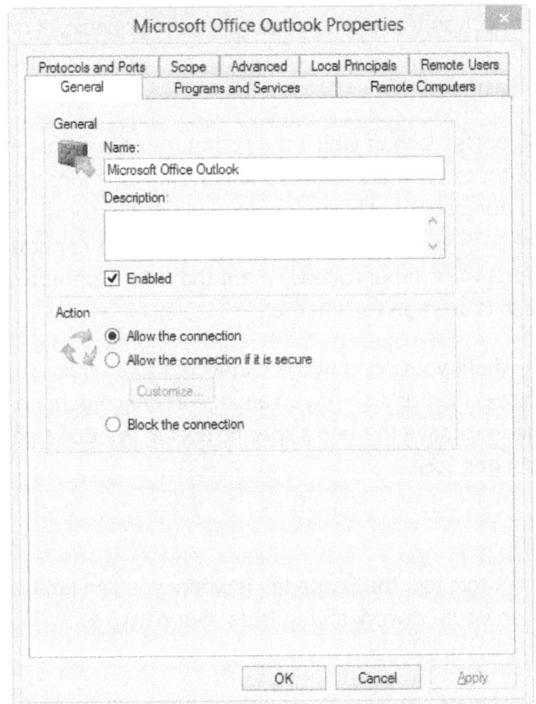

Figure 34-4 Managing the properties of a firewall rule.

General Tab

The General tab displays common information about the firewall rule along with controls for turning the rule on and off, or for blocking the connection completely. On this tab, you can set a rule to allow a connection only when certain security measures are in place, indicating a secure connection, for example, when a company network connection is encrypted. You can allow a connection only if that connection is secure.

Program And Services Tab

If the firewall rule applies to specific programs or Windows services, you can set and configure it on the Programs And Services tab.

Remote Computers Tab

On the Remote Computers tab, you can control firewall connections on organization networks, such as limit the connection to certain computers on your network only.

Protocols And Ports Tab

Your computer has 65,535 ports, each of which is a communications port into and out of your computer. Some of these ports are reserved for specific functions, some are used by Internet and other communications software on your computer (some are used exclusively by external hardware such as your router), and others are user-configurable. The protocols used by these ports to communicate vary, but the most common communication method is TCP/IP, which is used on the Internet.

In a business environment where your computer is connected to a server, you might want to open or block access to specific ports. Or, if you engage in online gaming or peer-to-peer file sharing, you sometimes have to open a specific port in Windows and/or in your router to allow communications access.

Scope Tab

Similar to the Remote Computers tab, the Scope tab is where you can limit access to or from specific IP addresses on your network and outside your network.

Advanced Tab

On the Advanced tab, you can specify profiles to apply to a rule. For example, you can specify that a rule applies only when you are connected to a public network with a certain type of connection, such as a wireless network.

Adding New Inbound or Outbound Firewall Rules

To create a new inbound or outbound firewall rule, perform the following steps, adapting the procedure to indicate the type of rule you are adding. In this example, you are creating a new outbound firewall rule.

1. In the left pane of the Windows Firewall With Advanced Security management console, click Outbound Rules. (If you wanted to create a new inbound firewall rule, you would click Inbound Rules and follow the same process.)
2. In the Actions pane, click New Rule to display the New Outbound Rule Wizard.
3. On the Rule Type page, click the type of firewall rule you want to create: a rule for a program, port, or Windows service, and then click Next (see Figure 34-5).

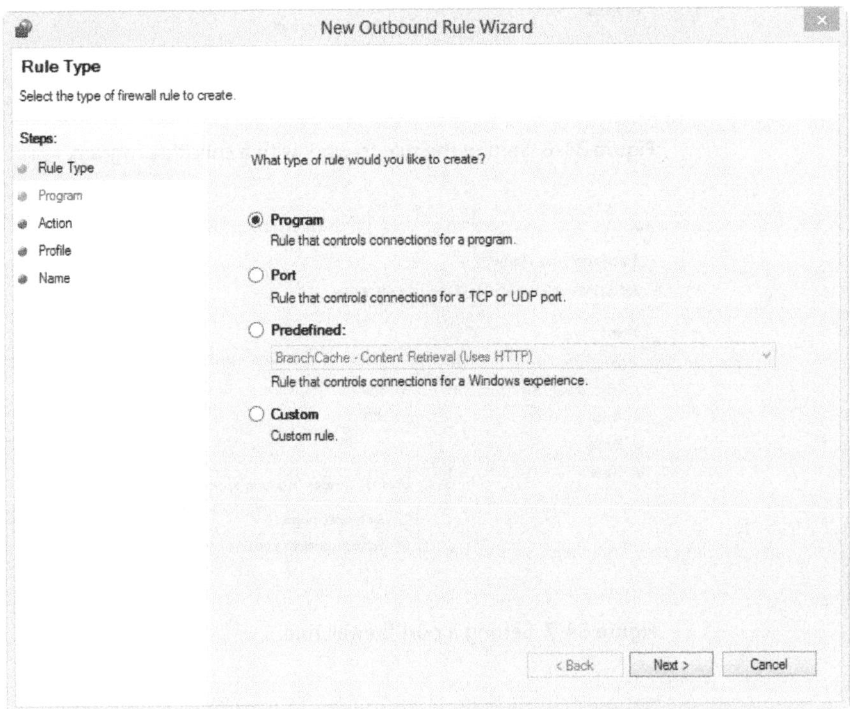

Figure 34-5 Creating a new firewall rule.

4. On the Program page, specify a particular program or allow all programs to which the rule will apply, and then click Next. Note that when configuring rules for Windows Firewall, you might want to set many different rule types. Figure 34-6 shows the options for programs, and Figure 34-7 shows the options for protocols and ports. These will be the most common types of rules you set.

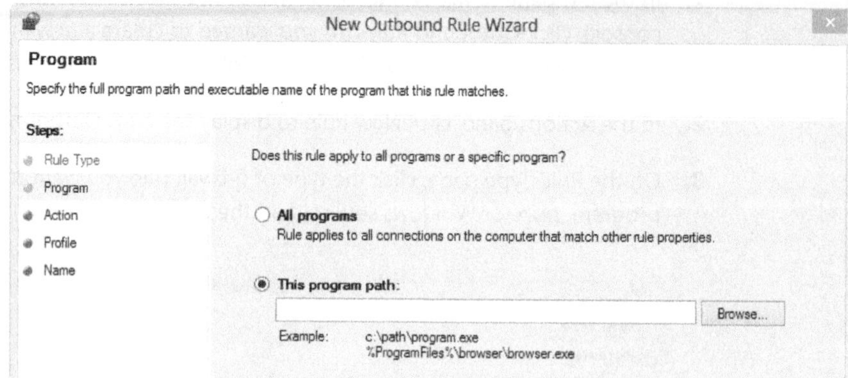

Figure 34-6 Setting the rule to work with a specific program.

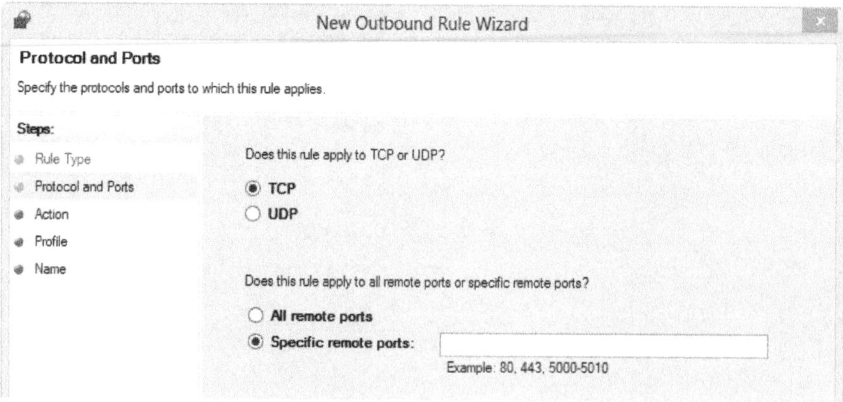

Figure 34-7 Setting a port firewall rule.

5. On the Action page (see Figure 34-8), set the firewall action, and then click Next. You can always allow the connection, allow it only when the connection is secure, or block it.

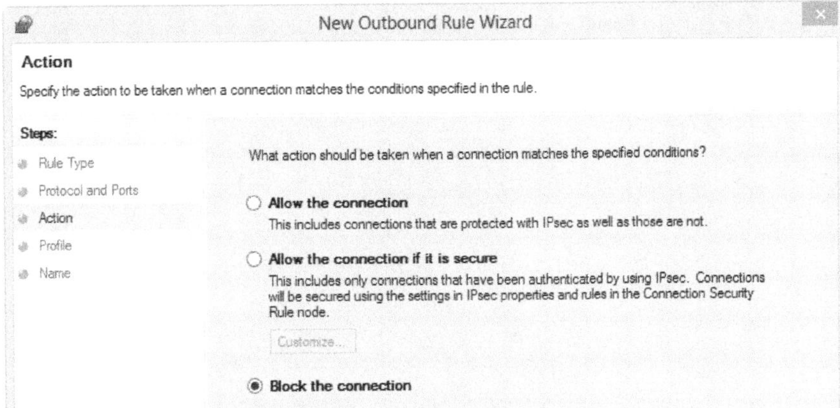

Figure 34-8 Setting a firewall action.

6. On the Profile page (see Figure 34-9), indicate to which network types this connection applies, and then click Next. You can apply it to all network types or perhaps just to the corporate network or public networks.

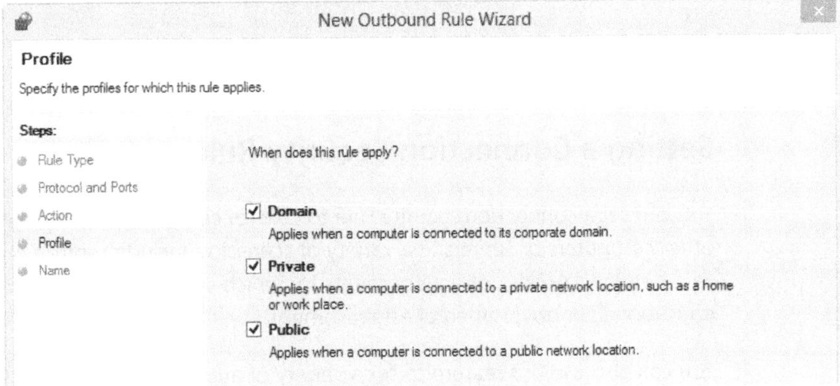

Figure 34-9 Setting to which networks the rule applies.

7. On the Name page (see Figure 34-10), give the rule a name, and optionally a description, and then click Finish.

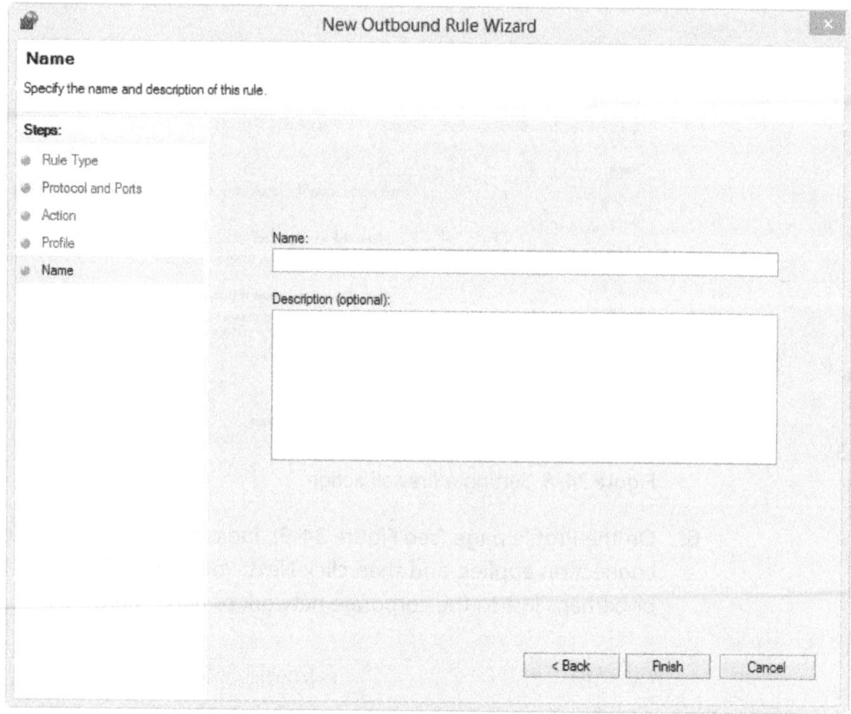

Figure 34-10 Giving the rule a name and description.

Setting a Connection Security Rule

You can set a connection security rule to control connections between your computer and other computers or servers in a variety of scenarios, including office scenarios, virtual private networks (VPNs), or environments for which security is critical, such as in a corporate, educational, or governmental establishment.

You can also use this feature to set a variety of authentication methods between two computers, including the use of root security certificates. With some options, you can select the encryption methods used to transmit data between computers.

To set new rules, in the left pane of the Windows Firewall With Advanced Security management console, click the Connection Security Rules node, and then on the Actions menu, click New to start the New Connection Security Rule Wizard (see Figure 34-11).

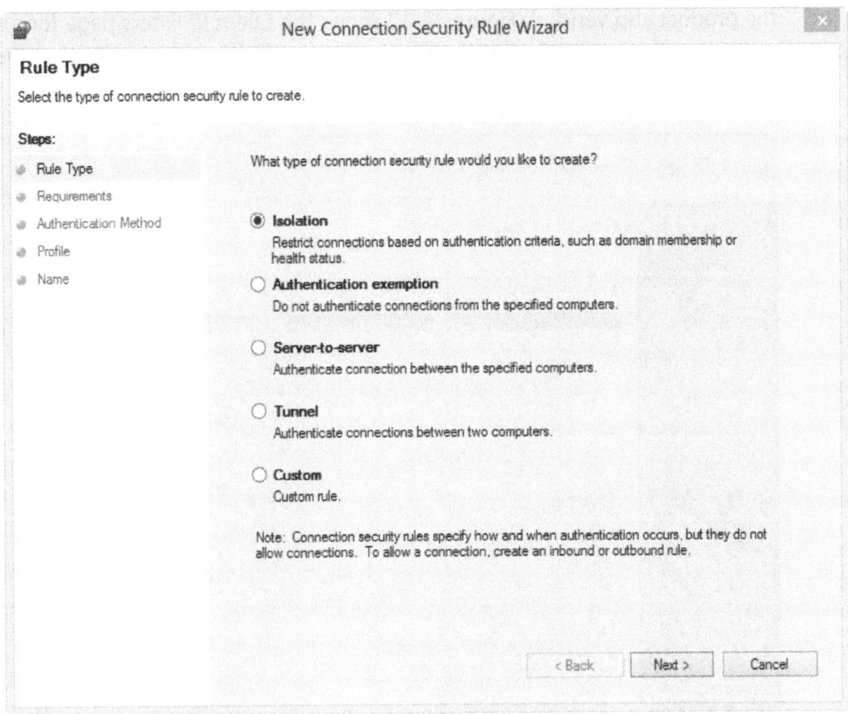

Figure 34-11 The New Connection Security Rule Wizard.

Monitoring

In the left pane of the Windows Firewall With Advanced Security management console, click the Monitoring node to access information about the current status of your firewall and any custom rules you have set up for it. Opening the Monitoring pane displays the results of the most recent activity of any particular firewall rule. You can check whether the rule is working correctly (such as whether it is accessing the correct port, for example), and see what it is allowing through the firewall and what it is blocking.

Checking Port Control for Routers

Some connection problems cannot be solved by using Windows Firewall to allow access to specific ports if these ports are blocked by the router you use to connect to the Internet. To see your router's firewall settings, you can log on to your router, typically by typing the address **192.168.0.1** or **192.168.1.1** into your web browser (although you should check the documentation that came with your router because this address differs depending on the product and vendor). Figure 34-12 shows the Client IP Filters page for a router. On this page, you can see which options you can set, or block port access for specific computers (IP addresses).

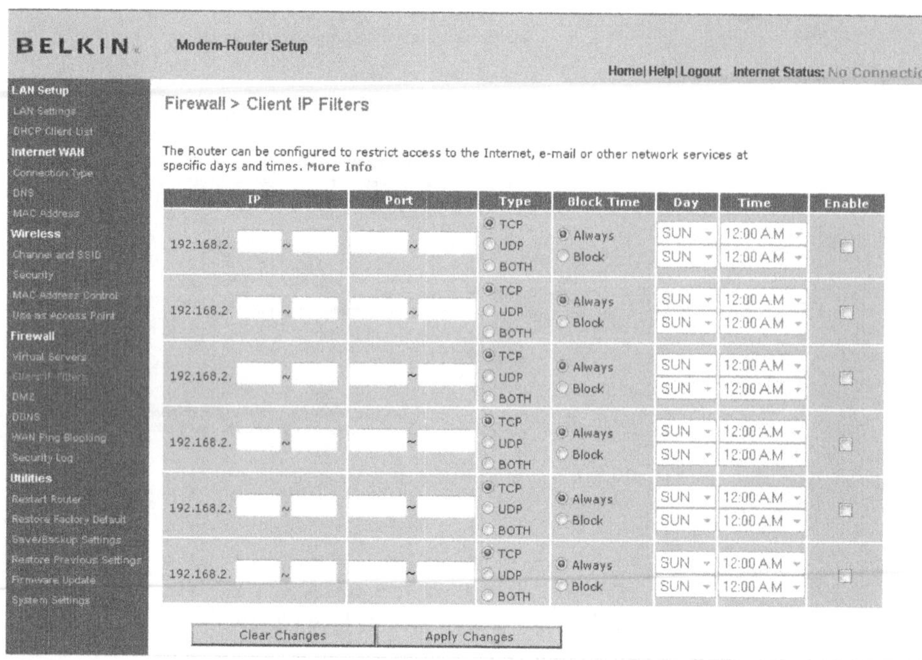

Figure 34-12 Router firewall control.

INSIDE OUT Troubleshooting router blocks

The router will assign your computer an IP address when it connects. This should always be the same, but sometimes the router assigns a different IP address for your computer, which can cause connection problems.

The router will have a section in its configuration software where you can see the IP addresses for all the computers on your network. If you have previously set a port unblocking rule and it is not working, check the configuration software to determine whether the IP address assigned to that rule still points to the correct computer.

CHAPTER 35

Working with the Registry

As you learned in Chapter 20, "Using Advanced Repair Methods," the registry is a database of settings and configuration options for Windows and all of your programs. On the Microsoft support website, Microsoft describes the operation of the registry as follows:

The registry contains information that Windows continually references during operation, such as profiles for each user, the applications installed on the computer and the types of documents that each can create, property sheet settings for folders and application icons, what hardware exists on the system, and the ports that are being used.

You might occasionally need to change a setting for Windows or for a program that is contained within the registry, perhaps because an error has occurred and a program or Windows component is malfunctioning, or because you are making (or undoing) a tweak to the operating system or a program to change behavior or performance. This chapter discusses the different sections of the registry and how to make changes to them.

Understanding the Registry Structure

To see the registry structure and ultimately work with the registry, access the Registry Editor (see Figure 35-1) by searching for **regedit** on the Start screen.

CAUTION!

This chapter describes how to modify the registry, but you need to know that serious problems might occur if you modify the registry incorrectly. Therefore, make sure that you follow the steps presented in this chapter carefully. For added protection, back up the registry before you modify it so that you can restore the registry if a problem occurs.

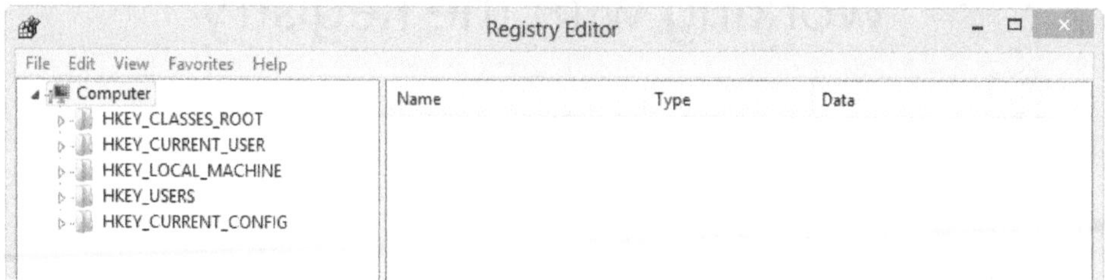

Figure 35-1 The Windows Registry Editor.

In addition to the main registry file for Windows, each user has their own individual registry file that contains the settings for their own user account. This is a hidden file stored in the root of the user's C:\Users\UserName folder.

The registry is split into five different primary keys, shown in Figure 35-1: two for the current user, two for the computer, and one for system startup:

- **HKEY_ CLASSES_ROOT** Subkey of HKEY_LOCAL_MACHINE\Software. This section stores all the information for registered applications, including file associations. If you write a registry key to HKEY_CLASSES_ROOT, and the key already exists under HKEY_CURRENT_USER\Software\Classes, Windows will use the information stored in the HKEY_CURRENT_USER\Software\Classes as the parent key. It is unlikely that you will need to make changes to this part of the registry. This subkey is sometimes abbreviated as HKCR.
- **HKEY_CURRENT_USER** Contains configuration options for the current user's profile, including the location pointers to the user's documents folders, display options, and Control Panel settings. This registry key is sometimes referred to as HKCU.
- **HKEY_LOCAL_MACHINE** Contains settings specific to the computer, including installed applications. This section is the most commonly altered. It is sometimes known as HKLM.
- **HKEY_USERS** Contains keys that are subkeys corresponding to HKEY_CURRENT_USER. It stores information for each user profile that is actively loaded. It is sometimes known as HKU.
- **HKEY_CURRENT_CONFIG** Includes information gathered at startup. Information and keys are stored here temporarily and are replaced when the computer is restarted.

Although the registry is large and complex, it is logically organized. Registry keys are sensibly named, so you should be able to find a specific setting fairly easily. You will find most of the Windows 8 settings, for instance, in the following key:

HKEY_LOCAL_MACHINE\SOFTWARE\Microsoft\Windows\CurrentVersion

Most of your software configuration options can be found in the following key:

HKEY_LOCAL_MACHINE\SOFTWARE

CAUTION!

You should always create a backup of the registry whenever you intend to work with it. Even the smallest, seemingly innocent change can cause Windows or one of your programs or hardware drivers to become unstable.

Registry Keys and Settings

There are different types of registry keys and entries, which are usually stored as string values, and as binary, decimal, and hexadecimal numbers. Table 35-1 describes them.

Table 35-1 **Registry Key Types**

Registry Key	Description
REG_BINARY	Raw binary data for storing hardware component information.
REG_DWORD	Data represented by a 4-byte number (32-bit integer). DWORDS are used as the parameters for many settings, including device drivers, and software and configuration options.
REG_EXPAND_SZ	A variable-length data string.
REG_MULTI_SZ	A multiple string; for example, a list of multiple values in a format that people can read. These are usually separated by commas or spaces.
REG_SZ	A fixed-length text string.
REG_RESOURCE_LIST	A resource list in a series of nested arrays. These are used by device drivers.
REG_RESOURCE_REQUIREMENTS_LIST	An array list of hardware resources required by device drivers.
REG_FULL_RESOURCE_DESCRIPTOR	Nested arrays used to store resource lists for physical hardware devices.
REG_NONE	Data without any particular type.
REG_LINK	A Unicode string that names a symbolic.
REG_QWORD	Data that is represented by a 64-bit integer.

> **Note**
>
> **In the same way that 64-bit versions of Windows 8 have two Program Files folders each for 32-bit and 64-bit programs, the registry contains different sections for 64-bit registry keys. You can find these in HKEY_LOCAL_MACHINE\Software\WOW6432Node.**

Backing Up and Restoring the Registry

Before you do any work in the registry, always back it up in case a change you make causes Windows 8 or one of your applications to become unstable or unresponsive. To back up the registry, in the Registry Editor, on the File menu (see Figure 35-2), click Export.

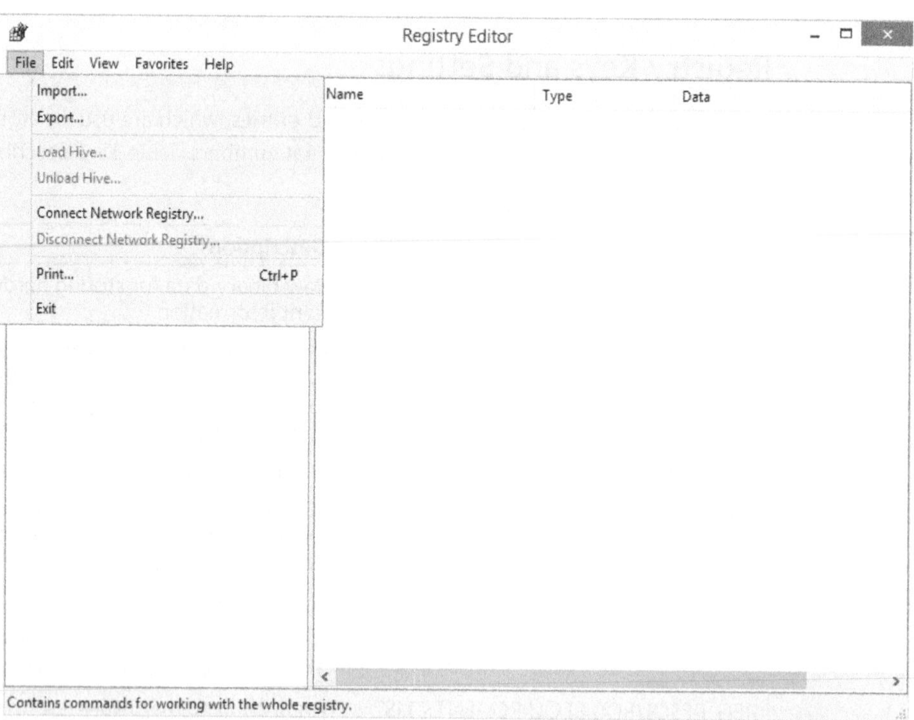

Figure 35-2 Backing up the Windows registry.

You can restore the registry by clicking the Import options on the File menu (see Figure 35-2). Always ensure that you select the correct part of the key to back up. If you need to back up a main registry key and have only a subkey selected, only that subkey will be backed up.

Note

If changes to the registry have made Windows 8 unresponsive, you might be able to boot into Safe Mode or use System Restore in the System Recovery options to restore the registry. See Chapter 14, "Easy Ways to Repair Windows 8," and Chapter 20, "Using Advanced Repair Methods," for more information about how to use System Restore and Safe Mode, respectively, to rescue your computer.

Strategies for Working with the Registry

Using the Registry Editor is just one way you can work with the registry. The following list describes some other methods that can be used for managing the Windows registry:

- **Group Policies and the Microsoft Management Console (MMC)** Use these to administer networks, your computer, services, or other operating system components.
- **Microsoft Visual Basic Scripting Edition (VBScript) or JScript scripts** Use these to work directly with Windows Script Host.
- **.reg files** These files contain registry keys that you can add to the registry by double-clicking them to open and run them.
- **Reg.exe** This is a command-line program. Type **reg /?** in a Command Prompt window to get a full list of supported commands. You will need to run the Command Prompt window as an administrator.
- **System Center Configuration Manager (SCCM)** Use this in a Windows Server environment to manage the registry across a domain.
- **Windows Management Instrumentation (WMI)** Use this enterprise-based tool for managing the Windows operating system to automate certain tasks.

Microsoft provides more information about using these methods at *http://support.microsoft.com/kb/256986*.

Editing, Deleting, or Adding Registry Keys

Right-click any registry key to modify, delete, or rename it (see Figure 35-3).

To create new registry keys of any type, right-click any blank space in the right pane of the Registry Editor, and then click New (see Figure 35-4).

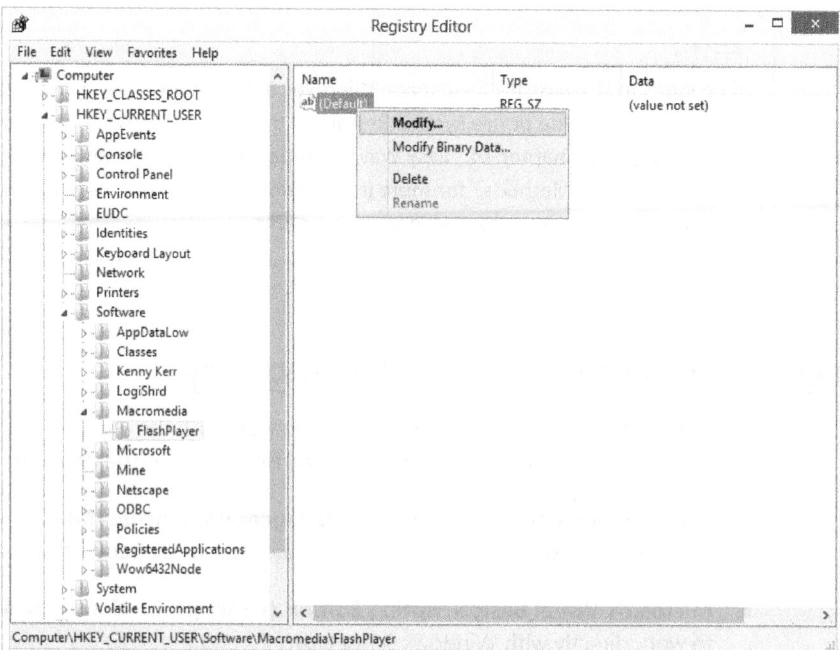

Figure 35-3 Editing or deleting a registry key.

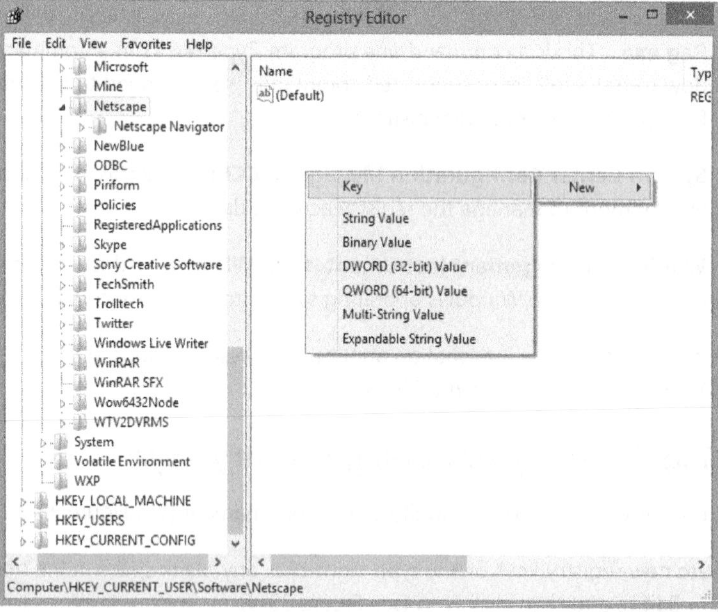

Figure 35-4 Adding a new registry key.

Backing Up Specific Registry Keys

You can also back up specific registry keys—or sets of keys—in the Registry Editor by right-clicking the folder in the left pane and then clicking Export (see Figure 35-5). This will create a .reg file that you can later reimport to the same computer or a different one.

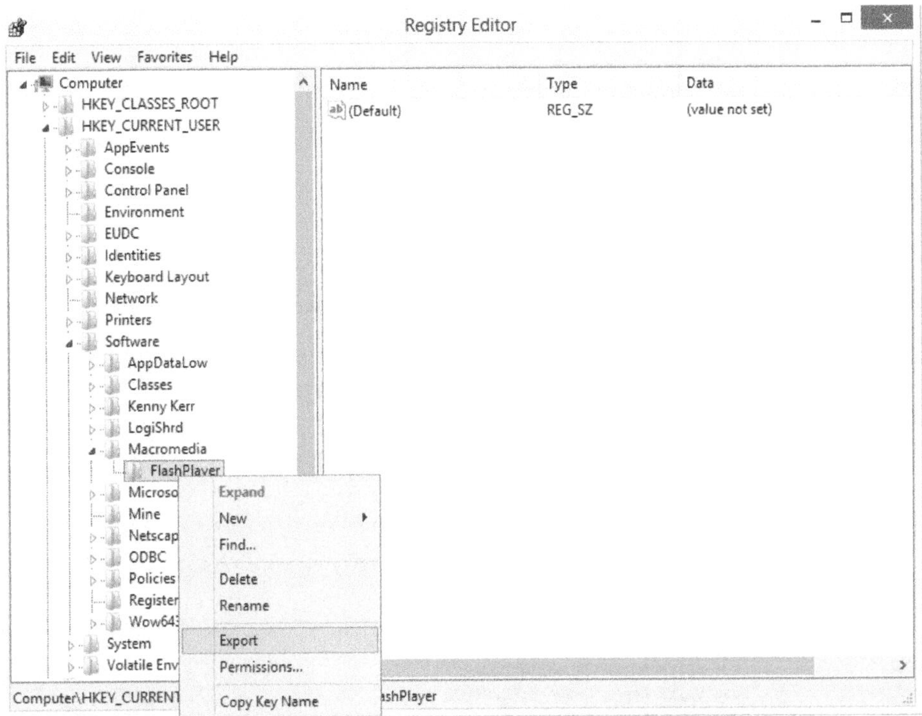

Figure 35-5 Backing up a specific registry key set.

Combining Exported Registry Keys

You can't import a registry from one computer into another, because so many keys such as the drive assignments, hardware drivers, and installed software will be different for each computer. It is quite reasonable, however, to export specific registry keys for distribution across multiple computers, such as keys for specific configuration settings that customize the look and feel of Windows 8, or keys for specific hardware.

You will want to avoid importing multiple .reg files to new computers, but you can edit these particular settings into a single file to import. To do this, in File Explorer, right-click the exported file, and then click Edit to open the registry file in Notepad (see Figure 35-6). You can then use this file to merge multiple registry files into a single file, which you can save as a new .reg file.

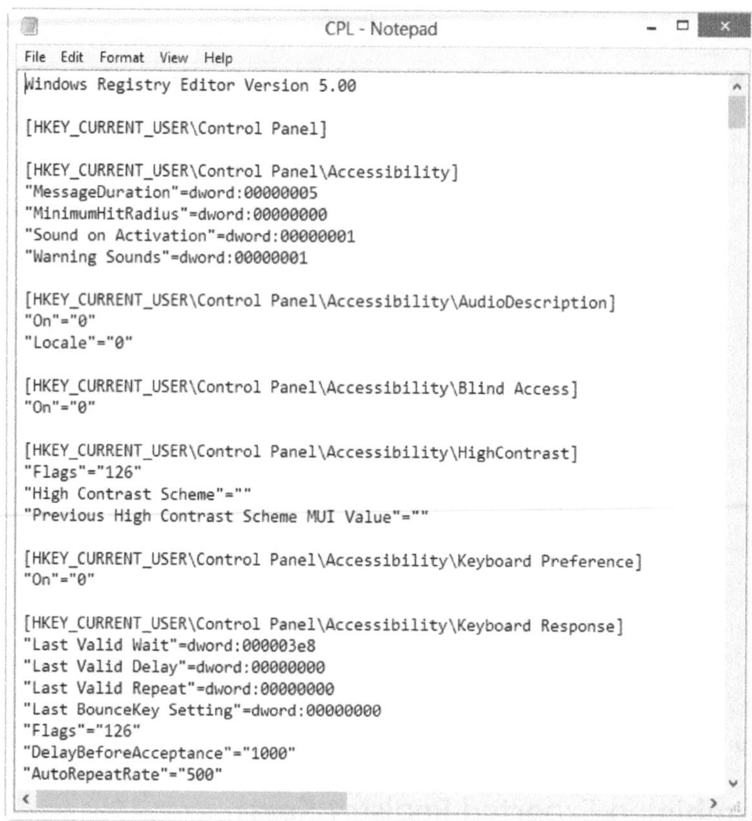

Figure 35-6 Editing a registry key by using Notepad.

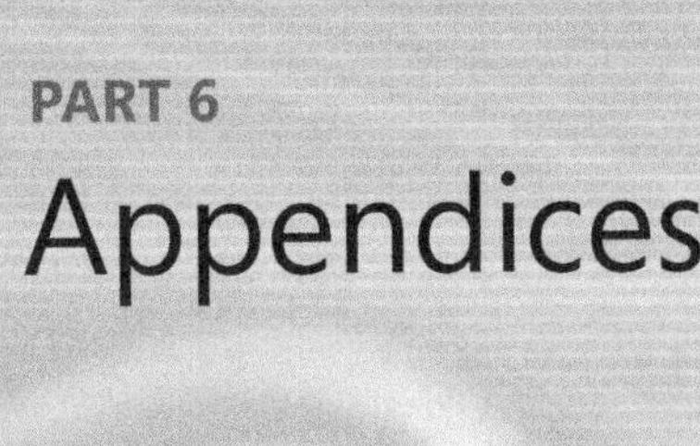

PART 6

Appendices

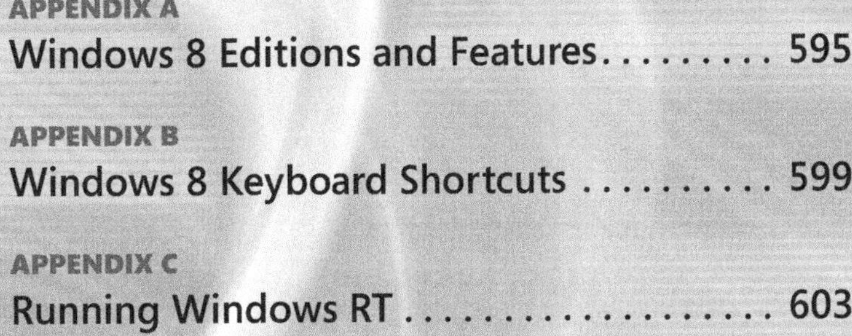

APPENDIX A

Windows 8 Editions and Features

When you move from one edition of an operating system to a new one, you need to pay attention to several requirements. For example, your computer system may need to support certain requirements regarding processor speed and available memory. The following table provides the system requirements for running the available Windows 8 editions.

Edition	32-Bit Memory Limit	64-Bit Memory Limit	Availability	Notes
Windows 8	4 GB	16 GB	Retail/OEMs	Can be upgraded to Windows 8 Pro
Windows 8 Pro	4 GB	192 GB	Retail/OEMs	Can be upgraded to include Windows Media Center
Windows 8 Enterprise	4 GB	192 GB	Volume Licensing	Cannot be upgraded to include Windows Media Center
Windows RT	4 GB	N/A	OEMs	Used in computers running Windows RT and in Windows Phone

GB refers to gigabytes.

A minimum of 768 vertical-pixel resolution is required for the Start screen; a minimum of 1,366 horizontal resolution is needed for side-by-side apps.

At the time of this writing, Windows 8 will be the final edition of the operating system to come in both 32-bit and 64-bit versions. Microsoft has stated that all future versions of Windows will be 64-bit only.

The following is a list of features offered by each Windows 8 edition.

Features in the Windows 8 Edition

- Upgrading permitted from Windows 7 Starter, Home Basic, and Home Premium
- Start screen, Semantic Zoom, Live Tiles
- Windows Store
- Apps (Mail, Calendar, People, Messaging, Photos, Microsoft SkyDrive, Reader, Music, Video, Weather, Microsoft Xbox Live, Finance, Travel, Sports)

- Windows Internet Explorer 10
- Connected standby (enabling fast startup times)
- Microsoft Account (formerly known as Live ID)
- Desktop
- File Explorer (formerly Windows Explorer)
- Windows Defender (a rebranded Microsoft Security Essentials antimalware package)
- SmartScreen (Internet security software)
- Windows Update
- Task Manager (updated)
- Language pack support
- Multiple monitor support
- Storage Spaces (software RAID equivalent)
- Microsoft Exchange ActiveSync
- File History (file versioning control)
- Mount ISO/VHD
- Mobile broadband (3G/4G)
- Picture password
- PlayTo
- Remote Desktop (Client)
- Refresh Your PC and Reset Your PC (backup and restore tools for Windows 8)
- Snap and Shake (usability tools for the desktop)
- Touch and Thumb keyboard
- Trusted Boot (UEFI-only boot security system)
- Virtual private network (VPN) client

Additional Features in Windows 8 Pro and Enterprise Editions

- Upgrading permitted from Windows 7 Professional and Enterprise
- Microsoft BitLocker and BitLocker To Go (full-disk encryption)
- Boot from VHD
- Client Hyper-V (virtualization client)
- Domain Join
- Encrypting File System (file/folder encryption)
- Group Policy
- Remote Desktop (Host)
- Additional features available through upgrade purchase:
  - Windows Media Center (available in Windows 8 Pro only)
  - DVD playback (available in Windows Media Center only)
  - Blu-ray disc playback (available in Windows Media Center only)

Additional Features in Windows 8 Enterprise Edition

- Windows To Go (bootable version of Windows 8 on a USB flash drive)

Windows 8 Features Absent in Windows RT

- Upgrading from earlier versions of Windows
- Storage Spaces

Features Unique to Windows RT

Windows RT contains some features that are unique and not available in Windows 8. These include some Microsoft Office apps that are not provided with Windows 8:

- Microsoft Office Home & Student 2013 RT (Word, Excel, PowerPoint, OneNote)
- Device encryption (uses BitLocker)

APPENDIX B

Windows 8 Keyboard Shortcuts

This appendix provides a handy list of keyboard shortcuts to help you work in Windows 8.

Table B-1 System Response to Keys Pressed Independently

Key	Result
Space	Select or clear active check box.
Tab	Move forward through options.
Esc	Cancel.
NumLock	Hold for five seconds to turn toggle keys on and off.
Del	Delete file (File Explorer).
Left arrow	Open previous menu or close submenu.
Right arrow	Open next menu or open submenu.
F1	Display Help (if available).
F2	Rename item.
F3	Search for file or folder.
F4	Display items in active list.
F5	Refresh.

Table B-2 System Response to Keys Pressed with the Windows Logo Key

Key pressed with Windows logo key	Result
Only Windows Logo key	Toggle between Start screen and most recently used app.
PrtScr	Capture screenshot (saved in Pictures as Screenshot.png).
C	Reveal charms.
D	Show desktop.
E	Open File Explorer.
F	Go to files in Search charm. (+Ctrl to find computers on a network).
G	Cycle through desktop gadgets.
H	Open Share charm.

Key pressed with Windows logo key	Result
I	Open Settings charm.
J	Switch focus between snapped and larger apps.
K	Open Devices charm.
L	Lock computer.
M	Minimize all windows (desktop).
O	Lock screen orientation.
P	Open Projection options.
Q	Open Search charm.
R	Run.
T	Set focus on taskbar and cycle through running desktop programs.
U	Open Ease of Access Center.
V	Cycle through notifications (+Shift to go backward).
W	Go to settings in Search charm.
X	Quick link to WinX menu commands (opens Windows Mobility Center if present).
Z	Open App bar.
1–9	Go to the app at the position on the taskbar.
+	Zoom in (Magnifier).
–	Zoom out (Magnifier).
, (comma)	Preview the desktop.
. (period)	Snap an app to the right (+Shift to snap an app to the left).
Enter	Open Narrator (+Alt to open Windows Media Center if installed).
Spacebar	Switch input language and keyboard layout.
Tab	Cycle through App History.
Esc	Exit Magnifier.
Home	Minimize nonactive desktop windows.
PgUp	Move Start screen to left monitor.
PgDn	Move Start screen to right monitor.
Left arrow	Snap desktop window to the left (+Shift to move to left monitor).
Right arrow	Snap desktop windows to the right (+Shift to move to right monitor).
Up arrow	Maximize desktop window (+Shift to keep width).
Down arrow	Restore/minimize desktop window (+Shift to keep width).
F1	Windows Help and Support.

Table B-3 **System Response to Keys Pressed with Ctrl**

Key Pressed with control	Result
Mouse wheel	Desktop: Change icon size; Start screen: Zoom in/out.
A	Select All.
C	Copy.
E	Select search box (File Explorer/Windows Internet Explorer).
N	Open new window (File/Internet Explorer).
R	Refresh.
V	Paste.
W	Close current window (File Explorer/Internet Explorer).
X	Cut.
Y	Redo.
Z	Undo.
Tab	Cycle through App History.
Esc	Open Start screen.
NumLock	Copy.
Left arrow	Go to previous word.
Right arrow	Go to next word.
Up arrow	Go to previous paragraph.
Down arrow	Go to next paragraph.
F4	Close active document.

Table B-4 **System Response to Keys Pressed with Alt**

Key Pressed with Alt	Result
D	Select address bar (File Explorer/Internet Explorer).
Enter	Open properties.
Spacebar	Open shortcut menu.
Tab	Switch between apps.
Left arrow	Open previous folder (File Explorer).
Up arrow	Go up one level (File Explorer).
F4	Close active item or app.

Table B-5 System Response to Keys Pressed with Shift

Key Pressed with Shift	Result
No other key	Press for 8 seconds: Filter keys open; Press 5 times: sticky keys open.
N	Open new folder (File Explorer).
Tab	Move backward through options.
Left arrow	Select a block of text.
Right arrow	Select a block of text.
Up arrow	Select a block of text.
Down arrow	Select a block of text.

Table B-6 System Response to Keys Pressed with Ctrl+Alt

Key pressed with Ctrl+Alt	Result
D	Switch to Docked mode (Magnifier).
I	Invert colors (Magnifier).
L	Switch to Lens mode (Magnifier).
Tab	Switch between apps by using mouse or cursor keys; stays on screen.

Table B-7 System Response to Keys Pressed with Alt+Shift

Key pressed with Alt+Shift	Result
PrtSc	Left Alt+Left Shift+PrtSc to turn on High Contrast (does not use keys on the right of the keyboard)
NumLock	Left Alt+Left Shift+NumLock to turn on mouse buttons (does not use keys on the right of the keyboard)

Table B-8 System Response to Key Pressed with Ctrl+Shift

Key pressed with Ctrl+Shift	Result
Esc	Task Manager

APPENDIX C

Running Windows RT

BOOKS LIKE THIS ONE EXIST BECAUSE YOUR COMPUTER isn't the same type of electronics device as is your microwave oven or your television. With those devices, the operating system—and yes, they do have one—is embedded on a chip and can't be changed (or at least not usually).

With Windows on your desktop computer, you can manually copy the operating system onto the disk file by file, and you can also make any changes to those files that you want. This has the effect of creating something that is very flexible and upgradeable, but ultimately not as robust as, say, a microwave or television.

ARM processors are different in this respect, though. What started as a small company in the United Kingdom grew into Acorn, which resulted in the creation of the BBC Micro and the Acorn Electron, and then ultimately ARM. You'll find ARM processors everywhere. In fact, there's an extremely good chance that the processors in your microwave and television were designed by ARM.

Unlike Intel, which designs and manufactures the chips to go into desktop computers, ARM simply designs chips that it then licenses to other companies to manufacture. The result is many chip manufacturers producing ARM chips.

It is the underlying architecture of ARM chips, though, that makes them special. They were developed from Acorn's Reduced Instruction Set Computing (RISC) processor, which was first seen in the Archimedes computer that was released in 1987. These chips were more efficient in the way they processed commands than the clunky 8088, 8086, and Z80 processors that had come before. Over the years, ARM refined the RISC processor, and the result of that reduced instruction set is a leaner, more efficient processor that consumes much less power overall and is therefore far better for mobile devices.

Introducing Windows RT

We've had embedded versions of Windows for years. You might remember using Windows CE (which stands for Consumer Electronics), which formed the basis of Windows Mobile for most of a decade. You might also have used Windows CE on a thin-client terminal at work.

Because the mainstream version of Windows has been specifically reengineered to work on low-power ARM processors, we have Windows RT. Windows RT is nearly identical to Windows 8.

Windows 8 inspired many Windows RT tablets, including the Microsoft Surface tablet (see Figure C-1). It is very likely that we will see Windows RT appearing in other devices also, including Ultrabooks, set top boxes, and even all-in-one computers for the home. This is because the low-power nature of the processors makes them attractive not only for mobile devices but also for ecologically sound devices in the home. The other reason is that as users use Windows apps more and desktop software less, home users do not need to have the full version of Windows, which is more prone to problematic issues than Windows RT and is more complex to administer and repair for the user.

Figure C-1 The Microsoft Surface RT tablet.

Windows RT is also the operating system in the latest generation of Windows Phones (see Figure C-2). Although it has a slightly different user interface, it has the same kernel.

Figure C-2 Windows Phone 8.

How Windows RT Differs from Windows 8

The most noticeable way that Windows RT differs from Windows 8 is regarding the desktop. Windows RT ships with full versions of Microsoft Word, Excel, PowerPoint, and OneNote programs, and these run on the desktop, which still exists in Windows RT (see Figure C-3).

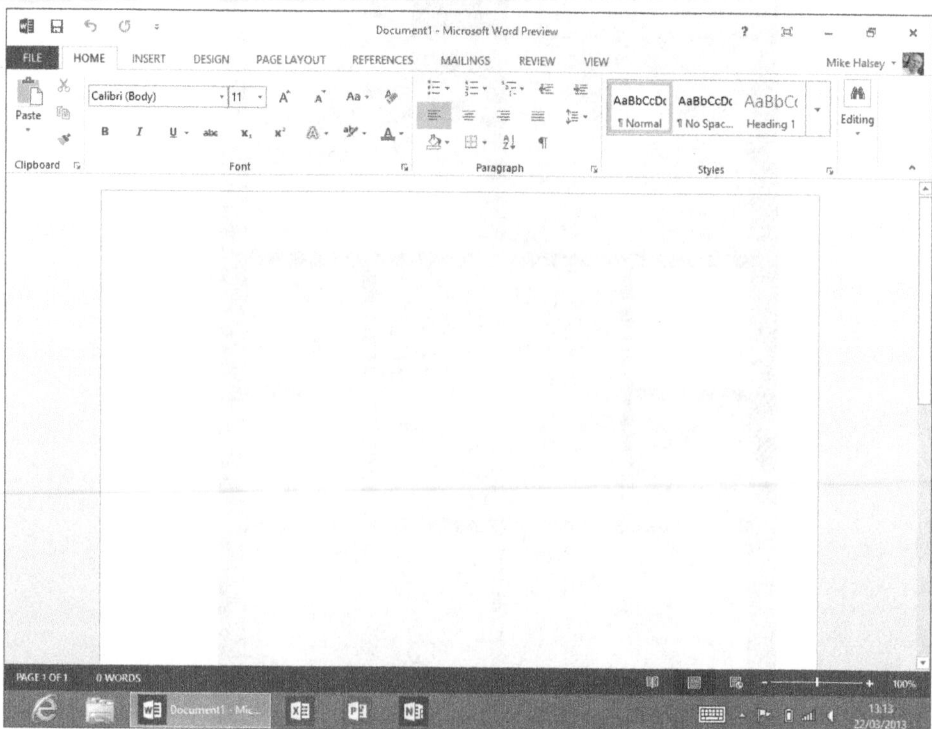

Figure C-3 A full version of Word 2013 running on Windows RT.

You'll notice the difference when you try to install anything else onto the desktop, because you can't install Windows desktop programs (see Figure C-4). This is because of some fundamental differences between Intel and ARM architecture that make software written for one platform incompatible with the other.

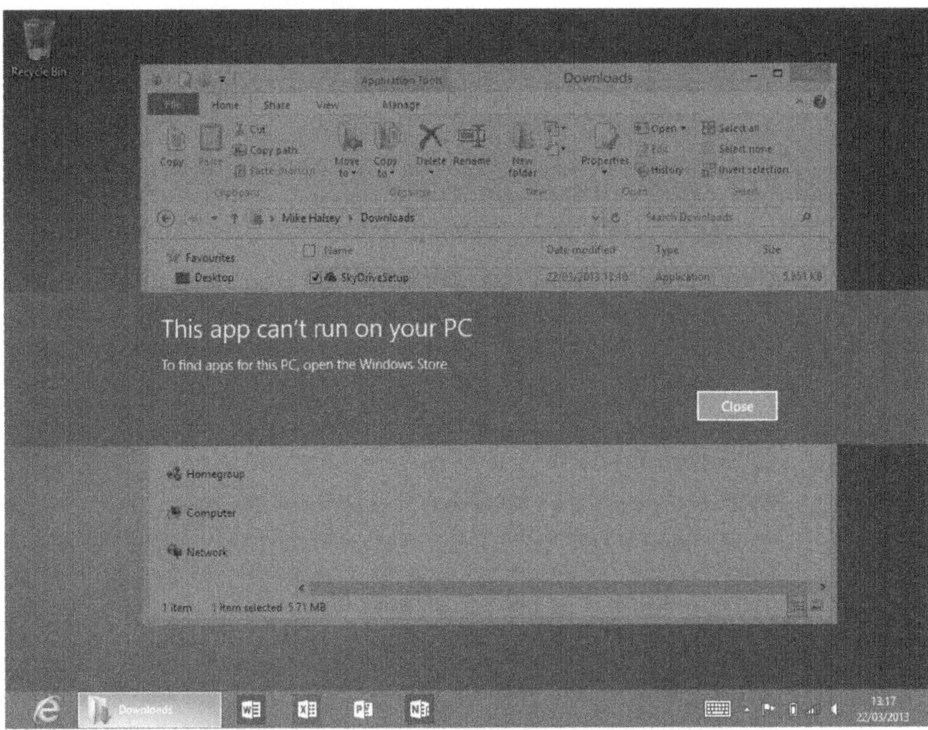

Figure C-4 You can't install desktop apps on a device running Windows RT.

"But, what about my Windows 8 apps?" I hear you ask. These are a new part of Windows; because Microsoft has strict policies and controls over how these apps can be written and what software language they must be written in, the development software has been designed in such a way as to allow the same app to be compiled for both processors. Regardless of the processor type, the development and coding language remains the same. However, you will need the correct version of the compiler.

Technically, this means that existing Windows desktop programs will be recompiled for ARM processors, and although it's possible you'll see a few Windows desktop programs, Microsoft is doing its best to discourage them. Also, software houses likely do not see the essentially consumer-only device market as being large enough to warrant the additional development time required to adapt earlier software.

So how else does Windows RT differ from Windows 8? Windows RT excludes the following Windows features:

- It cannot be installed by the user and will not be available for purchase on its own.
- It doesn't include the Windows 8 Storage Spaces feature.
- It doesn't include Windows Media Player.
- It doesn't include or support any Pro and Enterprise features, such as virtual hard disks (VHDs), Client Hyper-V, Domain Join, Encrypting File System (EFS), Group Policy, Remote Desktop (RD) hosting or Microsoft BitLocker (although it does include its own Device Encryption option in PC Settings).

Secure By Design

Windows RT is designed to be secure and resistant to malware. All apps submitted for the operating system are scanned for malware by Microsoft before being allowed into the Windows Store. Malware may still get through, but if it does, Microsoft is able to remotely stop the offending app when discovered.

That said, you shouldn't be complacent regarding security; antimalware software does exist for every mobile platform. It will also be available for Windows RT. Windows RT comes pre-loaded with the Windows Defender antimalware software provided with Windows 8, and this should always be kept up to date.

Jail Breaking

I mentioned earlier in this appendix that Microsoft is doing its best to discourage people from installing desktop software. This is where jail breaking comes in, and it's been extremely popular on iOS and Android devices. Jail breaking is the process of disabling the security of a device at the root operating system level so that you can install your own nonauthorized software, and even your own updates or customized versions of the operating system.

For many technical enthusiasts, jail breaking is tempting, although I would never recommend it personally. In fact, I would go so far as to actively discourage anybody from jail breaking their devices running Windows RT, because the security implications in potentially allowing malware onto the device create too much of a risk. And for the record, to potential jail breakers: I do not now, nor have I ever, jail broken one of my own devices.

Microsoft does allow devices to be unlocked if you have a software developer account, but even then, each developer account can only unlock three devices. This will allow you to load apps onto the devices that are not available in the Store for testing purposes. This is an officially authorized and sanctioned approach, but your warranty might be invalidated by doing so.

Troubleshooting Windows RT

If something goes wrong with Windows RT, you must use the options in PC Settings to fix the issue, because the full administration and management tools aren't included in Windows RT:

- **Windows Update** Windows Update works in the same way it does as in the desktop version of Windows 8. It is essential for providing security and stability updates for the platform.
- **Refresh Your PC** You won't be able to create a custom refresh image like you can with Windows 8, but you will be able to take the device back to a fully working copy of Windows 8 without deleting any files you have on the device.

Resetting Windows RT

All devices running Windows RT come with a way to reset the device. This process varies from one device to another but usually includes soft reset and hard reset options. A soft reset turns the machine off and on again, restarting the operating system. For most troubleshooting purposes, this will be effective for correcting problems.

A hard reset wipes the machine, including all of your installed apps and files, and takes the system back to its factory default settings. If you are encountering serious problems with your Windows RT device, you might need to perform a hard reset.

Updating Windows RT

The biggest challenges you'll have with Windows RT concern updating the operating system. Most updates are delivered through Windows Update and are installed in the same way they are on a desktop computer; in fact, you probably won't even notice updates are happening.

Larger service pack updates, however, completely rewrite the operating system core and require the device to restart. When something goes wrong with this process, such as losing power, the device is unable to start. This is called *bricking* a device.

INSIDE OUT **Always ensure that your battery is fully charged when updating**

When you are updating the Windows RT operating system on a mobile device, always ensure that the device is fully charged and plugged into an electric power source. This will give the device a solid battery to work from in the event of a power outage, and it significantly reduces the risk of bricking the device during the update.

Windows Phone has a good reputation with updates, but if your device is bricked, you might need to have the operating system reinstalled. I would recommend that before you perform an update of your device running Windows RT, back up all your files, music, and photos. You can do this by plugging the device into a computer running Windows 8 and copying the files to that computer.

Index

B

C

G

H

M

Q

R

S

U

V

X

Y

Z

About the Author

Mike Halsey is the author of several books about Microsoft operating systems, including *Troubleshooting Windows 7 Inside Out* (Microsoft Press, 2010), *Beginning Windows 8* (Apress, 2012), *Exam Ref 70-687 Configuring Windows 8* (Microsoft Press, 2013), and the best-selling *Windows 8: Out of the Box* (O'Reilly, 2012).

An English and Math teacher by trade, Mike is also a Microsoft Most Valuable Professional (MVP) awardee (2011, 2012, 2013) and recognized Windows expert. Mike has an open mailbag at *mike@MVPs.org* and can also be found on Facebook, Twitter, and YouTube as *HalseyMike*. He lives in Yorkshire (UK) with his rescue border collie, Jed.

Contacting the Author

http://www.facebook.com/HalseyMike

http://www.youtube.com/HalseyMike

http://www.twitter.com/HalseyMike

http://www.thelongclimb.com

How To Download Your eBook

Thank you for purchasing this Microsoft Press® title. Your companion PDF eBook is ready to download from O'Reilly Media, official distributor of Microsoft Press titles.

To download your eBook, go to

http://go.microsoft.com/FWLink/?Linkid=224345

and follow the instructions.

Please note: You will be asked to create a free online account and enter the access code below.

Your access code:

DGWRPNM

Troubleshoot and Optimize Windows 8®
Inside Out

Your PDF eBook allows you to:

- Search the full text
- Print
- Copy and paste

Best yet, you will be notified about free updates to your eBook.

If you ever lose your eBook file, you can download it again just by logging in to your account.

Need help? Please contact:
mspbooksupport@oreilly.com
or call 800-889-8969.

Please note: This access code is non-transferable and is void if altered or revised in any way. It may not be sold or redeemed for cash, credit, or refund.